50 Golden Years of Oscar

1927/28 Wings·Emil Jannings (The Last Command; The Way of All Flesh) Janet Gaynor (Seventh Heaven; Street Angel; Sunrise) 1928/29 Broadway Melody·Warner Baxter (In Old Arizona) Mary Pickford (Coquette) 1929/30 All Quiet on The Western Front·George Arliss (Disraeli) Norma Shearer (The Divorcee) 1930/31 Cimarron·Lionel Barrymore (A Free Soul) Marie Dressler (Min and Bill) 1931/32 Grand Hotel·Fredric March (Dr. Jekyll and Mr. Hyde) Wallace Beery (The Champ) Helen Hayes (The Sin of Madelon Claudet) 1932/33 Cavalcade·Charles Laughton (The Private Life of Henry VIII) Katharine Hepburn (Morning Glory) 1934 It Happened One Night·Clark Gable (It Happened One Night) Claudette Colbert (It Happened One Night) 1935 Mutiny on the Bounty·Victor McLaglen (The Informer) Bette Davis (Dangerous) 1936 The Great Ziegfeld·Paul Muni (Story of Louis Pasteur) Luise Rainer (The Great Ziegfeld) Walter Brennan (Come and Get It) Gale Sondergaard (Anthony Adverse) 1937 The Life of Emile Zola·Spencer Tracy (Captains Courageous) Luise Rainer (The Good Earth) Joseph Schildkraut (The Life of Emile Zola) Alice Brady (In Old Chicago) 1938 You Can't Take It With You·Spencer Tracy (Boys Town) Bette Davis (Jezebel) Walter Brennan (Kentucky) Fay Bainter (Jezebel) 1939 Gone With The Wind·Robert Donat (Goodbye, Mr. Chips) Vivien Leigh (Gone With The Wind) Thomas Mitchell (Stagecoach) Hattie McDaniel (Gone With The Wind) 1940 Rebecca·James Stewart (The Philadelphia Story) Ginger Rogers (Kitty Foyle) Walter Brennan (The Westerner) Jane Darwell (The Grapes of Wrath) 1941 How Green Was My Valley·Gary Cooper (Sergeant York) Joan Fontaine (Suspicion) Donald Crisp (How Green Was My Valley) Mary Astor (The Great Lie) 1942 Mrs. Miniver·James Cagney (Yankee Doodle Dandy) Greer Garson (Mrs. Miniver) Van Heflin (Johnny Eager) Teresa Wright (Mrs. Miniver) 1943 Casablanca·Paul Lukas (Watch on the Rhine) Jennifer Jones (Song of Bernadette) Charles Coburn (The More the Merrier) Katina Paxinou (For Whom the Bell Tolls) 1944 Going My Way·Bing Crosby (Going My Way) Ingrid Bergman (Gaslight) Barry Fitzgerald (Going My Way) Ethel Barrymore (None But the Lonely Heart) 1945 The Lost Weekend·Ray Milland (The Lost Weekend) Joan Crawford (Mildred Pierce) James Dunn (A Tree Grows In Brooklyn) Anne Revere (National Velvet) 1946 The Best Years of Our Lives·Fredric March (The Best Years of Our Lives) Olivia de Havilland (To Each His Own) Harold Russell (The Best Years of Our Lives) Anne Baxter (The Razor's Edge) 1947 Gentleman's Agreement·Ronald Colman (A Double Life) Loretta Young (The Farmer's Daughter) Edmund Gwenn (Miracle on 34th Street) Celeste Holm (Gentleman's Agreement) 1948 Hamlet·Laurence Olivier (Hamlet) Jane Wyman (Johnny Belinda) Walter Huston (Treasure of Sierra Madre) Claire Trevor (Key Largo) 1949 All The King's Men·Broderick Crawford (All The King's Men) Olivia de Havilland (The Heiress) Dean Jagger (Twelve O'Clock High) Mercedes McCambridge (All The King's Men) 1950 All About Eve·Jose Ferrer (Cyrano de Bergerac) Judy Holliday (Born Yesterday) George Sanders (All About Eve) Josephine Hull (Harvey) 1951 An American in Paris·Humphrey Bogart (The African Queen) Vivien Leigh (A Streetcar Named Desire) Karl Malden (A Streetcar Named Desire) Kim Hunter (A Streetcar Named Desire) 1952 The Greatest Show on Earth·Gary Cooper (High Noon) Shirley Booth (Come Back Little Sheba) Anthony Quinn (Viva Zapata) Gloria Grahame (The Bad and The Beautiful) 1953 From Here To Eternity·William Holden (Stalag 17) Audrey Hepburn (Roman Holiday) Frank Sinatra (From Here To Eternity) Donna Reed (From Here To Eternity) 1954 On the Waterfront·Marlon Brando (On the Waterfront) Grace Kelly (The Country Girl) Edmond O'Brien (The Barefoot Contessa) Eva Marie Saint (On the Waterfront) 1955 Marty·Ernest Borgnine (Marty) Anna Magnani (The Rose Tattoo) Jack Lemmon (Mr. Roberts) Jo Van Fleet (East of Eden) 1956 Around the World in 80 Days·Yul Brynner (The King and I) Ingrid Bergman (Anastasia) Anthony Quinn (Lust for Life) Dorothy Malone (Written On the Wind) 1957 The Bridge On the River Kwai·Alec Guinness (The Bridge On the River Kwai) Joanne Woodward (The Three Faces of Eve) Red Buttons (Sayonara) Miyoshi Umeki (Sayonara) 1958 Gigi·David Niven (Separate Tables) Susan Hayward (I Want to Live) Burl Ives (The Big Country) Wendy Hiller (Separate Tables) 1959 Ben-Hur·Charlton Heston (Ben-Hur) Simone Signoret (Room at the Top) Hugh Griffith (Ben-Hur) Shelley Winters (The Diary of Anne Frank) 1960 The Apartment·Burt Lancaster (Elmer Gantry) Elizabeth Taylor (Butterfield 8) Peter Ustinov (Spartacus) Shirley Jones (Elmer Gantry) 1961 West Side Story·Maximilian Schell (Judgment at Nuremberg) Sophia Loren (Two Women) George Chakiris (West Side Story) Rita Moreno (West Side Story) 1962 Lawrence of Arabia·Gregory Peck (To Kill a Mockingbird) Anne Bancroft (The Miracle Worker) Ed Begley (Sweet Bird of Youth) Patty Duke (The Miracle Worker) 1963 Tom Jones·Sidney Poitier (Lilies of the Field) Patricia Neal (Hud) Melvyn Douglas (Hud) Margaret Rutherford (V.I.P.s) 1964 My Fair Lady·Rex Harrison (My Fair Lady) Julie Andrews (Mary Poppins) Peter Ustinov (Topkapi) Lila Kedrova (Zorba the Greek) 1965 The Sound of Music·Lee Marvin (Cat Ballou) Julie Christie (Darling) Martin Balsam (A Thousand Clowns) Shelley Winters (A Patch of Blue) 1966 A Man for All Seasons·Paul Scofield (A Man for All Seasons) Elizabeth Taylor (Who's Afraid of Virginia Woolf?) Walter Matthau (The Fortune Cookie) Sandy Dennis (Who's Afraid of Virginia Woolf?) 1967 In the Heat of the Night·Rod Steiger (In the Heat of the Night) Katharine Hepburn (Guess Who's Coming to Dinner) George Kennedy (Cool Hand Luke) Estelle Parsons (Bonnie and Clyde) 1968 Oliver·Cliff Robertson (Charly) Katharine Hepburn (The Lion in Winter) Barbra Streisand (Funny Girl) Jack Albertson (The Subject Was Roses) Ruth Gordon (Rosemary's Baby) 1969 Midnight Cowboy·John Wayne (True Grit) Maggie Smith (The Prime of Miss Jean Brodie) Gig Young (They Shoot Horses, Don't They?) Goldie Hawn (Cactus Flower) 1970: Patton·George C. Scott (Patton) Glenda Jackson (Women in Love) John Mills (Ryan's Daughter) Helen Hayes (Airport) 1971 The French Connection·Gene Hackman (The French Connection) Jane Fonda (Klute) Ben Johnson (The Last Picture Show) Cloris Leachman (The Last Picture Show) 1972 The Godfather·Marlon Brando (The Godfather) Liza Minnelli (Cabaret) Joel Grey (Cabaret) Eileen Heckart (Butterflies are Free) 1973 The Sting·Jack Lemmon (Save the Tiger) Glenda Jackson (A Touch of Class) John Houseman (The Paper Chase) Tatum O'Neal (Paper Moon) 1974 The Godfather Part II·Art Carney (Harry and Tonto) Ellen Burstyn (Alice Doesn't Live Here Anymore) Robert De Niro (The Godfather Part II) Ingrid Bergman (Murder on the Orient Express) 1975 One Flew Over the Cuckoo's Nest·Jack Nicholson (One Flew Over the Cuckoo's Nest) Louise Fletcher (One Flew Over the Cuckoo's Nest) George Burns (The Sunshine Boys) Lee Grant (Shampoo) 1976 Rocky·Peter Finch (Network) Faye Dunaway (Network) Jason Robards (All The President's Men) Beatrice Straight (Network) 1977 Annie Hall·Richard Dreyfuss (The Goodbye Girl) Diane Keaton (Annie Hall) Jason Robards (Julia) Vanessa Redgrave (Julia)

1927 ~ 1977

Personal Copy for _____

Presented by _____

PUBLISHER

 **ESE California**
509 N. Harbor Boulevard, La Habra, Calif. 90631

In association with the
ACADEMY OF MOTION PICTURE ARTS AND SCIENCES

(T) ISBN-912076-30-5
(P) ISBN-912076-29-1

50 GOLDEN YEARS OF OSCAR

THE OFFICIAL HISTORY OF THE ACADEMY OF MOTION PICTURE ARTS & SCIENCES

by Robert Osborne

designed by
Ernest E. Schworck

Dedicated to the Founders of the Academy

whose individual creative talents and collective support of the motion picture helped make it the preeminent art form of the twentieth century.

April 3, 1978

A very special occasion

at the Dorothy Chandler Pavilion, Los Angeles Music Center

Oscar's

Fiftieth Birthday

Celebration...

Dorothy Chandler Pavilion

Mickey Mouse, Artoo-Detoo

Gale Sondergaard

Bette Davis, Gregory Peck

In the forecour

Mr. and Mrs. Richard Burton

"Nobody Does It Better": Aretha Franklin

Greer Garson, Henry Winkler

Sylvester Stallone

Debbie Reynolds

Farrah Fawcett-Majors, Marcello Mastroianni

Mr. and Mrs. Pat Boone

Richard Dreyfuss

Vanessa Redgrave

"Look How Far We've Come": Debbie Reynolds

et Gaynor, Diane Keaton

Olivia Newton-John, John Williams, John Green, Henry Mancini

Paddy Chayefsky

Richard Dreyfuss, Diane Keaton

"Come Light the Candles": Marvin Hamlisch, Sammy Davis, Jr.

"Candle on the Water": Sylvia Lorince

Paul Williams, Co-Headsman, Beverly Shaffer, Jodie Foster, Mickey Mouse

Raquel Welch, Kirk Douglas

Raymond Danone, Roger Christian, Eva Marie Saint, Jack Valenti

Charles H. Joffe, Jack Nicholson

"You Light Up My Life": Debby Boone

Maggie Smith, Michael Caine, Bob Hope

Janet Gaynor, the first Oscar-winning Actress

Natalie Wood, Bob Hope

Fred Astaire

"The Slipper and the Rose Waltz": Jane Powell

Grant McCune, Robert Blalack, John Dykstra, Richard Edlund, Joan Fontaine, John Stears

Margaret Booth, Olivia de Havilland

John Travolta

Walter Mirisch, Stanley Kramer

Garrett Brown, Ed Digiulio, John Jurgens, Billy Dee Williams

See Threepio (Anthony Daniels)

The Beginning...

In 1928, no one knew better than Mary Pickford how much the motion picture industry needed one all-encompassing organization as a focal point for unbiased judgments, coordination and cool thinking in the often-scrambled movie community known as Hollywood. Miss Pickford had been a part of the movie business almost from its beginning, watching the nickelodeon novelty grow with lightning speed into what had become, by the end of the 1920s, the fourth largest industry in America. The movies—silent but golden—had captured the imagination and the pocketbooks of the world, but until the Academy of Motion Picture Arts and Sciences was formed, no one had organized the moviemakers themselves into a single, cohesive force. And the time had come.

The 1920s had been, in fact, a time of great changes everywhere, a dynamic period of transition. After World War I ended in 1918, the United States had been undergoing an invigorating decade of technological and cultural breakthroughs, one after another, stockpiling inventions and creations faster than at any other period in the country's history. Growth was particularly swift in the area of mass communications and, by the end of the 1920s, all the current major communications media had attained some degree of maturity, except of course, for television.

Statistics on the motion picture industry itself were staggering. By 1928, the American film colony alone was producing over five hundred feature-length films (and hundreds of short subjects) each year for a weekly audience of one hundred million ticket-buyers in twenty-three thousand theaters across the nation. Hollywood, California—that little suburb which had mushroomed just outside of Los Angeles—had firmly established itself, without any premeditation, as the film capital of the world. That's when problems began, problems which brought about an organization encompassing all filmmakers.

World leadership in any field has distinct disadvantages, and Hollywood was getting all the slaps synonymous with success. The attacks came from everywhere. Church groups charged that the medium foisted harmful influences on unsuspecting patrons, and Parent-Teacher Associations criticized Hollywood's preoccupation with adult themes. Everyone had something to say about the personal conduct of the town's citizenry, often blown out of proportion for publicity purposes, then eagerly reported by the world's press, often encouraged on by aggressive studio publicity departments. The government, too, often cast a critical eye on Hollywood, eager to show the moviemakers how to use, or how not to use, their undeniable influence over the masses.

The handwriting was on the wall: outside censorship of the film industry was inevitable unless the industry took hasty steps to police itself. In order to head off the possibility of outside control, a group of film producers gathered together in 1922 and hired Will H. Hays, a former Postmaster General under President Warren Harding, to head up a new self-policing body for the industry. Hays was to set guidelines for films, censor the offenders of good taste and give a stamp of approval to acceptable products, all of which the film community was to accept en masse. Everyone hoped the distinguished Hays name would help alleviate

What The Academy Means To Me

The Academy is the League of Nations of the Motion Picture Industry. It is our open forum where all branches can meet and discuss constructive problems with which each is confronted. In the past we have never been able to get together as a common ground and in making this possible, the Academy has conferred a great service. The producer, star featured player, cinematographer—in fact, every individual can come into the Academy with any problem or proposal and feel that all barriers are leveled, that in this open court his voice carries the same weight as that of any other person, regardless of position or standing. There is no greater force for coordination, no greater avenue for constructive and intelligent cooperation for advancement than that offered by the Academy of Motion Picture Arts and Sciences.

Mary Pickford
Academy Bulletin, April 2, 1928

those outside criticisms, with the knowledge that the moviemakers themselves were doing something constructive to police the screen. Hays' leadership was the stimulus for the first movie production code, but it still didn't prevent all attempts at outside interference with films and filmmakers. Despite the good intentions and tough policies of Mr. Hays, a few states and several cities still decided to establish their own local censorship boards to pass on motion picture content, and these boards often rejected films previously cleared by Hays and his Hollywood code office.

There was another problem also plaguing the industry: a favorable trend towards unionism. Los Angeles had long been known as a haven for non-union employment, and pro-union organizers felt that the motion picture industry could be used as a tool to bring unions into the unorganized labor town. It started slowly at first. In November of 1926, a Studio Basic Agreement was signed between nine film studios and unions representing carpenters, painters, electricians, stagehands and musicians. At the same time, an attempt to form a screenwriter's guild was defeated, and a major effort to organize talent groups by Actors Equity Association, the stage union covering performers, had failed. Still, more change was inevitable, one way or another.

Public interest in silent films was also on the wane, and the motion picture industry was in a serious state of mechanical overhaul. Technological advances were being made by various studios, but each was keeping its knowledge a heavily guarded secret, leading to chaos in the manufacture and distribution of prints, even the silent ones to theaters. There were as many standards as there were studios, and in the face of a falling market, producers needed all the cooperation they could muster, particularly with the impending changeover to sound-on-film. They needed, first and foremost, a central clearinghouse and exchange for ideas, a common ground where the development of new equipment could be discussed, and procedures could be shared which would benefit the entire industry.

In January of 1927, just five weeks after the Studio Basic Agreement was a fact of Hollywood life, the first seed-idea for the Academy of Motion Picture Arts and Sciences was planted. It happened during a Sunday dinner at the Santa Monica beach home of M-G-M's powerful studio chief Louis B. Mayer, during a conversation between Mayer and three of his guests, actor Conrad Nagel, director Fred Niblo and producer Fred Beetson. The men agreed there should be one organized group which could benefit the entire industry, help solve technological problems, aid in arbitrating labor disputes, and assist Will Hays in policing screen content. Stimulated by the idea, the four men planned a dinner for the following week, which would be attended by representatives from all the creative branches of the motion picture industry whom, hopefully, would be equally willing to support such an organization.

The men meant business. On January 11, 1927, thirty-six people gathered at the Ambassador Hotel in Los Angeles, listened to the proposal, and applauded the whole idea. These film industry leaders became the official founders of the International Academy of Motion Picture Arts and Sciences (the "International" was later dropped during incorporation proceedings). The thirty-six, besides Mayer, Nagel, Niblo and Beetson, were J.A. Ball, Richard Barthelmess, Charles H. Christie, George Cohen, Cecil B. DeMille, Douglas Fairbanks, Joseph W. Farnham, Cedric Gibbons, Benjamin Glazer, Sid Grauman, Milton Hoffman, Jack Holt, Henry King, Jesse Lasky, M.C. Levee, Frank Lloyd,

INTRODUCTION

" It is sometimes hard to believe that the American film of today, with its technical advancements, sophisticated themes, and international repute, had its roots in the flickering images cast on the walls of storefront theaters catering to New York's East Side sweatshop employees.

The contrast between the early days of the Academy of Motion Picture Arts and Sciences and its position on the occasion of its Golden Anniversary is no less dramatic.

The 36 founders of the Academy prepared a small booklet which they distributed to the 300 film industry leaders in attendance at an organizational banquet, held May 11, 1927. The following statement summarized their goals for the new association: "The Academy proposes to do for the motion picture profession in all its branches what other great national and international constructive bodies have done for other arts and sciences and industries. To the end that the arts and sciences of the industry and the dignity and honor of profession may be advanced to their rightful standing among the creative institutions of mankind, we have sponsored the Academy of Motion Picture Arts and Sciences."

Those simple goals have remained basically unchanged since 1927, although the institution of the Academy has grown far beyond the scope of its pioneers.

Through the intervening half century, the Academy has promulgated industry technical standards, provided funds for scholarships and research grants, provided incentives for student filmmakers, carried out a wide variety of film-related cultural and educational activities, and accumulated what is possibly the finest library related to motion pictures in the world.

But shining above it all is Oscar.

Created in 1927 by art director Cedric Gibbons, and first awarded fifty years ago, Oscar has become an eight-and-a-half pound, thirteen-and-a-half-inch high symbol of technical and artistic achievement.

The idea behind Oscar was then—and is now—to promote film excellence by recognizing it. Oscar has become the symbol of recognition by one's peers, and, as such, the highest honor one can achieve.

As Oscar celebrates his Golden Anniversary, we proudly note that the list of films, filmmakers and artists he has honored constitute most of the greatest achievements of the motion picture art.

We dedicate this book, the story of the Academy's first fifty years, both to those who love the movies, and to all those who share our goal of providing constant incentives for continuing excellence in all fields of human endeavor.

Oscar, and the Academy he represents, will grow as long as men and women of talent and vision continue to make motion pictures. **"**

Howard W. Koch

Howard W. Koch, President
Academy of Motion Picture Arts and Sciences

Harold Lloyd, Edwin Loeb, Jeanie MacPherson, Bess Meredith, Mary Pickford, Roy Pomeroy, Harry Rapf, Joseph Schenck, Milton Sills, John Stahl, Irving Thalberg, Raoul Walsh, Harry Warner, Jack L. Warner, Carey Wilson and Frank Woods.

After that, things moved swiftly. Articles of incorporation were presented by mid-March, and the first officers were elected: Douglas Fairbanks (president), Fred Niblo (vice president), M.C. Levee (treasurer) and Frank Woods (secretary). On May 4, 1927, the state of California granted the Academy a charter as a non-profit corporation, and a week later, on May 11, 1927, a festive and official organizational banquet took place in the Crystal Ballroom of the Biltmore Hotel in Los Angeles with three hundred guests in attendance. That night, two hundred and thirty-one of them joined the new Academy as pioneer members, by signing a check for one hundred dollars. "Our purpose is positive, not negative," Fairbanks told them. "We are formed to do, not un-do."

On June 20, 1927, the Academy founders further committed the goals of the new organization in a statement, which declared:

> The Academy will take aggressive action in meeting outside attacks that are unjust.
>
> It will promote harmony and solidarity among the membership and among different branches.
>
> It will reconcile internal differences that may exist or arise.
>
> It will adopt such ways and means as are proper to further the welfare and protect the honor and good repute of the profession.
>
> It will encourage the improvement and advancement of the arts and sciences of the profession by the interchange of constructive ideas and by awards of merit for distinctive achievement.
>
> It will take steps to develop the greater power and influence of the screen.
>
> In a word, the Academy proposes to do for the motion picture profession in all its branches what other great national and international bodies have done for other arts and sciences and industries.

The organization of the Academy of Motion Picture Arts and Sciences consisted of different groups, each with equal representation on the Board of Directors (later changed to the Board of Governors), and each group with a semi-autonomous branch organization of its own. Initially, there were five main branches—Producers, Actors, Directors, Writers and Technicians—but the number of branches has gradually been increased over the years to reflect the greater diversity of activity and specialization in the production of motion pictures. More of that later.

The Academy was intended as an exclusive, invitational organization, and its opinions and actions were to be those of the organization, not necessarily of the entire industry. Still, in 1927, the Academy was (and still is, some fifty years later) used to initiate and solve industry-wide problems. From the beginning, no attempt at "membership drives" has ever been made. Membership in the Academy is by invitation only. Qualification for membership is based on distinctive achievements in one of the branches of motion picture production covered by the Academy.

In May, 1927, the Academy rented a suite of offices at 6912 Hollywood Boulevard to serve as temporary headquarters for the organization. The Golden Years had started.

The Academy's First Decade
1927-28 thru 1937

EDITOR'S NOTE
We wish to express our appreciation to the Academy Award winners who have responded to our request for their Oscar memories. More than one hundred and twenty have sent us their personal remembrances. All of these comments are presented below for the enjoyment of our readers.

JANET GAYNOR

❝*I was most impressed with the library at the new Academy building, for there immediately is the history of the film in all respects—available for students, researchers, or professionals—a highly valuable achievement, and one for the industry to point to with pride.*❞

Janet Gaynor
Best Actress, 1927-28

NORMA SHEARER

❝*I wish to take this glorious opportunity to express my deep affection and admiration for all those wonderful people in the motion picture business it has been my privilege to know and admire and to call my friends throughout the years.*❞

Norma Shearer
Best Actress, 1929-30

May, 1927: the same month the Academy of Motion Picture Arts and Sciences was officially born, air mail pilot Charles A. Lindbergh stunned the world by making the first non-stop New York-to-Paris flight, alone aboard his *Spirit of St. Louis* monoplane. In Washington, D.C., Calvin Coolidge was President of the United States, in New York Mae West was holding forth on Broadway in a play called *Sex* and across the country moviegoers were paying an average of 25¢ for a ticket each time they went to the movies, and were still mourning the death of Rudolph Valentino nine months before. Out in Hollywood, Grauman's Chinese Theatre opened its doors for the first time on May 18 (showing Cecil B. DeMille's *King of Kings* plus a spectacular stage presentation) and movie makers had their minds on a myriad of matters, one of them the worrisome possibility of talking pictures, launched by Warner Bros. with some Vitaphone short subjects the previous year.

At the Academy, the first order of business was a labor dispute that was threatening to erupt within the motion picture industry. The West Coast managers of the major motion picture studios—including Metro-Goldwyn-Mayer, Paramount, Fox, Universal, Warner Bros. and United Artists—were being severely pressured by their New York superiors and Manhattan bankers to impose a ten percent salary cut on all Hollywood studio personnel as a means of reducing production costs. A full-scale strike by studio employees was imminent; they were arguing that costs could—and should—be slashed elsewhere, not at the employee-salary level. The Producers Branch of the new Academy stepped in, effected a meeting with the other Academy branches to discuss the proposed cut and its ramifications, arbitrated the differences and ultimately managed to have the proposed salary cut withdrawn altogether.

Some Founders of the Academy: (Standing) Cedric Gibbons, J.A. Ball, Carey Wilson, George Cohen, Edwin Loeb, Fred Beetson, Frank Lloyd, Roy Pomeroy, John Stahl, Harry Rapf; (Seated) Louis B. Mayer, Conrad Nagel, Mary Pickford, Douglas Fairbanks, Frank Woods, M.C. Levee, Joseph M. Schenck, Fred Niblo.

Another early order of business was a search for larger headquarters. The Academy's office at 6912 Hollywood Boulevard was barely large enough for small committee meetings, much less for an organization with several hundred members. In June of 1927, one month after the Academy's official incorporation, the Building and Finance Committee submitted a proposal for construction of a new building, but the idea was rejected by the Board for a lack of funds. In November of the same year, the Academy found suitable office space on the mezzanine floor of the Roosevelt Hotel, located at 7010 Hollywood Boulevard. There the Academy began accumulating a complete file of professional periodicals from all over the world, and plans were made for an eventual library.

In May, 1928, the Board approved the installation of screening facilities in the Club Lounge of the hotel. The most complete and up-to-date equipment available was ordered, and the plan was for immediate installation. Seven months later, the "immediate installation" still had not taken place, due to the tremendous demand by theater owners all over the country for sound equipment to cash in on the sudden impact of talking pictures. An appeal was made to the equipment manufacturers

Douglas Fairbanks, Benjamin Glazer, Janet Gaynor, Karl Struss, Frank Borzage

and—finally—the desired facilities were completed six months later, in April, 1929. But it was worth the wait, as the Academy's screening room was equipped with Vitaphone, Movietone and every other sound system then used by the industry.

During the Academy's first decade, there were other moves, necessitated by the organization's rapid expansion. In June, 1930, a suite of offices in the Professional Building at 7046 Hollywood Boulevard was rented, where the Academy could have space for its increased staff of four executives, three assistants and six clerks. By December, the library was acknowledged as having one of the most complete collections of information on the motion picture industry anywhere in existence.

Moving again in 1935, the accounting and executive offices shifted to the Taft Building on the corner of Hollywood and Vine, right in the

HELEN HAYES

"Advice to young actors winning Oscars: Enjoy! Don't wait years to find out what that award can give you in comfort and confidence. As an actor grows older, no matter how long his memory, it is hard to hold on to that delicious feeling of his youth—of being best. That Oscar sitting on the mantel is a good reminder. I treasure mine for just that."

Helen Hayes
Best Actress, 1931-32
Best Supporting Actress, 1970

LEWIS MILESTONE

"From my first Oscar, handed me by Douglas Fairbanks in 1928, a small and (by today's standards) informal family celebration, to the present worldwide interest in the Oscar presentations, the growth of the Academy Awards proves indeed the cultural and educational benefits of these 50 Golden Years.

The Academy is the Supreme Court of the Screen."

Lewis Milestone
Best Director, 1927-28; 1929-30

BETTE DAVIS

"I have always felt proud of my Oscars and my numerous nominations. This pride is due to the fact it was the result of voters from the members of my own profession.

This, of course, is a great compliment for one's work. I hope each winner of an Oscar is as thrilled as I was when I received mine."

Bette Davis
Best Actress, 1935; 1938

CLAUDETTE COLBERT

"What can one say about receiving the Academy Award except, 'I was so happy, excited, etc., etc., etc.'

In my particular case, added to all these emotions was utter astonishment! I was convinced that we could not win because a comedy had never won—so convinced, that I was actually boarding the Santa Fe Super Chief for New York when I was whisked back to the Biltmore Hotel to accept the Oscar while they held the train. It was quite a scenario!!!"

Claudette Colbert
Best Actress, 1934

KATHARINE HEPBURN

**" ** *Prizes are given. Prizes are won. They are the result of competition. Any way you want to look at it, from birth to death we are competing.*

My first competition. A track meet. The three-legged race. I won it. My next was a diving contest. I was doing several very complicated dives badly. My friend and competitor was doing several very simple dives well. She won it. I resented it deeply. But there it was. There is a terrible agony in competition. You have to pretend that you don't care if you lose. We have home movies of all those early competitions. Cry at the beginning. Cry during the race. Cry when you win. Cry when you lose.

No way. Too much of a strain. I'll avoid that. But I didn't. I encountered The Super Cry.

I grew up. I went to work. And I found that I had entered a business which had a thing called—THE ACADEMY AWARD. People from all over the world see the different competitors do their stuff. The winning of the prize in any department is a boost to business. The winning of Best Picture. Best Director. Best Actor. Best Actress. This is a Super Boost.

The effort to win votes by advertising, selling, begging, organizing in full swing in all media. Then the terrible Night. Telecast worldwide. All dressed up. Here I am a competitor. And I care. I care desperately. Will I be the one to . . .

Oh dear me. Let's avoid that, I said to myself. So I never went. But I had to be honest enough with myself to wonder— What is it, Kathy? Are you afraid that you won't win?

One year when I was not in the running myself I was asked to present the Thalberg Award to Lawrence Weingarten. I just could not in all conscience refuse. So I rushed on. And then I rushed off. But do you know what—they all stood up. They stood up for me. All those people. Those people whose votes through the years had given me the prize. They had voted me in. Not once, but twice— and a half. They stood. They clapped. They gave me their respect and their affection. It was a revelation—the generous heart of the industry. The pat on the back from one's peers.

Continued on next page

center of Hollywood, while the library relocated to 1455 North Gordon Street. The library was growing so rapidly that in 1936, the Academy's first full-time librarian, Margaret Herrick, was hired to oversee its burgeoning collection of periodicals and other film materials.

During the initial decade, the Academy began initiating a few publications of its own, as a service to its members and the industry in general. In 1928, the Academy published its first book, *Report on Incandescent Illumination,* based on the contents of a series of Academy-sponsored seminars which had been given earlier in the year with the help of the American Society of Cinematographers and Producers Association. This had been attended by one hundred and fifty interested cinematographers. Another series of lectures on sound technique, sponsored by the Academy to help familiarize novices with the vast technical requirements of sound-on-film, was the basis for a second book, *Recording Sound for Motion Pictures,* which was published in 1931. In 1929, *Introduction to the Photoplay* was published, based on lectures given during a new film course at the University of Southern California in cooperation with the Academy's College Affairs Committee.

The Academy tried its hand at publishing a magazine, too, but without much success. During the period, *Motion Picture Arts and Sciences* was premiered, featuring Academy news and distributed only to Academy members. It was published in November, 1927, and lasted for the one issue. In 1928, the organization made plans to purchase an existing publication titled *Hollywood,* intending to circulate it nationally, but dropped the idea when the plans for wide-spread distribution were not feasible.

Other Academy efforts in the publications field have been more durable. In 1933, the *Screen Achievement Records Bulletin* was born, listing film production titles and complete credits for directors and writers; today it is still published, now three times each year, expanded to include complete motion picture credits of productions, cross-indexed by title, individual, production company and specific craft. The *Academy Players Directory* began in 1937, showing then—as now—photographs of actors, with the name of their agents or industry contacts, as a service to casting directors. Like the *Screen Achievement Records Bulletin,* the *Academy Players Directory* is still being published three times a year, now with over 10,000 performers in recent issues, all given the same amount of space, regardless of their credits or fame, and all available for assignment.

One of the primary reasons for the formation of the Academy was to counter the unfavorable publicity focusing on the film industry at the time, and through succeeding years continued to do powerful public relations work for the entire movie community. Some of its early attempts to improve the industry's image and create good will with the public included such efforts as Academy contributions to the Mississippi River Relief Fund. Prior to the official organization charter date, the Academy raised funds for the relief of suffering flood victims in the Mississippi Basin and on May 12, 1927, just one day after the organization dinner of May 11, the Academy presented a check to the Fund for over thirty-five thousand dollars, which was over one-quarter of the total donation from the entire city of Los Angeles.

As a further good will gesture, the Academy opened its facilities to outside organizations and groups for meetings. Advance screenings of as-yet-unreleased motion pictures were held for the benefit of opinion-makers from major churches in the community, plus certain educational and fraternal institutions. The value of having influential community

Henry B. Walthall, D.W. Griffith   Norma Shearer

GALE SONDERGAARD

"I came to Hollywood in 1935, not to seek a career in motion pictures but rather to accompany my husband, Herbert Biberman, New York Theater Guild director, who was about to embark on his new career as director of films.

Although I was already a stage actress and had played leading roles on Broadway, I sincerely believed that I did not belong in motion pictures.

Much to my amazement, it then happened that Mervyn LeRoy cast me as Faith Paleologue in Anthony Adverse— and then, to my even greater amazement, in 1936 I won the first Academy Award ever given to an actress in a supporting role.

My new career was on its way. I love the Academy of Motion Picture Arts and Sciences. **"**

Gale Sondergaard
Best Supporting Actress, 1936

HERMES PAN

"I am very happy to be able to participate in any way in the golden years of Oscar.

The Academy of Motion Picture Arts and Sciences is, and always has been, a great stimulus and encouragement to all involved in the film industry.

Needless to say, the highlight of my career was a night many years ago at the old Biltmore Hotel ballroom, when I heard a voice saying, 'And the winner is— Hermes Pan. **"**

Hermes Pan
Dance Direction, 1937

leaders approve Hollywood product was, at the time, of inestimable help to the industry. Though the Academy was never intended to be the official spokesman for the entire film community, it often served as a clearinghouse for inquiries from the press, private individuals, civic organizations and others.

Another public relations "first" came when the Academy began arranging visits with studio personnel from foreign nations, as in 1930 when leading representatives from the Russian film industry met with Hollywood executives and technicians to exchange ideas and knowledge. In November of the same year, the Academy began a successful practice of having some of its members tour to various cities in the United States, talking to civic groups, schools and leaders of industry.

Through the early years, the Academy often became involved in studio problems and union matters, but it was never its strongest suit, despite its being one of the original reasons for the formation of the organization. By the time the first decade of the Academy of Motion Picture Arts and Sciences was over, it was out of the arbitration business. But it had tried to help, many times and in many ways.

A troublesome period loomed with the launching of sound films. Talking pictures had done a great deal to revive and sustain some weighty box office problems which had been plaguing the industry, but the national Depression in 1931 was another crippler. It pushed several studios to the brink of bankruptcy and sent Universal and RKO Radio into receivership. In March of 1933 came the final blow: from Washington, D.C., the new President, Franklin D. Roosevelt, declared a bank holiday. In order to survive, Hollywood studios had frenzied meetings, uncertain if they should continue, scratch production plans or shut their gates altogether. In the meantime, several companies suspended salaries.

LUISE RAINER

" *The Academy Award—what shall I say? Surely I'd like to be included in the 50 Golden Years of Oscar. Were they golden? Only gilded anyway. I shall jot down, quickly, as it comes to my mind:*

Still in my early twenties, only a few months in Hollywood, I made my first film. It made me a star. It was then I first heard of 'the Academy Award.' What was it? I should soon learn. I never had much thought of any award beyond the wondrous contact and the warmth that I was fortunate to receive from many while spending my teens on the stage in Vienna and Berlin; my driving force was love and enthusiasm for my work and great hope to develop as an actress.

In my first year in Hollywood I started and finished my second film, The Great Ziegfeld. *Mr. Louis B. Mayer did not want me to do the film: 'Anna Held is out of it before the film is halfway through,' he said. 'You are a star now and you can't do it!' I hoped to make something of the two-minute telephone scene. It brought me my first Academy Award.*

Immediately after, I started The Good Earth. *Irving Thalberg cast me. Mr. Mayer was against that, too: 'She has to be a dismal-looking slave and grow old; but Luise is a young girl; we just have made her glamorous—what are you doing?' It brought me my second Academy Award as the best actress of the year. It happened in two successive years.*

How did I feel about it? As often in life, big events or the importance of them are felt less at the time than later. There was a great deal of photographing, much clamour, more so than the 'glamour' it is believed to be. Above all, a change of one's image felt by others but not by oneself. One was acclaimed, now; therefore one's doings, one's motives, one's every utterance seemed to have greater dimension and therefore suddenly became suspect. It seemed harder to continue one's work quietly. Shortly later I left Hollywood.

I have often heard the Academy Award to be a bad omen. I don't think it need be. Except, maybe, that the industry seemed to feel that having an Academy Award-winner on their hands was sufficient to overcome bad story material as was, often, handed out afterwards to stars under long-term contract. However, to build anything good it needs solid material, so it does not slip through your fingers like sand. This is what I felt then. Now I feel that it is wonderful to have received two Academy Awards! "

Luise Rainer
Best Actress, 1936; 1937

Fredric March, wife Florence Eldridge

The Academy did what it could to help a difficult situation by forming an Emergency Committee and recommended a temporary pay cut of 50% for studio employees as opposed to total shutdown which, they feared, would be a death blow to several of the troubled companies. An adjusted scale was also devised by the Emergency Committee to provide additional aid for low-salaried employees. The plan was to remain in effect for a limited, eight-week period (March 6-April 30, 1933). One provision was that the Academy be given permission to inspect companies' financial records to ensure that all was conducted fairly, as agreed. The accounting firm of Price Waterhouse & Co. was hired for auditing; it was the Academy's first utilization of the company which in 1936 took charge of officially tabulating results of Academy Awards balloting.

Basically, the Academy's aid in the 1933 crisis was a success— both in helping to get a badly bruised industry moving again, and by demonstrating the value of the Academy in producing measures for the industry-at-large. At the end of the "freeze" period, the crisis had ebbed, the panic had given way to optimism and all studios returned their employees to full salary as promised, with the exception of the Warner Bros. company. Its failure to do so enraged Darryl F. Zanuck, one of the studio's production heads, and he quit the company in protest.

Zanuck subsequently formed his own 20th Century Productions, which initially released through United Artists distribution channels, then merged in 1936 with the Fox Film Corporation. The Warner Bros. action also had an effect on the Academy hierarchy. Academy President Conrad Nagel was accused by some of supporting the studio in its action, and received a vote of no confidence from the Academy Board of Directors and consequently resigned, succeeded by J. Theodore Reed.

The incident proved to be a taint on the Academy's ability to hold its constituents' faith as an impartial arbiter and was one reason the Academy began easing away from involvement in labor relations. Reed took upon himself—as a first order of Academy business—the job of drafting a new constitution, one free of politics and any self-serving interests which might apply to any Academy officer in the future.

There was more trouble ahead. Union militancy again presented itself in June, 1933, when President Roosevelt introduced his National Industrial Recovery Act, a further effort of Washington to loosen the binds imposed by the Depression. The main thrust of the National

Recovery Act was to suspend various anti-trust laws, allowing industries such as the motion picture business to regulate itself, following self-imposed codes. The lengthy code, drawn up by the Motion Pictures Code Committee, infuriated almost everyone, especially performers. They were without a union, or organization, and they eyed the code as another example of dictatorship by the major studio executives. Since the Academy numbered many of those executives among its membership and—at the same time—made rather weak protestations at code hearings, suspicions grew that the Academy was on the side of the "enemy" and was no longer inclined to act in the best interests of actors, as it had often done in the past.

In July, 1933, a number of actors dropped their Academy membership and broke away to form the Screen Actors Guild union. A mass defection began when the specific rules in the code were released and discovered to contain such irritating items as strict salary controls, licensing of agencies, and other dominating provisions. Important names such as Paul Muni, Gary Cooper, Fredric March, James Cagney and George Raft were among the defectors, additionally angered because Academy President Reed had been one of the authors of the code. By November, over 1,000 actors had joined the new Screen Actors Guild. The strong anti-Academy resentments lasted even after the National Recovery Administration was declared unconstitutional by

Louis B. Mayer, Helen Hayes, Lionel Barrymore

the United States Supreme Court on May 27, 1935. It continued even through 1936, including the eighth Academy Awards presentation banquet on March 5, 1936, when several guilds and unions boycotted the annual dinner, causing many actors, writers and craftsmen to be absent. Because of the boycott, screenwriter Dudley Nichols became the first individual to refuse an Academy Award. After his name was announced as winner of the 1935 Screenplay Award (for *The Informer*), he announced that he could not accept because to do so would imply tacit approval of the Academy, and therefore weaken his own union or guild.

FRANK CAPRA

❝ *Late in 1935 (during the preparation of* Mr. Deeds*), the Board of Governors of the Academy of Motion Picture Arts and Sciences bestowed on me the dubious honor of electing me president.*

I say 'dubious' because the president would be presiding at a deathwatch. The Academy had become the favorite whipping boy of Hollywood. Its membership slashed from six hundred to four hundred, its officers to one, loyal, underpaid, executive secretary Margaret Herrick—the Academy's alter ego. With few dollars in its treasury—and fewer in sight—the odds were ten to one the Academy would fold and Oscar would acquire the patina of a collector's item.

Why? Because the polyarchic Academy —governed by management, technicians, and creative talent—was caught in the middle of Hollywood's first labor war between management and talent. The producing companies did everything short of asking for the National Guard to prevent actors, writers, and directors from organizing into guilds. The guilds were organized. But their siege of company ramparts was to last five long years— years of strife and strikes—before management capitulated and accepted the guilds as the bargaining agents for talent.

However, in 1935 the labor war was in full cry. Actor Ronald Reagan, writer John Howard Lawson, and director King Vidor led the fight for their respective guilds.

Part of talent's strategy was to wreck the Academy in order to deny management the box office promotional values of the Oscars. Oddly enough, short-sighted company heads couldn't care less. The Academy had failed them as an instrument of salary cuts during the bank-closing crisis. They withdrew their memberships and financial support, leaving the derelict organization in the care of a few staunch Academy-oriented

Continued on next page

Continued from previous page

visionaries dedicated to the cultural advancement of the arts and sciences of filmmaking, and to the continuance of the Awards—the most valuable, but least expensive, item of worldwide public relations ever invented by any industry.

It is an honor to name the few unsung idealists who crossed all economic battle lines to prevent the destruction of Hollywood's lone bastion of culture:

Writers: Howard Estabrook, Jane Murfin, Waldemar Young, Edwin Burke;

Producers: David O. Selznick, Darryl F. Zanuck, Sam Briskin, Fred Leahy, DeWitt Jennings, Graham Baker;

Technicians: Nathan Levinson, John Arnold, Van Nest Polglase;

Directors: Cecil B. DeMille, Frank Lloyd.

This group elected me to lead them in the Academy's fight for survival. What motivated my instant acceptance—pride or service? I am not sure. But I was sure that the upcoming Academy Awards banquet of March, 1936, loomed dark and discouraging; that things could get worse before they got 'worser.'

Boycott rumors were rife. Officers of the Screen Actors and Screen Writers Guilds sent telegrams to all members urging them not to attend the Academy dinner, and not to accept any Oscars.

To keep the Academy's head above water, we grabbed at the following straws: for the first time, we allowed films made in England to compete for the Oscars; we established the Supporting Actor and Supporting Actress categories; we also established the 'Irving G. Thalberg Memorial Award' for outstanding contribution in the production of films. But our top caper to hypo the attendance was to persuade the giant of all filmmakers, D.W. Griffith, to come out of his retired oblivion and accept from the Academy a special statuette for his legendary pioneering in films.

Griffith's name was magic. The boycott fizzled. Bette Davis was present to receive her Best Actress trophy for Dangerous; *Victor McLaglen was there to clutch a Best Actor award for* The Informer.

But neither John Ford nor Dudley Nichols showed up for their Best Directing and Best Writing Oscars awarded The Informer. *Ford accepted the trophy later. Nichols did not. He was quoted in a trade paper as having said: 'To accept it would be to turn my back on nearly a thousand members of the Writers Guild . . .'*

Continued on next page

In 1937, while Frank Capra presided over the Academy, the bylaws were again rewritten and the Academy withdrew from involvement in labor-management arbitrations and negotiations. It hadn't been a successful foray, but it couldn't be dismissed as a weakening disaster for the Academy, either. The Academy had achieved success in settling many disputes that plagued the industry from time to time; it helped introduce collective bargaining to the industry and, intended or not, aided in the development of strong labor unions.

During its early years, the Academy experienced several erratic shifts in the size of its membership. Going from an initial enrollment of 261 members, the Academy roll expanded to 374 members in November, 1928, mushrooming to over 800 members in 1932, dropped drastically to just 400 members after the 1933 protest, then grew again by the end of the first decade.

If labor relations had temporarily caused the Academy's membership lists to shrink, the Awards of Merit always caused public interest to grow. And nothing would probably have surprised the Academy founders more. When the Academy was first organized in 1927, the Awards of Merit committee was only one of several general committees dispatched, and the presentation of Awards originally a secondary matter.

The original seven members of the committee were Richard Barthelmess, D.W. Griffith, Henry King, Sid Grauman, Bess Meredyth, J. Stuart Blackton and Cedric Gibbons. Gibbons served as chairman. Griffith and Barthelmess were later replaced by Charles Roshner and George Fawcett. During its initial meetings, the committee gave thoughts to the development of some sort of Academy Awards presentation, but the idea was put aside due to more urgent matters. In May, 1928—a full year after the Academy was organized—the subject was again brought up and actively pursued. By July, it was suggested by the committee and approved by the Board to present awards in twelve categories:

Most outstanding production
Achievement by an actor
Achievement by an actress
Achievement in dramatic directing
Achievement in comedy directing
Achievement in cinematography
Achievement in art directing
Achievement in engineering effects
Achievement in original story writing
Achievement in writing adaptation
Achievement in title writing
Most artistic or unique production

The first awards, it was agreed, would be for motion pictures which had been released in the Los Angeles area between August 1, 1927, and July 31, 1928. In order to consider properly all qualifying films, studios were asked to supply the Academy with a list of pictures released within those dates, and the reminder list was sent on to the membership from which they were to make the initial nominations for Awards. The deadline was August 15, 1928, after which five Boards of Judges (one from each of the Academy's branches) were appointed to consider the ten achievements in each category accumulating the largest vote totals, narrowing those ten finalists down to three recommendations. Then came a Central Board of Judges—made up of *one* member from each branch—who made the final decision as to who would be the winner. The two remaining finalists would be singled out for "honorable mention."

The five men who made the decision on the first Academy Awards were Frank Lloyd (representing the Directors Branch), Sid Grauman (Producers Branch), Alec Francis (Actors Branch), Tom Geraghty (Writers Branch) and A. George Volck (Technicians Branch).

Unlike in later years, nominees were not publicly announced in advance of the final balloting. The decision on winners was made at an Academy conclave on Friday, February 15, 1929, a full six months after the closing date for submission of nominations, and the results were announced to the press the following Monday. The Awards themselves were officially presented months later, on May 16, 1929.

The second Awards year, only seven categories were honored: Production, Performance by an Actor, Performance by an Actress, Direction, Writing Achievement, Cinematography and Art Direction. Sound pictures became eligible for the first time, having been excluded from consideration the first time around, primarily because the Academy judges weren't sure how to evaluate the new phenomenon of talking pictures on a yardstick with silents. The period of eligibility remained seasonal—August 1 to July 31—and remained so until the sixth Awards. In 1933, it was decided to begin using the calendar year (January 1 to December 31) as the Academy's eligibility period for Awards consideration, but since the preceding cut-off date had been July 31, 1932, all the films released in Los Angeles between August 1-December 31, 1932, would be left unjudged unless the Academy incorporated them into the 1933 "calendar" year. They did. The sixth Awards eligibility period, therefore, incorporated seventeen months, from August 1, 1932 through December 31, 1933. Since 1934, the Academy's official year is a calendar one, and eligibility limited to films exhibited theatrically in the Los Angeles area.

Through the years, there have been constant changes in other areas of voting, as well. The process by which winners are selected remained the same for the second Awards year, but was broadened the third year (and remained so through the eighth Awards year) so that both the nomination procedure and the final voting was done by the full Academy membership. In 1936, the nominations were made by a special Awards Nominating Committee, appointed by President Frank Capra, with the final vote then done by the full Academy membership.

New categories have been adopted, then dropped or honed at the discretion of the Academy, such as awards for Dance Direction, One-reel and Two-reel short subjects, and awards distinguishing between color films and black-and-white ones. Two significant—and long-lasting—Awards were introduced near the end of the Academy's first decade: awards for Performance by an Actor in a Supporting Role, and Performance by an Actress in a Supporting Role. Like other aspects of the voting structure, the designation of a "supporting role" as opposed to a "leading role" has changed through the years. Originally it was decided by the studios, who based it on a performer's billing status. At times, studios have made the decision, but arbitrarily; other years, it has been left to the discretion of the performer himself. As of the Academy's fiftieth year, it was left to the discretion of the Academy member doing the voting.

The original constitution and bylaws provided for the conferring of honorary Academy memberships to "any person distinguished for public service or eminence in the industry, or by reason of any contribution made thereto." The first honorary membership was given to Thomas Edison at the organizational banquet on May 11, 1927; the second went

By prayers and incantations, and the Board members putting up their own money for the statuettes, plus some fancy begging on my part (each year I had to plead with the officers of the talent guilds to allow me to mail Academy ballots to their Guild members) the Academy deathwatch kept the grim reaper away until 1939.

Then came a massive transfusion of new blood. The writers, actors, and directors, having signed their newly won basic agreements with management, returned to the Academy fold virtually en masse. The Academy was reorganized into a self-supporting institution dedicated solely to cultural goals. And it was off and running! Today, its Oscars are the world's number one news event of the year. **"**

Frank Capra
Best Director, 1934; 1936; 1938

BOB HOPE

"*Being invited to add my comments to the others in this important, fascinating and unique book is the realization of a lifelong dream. At long last, I take my place among a galaxy of Oscar winners! And I consider this request from the Academy as an apology for not giving me an award for my acting.*

My spectacular lack of success in winning an Oscar is too well known to be repeated here. Though I've tried every conceivable way to win one of those coveted little yellow kids, I've had about as much luck as the guy who tried to sell a case of Brylcreem to Telly Savalas.

Once I came close to getting one. In fact, I was going to reach out and grab it. But the foresight of the Academy defeated me. My chain was just a couple of links too short!

Nonetheless, I consider myself eminently qualified to air my thoughts and feelings about movies because like just about everyone else, I'm a movie fan. I love pictures . . . and everything about them . . . making them, and even more, watching them.

Music, literature, painting, and all the other arts have made incalculable contributions to the world. But, in my view, movies are the most influential, the most marvelous, and the most universal art form known to man!

When you consider that movies are a product of this century, the growth and

Continued on next page

Continued from previous page

accomplishments of the film industry have been nothing less than miraculous.

Just by shelling out the price of a ticket, you can escape from the cares and problems of real life, and be transported to another wondrous world, a magical world where nothing is impossible. A world inhabited by the most diverse, the most gifted and the most beautiful people ever assembled in such profusion, whose only mission is to thrill, charm and entertain us.

A trip to a movie theater is the greatest travel bargain ever known. Via the silver screen we've been able to travel from Shangri-la to the moon. (In fact, we had a chance to visit the moon twenty-five years before Neil Armstrong.) And now, with Star Wars *and* Close Encounters, *movies have taken us into the limitless and spellbinding reaches of outer space. And even more wonderful, upon our return, we don't have to spend time searching for our luggage!*

And what a stupendous multitude of players movies have given us! The regal elegance of Greer Garson, the grace and gentility of Ronald Colman, the savoire faire of Cary Grant, the electrifying dancing of Fred Astaire, the incredible beauty of Garbo, the royal family of acting —the Barrymores, Bogart, Harlow, Cooper, Tracy, Hepburn, Laughton, Valentino, Garland, and the inimitable and greatest clown the world has ever known, Charlie Chaplin, whose comic genius broke your heart—and your funnybone! And those are just a few of the magnificent and scintillating stars who captivated us, thrilled us, and illuminated and enriched the lives of numberless millions, not only in America but in every far-flung corner of the world.

The film industry has survived every change, every crisis, and, despite the inevitable prophets of doom, movies are more alive, more innovative, and more marvelous than ever. No other medium can match its scope, its magnetism, or the masterful way in which it has made come alive for us every facet of human experience. What other medium has entranced and delighted us with such masterpieces as Fantasia, Snow White and the Seven Dwarfs, *and all the other amazing, lovable and astounding characters born through the prodigious genius of Walt Disney?*

And in the area of comedy, which has a special interest for me, movies have produced the greatest array of giants and peerless laughter-makers in history.

Just the mention of their names inspires awe, admiration and wonder. In addition to the comic genius of Chaplin,

Continued on next page

to George Eastman at the 1930 Awards ceremony.

With the Academy's growing involvement in research through the years, the category for Scientific or Technical Achievement was established for the 1930-31 Awards. This Award may be given in any of three classes:

> Class I— for basic achievements which influence the advancement of the industry as a whole.
>
> Class II— for high level of engineering or technical merit.
>
> Class III—for accomplishments which are valuable contributions to the progress of the industry.

The Irving G. Thalberg Memorial Award, given for consistently high quality of production and presented in the form of a bronze likeness of Thalberg's head, was first bestowed at the 1937 Awards ceremony, held March 10, 1938. The former production chief of Metro-Goldwyn-Mayer studios had died in September, 1936.

The Awards themselves are presented in several forms and, like the various rules and categories themselves, have changed through the years, only becoming somewhat standarized in the middle 1940s. Actor and actress winners have always received full-sized statuettes. Winners in the Supporting Actor and Supporting Actress divisions only began receiving statuettes at the March 2, 1944, ceremony; for the first seven years honoring that category, recipients received Academy plaques.

Initially, film editors chosen for recognition received certificates of merit (1934-1935), then Academy plaques (1936 thru 1943), then statuettes (beginning in 1944). Most of the other categories honored by the Academy have had equally varied histories in respect to the form of Award given each winner. Basically, they are given either as (a) full-size statuettes, representing a knight holding a crusader's sword and standing on a reel of film whose spokes signify the five original branches of the Academy—Actors, Writers, Directors, Producers and Technicians; (b) Academy plaques, containing a small replica of the Academy symbol, or (c) certificates of merit, or scrolls. In the technical division, Class I Award winners receive a statuette, Class II winners receive an Academy plaque and Class III winners are given a certificate of merit. Honorary Awards may be given in the form of a statuette, a scroll, a life membership or any design ordered by the Board of Governors. For several years, beginning with the 1934 Awards year, juvenile players received miniature replicas of the Academy statuette. Edgar Bergen, at the 1937 Awards year ceremony, was presented a miniature wooden

Bette Davis, Victor McLaglen

Bob Hope

statuette with a moveable mouth, in honor of his creation of Charlie McCarthy. All nominees receive certificates of nomination.

The Academy statuette was designed in 1928 by M-G-M's art director Cedric Gibbons and hasn't been altered since, except in later years when it was given a higher pedestal on which to stand. It stands thirteen and one-half inches tall, weighs eight and one-half pounds and is made of britannium and is gold plated. Since 1949, the statuettes have been numbered, starting with #501. Sculptor George Stanley received a fee of $500 to execute the original statue from Gibbons design. Sometime during the first decade, the nickname of "Oscar" was born and, at various times, three people have been credited with the abbreviation: Margaret Herrick, at the time the Academy's librarian, and later its executive director, actress Bette Davis and columnist Sidney Skolsky. The actual author isn't as clear as the fact the nickname caught on like wildfire, warmly embraced by newsmen, fans and Hollywood citizenry who were finding it increasingly cumbersome to refer to the Academy's Award of Merit as "the Academy's gold statue," "the Academy Award statuette" or, worse, "the trophy."

Under any name, the Academy Awards and the Academy itself had become prestigious parts of the film community by the end of the first decade, and the organization had been internally strengthened by growing pains and the ability to adapt in a changing world and industry. More problems were ahead, but the beginning years of the new organization had created a firm foundation on which to build. And the presentation of the Academy Awards themselves had already become an indelible part of the public's consciousness far beyond any invisible walls called Hollywood.

ACADEMY PRESIDENTS, THE FIRST DECADE

May 1927-October 1927	DOUGLAS FAIRBANKS
October 1927-October 1928	DOUGLAS FAIRBANKS
October 1928-October 1929	DOUGLAS FAIRBANKS
October 1929-October 1930	WILLIAM C. DEMILLE
October 1930-October 1931	WILLIAM C. DEMILLE
October 1931-October 1932	M.C. LEVEE
October 1931-April 1933	CONRAD NAGEL
April 1933-August 1933	J. THEODORE REED
August 1933-October 1934	J. THEODORE REED
October 1934-October 1935	FRANK LLOYD
October 1935-October 1936	FRANK CAPRA
October 1936-October 1937	FRANK CAPRA

there was Harold Lloyd—the Evel Knievel of his day. The incredibly inventive Buster Keaton, the immensely comical bumbling of Laurel and Hardy, the unforgettable 'Our Gang' kids, Ben Turpin and Harry Langdon, the comedy explosion called the Marx Brothers and so many others. More recently, the great tradition of movie comedy has been carried on by such worthy exponents of perhaps the most difficult of all the arts as Jack Lemmon, George Segal, Goldie Hawn, Walter Matthau—the endlessly resourceful and gifted Woody Allen and the incisive and brilliant Lily Tomlin.

All of them, and others too numerous to mention in one book, have brought us the great gift of laughter, which Sean O'Casey so aptly called 'wine for the soul . . . the hilarious declaration made by man that life is worth living.'

And in a world in which anxieties seem to increase with each day's newscasts, laughter is more precious than ever . . . without it, we might not have been able to survive inflation, wars, taxes, floods, droughts, and all the other problems—including reviews. In my view, laughter is a greater boon than all the 'wonder drugs' ever compounded. It is the world's most effective survival kit!

And it's reassuring to know that we'll never run out of laughs . . . they're going to televise congress!

Thankfully, movies will be around to thrill, dazzle and broaden the horizons of generations yet unborn. Because, by some indefinable alchemy, movies fill a need in our souls and psyches no other medium can equal. There never has been, nor ever will be, anything quite like them. I hasten to add, movies have even given actors the secret of eternal youth. It's called—The Late Show.

It is fitting that we pay this tribute to the movies . . . the fabulous art that has given us great drama, mystery, superb comedy that has inspired us, lifted our spirits, and brought us all those dedicated, brilliant and beautiful people. All that and popcorn, too!

I'm proud and privileged to have been a part of the magical, mystical and marvelous illusion called . . . movies.

And to all who made them possible, the wizards behind the scenes, the sorcerers on the screen, all of them, from the stars to the stand-ins, the bit players, the stuntmen and women, and those who dreamed up the lines . . . my gratitude, my admiration, and my affection. "

Bob Hope
Special Award, 1940; 1944
Honorary Award, 1952; 1965
Jean Hersholt Humanitarian Award, 1959

1927-28 The First Year

Nineteen hundred and twenty-nine was a year of transition and activity all across the United States. Herbert Hoover succeeded Calvin Coolidge as president, construction began on the Empire State Building, Knute Rockne's Notre Dame football team became the year's national champion, Wall Street had its thundering crash, and the motion picture industry began wiring for sound. In the midst of it all, on May 16, 1929 (postponed from May 9), the first Academy Awards were presented at a black-tie dinner, held in the Blossom Room of the Hollywood Roosevelt Hotel, a full three months after the winners had been announced to the press, industry and public. The dinner also marked the second anniversary of the Academy's organization, but little business was done that night beyond the presentation of the Academy's Awards of Merit and Certificates of Honorable Mention. It was a relaxed, festive "family" evening, attended by two hundred and seventy, most of them Academy members, along with guests of members who were invited to attend (at a slight charge of five dollars to their hosts).

After a dinner of Jumbo Squab Perigeaux, Lobster Eugenie, Los Angeles Salad, Clear Terrapin and Fruit Supreme, Academy President Douglas Fairbanks explained to the gathering how the Awards selections had been made: after Academy members made initial suggestions, twenty Academy-appointed judges designated official nominees and five other judges made the final decisions. Fairbanks then made the official presentations while William C. deMille called the winners to the head table. In explaining the difficulty the five final judges had in making their selections, he commented, "It is a bit like asking, 'Does this man play checkers better than that man plays chess?' "

Twelve awards were presented at this first dinner, and twenty additional certificates of honorable mention were given to runners-up in each of the Awards categories. Most of the winners were present, except Best Actor winner Emil Jannings (for *The Last Command* and *The Way of All Flesh*) who had left Hollywood for his home in Europe. Said deMille, "Mr. Jannings arrives in Berlin today; he was presented with

Best Actress: Janet Gaynor in *Seventh Heaven* (below, left; directed by Frank Borzage), *Street Angel* (below, middle; directed by Borzage) and *Sunrise* (below, right; directed by F.W. Murnau), all Fox films. New to the screen, Janet Gaynor was the Academy's first Award-winning actress, chosen on the basis of three films, all of them silent. Later, she smoothly adjusted to the coming of sound films and was again nominated in 1937, for her performance in *A Star is Born*.

Best Picture: Wings (Paramount; produced by Lucien Hubbard) was the story of World War I aviation and, specifically, two American aviators (Charles 'Buddy' Rogers and Richard Arlen) both in love with the same hometown beauty (Clara Bow). It was a silent film, directed by William A. Wellman, accompanied in many engagements by a musical score composed and synchronized by John S. Zamecnick. *Wings* was also visual, touching, great fun and the kind of red-blooded entertainment with which the motion picture industry first found its mass audience and support.

Best Actor: Emil Jannings in *The Last Command* (Paramount; directed by Josef Von Sternberg) and *The Way of All Flesh* (Paramount; directed by Victor Fleming). Jannings was born in Brooklyn but raised in Germany; at the peak of his career as a great figure in the German film industry, he went to Hollywood and stayed until the advent of talking pictures. He was not only the first actor to win an Academy Award, but the first person ever presented an Academy statuette. After being announced as a winner, he was photographed with his Award, then left for Europe and never again returned to the United States.

Nominations
1927-28

PICTURE

THE LAST COMMAND, Paramount. Produced by J.G. Bachmann, with B.P. Shilberg.

THE RACKET, Caddo, UA. Produced by Howard Hughes.

SEVENTH HEAVEN, Fox. Produced by William Fox.

THE WAY OF ALL FLESH, Paramount. Produced by Adolph Zukor and Jesse L. Lasky.

★ **WINGS**, Paramount. Produced by Lucien Hubbard.

ACTOR

RICHARD BARTHELMESS in *The Noose* (First National) and *The Patent Leather Kid* (First National).

CHARLES CHAPLIN in *The Circus* (Chaplin, UA).

★ **EMIL JANNINGS** in *The Last Command* (Paramount) and *The Way of All Flesh* (Paramount).

ACTRESS

LOUISE DRESSER in *A Ship Comes In*, Pathe-RKO Radio.

★ **JANET GAYNOR** in *Seventh Heaven* (Fox), *Street Angel* (Fox) and *Sunrise* (Fox).

GLORIA SWANSON in *Sadie Thompson* (United Artists).

DIRECTION

★ **FRANK BORZAGE** for *Seventh Heaven*, Fox.

HERBERT BRENON for *Sorrell and Son*, United Artists.

KING VIDOR for *The Crowd*, M-G-M.

(Comedy Direction)
(Note: Award not given after this year)

CHARLES CHAPLIN for *The Circus*, Chaplin, UA.

★ **LEWIS MILESTONE** for *Two Arabian Knights*, United Artists.

TED WILDE for *Speedy*, Paramount.

WRITING

(Adaptation)

GLORIOUS BETSY, Warner Bros. Anthony Coldeway.

THE JAZZ SINGER, Warner Bros. Alfred Cohn.

★ **SEVENTH HEAVEN**, Fox. Benjamin Glazer.

(Original Story)

THE LAST COMMAND, Paramount. Lajos Biro.

THE PATENT LEATHER KID, First National. Rupert Hughes.

★ **UNDERWORLD**, Paramount. Ben Hecht.

(Title Writing)
(Note: Award not given after this year)

THE PRIVATE LIFE OF HELEN OF TROY, First National. Gerald Duffy.

THE FAIR CO-ED, M-G-M. Joseph Farnham.

LAUGH, CLOWN, LAUGH, M-G-M. Joseph Farnham.

★ **TELLING THE WORLD**, M-G-M. Joseph Farnham.

OH KAY!, First National. George Marion, Jr.

CINEMATOGRAPHY

DEVIL DANCER, United Artists. George Barnes.

DRUMS OF LOVE, United Artists. Karl Struss.

MAGIC FLAME, United Artists. George Barnes.

MY BEST GIRL, Pickford, UA. Charles Rosher.

SADIE THOMPSON, United Artists. George Barnes.

★ **SUNRISE**, Fox. Charles Rosher and Karl Struss.

THE TEMPEST, United Artists. Charles Rosher.

ART DIRECTION

★ **THE DOVE**, United Artists. William Cameron Menzies.

SEVENTH HEAVEN, Fox. Harry Oliver.

SUNRISE, Fox. Rochus Gliese.

THE TEMPEST, United Artists. William Cameron Menzies.

ARTISTIC QUALITY OF PRODUCTION
(Note: Award not given after this year)

CHANG, Paramount.

THE CROWD, M-G-M.

★ **SUNRISE**, Fox.

ENGINEERING EFFECTS
(Note: Award not given after this year)

THE JAZZ SINGER, Warner Bros. Nugent Slaughter.

THE PRIVATE LIFE OF HELEN OF TROY, First National. Ralph Hammeras.

★ **WINGS**, Paramount. Roy Pomeroy.

SPECIAL AWARDS

TO WARNER BROS. for producing *The Jazz Singer*, the outstanding pioneer talking picture, which has revolutionized the industry. (statuette)

TO CHARLES CHAPLIN for versatility and genius in writing, acting, directing and producing *The Circus*. (statuette)

★ **INDICATES WINNER**

Best Comedy Direction: Lewis Milestone for *Two Arabian Knights* (United Artists) with William Boyd and Mary Astor (above). For the first and only year, the Academy distinguished between comedy direction and dramatic direction, in two separate voting categories; hereafter, they were judged as one body. Milestone won a second Academy Award two years later for his very dramatic *All Quiet on the Western Front*.

Best Dramatic Director: Frank Borzage (left, with Charles Farrell sitting in the trench) for *Seventh Heaven* (Fox). Borzage made a bona fide classic, in the best tradition of silent screen romance, with his adaptation of Austin Strong's stage play about a young Montmartre waif whose faith and loyalty brings her lover back from the World War I battlefield. The film was additionally honored for Benjamin Glazer's Writing Adaptation.

his statuette before he left, and carried it with him to Germany." (He thus became the first individual to actually receive an Academy statuette, later called an "Oscar.") All the honored films were silent ones, and *Wings* was chosen the outstanding picture of the year, Janet Gaynor was named Best Actress for her work in three films (*Seventh Heaven, Street Angel* and *Sunrise*) and the Academy, for the first and only time, gave Awards for both Dramatic Direction (presented to Frank Borzage for *Seventh Heaven*) and Comedy Direction (Lewis Milestone for *Two Arabian Knights*). Special Awards went to Warner Bros. for producing *The Jazz Singer* (accepted by Warner Bros.' executive Darryl F. Zanuck) and to Charles Chaplin for writing, producing, acting and directing *The Circus*. Said deMille, "Mr. Chaplin is not here tonight, due to cold feet, but he has wired his high appreciation of the honor."

Once the Awards were presented, there were addresses by Mary Pickford, Professor Walter R. Miles (of Stanford University), Dean Waugh (of the University of Southern California), Mrs. Edward Jacobs (of the Federated Women's Clubs), Sir Gilbert Parker, Cecil B. DeMille, and three of the original thirty-six Academy founders: Fred Niblo, Conrad Nagel and Louis B. Mayer. After that, a reel of talking film, photographed at Paramount's Long Island, New York, studios and showing Adolph Zukor visiting with Douglas Fairbanks, was shown, then Al Jolson—in person—brought the evening to a close.

Years later, Miss Gaynor recalled the evening. "Naturally, I was thrilled," she said. "But being the first year, the Academy had no background or tradition and it naturally didn't mean what it has come to mean. Had I known then what it would come to mean in the next few years, I'm sure I would have been overwhelmed. But I still remember that night as very special, a warm evening, and a room filled with important people and nice friends."

Special Award: Charles Chaplin in *The Circus*. Chaplin was very much in evidence during the Academy's first Awards year, personally nominated for acting and comedy direction and voted a Special Award by the Academy Board of Governors for "versatility and genius in writing, acting, directing and producing *The Circus*." Forty three years later, in a far different world and industry, he again received a Special Award from the Academy.

Special Award: to Warner Bros. for producing *The Jazz Singer* (right, with Al Jolson), "the pioneer outstanding talking picture which has revolutionized the industry." The film opened during the Academy's initial (and basically silent) eligibility year, August 1, 1927 to August 1, 1928; by the time the Awards were actually presented in May of 1929, sound-on-film had become a country-wide sensation, and silent films were suddenly passé.

1928-29
The Second Year

Talking pictures were firmly established as a Hollywood fact of life by the time the second Academy Awards were presented April 3, 1930, six months after the stock market crash, covering motion pictures exhibited in the Los Angeles area during the eligibility period of August 1, 1928, to July 31, 1929. Still, enough silent films were being made, or in release, to cause some confusion at the Academy office as to whether there should be separate Awards categories for silent films *and* sound films. "The development of talking pictures has made individual achievement of artists more difficult to judge," said Academy Secretary Frank Woods, adding, "Sound has brought in a new element of screen art and a host of new people." After considerable discussion, it was decided no special distinction would be made in voting between the new talking pictures and silent ones.

Once again, as in the first voting year, only five individuals made the final selection of Award winners. M-G-M's first all-talking picture, *The Broadway Melody,* was chosen Best Picture, Warner Baxter was chosen Best Actor for *In Old Arizona,* the screen's first outdoor talkie, Mary Pickford, one of the Academy founders, was named Best Actress for *Coquette,* which had been her initiation to sound films, and Frank Lloyd was named Best Director. In total, only seven Awards were given, seven less than in the previous year. All the presentations were made by the new Academy President William C. deMille, and the banquet was held, not at the Biltmore Hotel or the Hollywood Roosevelt as before, but at the splendid Cocoanut Grove of the Ambassador Hotel in Los Angeles.

For the next formative years, it was inevitable the Awards structure would undergo changes while the Academy leaders experimented with the best ways to utilize the Awards of Merit as a constructive arm of the Academy organization, and a worthwhile complement to the entire motion picture industry.

It was just as inevitable that the early years would also be inundated with "firsts." It was at the Academy banquet honoring the 1928-29 achievements that the first radio broadcast of an Academy Awards ceremony took place. A local Los Angeles radio station, KNX, did on-the-spot coverage of the festivities for one hour, beginning at 10:30 p.m. Pacific Standard Time. The annual presentation has been broadcast ever since, either on radio, or television, or both.

Best Actress: Mary Pickford as Norma Beasant (above, with Johnny Mack Brown) in *Coquette* (United Artists; directed by Sam Taylor). It was quite an event for moviegoers when Mary Pickford's voice was heard on screen for the first time; her introduction to sound also gave her an intense, adult role to play, as a small-town Southern flirt who wrecks havoc on all the men in her life.

Best Actor: Warner Baxter as The Cisco Kid in *In Old Arizona* (Fox; directed by Irving Cummings). Baxter was a last-minute replacement to play O. Henry's troubadouring bandido who robs the rich and aids the poor; Raoul Walsh had been first choice but was injured in a Utah location accident during early filming. Baxter again played the Kid in two sequels, *The Cisco Kid* (1931) and *The Return of the Cisco Kid* (1939).

Nominations 1928-29

PICTURE

ALIBI, Feature Productions, UA. Produced by Roland West.

★ THE BROADWAY MELODY, M-G-M. Produced by Harry Rapf.

THE HOLLYWOOD REVUE, M-G-M. Produced by Harry Rapf.

IN OLD ARIZONA, Fox. Winfield Sheehan, studio head.

THE PATRIOT, Paramount. Produced by Ernst Lubitsch.

ACTOR

GEORGE BANCROFT in *Thunderbolt*, Paramount.

★ WARNER BAXTER in *In Old Arizona*, Fox.

CHESTER MORRIS in *Alibi*, Feature Productions, UA.

PAUL MUNI in *The Valiant*, Fox.

LEWIS STONE in *The Patriot*, Paramount.

ACTRESS

RUTH CHATTERTON in *Madame X*, M-G-M.

BETTY COMPSON in *The Barker*, First National.

JEANNE EAGELS in *The Letter*, Paramount.

BESSIE LOVE in *The Broadway Melody*, M-G-M.

★ MARY PICKFORD in *Coquette*, Pickford, UA.

DIRECTION

LIONEL BARRYMORE for *Madame X*, M-G-M.

HARRY BEAUMONT for *Broadway Melody*, M-G-M.

IRVING CUMMINGS for *In Old Arizona*, Fox.

★ FRANK LLOYD for *The Divine Lady* (First National), *Weary River* (First National) and *Drag* (First National)

ERNST LUBITSCH for *The Patriot*, Paramount.

WRITING

(Achievement)

IN OLD ARIZONA, Fox. Tom Barry.

THE LEATHERNECK, Pathe. Elliott Clawson.

OUR DANCING DAUGHTERS, M-G-M. Josephine Lovett.

★ THE PATRIOT, Paramount. Hans Kraly.

THE VALIANT, Fox. Tom Barry.

WONDER OF WOMEN, M-G-M. Bess Meredyth.

CINEMATOGRAPHY

THE DIVINE LADY, First National. John Seitz.

FOUR DEVILS, Fox. Ernest Palmer.

IN OLD ARIZONA, Fox. Arthur Edeson.

OUR DANCING DAUGHTERS, M-G-M. George Barnes.

STREET ANGEL, Fox. Ernest Palmer.

★ WHITE SHADOWS IN THE SOUTH SEAS, M-G-M. Clyde De Vinna.

ART DIRECTION

★ THE BRIDGE OF SAN LUIS REY, M-G-M. Cedric Gibbons.

DYNAMITE, Pathe. Mitchell Leisen.

HOLLYWOOD REVUE, M-G-M. Cedric Gibbons.

THE IRON MASK, United Artists. William Cameron Menzies.

THE PATRIOT, Paramount. Hans Dreier.

STREET ANGEL, Fox. Harry Oliver.

SPECIAL AWARDS

None given this year.

★ INDICATES WINNER

Best Director: Frank Lloyd (at right, sitting in lower chair with Corrine Griffith on the set of *The Divine Lady*) for three films: *The Divine Lady* with Miss Griffith and Marie Dressler, *Drag* with Richard Barthelmess and *Weary River* with Barthelmess and Betty Compson. Lloyd was again an Academy Award winner in 1932-33 for *Cavalcade,* and served one term as Academy President, in 1934-35.

Best Picture: The Broadway Melody (M-G-M; produced by Harry Rapf) starred (left) Bessie Love, Charles King and Anita Page, and was the first sound film to win the Academy's Best Picture statuette. The story was conventional by later yardsticks (two sisters, working in vaudeville, both fall in love with a successful Broadway song-and-dance man) but was particularly impressive in its day, surrounded by the novelty of sound on film. It contained a big "Wedding of the Painted Doll" musical sequence in color hues, and prompted M-G-M to produce three more musicals with the *Broadway Melody* label during the next ten years, all of them starring Eleanor Powell.

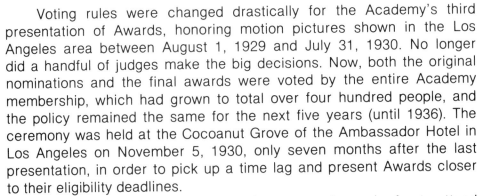

1929-30
The Third Year

Voting rules were changed drastically for the Academy's third presentation of Awards, honoring motion pictures shown in the Los Angeles area between August 1, 1929 and July 31, 1930. No longer did a handful of judges make the big decisions. Now, both the original nominations and the final awards were voted by the entire Academy membership, which had grown to total over four hundred people, and the policy remained the same for the next five years (until 1936). The ceremony was held at the Cocoanut Grove of the Ambassador Hotel in Los Angeles on November 5, 1930, only seven months after the last presentation, in order to pick up a time lag and present Awards closer to their eligibility deadlines.

Academy members, for the first time, were charged a fee to attend the banquet (ten dollars per person) and it was a complete sellout. Guests listened to a pre-dinner address by Will H. Hays, president of the Motion Picture Producers and Distributors Organization, and a post-dinner talk by Thomas A. Edison. Edison and George Eastman were both given honorary Academy memberships for their pioneering in the film medium. Academy Vice President Conrad Nagel presided over the evening and Awards were presented by Louis B. Mayer, Lawrence Grant and John Cromwell. Eight Awards were given, and it was the last year so few would be dispersed.

All Quiet on the Western Front and *The Big House* were the most honored films, with two Awards each. *All Quiet* was named as Best Picture, and for its director Lewis Milestone; *The Big House* was honored for Frances Marion's writing achievement and in a new category, Sound Recording, won by Norma Shearer's brother, Douglas Shearer. Norma Shearer was named Best Actress, officially for *The Divorcee,* and George Arliss was chosen Best Actor for *Disraeli.* The Arliss win marked another Academy "first:" it was the first time a performer was honored by Academy voters for re-creating a role on screen which he or she had performed previously on the legitimate stage. Other Awards went to *With Byrd at the South Pole* for its cinematography and *King of Jazz* for its art direction.

Sound on film now fully dominated the industry; the transitional period from the silent era was over. Interestingly, talking pictures had severely curbed the careers of several silent screen stars, but others were enhanced by the spoken word, and flourished, a fact underscored by the 1929-30 Awards. Three of the year's nominees—Ronald Colman, Greta Garbo and Gloria Swanson—were stars who had bridged the gap successfully and were honored for performances in their initial sound films.

Best Actor: George Arliss as Benjamin Disraeli (above, with Joan Bennett) in *Disraeli* (Warner Bros.; directed by Alfred E. Green). Arliss was a successful stage actor who popularly became known as the First Gentleman of the Talking Screen, and he was also the screen's dean of biography. He played *Disraeli* in the legitimate theater for five years before it became an early sound feature; predominently set at No. 10 Downing Street in London, it covered the political manipulations of Prime Minister Disraeli to acquire the Suez Canal for England and Queen Victoria by outwitting Russia, concentrated on characterization and ideas rather than action.

Best Picture: All Quiet on the Western Front
(Universal; produced by Carl Laemmle, Jr.)
and **Best Director: Lewis Milestone**
for *All Quiet on the Western Front.* Erich
Maria Remarque's savage anti-war novel
traced the steps of seven German
schoolboys of 1914 as they come to face
fear, filth, death and other horrors
of battle during four years of World War I
combat, a daring subject for the screen and
dubious commercial material for
audiences concerned with a national
Depression. But it was an enormous
success, skillfully made, won Academy
Awards for producer Laemmle and director
Milestone, and gave stimulus to the
careers of its cast, including (above)
Lew Ayres and Louis Wolheim.

PICTURE

★ **ALL QUIET ON THE WESTERN FRONT,**
Universal. Produced by Carl
Laemmle, Jr.
THE BIG HOUSE, M-G-M. Produced by
Irving G. Thalberg.
DISRAELI, Warner Bros. Produced by
Jack L. Warner, with Darryl F. Zanuck.
THE DIVORCEE, M-G-M. Produced by
Robert Z. Leonard.
THE LOVE PARADE, Paramount.
Produced by Ernst Lubitsch.

ACTOR

† ★ **GEORGE ARLISS** in *Disreali* (Warner
Bros.) and *The Green Goddess*
(Warner Bros.)
WALLACE BEERY in *The Big House*
(M-G-M).
MAURICE CHEVALIER in *The Love
Parade* (Paramount) and *The Big
Pond* (Paramount).
RONALD COLMAN in *Bulldog
Drummond* (Goldwyn, UA) and
Condemned (Goldwyn, UA).
LAWRENCE TIBBETT in *The Rogue
Song* (M-G-M).
†*Note: On the official Academy ballot
for 1929-30, Mr. Arliss was given a
single nomination involving two
achievements, as listed; however,
he is officially credited as having
won his Academy Award only for
the first-named film, Disraeli.*

ACTRESS

NANCY CARROLL in *The Devil's
Holiday* (Paramount).
RUTH CHATTERTON in *Sarah and Son*
(Paramount).
GRETA GARBO in *Anna Christie*
(M-G-M) and *Romance* (M-G-M).
† ★ **NORMA SHEARER** in *The Divorcee*
(M-G-M) and *Their Own Desire*
(M-G-M).
GLORIA SWANSON in *The Trespasser*
(Kennedy, UA).
†*Note: On the official Academy ballot
for 1929-30, Miss Shearer was given
a single nomination involving the
two achievements as listed;
however, she is officially credited
as having won her Academy Award
only for the first-named film,
The Divorcee.*

DIRECTION

CLARENCE BROWN for *Anna Christie*
(M-G-M) and *Romance* (M-G-M).
ROBERT LEONARD for *The Divorcee*
(M-G-M).
ERNST LUBITSCH for *The Love Parade*
(Paramount).

★ **LEWIS MILESTONE** for *All Quiet on the
Western Front,* Universal.
KING VIDOR, for *Hallelujah,* M-G-M.

WRITING

(Achievement)
ALL QUIET ON THE WESTERN FRONT,
Universal. George Abbott, Maxwell
Anderson and Dell Andrews.
★ **THE BIG HOUSE,** M-G-M. Frances
Marion.
DISRAELI, Warner Bros. Julian
Josephson.
THE DIVORCEE, M-G-M. John Meehan.
STREET OF CHANCE, Paramount.
Howard Estabrook.

CINEMATOGRAPHY

ALL QUIET ON THE WESTERN FRONT,
Universal. Arthur Edeson.
ANNA CHRISTIE, M-G-M. William
Daniels.
HELL'S ANGELS, United Artists.
Gaetano Gaudio and Harry Perry.
THE LOVE PARADE, Paramount. Victor
Milner.
★ **WITH BYRD AT THE SOUTH POLE,**
Paramount. Joseph T. Rucker and
Willard Van Der Veer.

ART DIRECTION

BULLDOG DRUMMOND, Goldwyn, UA.
William Cameron Menzies.
★ **KING OF JAZZ,** Universal. Herman
Rosse.
THE LOVE PARADE, Paramount. Hans
Dreier.
SALLY, First National. Jack Okey.
THE VAGABOND KING, Paramount.
Hans Dreier.

SOUND RECORDING

(New category)
★ **THE BIG HOUSE,** M-G-M. Douglas
Shearer.
THE CASE OF SERGEANT GRISCHA,
RKO Radio. John Tribby.
THE LOVE PARADE, Paramount. Frank-
lin Hansen.
RAFFLES, Goldwyn, UA. Oscar
Lagerstrom.
SONG OF THE FLAME, First National.
George Groves.

SPECIAL AWARDS

None given this year.

★ INDICATES WINNER

Best Actress: Norma Shearer as Jerry (left,
with Conrad Nagel) in *The Divorcee*
(M-G-M; directed by Robert Leonard).
The official Academy voting ballot for
1929-30 lists Miss Shearer with a single
nomination encompassing two
achievements (*The Divorcee* and *Their Own
Desire*) but her Award was officially
presented solely for the first-named film, in
which she played a free-spirited woman
involved with a broken marriage and her
ex-husband's best friend. How, or why, the
single designation was made is now a
mystery to everyone, including Academy
researchers and Miss Shearer herself. But
the following year, a 1931 rule change
stated that in the future "no performer shall
be entitled to more than one nomination,
with the achievement polling the highest
vote to be listed in case the individual may
have received enough votes for different
achievements to be entitled to more
than one nomination."

Best Actor: Lionel Barrymore as Stephen Ashe (above, with Norma Shearer) in *A Free Soul* (M-G-M; directed by Clarence Brown). They didn't make actors any better, or better liked, than Lionel Barrymore, and he always claimed *A Free Soul* was his favorite screen role. In it, he played a heavy-drinking, free-thinking criminal lawyer whose unconventional behavior is adopted by his spoiled daughter; at the finale, he delivered a courtroom soliloquy that was considered a high mark in screen acting for the period. Earlier, Barrymore was nominated for a 1928-29 Academy Award as Best Director of *Madame X,* starring Ruth Chatterton.

Best Director: Norman Taurog for *Skippy* (Paramount), adapted from Percy Crosby's widely read comic strip of the day. Jackie Cooper was Skippy and Robert Coogan played Sooky (above), a couple of kids endeavoring to acquire enough money to buy Sooky's mongrel dog back from the local dogcatcher, to no avail. Taurog, Cooper and Coogan reteamed later in 1931 for a sequel, *Sooky,* and Taurog was again nominated in 1938 for his direction of *Boys Town.*

1930-31
The Fourth Year

The Academy had gained a solid, national reputation by its fifth anniversary, at the same time the fourth year of presenting Awards for screen achievement. From Washington, D.C., President Herbert Hoover sent Vice President Charles Curtis to attend the 1930-31 Awards banquet, held November 10, 1931, at the Biltmore Hotel in Los Angeles. Curtis, attending with his socially prominent sister Mrs. Dolly Gann, told the Academy members and guests, "I have come to you tonight from the capital of our country to pay my respects to the creative minds of the world's greatest and most influential enterprise, the motion picture." Movies had been a great morale booster during the year, which had been one of massive unemployment and a nationwide Depression. The Academy had also solidified its public image by establishing an extensive library dealing solely with motion pictures, helping inaugurate college film courses, organizing lectures on mechanical innovations and other activities.

Lawrence Grant was the master of ceremonies and speakers joining Vice President Curtis included new Academy President M.C. Levee, past President William C. deMille, Louis B. Mayer, Conrad Nagel and California Governor James Rolph, Jr.; non-member guests included eastern film executives and visiting journalists from all over the United States, the first time the nation's news media paid rapt attention to an Academy Awards function. It was carried on a local radio station (KHJ) plus the entire Don Lee-Columbia radio network on the Pacific Coast.

Cimarron received three Awards: for Best Picture, Writing Adaptation and Art Direction. Norman Taurog was named Best Director for *Skippy.* Lionel Barrymore was saluted as Best Actor for *A Free Soul,* and Marie Dressler won the Best Actress statuette for *Min and Bill.* Norma Shearer, the previous year's Best Actress winner, was asked to present the latter award and did so. Later, the program planners realized she inadvertently could have been placed in the embarrassing position of announcing herself as the winner, since she was again a nominee. Since that night, there has been an unwritten rule that previous *Actress* honorees would present awards to winning *Actors,* and vice versa. Also, the outcome of the balloting had always been disclosed a week or more in advance of the actual presentation; this year, Academy officials took extra precautions to keep the results of voting a secret, not giving names of winners to the press until late in the day of the Awards.

One of the nominees drew attention when he fell asleep during the festivities. As the speeches wore on, ten-year-old Jackie Cooper, nominated as Best Actor for *Skippy,* snoozed with his head resting on the ample shoulder of Marie Dressler. When she was called to receive her Award, young Cooper, still sleeping, had to be eased onto his mother's lap.

Best Actress: Marie Dressler as Min (left, with Wallace Beery) in *Min and Bill* (M-G-M; directed by George Hill. She had a bulky figure, unforgettable face and enormous talent, and in *Min and Bill* Marie Dressler walked the treacherous line between comedy and pathos with enormous distinction. As Min, she was a good-hearted old boozer who runs a broken-down waterfront hotel, works hard, constantly battles with a hulking beau (Beery), raises a foundling and ultimately gets led off to jail for killing the foundling's wayward mother. She was again nominated in 1931-32 for her performance in *Emma*.

Best Picture: Cimarron (RKO Radio; produced by William LeBaron) covered the rise of Oklahoma from early pioneer days to statehood, based on Edna Ferber's sweeping novel. Richard Dix (below, with Irene Dunne) was a homesteader in the great Oklahoma landrush of 1888 who lost his claim, became a newspaper editor and during the next four decades helped turn the overnight camp of Osage into a respectable town. *Cimarron* also won Academy Awards for Writing Adaptation (by Howard Estabrook) and Art Direction (by Max Ree) and is the only motion picture with a distinctly western flavor to have won a Best Picture Award during the Academy's first fifty years.

Nominations

1930-31

PICTURE

★ **CIMARRON**, RKO Radio. Produced by William LaBaron.
EAST LYNNE, Fox. Winfield Sheehan, studio head.
THE FRONT PAGE, Cado, UA. Produced by Howard Hughes.
SKIPPY, Paramount. Adolph Zukor, studio head.
TRADER HORN, M-G-M. Produced by Irving G. Thalberg.

ACTOR

★ **LIONEL BARRYMORE** in *A Free Soul*, M-G-M.
JACKIE COOPER in *Skippy*, Paramount.
RICHARD DIX in *Cimarron*, RKO Radio.
FREDRIC MARCH in *The Royal Family of Broadway*, Paramount.
ADOLPHE MENJOU in *The Front Page*, Caddo, UA.

ACTRESS

MARLENE DIETRICH in *Morocco*, Paramount.
★ **MARIE DRESSLER** in *Min and Bill*, M-G-M.
IRENE DUNNE in *Cimarron*, RKO Radio.
ANN HARDING in *Holiday*, RKO Pathe.
NORMA SHEARER in *A Free Soul*, M-G-M.

DIRECTION

CLARENCE BROWN for *A Free Soul*, M-G-M.
LEWIS MILESTONE for *The Front Page*, Caddo, UA.
WESLEY RUGGLES for *Cimarron*, RKO Radio.
★ **NORMAN TAUROG** for *Skippy*, Paramount.
JOSEF VON STERNBERG for *Morocco*, Paramount.

WRITING

(Adaptation)
★ **CIMARRON**, RKO Radio. Howard Estabrook.
THE CRIMINAL CODE, Columbia. Seton Miller and Fred Niblo, Jr.
HOLIDAY, RKO Pathe. Horace Jackson.
LITTLE CAESAR, Warner Bros. Francis Faragoh and Robert N. Lee.
SKIPPY, Paramount. Joseph Mankiewicz and Sam Mintz.

(Original Story)
★ **THE DAWN PATROL**, Warner Bros., First National. John Monk Saunders.
DOORWAY TO HELL, Warner Bros.-First National. Rowland Brown.

LAUGHTER, Paramount. Harry d'Abbadie d'Arrast, Douglas Doty and Donald Ogden Stewart.
THE PUBLIC ENEMY, Warner Bros.-First National. John Bright and Kubec Glasmon.
SMART MONEY, Warner Bros.-First National. Lucien Hubbard and Joseph Jackson.

CINEMATOGRAPHY

CIMARRON, RKO Radio. Edward Cronjager.
MOROCCO, Paramount. Lee Garmes.
THE RIGHT TO LOVE, Paramount. Charles Lang.
SVENGALI, Warner Bros.-First National. Barney ''Chick'' McGill.
★ **TABU**, Paramount. Floyd Crosby.

ART DIRECTION

★ **CIMARRON**, RKO Radio. Max Ree.
JUST IMAGINE, Fox. Stephen Goosson and Ralph Hammeras.
MOROCCO, Paramount. Hans Dreier.
SVENGALI, Warner Bros.-First National. Anton Grot.
WHOOPEE, Goldwyn, UA. Richard Day.

SOUND RECORDING

M-G-M STUDIO SOUND DEPT.
★ **PARAMOUNT STUDIO SOUND DEPT.**
RKO RADIO STUDIO SOUND DEPT.
SAMUEL GOLDWYN SOUND DEPT.

SPECIAL AWARD

None given this year.

SCIENTIFIC OR TECHNICAL

(New category)

CLASS I (statuette)
ELECTRICAL RESEARCH PRODUCTS, INC., RCA-PHOTOPHONE, INC., and **RKO RADIO PICTURES, INC.,** for noise reduction recording equipment.
DuPONT FILM MANUFACTURING CORP. and **EASTMAN KODAK CO.** for super-sensitive panchromatic film.

CLASS II (plaque)
FOX FILM CORP. for effective use of synchro-projection composite photography.

CLASS III (citation)
ELECTRICAL RESEARCH PRODUCTS, INC.;
RKO RADIO PICTURES, INC.;
RCA-PHOTOPHONE, INC.

★ **INDICATES WINNER**

Best Actress: Helen Hayes as Madelon (above, with Neil Hamilton) in *The Sin of Madelon Claudet* (M-G-M; directed by Edgar Selwyn). Helen Hayes had made a few film appearances as a juvenile during the movies' silent era, but *The Sin of Madelon Claudet* was her much-heralded introduction to screen audiences after she'd made a notable success as a Broadway star. It was also a tear-jerker of the dampest sort, based on Edward Knoblock's play *The Lullaby,* about a young Parisian girl who falls in love with an American artist, bears an illegitimate child, then goes from mistress to party girl to barfly to street-walker to scrubwoman, in an effort to raise money so her unsuspecting son can have a good life. Audiences in 1931 reveled in it, and in Miss Hayes' rich performance. She was again an Academy Award winner 38 years later, as 1970's Best Supporting Actress in *Airport.*

1931-32 The Fifth Year

A tie occurred for the first time at the 1931-32 Awards ceremony, honoring films released between August 1, 1931 and July 31, 1932 in the Los Angeles area. Academy rules stated that duplicate Awards were to be given when any contender came within three votes of a winner on the final ballot, and Wallace Beery, for his performance in *The Champ,* received only one less vote than Fredric March who starred in *Dr. Jekyll and Mr. Hyde,* so both officially shared recognition as the year's Best Actor. Later, rules were changed so that a tie is declared only when nominees receive the *exact* same number of final votes.

The banquet was held November 18, 1932, in the Ambassador Hotel's Cocoanut Grove, just eight days after Franklin D. Roosevelt's election as the thirty-second President of the United States in a landslide victory. The previous year's Best Actor winner, Lionel Barrymore, was master of ceremonies, and the most-honored films were *The Champ* and *Bad Girl* with two Awards each. *Grand Hotel* was named Best Picture, Helen Hayes was Best Actress for *The Sin of Madelon Claudet,* and Frank Borzage won his second Award as Director, for *Bad Girl.* The Awards categories themselves had increased to a total of ten, with the addition of a new division honoring short subjects and won by Walt Disney for his cartoon *Flowers and Trees.* Disney also was given an Honorary Award for his creation of Mickey Mouse and, during the next five decades, was destined to win more Academy Awards than any other individual.

The year caused two particularly interesting happenings. The Academy, attempting to stimulate excellence in motion picture achievements from all countries and all sources, had previously welcomed non-Hollywood product in its Awards lists. However, some voters had been disturbed that the preceding year *Tabu,* filmed in the South Seas by the late German director F.W. Murnau, had received the Academy's Cinematography Award, over a home-town achievement, so the Academy was asked to qualify the requirements for its 1931-32 Cinematography Award to read, ''for the best achievement in cinematography of a black-and-white picture photographed in America under normal production conditions.'' The 1931-32 nomination for the French-made *A Nous la Liberté* in the Art Direction category caused a similar qualification in 1932-33. In later years, however, as industry sentiments matured, the Academy again showed its respect for foreign-made films by according them equal status with domestic product.

The Fredric March-Wallace Beery tie also triggered the first of many ''quotable quotes'' given by Academy winners throughout the years. By coincidence, both actors had adopted children shortly before winning their Awards. ''It seems a little odd,'' said Mr. March during his acceptance speech, ''that Wally and I were both given Awards for the best male performance of the year.''

Best Actor: Fredric March as Henry Jekyll and as Mr. Hyde (left) in *Dr. Jekyll and Mr. Hyde* (Paramount; directed by Rouben Mamoulian). Many distinguished actors have had a field day playing the two-faced doctor created by Robert Louis Stevenson in his fascinating tale of a man who dreams of releasing the evil desires in every man's subconscious. James Cruze, Sheldon Lewis, John Barrymore, Spencer Tracy and Paul Massie are among those who have had a go at it on screen; none, however, has been more successful than Fredric March in the first sound version of the horror story. Virtually unrecognizable as the alter-ego Hyde, wearing false teeth, putty nose, gorilla hands and makeup which took three hours to apply, March won the Academy Award for his performance. He won again in 1946 for *The Best Years of Our Lives* and received five Award nominations during his lifetime.

Best Actor: Wallace Beery as Champ (below, with Jackie Cooper) in *The Champ* (M-G-M; directed by King Vidor) Beery once said, "I have no art in my soul, I don't try to be different. I'm just plain me in every picture and the public continues to accept me." However, Beery was seen in two widely divergent roles during the 1931-32 Awards year, as the crooked industrialist in *Grand Hotel* and as a drunken, ex-champion prizefighter in *The Champ*, and showed his enormous power as an actor in both. When Academy Award votes were counted, Beery's performance in the latter film had come within one vote of Fredric March in *Dr. Jekyll and Mr. Hyde*, so under Academy rules of the day, both officially shared honors and received statuettes as the year's Best Actor.

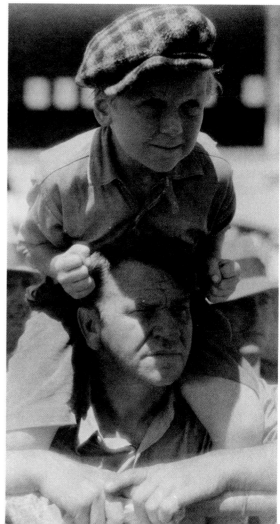

Transatlantic (Fox) took place on an elegant transatlantic steamer, stern to bow, all meticulously recreated on the Fox studio lot. It starred Edmund Lowe (above) with Jean Hersholt, John Halliday, Myrna Loy and others, and won for the Art Direction of Gordon Wiles.

(left) **Best Picture: Grand Hotel** (M-G-M; produced by Irving Thalberg) created a new screen formula in which all-star casts and unrelated characters were brought together in a common and dramatic environment. In the case of *Grand Hotel,* it was a plush Berlin hotel during a 48-hour period, based on a Vicki Baum novel and subsequent play which had been financed by M-G-M. Edmund Goulding directed the film and the cast included Greta Garbo, John Barrymore, Joan Crawford, Wallace Beery and Lionel Barrymore, each of whom usually was the solo star of his or her own Metro film. It was later updated as *Week-end at the Waldorf* in 1945, and remade in Germany as *Menschen Im Hotel* in 1960.

Nominations
1931-32

PICTURE

ARROWSMITH, Goldwyn, UA. Produced by Samuel Goldwyn.
BAD GIRL, Fox. Winfield Sheehan, studio head.
THE CHAMP, M-G-M. Produced by King Vidor.
FIVE STAR FINAL, First National. Produced by Hal B. Wallis.
* GRAND HOTEL, M-G-M. Produced by Irving Thalberg.
ONE HOUR WITH YOU, Paramount. Produced by Ernst Lubitsch.
SHANGHAI EXPRESS, Paramount. Adolph Zukor, studio head.
THE SMILING LIEUTENANT, Paramount. Produced by Ernst Lubitsch.

ACTOR

* WALLACE BEERY in *The Champ*, M-G-M.
ALFRED LUNT in *The Guardsman*, M-G-M.
* FREDRIC MARCH in *Dr. Jekyll and Mr. Hyde*, Paramount.

ACTRESS

MARIE DRESSLER in *Emma*, M-G-M.
LYNN FONTANNE in *The Guardsman*, M-G-M.
* HELEN HAYES in *The Sin of Madelon Claudet*, M-G-M.

DIRECTION

* FRANK BORZAGE for *Bad Girl*, Fox.
KING VIDOR for *The Champ, M-G-M.*
JOSEF VON STERNBERG for *Shanghai Express*, Paramount.

WRITING

(Adaptation)
ARROWSMITH, Goldwyn, UA. Sidney Howard.
* BAD GIRL, Fox. Edwin Burke.
DR. JEKYLL AND MR. HYDE, Paramount. Percy Heath and Samuel Hoffenstein.

(Original Story)
* THE CHAMP, M-G-M. Frances Marion.
LADY AND GENT, Paramount. Grover Jones and William Slavens McNutt.
STAR WITNESS, Warner Bros. Lucien Hubbard.
WHAT PRICE HOLLYWOOD, RKO Radio. Adela Rogers St. John.

CINEMATOGRAPHY

ARROWSMITH, Goldwyn, UA. Ray June.
DR. JEKYLL AND MR. HYDE, Paramount. Karl Struss.
* SHANGHAI EXPRESS, Paramount. Lee Garmes.

ART DIRECTION

A NOUS LA LIBERTE (French). Lazare Meerson.
ARROWSMITH, Goldwyn, UA. Richard Day.
* TRANSATLANTIC, Fox. Gordon Wiles.

SOUND RECORDING

PARAMOUNT STUDIO SOUND DEPT.

SHORT SUBJECTS

(New category)

(Cartoons)
* FLOWERS AND TREES, Disney, UA.
MICKEY'S ORPHANS, Disney, Columbia.
IT'S GOT ME AGAIN, Schlesinger, Warner Bros.

(Comedy)
THE LOUD MOUTH, Mack Sennett.
* THE MUSIC BOX, Roach, M-G-M. (Laurel & Hardy)
STOUT HEARTS AND WILLING HANDS, RKO Radio. (Masquers Comedies)

(Novelty)
SCREEN SOUVENIRS, Paramount.
SWING HIGH, M-G-M. (Sport Champion)
* WRESTLING SWORDFISH, Mack Sennett, Educational. (Cannibals Of The Deep)

SPECIAL AWARD

TO WALT DISNEY for the creation of Mickey Mouse. (statuette)

SCIENTIFIC OR TECHNICAL

CLASS I (statuette)
None.

CLASS II (plaque)
TECHNICOLOR MOTION PICTURE CORP. for their color cartoon process.

CLASS III (citation)
EASTMAN KODAK CO.

* INDICATES WINNER

Shanghai Express (Paramount), starred Marlene Dietrich and Clive Brook (above) as two passengers on a train journey to Shanghai, amid rebel unrest in China, sharing secrets and staterooms with the likes of Anna May Wong, Warner Oland, Eugene Pallette and others. It won an Academy Award for Lee Garmes' atmospheric cinematography; Garmes had also photographed Miss Dietrich's two previous American-made films, *Morocco* and *Dishonored.*

Best Director: Frank Borzage for *Bad Girl* (Fox) starring James Dunn and Sally Eilers (left). Strangely mistitled, *Bad Girl* covered a year in the life of a likable fellow and girl, from their first meeting, through marriage, to the birth of a son, set against a background of New York tenement life. Borzage, a specialist in directing effective, sentimental stories, had earlier won the Academy Award for his direction of *Seventh Heaven* during the first Awards year.

1932-33 The Sixth Year

Some befuddled confusion accompanied the 1932-33 Academy party, the type of unrehearsed fun which has added to the folklore of Hollywood's annual Awards night. Will Rogers, already a legendary humorist and sometime actor, was host and, in presenting the Award for Director of the year, drawled on at length about "my good friend Frank," and "Frank's rise to prominence," finally finishing his introduction by commanding, "Come and get it, Frank." Nominee Frank Capra was out of his seat and halfway to the podium when he realized another nominee, Frank Lloyd for *Cavalcade,* was the actual winner. Capra later returned to his seat from what he later described good-naturedly as "the longest crawl in history." During the festivities, host Rogers also invited Actress nominees May Robson and Diana Wynyard to the speakers' table, leading many people to anticipate there had been a tie; Rogers kissed them both, told them they had delivered "sparkling performances," and announced the absent Katharine Hepburn as the winner, for *Morning Glory.*

During the evening, March 16, 1934, in the Cocoanut Grove of the Ambassador Hotel, fourteen Awards categories were honored, including a new one for Assistant Directors. *Cavalcade,* with its trio of Awards, including Best Picture, won the most honors from Academy voting. Charles Laughton was named Best Actor for *The Private Life of Henry VIII,* the first time a performer in a British-made film had been an Academy Award winner. Also, second and third place runners-up in all categories were announced, a practice later discontinued shortly after the certified public accounting firm of Price Waterhouse & Co. began tabulating ballots for the Academy. *Cavalcade* was followed by *A Farewell to Arms,* then *Little Women,* in number of votes as the Best Picture; Paul Muni and May Robson were first runners-up for acting Awards, and Leslie Howard and Diana Wynyard were second runners-up. Frank Capra was the second choice for Director, and George Cukor was third choice.

For the first and only time, more than a twelve-month span was used as the Awards eligibility period; instead, the 1932-33 Awards covered seventeen months, from August 1, 1932, to December 31, 1933, in order to allow future Academy Awards to be based on a calendar year, rather than a seasonal one. The Awards have remained on a calendar basis ever since.

Best Actor: Charles Laughton as King Henry (above) in *The Private Life of Henry VIII* (United Artists; directed in England by Alexander Korda). Laughton's performance was the first in a non-Hollywood film to win the Academy Award, and a vastly good-natured portrait of England's bulky monarch (1491-1547) whose six marriages complicated the future reigns of his country and brought about the independence of the Church of England. Laughton played it with flamboyant spice and among his most memorable moments was a scene when he dined a la Henry, ripping a chicken apart with his hands, devouring the food, belching and generally having a grand gastronomical time.

Best Actress: Katharine Hepburn as Eva Lovelace (left, with C. Aubrey Smith) in *Morning Glory* (RKO Radio; directed by Lowell Sherman). A year after her striking screen debut in *Morning Glory,* and concurrent with another 1933 success, *Little Women,* Miss Hepburn played a stage-struck young actress, self-confident, talkative and ambitiously determined to become 'the finest actress in the world,' with Adolphe Menjou and Douglas Fairbanks, Jr. as two important men in her private-public life.

Best Picture: Calvalcade (Fox Film Corporation) and **Best Director: Frank Lloyd** for *Calvalcade.* Based on the play by Noel Coward, with a screenplay by Reginald Berkeley, *Cavalcade* was a sweeping, episodic composition with a British flavor and British cast, but filmed in Hollywood. It told of the effect of world events on the home life and family of a married couple (Diane Wynyard and Clive Brook, below) during the decades between New Year's Eve 1899 and the same evening 33 years later, a patriotic pageant with a universal theme and appeal for families of any country. William S. Darling was also honored for his Art Direction.

Little Women (RKO Radio; produced by Merian C. Cooper, with Kenneth MacGowan) was Louisa May Alcott wrapped up in the persona of (above) Joan Bennett as Amy, Spring Byington as Marmee, Frances Dee as Meg, Jean Parker (at piano) as Beth and Katharine Hepburn as Jo. It won for the writing adaptation of Miss Alcott's popular novel by screenwriters Victor Heerman and Sarah Y. Mason. George Cukor directed.

Nominations 1932-33

PICTURE

★ **CAVALCADE**, Fox. Winfield Sheehan, studio head.
A FAREWELL TO ARMS, Paramount. Adolph Zukor, studio head.
42nd STREET, Warner Bros. Produced by Darryl F. Zanuck.
I AM A FUGITIVE FROM A CHAIN GANG, Warner Bros. Produced by Hal B. Wallis.
LADY FOR A DAY, Columbia. Produced by Frank Capra.
LITTLE WOMEN, RKO Radio. Produced by Merian C. Cooper, with Kenneth MacGowan.
THE PRIVATE LIFE OF HENRY VIII, London Films, UA (British). Produced by Alexander Korda.
SHE DONE HIM WRONG, Paramount. Produced by William Le Baron.
SMILIN' THRU, M-G-M. Produced by Irving Thalberg.
STATE FAIR, Fox. Winfield Sheehan, studio head.

ACTOR

LESLIE HOWARD in *Berkeley Square*, Fox.
★ **CHARLES LAUGHTON** in *The Private Life of Henry VIII*, London Films, UA (British).
PAUL MUNI in *I Am a Fugitive from a Chain Gang*, Warner Bros.

ACTRESS

★ **KATHARINE HEPBURN** in *Morning Glory*, RKO Radio.

MAY ROBSON in *Lady for a Day*, Columbia.
DIANA WYNYARD in *Cavalcade*, Fox.

DIRECTION

FRANK CAPRA in *Lady for a Day*, Columbia.
GEORGE CUKOR for *Little Women*, RKO Radio.
★ **FRANK LLOYD** for *Cavalcade*, Fox.

WRITING

(Adaptation)
LADY FOR A DAY, Columbia. Robert Riskin.
★ **LITTLE WOMEN**, RKO Radio. Victor Heerman and Sarah Y. Mason.
STATE FAIR, Fox. Paul Green and Sonya Levien.

(Original Story)
★ **ONE WAY PASSAGE**, Warner Bros. Robert Lord.
THE PRIZEFIGHTER AND THE LADY, M-G-M. Frances Marion.
RASPUTIN AND THE EMPRESS, M-G-M. Charles MacArthur.

CINEMATOGRAPHY

★ **A FAREWELL TO ARMS**, Paramount. Charles Bryant Lang, Jr.
REUNION IN VIENNA, M-G-M. George J. Folsey, Jr.
THE SIGN OF THE CROSS, Paramount. Karl Struss.

ART DIRECTION

★ **CAVALCADE**, Fox. William S. Darling.
A FAREWELL TO ARMS, Paramount. Hans Dreier and Roland Anderson.
WHEN LADIES MEET, M-G-M. Cedric Gibbons.

SOUND RECORDING

★ **A FAREWELL TO ARMS**, Paramount, Harold C. Lewis.
FORTY-SECOND STREET, Warner Bros. Nathan Levinson.
GOLDDIGGERS OF 1933, Warner Bros. Nathan Levinson.
I AM A FUGITIVE FROM A CHAIN GANG, Warner Bros. Nathan Levinson.

ASSISTANT DIRECTOR
(New category)

★ **CHARLES BARTON**, Paramount.
★ **SCOTT BEAL**, Universal.
★ **CHARLES DORIAN**, M-G-M.
★ **FRED FOX**, United Artists.
★ **GORDON HOLLINGSHEAD**, Warner Bros.
★ **DEWEY STARKEY**, RKO Radio.
★ **WILLIAM TUMMEL**, Fox.
(Note: Multiple award given this year only.)

SHORT SUBJECTS

(Cartoons)
BUILDING A BUILDING, Disney, UA.
THE MERRY OLD SOUL, Lantz, Universal.

★ **THE THREE LITTLE PIGS**, Disney, UA.

(Comedy)
MISTER MUGG, Universal. (Comedies)
PREFERRED LIST, RKO Radio. (Head-liner Series #5)
★ **SO THIS IS HARRIS**, RKO Radio. (Special)

(Novelty)
★ **KRAKATOA**, Educational. (Three-reel Special)
MENU, Pete Smith, M-G-M. (Oddities)
THE SEA, Educational. (Battle For Life)

SPECIAL AWARDS

None given this year.

SCIENTIFIC OR TECHNICAL

CLASS I (statuette)
None.

CLASS II (plaque)
ELECTRICAL RESEARCH PRODUCTS, INC., for their wide range recording and reproducing system.
RCA-VICTOR CO., INC., for their high-fidelity recording and reproducing system.

CLASS III (citation)
FOX FILM CORP., FRED JACKMAN and WARNER BROS. PICTURES, INC., and **SIDNEY SANDERS** of RKO Studios, Inc.

★ **INDICATES WINNER**

One Way Passage (Warner Bros.; supervised by Hal B. Wallis) told one of the screen's best remembered love stories of the 1930s: she's incurably ill, he's going to prison; they meet on a Hong Kong-to-San Francisco oceanliner, fall in love but keep their secrets, promising to meet on New Year's Eve which neither is able to do. William Powell and Kay Francis (right) starred, and Robert Lord won an Academy Award for Original Story. It was remade in 1940 as *'Til We Meet Again* with Merle Oberon and George Brent.

A Farewell to Arms (Paramount) received two Awards: for Cinematography (by Charles Bryant Lang, Jr.) and Sound Recording (by Harold C. Lewis). It was based on the 1930 Ernest Hemingway book and directed by Frank Borzage, with (left) Gary Cooper as the American lieutenant serving with the Italian ambulance corps who falls in love with Helen Hayes as an English nurse, during wartime. The film opted for a happy ending, as opposed to Hemingway's more tragic one, something audiences often demanded in the 1930s. It was a distinguished, well-admired film and inspired two later versions: a revamped adaptation called *Force of Arms* (1950) with William Holden and Nancy Olson, and a remake in 1957 with Rock Hudson and Jennifer Jones, produced by David O. Selznick.

1934 The Seventh Year

When the nominees for the 1934 Awards were announced, the Academy was bombarded with protests, the first time there had been such massive critical argument with the selections. The crux of the irritation was the fact that in the Best Actress category the names of Bette Davis (for *Of Human Bondage*) and Myrna Loy (in *The Thin Man*), two of the year's most respected performances, were missing. Newspaper editorials, telegrams and telephone calls assailed the Academy, reaching a high enough pitch that voting rules were temporarily abandoned and the Academy announced, on January 16, 1935, that voters would be allowed to disregard the printed ballot and write in any name they preferred.

On the night of the Awards, February 27, 1935, nearly a thousand guests jammed into the Biltmore Bowl of the Los Angeles Biltmore Hotel to hear the outcome, realizing there was a good chance none of the original nominees would ultimately be declared the winners, despite the fact that many members had marked their ballots before the ''write-in'' free-for-all was allowed. When the final results were announced, everyone had reason to be surprised. The ''overlooked'' performers, including Bette Davis and Myrna Loy, did not win, place or show. A single picture, *It Happened One Night,* walked off with five of the evening's Awards, including Best Picture, Actor (Clark Gable), Actress (Claudette Colbert), Director (Frank Capra) and Writing Adaptation (Robert Riskin), the first time one picture had been so prominent in a single Awards year.

Claudette Colbert, not expecting to win, was in the process of boarding a train to New York when Academy officials found her and informed her of the results. Santa Fe officials held up the locomotive as she was rushed off to collect her prize, dressed in a tailored suit for travel. She arrived at the banquet, received her Award from host-presenter Irvin S. Cobb, posed for photographers, then was whisked back to the train. Later, when the voting order was officially made known, Miss Colbert's runners-up were Norma Shearer, then Grace Moore, all of them official nominees. Clark Gable was followed by Frank Morgan and William Powell, also official nominees.

Music was honored for the first year, in two categories (Song and Music Score), and a Film Editing division was also inaugurated. Shirley Temple received a Special Award in the form of a miniature statuette, in recognition of her contributions during the year as a screen juvenile. And for the first time, the eligibility period for Awards consideration was based on a calendar year (January 1 to December 31, 1934) rather than a seasonal period.

Best Picture: It Happened One Night (Columbia; produced by Harry Cohn), **Best Director: Frank Capra** (above), **Best Actor: Clark Gable** as Peter Warne and **Best Actress: Claudette Colbert** as Ellie Andrews (right) in *It Happened One Night.* It was one of those happy celluloid accidents, difficult to analyze and impossible to reproduce intentionally. *Night Bus,* the original script, had been kicking around studios for several months; M-G-M bought it, then traded it and the services of Clark Gable to Columbia in exchange for the services of Frank Capra for a picture that never materialized. No one expected it to be such a runaway hit, but it was exactly the kind of entertainment that appealed to a Depression-weary country, and its appeal is just as potent today. It marked Gable's first go at playing comedy, and was one of three strong 1934 roles for Miss Colbert, along with *Cleopatra* and *Imitation of Life;* it was also the first of Capra's three Awards as Best Director. For the next 41 years, it would also remain the only film to win the Academy's prizes for Picture, Actor, Actress and Director. It also won a fifth Award, for Robert Riskin's invaluable Writing Adaptation.

Cleopatra (Paramount; produced by Cecil B. DeMille) was DeMillian spectacle at its showiest, a superb example of the kind of eye-feast which the motion picture medium could serve better than any other. Claudette Colbert (left) played the Egyptian Queen, involved with court intrigue, Julius Caesar, Marc Antony and a thousand extras, and the film won the Academy Award for Victor Milner's Cinematography.

The Merry Widow (M-G-M; produced by Ernst Lubitsch) was based on Franz Lehar's sturdy operetta, earlier done as a silent film in 1924, directed by Erich Von Stroheim and starring Mae Murray and John Gilbert. This version belonged to director Ernst Lubitsch and his stars Jeannette MacDonald and Maurice Chevalier (right) and received its Award for the Art Direction of Cedric Gibbons and Frederic Hope, who created the mythical kingdom of Marshovia and an idealized Paris on sound stages in Culver City.

Special Award: Shirley Temple (right, with Irvin S. Cobb). "When Santa Claus brought you down Creation's chimney, he brought the loveliest Christmas present that has ever been given to the world," said Cobb as he presented a miniature statuette to Shirley Temple for her contributions during the year to screen entertainment. There were nine Temple features in 1934, including *Little Miss Marker* which had made her a major screen attraction, and America's favorite tot.

Nominations 1934

PICTURE

THE BARRETTS OF WIMPOLE STREET, M-G-M. Produced by Irving Thalberg.
CLEOPATRA, Paramount. Produced by Cecil B. DeMille.
FLIRTATION WALK, First National. Produced by Jack L. Warner and Hal Wallis, with Robert Lord.
THE GAY DIVORCEE, RKO Radio. Produced by Pandro S. Berman.
HERE COMES THE NAVY, Warner Bros. Produced by Lou Edelman.
THE HOUSE OF ROTHSCHILD, 20th Century, UA. Produced by Darryl F. Zanuck, with William Goetz and Raymond Griffith.
IMITATION OF LIFE, Universal. Produced by John M. Stahl.
★ **IT HAPPENED ONE NIGHT,** Columbia. Produced by Harry Cohn.
ONE NIGHT OF LOVE, Columbia. Produced by Harry Cohn, with Everett Riskin.
THE THIN MAN, M-G-M. Produced by Hunt Stromberg.
VIVA VILLA, M-G-M. Produced by David O. Selznick.
THE WHITE PARADE, Fox. Produced by Jesse L. Lasky.

ACTOR

★ **CLARK GABLE** in *It Happened One Night*, Columbia.
FRANK MORGAN in *Affairs of Cellini*, 20th Century, UA.
WILLIAM POWELL in *The Thin Man*, M-G-M.

ACTRESS

★ **CLAUDETTE COLBERT** in *It Happened One Night*, Columbia.
GRACE MOORE in *One Night of Love*, Columbia.
NORMA SHEARER in *The Barretts of Wimpole Street*, M-G-M.

DIRECTION

★ **FRANK CAPRA** for *It Happened One Night*, Columbia.
VICTOR SCHERTZINGER for *One Night of Love*, Columbia.
W.S. VAN DYKE for *The Thin Man*, M-G-M.

WRITING

(Adaptation)
★ **IT HAPPENED ONE NIGHT,** Columbia. Robert Riskin.
THE THIN MAN, M-G-M. Frances Goodrich and Albert Hackett.
VIVA VILLA, M-G-M. Ben Hecht.

(Original Story)
HIDE-OUT, M-G-M. Mauri Grashin.
★ **MANHATTAN MELODRAMA,** M-G-M. Arthur Caesar.
THE RICHEST GIRL IN THE WORLD, RKO Radio. Norman Krasna.

CINEMATOGRAPHY

THE AFFAIRS OF CELLINI, 20th Century, UA. Charles Rosher.
★ **CLEOPATRA,** Paramount. Victor Milner.
OPERATION 13, M-G-M. George Folsey.

ART DIRECTION

AFFAIRS OF CELLINI, 20th Century, UA. Richard Day.
THE GAY DIVORCEE, RKO Radio. Van Nest Polglase and Carroll Clark.
★ **THE MERRY WIDOW,** M-G-M. Cedric Gibbons and Frederic Hope.

SOUND RECORDING

AFFAIRS OF CELLINI, 20th Century, UA. Thomas T. Moulton.
CLEOPATRA, Paramount. Franklin Hansen.
FLIRTATION WALK, First National. Nathan Levinson.
THE GAY DIVORCEE, RKO Radio. Carl Dreher.

IMITATION OF LIFE, Universal. Gilbert Kurland.
★ **ONE NIGHT OF LOVE,** Columbia. Paul Neal.
VIVA VILLA, M-G-M. Douglas Shearer.

FILM EDITING
(New category)

CLEOPATRA, Paramount. Anne Bauchens.
★ **ESKIMO,** M-G-M. Conrad Nervig.
ONE NIGHT OF LOVE, Columbia. Gene Milford.

MUSIC
(New category)

(Song)
CARIOCA (*Flying Down to Rio*, RKO Radio); Music by Vincent Youmans. Lyrics by Edward Eliscu and Gus Kahn.
★ **THE CONTINENTAL** (*The Gay Divorcee*, RKO Radio); Music by Con Conrad. Lyrics by Herb Magidson.
LOVE IN BLOOM (*She Loves Me Not*, Paramount); Music by Ralph Rainger. Lyrics by Leo Robin.

(Score)
THE GAY DIVORCEE, RKO Radio. RKO Radio Studio Music Dept.; Max Steiner, head. Score by Kenneth Webb and Samuel Hoffenstein.
THE LOST PATROL, RKO Radio. RKO Radio Studio Music Dept.; Max Steiner, head. Score by Max Steiner.
★ **ONE NIGHT OF LOVE,** Columbia. Columbia Studio Music Dept.; Louis Silvers, head. Thematic music by Victor Schertzinger and Gus Kahn.
(Note: from 1934-1937, Best Score was considered a music department achievement and award was presented to department head instead of to the composer.)

ASSISTANT DIRECTOR

SCOTT BEAL for *Imitation of Life*, Universal.

CULLEN TATE for *Cleopatra*, Paramount.
★ **JOHN WATERS** for *Viva Villa*, M-G-M.

SHORT SUBJECTS

(Cartoons)
HOLIDAY LAND, Mintz, Columbia.
JOLLY LITTLE ELVES, Universal.
★ **THE TORTOISE AND THE HARE,** Disney, UA.

(Comedy)
★ **LA CUCARACHA,** RKO Radio. (Special)
MEN IN BLACK, Columbia. (Broadway Comedies)
WHAT, NO MEN!, Warner Bros. (Broadway Brevities)

(Novelty)
BOSOM FRIENDS, Educational. (Treasure Chest)
★ **CITY OF WAX,** Educational. (Battle For Life)
STRIKES AND SPARES, M-G-M. (Oddities)

SPECIAL AWARD

TO SHIRLEY TEMPLE, in grateful recognition of her outstanding contribution to screen entertainment during the year 1934. (miniature statuette)

SCIENTIFIC OR TECHNICAL

CLASS I (statuette)
None.

CLASS II (plaque)
ELECTRICAL RESEARCH PRODUCTS, INC., for their development of the vertical cut disc method of recording sound for motion pictures (hill and dale recording).

CLASS III (citation
COLUMBIA PICTURES CORP.;
BELL AND HOWELL CO.

★ INDICATES WINNER

1935 The Eighth Year

Sometime in 1935, or thereabouts, the Academy Award statuette acquired an indelible nickname. For years, industry members and newspaper reporters had been forced to refer clumsily to "the Academy statuette" or "the golden trophy" or "the statue of merit," but suddenly it became widely known as, simply, "Oscar." The name of the person responsible for initiating the new name is not conclusively documented, but through the years, three people have been credited. Margaret Herrick, then the Academy's librarian and later its executive director, is said to have named the statue after an uncle, a Mr. Oscar Pierce. Hollywood columnist Sidney Skolsky claims to have first called it Oscar after an old vaudeville joke ("Will you have a cigar, Oscar?") because he was weary of finding synonyms when writing about Academy Award winners. Bette Davis is also said to have been the originator, naming the Award after her husband, Harmon Oscar Nelson, Jr., whom, she claimed, the statuette resembled. Only one thing is certain: sometime in the mid-1930s, the name "Oscar" arrived. And stayed.

The 1935 Awards were held March 5, 1936, at the Biltmore Hotel and, as in the preceding year, write-in votes were allowed by the Academy which, during the year, had retained the public accounting firm of Price Waterhouse & Co. to tabulate ballots, a job earlier left to the staff and judges at the Academy headquarters. Cinematographer Hal Mohr became the first, and only, write-in Oscar winner. Mr. Mohr later said, "I think there had been some industry antagonism towards me because I had been very active in a 1933 strike, and I wasn't nominated for *A Midsummer Night's Dream*. But write-ins were allowed then, and I was unshaven, sitting at home in my work clothes and the phone rang. It was Eddie Blackburn, a friend, at the Biltmore Bowl and he told me I'd won and to get the hell down there. I shaved, threw on a tux, and with my wife jumped in a cab and was there in an hour. I'm very proud of that Award."

Pioneer director D.W. Griffith received a Special Award from the Academy and, in turn, he presented the acting Awards. As in previous years, runners-up were again disclosed. Bette Davis was named Best Actress for *Dangerous,* with Katharine Hepburn and Elisabeth Bergner as her runners-up. Victor McLaglen was named Best Actor for *The Informer,* competing with three actors from *Mutiny on the Bounty:* Clark Gable, Charles Laughton and Franchot Tone. Paul Muni, not a nominee, came in second on the ballots (for *Black Fury*) and Laughton came in third. *Mutiny on the Bounty* was named Best Picture, followed by *The Informer* and *Captain Blood.* John Ford was named Best Director for *The Informer,* followed by *Captain Blood*'s Michael Curtiz, who had not been an official nominee, then Henry Hathaway for *The Lives of a Bengal Lancer.* It was the last year write-in votes were allowed by the Academy.

Writer Dudley Nichols, voted the Oscar for his screenplay of *The Informer,* also became the first to decline an Academy Award. He took the stand, he said, not to demean the honor, but because of antagonism between several industry guilds and the Academy over union matters, which resulted in many members boycotting the 1935 Awards party. It was not the last time an Academy Awards night would be used to underline either a political or a personal stand.

Best Actor: Victor McLaglen as Gypo and **Best Director: John Ford** for *The Informer* (RKO Radio). RKO bosses had been reluctant to film writer Liam O'Flaherty's story about a drunken, boastful Irishman in Dublin during the Irish Revolutionary troubles of 1922 who sells out his best pal to the police for a 20-pound note, then spends the money on a drunken spree, and is eventually "executed" by his fellow Revolutionists. They relented only after endless badgering by director Ford, who then made what many regard as one of the genuine screen masterpieces, dominated by the towering performance of McLaglen as the tragic Gypo. *The Informer* is the first film to noticeably benefit financially from winning Academy Awards; it was not a box office success during its original release, but after winning four Awards (including one for Dudley Nichols' screenplay and another for Max Steiner's score) was rebooked into theaters and attracted a sizable audience.

Best Picture: Mutiny on the Bounty
(M-G-M; produced by Irving Thalberg, with Albert Lewin). Charles Laughton was the hateful Captain Bligh. Clark Gable was "MIST-AH Christian!" and Frank Lloyd directed this rousing version of the actual 1789 Bounty case in which a master's mate led a mutiny against a sadistic commander of a British vessel while transporting breadfruit plants from Tahiti to the West Indies. It remains one of the best photoplays ever done about the sea.

Best Actress: Bette Davis as Joyce Heath (right, with Franchot Tone) in *Dangerous* (Warner Bros.; directed by Alfred E. Green). Legend has it that Bette Davis received her 1935 Oscar because voters had overlooked her performance in *Of Human Bondage* the preceding Awards year; Miss Davis herself has said she suspects it was so. Nevertheless, her *Dangerous* performance as a self-centered, neurotic and destructive ex-Broadway star is eminently Oscar-worthy, and elevates a short (78 minutes) and relatively undistinguished film into a substantial, crackling drama.

Broadway Melody of 1936 (M-G-M; produced by John W. Considine) contained a musical sequence with (right) Robert Taylor, June Knight and hardtapping accomplices singing and dancing to "I've Got a Feeling You're Fooling," for which choreographer Dave Gould received an Award in a new category, honoring Dance Direction. Choreography in motion pictures was similarly honored for the next two years, then discontinued as a yearly Award.

Nominations 1935

PICTURE

ALICE ADAMS, RKO Radio. Produced by Pandro S. Berman.
BROADWAY MELODY OF 1936, M-G-M. Produced by John W. Considine, Jr.
CAPTAIN BLOOD, Warner Bros.-Cosmopolitan. Produced by Hal Wallis, with Harry Joe Brown and Gordon Hollingshead.
DAVID COPPERFIELD, M-G-M. Produced by David O. Selznick.
THE INFORMER, RKO Radio. Produced by Cliff Reid.
LES MISERABLES, 20th Century, UA. Produced by Darryl F. Zanuck.
THE LIVES OF A BENGAL LANCER, Paramount. Produced by Louis D. Lighton.
A MIDSUMMER NIGHT'S DREAM, Warner Bros. Produced by Henry Blanke.
★ MUTINY ON THE BOUNTY, M-G-M. Produced by Irving Thalberg, with Albert Lewin.
NAUGHTY MARIETTA, M-G-M. Produced by Hunt Stromberg.
RUGGLES OF RED GAP, Paramount. Produced by Arthur Hornblow, Jr.
TOP HAT, RKO Radio. Produced by Pandro S. Berman.

ACTOR

CLARK GABLE in Mutiny on the Bounty, M-G-M.
CHARLES LAUGHTON in Mutiny on the Bounty, M-G-M.
★ VICTOR McLAGLEN in The Informer, RKO Radio.
FRANCHOT TONE in Mutiny on the Bounty, M-G-M.

ACTRESS

ELISABETH BERGNER in Escape Me Never, Wilcox, UA (British).
CLAUDETTE COLBERT in Private Worlds, Paramount.
★ BETTE DAVIS in Dangerous, Warner Bros.
KATHARINE HEPBURN in Alice Adams, RKO Radio.
MIRIAM HOPKINS in Becky Sharp, Pioneer, RKO Radio.
MERLE OBERON in The Dark Angel, Goldwyn, UA.

DIRECTION

★ JOHN FORD for The Informer, RKO Radio.
HENRY HATHAWAY for Lives of a Bengal Lancer, Paramount.
FRANK LLOYD for Mutiny on the Bounty, M-G-M.

WRITING

(Original Story)
BROADWAY MELODY OF 1936, M-G-M. Moss Hart.
THE GAY DECEPTION, Lasky, Fox. Don Hartman and Stephen Avery.
★ THE SCOUNDREL, Paramount. Ben Hecht and Charles MacArthur.

(Screenplay)
★ THE INFORMER, RKO Radio. Dudley Nichols.
LIVES OF A BENGAL LANCER, Paramount. Achmed Abdullah, John L. Balderston, Grover Jones, William Slavens McNutt and Waldemar Young.
MUTINY ON THE BOUNTY, M-G-M. Jules Furthman, Talbot Jennings and Carey Wilson.

CINEMATOGRAPHY

BARBARY COAST, Goldwyn, UA. Ray June.
THE CRUSADES, Paramount. Victor Milner.
LES MISERABLES, 20th Century, UA. Gregg Toland.
★ A MIDSUMMER NIGHT'S DREAM, Warner Bros. Hal Mohr.

ART DIRECTION

★ THE DARK ANGEL, Goldwyn, UA. Richard Day.
LIVES OF A BENGAL LANCER, Paramount. Hans Dreier and Roland Anderson.
TOP HAT, RKO Radio. Carroll Clark and Van Nest Polglase.

SOUND RECORDING

THE BRIDE OF FRANKENSTEIN, Universal. Gilbert Kurland.
CAPTAIN BLOOD, Warner Bros. Nathan Levinson.
THE DARK ANGEL, Goldwyn, UA. Goldwyn Sound Dept. Thomas T. Moulton.
I DREAM TOO MUCH, RKO Radio. Carl Dreher.
LIVES OF A BENGAL LANCER, Paramount. Franklin Hansen.
LOVE ME FOREVER, Columbia. John Livadary.
★ NAUGHTY MARIETTA, M-G-M. Douglas Shearer.
1,000 DOLLARS A MINUTE, Republic. Republic Sound Dept.
THANKS A MILLION, 20th Century-Fox. E.H. Hansen.

FILM EDITING

DAVID COPPERFIELD, M-G-M. Robert J. Kern.
THE INFORMER, RKO Radio. George Hively.
LES MISERABLES, 20th Century, UA. Barbara McLean.
LIVES OF A BENGAL LANCER, Paramount. Ellsworth Hoagland.
★ A MIDSUMMER NIGHT'S DREAM, Warner Bros. Ralph Dawson.
MUTINY ON THE BOUNTY, M-G-M. Margaret Booth.

MUSIC

(Song)
CHEEK TO CHEEK (Top Hat, RKO Radio); Music and Lyrics by Irving Berlin.
LOVELY TO LOOK AT (Roberta, RKO Radio); Music by Jerome Kern. Lyrics by Dorothy Fields and Jimmy McHugh.
★ LULLABY OF BROADWAY (Gold Diggers of 1935, Warner Bros.); Music by Harry Warren. Lyrics by Al Dubin.

(Score)
★ THE INFORMER, RKO Radio. RKO Radio Studio Music Dept.; Max Steiner, head. Score by Max Steiner.
MUTINY ON THE BOUNTY, M-G-M. M-G-M Studio Music Dept.; Nat W. Finston, head. Score by Herbert Stothart.
PETER IBBETSON, Paramount. Paramount Studio Music Dept.; Irvin Talbot, head. Score by Ernst Toch.
(Note: Until 1938, Best Score was considered a music department achievement and award was presented to department head instead of to composer)

ASSISTANT DIRECTOR

★ CLEM BEAUCHAMP for Lives of a Bengal Lancer, Paramount.
ERIC STACEY for Les Miserables, 20th Century, UA.
★ PAUL WING for Lives of a Bengal Lancer, Paramount.
JOSEPH NEWMAN for David Copperfield, M-G-M.

DANCE DIRECTION

(New category)
BUSBY BERKELEY for "Lullaby of Broadway" number and "The Words Are in My Heart" number from Gold Diggers of 1935, (Warner Bros.).
BOBBY CONNOLLY for "Latin from Manhattan" number from Go into Your Dance (Warner Bros.) and "Play-boy from Paree" number from Broadway Hostess (Warner Bros.).
★ DAVE GOULD for "I've Got a Feeling You're Fooling" number from Broadway Melody of 1936 (M-G-M and "Straw Hat" number from Folies Bergere (20th Century, UA).
SAMMY LEE for "Lovely Lady" number and "Too Good to be True" number from King of Burlesque (20th Century-Fox).

HERMES PAN for "Piccolino" number and "Top Hat" number from Top Hat (RKO Radio).
LEROY PRINZ for "Elephant Number—It's the Animal in Me" from Big Broadcast of 1936 (Paramount) and "Viennese Waltz" number from All the King's Horses (Paramount).
B. ZEMACH for "Hall of Kings" number from She (RKO Radio).

SHORT SUBJECTS

(Cartoons)
THE CALICO DRAGON, Harman-Ising, M-G-M.
★ THREE ORPHAN KITTENS, Disney, UA.
WHO KILLED COCK ROBIN?, Disney, UA.

(Comedy)
★ HOW TO SLEEP, M-G-M. (Miniature)
OH, MY NERVES, Columbia. (Broadway Comedies)
TIT FOR TAT, Roach, M-G-M. (Laurel & Hardy)

(Novelty)
AUDIOSCOPIKS, M-G-M.
CAMERA THRILLS, Universal.
★ WINGS OVER MT. EVEREST, Educational.

SPECIAL AWARDS

TO DAVID WARK GRIFFITH, for his distinguished creative achievements as director and producer and his invaluable initiative and lasting contributions to the progress of the motion picture arts. (statuette)

SCIENTIFIC OR TECHNICAL

CLASS I (statuette)
None.

CLASS II (plaque)
AGFA ANSCO CORP. for their development of the Agfa infra-red film.
EASTMAN KODAK CO. for their development of the Eastman Pola-Screen.

CLASS III (citation)
METRO-GOLDWYN-MAYER STUDIO;
WILLIAM A. MUELLER of Warner Bros.-First National Studio Sound Dept.;
MOLE-RICHARDSON CO.;
DOUGLAS SHEARER and M-G-M STUDIO SOUND DEPT.;
ELECTRICAL RESEARCH PRODUCTS, INC.;
PARAMOUNT PRODUCTIONS, INC.;
NATHAN LEVINSON, director of Sound Recording for Warner Bros.-First National Studio.

★ INDICATES WINNER

1936

The Ninth Year

Prior to 1936, acting done by supporting performers, or "featured players," was either judged by Academy voters alongside the work of leading actors, or ignored totally. During Oscar's initial eight years, the only supporting performances which managed to earn Academy nominations were those of Lewis Stone in *The Patriot* (1928-29), Frank Morgan in *Affairs of Cellini* (1934) and Franchot Tone in *Mutiny on the Bounty* (1935), and each of them lost to work done by starring players with considerably more on-screen time. In the Academy's ninth year, the unintentional slighting was corrected and the organization began honoring an actor and an actress for their work in that area each year thereafter. Walter Brennan in *Come and Get It* and Gale Sondergaard in *Anthony Adverse* were the first supporting winners, and they were presented Academy Award plaques. Full-sized Oscar statuettes were not given Supporting winners until the 1943 Awards year.

Voting rules again changed, after six years. Nominations for Awards were made by a special committee of fifty individuals appointed by Academy President Frank Capra, with equal representation from each of the Academy's branches, and the final decisions were made by a vote of all Academy members. The big winner of the year was *Anthony Adverse* with four Awards, including the one for Miss Sondergaard, plus Cinematography, Music Score and Film Editing. Paul Muni was chosen Best Actor for *The Story of Louis Pasteur,* Luise Rainer won as Best Actress for *The Great Ziegfeld,* and the latter was also named the year's Best Picture. Frank Capra won his second Oscar as Director, for *Mr. Deeds Goes to Town. The March of Time,* a unique short subject series, received a Special Award statuette for its "significance and for having revolutionized one of the most important branches of the industry, the newsreel." Outside the regular Cinematography category, W. Howard Greene and Harold Rosson were given Special Award plaques for their color cinematography of *The Garden of Allah* starring Marlene Dietrich, the first time the Academy had acknowledged the use of color in a motion picture.

The Awards ceremony itself was held March 4, 1937, at the Biltmore Hotel, attended by over fifteen hundred Academy members and guests, with George Jessel as master of ceremonies. Except for Victor McLaglen's presentation of the Actor Award to Paul Muni (wearing a beard for his current filming of *The Life of Emile Zola*), all the Awards were presented by Jessel. Norma Shearer, nominated for *Romeo and Juliet,* attended the festivities with Louis B. Mayer; it was her first public appearance following the death of her husband, Irving G. Thalberg, on September 14, 1936. Among the winners was Walt Disney, who picked up his fifth straight Oscar for producing the Best Cartoon of the year. In the Writing category, Pierre Collings and Sheridan Gibney of *The Story of Louis Pasteur* won the Awards in both the Original Story and the Screenplay divisions, the only time such a double win ever occurred.

Best Actor: Paul Muni as Louis Pasteur in *The Story of Louis Pasteur* (Warner Bros.; directed by William Dieterle). *Pasteur* deviated from the Hollywood formula for biographies, skipping the early life of the famous French medical genius and concentrating on his battles with the French Academy of Medicine over sterilization of medical instruments, and search for a rabies cure. It was unlikely screen material, but in the hands of director Dieterle and actor Muni, was an unqualified success, critically and commercially. Muni, despite a limited catalog of screen roles, received five Oscar nominations including ones for *The Valiant* (1928-29), *I Am a Fugitive from a Chain Gang* (1832-33), *The Life of Emile Zola* (1937) and *The Last Angry Man* (1959).

Best Supporting Actor: Walter Brennan as Swan Bostrom (right, with Edward Arnold) in *Come and Get It* (United Artists; directed by Howard Hawks and William Wyler). Brennan became the first male winner of the Academy's new Award designation for supporting performances, as the Swedish lumberjack pal of Arnold in the adaptation of Edna Ferber's novel about a Wisconsin lumber dynasty; later, Brennan marries a saloon singer (Frances Farmer) whom Arnold has jilted. During the next four years, Brennan won two more Supporting Actor Awards, a remarkable Academy record.

Best Picture: The Great Ziegfeld (M-G-M; produced by Hunt Stromberg) and **Best Actress: Luise Rainer** as Anna Held (left, with William Powell) in *The Great Ziegfeld*. Universal studios spent a year planning a film based on the life of Broadway's spectacular showman Florenz Ziegfeld, then sold the project to M-G-M who used the full resources of that studio to produce a gargantuan, lavish entertainment. It was directed by Robert Z. Leonard with Powell as Ziegfeld, rising from an 1893 sideshow promoter to his eventual success as a New York impressario, and Miss Rainer as Anna Held, the famous stage beauty with whom he had a stormy marriage and divorce, but continued to love. The cast included Myrna Loy as Billie Burke (Ziegfeld's later wife, and widow), Fannie Brice, Frank Morgan, Gilda Gray, Ray Bolger, Leon Errol, and encompassed some 23 songs and seven spectacular production numbers. Still, it is best remembered for one simple scene of a woman and a telephone, as Miss Rainer playing Anna calls her ex-husband to congratulate him on his forthcoming marriage and emotionally begins, "Hello, Flo? . . . yes, this is Anna . . ."

Best Supporting Actress: Gale Sondergaard as Faith Paleologue (above, greeting Fredric March) in *Anthony Adverse* (Warner Bros.; directed by Mervyn LeRoy). Miss Sondergaard was the first winner of an Oscar for a supporting performance by an actress, playing a woman scheming for wealth and position in the time of Napoleon, and a thorn to Anthony, played by March. The film was based on Hervey Allen's massive adventure novel, and won more Academy Awards than any other film of the year, including Oscars for Cinematography (Gaetano Gaudio), Music Score (Leo Forbstein) and Film Editing (Ralph Dawson). The cast included, besides March and Miss Sondergaard, Olivia de Havilland, Claude Rains, Edmund Gwenn, Louis Hayward, Akim Tamiroff, Anita Louise, Donald Woods and Billy Mauch.

Nominations 1936

PICTURE

ANTHONY ADVERSE, Warner Bros. Produced by Henry Blanke.
DODSWORTH, Goldwyn, UA. Produced by Samuel Goldwyn, with Merritt Hulbert.
★ THE GREAT ZIEGFELD, M-G-M. Produced by Hunt Stromberg.
LIBELED LADY, M-G-M. Produced by Lawrence Weingarten.
MR. DEEDS GOES TO TOWN, Columbia. Produced by Frank Capra.
ROMEO AND JULIET, M-G-M. Produced by Irving Thalberg.
SAN FRANCISCO, M-G-M. Produced by John Emerson and Bernard H. Hyman.
THE STORY OF LOUIS PASTEUR, Warner Bros. Produced by Henry Blanke.
A TALE OF TWO CITIES, M-G-M. Produced by Joseph Pasternak, with Charles R. Rogers.

ACTOR

GARY COOPER in *Mr. Deeds Goes to Town*, Columbia.
WALTER HUSTON in *Dodworth*, Goldwyn, UA.
★ PAUL MUNI in *The Story of Louis Pasteur*, Warner Bros.
WILLIAM POWELL in *My Man Godfrey*, Universal.
SPENCER TRACY in *San Francisco*, M-G-M.

ACTRESS

IRENE DUNNE in *Theodora Goes Wild*, Columbia.
GLADYS GEORGE in *Valiant Is the Word for Carrie*, Paramount.
CAROLE LOMBARD in *My Man Godfrey*, Universal.
★ LUISE RAINER in *The Great Ziegfeld*, M-G-M.
NORMA SHEARER in *Romeo and Juliet*, M-G-M.

SUPPORTING ACTOR
(new catagory)

MISCHA AUER in *My Man Godfrey*, Universal.
★ WALTER BRENNAN in *Come and Get It*, Goldwyn, UA.
STUART ERWIN in *Pigskin Parade*, 20th Century-Fox.
BASIL RATHBONE in *Romeo and Juliet*, M-G-M.
AKIM TAMIROFF in *The General Died at Dawn*, Paramount.

SUPPORTING ACTRESS
(new category)

BEULAH BONDI in *The Gorgeous Hussy*, M-G-M.
ALICE BRADY in *My Man Godfrey*, Universal.
BONITA GRANVILLE in *These Three*, Goldwyn, UA.
MARIA OUSPENSKAYA in *Dodsworth*, Goldwyn, UA.
★ GALE SONDERGAARD in *Anthony Adverse*, Warner Bros.

DIRECTION

★ FRANK CAPRA for *Mr. Deeds Goes to Town*, Columbia.
GREGORY LACAVA for *My Man Godfrey*, Universal.
ROBERT Z. LEONARD for *The Great Ziegfeld*, M-G-M.
W.S. VAN DYKE for *San Francisco*, M-G-M.
WILLIAM WYLER for *Dodsworth*, UA.

WRITING

(Original Story)
FURY, M-G-M. Norman Krasna.
THE GREAT ZIEGFELD, M-G-M. William Anthony McGuire.
SAN FRANCISCO, M-G-M. Robert Hopkins.
★ THE STORY OF LOUIS PASTEUR, Warner Bros. Pierre Collings and Sheridan Gibney.
THREE SMART GIRLS, Universal. Adele Commandini.

(Screenplay)
AFTER THE THIN MAN, M-G-M. Frances Goodrich and Albert Hackett.
DODSWORTH, Goldwyn, UA. Sidney Howard.
MR. DEEDS GOES TO TOWN, Columbia. Robert Riskin.
MY MAN GODFREY, Universal. Eric Hatch and Morris Ryskind.
★ THE STORY OF LOUIS PASTEUR, Warner Bros. Pierre Collings and Sheridan Gibney.

CINEMATOGRAPHY

★ ANTHONY ADVERSE, Warner Bros. Gaetano Gaudio.
THE GENERAL DIED AT DAWN, Paramount. Victor Milner.
THE GORGEOUS HUSSY, M-G-M. George Folsey.

ART DIRECTION

ANTHONY ADVERSE, Warner Bros. Anton Grot.
★ DODSWORTH, Goldwyn, UA. Richard Day.
THE GREAT ZIEGFELD, M-G-M. Cedric Gibbons, Eddie Imazu and Edwin B. Willis.
LLOYDS OF LONDON, 20th Century-Fox. William S. Darling.
THE MAGNIFICENT BRUTE, Universal. Albert S. D'Agostino and Jack Otterson.
ROMEO AND JULIET, M-G-M. Cedric Gibbons, Frederic Hope and Edwin B. Willis.
WINTERSET, RKO Radio. Perry Ferguson.

SOUND RECORDING

BANJO ON MY KNEE, 20th Century-Fox. E.H. Hansen.
THE CHARGE OF THE LIGHT BRIGADE, Warner Bros. Nathan Levinson.
DODSWORTH, Goldwyn, UA. Oscar Lagerstrom.
GENERAL SPANKY, Roach, M-G-M. Elmer A. Raguse.
MR. DEEDS GOES TO TOWN, Columbia. John Livadary.
★ SAN FRANCISCO, M-G-M. Douglas Shearer.

Best Director: Frank Capra (right with Gary Cooper) for *Mr. Deeds Goes to Town* (Columbia). Capra had previously won an Oscar two years before for 1934's *It Happened One Night,* and had another one in his future for 1938's *You Can't Take It With You.* With *Mr. Deeds,* he again tackled a favorite Capra topic: what happened when an average American guy gets thrown in with devious sophisticates, in this case a small town fellow named Longfellow Deeds (Cooper) who has just inherited $20 million and gets taken, at least, temporarily, by New Yorkers such as Jean Arthur, George Bancroft and Douglas Dumbrille.

THE TEXAS RANGERS, Paramount. Franklin Hansen.
THAT GIRL FROM PARIS, RKO Radio. J.O. Aalberg.
THREE SMART GIRLS, Universal. Homer G. Tasker.

FILM EDITING

* ANTHONY ADVERSE, Warner Bros. Ralph Dawson.
COME AND GET IT, Goldwyn, UA. Edward Curtiss.
THE GREAT ZIEGFELD, M-G-M. William S. Gray.
LLOYDS OF LONDON, 20th Century-Fox. Barbara McLean.
A TALE OF TWO CITIES, M-G-M. Conrad A. Nervig.
THEODORA GOES WILD, Columbia. Otto Meyer.

MUSIC
(Song)
DID I REMEMBER (*Suzy,* M-G-M); Music by Walter Donaldson. Lyrics by Harold Adamson.
I'VE GOT YOU UNDER MY SKIN (*Born to Dance,* M-G-M); Music and Lyrics by Cole Porter.
A MELODY FROM THE SKY (*Trail of the Lonesome Pine,* Paramount); Music by Louis Alter. Lyrics by Sidney Mitchell.
PENNIES FROM HEAVEN (*Pennies from Heaven,* Columbia); Music by Arthur Johnston. Lyrics by Johnny Burke.
* THE WAY YOU LOOK TONIGHT (*Swing Time,* RKO Radio); Music by Jerome Kern. Lyrics by Dorothy Fields.
WHEN DID YOU LEAVE HEAVEN (*Sing Baby Sing,* 20th Century-Fox); Music by Richard A. Whiting. Lyrics by Walter Bullock.

(Score)
* ANTHONY ADVERSE, Warner Bros. Warner Bros. Studio Music Dept.; Leo Forbstein, head. Score by Erich Wolfgang Korngold.
THE CHARGE OF THE LIGHT BRIGADE, Warner Bros. Warner Bros. Studio Music Dept.; Leo Forbstein, head. Score by Max Steiner.
THE GARDEN OF ALLAH, Selznick, UA. Selznick International Pictures Music Dept.; Max Steiner, head. Score by Max Steiner.
THE GENERAL DIED AT DAWN, Paramount. Paramount Studio Music Dept.; Boris Morros, head. Score by Werner Janssen.
WINTERSET, RKO Radio. RKO Radio Studio Music Dept.; Nathaniel Shilkret, head. Score by Nathaniel Shilkret.
(NOTE: Through 1937, Best Score was considered a music department achievement and award was presented to department head instead of composer.)

ASSISTANT DIRECTOR

CLEM BEAUCHAMP for *Last of the Mohicans,* Reliance, UA.
WILLIAM CANNON for *Anthony Adverse,* Warner Bros.
JOSEPH NEWMAN for *San Francisco,* M-G-M.
ERIC G. STACEY for *Garden of Allah,* Selznick, UA.
* JACK SULLIVAN for *The Charge of the Light Brigade,* Warner Bros.

DANCE DIRECTION

BUSBY BERKELEY for "Love and War" number from *Gold Diggers of 1937,* (Warner Bros.).
BOBBY CONNOLLY for "1000 Love Songs" number from *Cain and Mabel,* (Warner Bros.).
* SEYMOUR FELIX for "A Pretty Girl Is Like a Melody" number from *The Great Ziegfeld,* (M-G-M).
DAVE GOULD for "Swingin' the Jinx" number from *Born to Dance,* (M-G-M).
JACK HASKELL for "Skating Ensemble" number from *One in a Million,* (20th Century-Fox).
RUSSELL LEWIS for "The Finale" number from *Dancing Pirate,* (RKO Radio).
HERMES PAN for "Bo Jangles" number from *Swing Time,* (RKO Radio).

SHORT SUBJECTS
(Cartoons)
* COUNTRY COUSIN, Disney, UA.
OLD MILL POND, Harman-Ising, M-G-M.
SINBAD THE SAILOR, Paramount.

(One-reel)
* BORED OF EDUCATION, Roach, M-G-M. (Our Gang)
MOSCOW MOODS, Paramount. (Headliners)
WANTED, A MASTER, M-G-M. (Pete Smith Specialties)

(Two-reel)
DOUBLE OR NOTHING, Warner Bros. (Broadway Brevities)
DUMMY ACHE, RKO Radio. (Edgar Kennedy Comedies)
* THE PUBLIC PAYS, M-G-M. (Crime Doesn't Pay)

(Color)
* GIVE ME LIBERTY, Warner Bros. (Broadway Brevities)
LA FIESTA DE SANTA BARBARA, M-G-M. (Musical Revues)
POPULAR SCIENCE J-6-2, Paramount.

SPECIAL AWARDS

TO MARCH OF TIME for its significance to motion pictures and for having revolutionized one of the most important branches of the industry—the newsreel. (statuette)
TO W. HOWARD GREENE and HAROLD ROSSON for the color cinematography of the Selznick International Production, *The Garden of Allah.* (plaques)

SCIENTIFIC OR TECHNICAL

CLASS I (statuette)
DOUGLAS SHEARER and the M-G-M STUDIO SOUND DEPARTMENT for the development of a practical two-way horn system and a biased Class A push-pull recording system.

CLASS II (plaque)
E.C. WENTE and the BELL TELEPHONE LABORATORIES for their multi-cellular high-frequency horn and receiver.

CLASS III (citations)
RCA MANUFACTURING CO., INC. (3 citations)
ELECTRICAL RESEARCH PRODUCTS, INC.;
UNITED ARTISTS STUDIO CORP.

* INDICATES WINNER

Swing Time (RKO Radio) marked the sixth screen teaming of top box office favorites Fred Astaire and Ginger Rogers, and the second time they introduced an Oscar-winning Song. The first was "The Continental" from 1934's *The Gay Divorcee;* this year, the song was "The Way You Look Tonight" by Jerome Kern and Dorothy Fields. Fred and Ginger also received Academy Awards of their own; she was chosen Best Actress of 1940 (for *Kitty Foyle*), he was voted a Special Award in 1949.

1937 The Tenth Year

Luise Rainer became the first performer to win a second Academy Award; at the same time, she also was the first actor or actress to win two Awards in succession. At the 1937 Oscar ceremony, she was named Best Actress for *The Good Earth,* and other Oscars went to Best Actor Spencer Tracy in *Captains Courageous,* Director Leo McCarey for *The Awful Truth,* Supporting Actor Joseph Schildkraut for *The Life of Emile Zola* and Supporting Actress Alice Brady for *In Old Chicago. Zola* won three Awards, the highest total of the evening, including Best Picture and Screenplay.

The actual presentation banquet was delayed one week (to March 10, 1938), due to a major rain and flood which had incapacitated the Los Angeles area. When the party finally took place at the Biltmore Hotel, more than thirteen hundred guests attended, the largest turnout to date at an Academy Awards function. Comedian Bob Burns was the master of ceremonies and, during the evening, W.C. Fields presented a Special Award to Mack Sennett for his contributions to screen comedy. Darryl F. Zanuck of the recently merged 20th Century-Fox studios received the first Irving G. Thalberg Memorial Award, established in the name of the late M-G-M producer, which is given to a creative producer whose work reflects a consistently high quality of motion picture production. Ventriloquist Edgar Bergen was also called to the podium to receive a special miniature wooden Oscar statuette, with a hinged and movable mouth, on behalf of his wooden comedy creation Charlie McCarthy. The Award for Dance Direction was given for the last time, to Hermes Pan; since 1937, choreography in motion pictures has been honored only on an occasional basis, in the form of a Special Award.

In its continuing attempt to find the most democratic means of selecting winners, the Academy again changed its voting rules and, for the first time, invited members of *all* industry-related guilds and unions, including the Screen Extras Guild, to join with Academy members in selecting both the Award nominees and final winners, with the result that twelve thousand people now participated in the voting. This policy continued for eight years, until 1944, when the Screen Extras were disqualified from participation.

There was another first in 1937: John Lee Mahin became the first individual to refuse an Academy nomination, for his co-authorship of the *Captains Courageous* screenplay, in protest over the way the Writers Branch of the Awards committee had been selected.

As before, newspapers in the area had been furnished with the names of Award winners at 8:30 p.m. on the evening of the presentations, but were pledged to keep the news secret until late editions. Luise Rainer was at home in house slippers when the Academy committee noted her absence and phoned to tell her she had won for the second year in a row. She hastily changed into an evening gown and hurried to the Biltmore with husband Clifford Odets. Winner Alice Brady was confined at home with a broken ankle, and Mrs. Spencer Tracy accepted the Award for her husband, who was recovering from a major operation at Good Samaritan Hospital. When his Oscar was later sent to be inscribed, it came back incorrectly engraved to "Dick Tracy." Luckily, the error was caught before the statuette was sent on to Spencer Tracy and it was corrected.

Best Actress: Luise Rainer as O-Lan in *The Good Earth* (M-G-M; directed by Sidney Franklin). Miss Rainer won her second Academy Award in succession as the passive but earth-strong farm wife to Wang (played by Paul Muni), characters originally created by Pearl S. Buck in her epic 1931 novel. *Earth* also won an Oscar for Karl Freund's Cinematography, and was dedicated to production genius Irving Thalberg who died shortly after filming had been completed.

Best Picture: The Life of Emile Zola
(Warner Bros.; produced by Henry Blanke)
with Paul Muni, above. Directed by William
Dieterle, *Zola* followed 1936's *The Story of
Louis Pasteur* as another meticulous
Muni-Dieterle-Warners screen biography,
and covered the early career of the brilliant
French novelist, but concentrated the
majority of its footage on Zola's fight for
the underdog in the famous Dreyfus case.
The cast included Gale Sondergaard,
Donald Crisp, Gloria Holden, Louis Calhern,
Erin O'Brien-Moore (as the real-life *Nana*)
and Joseph Schildkraut, who also won an
Oscar as Dreyfus.

Best Actor: Spencer Tracy as Manuel in
Captains Courageous (M-G-M; directed by
Victor Fleming). Tracy portrayed Rudyard
Kipling's happy-go-lucky, simple Portuguese
fisherman who befriends a spoiled
English lad (played by Freddie Bartholomew,
right with Tracy) and teaches him the
values of honesty and obedience to orders.
The role required the actor to sing several
old-time sea chants and speak with
a Portuguese accent, both of which he
claimed made him extremely nervous. His
talented shipmates included Lionel
Barrymore, Charles Grapewin, Mickey
Rooney, John Carradine, Jack LaRue and
(on shore) Melvyn Douglas, and the film
brought him his first Academy Award.
The following year he won a second
one for *Boys Town.*

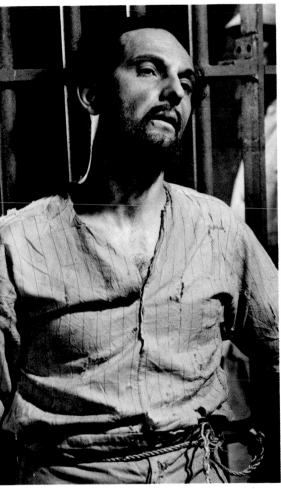

Nominations 1937

PICTURE

THE AWFUL TRUTH, Columbia. Produced by Leo McCarey, with Everett Riskin.
CAPTAINS COURAGEOUS, M-G-M. Produced by Louis D. Lighton.
DEAD END, Goldwyn, UA. Produced by Samuel Goldwyn, with Merritt Hulbert.
THE GOOD EARTH, M-G-M. Produced by Irving Thalberg, with Albert Lewin.
IN OLD CHICAGO, 20th Century-Fox. Produced by Darryl F. Zanuck, with Kenneth MacGowan.
★ **THE LIFE OF EMILE ZOLA**, Warner Bros. Produced by Henry Blanke.
LOST HORIZON, Columbia. Produced by Frank Capra.
100 MEN AND A GIRL, Universal. Produced by Charles R. Rogers, with Joe Pasternak.
STAGE DOOR, RKO Radio. Produced by Pandro S. Berman.
A STAR IS BORN, Selznick International, UA. Produced by David O. Selznick.

ACTOR

CHARLES BOYER in *Conquest*, M-G-M.
FREDRIC MARCH in *A Star Is Born*, Selznick, UA.
ROBERT MONTGOMERY in *Night Must Fall*, M-G-M.
PAUL MUNI in *The Life of Emile Zola*, Warner Bros.
★ **SPENCER TRACY** in *Captains Courageous*, M-G-M.

ACTRESS

IRENE DUNNE in *The Awful Truth*, Columbia.
GRETA GARBO in *Camille*, M-G-M.
JANET GAYNOR in *A Star Is Born*, Selznick, UA.
★ **LUISE RAINER** in *The Good Earth*, M-G-M.
BARBARA STANWYCK in *Stella Dallas*, Goldwyn, UA.

SUPPORTING ACTOR

RALPH BELLAMY in *The Awful Truth*, Columbia.
THOMAS MITCHELL in *Hurricane*, Goldwyn, UA.
★ **JOSEPH SCHILDKRAUT** in *The Life of Emile Zola*, Warner Bros.
H.B. WARNER in *Lost Horizon*, Columbia.
ROLAND YOUNG in *Topper*, Roach, M-G-M.

SUPPORTING ACTRESS

★ **ALICE BRADY** in *In Old Chicago*, 20th Century-Fox.
ANDREA LEEDS in *Stage Door*, RKO Radio.
ANNE SHIRLEY in *Stella Dallas*, Goldwyn, UA.
CLAIRE TREVOR in *Dead End*, Goldwyn, UA.
DAME MAY WHITTY in *Night Must Fall*, M-G-M.

DIRECTION

WILLIAM DIETERLE for *The Life of Emile Zola*, Warner Bros.
SIDNEY FRANKLIN for *The Good Earth*, M-G-M.
GREGORY LaCAVA for *Stage Door*, RKO Radio.
★ **LEO McCAREY** for *The Awful Truth*, Columbia.
WILLIAM WELLMAN for *A Star Is Born*, Selznick, UA.

WRITING

(Original Story)
BLACK LEGION, Warner Bros. Robert Lord.
IN OLD CHICAGO, 20th Century-Fox. Niven Busch.
THE LIFE OF EMILE ZOLA, Warner Bros. Heinz Herald and Geza Herczeg.

100 MEN AND A GIRL, Universal. Hans Kraly.
★ **A STAR IS BORN**, Selznick, UA. William A. Wellman and Robert Carson.

(Screenplay)
THE AWFUL TRUTH, Columbia. Vina Delmar.
CAPTAINS COURAGEOUS, M-G-M. Marc Connolly, John Lee Mahin and Dale Van Every.
★ **THE LIFE OF EMILE ZOLA**, Warner Bros. Heinz Herald, Geza Herczeg and Norman Reilly Raine.
STAGE DOOR, RKO Radio. Morris Ryskind and Anthony Veiller.
A STAR IS BORN, Selznick, UA. Alan Campbell, Robert Carson and Dorothy Parker.

CINEMATOGRAPHY

DEAD END, Goldwyn, UA. Gregg Toland.
★ **THE GOOD EARTH**, M-G-M. Karl Freund.
WINGS OVER HONOLULU, Universal. Joseph Valentine.

ART DIRECTION

CONQUEST, M-G-M. Cedric Gibbons and William Horning.
A DAMSEL IN DISTRESS, RKO Radio. Carroll Clark.
DEAD END, Goldwyn, UA. Richard Day.
EVERY DAY'S A HOLIDAY, Major Prods., Paramount. Wiard Ihnen.
THE LIFE OF EMILE ZOLA, Warner Bros. Anton Grot.
★ **LOST HORIZON**, Columbia. Stephen Goosson.
MANHATTAN MERRY-GO-ROUND, Republic. John Victor Mackay.
THE PRISONER OF ZENDA, Selznick, UA. Lyle Wheeler.
SOULS AT SEA, Paramount. Hans Dreier and Roland Anderson.
VOGUES OF 1938, Wanger, UA. Alexander Toluboff.

Best Supporting Actor: Joseph Schildkraut as Capt. Alfred Dreyfus in *The Life of Emile Zola*. A major asset to the year's Best Picture, Schildkraut portrayed the real-life French Army officer who was disgraced and unjustly accused of treason in 1894 and sentenced to life imprisonment on Devil's Island, a penalty comparable to death. William Dieterle was his director.

A Star is Born (United Artists; produced by David O. Selznick) received an Academy Award for its Original Story by William Wellman and Robert Carson, plus a Special Award plaque to W. Howard Greene for Color Cinematography; the latter award was recommended by a committee of leading cinematographers after viewing all the color pictures made during 1937. Wellman also directed the film, which starred (at right) Janet Gaynor, Fredric March and Adolphe Menjou.

Best Supporting Actress: Alice Brady as Molly O'Leary in *In Old Chicago* (20th Century-Fox; directed by Henry King). Miss Brady, a famous stage actress best known for playing flittery society ladies, won her Academy trophy for playing the decidedly unflittery Mrs. O'Leary, a lady with three sons (Tyrone Power, Don Ameche and Tom Brown) and the cow who accidentally started the great Chicago fire of 1871.

Best Director: Leo McCarey for *The Awful Truth* (Columbia; produced by McCarey, with Everett Riskin) with Irene Dunne and Cary Grant (below). One of the best (and most timeless) of the screwball comedy genre, *Truth* won McCarey the first of two Oscars as Best Director. He won his second in 1944 for directing *Going My Way.*

WEE WILLIE WINKIE, 20th Century-Fox. William S. Darling and David Hall.
YOU'RE A SWEETHEART, Universal. Jack Otterson.

MUSIC

(Song)
REMEMBER ME (*Mr. Dodd Takes the Air,* Warner Bros.); Music by Harry Warren. Lyrics by Al Dubin.
* SWEET LEILANI (*Waikiki Wedding,* Paramount); Music and Lyrics by Harry Owens.
THAT OLD FEELING (*Vogues of 1938,* Wanger, UA); Music by Sammy Fain. Lyrics by Lew Brown.
THEY CAN'T TAKE THAT AWAY FROM ME (*Shall We Dance,* RKO Radio); Music by George Gershwin. Lyrics by Ira Gershwin.
WHISPERS IN THE DARK (*Artists and Models,* Paramount); Music by Frederick Hollander. Lyrics by Leo Robin.

(Score)
HURRICANE, Goldwyn, UA. Samuel Goldwyn Studio Music Dept.; Alfred Newman, head. Score by Alfred Newman.
IN OLD CHICAGO, 20th Century-Fox. 20th Century-Fox Studio Music Dept.; Louis Silvers, head. (No composer credit)
THE LIFE OF EMILE ZOLA, Warner Bros. Warner Bros. Studio Music Dept.; Leo Forbstein, head. Score by Max Steiner.
LOST HORIZON, Columbia. Columbia Studio Music Dept.; Morris Stoloff, head. Score by Dimitri Tiomkin.
MAKE A WISH, Lesser, RKO Radio. Dr. Hugo Riesenfeld, musical director. Score by Dr. Hugo Riesenfeld.
MAYTIME, M-G-M. M-G-M Studio Music Dept.; Nat W. Finston, head. Score by Herbert Stothart.
* 100 MEN AND A GIRL, Universal. Universal Studio Music Dept.; Charles Previn, head. (No composer credit)
PORTIA ON TRIAL, Republic. Republic Studio Music Dept.; Alberto Colombo, head. Score by Alberto Colombo.
THE PRISONER OF ZENDA, Selznick, UA. Selznick International Pictures Music Dept.; Alfred Newman, musical director. Score by Alfred Newman.
QUALITY STREET, RKO Radio. RKO Radio Studio Music Dept.; Roy Webb, musical director. Score by Roy Webb.
SNOW WHITE AND THE SEVEN DWARFS, Disney, RKO Radio. Walt Disney Studio Music Dept.; Leigh Harline, head. Score by Frank Churchill, Leigh Harline and Paul J. Smith.
SOMETHING TO SING ABOUT, Grand National. Grand National Studio Music Dept.; C. Bakaleinikoff, musical director. Score by Victor Schertzinger.
SOULS AT SEA, Paramount. Paramount Studio Music Dept.; Boris Morros, head. Score by W. Franke Harling and Milan Roder.

WAY OUT WEST, Roach, M-G-M. Roach Studio Music Dept.; Marvin Hatley, head. Score by Marvin Hatley.
(NOTE: Through 1937, Best Score was considered a music department achievement and award was presented to department head instead of to composer.)

SOUND RECORDING
THE GIRL SAID NO, Grand National. A.E. Kaye.
HITTING A NEW HIGH, RKO Radio. John Aalberg.
* THE HURRICANE, Goldwyn, UA. Thomas Moulton.
IN OLD CHICAGO, 20th Century-Fox. E.H. Hansen.
THE LIFE OF EMILE ZOLA, Warner Bros. Nathan Levinson.
LOST HORIZON, Columbia. John Livadary.
MAYTIME, M-G-M. Douglas Shearer.
100 MEN AND A GIRL, Universal. Homer Tasker.
TOPPER, Roach, M-G-M. Elmer Raguse.
WELLS FARGO, Paramount. L.L. Ryder.

FILM EDITING
THE AWFUL TRUTH, Columbia. Al Clark.
CAPTAINS COURAGEOUS, M-G-M. Elmo Vernon.
THE GOOD EARTH, M-G-M. Basil Wrangell.
* LOST HORIZON, Columbia. Gene Havlick and Gene Milford.
100 MEN AND A GIRL, Universal. Bernard W. Burton.

ASSISTANT DIRECTOR
(Not given after this year)
C.C. COLEMAN, JR. for *Lost Horizon,* Columbia.
RUSS SAUNDERS for *The Life of Emile Zola,* Warner Bros.
ERIC STACEY for *A Star Is Born,* Selznick, UA.
HAL WALKER for *Souls at Sea,* Paramount.
* ROBERT WEBB for *In Old Chicago,* 20th Century-Fox.

DANCE DIRECTION
(Not given after this year)
BUSBY BERKELEY for "The Finale" number from *Varsity Show* (Warner Bros.).
BOBBY CONNOLLY for "Too Marvelous for Words" number from *Ready, and Able* (Warner Bros.).
DAVE GOULD for "All God's Children Got Rhythm" number from *A Day at the Races* (M-G-M.).
SAMMY LEE for "Swing Is Here to Stay" number from *Ali Baba Goes to Town* (20th Century-Fox).
HARRY LOSEE for "Prince Igor Suite" number from *Thin Ice* (20th Century-Fox).
* HERMES PAN for "Fun House" number from *Damsel in Distress* (RKO Radio).
LEORY PRINZ for "Luau" number from *Waikiki Wedding* (Paramount).

SHORT SUBJECTS

(Cartoons)
EDUCATED FISH, Paramount.
THE LITTLE MATCH GIRL, Mintz, Columbia.
* THE OLD MILL, Disney, RKO Radio.

(One-reel)
A NIGHT AT THE MOVIES, M-G-M. (Robert Benchley)
* PRIVATE LIFE OF THE GANNETS, Educational.
ROMANCE OF RADIUM, M-G-M. (Pete Smith Specialties)

(Two-reel)
DEEP SOUTH, RKO Radio. (Radio Musical Comedies)
SHOULD WIVES WORK, RKO Radio. (Leon Errol Comedies)
* TORTURE MONEY, M-G-M. (Crime Doesn't Pay)

(Color)
THE MAN WITHOUT A COUNTRY, Warner Bros. (Broadway Brevities)
* PENNY WISDOM, M-G-M. (Pete Smith Specialties)
POPULAR SCIENCE J-7-1, Paramount.

SPECIAL AWARDS
TO MACK SENNETT "for his lasting contribution to the comedy technique of the screen, the basic principles of which are as important today as when they were first put into practice, the Academy presents a Special Award to that master of fun, discoverer of stars, sympathetic, kindly, understanding comedy genius, Mack Sennett." (statuette)
TO EDGAR BERGEN for his outstanding comedy creation, Charlie McCarthy. (wooden statuette)
TO THE MUSEUM OF MODERN ART FILM LIBRARY for its significant work in collecting films dating from 1895 to the present and for the first time making available to the public the means of studying the historical and aesthetic development of the motion picture as one of the major arts. (scroll certificate)
TO W. HOWARD GREENE for the color photography of *A Star Is Born.* (This Award was recommended by a committee of leading cinematographers after viewing all the color pictures made during the year). (plaque)

1937 IRVING G. THALBERG MEMORIAL AWARD
(First year presented)
TO DARRYL F. ZANUCK.

SCIENTIFIC OR TECHNICAL

CLASS I (statuette)
AGFA ANSCO CORP. for Agfa Supreme and Agfa Ultra Speed pan motion picture negatives.

CLASS II (plaque)
WALT DISNEY PRODS., LTD., for the design and application to production of the Multi-Plane Camera;
EASTMAN KODAK CO. for two fine-grain duplicating film stocks;
FARCIOT EDOUART and PARAMOUNT PICTURES, INC., for the development of the Paramount dual screen transparency camera setup;
DOUGLAS SHEARER and the M-G-M STUDIO SOUND DEPT. for a method of varying the scanning width of variable density sound tracks (squeeze tracks) for the purpose of obtaining an increased amount of noise reduction.

CLASS III (citation)
JOHN ARNOLD and the M-G-M STUDIO CAMERA DEPT.;
JOHN LIVADARY, director of Sound Recording for Columbia Pictures Corp.;
THOMAS T. MOULTON and the UNITED ARTISTS STUDIO SOUND DEPT.;
RCA MANUFACTURING CO., INC.;
JOSEPH E. ROBBINS and PARAMOUNT PICTURES, INC.;
DOUGLAS SHEARER and the M-G-M STUDIO SOUND DEPARTMENT.

* INDICATES WINNER

The Academy's Second Decade

DEANNA DURBIN DAVID

"Dear Oscar,
You were only ten years old when we met, and here you are celebrating your fiftieth birthday! All my best wishes to you and to the many members of our big family.
Sincerely,"

Deanna Durbin David
Special Award, 1938

IRVING BERLIN

" I'm glad to present the award. I've known the fellow for a long time. "

Irving Berlin
Music (Best Song), 1942

EDITORS NOTE: Mr. Berlin requested, as his contribution, that we print his remarks at the 1942 Awards ceremony when he presented an Oscar to himself, for Best Song (''White Christmas'').

MICKEY ROONEY

" My first Oscar was a little Oscar, not because I am a little guy, but because I was honored as a first Oscar-winning child. It meant so much to me that I had it re-created for me for my birthday only last September, having relinquished it as part of alimony payments to a former wife. (Is that how to spell 'alimoney?' To me it means ALL-MONEY!) I love children . . . mine and all the rest of them in the world, and I am presently realizing a cherished dream I have always had: to be able to go into the homes and hearts of children through my S.S.A.C., The World Entertainment Guild. These are Self-Study Acting Courses on tapes, in which I advise my students to never lose the naturalness and joy of childhood. I feel it is a key to the success of all great performers.

I am grateful and proud to be a part of the wonderful work of the Academy of Motion Picture Arts and Sciences and the 50 Golden Years of Oscar. "

Mickey Rooney
Special Award, 1938

GINGER ROGERS

" In 1940 there were no television cameras to record my gratitude when I received an 'Oscar' for my performance in Kitty Foyle. *Now 50 Golden Years of Oscar gives me—at long last—the opportunity to say to my peers of the Academy—thank you for that marvelous tribute. "*

Ginger Rogers
Best Actress, 1940

The outbreak of World War II, outside Hollywood's boundaries but certainly within its consciousness, had a distinct effect on all elements connected with the motion picture industry and the Academy of Motion Picture Arts and Sciences, as well.

It was not the first introduction the Academy had to the world of the military. Back in 1930, at the government's request, the Academy had been called upon to help pave the way for a training program in which Signal Corps officers could learn about motion picture production in order to produce military training films. Sponsored and planned by the Academy, one Signal Corps officer per year for eight years was trained in the intricacies of photography, editing, mixing, sound and other elements, by visiting actual film departments at work. With the outbreak of World War II, the studios opened their doors even wider to aid the war effort.

Darryl F. Zanuck, head of 20th Century-Fox studios and chairman of the Academy's Research Council, recognized the need for well-made training films for newly inducted military personnel, and he immediately

Judy Garland, Mickey Rooney

Ginger Rogers, Lynn Fontanne, Alfred Lunt

volunteered the Council's complete cooperation. Approved by the Academy's Board of Governors, the Council set to work arranging for major motion picture studios, including 20th Century-Fox, Metro-Goldwyn-Mayer, Paramount and Warner Bros., to produce training films of all kinds, on a non-profit basis. The studios used existing equipment and facilities to do the work, and charged the government only for film stock and film processing and a few labor salaries not waived by unions. From the start of the war until mid-1943, over four hundred training shorts and related featurettes were delivered to the armed services, covering a wide range of subjects, including *Combat Counter-Intelligence* and *The Articles of War,* as well as *Sex Hygiene* and *Safeguarding Military Information.*

The war also had an effect on the Academy's actual Awards-night galas, to that time held in posh dining rooms of Los Angeles and Hollywood hotels, such as the Hollywood Roosevelt, the Ambassador or the Biltmore. Not only was ever-increasing attendance causing space problems and overcrowded conditions, but Academy officials also reasoned it was not in the best interests of the organization to dispense industry Oscars at elegant banquets at a time when much of the world was suffering a lack of food and the indignities of a calamitous war. On March 2, 1944, honoring film achievements during the calendar year of 1943, the festivities were held for the first time in an actual theater, Grauman's Chinese in Hollywood, without an accompanying gala dinner-dance.

DORE SCHARY

" *Herewith—some memories:*

I remember Frank Capra's face when it was announced: 'And the winner is Frank Capra!'

I remember Eric Johnston, who in 1942 presented: 'As an honored guest, the distinguished Ambassador from Japan— I mean China.'

I remember Clare Booth Luce saying as she presented the writers award: 'And the winner is John Husston!'

A moment later John, in accepting, said 'Thank you, Miss Looka!'

I remember the year the program simply ran out of TV time.

I remember the night that Frank Lloyd and Frank Capra were both nominated— and as the announcer said, 'And the winner is Frank . . .' both Franks got up. But the winner was Lloyd.

And finally I remember when I got my Oscar. It was a golden moment—just as golden as shining Oscar.

Warmest and best wishes. "

Dore Schary
Writing (Original Story), 1938

MARY ASTOR

" *It was war time when I received my award. And since metal was precious, all the winners in other than Best Actor, Best Actress and Best Picture were given small metal plaques. Of course I was delighted with the honor, and I thanked everyone with a pretty little speech. (I'm grateful now that we had no TV coverage then!)*

Over the years and after my retirement, I felt something was lacking. I had won an Oscar—and yet I hadn't.

In my book, A Life On Film, I describe my feelings, and in parentheses I wrote: (Hey Academy! I would dearly love to have a real Oscar!)

So now I have my real Golden Boy standing on my bookshelf beside the faded little plaque of 1942. "

Mary Astor
Best Supporting Actress, 1941

RICHARD RODGERS

" *Oscar Hammerstein II and I won an Oscar for 'It Might As Well Be Spring' in 1945. The only thing that could have made me happier than this award was the song itself.* "

Richard Rodgers
Music (Song), 1945

CLAUDE JARMAN JR.

" *Even at the age of twelve, it was an overwhelming experience to receive an Oscar. Thirty-one years later I still feel the same way.* "

Claude Jarman, Jr.
Special Award, 1946

GREER GARSON

"*On the night I was given my Oscar I tried impulsively to express not only thanks but some honest thoughts about the Awards system. Hardly tactful timing, perhaps. I was said to have given the longest acceptance speech ever. It wasn't, really. It just seemed that way to a roomful of weary listeners at midnight. However, maybe I can claim modestly to have triggered a needed overhaul of the Awards program, that gradually transformed it from the original rather loosely organized informal dinner-dance evening for Industry members, to a split-second, elaborately staged, spectacular gala for an audience of millions.*

Of course I treasure my statuette. And I treasure several nominations just as much, because I have always thought the nominations themselves should be considered the Awards. For actors, acting is not a competition but a sharing and blending of experiences and imaginings.

I am forever proud of being part of this Industry and this Academy. "

Greer Garson
Best Actress, 1942

ALEXANDER GOLITZEN

" *To be nominated (and as many times as I have) comes always as a surprise and with great appreciation as one realizes that it was approved by one's own kind.*

Then comes the 'day' —and winning an 'Oscar' (whether the first, second, etc., etc. is always a 'thrill').

In the 'old' days there was no celebration, ball, etc., so one merely collected one's statuette and celebrated with close friends. In my case (when I won the first one) we all met at Jimmy Wong Howe's Restaurant (he was a great cameraman), and this is where I made my acceptance speech. "

Alexander Golitzen
Art Direction (Color), 1943; 1960
Art Direction (Black-and-white), 1962

There was also another major change in Oscar during the second decade of existence: beginning with the 1940 Awards, presented February 27, 1941, winners were no longer divulged in advance, and the names of recipients were kept completely secret in sealed and guarded envelopes, until the statuettes were formally handed to the winners.

Change has always been an integral part of the Academy story, then as now. There has been a determination on the part of the Academy to stay in step with changing industry styles and technological innovations, the need for expanding or deleting requirements in certain Awards categories. These were necessitated by actualities, such as the increased use of color in the making of films. Rules change yearly— as have voting requirements and category designations—all in an attempt to do right by the industry and the Academy itself. Among the important changes made between 1938 and 1947 were several Academy constitutional bylaws. In December of 1939, for example, the bylaws were revised to group the five existing Academy branches—Producers, Directors, Actors, Writers and Technicians—into two main categories, the Arts Branches and the Sciences Branches. In 1946, memberships were defined into three specific types: active, honorary and life; earlier, they had also included fellowship memberships and foundation memberships. The number of Academy branches were also increased from five to eight, with the addition of branches for Music, Short Subjects and Public Relations, then later it was increased to a total of twelve. The Technicians branch was retired in favor of more specifically defined branches for Cinematographers, Film Editors, Art Directors (which

Greer Garson, James Cagney

Joan Crawford

Teresa Wright

includes Costume Designers), Sound and Miscellaneous, the latter to cover those not included elsewhere.

There was another significant rule change in 1941: unlike times past, an Academy Award winner was no longer able to sell "or otherwise dispose of (an Oscar statuette), nor permit it to be sold or disposed of by operation of law without first offering to sell it back to the Academy for ten dollars." This protection was sealed when the Academy Award design was officially copyrighted on September 2, 1941.

As the importance, prestige and fame of the Academy Awards presentation ceremonies continued to grow, other Academy functions also continued to expand, and with far-reaching effects. By 1941, the archival and reference library facilities of the Academy had grown to such an extent it was ranked as one of the most complete collections on motion pictures anywhere in the world. The library now included almost every book published in English about motion pictures, production information on nearly 20,000 motion pictures produced since 1896, plus still photographs and scripts from many significant productions. The library continued to develop its extensive biography files of clippings and still photographs on actors, actresses, directors and other film people.

There was a special clipping file established dealing solely with the effects of the war on the motion picture industry, and in the archives there was the Academy's own growing collection of motion picture prints, in both 35mm and 16mm, encompassing features and short subjects. In order to provide a tangible record of Oscar's screen achievements, the Academy also began a project to acquire a print from studios of every film which has received an Academy Award nomination.

TERESA WRIGHT

" The Academy Award ceremonies of 1942, our first war year, was an evening of mixed emotions for all of us who had worked on Mrs. Miniver. *Willie Wyler, in service overseas, could not be with us to share the thrill of* Miniver *winning six awards. It was also an unbelievably exciting night for me, as I had been nominated for two awards, for my second and third films: Best Performance by an Actress in a Starring Role in* Pride of the Yankees, *as well as the supporting role in* Mrs. Miniver.

A memory that I recall with affection was an evening when I had been asked to present an award. I was sitting in a dark corner backstage at Grauman's Chinese Theatre as nervous as if I had to perform. Suddenly I realized I shared the darkness with a beautiful man: white curly hair, sad-comic face, huge harp; my favorite Marx brother. I was so delighted to see him that I couldn't keep my eyes off him; a fact which he noticed because he broke his famous silence to say, 'Young lady, are you flirting with me?'"

Teresa Wright
Best Supporting Actress, 1942

ANNE REVERE

" The nomination for my 'Mrs. Brown' in National Velvet *brought me great joy, but as an orphan with no studio to champion my cause, I had little hope of winning the Oscar.*

On the eve of the great day, the odds-on favorite was Warner Bros.' talented young starlet Ann Blyth, for her notable performance in Mildred Pierce.

Next morning the papers reported the surprising winner: ANNE REVERE, the talented young Warner Bros.' starlet!

The surprise, I think, doubled my pleasure."

Anne Revere
Best Supporting Actress, 1945

HAROLD RUSSELL

❝*Winning two 'Oscars' for my first commercial motion picture is and was a thrill almost beyond description. The Best Years of Our Lives was Hollywood's tribute to the servicemen and women of World War II and the awards it won reflected that feeling. Personally, my Oscars brought me in contact with the field of rehabilitation and the opportunity to work with disabled people in the areas of education and employment. For all of this, I am very grateful to the wonderful people of the motion picture industry.*❞

Harold Russell
Best Supporting Actor, 1946
Honorary Award, 1946

ANNE BAXTER

❝*Oscar, Oscar, wherefore art thou, Oscar? It's easy to lose things when you move. I lost my Oscar. He vanished between van and new threshold or fell prey to the sticky fingers of a souvenir-happy moving man, but in either case— gone. Getting his duplicate was a polite hassle, complete with affidavits, details, descriptions and seventy-five dollars.*

I moved yet again, under particularly horrendous circumstances, and undid the royal blue, golden-corded felt bag cradling Oscar's stand-in, only to watch him crash out in two gleaming hunks—not lost or stolen this time. Broken. Will I try, try again? Yes. Because nothing else will so sharply bring into focus an emotional peak.

Through the years, awards have mushroomed as after a cloudburst, but there is only one Oscar. Belittle, scoff at or denigrate him as you will, when your name comes bounding out of that microphone I defy adrenal glands of marble not to quiver. In memoriam, I still cringe at my acceptance mumbles and leaky eyes and at looking fatly stuffed into a pompous navy blue lace dress, but it's a moment impossible to plan.

The best response I can remember was Jimmy Cagney's. He won for Yankee Doodle Dandy at the last monkey-draped Cocoanut Grove Awards Dinner. I can see him now, stepping energetically up to the mike and carving the hush neatly with:

'It's nice to know some people think a job has been well done. Thank you.' Wish I'd said that.❞

Anne Baxter
Best Supporting Actress, 1946

Harold Russell, Shirley Temple, Claude Jarman, Jr.

With such an extensive collection of tangible material, the Academy was also able to aid and support film research under the guidance of the Academy Foundation, created during this period to take charge of the educational and cultural activities of the Academy.

The Foundation was officially incorporated on January 31, 1944, as a separate unit from the Academy, in order to be eligible to receive gifts of private funding and certain tax-exemption privileges. The Foundation accepts bequests and donations from estates, governmental agencies, other foundations, the motion picture industry and the general public, and uses the funds to administer educational, cultural and film archival activities.

The ties between the Academy and educational groups actually started long before the Academy Foundation came into being on May 24, 1927, only days after that initial organizational banquet. Cecil B. DeMille and Milton Sills, representing the Academy, met with the then-president of the University of Southern California regarding the establishment of cinema classes at the school, with the Academy's assistance. Further aid was later given to such schools as Yale, Purdue, Columbia, the University of Oregon and others. In 1943, the Academy helped the

University of California at Los Angeles (UCLA) organize extensive courses on the motion picture field, and later remained closely affiliated with the school in an advisory capacity.

The cooperation with schools and educational institutions continued. The Academy supplied a constant flow of information on the movie spectrum to students around the world, in the form of clippings, still photographs, scripts, journal references and other kinds of requested information. Later, in 1972, the Academy, in conjunction with the Academy Foundation, established the National Film Information Service to offer access, by mail, to the extensive holdings of the library, so historians, students, scholars, teachers and film programmers living outside the Los Angeles area could also take advantage of the library's fund of knowledge.

The Academy Foundation was also deeply involved in restoring an invaluable collection of Paper Prints at the Library of Congress. From 1894 to 1912, all motion pictures had been copyrighted via a series of still photographs, made by paper prints of the originals on celluloid which were then stored in the Copyright Office in Washington, D.C., and forgotten. In the 1940s, Howard Walls, a Library of Congress employee, discovered over two and one-half million feet of dusty copies stored there, including newsreels with priceless footage of early presidential inaugurations, coverage of the Boer and Spanish-American wars, and other films of historical interest no longer available from other sources. There were also many theatrical features in the collection, long since assumed to have been lost. Walls was immediately appointed curator of the collection for the Library of Congress and began the task of transferring the positive paper prints to motion picture film, but was soon stopped when Congress abruptly voted to end the Motion Picture Division, due to wartime cutbacks. The Academy Foundation then took over, hired Walls to continue as curator. Walls was eventually succeeded by Kemp Niver, a film restoration specialist, and the job was completed ten years later.

Edmund Gwenn, Anne Baxter

David O. Selznick, Vivien Leigh

MARGARET O'BRIEN

“ The Academy Awards have the same mystique for actors as for audiences and I must admit it was a delightful assignment to look back and recollect when my mother told me we would be attending the Academy Awards and that there was a possibility that I might receive an Oscar for my performance in Meet Me In St. Louis *I was typically excited and apprehensive. I think my reaction pleased my mother, but what she didn't realize was that my excitement was the possibility of receiving the award from my very secret heartthrob, Bob Hope, and my apprehension was the possibility that one of the false teeth that the studio made me wear to cover my missing baby teeth might fall out as they often did while we were making the film. Nevertheless, all went well. My false teeth held fast, I received the Oscar, and the handsome Bob Hope presented it to me. As a matter of fact, he even hugged me; he hugged most of the other actresses too, but I was the only one he both hugged and lifted.* ”

Margaret O'Brien
Honorary Award, 1944

JACK CARDIFF

“ When Madame Curie *received the Nobel Prize and Churchill was knighted by the Queen, they must have felt the same orbital elation I experienced when I won my Oscar.*

I am unashamedly conceited about it. It would be most difficult for any visitor to my house to avoid seeing it, shimmering its golden glow, beckoning homage like a god.

The visitor says, 'Is that really an Oscar?' and I take it off the shelf with a Peter Sellers smirk and condescendingly let it be handled. They weigh it and stroke it reverently, murmuring the usual things — 'Never thought I'd hold a real Oscar . . . is it real gold, etc.' and then it goes back in the middle of my other trophies.

But proud as I am of my Golden Globes, the New York Film Critics' Award and others, my Oscar stands out in Olympian detachment like a dazzling beacon to artistic endeavour, and whenever I gaze at it I always seem to grow a few inches taller. ”

Jack Cardiff
Cinematography (Color), 1947

LAURENCE OLIVIER

" *My thoughts for a special award for Henry V in 1947 and for Hamlet in '48 for performance and best picture were for each and both of the most delighted kind, and my gratitude of the heartfelt fullest.* "

Laurence Olivier
Special Award, 1946
Best Actor, 1948

MIKLOS ROZSA

" *At the time I received my Oscars, they meant a great deal to me careerwise, and I am very grateful for them.* "

Miklos Rozsa
Music (Scoring Dramatic or
Comedy Picture), 1945; 1947; 1959

LORETTA YOUNG

" *There is something about a dark horse winning that brings the house down. In 1947, I was the dark horse, the house was the Shrine Auditorium! All those hands clapping made lots of noise. Beautiful noise! And I allowed myself the luxury of believing it was indeed all for me. For over twenty years, I'd been more than satisfied with the work itself, without a nod from the Academy—now the 'jackpot'!*

I guess primarily it was a good night for me because it meant the industry looked at me as more than just 'pretty as usual. Period.' Acceptance! A great word, great for the heart and soul. Great for the ego, the actor's source. My self-confidence soared and in a strange way it has never wavered since, at least not in any serious way.

Soon, wise friends were reminding me 'the Oscar is only the icing on the cake.' I agreed with them, I still do. But, my, oh, my, what a lovely taste that icing had, and still has!

Every time I open the guest coat closet, in my front hall, and see Oscar residing on a shelf, all by himself, with the automatic door light shining down on him, I enjoy a small wave of gratitude and I'm delighted all over again to have been chosen a winner.

In my professional life, more than once, it's occurred to me there are only two material things in my life that I've never gotten used to. One, the Oscar statuette residing in my home, with my name on it. The other, for no sensible reason I know of, is my Rolls-Royce car. Unless it's because they both make me feel like a movie star, and I like that. I like it a lot! "

Loretta Young
Best Actress, 1947

Academy headquarters, 1946-1975

In 1946, the Academy again found itself in need of more room. A twenty-five-year-old building, known as the Marquis Theater and functioning as a neighborhood cinema, located at 9038 Melrose Avenue, was purchased from the West Coast theater chain and became the new Academy of Motion Picture Arts and Sciences' headquarters. The main floor of the building housed a 950-seat theater, and allowed greater seating capacity for members than the Academy had earlier enjoyed; its projection booth and sound facilities were soon redesigned by the Research Council to make it one of the most acoustically perfect theaters anywhere. The upper floor, designed for executive offices and the library, allowed sorely needed room for those ever-expanding files and other material. By the end of the decade, the library was averaging three hundred visiting researchers per week, including studio personnel, Academy members, college students and others needing assistance. Several thousand phone calls were also coming in each month, asking for specific pieces of information on some facet or another of the movie world, or the Academy operation.

By 1947, Academy membership had reached a new high of 1600, the war was over, Oscar was in a new home, and there were new challenges and projects ahead. One of them was an attempt to set into motion a series of twelve documentary featurettes which would help inform the public about specific facets of film production and industry life, plus concurrently improve the public image of the industry, something Hollywood always seemed to need. Spearheaded by the Academy, and underwritten by the Producers Association, the films were made at various cooperating studios, and budgeted so that the financial returns from the distribution of the first five made would pay the costs of the entire dozen planned. The series, including *The Actor, The Writer, The Director, The Sound Man, The Cinematographer, The Costume Designer, Moments in Music, History Brought to Life, Movies Are Adventure, Let's Go to the Movies* and *This Theater and You,* were not finished until into the Academy's third decade, but in later years, through distribution in 16mm to schools, libraries and universities, it proved to be one of the Academy's most worthwhile legacies to the understanding of Hollywood and its work.

Fredric March, Loretta Young, Price Waterhouse & Co. representative

ACADEMY PRESIDENTS, THE SECOND DECADE

October 1937-October 1938	FRANK CAPRA
October 1938-December 1939	FRANK CAPRA
December 1939-December 1940	WALTER WANGER
January 1941-October 1941	WALTER WANGER
October 1941-December 1941	BETTE DAVIS*
December 1941-October 1942	WALTER WANGER
October 1942-October 1943	WALTER WANGER
October 1943-October 1944	WALTER WANGER
October 1944-October 1945	WALTER WANGER
October 1945-May 1947	JEAN HERSHOLT

*Resigned during first term

CELESTE HOLM

"When I was making my first film in 1946, I met a dear man named Gabe York who was in the publicity department. I never knew his title—but he came down on the set to talk to me, and before I knew it we were talking about the films that had meant a great deal to us personally, and why. There weren't a whole lot of them—some of them were foreign, which seemed heretical, seated as we were on the back lot at 20th Century-Fox. But all of them had shown people as not only fascinating, but valuable—that to be human was a wonderful thing to be.

'I want to make movies that say something,' I said, 'for people to keep.'

Gabe York wore glasses that made his eyes look enormous. 'From Hollywood?' he asked, and his eyes looked even bigger.

'Well,' I said, 'I can try.'

Two years later I was sitting in my assigned seat at the Academy Awards presentations in the old Shrine Auditorium (which always smelled softly of elephants). Quite early in the proceedings I heard, '. . . and the winner,' spoken by Donald Crisp, 'for her role in Gentleman's Agreement, Celeste Holm.'

I literally could not move, the lights were so sudden and so intense. My husband muttered, 'Get up, get up.'

I didn't, so he and the man on my right hoisted me to my feet. I had not expected to win; Ethel Barrymore was also in the same category.

In a dream I walked toward the stage, and as I started up the steps, I hoped I would not stumble up the inside of my ruffled petticoat. I didn't, and I found myself facing that huge, warm ocean of appreciation. And then I was supposed to say something. I hadn't prepared anything because I was sure I would not win. And I suddenly thought of Gabe York.

'I thought,' I said slowly, looking for the words from a full heart, 'that I'd already received the greatest reward an actress can have—of being in a picture that brings understanding, in a world that seems to need it so much.' As I left the dazzle of the stage, into the dark wings, there was Gabe. 'You did it!' he said.

And I leaked happy tears all over his tuxedo."

Celeste Holm
Best Supporting Actress, 1947

Best Actor: Spencer Tracy as Father Flanagan in *Boys Town* (M-G-M; directed by Norman Taurog). An Academy Award winner for the second consecutive year, Tracy played the real-life Flanagan, a man who founded a community 12 miles outside Omaha in 1920 to help turn juvenile delinquents into responsible citizens. Mickey Rooney co-starred, and the film's success inspired a sequel in 1941, *Men of Boys Town,* again with Tracy as Father Flanagan plus Rooney.

1938 The Eleventh Year

Across the world, grim war clouds continued to cover Europe as the Academy of Motion Picture Arts and Sciences entered its second decade, and Hollywood itself was having some troubled times, as well. Box office attendance had taken an alarming dip which—coupled with possible revenue losses from the dwindling European film market—caused jitters within the industry. Oscar night, however, was an unparalleled success, the biggest to date, held on February 3, 1939, in the Biltmore Bowl of the Los Angeles Biltmore Hotel.

For the second year, both the nominations and the final vote for Award winners was made by 12,000 Hollywood citizens (Academy members, plus members of various industry guilds and unions). Three of the four acting winners (Spencer Tracy, Bette Davis, Walter Brennan) had won before, so they were familiar faces in the winners' circle, as was director Frank Capra, who collected his third Oscar in that luminous category. There was no official master of ceremonies at the Award banquet, and most of the acting statuettes were presented by character actor Cedric Hardwicke and new matinee idol Tyrone Power. Shirley Temple, ten years old and Hollywood's boxoffice queen, presented Walt Disney with one large Honorary Oscar and seven miniature ones on behalf of his animated feature *Snow White and the Seven Dwarfs.* Miniature-sized Academy Awards also went to Universal's Deanna Durbin (age seventeen) and M-G-M's Mickey Rooney (age eighteen) for their juvenile performances during the preceding year. Biggest single winner of all 1938 films was Warner Bros.' colorful *The Adventures of Robin Hood,* which won three Academy Awards, but the Best Picture prize itself went to Mr. Capra's infectious *You Can't Take It With You,* just the kind of warm and comical entertainment to take everyone's mind off uneasy ledger sheets in the bookkeeping departments, and that impending crisis overseas.

Best Picture: You Can't Take It With You (Columbia; produced and directed by Frank Capra). The zany story of an eccentric clan by the name of Vanderhof (with some Sycamores thrown in), it was based on the Pulitzer Prize-winning play by George S. Kaufman and Moss Hart, and starred (left to right) Lionel Barrymore, James Stewart, Jean Arthur and Edward Arnold, plus scene-stealers like Mischa Auer, Spring Byington, Donald Meek, Ann Miller, H.B. Warner and Eddie (Rochester) Anderson. As with most Capra capers, it had a generous supply of cracker-barrel philosophy mixed in with its daffy doings and comedy.

(above)
Best Actress: Bette Davis as Julie Marsden, and **Best Supporting Actress Fay Bainter** as Aunt Belle (with Henry Fonda, at right) in *Jezebel* (Warner Bros.; produced by Henry Blanke). Under the meticulous direction of William Wyler, Bette Davis won her second Oscar as a willful, headstrong Southern belle in pre-Civil War New Orleans who ultimately sacrifices herself for the man she loves; Miss Bainter—also a 1938 nominee as Best Actress for *White Banners*—received the Supporting Actress Award as Julie's stern but sympathetic friend.

(left)
Best Director: Frank Capra for *You Can't Take It With You.* It was the third win for Capra (here adjusting the lapel of Lionel Barrymore, as Ann Miller watches) after previous Oscars in 1934 and 1936. He also served four terms (October 1935 through October 1938) as president of the Academy.

The Adventures of Robin Hood (Warner Bros., produced by Hal B. Wallis, with Henry Blanke) won the most Oscars in 1938. Starring Errol Flynn, Olivia de Havilland, Basil Rathbone and Claude Rains, it won three Academy Awards, one each for Original Music Score, Art Direction and Film Editing.

(below)
Best Supporting Actor: Walter Brennan as Peter Goodwin in *Kentucky* (20th Century-Fox; produced by Darryl F. Zanuck). Supporting Loretta Young, Richard Greene and some Technicolored and thoroughbred racehorses, Brennan helped beautiful Loretta save her family plantation with a long-shot race at the Kentucky Derby. Directed by David Butler, it brought Brennan his second Academy Award in three years.

Nominations 1938

PICTURE

THE ADVENTURES OF ROBIN HOOD, Warner Bros. Produced by Hal B. Wallis, with Henry Blanke.
ALEXANDER'S RAGTIME BAND, 20th Century-Fox. Produced by Darryl F. Zanuck, with Harry Joe Brown.
BOYS TOWN, M-G-M. Produced by John W. Considine, Jr.
THE CITADEL, M-G-M (British). Produced by Victor Saville.
FOUR DAUGHTERS, Warner Bros.-First National. Produced by Hal B. Wallis, with Henry Blanke.
GRAND ILLUSION, R.A.O., World Pictures (French). Produced by Frank Rollmer and Albert Pinkovitch.
JEZEBEL, Warner Bros. Produced by Hal B. Wallis, with Henry Blanke.
PYGMALION, M-G-M (British). Produced by Gabriel Pascal.
TEST PILOT, M-G-M. Produced by Louis D. Lighton.
★ YOU CAN'T TAKE IT WITH YOU, Columbia. Produced by Frank Capra.

ACTOR

CHARLES BOYER in *Algiers*, Wanger, UA.
JAMES CAGNEY in *Angels With Dirty Faces*, Warner Bros.
ROBERT DONAT in *The Citadel*, M-G-M (British).
LESLIE HOWARD in *Pygmalion*, M-G-M (British).
★ SPENCER TRACY in *Boys Town*, M-G-M.

ACTRESS

FAY BAINTER in *White Banners*, Warner Bros.
★ BETTE DAVIS in *Jezebel*, Warner Bros.
WENDY HILLER in *Pygmalion*, M-G-M (British).
NORMA SHEARER in *Marie Antoinette*, M-G-M.
MARGARET SULLAVAN in *Three Comrades*, M-G-M.

SUPPORTING ACTOR

★ WALTER BRENNAN in *Kentucky*, 20th Century-Fox.
JOHN GARFIELD in *Four Daughters*, Warner Bros.
GENE LOCKHART in *Algiers*, Wanger UA.
ROBERT MORLEY in *Marie Antoinette*, M-G-M.
BASIL RATHBONE in *If I Were King*, Paramount.

SUPPORTING ACTRESS

★ FAY BAINTER in *Jezebel*, Warner Bros.
BEULAH BONDI in *Of Human Hearts*, M-G-M.
BILLIE BURKE in *Merrily We Live*, Roach, M-G-M.
SPRING BYINGTON in *You Can't Take It With You*, Columbia.
MILIZA KORJUS in *The Great Waltz*, M-G-M.

DIRECTION

★ FRANK CAPRA for *You Can't Take It With You*, Columbia.
MICHAEL CURTIZ for *Angels With Dirty Faces*, Warner Bros.
MICHAEL CURTIZ for *Four Daughters*, Warner Bros.
NORMAN TAUROG for *Boys Town*, M-G-M.
KING VIDOR for *The Citadel*, M-G-M (British).

WRITING

(Original Story)
ALEXANDER'S RAGTIME BAND, 20th Century-Fox. Irving Berlin.
ANGELS WITH DIRTY FACES, Warner Bros. Rowland Brown.
BLOCKADE, Wanger, UA. John Howard Lawson.
★ BOYS TOWN, M-G-M. Eleanore Griffin and Dore Schary.
MAD ABOUT MUSIC, Universal. Marcella Burke and Frederick Kohner.
TEST PILOT, M-G-M. Frank Wead.

(Screenplay)
BOYS TOWN, M-G-M. John Meehan and Dore Schary.
THE CITADEL, M-G-M (British). Ian Dalrymple, Elizabeth Hill and Frank Wead.
FOUR DAUGHTERS, Warner Bros. Lenore Coffee and Julius J. Epstein.
★ PYGMALION, M-G-M (British). George Bernard Shaw; adaptation by Ian Dalrymple, Cecil Lewis and W.P. Lipscomb.
YOU CAN'T TAKE IT WITH YOU, Columbia. Robert Riskin.

CINEMATOGRAPHY

ALGIERS, Wanger, UA. James Wong Howe.
ARMY GIRL, Republic. Ernest Miller and Harry Wild.
THE BUCCANEER, Paramount. Victor Milner.
★ THE GREAT WALTZ, M-G-M. Joseph Ruttenberg.
JEZEBEL, Warner Bros. Ernest Haller.
MAD ABOUT MUSIC, Universal. Joseph Valentine.
MERRILY WE LIVE, Roach, M-G-M. Norbert Brodine.
SUEZ, 20th Century-Fox. Peverell Marley.
VIVACIOUS LADY, RKO Radio. Robert de Grasse.
YOU CAN'T TAKE IT WITH YOU, Columbia. Joseph Walker.
THE YOUNG IN HEART, Selznick, UA. Leon Shamroy.

ART DIRECTION

★ THE ADVENTURES OF ROBIN HOOD, Warner Bros. Carl J. Weyl.
THE ADVENTURES OF TOM SAWYER, Selznick, UA. Lyle Wheeler.
ALEXANDER'S RAGTIME BAND, 20th Century-Fox. Bernard Herzbrun and Boris Leven.
ALGIERS, Wanger, UA. Alexander Toluboff.
CAREFREE, RKO Radio. Van Nest Polglase.
GOLDWYN FOLLIES, Goldwyn, UA. Richard Day.
HOLIDAY, Columbia. Stephen Goosson and Lionel Banks.
IF I WERE KING, Paramount. Hans Dreier and John Goodman.
MAD ABOUT MUSIC, Universal. Jack Otterson.
MARIE ANTOINETTE, M-G-M. Cedric Gibbons.
MERRILY WE LIVE, Roach, M-G-M. Charles D. Hall.

SOUND RECORDING

ARMY GIRL, Republic. Charles Lootens.
★ THE COWBOY AND THE LADY, Goldwyn, UA. Thomas Moulton.
FOUR DAUGHTERS, Warner Bros. Nathan Levinson.
IF I WERE KING, Paramount. L.L. Ryder.
MERRILY WE LIVE, Roach, M-G-M. Elmer Raguse.
SWEETHEARTS, M-G-M. Douglas Shearer.
SUEZ, 20th Century-Fox. Edmund Hansen.
THAT CERTAIN AGE, Universal. Bernard B. Brown.
VIVACIOUS LADY, RKO Radio. James Wilkinson.
YOU CAN'T TAKE IT WITH YOU, Columbia. John Livadary.

FILM EDITING

* **THE ADVENTURES OF ROBIN HOOD**, Warner Bros. Ralph Dawson.
ALEXANDER'S RAGTIME BAND, 20th Century-Fox. Barbara McLean.
THE GREAT WALTZ, M-G-M. Tom Held.
TEST PILOT, M-G-M. Tom Held.
YOU CAN'T TAKE IT WITH YOU, Columbia. Gene Havlick.

MUSIC
(New classifications)

(Song)

ALWAYS AND ALWAYS (*Mannequin*, M-G-M); Music by Edward Ward. Lyrics by Chet Forrest and Bob Wright.
CHANGE PARTNERS AND DANCE WITH ME (*Carefree*, RKO Radio); Music and Lyrics by Irving Berlin.
THE COWBOY AND THE LADY (*The Cowboy and the Lady*, Goldwyn, UA); Music by Lionel Newman. Lyrics by Arthur Quenzer.
DUST (*Under Western Stars*, Republic); Music and Lyrics by Johnny Marvin.
JEEPERS CREEPERS (*Going Places*, Warner Bros.); Music by Harry Warren. Lyrics by Johnny Mercer.
MERRILY WE LIVE (*Merrily We Live*, Roach, M-G-M); Music by Phil Craig. Lyrics by Arthur Quenzer.
A MIST OVER THE MOON (*The Lady Objects*, Columbia); Music by Ben Oakland. Lyrics by Oscar Hammerstein II.
MY OWN (*That Certain Age*, Universal); Music by Jimmy McHugh. Lyrics by Harold Adamson.
NOW IT CAN BE TOLD (*Alexander's Ragtime Band*, 20th Century-Fox); Music and Lyrics by Irving Berlin.
* **THANKS FOR THE MEMORY** (*Big Broadcast of 1938*, Paramount); Music by Ralph Rainger. Lyrics by Leo Robin.

(Scoring)

* **ALEXANDER'S RAGTIME BAND**, 20th Century-Fox. Alfred Newman.
CAREFREE, RKO Radio. Victor Baravalle.
GIRLS SCHOOL, Columbia. Morris Stoloff and Gregory Stone.
GOLDWYN FOLLIES, Goldwyn, UA. Alfred Newman.
JEZEBEL, Warner Bros. Max Steiner.
MAD ABOUT MUSIC, Universal. Charles Previn and Frank Skinner.
STORM OVER BENGAL, Republic. Cy Feuer.
SWEETHEARTS, M-G-M. Herbert Stothart.
THERE GOES MY HEART, Hal Roach, UA. Marvin Hatley.
TROPIC HOLIDAY, Paramount. Boris Morros.
THE YOUNG IN HEART, Selznick, UA. Franz Waxman.

(Original Score)

* **THE ADVENTURES OF ROBIN HOOD**, Warner Bros. Erich Wolfgang Korngold.
ARMY GIRL, Republic. Victor Young.
BLOCKADE, Wanger, UA. Werner Janssen.
BLOCKHEADS, Roach, UA. Marvin Hatley.
BREAKING THE ICE, RKO Radio. Victor Young.
THE COWBOY AND THE LADY, Goldwyn, UA. Alfred Newman.
IF I WERE KING, Paramount. Richard Hageman.
MARIE ANTOINETTE, M-G-M. Herbert Stothart.
PACIFIC LINER, RKO Radio. Russell Bennett.
SUEZ, 20th Century-Fox. Louis Silvers.
THE YOUNG IN HEART, Selznick, UA. Franz Waxman.

Pygmalion (released by M-G-M; produced in England by Gabriel Pascal) starred Leslie Howard and Wendy Hiller, and won an Academy Award for Best Screenplay. Recipient George Bernard Shaw feigned indignance when informed of the honor. "To offer me an award of this sort is an insult, as if they've never heard of me in Hollywood before!" the 82-year-old playwright bellowed. But friends of Shaw say he always displayed his Oscar with affectionate pride to anyone who visited his home thereafter.

Snow White and the Seven Dwarfs (released by RKO Radio; produced by Walt Disney) received a Special Honorary Award salute in 1938: one full-size statuette and seven miniature ones to the man who pioneered the animated feature.

SPECIAL AWARDS

TO DEANNA DURBIN and **MICKEY ROONEY** for their significant contribution in bringing to the screen the spirit and personification of youth, and as juvenile players setting a high standard of ability and achievement. (miniature statuette trophies)

TO HARRY M. WARNER in recognition of patriotic service in the production of historical short subjects presenting significant episodes in the early struggle of the American people for liberty. (scroll)

TO WALT DISNEY for *Snow White and the Seven Dwarfs*, recognized as a significant screen innovation which has charmed millions and pioneered a great new entertainment field for the motion picture cartoon. (one statuette —seven miniature statuettes)

TO OLIVER MARSH and **ALLEN DAVEY** for the color cinematography of the M-G-M production *Sweethearts*. (plaques)

For outstanding achievement in creating special photographic and sound effects in the Paramount production *Spawn of the North*: special effects by **GORDON JENNINGS**, assisted by **JAN DOMELA, DEV JENNINGS, IRMIN ROBERTS** and **ART SMITH**: transparencies by **FARCIOT EDOUART**, assisted by **LOYAL GRIGGS**; sound effects by **LOREN RYDER**, assisted by **HARRY MILLS, LOUIS H. MESENKOP** and **WALTER OBERST**. (plaques)

TO J. ARTHUR BALL for his outstanding contributions to the advancement of color in motion picture photography. (scroll)

SHORT SUBJECTS

(Cartoons)

BRAVE LITTLE TAILOR, Disney, RKO Radio.
MOTHER GOOSE GOES HOLLYWOOD, Disney, RKO Radio.
* **FERDINAND THE BULL**, Disney, RKO Radio.
GOOD SCOUTS, Disney, RKO Radio.
HUNKY AND SPUNKY, Paramount.

(One-reel)

THE GREAT HEART, M-G-M. (Miniature)
* **THAT MOTHERS MIGHT LIVE**, M-G-M. (Miniature)
TIMBER TOPPERS, 20th Century-Fox. (Ed Thorgensen-Sports)

(Two-reel)

* **DECLARATION OF INDEPENDENCE**, Warner Bros. (Historical Featurette)
SWINGTIME IN THE MOVIES, Warner Bros. (Broadway Brevities)
THEY'RE ALWAYS CAUGHT, M-G-M. (Crime Doesn't Pay)

1938 IRVING G. THALBERG MEMORIAL AWARD

TO HAL B. WALLIS

SCIENTIFIC OR TECHNICAL

CLASS I (statuette)
None.

CLASS II (plaque)
None.

CLASS III (citation)
JOHN AALBERG and the **RKO RADIO STUDIO SOUND DEPT.**;
BYRON HASKIN and the **SPECIAL EFFECTS DEPT. of WARNER BROS. STUDIO.**

★ INDICATES WINNER

1939 The Twelfth Year

From start (with the January release of *Gunga Din*) to finish (with the December unveiling of *The Light That Failed*), the calendar year of 1939 produced probably more bona fide great entertainments and classics than any similar period in moviemaking annals. At Academy Award time, the competition was unintentionally outlandish, but eight of the features survived to win Oscars: *Gone With the Wind*, *The Wizard of Oz*, *Stagecoach*, *Wuthering Heights*, *The Rains Came*, *Mr. Smith Goes to Washington*, *When Tomorrow Comes* and *Goodbye, Mr. Chips*.

Gone With the Wind, in fact, set a new Oscar numbers record, with eight Awards, plus the Irving G. Thalberg Award for its producer David O. Selznick. Winning writer Sidney Howard, credited with sole authorship of the final *G.W.T.W.* script, became the Academy's first posthumous winner. He had died in a Massachusetts farm accident in August, 1939, while the film was still in production. Douglas Fairbanks, Sr., the first president of the Academy, was also posthumously honored at the 1939 Award ceremony, held February 29, 1940, at the Cocoanut Grove of the Los Angeles Ambassador Hotel; Fairbanks had died two months before, and his Special Award was accepted by his son, Douglas, Jr.

For the first time, Bob Hope was an Oscar night master of ceremonies ("What a wonderful thing, this benefit for David Selznick," he said), but it was the last year the names of winners were told to the press prior to the actual presentation of Awards. As in previous times, the Academy tipped off journalists in advance of the festivities, but under strict instructions the results were not to be printed prior to the ceremonial handing out of Oscars. The *Los Angeles Times,* however, jumped the gun and heralded the winners' names in their 8:45 p.m. edition, which could be easily read by nominees and guests on their way to the Award banquet. It brought on an Academy decision that holds to this day: ever after, the names of the winners would be kept a stony secret from *everyone*—except one representative of a tight-lipped tabulating firm—until the actual moment of presentation. Thus, "The envelope please . . ." was born.

Best Director: Victor Fleming for *Gone With the Wind.* Fleming (left, directing William Bakewell as a dispatch rider and Vivien Leigh) took over direction on the Selznick epic after the film began with George Cukor in charge; later, both Sam Wood and William Cameron Menzies helmed certain scenes, but Fleming was the only director officially credited when the film was released.

Best Picture: Gone With the Wind and **Best Actress: Vivien Leigh** as Scarlett O'Hara in *Gone With the Wind* (Released by M-G-M; produced by David O. Selznick). Long-winded by 1939 standards at 222 minutes, with intermission, Margaret Mitchell's famous novel about a Southern belle and Civil War survival became the epic of the year and—unknown at the time—probably the most famous motion picture of all time. One of the great reasons for its popularity can be summed up simply: it *moves.* Another reason: the performance of 26-year-old Vivien Leigh (above with Thomas Mitchell) as the determined O'Hara girl, one of the best-liked and most durable pieces of acting committed to film.

Best Supporting Actress: Hattie McDaniel as Mammy (at left with Olivia de Havilland) in *Gone With the Wind.* Entering films in 1931, Hattie McDaniel had become a welcome staple by the time she played Scarlett O'Hara's no-nonsense Mammy. Via her performance, she became the first Negro ever nominated for an Academy Award, and the first subsequently to win. Among her competition was co-worker de Havilland.

The Wizard of Oz (M-G-M; produced by Mervyn LeRoy) won Oscars for Original Music Score, Song ("Over the Rainbow") plus a special miniature statuette for Judy Garland (at left on the yellow brick road with Jack Haley as the Tin Man and Ray Bolger as the Straw Man). It was also nominated for Art Direction (but lost to *Gone With the Wind*) and in a new category honoring Special Effects (where *The Rains Came* was the final winner).

Nominations 1939

PICTURE

DARK VICTORY, Warner Bros. Produced by David Lewis.
★ GONE WITH THE WIND, Selznick, M-G-M. Produced by David O. Selznick.
GOODBYE, MR. CHIPS, M-G-M (British). Produced by Victor Saville.
LOVE AFFAIR, RKO Radio. Produced by Leo McCarey.
MR. SMITH GOES TO WASHINGTON, Columbia. Produced by Frank Capra.
NINOTCHKA, M-G-M. Produced by Sidney Franklin.
OF MICE AND MEN, Hal Roach, UA. Produced by Lewis Milestone.
STAGECOACH, Wanger, UA. Produced by Walter Wanger.
THE WIZARD OF OZ, M-G-M. Produced by Mervyn LeRoy.
WUTHERING HEIGHTS, Goldwyn, UA. Produced by Samuel Goldwyn.

ACTOR

★ ROBERT DONAT in *Goodbye, Mr. Chips*, M-G-M (British).
CLARK GABLE in *Gone With the Wind*, Selznick, M-G-M.
LAURENCE OLIVIER in *Wuthering Heights*, Goldwyn, UA.
MICKEY ROONEY in *Babes in Arms*, M-G-M.
JAMES STEWART in *Mr. Smith Goes to Washington*, Columbia.

ACTRESS

BETTE DAVIS in *Dark Victory*, Warner Bros.
IRENE DUNNE in *Love Affair*, RKO Radio.
GRETA GARBO in *Ninotchka*, M-G-M.
GREER GARSON in *Goodbye, Mr. Chips*, M-G-M (British).
★ VIVIEN LEIGH in *Gone With the Wind*, Selznick, M-G-M.

SUPPORTING ACTOR

BRIAN AHERNE in *Juarez*, Warner Bros.
HARRY CAREY in *Mr. Smith Goes to Washington*, Columbia.
BRIAN DONLEVY in *Beau Geste*, Paramount.
★ THOMAS MITCHELL in *Stagecoach*, Wanger, UA.
CLAUDE RAINS in *Mr. Smith Goes to Washington*, Columbia.

SUPPORTING ACTRESS

OLIVIA DE HAVILLAND in *Gone With the Wind*, Selznick, M-G-M.
GERALDINE FITZGERALD in *Wuthering Heights*, Goldwyn, UA.
★ HATTIE McDANIEL in *Gone With the Wind*, Selznick, M-G-M.

EDNA MAY OLIVER in *Drums Along the Mohawk*, 20th Century-Fox.
MARIA OUSPENSKAYA in *Love Affair*, RKO Radio.

DIRECTION

FRANK CAPRA for *Mr. Smith Goes to Washington*, Columbia.
★ VICTOR FLEMING for *Gone With the Wind*, Selznick, M-G-M.
JOHN FORD for *Stagecoach*, Wanger, UA.
SAM WOOD for *Goodbye, Mr. Chips*, M-G-M (British).
WILLIAM WYLER for *Wuthering Heights*, Goldwyn, UA.

SHORT SUBJECTS

(Cartoons)
DETOURING AMERICA, Warner Bros.
PEACE ON EARTH, M-G-M.
THE POINTER, Disney, RKO Radio.
★ THE UGLY DUCKLING, Disney, RKO Radio.

(One-reel)
★ BUSY LITTLE BEARS, Paramount. (Paragraphics)
INFORMATION PLEASE, RKO Radio.
PROPHET WITHOUT HONOR, M-G-M. (Miniature)
SWORD FISHING, Warner Bros. (Vitaphone Varieties)

(Two-reel)
DRUNK DRIVING, M-G-M. (Crime Doesn't Pay)
FIVE TIMES FIVE, RKO Radio. (Special)
★ SONS OF LIBERTY, Warner Bros. (Historical Featurette)

FILM EDITING

★ GONE WITH THE WIND, Selznick, M-G-M. Hal C. Kern and James E. Newcom.
GOODBYE, MR. CHIPS, M-G-M (British). Charles Frend.
MR. SMITH GOES TO WASHINGTON, Columbia. Gene Havlick and Al Clark.
THE RAINS CAME, 20th Century-Fox. Barbara McLean.
STAGECOACH, Wanger, UA. Otho Lovering and Dorothy Spencer.

ART DIRECTION

BEAU GESTE, Paramount. Hans Dreier and Robert Odell.
CAPTAIN FURY, Roach, UA. Charles D. Hall.
FIRST LOVE, Universal. Jack Otterson and Martin Obzina.
★ GONE WITH THE WIND, Selznick, M-G-M. Lyle Wheeler.

LOVE AFFAIR, RKO Radio. Van Nest Polglase and Al Herman.
MAN OF CONQUEST, Republic. John Victor Mackay.
MR. SMITH GOES TO WASHINGTON, Columbia. Lionel Banks.
THE PRIVATE LIVES OF ELIZABETH AND ESSEX, Warner Bros. Anton Grot.
THE RAINS CAME, 20th Century-Fox. William Darling and George Dudley.
STAGECOACH, Wanger, UA. Alexander Toluboff.

Best Actor: Robert Donat as Mr. Chipping in *Goodbye, Mr. Chips* (M-G-M; produced by Victor Saville). The touching tribute to teachers everywhere, Donat played a shy and scholarly schoolmaster in England who builds careers and character during several generations of Brookfield schoolboys. Conceived in Hollywood, the film was made in England at the M-G-M studios there, and co-starred Greer Garson as the ill-fated Mrs. Chips. Sam Wood, who also helped out on *Gone With the Wind*, directed.

THE WIZARD OF OZ, M-G-M. Cedric Gibbons and William A. Horning.
WUTHERING HEIGHTS, Goldwyn, UA. James Basevi.

MUSIC
(Song)
FAITHFUL FOREVER (*Gulliver's Travels*, Paramount); Music by Ralph Rainger. Lyrics by Leo Robin.
I POURED MY HEART INTO A SONG (*Second Fiddle*, 20th Century-Fox); Music and Lyrics by Irving Berlin.
★ OVER THE RAINBOW (*The Wizard of Oz*, M-G-M); Music by Harold Arlen. Lyrics by E.Y. Harburg.
WISHING (*Love Affair*, RKO Radio); Music and Lyrics by Buddy de Sylva.

(Scoring)
BABES IN ARMS, M-G-M. Roger Edens and George E. Stoll.
FIRST LOVE, Universal. Charles Previn.
THE GREAT VICTOR HERBERT, Paramount. Phil Boutelje and Arthur Lange.
THE HUNCHBACK OF NOTRE DAME, RKO Radio. Alfred Newman.
INTERMEZZO, Selznick, UA. Lou Forbes.
MR. SMITH GOES TO WASHINGTON, Columbia. Dimitri Tiomkin.
OF MICE AND MEN, Roach, UA. Aaron Copland.
THE PRIVATE LIVES OF ELIZABETH AND ESSEX, Warner Bros. Erich Wolfgang Korngold.
SHE MARRIED A COP, Republic. Cy Feuer.
★ STAGECOACH, Wanger, UA. Richard Hageman, Frank Harling, John Leipold and Leo Shuken.
SWANEE RIVER, 20th Century-Fox. Louis Silvers.
THEY SHALL HAVE MUSIC, Goldwyn, UA. Alfred Newman.
WAY DOWN SOUTH, Lesser, RKO Radio. Victor Young.

(Original Score)
DARK VICTORY, Warner Bros. Max Steiner.
ETERNALLY YOURS, Wanger, UA. Werner Janssen.
GOLDEN BOY, Columbia. Victor Young.
GONE WITH THE WIND, Selznick, M-G-M. Max Steiner.
GULLIVER'S TRAVELS, Paramount. Victor Young.
THE MAN IN THE IRON MASK, Small, UA. Lud Gluskin and Lucien Moraweck.
MAN OF CONQUEST, Republic. Victor Young.
NURSE EDITH CAVELL, RKO Radio. Anthony Collins.
OF MICE AND MEN, Roach, UA. Aaron Copland.
THE RAINS CAME, 20th Century-Fox. Alfred Newman.
★ THE WIZARD OF OZ, M-G-M. Herbert Stothart.
WUTHERING HEIGHTS, Goldwyn, UA. Alfred Newman.

SOUND RECORDING
BALALAIKA, M-G-M. Douglas Shearer.
GONE WITH THE WIND, Selznick, M-G-M. Thomas T. Moulton.
GOODBYE, MR. CHIPS, M-G-M (British). A.W. Watkins.

THE GREAT VICTOR HERBERT, Paramount. Loren Ryder.
THE HUNCHBACK OF NOTRE DAME, RKO Radio. John Aalberg.
MAN OF CONQUEST, Republic. C.L. Lootens.
MR. SMITH GOES TO WASHINGTON, Columbia. John Livadary.
OF MICE AND MEN, Roach, M-G-M. Elmer Raguse.
THE PRIVATE LIVES OF ELIZABETH AND ESSEX, Warner Bros. Nathan Levinson.
THE RAINS CAME, 20th Century-Fox. E.H. Hansen.
★ WHEN TOMORROW COMES, Universal. Bernard B. Brown.

WRITING
(Original Story)
BACHELOR MOTHER, RKO Radio. Felix Jackson.
LOVE AFFAIR, RKO Radio. Mildred Cram and Leo McCarey.
★ MR. SMITH GOES TO WASHINGTON, Columbia. Lewis R. Foster.
NINOTCHKA, M-G-M. Melchior Lengyel.
YOUNG MR. LINCOLN, 20th Century-Fox. Lamar Trotti.

(Screenplay)
★ GONE WITH THE WIND, Selznick, M-G-M. Sidney Howard.
GOODBYE, MR. CHIPS, M-G-M (British). Eric Maschwitz, R.C. Sherriff and Claudine West.
MR. SMITH GOES TO WASHINGTON, Columbia. Sidney Buchman.
NINOTCHKA, M-G-M. Charles Brackett Walter Reisch and Billy Wilder.
WUTHERING HEIGHTS, Goldwyn, UA. Ben Hecht and Charles MacArthur.

CINEMATOGRAPHY
(New classifications)
(Black-and-White)
STAGECOACH, Wanger, UA. Bert Glennon.
★ WUTHERING HEIGHTS, Goldwyn, UA. Gregg Toland.

(Color)
★ GONE WITH THE WIND, Selznick, M-G-M. Ernest Haller and Ray Rennahan.
THE PRIVATE LIVES OF ELIZABETH AND ESSEX, Warner Bros. Sol Polito and W. Howard Greene.

SPECIAL EFFECTS
(New Category)
GONE WITH THE WIND, Selznick, M-G-M. John R. Cosgrove, Fred Albin and Arthur Johns.
ONLY ANGELS HAVE WINGS, Columbia. Roy Davidson and Edwin C. Hahn.
THE PRIVATE LIVES OF ELIZABETH AND ESSEX, Warner Bros. Byron Haskin and Nathan Levinson.
★ THE RAINS CAME, 20th Century-Fox. E.H. Hansen and Fred Sersen.
TOPPER TAKES A TRIP, Roach, UA. Roy Seawright.
UNION PACIFIC, Paramount. Farciot Edouart, Gordon Jennings and Loren Ryder.
THE WIZARD OF OZ, M-G-M. A. Arnold Gillespie and Douglas Shearer.

SPECIAL AWARDS
TO DOUGLAS FAIRBANKS (Commemorative Award)—recognizing the unique and outstanding contribution of Douglas Fairbanks, first president of the Academy, to the international development of the motion picture. (statuette)
TO THE MOTION PICTURE RELIEF FUND—acknowledging the outstanding services to the industry during the past year of the Motion Picture Relief Fund and its progressive leadership. Presented to JEAN HERSHOLT, President; RALPH MORGAN, Chairman of the Executive Committee; RALPH BLOCK, First Vice-President; CONRAD NAGEL. (plaques)
TO JUDY GARLAND for her outstanding performance as a screen juvenile during the past year. (miniature statuette)
TO WILLIAM CAMERON MENZIES for outstanding achievement in the use of color for the enhancement of dramatic mood in the production of *Gone With the Wind*. (plaque)
TO TECHNICOLOR COMPANY for its contributions in successfully bringing three-color feature production to the screen. (statuette)

1939 IRVING G. THALBERG MEMORIAL AWARD
TO DAVID O. SELZNICK

SCIENTIFIC OR TECHNICAL

CLASS I (statuette)
None.

CLASS II (plaque)
None.

CLASS III (citation)
GEORGE ANDERSON of Warner Bros. Studio;
JOHN ARNOLD of Metro-Goldwyn-Mayer Studio;
THOMAS T. MOULTON, FRED ALBIN and the SOUND DEPARTMENT of the SAMUEL GOLDWYN STUDIO;
FARCIOT EDOUART, JOSEPH E. ROBBINS, WILLIAM RUDOLPH and PARAMOUNT PICTURES, INC.;
EMERY HUSE and RALPH B. ATKINSON of Eastman Kodak Co.;
HAROLD NYE of Warner Bros. Studio;
A.J. TONDREAU;
F.R. ABBOTT, HALLER BELT, ALAN COOK and BAUSCH & LOMB OPTICAL CO.;
MITCHELL CAMERA CO.;
MOLE-RICHARDSON CO.;
CHARLES HANDLEY, DAVID JOY and NATIONAL CARBON CO.;
WINTON HOCH and TECHNICOLOR MOTION PICTURE CORP.;
DON MUSGRAVE and SELZNICK INTERNATIONAL PICTURES, INC.

★ INDICATES WINNER

Best Supporting Actor: Thomas Mitchell as Doc Boone in *Stagecoach* (United Artists; produced by Walter Wanger). Mitchell, also a veteran of the *Gone With the Wind* cast, won his Oscar for another 1939 triumph: as a heavy-drinking doctor who rises to his finest hour delivering a baby during a stagecoach trek. Claire Trevor (right, with Mitchell) helped with the delivery; John Ford directed, and made a bona fide western classic at the same time.

Best Actress: Ginger Rogers as Kitty in *Kitty Foyle* (RKO Radio; directed by Sam Wood). Taking leave of her dancing shoes, Ginger Rogers (right) won the Oscar as the heroine of a popular Christopher Morley novel about a white-collar worker who has to choose between a rich married socialite (Dennis Morgan) and an industrious young doctor (James Craig). She also had a second major 1940 success as an actress in *Primrose Path,* directed by Gregory La Cava.

Best Director: John Ford (below, with Henry Fonda) for *The Grapes of Wrath* (20th Century-Fox; produced by Darryl F. Zanuck, with Nunnally Johnson). It was the second Academy Award for Ford (after 1935's *The Informer*), and his picture remains one of the enduring pieces of cinema storytelling; John Steinbeck's saga of the Joad family's migration from the dust bowl of Oklahoma to a new beginning in California.

1940 The Thirteenth Year

Since the early nickelodeon days, movies had been an important entertainment toy for audiences, but as a new World War erupted in Europe, the toy began to gain recognition as a powerful tool for aiding the national defense and solidarity. President Franklin D. Roosevelt underscored that fact at the thirteenth Academy Awards banquet, held February 21, 1941, by giving a six-minute direct-line radio address from the White House in Washington, D.C., to the 1400 guests gathered at the Biltmore Bowl of the Los Angeles Biltmore Hotel, paying tribute to the work being done by Hollywood's citizenry. It was the first time an American president had participated in an Oscar evening, even indirectly, and the town was justifiably pleased and impressed.

Most of the guests were justifiably nervous, too. For the first time, the names of all the evening's winners were kept a mute secret until the actual moment statuettes were placed in the hands of the winners. The Academy had hired Price Waterhouse & Co., a certified public accounting firm, to count the ballots, insure secrecy and thus avoid any future embarrassment of press leaks as had occurred in the past. So, to the fellowship and glamor synonymous with Oscars, the "surprise element" was now added.

For the second year in a row, independent producer David O. Selznick produced the picture honored as Best of the year, *Rebecca*. The biggest single winner—with three awards—was also independently produced, Alexander Korda's *The Thief of Bagdad*. Walter Brennan became the first performer to win three Academy Awards for acting, this time for Samuel Goldwyn's *The Westerner*. James Stewart was awarded as Best Actor for *The Philadelphia Story*, Ginger Rogers was named Best Actress for *Kitty Foyle*, and Jane Darwell was chosen Best Supporting Actress for *The Grapes of Wrath*. Also for *Grapes*, John Ford won his second Oscar as Best Director. Bob Hope, the evening's master of ceremonies, received his first official Academy recognition: a special silver plaque, in recognition of "his unselfish services to the motion picture industry." The acting awards were presented that night by the theater's most luminous acting couple, Alfred Lunt and Lynn Fontanne.

Best Actor: James Stewart as Mike Connor in *The Philadelphia Story* (M-G-M). produced by Joseph L. Mankiewicz). Stewart, directed by George Cukor, was a Spy magazine reporter assigned to cover the upcoming society marriage of a Philadelphia mainliner (Katharine Hepburn, above) only to fall in love with the lady himself. Said Stewart later: "Very early in the morning after I won, the phone rang. My father in Indiana, Pennsylvania, told me he'd heard on the radio that they'd given me some sort of prize. He said, 'What was it? A plaque? A cup? Or what?' I described the Oscar to him and he said that he thought I'd better send it back to Indiana and he'd put it in the window of the hardware store which he and his father had been running for almost a hundred years. So that's what I did, and it stayed there for almost twenty years, until he died."

Best Picture: Rebecca (United Artists; produced by David O. Selznick). From the atmospheric suspense novel by Daphne du Maurier, *Rebecca* was producer Selznick's first film following *Gone With the Wind*, and marked the Hollywood directorial debut of England's Alfred Hitchcock. The film opened with the famous line from the du Maurier novel ("Last night I dreamt I went to Manderley again . . .") and at Selznick's insistence included all the famous passages from the well-read story, including (at left) the moment Maxim de Winter (Laurence Olivier) introduces his meek second wife (Joan Fontaine) to the Manderley staff, including the mysterious housekeeper Mrs. Danvers (Judith Anderson).

Best Supporting Actor: Walter Brennan as Judge Roy Bean in *The Westerner* (United Artists; directed by William Wyler). Brennan, a previous award recipient in 1936 and 1938, became the Academy's first three-time winner among performers with his performance as the feisty, real-life judge who held his court from behind the bar of a saloon in Vinegaroon, Texas, in the 1880s. He was nominated again in 1941.

(below) **The Thief of Bagdad** (United Artists; produced by Alexander Korda) received the most Academy Awards of 1940: three, including statuettes for Special Effects (Lawrence Butler, Jack Whitney), Color Cinematography (George Perinal) and Color Art Direction (Vincent Korda). Made in England, the cast included Sabu, Conrad Veidt, John Justin, June Duprez and, pictured below, Rex Ingram as an ill-tempered genie.

PICTURE

ALL THIS, AND HEAVEN TOO, Warner Bros. Produced by Jack L. Warner and Hal Wallis, with David Lewis.
FOREIGN CORRESPONDENT, Wanger, UA. Produced by Walter Wanger.
THE GRAPES OF WRATH, 20th Century-Fox. Produced by Darryl F. Zanuck, with Nunnally Johnson.
THE GREAT DICTATOR, Chaplin, UA. Produced by Charles Chaplin.
KITTY FOYLE, RKO Radio. Produced by David Hempstead.
THE LETTER, Warner Bros. Produced by Hal B. Wallis.
THE LONG VOYAGE HOME, Wanger, UA. Produced by John Ford.
OUR TOWN, Lesser, UA. Produced by Sol Lesser.
THE PHILADELPHIA STORY, M-G-M. Produced by Joseph L. Mankiewicz.
* **REBECCA**, Selznick, UA. Produced by David O. Selznick.

ACTOR

CHARLES CHAPLIN in *The Great Dictator*, Chaplin, UA.
HENRY FONDA in *The Grapes of Wrath*, 20th Century-Fox.
RAYMOND MASSEY in *Abe Lincoln in Illinois*, RKO Radio.
LAURENCE OLIVIER in *Rebecca*, Selznick, UA.
* **JAMES STEWART** in *The Philadelphia Story*, M-G-M.

ACTRESS

BETTE DAVIS in *The Letter*, Warner Bros.
JOAN FONTAINE in *Rebecca*, Selznick, UA.
KATHARINE HEPBURN in *The Philadelphia Story*, M-G-M.
* **GINGER ROGERS** in *Kitty Foyle*, RKO Radio.
MARTHA SCOTT in *Our Town*, Lesser, UA.

SUPPORTING ACTOR

ALBERT BASSERMAN in *Foreign Correspondent*, Wanger, UA.
* **WALTER BRENNAN** in *The Westerner*, Goldwyn, UA.
WILLIAM GARGAN in *They Knew What They Wanted*, RKO Radio.
JACK OAKIE in *The Great Dictator*, Chaplin, UA.
JAMES STEPHENSON in *The Letter*, Warner Bros.

SUPPORTING ACTRESS

JUDITH ANDERSON in *Rebecca*, Selznick, UA.
* **JANE DARWELL** in *The Grapes of Wrath*, 20th Century-Fox.
RUTH HUSSEY in *The Philadelphia Story*, M-G-M.
BARBARA O'NEIL in *All This, and Heaven Too*, Warner Bros.
MARJORIE RAMBEAU in *Primrose Path*, RKO Radio.

DIRECTION

GEORGE CUKOR for *The Philadelphia Story*, M-G-M.
* **JOHN FORD** for *The Grapes of Wrath*, 20th Century-Fox.
ALFRED HITCHCOCK for *Rebecca*, Selznick, UA.
SAM WOOD for *Kitty Foyle*, RKO Radio.
WILLIAM WYLER for *The Letter*, Warner Bros.

Best Supporting Actress: Jane Darwell as Ma Joad in *The Grapes of Wrath.* Long a staple in Hollywood's ranks of familiar character faces, Miss Darwell had her finest screen hour as Steinbeck's indomitable Ma Joad, the undeviating strength at the core of the Joad clan. Among her most memorable scenes: saying goodbye, perhaps forever, to her son Tom (Henry Fonda, above), near the conclusion of the drama directed by John Ford.

SPECIAL EFFECTS

THE BLUE BIRD, 20th Century-Fox. Fred Sersen and E.H. Hansen.
BOOM TOWN, M-G-M. A. Arnold Gillespie and Douglas Shearer.
THE BOYS FROM SYRACUSE, Universal. John P. Fulton, Bernard B. Brown and Joseph Lapis.
DR. CYCLOPS, Paramount. Farciot Edouart and Gordon Jennings.
FOREIGN CORRESPONDENT, Wanger, UA. Paul Eagler and Thomas T. Moulton.
THE INVISIBLE MAN RETURNS, Universal. John P. Fulton, Bernard B. Brown and William Hedgecock.
THE LONG VOYAGE HOME, Argosy-Wanger, UA. R.T. Layton, R.O. Binger and Thomas T. Moulton.
ONE MILLION B.C., Roach, UA. Roy Seawright and Elmer Raguse.
REBECCA, Selznick, UA. Jack Cosgrove and Arthur Johns.
THE SEA HAWK, Warner Bros. Byron Haskin and Nathan Levinson.
SWISS FAMILY ROBINSON, RKO Radio. Vernon L. Walker and John O. Aalberg.
★ **THE THIEF OF BAGDAD**, Korda, UA. Lawrence Butler and Jack Whitney.
TYPHOON, Paramount. Farciot Edouart, Gordon Jennings and Loren Ryder.
WOMEN IN WAR, Republic. Howard J. Lydecker, William Bradford, Ellis J. Thackery and Herbert Norsch.

WRITING
(Slight alteration of classifications)

(Original Story)
★ **ARISE, MY LOVE**, Paramount. Benjamin Glazer and John S. Toldy.
COMRADE X, M-G-M. Walter Reisch.
EDISON THE MAN, M-G-M. Hugo Butler and Dore Schary.
MY FAVORITE WIFE, RKO Radio. Leo McCarey, Bella Spewack and Samuel Spewack.
THE WESTERNER, Goldwyn, UA. Stuart N. Lake.

(Original Screenplay)
ANGELS OVER BROADWAY, Columbia. Ben Hecht.

DR. EHRLICH'S MAGIC BULLET, Warner Bros. Norman Burnside, Heinz Herald and John Huston.
FOREIGN CORRESPONDENT, Wanger, UA. Charles Bennett and Joan Harrison.
THE GREAT DICTATOR, Chaplin, UA. Charles Chaplin.
★ **THE GREAT McGINTY**, Paramount. Preston Sturges.

(Screenplay)
THE GRAPES OF WRATH, 20th Century-Fox. Nunnally Johnson.
KITTY FOYLE, RKO Radio. Dalton Trumbo.
THE LONG VOYAGE HOME, Argosy-Wanger, UA. Dudley Nichols.
★ **THE PHILADELPHIA STORY**, M-G-M. Donald Ogden Stewart.
REBECCA, Selznick, UA. Robert E. Sherwood and Joan Harrison.

FILM EDITING

THE GRAPES OF WRATH, 20th Century-Fox. Robert E. Simpson.
THE LETTER, Warner Bros. Warren Low.
THE LONG VOYAGE HOME, Argosy-Wanger, UA. Sherman Todd.
★ **NORTH WEST MOUNTED POLICE**, DeMille, Paramount. Anne Bauchens.
REBECCA, Selznick, UA. Hal C. Kern.

CINEMATOGRAPHY

(Black-and-White)
ABE LINCOLN IN ILLINOIS, RKO Radio. James Wong Howe.
ALL THIS, AND HEAVEN TOO, Warner Bros. Ernest Haller.
ARISE, MY LOVE, Paramount. Charles B. Lang, Jr.
BOOM TOWN, M-G-M. Harold Rosson.
FOREIGN CORRESPONDENT, Wanger, UA. Rudolph Mate.
THE LETTER, Warner Bros. Gaetano Gaudio.
THE LONG VOYAGE HOME, Argosy-Wanger, UA. Gregg Toland.
★ **REBECCA**, Selznick, UA. George Barnes.
SPRING PARADE, Universal. Joseph Valentine.
WATERLOO BRIDGE, M-G-M. Joseph Ruttenberg.

(Color)
BITTER SWEET, M-G-M. Oliver T. Marsh AND Allen Davey.
THE BLUE BIRD, 20th Century-Fox. Arthur Miller and Ray Rennahan.
DOWN ARGENTINE WAY, 20th Century-Fox. Leon Shamroy and Ray Rennahan.
NORTH WEST MOUNTED POLICE, DeMille, Paramount. Victor Milner and W. Howard Greene.
NORTHWEST PASSAGE, M-G-M. Sidney Wagner and William V. Skall.
★ **THE THIEF OF BAGDAD**, Korda, UA (British). George Perinal.

SOUND RECORDING

BEHIND THE NEWS, Republic. Charles Lootens.
CAPTAIN CAUTION, Roach, UA. Elmer Raguse.
THE GRAPES OF WRATH, 20th Century-Fox. E.H. Hansen.
THE HOWARDS OF VIRGINIA, Columbia. Jack Whitney, General Service.
KITTY FOYLE, RKO Radio. John Aalberg.
NORTH WEST MOUNTED POLICE, DeMille, Paramount. Loren Ryder.
OUR TOWN, Lesser, UA. Thomas Moulton.
THE SEA HAWK, Warner Bros. Nathan Levinson.
SPRING PARADE, Universal. Bernard B. Brown.
★ **STRIKE UP THE BAND**, M-G-M. Douglas Shearer.
TOO MANY HUSBANDS, Columbia. John Livadary.

ART DIRECTION
(New classifications)

(Black-and-White)
ARISE, MY LOVE, Paramount. Hans Dreier and Robert Usher.
ARIZONA, Columbia. Lionel Banks and Robert Peterson.
THE BOYS FROM SYRACUSE, Universal. John Otterson.
DARK COMMAND, Republic. John Victor Mackay.
FOREIGN CORRESPONDENT, Wanger, UA. Alexander Golitzen.
LILLIAN RUSSELL, 20th Century-Fox. Richard Day and Joseph C. Wright.
MY FAVORITE WIFE, RKO Radio. Van Nest Polglase and Mark-Lee Kirk.
MY SON, MY SON, Small, UA. John DuCasse Schulze.
OUR TOWN, Lesser, UA. Lewis J. Rachmil.
★ **PRIDE AND PREJUDICE**, M-G-M. Cedric Gibbons and Paul Groesse.
REBECCA, Selznick, UA. Lyle Wheeler.
SEA HAWK, Warner Bros. Anton Grot.
THE WESTERNER, Goldwyn, UA. James Basevi.

(Color)
BITTER SWEET, M-G-M. Cedric Gibbons and John S. Detlie.
DOWN ARGENTINE WAY, 20th Century-Fox. Richard Day and Joseph C. Wright.
NORTH WEST MOUNTED POLICE, DeMille, Paramount. Hans Dreier and Roland Anderson.
★ **THE THIEF OF BAGDAD**, Korda, UA. Vincent Korda.

MUSIC
(Song)
DOWN ARGENTINE WAY (*Down Argentine Way*, 20th Century-Fox); Music by Harry Warren. Lyrics by Mack Gordon.
I'D KNOW YOU ANYWHERE (*You'll Find Out*, RKO Radio); Music by Jimmy McHugh. Lyrics by Johnny Mercer.
IT'S A BLUE WORLD (*Music in My Heart*, Columbia); Music and Lyrics by Chet Forrest and Bob Wright.
LOVE OF MY LIFE (*Second Chorus*, Paramount); Music by Artie Shaw. Lyrics by Johnny Mercer.
ONLY FOREVER (*Rhythm on the River*, Paramount); Music by James Monaco. Lyrics by John Burke.
OUR LOVE AFFAIR (*Strike Up the Band*, M-G-M); Music and Lyrics by Roger Edens and Georgie Stoll.
WALTZING IN THE CLOUDS (*Spring Parade*, Universal); Music by Robert Stolz. Lyrics by Gus Kahn.
★ **WHEN YOU WISH UPON A STAR** (*Pinocchio*, Disney, RKO Radio); Music by Leigh Harline. Lyrics by Ned Washington.
WHO AM I? (*Hit Parade of 1941*, Republic); Music by Jule Styne. Lyrics by Walter Bullock.

(Score)
ARISE, MY LOVE, Paramount. Victor Young.
HIT PARADE OF 1941, Republic. Cy Feuer.
IRENE, Imperadio, RKO Radio. Anthony Collins.

OUR TOWN, Lesser, UA. Aaron Copland.
THE SEA HAWK, Warner Bros. Erich Wolfgang Korngold.
SECOND CHORUS, Paramount. Artie Shaw.
SPRING PARADE, Universal. Charles Previn.
STRIKE UP THE BAND, M-G-M. Georgie Stoll and Roger Edens.
★ **TIN PAN ALLEY**, 20th Century-Fox. Alfred Newman.

(Original Score)
ARIZONA, Columbia. Victor Young.
DARK COMMAND, Republic. Victor Young.
THE FIGHT FOR LIFE, U.S. Government-Columbia. Louis Gruenberg.
THE GREAT DICTATOR, Chaplin, UA. Meredith Willson.
THE HOUSE OF SEVEN GABLES, Universal. Frank Skinner.
THE HOWARDS OF VIRGINIA, Columbia. Richard Hageman.
THE LETTER, Warner Bros. Max Steiner.
THE LONG VOYAGE HOME, Argosy-Wanger, UA. Richard Hageman.
THE MARK OF ZORRO, 20th Century-Fox. Alfred Newman.
MY FAVORITE WIFE, RKO Radio. Roy Webb.
NORTH WEST MOUNTED POLICE, DeMille, Paramount. Victor Young.
ONE MILLION B.C., Roach, UA. Werner Heymann.
OUR TOWN, Lesser, UA. Aaron Copland.
★ **PINOCCHIO**, Disney, RKO Radio. Leigh Harline, Paul J. Smith and Ned Washington.
REBECCA, Selznick, UA. Franz Waxman.
THE THIEF OF BAGDAD, Korda, UA. Miklos Rozsa.
WATERLOO BRIDGE, M-G-M. Herbert Stothart.

SHORT SUBJECTS

(Cartoons)
★ **MILKY WAY**, M-G-M. (Rudolph Ising Series)
PUSS GETS THE BOOT, M-G-M. (Cat and Mouse Series)
A WILD HARE, Schlesinger, Warner Bros.

(One-reel)
LONDON CAN TAKE IT, Warner Bros. (Vitaphone Varieties)
MORE ABOUT NOSTRADAMUS, M-G-M.
★ **QUICKER 'N A WINK**, Pete Smith, M-G-M.
SIEGE, RKO Radio. (Reelism)

(Two-reel)
EYES OF THE NAVY, M-G-M. (Crime Doesn't Pay)
SERVICE WITH THE COLORS, Warner Bros. (National Defense Series)
★ **TEDDY, THE ROUGH RIDER**, Warner Bros. (Historical Featurette)

SPECIAL AWARDS

TO BOB HOPE, in recognition of his unselfish services to the motion picture industry. (special silver plaque)
TO COLONEL NATHAN LEVINSON for his outstanding service to the industry and the Army during the past nine years, which has made possible the present efficient mobilization of the motion picture industry facilities for the production of Army training films. (statuette)

1940 IRVING G. THALBERG MEMORIAL AWARD

None given.

SCIENTIFIC OR TECHNICAL

CLASS I (statuette)
20TH CENTURY-FOX FILM CORP. for the design and construction of the 20th Century Silenced Camera, developed by **DANIEL CLARK**, **GROVER LAUBE**, **CHARLES MILLER** and **ROBERT W. STEVENS**.

CLASS II (plaque)
None.

CLASS III (citation)
WARNER BROS. STUDIO ART DEPARTMENT AND **ANTON GROT**.

★ INDICATES WINNER

1941 The Fourteenth Year

War was now a grim reality. Just two months before the Academy was scheduled to hold the Oscar Award banquet honoring achievements for the calendar year 1941, World War II for the United States erupted with the Japanese attack at Pearl Harbor. Then, on January 16, 1942, Carole Lombard—one of the town's top stars and most popular citizens—was killed in an airplane accident returning from a bond-selling tour. Initially, Academy officials decided it best to cancel the Oscar festivities altogether. Bette Davis, newly-elected Academy president, suggested they be held, but in a large auditorium instead of a banquet hall, with the public invited to buy tickets, and those proceeds turned over to the Red Cross. After some discussion, the Academy governors vetoed the Davis plan, but decided to go ahead with the awarding of Oscars, under modified conditions. Formal attire was banned, the ceremony was labeled a ''dinner'' rather than a banquet and there were no search-lights fanning through the skies outside the Biltmore Hotel that night, February 26, 1942.

There was no official master of ceremonies, but the principal speaker was Wendell L. Wilkie, the top man in the Republican party, allowing the GOP equal time among the film folk after the participation of President Roosevelt, a Democrat, the previous year. Biggest single winner of the evening was 20th Century-Fox's *How Green Was My Valley* with five awards, including Best Picture, Best Supporting Actor Donald Crisp, and Best Director John Ford. It was Ford's third win, and his second one in two years. For the first time, two real-life sisters were among the nominees for Best Actress of the year, Olivia de Havilland for *Hold Back the Dawn* and—the winner—Joan Fontaine for *Suspicion.* Mary Astor received her plaque as Best Supporting Actress for *The Great Lie;* she'd also been prominent in another major 1941 success, *The Maltese Falcon.* Orson Welles was personally nominated for four Oscars (as actor, director, producer and co-writer of *Citizen Kane*) and won in the Original Screenplay division, along with Herman J. Mankiewicz. Harry Segall won the Best Original Story award for *Here Comes Mr. Jordan,* based on his play *Heaven Can Wait;* it was eligible as an ''original'' because the play had not yet been produced anywhere.

For the first time, the Academy recognized documentary film production; it would be an increasingly important genre in the war years ahead. It was also the last year for a while that the themes of Holly-wood's productions would be an equal balance of romantic dramas, infectious musicals, warm comedies, dashing adventure stories and pure escapist fare. For the next several seasons, war would dominate the movies just as it did real life.

Best Actress: Joan Fontaine as Lina Laidlaw in *Suspicion* (RKO Radio). Will he or won't he? As a shy British girl who entered into a hasty marriage with a mysterious charmer (Cary Grant, above at left), Miss Fontaine had growing reasons to believe her husband was possibly a murderer, with herself intended as a victim. The thriller, based on Frances Iles' *Before the Fact,* reunited the actress with her *Rebecca* director, Alfred Hitchcock.

Best Director: John Ford (at right, wearing dark glasses, with his company) for *How Green Was My Valley.* For the second year in a row, Ford won the Academy's statuette for direction, this time for his warm, human and episodic story of Welsh coal-mining life. It was his third Academy Award; in 1952, he won a fourth one, for *The Quiet Man,* again with Maureen O'Hara.

DONALD CRISP
How Green Was My Valley

Best Picture: How Green Was My Valley (20th Century-Fox; produced by Darryl F. Zanuck) was based on the novel by Richard Llewellyn, and was told through the eyes of a grown man relating the story of the Morgans, a family of miners, through their conflicts with employers, romances, achievements and personal heartbreaks. The cast, an example of superb ensemble actors, included Walter Pidgeon and 13-year-old Roddy McDowall (at left), and Maureen O'Hara, Donald Crisp, Sara Allgood, Anna Lee, Barry Fitzgerald, John Loder and Patric Knowles.

Best Actor: Gary Cooper as Alvin York in *Sergeant York* (Warner Bros.; directed by Howard Hawks). York was a real-life Tennessee farmer who became a conscientious objector during World War I, then won fame as a soldier who singlehandedly captured 132 German soldiers in the Argonne Forest on October 6, 1918, armed only with a Springfield rifle. As a movie, it was a perfect matching of actor and role. Below, Cooper is the backwoods York at a local bar with cohorts Buck (Noah Beery, Jr.) and Ike (Ward Bond).

Best Supporting Actor: Donald Crisp as Mr. Morgan in *How Green Was My Valley.* Crisp was one of the founding fathers of the entire motion picture industry, and one of its finest actors. He played General Grant in D.W. Griffith's *Birth of a Nation* (1915), became a silent screen director (among his successes: Buster Keaton's *The Navigator*), then devoted his time exclusively to character acting. In his Oscar-winning role, he played the patriarchal head of a closely knit coal-mining clan.

Best Supporting Actress: Mary Astor as Sandra Kovack in *The Great Lie* (Warner Bros.) Like Crisp, Miss Astor was also a screen contributor whose work stretched back to silent days, when she was usually cast as a sweet ingenue to John Barrymore, Douglas Fairbanks and others. In *The Great Lie,* directed by Edmund Goulding, she was no longer playing a softie but instead a brittle, spoiled concert pianist who creates mayhem in the lives of Bette Davis and George Brent.

Nominations 1941

PICTURE

BLOSSOMS IN THE DUST, M-G-M. Produced by Irving Asher.
CITIZEN KANE, RKO Radio. Produced by Orson Welles.
HERE COMES MR. JORDAN, Columbia. Produced by Everett Riskin.
HOLD BACK THE DAWN, Paramount. Produced by Arthur Hornblow, Jr.
★ **HOW GREEN WAS MY VALLEY**, 20th Century-Fox. Produced by Darryl F. Zanuck.
THE LITTLE FOXES, Goldwyn, RKO Radio. Produced by Samuel Goldwyn.
THE MALTESE FALCON, Warner Bros. Produced by Hal B. Wallis.
ONE FOOT IN HEAVEN, Warner Bros. Produced by Hal B. Wallis.
SERGEANT YORK, Warner Bros. Produced by Jesse L. Lasky and Hal B. Wallis.
SUSPICION, RKO Radio. Produced by RKO Radio.

ACTOR

★ **GARY COOPER** in *Sergeant York*, Warner Bros.
CARY GRANT in *Penny Serenade*, Columbia.
WALTER HUSTON in *All That Money Can Buy* (aka *The Devil and Daniel Webster*), RKO Radio.
ROBERT MONTGOMERY in *Here Comes Mr. Jordan*, Columbia.
ORSON WELLES in *Citizen Kane*, RKO Radio.

ACTRESS

BETTE DAVIS in *The Little Foxes*, Goldwyn, RKO Radio.
★ **JOAN FONTAINE** in *Suspicion*, RKO Radio.
GREER GARSON in *Blossoms in the Dust*, M-G-M.
OLIVIA DE HAVILLAND in *Hold Back the Dawn*, Paramount.
BARBARA STANWYCK in *Ball of Fire*, Goldwyn, RKO Radio.

SUPPORTING ACTOR

WALTER BRENNAN in *Sergeant York*, Warner Bros.
CHARLES COBURN in *The Devil and Miss Jones*, RKO Radio.
★ **DONALD CRISP** in *How Green Was My Valley*, 20th Century-Fox.
JAMES GLEASON in *Here Comes Mr. Jordan*, Columbia.
SYNDEY GREENSTREET, in *The Maltese Falcon*, Warner Bros. ·

SUPPORTING ACTRESS

SARA ALLGOOD in *How Green Was My Valley*, 20th Century-Fox.
★ **MARY ASTOR** in *The Great Lie*, Warner Bros.
PATRICIA COLLINGE in *The Little Foxes*, Goldwyn, RKO Radio.
TERESA WRIGHT in *The Little Foxes*, Goldwyn, RKO Radio.
MARGARET WYCHERLY in *Sergeant York*, Warner Bros.

DIRECTION

★ **JOHN FORD** for *How Green Was My Valley*, 20th Century-Fox.
ALEXANDER HALL for *Here Comes Mr. Jordan*, Columbia.
HOWARD HAWKS for *Sergeant York*, Warner Bros.
ORSON WELLES for *Citizen Kane*, Mercury, RKO Radio.
WILLIAM WYLER for *The Little Foxes*, Goldwyn, RKO Radio.

MUSIC
(New Classifications)
(Song)

BABY MINE (*Dumbo,* Disney, RKO Radio); Music by Frank Churchill. Lyrics by Ned Washington.
BE HONEST WITH ME (*Ridin' on a Rainbow,* Republic); Music and Lyrics by Gene Autry and Fred Rose.
BLUES IN THE NIGHT (*Blues in the Night,* Warner Bros.); Music by Harold Arlen. Lyrics by Johnny Mercer.
BOOGIE WOOGIE BUGLE BOY OF COMPANY B (*Buck Privates,* Universal); Music by Hugh Prince. Lyrics by Don Raye.
CHATTANOOGA CHOO CHOO (*Sun Valley Serenade,* 20th Century-Fox); Music by Harry Warren. Lyrics by Mack Gordon.
DOLORES (*Las Vegas Nights,* Paramount); Music by Lou Alter. Lyrics by Frank Loesser.
★ **THE LAST TIME I SAW PARIS** (*Lady Be Good,* M-G-M); Music by Jerome Kern. Lyrics by Oscar Hammerstein II.
OUT OF THE SILENCE (*All American Co-Ed,* Roach, UA); Music and Lyrics by Lloyd B. Norlind.
SINCE I KISSED BY BABY GOODBYE (*You'll Never Get Rich,* Columbia); Music and Lyrics by Cole Porter.

(Scoring of a Dramatic Picture)

★ **ALL THAT MONEY CAN BUY**, RKO Radio. Bernard Herrmann.
BACK STREET, Universal. Frank Skinner.
BALL OF FIRE, Goldwyn, RKO Radio. Alfred Newman.
CHEERS FOR MISS BISHOP, Rowland, UA. Edward Ward.
CITIZEN KANE, Mercury, RKO Radio. Bernard Herrmann.
DR. JEKYLL AND MR. HYDE, M-G-M. Franz Waxman.
HOLD BACK THE DAWN, Paramount. Victor Young.
HOW GREEN WAS MY VALLEY, 20th Century-Fox. Alfred Newman.
KING OF THE ZOMBIES, Monogram. Edward Kay.
LADIES IN RETIREMENT, Columbia. Morris Stoloff and Ernst Toch.
THE LITTLE FOXES, Goldwyn, RKO Radio. Meredith Willson.
LYDIA, Korda, UA. Miklos Rozsa.
MERCY ISLAND, Republic. Cy Feuer and Walter Scharf.
SERGEANT YORK, Warner Bros. Max Steiner.
SO ENDS OUR NIGHT, Loew-Lewin, UA. Louis Gruenberg.
SUNDOWN, Wanger, UA. Miklos Rozsa.
SUSPICION, RKO Radio. Franz Waxman.
TANKS A MILLION, Roach, UA. Edward Ward.
THAT UNCERTAIN FEELING, Lubitsch, UA. Werner Heymann.
THIS WOMAN IS MINE, Universal. Richard Hageman.

(Scoring of a Musical Picture)

ALL AMERICAN CO-ED, Roach, UA. Edward Ward.
BIRTH OF THE BLUES, Paramount. Robert Emmett Dolan.
BUCK PRIVATES, Universal, Charles Previn.
THE CHOCOLATE SOLDIER, M-G-M. Herbert Stothart and Bronislau Kaper.
★ **DUMBO**, Disney, RKO Radio. Frank Churchill and Oliver Wallace.
ICE CAPADES, Republic. Cy Feuer.
THE STRAWBERRY BLONDE, Warner Bros. Heinz Roemheld.
SUN VALLEY SERENADE, 20th Century-Fox. Emil Newman.
SUNNY, RKO Radio. Anthony Collins.
YOU'LL NEVER GET RICH, Columbia. Morris Stoloff.

Citizen Kane (RKO Radio; produced by Orson Welles) won one Academy Award, for the Original Screenplay by Welles and Herman J. Mankiewicz, and has become one of the most famous of all films in the 1941 catalog. Loosely based on the career of newspaper tycoon William Randolph Hearst, it marked the motion picture debut of Welles and many of his Mercury Players cast (including Joseph Cotten, Ruth Warrick, Everett Sloane, Paul Stewart and Agnes Moorehead).

WRITING

(Original Story)
BALL OF FIRE, Goldwyn, RKO Radio. Thomas Monroe and Billy Wilder.
★ HERE COMES MR. JORDAN, Columbia. Harry Segall.
THE LADY EVE, Paramount. Monckton Hoffe.
MEET JOHN DOE, Warner Bros. Richard Connell and Robert Presnell.
NIGHT TRAIN, 20th Century-Fox (British). Gordon Wellesley.

(Original Screenplay)
★ CITIZEN KANE, Mercury, RKO Radio. Herman J. Mankiewicz and Orson Welles.
THE DEVIL AND MISS JONES, RKO Radio. Norman Krasna.
SERGEANT YORK, Warner Bros. Harry Chandlee, Abem Finkel, John Huston and Howard Koch.
TALL, DARK AND HANDSOME, 20th Century-Fox. Karl Tunberg and Darrell Ware.
TOM, DICK AND HARRY, RKO Radio. Paul Jarrico.

(Screenplay)
★ HERE COMES MR. JORDAN, Columbia. Sidney Buchman and Seton I. Miller.
HOLD BACK THE DAWN, Paramount. Charles Brackett and Billy Wilder.
HOW GREEN WAS MY VALLEY, 20th Century-Fox. Philip Dunne.
THE LITTLE FOXES, Goldwyn, RKO Radio. Lillian Hellman.
THE MALTESE FALCON, Warner Bros. John Huston.

SPECIAL EFFECTS

ALOMA OF THE SOUTH SEAS, Paramount. Farciot Edouart, Gordon Jennings and Louis Mesenkop.
FLIGHT COMMAND, M-G-M. A. Arnold Gillespie and Douglas Shearer.
★ I WANTED WINGS, Paramount. Farciot Edouart, Gordon Jennings and Louis Mesenkop.
THE INVISIBLE WOMAN, Universal. John Fulton and John Hall.
THE SEA WOLF, Warner Bros. Bryon Haskin and Nathan Levinson.
THAT HAMILTON WOMAN, Korda, UA. Lawrence Butler and William H. Wilmarth.
TOPPER RETURNS, Roach, UA. Roy Seawright and Elmer Raguse.
A YANK IN THE R.A.F., 20th Century-Fox. Fred Sersen and E.H. Hansen.

CINEMATOGRAPHY

(Black-and-White)
THE CHOCOLATE SOLDIER, M-G-M. Karl Freund.
CITIZEN KANE, Mercury, RKO Radio. Gregg Toland.
DR. JEKYLL AND MR. HYDE, M-G-M. Joseph Ruttenberg.
HERE COMES MR. JORDAN, Columbia. Joseph Walker.

HOLD BACK THE DAWN, Paramount. Leo Tover.
★ HOW GREEN WAS MY VALLEY, 20th Century-Fox. Arthur Miller.
SERGEANT YORK, Warner Bros. Sol Polito.
SUN VALLEY SERENADE, 20th Century-Fox. Edward Cronjager.
SUNDOWN, Wanger, UA. Charles Lang.
THAT HAMILTON WOMAN, Korda, UA. Rudolph.Mate.

(Color)
ALOMA OF THE SOUTH SEAS, Paramount. Wilfred M. Cline, Karl Struss and William Snyder.
BILLY THE KID, M-G-M. William V. Skall and Leonard Smith.
★ BLOOD AND SAND, 20th Century-Fox. Ernest Palmer and Ray Rennahan.
BLOSSOMS IN THE DUST, M-G-M. Karl Freund and W. Howard Greene.
DIVE BOMBER, Warner Bros. Bert Glennon.
LOUISIANA PURCHASE, Paramount. Harry Hallenberger and Ray Rennahan.

SHORT SUBJECTS

(Cartoons)
BOOGIE WOOGIE BUGLE BOY OF COMPANY B, Lantz, Universal.
HIAWATHA'S RABBIT HUNT, Schlesinger, Warner Bros.
HOW WAR CAME, Columbia. (Raymond Gram Swing Series)
★ LEND A PAW, Disney, RKO Radio.
THE NIGHT BEFORE CHRISTMAS, M-G-M. (Tom and Jerry Series)
RHAPSODY IN RIVETS, Schlesinger, Warner Bros.
THE ROOKIE BEAR, M-G-M. (Bear Series)
RHYTHM IN THE RANKS, Paramount. (George Pal Puppetoon Series)
SUPERMAN NO. 1, Paramount.
TRUANT OFFICER DONALD, Disney, RKO Radio. (Donald Duck)

(One-reel)
ARMY CHAMPIONS, Pete Smith, M-G-M. (Pete Smith Specialties)
BEAUTY AND THE BEACH, Paramount. (Headliner Series)
DOWN ON THE FARM, Paramount. (Speaking of Animals)
FORTY BOYS AND A SONG, Warner Bros. (Melody Master Series)
KINGS OF THE TURF, Warner Bros. (Color Parade Series)
★ OF PUPS AND PUZZLES, M-G-M. (Passing Parade Series)
SAGEBRUSH AND SILVER, 20th Century-Fox. (Magic Carpet Series)

(Two-reel)
ALIVE IN THE DEEP, Woodard Productions, Inc.
FORBIDDEN PASSAGE, M-G-M. (Crime Doesn't Pay)
THE GAY PARISIAN, Warner Bros. (Miniature Featurette Series)
★ MAIN STREET ON THE MARCH, M-G-M. (Special)
THE TANKS ARE COMING, Warner Bros. (National Defense Series)

ART DIRECTION-INTERIOR DECORATION

(For the first year, certificates of merit given to the Interior Decorators of the film receiving award for Art Direction)

(Black-and-White)
CITIZEN KANE, Mercury, RKO Radio. Perry Ferguson and Van Nest Polglase; Al Fields and Darrell Silvera.
FLAME OF NEW ORLEANS, Universal. Martin Obzina and Jack Otterson; Russell A. Gausman.
HOLD BACK THE DAWN, Paramount. Hans Dreier and Robert Usher; Sam Comer.
★ HOW GREEN WAS MY VALLEY, 20th Century-Fox. Richard Day and Nathan Juran; Thomas Little.
LADIES IN RETIREMENT, Columbia. Lionel Banks; George Montgomery.
THE LITTLE FOXES, Goldwyn, RKO Radio. Stephen Goosson; Howard Bristol.
SERGEANT YORK, Warner Bros. John Hughes; Fred MacLean.
SON OF MONTE CRISTO, Small, UA. John DuCasse Schulze; Edward G. Boyle.
SUNDOWN, Wanger, UA. Alexander Golitzen; Richard Irvine.
THAT HAMILTON WOMAN, Korda, UA. Vincent Korda; Julia Heron.
WHEN LADIES MEET, M-G-M. Cedric Gibbons and Randall Duell; Edwin B. Willis.

(Color)
BLOOD AND SAND, 20th Century-Fox. Richard Day and Joseph C. Wright; Thomas Little.
★ BLOSSOMS IN THE DUST, M-G-M. Cedric Gibbons and Urie McCleary; Edwin B. Willis.
LOUISIANA PURCHASE, Paramount. Raoul Pene du Bois; Stephen A. Seymour.

SOUND RECORDING

APPOINTMENT FOR LOVE, Universal. Bernard B. Brown.
BALL OF FIRE, Goldwyn, RKO Radio. Thomas Moulton.
THE CHOCOLATE SOLDIER, M-G-M. Douglas Shearer.
CITIZEN KANE, Mercury, RKO Radio. John Aalberg.
THE DEVIL PAYS OFF, Republic. Charles Lootens.
HOW GREEN WAS MY VALLEY, 20th Century-Fox. E.H. Hansen.
THE MEN IN HER LIFE, Columbia. John Livadary.
SERGEANT YORK, Warner Bros. Nathan Levinson.
SKYLARK, Paramount. Loren Ryder.
★ THAT HAMILTON WOMAN, Korda, UA. Jack Whitney, General Service.
TOPPER RETURNS, Roach, UA. Elmer Raguse.

FILM EDITING

CITIZEN KANE, Mercury, RKO Radio. Robert Wise.
DR. JEKYLL AND MR. HYDE, M-G-M. Harold F. Kress.
HOW GREEN WAS MY VALLEY, 20th Century-Fox. James B. Clark.
THE LITTLE FOXES, Goldwyn, RKO Radio. Daniel Mandell.
★ SERGEANT YORK, Warner Bros. William Holmes.

DOCUMENTARY

(New category)
ADVENTURES IN THE BRONX, Film Assocs.
BOMBER, U.S. Office for Emergency Management Film Unit.
CHRISTMAS UNDER FIRE, British Ministry of Information, Warner Bros.
★ CHURCHILL'S ISLAND, Canadian Film Board, UA.
LETTER FROM HOME, British Ministry of Information.
LIFE OF A THOROUGHBRED, 20th Century-Fox.
NORWAY IN REVOLT, March of Time, RKO Radio.
SOLDIERS OF THE SKY, 20th Century-Fox.
WAR CLOUDS IN THE PACIFIC, Canadian Film Board.

SPECIAL AWARDS

TO REY SCOTT for his extraordinary achievement in producing *Kukan*, the film record of China's struggle, including its photography with a 16mm camera under the most difficult and dangerous conditions. (certificate)
TO THE BRITISH MINISTRY OF INFORMATION for its vivid and dramatic persentation of the heroism of the RAF in the documentary film *Target For Tonight*. (certificate)
TO LEOPOLD STOKOWSKI and his associates for their unique achievement in the creation of a new form of visualized music in Walt Disney's production *Fantasia*, thereby widening the scope of the motion picture as entertainment and as an art form. (certificate)
TO WALT DISNEY, WILLIAM GARITY, JOHN N.A. HAWKINS and the RCA MANUFACTURING COMPANY, for their outstanding contribution to the advancement of the use of sound in motion pictures through the production of *Fantasia*. (certificates)

1941 IRVING G. THALBERG MEMORIAL AWARD

TO WALT DISNEY

SCIENTIFIC OR TECHNICAL

CLASS I (statuette)
None.

CLASS II (plaque)
ELECTRICAL RESEARCH PRODUCTS DIVISION OF WESTERN ELECTRIC CO., INC., for the development of the precision integrating sphere densitometer.
RCA MANUFACTURING CO. for the design and development of the MI-3043 Uni-directional microphone.

CLASS III (citation)
RAY WILKINSON and the PARAMOUNT STUDIO LABORATORY; CHARLES LOOTENS and the REPUBLIC STUDIO SOUND DEPT.;
WILBUR SILVERTOOTH and the PARAMOUNT STUDIO ENGINEERING DEPT.;
PARAMOUNT PICTURES, INC., and 20TH CENTURY-FOX FILM CORP.;
DOUGLAS SHEARER and the METRO-GOLDWYN-MAYER STUDIO SOUND DEPT. and to LOREN RYDER and the PARAMOUNT STUDIO SOUND DEPARTMENT.

★ INDICATES WINNER

1942 The Fifteenth Year

At the 1942 Academy Awards banquet, held March 4, 1943, at the Cocoanut Grove in the Los Angeles Ambassador Hotel, Greer Garson received the Oscar as Best Actress of the year for *Mrs. Miniver* and gave a speech which is still a subject for discussion. Legend has it that her "thank you" oratory lasted nearly an hour, causing Academy officials thereafter to put a time limit on all Academy acceptance speeches. As sometimes happens in Hollywood, the facts may have been devoured by exaggeration. Says Miss Garson good-naturedly, "Reports on the length of my speech that night seem to be a bit like that one report of Mark Twain's death: slightly exaggerated. Actually, it was clocked at about five-and-a-half minutes, but I think the reason people remembered it is because I somewhat fractured a long-standing rule which was that a winner should simply say 'thank you' and then dissolve into a flood of tears and sit down. I felt very sincerely about what I had to say, that there were no losers in the room that night, that we were all winners, but I know I didn't do a long, one-woman fillibuster as the reports now have it. I admit I do have a gift of gab, and it seems to have gotten me in hot water that time, but I did use it to advantage later while selling war bonds all over the country." And the Academy did *not* put a limit to the length of acceptance speeches.

Mrs. Miniver also won five other Academy Awards, including those for Best Picture, Best Director William Wyler and Best Supporting Actress Teresa Wright. It was a big year for Miss Wright; she was also nominated in the Best Actress category, for *The Pride of the Yankees.* James Cagney was named Best Actor for *Yankee Doodle Dandy* and Van Heflin was chosen Best Supporting Actor for *Johnny Eager.* Four winners were chosen in the Best Documentary division, and thereafter that category was more clearly defined between "Short Subjects" and "features." Best Song of the year was Irving Berlin's "White Christmas," introduced in *Holiday Inn* by Bing Crosby and Marjorie Reynolds. Berlin himself announced the winner in that category; when he opened the sealed envelope bearing his name, he told the on-lookers, "I'm glad to present the award. I've known the fellow for a long time."

Bob Hope was again master of ceremonies for the evening, Jeanette MacDonald sang the National Anthem, and the Oscar ceremony itself carried a distinctly military flavor, with honor guests from all branches of the military services. Before the actual winners were announced, Marine private Tyrone Power and Air Force private Alan Ladd unfurled an industry flag disclosing that 27,677 members of the motion picture industry were in uniform. For the first time, the usual bronze-filled, gold-plated Oscar statues were also made out of plaster, due to wartime shortages; they were all replaced by the real thing when the war was over. It was also the last time Academy Awards were handed out at small, industry banquets. With a world at war and many facing starvation, it seemed insensitive to continue presenting awards at elegant dinner parties, so Oscar moved into a theater.

(above) **Best Actor: James Cagney** as
George M. Cohan in *Yankee Doodle Dandy*
(Warner Bros.; directed by Michael Curtiz).
Cagney became the first actor to win an
Academy Award for a musical performance,
playing the theater's prolific
actor-writer-musician Cohan, born on the
fourth of July and a perennial flagwaver.

(left) **Best Director: William Wyler** for
Mrs. Miniver (M-G-M; produced by Sidney
Franklin). Wyler was in military action
overseas when he was announced as
1942's Oscar winner as Director; his
award was accepted by his wife. His film
had a profound effect on Americans, newly
plunged into war, giving them insight (and
courage) in meeting demands forced on
them by the world's conflicts.

(right) **Best Picture: Mrs. Miniver** (M-G-M;
produced by Sidney Franklin), **Best Actress:
Greer Garson** as Mrs. Miniver and **Best
Supporting Actress: Teresa Wright**
as Carol Beldon Miniver in *Mrs. Miniver*.
It was a war picture without a battle
scene, but showed an English family's
everyday adjustments to wartime problems
with courage and warmth, and it could
not have come to the screen at a more
apt time. Walter Pidgeon, Dame May Whitty
and Richard Ney were also prominent, and
there was a sequel in 1950 called *The
Miniver Story*, again starring Miss Garson
and Pidgeon.

Best Supporting Actor: Van Heflin as Jeff Hartnett in *Johnny Eager* (M-G-M; directed by Mervyn Le Roy). At age 32, Heflin became the youngest actor to date to win an Academy Award. He played a booze-soaked friend and conscience to an underworld tough guy (Robert Taylor) who was using the D.A.'s daughter (Lana Turner) to his own advantage.

Nominations 1942

PICTURE

THE INVADERS, Ortus, Columbia (British). Produced by Michael Powell.
KINGS ROW, Warner Bros. Produced by Hal B. Wallis.
THE MAGNIFICENT AMBERSONS, Mercury, RKO Radio. Produced by Orson Welles.
✶ **MRS. MINIVER**, M-G-M. Produced by Sidney Franklin.
THE PIED PIPER, 20th Century-Fox. Produced by Nunnally Johnson.
THE PRIDE OF THE YANKEES, Goldwyn, RKO Radio. Produced by Samuel Goldwyn.
RANDOM HARVEST, M-G-M. Produced by Sidney Franklin.
THE TALK OF THE TOWN, Columbia. Produced by George Stevens.
WAKE ISLAND, Paramount. Produced by Joseph Sistrom.
YANKEE DOODLE DANDY, Warner Bros. Produced by Jack Warner and Hal B. Wallis, with William Cagney.

ACTOR

✶ **JAMES CAGNEY** in *Yankee Doodle Dandy*, Warner Bros.
RONALD COLMAN in *Random Harvest*, M-G-M.
GARY COOPER in *The Pride of the Yankees*, Goldwyn, RKO Radio.
WALTER PIDGEON in *Mrs. Miniver*, M-G-M.
MONTY WOOLLEY in *The Pied Piper*, 20th Century-Fox.

ACTRESS

BETTE DAVIS in *Now, Voyager*, Warner Bros.
✶ **GREER GARSON** in *Mrs. Miniver*, M-G-M.
KATHARINE HEPBURN in *Woman of the Year*, M-G-M.
ROSALIND RUSSELL in *My Sister Eileen*, Columbia.
TERESA WRIGHT in *The Pride of the Yankees*, Goldwyn, RKO Radio.

SUPPORTING ACTOR

WILLIAM BENDIX in *Wake Island*, Paramount.
✶ **VAN HEFLIN** in *Johnny Eager*, M-G-M.
WALTER HUSTON in *Yankee Doodle Dandy*, Warner Bros.
FRANK MORGAN in *Tortilla Flat*, M-G-M.
HENRY TRAVERS in *Mrs. Miniver*, M-G-M.

SUPPORTING ACTRESS

GLADYS COOPER in *Now, Voyager*, Warner Bros.
AGNES MOOREHEAD in *The Magnificent Ambersons*, Mercury, RKO Radio.
SUSAN PETERS in *Random Harvest*, M-G-M.
DAME MAY WHITTY in *Mrs. Miniver*, M-G-M.
✶ **TERESA WRIGHT** in *Mrs. Miniver*, M-G-M.

DIRECTION

MICHAEL CURTIZ for *Yankee Doodle Dandy*, Warner Bros.
JOHN FARROW for *Wake Island*, Paramount.
MERVYN LeROY for *Random Harvest*, M-G-M.
SAM WOOD for *Kings Row*, Warner Bros.
✶ **WILLIAM WYLER** for *Mrs. Miniver*, M-G-M.

WRITING

(Original Story)

HOLIDAY INN, Paramount. Irving Berlin.
✶ **THE INVADERS**, Ortus, Columbia (British). Emeric Pressburger.
THE PRIDE OF THE YANKEES, Goldwyn, RKO Radio. Paul Gallico.
THE TALK OF THE TOWN, Columbia. Sidney Harmon.
YANKEE DOODLE DANDY, Warner Bros. Robert Buckner.

(Original Screenplay)

ONE OF OUR AIRCRAFT IS MISSING, Powell, UA (British). Michael Powell and Emeric Pressburger.
THE ROAD TO MOROCCO, Paramount. Frank Butler and Don Hartman.
WAKE ISLAND, Paramount. W.R. Burnett and Frank Butler.
THE WAR AGAINST MRS. HADLEY, M-G-M. George Oppenheimer.
✶ **WOMAN OF THE YEAR**, M-G-M. Michael Kanin and Ring Lardner, Jr.

(Screenplay)

THE INVADERS, Ortus, Columbia (British). Rodney Ackland and Emeric Pressburger.
✶ **MRS. MINIVER**, M-G-M. George Froeschel, James Hilton, Claudine West and Arthur Wimperis.
THE PRIDE OF THE YANKEES, Goldwyn, RKO Radio. Herman J. Mankiewicz and Jo Swerling.
RANDOM HARVEST, M-G-M. George Froeschel, Claudine West and Arthur Wimperis.
THE TALK OF THE TOWN, Columbia. Sidney Buchman and Irwin Shaw.

CINEMATOGRAPHY

(Black-and-White)

KINGS ROW, Warner Bros. James Wong Howe.
THE MAGNIFICENT AMBERSONS, Mercury, RKO Radio. Stanley Cortez.
✶ **MRS. MINIVER**, M-G-M. Joseph Ruttenberg.
MOONTIDE, 20th Century-Fox. Charles Clarke.
THE PIED PIPER, 20th Century-Fox. Edward Cronjager.
THE PRIDE OF THE YANKEES, Goldwyn, RKO Radio. Rudolph Mate.
TAKE A LETTER, DARLING, Paramount. John Mescall.
THE TALK OF THE TOWN, Columbia. Ted Tetzlaff.
TEN GENTLEMEN FROM WEST POINT, 20th Century-Fox. Leon Shamroy.
THIS ABOVE ALL, 20th Century-Fox. Arthur Miller.

(Color)

ARABIAN KNIGHTS, Wanger, Universal. Milton Krasner, William V. Skall and W. Howard Greene.
✶ **THE BLACK SWAN**, 20th Century-Fox. Leon Shamroy.
CAPTAINS OF THE CLOUDS, Warner Bros. Sol Polito.
JUNGLE BOOK, Korda, UA. W. Howard Greene.
REAP THE WILD WIND, DeMille, Paramount. Milner and William V. Skall.
TO THE SHORES OF TRIPOLI, 20th Century-Fox. Edward Cronjager and William V. Skall.

ART DIRECTION-INTERIOR DECORATION

(Black-and-White)

GEORGE WASHINGTON SLEPT HERE, Warner Bros. Max Parker and Mark-Lee Kirk; Casey Roberts.
THE MAGNIFICENT AMBERSONS, Mercury, RKO Radio. Albert S. D'Agostino; Al Fields and Darrell Silvera.
THE PRIDE OF THE YANKEES, Goldwyn, RKO Radio. Perry Ferguson; Howard Bristol.
RANDOM HARVEST, M-G-M. Cedric Gibbons and Randall Duell; Edwin B. Willis and Jack Moore.
THE SHANGHAI GESTURE, Arnold, UA. Boris Leven.
SILVER QUEEN, Sherman, UA. Ralph Berger; Emile Kuri.
THE SPOILERS, Universal. John B. Goodman and Jack Otterson; Russell A. Gausman and Edward R. Robinson.
TAKE A LETTER, DARLING, Paramount. Hans Dreier and Roland Anderson; Sam Comer.
THE TALK OF THE TOWN, Columbia. Lionel Banks and Rudolph Sternad; Fay Babcock.
✶ **THIS ABOVE ALL**, 20th Century-Fox. Richard Day and Joseph Wright; Thomas Little.

(Color)

ARABIAN NIGHTS, Wanger, Universal. Alexander Golitzen and Jack Otterson; Russell A. Gausman and Ira S. Webb.
CAPTAINS OF THE CLOUDS, Warner Bros. Ted Smith; Casey Roberts.
JUNGLE BOOK, Korda, UA. Vincent Korda; Julia Heron.
✶ **MY GAL SAL**, 20th Century-Fox. Richard Day and Joseph Wright; Thomas Little.
REAP THE WILD WIND, DeMille, Paramount. Hans Dreier and Roland Anderson; George Sawley.

SOUND RECORDING

ARABIAN NIGHTS, Wanger, Universal. Bernard Brown.
BAMBI, Disney, RKO Radio. Sam Slyfield.
FLYING TIGERS, Republic, Daniel Bloomberg.
FRIENDLY ENEMIES, Small, UA. Jack Whitney, Sound Service, Inc.
THE GOLD RUSH, Chaplin, UA. James Fields, RCA Sound.
MRS. MINIVER, M-G-M. Douglas Shearer.
ONCE UPON A HONEYMOON, RKO Radio. Steve Dunn.
THE PRIDE OF THE YANKEES, Goldwyn, RKO Radio. Thomas Moulton.
ROAD TO MOROCCO, Paramount. Loren Ryder.
THIS ABOVE ALL, 20th Century-Fox. E.H. Hansen.
✶ **YANKEE DOODLE DANDY**, Warner Bros. Nathan Levinson.
YOU WERE NEVER LOVELIER, Columbia. John Livadary.

FILM EDITING

MRS. MINIVER, M-G-M. Harold F. Kress.
✶ **THE PRIDE OF THE YANKEES**, Goldwyn, RKO Radio. Daniel Mandell.
THE TALK OF THE TOWN, Columbia. Otto Meyer.
THIS ABOVE ALL, 20th Century-Fox. Walter Thompson.
YANKEE DOODLE DANDY, Warner Bros. George Amy.

SPECIAL EFFECTS

THE BLACK SWAN, 20th Century-Fox. Fred Sersen, Roger Heman and George Leverett.
DESPERATE JOURNEY, Warner Bros. Byron Haskin and Nathan Levinson.
FLYING TIGERS, Republic. Howard Lydecker and Daniel J. Bloomberg.
INVISIBLE AGENT, Universal. John Fulton and Bernard B. Brown.
JUNGLE BOOK, Korda, UA. Lawrence Butler and William H. Wilmarth.
MRS. MINIVER, M-G-M. A. Arnold Gillespie, Warren Newcombe and Douglas Shearer.
THE NAVY COMES THROUGH, RKO Radio. Vernon L. Walker and James G. Stewart.
ONE OF OUR AIRCRAFT IS MISSING, Powell, UA (British). Ronald Neame and C.C. Stevens.
THE PRIDE OF THE YANKEES, Goldwyn, RKO Radio. Jack Cosgrove, Ray Binger and Thomas T. Moulton.
✶ **REAP THE WILD WIND**, DeMille, Paramount. Farciot Edouart, Gordon Jennings, William L. Pereira and Louis Mesenkop.

SHORT SUBJECTS

(Cartoons)

ALL OUT FOR V, 20th Century-Fox.
THE BLITZ WOLF, M-G-M.
✶ **DER FUEHRER'S FACE**, Disney, RKO Radio.
JUKE BOX JAMBOREE, Lantz, Universal.
PIGS IN A POLKA, Schlesinger, Warner Bros.
TULIPS SHALL GROW, Paramount. (George Pal Puppetoon)

(One-reel)

DESERT WONDERLAND, 20th Century-Fox. (Magic Carpet Series)
MARINES IN THE MAKING, M-G-M. (Pete Smith Specialties)
✶ **SPEAKING OF ANIMALS AND THEIR FAMILIES**. Paramount. (Speaking of Animals)
UNITED STATES MARINE BAND, Warner Bros. (Melody Master Bands)

(Two-reel)

✶ **BEYOND THE LINE OF DUTY**, Warner Bros. (Broadway Brevities)
DON'T TALK, M-G-M. (Two-reel Special)
PRIVATE SMITH OF THE U.S.A., RKO Radio. (This Is America Series)

MUSIC

(Song)

ALWAYS IN MY HEART (*Always in My Heart,* Warner Bros.); Music by Ernesto Lecuona. Lyrics by Kim Gannon.

DEARLY BELOVED (*You Were Never Lovelier,* Columbia); Music by Jerome Kern. Lyrics by Johnny Mercer.

HOW ABOUT YOU? (*Babes on Broadway,* M-G-M); Music by Burton Lane. Lyrics by Ralph Freed.

IT SEEMS I HEARD THAT SONG BEFORE (*Youth on Parade,* Republic); Music by Jule Styne. Lyrics by Sammy Cahn.

I'VE GOT A GAL IN KALAMAZOO (*Orchestra Wives,* 20th Century-Fox); Music by Harry Warren. Lyrics by Mack Gordon.

LOVE IS A SONG (*Bambi,* Disney, RKO Radio); Music by Frank Churchill. Lyrics by Larry Morey.

PENNIES FOR PEPPINO (*Flying With Music,* Roach, UA); Music by Edward Ward. Lyrics by Chet Forrest and Bob Wright.

PIG FOOT PETE (*Hellzapoppin',* Universal); Music by Gene de Paul. Lyrics by Don Raye.

THERE'S A BREEZE ON LAKE LOUISE (*The Mayor of 44th Street,* RKO Radio); Music by Harry Revel. Lyrics by Mort Greene.

★ WHITE CHRISTMAS (*Holiday Inn,* Paramount); Music and Lyrics by Irving Berlin.

(Scoring of a Dramatic or Comedy Picture)
(Slight alteration of classification)

ARABIAN NIGHTS, Universal. Frank Skinner.

BAMBI, Disney, RKO Radio. Frank Churchill and Edward Plumb.

THE BLACK SWAN, 20th Century-Fox. Alfred Newman.

THE CORSICAN BROTHER, Small, UA. Dimitri Tiomkin.

FLYING TIGERS, Republic. Victor Young.

THE GOLD RUSH, Chaplin, UA. Max Terr.

I MARRIED A WITCH, Cinema Guild, UA. Roy Webb.

JOAN OF PARIS, RKO Radio. Roy Webb.

JUNGLE BOOK, Korda, UA. Miklos Rozsa.

KLONDIKE FURY, Monogram. Edward Kay.

★ NOW, VOYAGER, Warner Bros. Max Steiner.

THE PRIDE OF THE YANKEES, Goldwyn, RKO Radio. Leigh Harline.

RANDOM HARVEST, M-G-M. Herbert Stothart.

THE SHANGHAI GESTURE, Arnold, UA. Richard Hageman.

SILVER QUEEN, Sherman, UA. Victor Young.

TAKE A LETTER, DARLING, Paramount. Victor Young.

THE TALK OF THE TOWN, Columbia. Frederick Hollander and Morris Stoloff.

TO BE OR NOT TO BE, Lubitsch, UA. Werner Heymann.

(Scoring of a Musical Picture)

FLYING WITH MUSIC, Roach, UA. Edward Ward.

FOR ME AND MY GAL, M-G-M. Roger Edens and Georgie Stoll.

HOLIDAY INN, Paramount. Robert Emmett Dolan.

IT STARTED WITH EVE, Universal. Charles Previn and Hans Salter.

JOHNNY DOUGHBOY, Republic. Walter Scharf.

MY GAL SAL, 20th Century-Fox. Alfred Newman.

★ YANKEE DOODLE DANDY, Warner Bros. Ray Heindorf and Heinz Roemheld.

YOU WERE NEVER LOVELIER, Columbia. Leigh Harline.

DOCUMENTARY

A SHIP IS BORN, U.S. Merchant Marine, Warner Bros.

AFRICA, PRELUDE TO VICTORY, March of Time, 20th Century-Fox.

★ BATTLE OF MIDWAY, U.S. Navy, 20th Century-Fox.

COMBAT REPORT, U.S. Army Signal Corps.

CONQUER BY THE CLOCK, Office of War Information, RKO Pathe. Frederic Ullman, Jr.

THE GRAIN THAT BUILT A HEMISPHERE, Coordinator's Office, Motion Picture Society for the Americas. Walt Disney.

HENRY BROWNE, FARMER, U.S. Department of Agriculture, Republic.

HIGH OVER THE BORDERS, Canadian National Film Board.

HIGH STAKES IN THE EAST, Netherlands Information Bureau.

INSIDE FIGHTING CHINA, Canadian National Film Board.

IT'S EVERYBODY'S WAR, Office of War Information, 20th Century-Fox.

★ KOKODA FRONT LINE, Australian News Information Bureau.

LISTEN TO BRITAIN, British Ministry of Information.

LITTLE BELGIUM, Belgian Ministry of Information.

LITTLE ISLES OF FREEDOM, Warner Bros. Victor Stoloff and Edgar Loew.

★ MOSCOW STRIKES BACK, Artkino (Russian).

MR. BLABBERMOUTH, Office of War Information, M-G-M.

MR. GARDENIA JONES, Office of War Information, M-G-M.

NEW SPIRIT, U.S. Treasury Department. Walt Disney.

★ PRELUDE TO WAR, U.S. Army Special Services.

THE PRICE OF VICTORY, Office of War Information, Paramount. Pine-Thomas.

TWENTY-ONE MILES, British Ministry of Information.

WE REFUSE TO DIE, Office of War Information, Paramount. William C. Thomas.

WHITE EAGLE, Cocanen Films.

WINNING YOUR WINGS, U.S. Army Air Force, Warner Bros.
(NOTE: four winners this year only.)

SPECIAL AWARDS

TO CHARLES BOYER for his his progressive cultural achievement in establishing the French Research Foundation in Los Angeles as a source of reference for the Hollywood motion picture industry. (certificate)

TO NOEL COWARD for his outstanding production achievement in *In Which We Serve.* (certificate)

TO METRO-GOLDWYN-MAYER STUDIO for its achievement in representing the American way of life in the production of the *Andy Hardy* series of films. (certificate)

1942 IRVING G. THALBERG MEMORIAL AWARD

TO SIDNEY FRANKLIN

SCIENTIFIC OR TECHNICAL

CLASS I (statuette)
None.

CLASS II (plaque)

CARROLL CLARK, F. THOMAS THOMPSON and the RKO RADIO STUDIO ART and MINIATURE DEPARTMENTS for the design and construction of a moving cloud and horizon machine.

DANIEL B. CLARK and the 20TH CENTURY-FOX FILM CORP. for the development of a lens calibration system and the application of this system to exposure control in cinematography.

CLASS III (citation)

ROBERT HENDERSON and the PARAMOUNT STUDIO ENGINEERING and TRANSPARENCY DEPARTMENTS;

DANIEL J. BLOOMBERG and the REPUBLIC STUDIO SOUND DEPARTMENT.

★ INDICATES WINNER

Woman of the Year (M-G-M; produced by Joseph L. Mankiewicz) marked the first screen teaming of Katharine Hepburn and Spencer Tracy (above), and won the Original Screenplay award for Michael Kanin and Ring Lardner, Jr. It was directed by George Stevens and matched a tough New York sportswriter (Tracy) with a society columnist (Hepburn); the Hepburn-Tracy chemistry was contagious, and inspired seven more pairings from *Keeper of the Flame* (1942) through *Guess Who's Coming to Dinner* (1967), twenty-five years later.

The Black Swan (20th Century-Fox; produced by Robert Bassler) starred Tyrone Power and Maureen O'Hara (below) in the dazzling kind of Technicolor swashbuckling adventure which was a common (and always welcome) screen commodity in the 1940s. *Swan* was a cut above most; directed by Henry King and based on a Rafael Sabatini novel (with a Ben Hecht screenplay), it received an Oscar for its Color Cinematography by Leon Shamroy.

Best Picture: Casablanca (Warner Bros.; produced by Hal B. Wallis) and **Best Director: Michael Curtiz** for *Casablanca.* Filled with the kind of punchy, hard-boiled melodrama for which Warner Bros. was most famous in the 1940s, *Casablanca* also reaped an unexpected publicity landfall during its initial release when World War II events splashed the name of the French African seaport town in headlines all over the world. But besides the topical title, it had a wealth of other qualities going for it too, including timeless characters colorfully played by Humphrey Bogart and Ingrid Bergman (right, in the climactic farewell scene) and a knockout supporting cast consisting of Paul Henreid, Claude Rains, Conrad Veidt, Sydney Greenstreet, Peter Lorre, Dooley Wilson and S.Z. ("Cuddles") Sakall—plus a haunting Max Steiner score.

Best Actress: Jennifer Jones as Bernadette in *The Song of Bernadette* (20th Century-Fox; directed by Henry King). A 24-year-old screen newcomer, Jennifer Jones (left) was luminous as the simple peasant girl of Lourdes who became the center of a spiritual tornado in the mid-1800s when she claimed to have seen a vision of the Virgin Mary while gathering firewood. Based on the novel by Franz Werfel, *Bernadette* was one of the year's most distinguished successes, and the year's biggest Oscar winner, with additional awards for Cinematography, Art Direction and Music Score.

Best Actor: Paul Lukas as Kurt Muller in *Watch on the Rhine* (Warner Bros.; directed by Herman Shumlin). Lukas (below, with Janis Wilson and Eric Roberts) re-created his Broadway role of a gentle German engineer, married to an American (Bette Davis) and a member of the German Underground fighting Fascism. Lillian Hellman wrote the original play—a topical warning about the threat of Fascism infiltrating American homes.

1943 The Sixteenth Year

The Oscar ceremony moved from a banquet setting into a theater for the first time on March 2, 1944, when awards were given for movie world achievement during 1943. The site of the new-style gala was the large and legendary Grauman's Chinese Theatre on Hollywood Boulevard with a seating capacity of 2,258; increased attendance at the Academy's big night had made further banquets impractical so, after 15 years, the intimate little industry dinners became a thing of the past. The extra space afforded by Grauman's not only gave Oscar a new look but also gave the industry a chance to invite a large number of servicemen and women from all military branches to come share in the excitement.

Something else new was added, too. For the first time since the Supporting Actor and Supporting Actress categories were inaugurated in 1936, winners in those divisions were given full-size statues instead of plaques (and, so no one would feel slighted, the Academy in later years replaced earlier plaques with statuettes for all acting award winners). The two most honored motion pictures of the year were *The Song of Bernadette* with four Awards, including Best Actress (Jennifer Jones), and *Casablanca* with three, including Best Picture and Best Director (Michael Curtiz). Photographers had a field day when Miss Jones arrived at the theater with Ingrid Bergman, both of them under contract to David O. Selznick, close friends and leading nominees for that Best Actress trophy.

Despite the fact the number of award categories had swelled to twenty-seven, as compared to seven in Oscar's first year, the only other movie to receive more than one award was *The Phantom of the Opera,* with nods for Color Cinematography and Color Art Direction. Paul Lukas was chosen Best Actor for *Watch on the Rhine,* a role he created on the Broadway stage with great success, and the Supporting Award statuettes went to Charles Coburn in *The More the Merrier* and Katina Paxinou in *For Whom the Bell Tolls.* Warner Bros.' Hal Wallis received the Irving G. Thalberg Award and, soon after, moved from Burbank over to Paramount to become an independent producer, one of the industry's most prolific and prestigious.

Awards for the evening were presented by Academy President Walter Wanger, producer Sidney Franklin, writer James Hilton, radio star Dinah Shore and actresses Greer Garson, Teresa Wright, Rosalind Russell and Carole Landis. Jack Benny was the master of ceremonies for a radio broadcast of the ceremony sent to Armed Forces fighting overseas. And that fighting was nearing an important campaign. Just three months after Oscar's sixteenth celebration, on D-Day, the sixth of June, 1944, the Allied invasion of Nazi-occupied West Europe would begin in Normandy, and World War II would be entering its final chapters.

Best Supporting Actress: Katina Paxinou as Pilar (below, overseeing Ingrid Bergman and Gary Cooper) in *For Whom the Bell Tolls* (Paramount; directed by Sam Wood). Long recognized as the first lady of Greek theater and a vital force in that nation's Royal Theatre of Athens, Katina Paxinou made her first Hollywood film appearance —and won the Academy Award—as a powerful, strong-willed hill woman and guerrilla fighter in the Spanish Civil War.

Nominations 1943

PICTURE

★ **CASABLANCA**, Warner Bros. Produced by Hal B. Wallis.
FOR WHOM THE BELL TOLLS, Paramount. Produced by Sam Wood.
HEAVEN CAN WAIT, 20th Century-Fox. Produced by Ernst Lubitsch.
IN WHICH WE SERVE, Two Cities, UA (British). Produced by Noel Coward.
MADAME CURIE, M-G-M. Produced by Sidney Franklin.
THE MORE THE MERRIER, Columbia. Produced by George Stevens.
THE OX-BOW INCIDENT, 20th Century-Fox. Produced by Lamar Trotti.
THE SONG OF BERNADETTE, 20th Century-Fox. Produced by William Perlberg.
WATCH ON THE RHINE, Warner Bros. Produced by Hal B. Wallis.

ACTOR

HUMPHREY BOGART in *Casablanca*, Warner Bros.
GARY COOPER in *For Whom the Bell Tolls*, Paramount.
★ **PAUL LUKAS** in *Watch on the Rhine*, Warner Bros.
WALTER PIDGEON in *Madame Curie*, M-G-M.
MICKEY ROONEY in *The Human Comedy*, M-G-M.

ACTRESS

JEAN ARTHUR in *The More the Merrier*, Columbia.
INGRID BERGMAN in *For Whom the Bell Tolls*, Paramount.
JOAN FONTAINE in *The Constant Nymph*, Warner Bros.
GREER GARSON in *Madame Curie*, M-G-M.
★ **JENNIFER JONES** in *The Song of Bernadette*, 20th Century-Fox.

SUPPORTING ACTOR

CHARLES BICKFORD in *The Song of Bernadette*, 20th Century-Fox.
★ **CHARLES COBURN** in *The More the Merrier*, Columbia.
J. CARROL NAISH in *Sahara*, Columbia.
CLAUDE RAINS in *Casablanca*, Warner Bros.
AKIM TAMIROFF in *For Whom the Bell Tolls*, Paramount.

SUPPORTING ACTRESS

GLADYS COOPER in *The Song of Bernadette*, 20th Century-Fox.
PAULETTE GODDARD in *So Proudly We Hail*, Paramount.
★ **KATINA PAXINOU** in *For Whom the Bell Tolls*, Paramount.
ANNE REVERE in *The Song of Bernadette*, 20th Century-Fox.
LUCILE WATSON in *Watch on the Rhine*, Warner Bros.

DIRECTION

CLARENCE BROWN for *The Human Comedy*, M-G-M.
★ **MICHAEL CURTIZ** for *Casablanca*, Warner Bros.
HENRY KING for *The Song of Bernadette*, 20th Century-Fox.
ERNST LUBITSCH for *Heaven Can Wait*, 20th Century-Fox.
GEORGE STEVENS for *The More the Merrier*, Columbia.

WRITING

(Original Story)
ACTION IN THE NORTH ATLANTIC, Warner Bros. Guy Gilpatric.
DESTINATION TOKYO, Warner Bros. Steve Fisher.
★ **THE HUMAN COMEDY**, M-G-M. William Saroyan.
THE MORE THE MERRIER, Columbia. Frank Ross and Robert Russell.
SHADOW OF A DOUBT, Universal, Gordon McDonell.

(Original Screenplay)
AIR FORCE, Warner Bros. Dudley Nichols.
IN WHICH WE SERVE, Two Cities-UA (British). Noel Coward.
THE NORTH STAR, Goldwyn, RKO Radio. Lillian Hellman.
★ **PRINCESS O'ROURKE**, Warner Bros. Norman Krasna.
SO PROUDLY WE HAIL, Paramount. Allan Scott.

(Screenplay)
★ **CASABLANCA**, Warner Bros. Julius J. Epstein, Philip G. Epstein and Howard Koch.
HOLY MATRIMONY, 20th Century-Fox. Nunnally Johnson.
THE MORE THE MERRIER, Columbia. Richard Flournoy, Lewis R. Foster, Frank Ross and Robert Russell.
THE SONG OF BERNADETTE, 20th Century-Fox. George Seaton.
WATCH ON THE RHINE, Warner Bros. Lillian Hellman and Dashiell Hammett.

CINEMATOGRAPHY

(Black-and-White)
AIR FORCE, Warner Bros. James Wong Howe, Elmer Dyer and Charles Marshall.
CASABLANCA, Warner Bros. Arthur Edeson.
CORVETTE K-225, Universal. Tony Gaudio.
FIVE GRAVES TO CAIRO, Paramount. John Seitz.
THE HUMAN COMEDY, M-G-M. Harry Stradling.
MADAME CURIE, M-G-M. Joseph Ruttenberg.
THE NORTH STAR, Goldwyn, RKO Radio. James Wong Howe.
SAHARA, Columbia. Rudolph Mate.
SO PROUDLY WE HAIL, Paramount. Charles Lang.
★ **THE SONG OF BERNADETTE**, 20th Century-Fox. Arthur Miller.

(Color)
FOR WHOM THE BELL TOLLS, Paramount. Ray Rennahan.
HEAVEN CAN WAIT, 20th Century-Fox. Edward Cronjager.
HELLO, FRISCO, HELLO, 20th Century-Fox. Charles G. Clarke and Allen Davey.
LASSIE COME HOME, M-G-M. Leonard Smith.
★ **THE PHANTOM OF THE OPERA**, Universal. Hal Mohr and W. Howard Greene.
THOUSANDS CHEER, M-G-M. George Folsey.

ART DIRECTION-INTERIOR DECORATION

(Black-and-White)
FIVE GRAVES TO CAIRO, Paramount. Hans Dreier and Ernst Fegte; Bertram Granger.
FLIGHT FOR FREEDOM, RKO Radio. Albert S. D'Agostino and Carroll Clark; Darrell Silvera and Harley Miller.
MADAME CURIE, M-G-M. Cedric Gibbons and Paul Groesse; Edwin B. Willis and Hugh Hunt.
MISSION TO MOSCOW, Warner Bros. Carl Weyl; George J. Hopkins.
THE NORTH STAR, Goldwyn, RKO Radio. Perry Ferguson; Howard Bristol.
★ **THE SONG OF BERNADETTE**, 20th Century-Fox. James Basevi and William Darling; Thomas Little.

(Color)
FOR WHOM THE BELL TOLLS, Paramount. Hans Dreier and Haldane Douglas; Bertram Granger.
THE GANG'S ALL HERE, 20th Century-Fox. James Basevi and Joseph C. Wright; Thomas Little.

The Human Comedy (M-G-M; produced and directed by Clarence Brown) was the sentimental and low-key story of a small California town and how its citizenry was affected by World War II, being waged a world away. It won the Best Original Story award for author William Saroyan, and starred Mickey Rooney as the town's messenger boy and Butch Jenkins (above, waving at the passing trainman) as his freckle-faced kid brother.

(below) **Best Supporting Actor: Charles Coburn** as Benjamin Dingle (flanked by Joel McCrea and Jean Arthur) in *The More the Merrier* (Columbia; directed by George Stevens). The setting was overcrowded, wartime Washington, D.C., and Coburn played a delightful old sharpie looking for a room to rent, which Jean Arthur happened to have. In 1966, the famous Coburn role reappeared in *Walk, Don't Run* and was played by Cary Grant.

The Phantom of the Opera (Universal; produced by George Waggner) featured Claude Rains (above) as the mad musician who secretly lives in the catacombs under the Paris Opera House and saws down a crystal chandelier during a sold-out performance, and it won two Academy Awards: for Color Cinematography and Color Art Direction. Universal was a specialist in the horror genre, but this remake of Lon Chaney's *Phantom* marked only the third time the studio had worked in the three-strip Technicolor genre (following 1942's *Arabian Nights* and 1943's *White Savage*).

* THE PHANTOM OF THE OPERA, Universal. Alexander Golitzen and John B. Goodman; Russell A. Gausman and Ira S. Webb.
THIS IS THE ARMY, Warner Bros. John Hughes and Lt. John Koenig; George J. Hopkins.
THOUSANDS CHEER, M-G-M. Cedric Gibbons and Daniel Cathcart; Edwin B. Willis and Jacques Mersereau.

SOUND RECORDING

HANGMEN ALSO DIE, Pressburger, UA. Jack Whitney, Sound Service, Inc.
IN OLD OKLAHOMA, Republic. Daniel J. Bloomberg.
MADAME CURIE, M-G-M. Douglas Shearer.
THE NORTH STAR, Goldwyn, RKO Radio. Thomas Moulton.
THE PHANTOM OF THE OPERA, Universal. Bernard B. Brown.
RIDING HIGH, Paramount. Loren L. Ryder.
SAHARA, Columbia. John Livadary.
SALUDOS AMIGOS, Disney, RKO Radio. C.O. Slyfield.
SO THIS IS WASHINGTON, RKO Radio. J.L. Fields, RCA Sound.
THE SONG OF BERNARDETTE, 20th Century-Fox. E.H. Hansen.
THIS IS THE ARMY, Warner Bros. Nathan Levinson.
* THIS LAND IS MINE, RKO Radio. Stephen Dunn.

FILM EDITING

* AIR FORCE, Warner Bros. George Amy.
CASABLANCA, Warner Bros. Owen Marks.
FIVE GRAVES TO CAIRO, Paramount. Doane Harrison.
FOR WHOM THE BELL TOLLS, Paramount. Sherman Todd and John Link.

THE SONG OF BERNADETTE, 20th Century-Fox. Barbara McLean.

SPECIAL EFFECTS

AIR FORCE, Warner Bros. Hans Koenekamp, Rex Wimpy and Nathan Levinson.
BOMBARDIER, RKO Radio. Vernon L. Walker, James G. Stewart and Roy Granville.
* CRASH DIVE, 20th Century-Fox. Fred Sersen and Roger Heman.
THE NORTH STAR, Goldwyn, RKO Radio. Clarence Slifer, R.O. Binger and Thomas T. Moulton.
SO PROUDLY WE HAIL, Paramount. Farciot Edouart; Gordon Jennings and George Dutton.
STAND BY FOR ACTION, M-G-M. A. Arnold Gillespie, Donald Jahraus and Michael Steinore.

MUSIC

(Song)
CHANGE OF HEART (*Hit Parade of 1943*, Republic); Music by Jule Styne. Lyrics by Harold Adamson.
HAPPINESS IS A THING CALLED JOE (*Cabin in the Sky*, M-G-M); Music by Harold Arlen. Lyrics by E.Y. Harburg.
MY SHINING HOUR (*The Sky's the Limit*, RKO Radio); Music by Harold Arlen. Lyrics by Johnny Mercer.
SALUDOS AMIGOS (*Saludos Amigos*, Disney, RKO Radio); Music by Charles Wolcott. Lyrics by Ned Washington.
SAY A PRAYER FOR THE BOYS OVER THERE (*Hers to Hold*, Universal); Music by Jimmy McHugh. Lyrics by Herb Magidson.

THAT OLD BLACK MAGIC (*Star Spangled Rhythm*, Paramount); Music by Harold Arlen. Lyrics by Johnny Mercer.
THEY'RE EITHER TOO YOUNG OR TOO OLD (*Thank Your Lucky Stars*, Warner Bros); Music by Arthur Schwartz. Lyrics by Frank Loesser.
WE MUSTN'T SAY GOOD BYE (*Stage Door Canteen*, Lesser, UA); Music by James Monaco. Lyrics by Al Dubin.
YOU'D BE SO NICE TO COME HOME TO (*Something to Shout About*, Columbia); Music and Lyrics by Cole Porter.
* YOU'LL NEVER KNOW (*Hello, Frisco, Hello*, 20th Century-Fox); Music by Harry Warren. Lyrics by Mack Gordon.

(Scoring of a Dramatic or Comedy Picture)
THE AMAZING MRS. HOLLIDAY, Universal. Hans J. Salter and Frank Skinner.
CASABLANCA, Warner Bros. Max Steiner.
THE COMMANDOS STRIKE AT DAWN, Columbia. Louis Gruenberg and Morris Stoloff.
THE FALLEN SPARROW, RKO Radio. C. Bakaleinikoff and Roy Webb.
FOR WHOM THE BELL TOLLS, Paramount. Victor Young.
HANGMEN ALSO DIE, Arnold, UA. Hanns Eisler.
HI DIDDLE DIDDLE, Stone UA. Phil Boutelje.
IN OLD OKLAHOMA, Republic. Walter Scharf.
JOHNNY COME LATELY, Cagney, UA. Leigh Harline.
THE KANSAN, Sherman, UA. Gerard Carbonara.
LADY OF BURLESQUE, Stromberg, UA. Arthur Lange.
MADAME CURIE, M-G-M. Herbert Stothart.
THE MOON AND SIXPENCE, Loew-Lewin, UA. Dimitri Tiomkin.
THE NORTH STAR, Goldwyn, RKO Radio. Aaron Copland.
* THE SONG OF BERNADETTE, 20th Century-Fox. Alfred Newman.
VICTORY THROUGH AIR POWER, Disney, UA. Edward H. Plumb, Paul J. Smith and Oliver G. Wallace.

(Scoring of a Musical Picture)
CONEY ISLAND, 20th Century-Fox. Alfred Newman.
HIT PARADE OF 1943, Republic. Walter Scharf.
THE PHANTOM OF THE OPERA, Universal. Edward Ward.
SALUDOS AMIGOS, Disney, RKO Radio. Edward H. Plumb, Paul J. Smith and Charles Wolcott.
THE SKY'S THE LIMIT, RKO Radio. Leigh Harline.
SOMETHING TO SHOUT ABOUT, Columbia. Morris Stoloff.
STAGE DOOR CANTEEN, Lesser, UA. Frederic E. Rich.
STAR SPANGLED RHYTHM, Paramount. Robert Emmett Dolan.
* THIS IS THE ARMY, Warner Bros. Ray Heindorf.
THOUSANDS CHEER, M-G-M. Herbert Stothart.

SHORT SUBJECTS

(Cartoons)
THE DIZZY ACROBAT, Universal. Walter Lantz, producer.
THE FIVE HUNDRED HATS OF BARTHOLOMEW CUBBINS, Paramount (Puppetoon). George Pal, producer.
GREETINGS, BAIT, Warner Bros. Leon Schlesinger, producer.
IMAGINATION, Columbia. Dave Fleischer, producer.
REASON AND EMOTION, Disney, RKO Radio. Walt Disney, producer.
* YANKEE DOODLE MOUSE, M-G-M. Frederick Quimby, producer.

(One-reel)
* AMPHIBIOUS FIGHTERS, Paramount. Grantland Rice, producer.
CAVALCADE OF THE DANCE WITH VELOZ AND YOLANDA, Warner Bros. (Melody Master Bands). Gordon Hollingshead, producer.

CHAMPIONS CARRY ON, 20th Century-Fox. (Sports Reviews). Edmund Reek, producer.
HOLLYWOOD IN UNIFORM, Columbia. (Screen Snapshots). Ralph Staub, producer.
SEEING HANDS, M-G-M. (Pete Smith Specialty). Pete Smith, producer.

(Two-reel)
* HEAVENLY MUSIC, M-G-M. Jerry Bresler and Sam Coslow, producers.
LETTER TO A HERO, RKO Radio. (This Is America). Fred Ullman, producer.
MARDI GRAS, Paramount. (Musical Parade). Walter MacEwen, producer.
WOMEN AT WAR, Warner Bros. (Technicolor Special). Gordon Hollingshead, producer.

DOCUMENTARY

(Short Subjects)
CHILDREN OF MARS, This Is America Series, RKO Radio.
* DECEMBER 7TH, U.S. Navy, Field Photographic Branch, Office of Strategic Services.
PLAN FOR DESTRUCTION, M-G-M.
SWEDES IN AMERICA, Office of War Information, Overseas Motion Picture Bureau.
TO THE PEOPLE OF THE UNITED STATES, U.S. Public Health Service, Walter Wanger, Prods.
TOMORROW WE FLY, U.S. Navy, Bureau of Aeronautics.
YOUTH IN CRISIS, March of Time, 20th Century-Fox.

(Features)
BATTLE OF RUSSIA, Special Service Division of the War Department.
BAPTISM OF FIRE, U.S. Army, Fighting Men Series.
* DESERT VICTORY, British Ministry of Information.
REPORT FROM THE ALEUTIANS, U.S. Army Pictorial Service, Combat Film Series.
WAR DEPARTMENT REPORT, Field Photographic Branch, Office of Strategic Services.

SPECIAL AWARDS

TO GEORGE PAL for the development of novel methods and techniques in the production of short subjects known as Puppetoons. (plaque)

1943 IRVING G. THALBERG MEMORIAL AWARD

TO HAL B. WALLIS

SCIENTIFIC OR TECHNICAL

CLASS I (statuette)
None.

CLASS II (plaque)
FARCIOT EDOUART, EARLE MORGAN, BARTON THOMPSON and the PARAMOUNT STUDIO ENGINEERING and TRANSPARENCY DEPARTMENTS for the development and practical application to motion picture production of a method of duplicating and enlarging natural color photographs, transferring the image emulsions to glass plates and projecting these slides by especially designed stereopticon equipment.
PHOTO PRODUCTS DEPARTMENT, E.I. duPONT de NEMOURS AND CO., INC. for the development of fine-grain motion picture films.

CLASS III (citation)
DANIEL J. BLOOMBERG and the REPUBLIC STUDIO SOUND DEPARTMENT;
CHARLES GALLOWAY CLARKE and the 20TH CENTURY-FOX STUDIO CAMERA DEPARTMENT;
FARCIOT EDOUART and the PARAMOUNT STUDIO TRANSPARENCY DEPARTMENT;
WILLARD H. TURNER and the RKO RADIO STUDIO SOUND DEPARTMENT.

* INDICATES WINNER

1944
The Seventeenth Year

Hollywood was in the midst of a labor strike on March 15, 1945, when the Academy honors for 1944 were handed out. The setting again was broadcast over network radio, via the American Broadcasting Company system. It was also the last time plaster statuettes were given to the winners. Wartime austerity still had its effect on Oscar but—happily—the news from Europe was optimistic. Within two months, Germany would surrender and the European siege would be over; by August, 1945, the Japanese would follow suit.

Once again, Bob Hope was master of ceremonies for the Academy party, sharing the job with director John Cromwell, whose *Since You Went Away* had been nominated in nine award categories. The two most honored films of the year were Darryl F. Zanuck's mammoth *Wilson* and Leo McCarey's gentle *Going My Way,* each nominated for ten Awards. Ultimately, *Wilson* won five Oscars and *Going My Way* received seven, including those for Best Picture, Best Actor (Bing Crosby), Best Supporting Actor (Barry Fitzgerald), Best Director (Leo McCarey) and Best Song ("Swinging on a Star" by James Van Heusen and Johnny Burke). It was a particular triumph for Crosby, best known not as an actor, but as the country's best-selling crooner.

Ingrid Bergman was named Best Actress for *Gaslight,* and Ethel Barrymore was chosen Best Supporting Actress for *None But The Lonely Heart,* her first film since *Rasputin and the Empress* in 1932. She was absent, but Miss Barrymore's Award was accepted by RKO's Charles Koerner. Norma Shearer, retired from the screen for three years, presented the Irving G. Thalberg Memorial Award to Darryl F. Zanuck; it was the first time Thalberg's widow had presented the Award herself.

Margaret O'Brien, age eight and a new star via four 1944 releases (*Jane Eyre, Lost Angel, The Canterville Ghost,* and *Meet Me in St. Louis*), received a miniature statuette as the year's outstanding child actress and, years later, recalled the evening warmly. "I was very excited and apprehensive," she said. "Excited because I received the award from Bob Hope, who was my secret heartthrob, and apprehensive because I was afraid one of the false teeth the studio made me wear to cover my missing baby teeth might fall out, as they often did when I was working. Nevertheless, all went well. I was *thrilled* when Bob Hope later hugged me. As a matter of fact, he hugged most of the other actresses, too, but I felt special because I was the only one he both hugged *and* lifted."

Best Actress: Ingrid Bergman as Paula Alquist Anton (above, with Charles Boyer) in *Gaslight* (M-G-M; directed by George Cukor). It was a choice role, flawlessly played: a helpless, frightened young bride returns to the home where her aunt has been murdered, only to discover her new husband is attempting to drive her insane. Based on a play by Patrick Hamilton called *Angel Street,* the story had also been filmed as a 1940 British thriller starring Diana Wynyard, but was withheld from showing in the United States until 1952 due to Ingrid Bergman's Oscar-winning version.

Best Picture: Going My Way (Paramount; produced and directed by Leo McCarey), **Best Director: Leo McCarey** and (pictured at left) **Best Actor: Bing Crosby** as Father O'Malley and **Best Supporting Actor: Barry Fitzgerald** as Father Fitzgibbon in *Going My Way.* A warm and inspiring story of a frisky young priest on his first assignment in an insolvent New York parish, it provided Crosby with a challenging change of pace and gave Fitzgerald a unique niche in Oscar history: he became the first (and only) performer to be nominated both as Best Actor and as Best Supporting Actor for the same performance, something no longer possible under present voting rules.

Best Supporting Actress: Ethel Barrymore as Ma Mott (left with Cary Grant) in *None But the Lonely Heart* (RKO Radio; directed by Clifford Odets). Long regarded as one of the genuine great ladies of the American stage, Miss Barrymore hadn't made a motion picture since 1932's *Rasputin and the Empress* when she played the sympathetic and terminally ill mother of cynical Ernie Mott (Grant), living in London's pre-World War II slums and destined to finally die of cancer in a prison hospital. Miss Barrymore also received Oscar nominations in 1946 (for *The Spiral Staircase*), 1947 (for *The Paradine Case*) and 1949 (for *Pinky*).

Nominations 1944

PICTURE

DOUBLE INDEMNITY, Paramount. Produced by Joseph Sistrom.
GASLIGHT, M-G-M. Produced by Arthur Hornblow, Jr.
★ GOING MY WAY, Paramount. Produced by Leo McCarey.
SINCE YOU WENT AWAY, Selznick, UA. Produced by David O. Selznick.
WILSON, 20th Century-Fox. Produced by Darryl F. Zanuck.

ACTOR

CHARLES BOYER in *Gaslight*, M-G-M.
★ BING CROSBY in *Going My Way*, Paramount.
BARRY FITZGERALD in *Going My Way*, Paramount.
CARY GRANT in *None But the Lonely Heart*, RKO Radio.
ALEXANDER KNOX in *Wilson*, 20th Century-Fox.

ACTRESS

★ INGRID BERGMAN in *Gaslight*, M-G-M.
CLAUDETTE COLBERT in *Since You Went Away*, Selznick, UA.
BETTE DAVIS in *Mr. Skeffington*, Warner Bros.
GREER GARSON in *Mrs. Parkington*, M-G-M.
BARBARA STANWYCK in *Double Indemnity*, Paramount.

SUPPORTING ACTOR

HUME CRONYN in *The Seventh Cross*, M-G-M.
★ BARRY FITZGERALD in *Going My Way*, Paramount.
CLAUDE RAINS in *Mr. Skeffington*, Warner Bros.
CLIFTON WEBB in *Laura*, 20th Century-Fox.
MONTY WOOLLEY in *Since You Went Away*, Selznick, UA.

SUPPORTING ACTRESS

★ ETHEL BARRYMORE in *None But the Lonely Heart*, RKO Radio.
JENNIFER JONES in *Since You Went Away*, Selznick, UA.
ANGELA LANSBURY in *Gaslight*, M-G-M.
ALINE MacMAHON in *Dragon Seed*, M-G-M.
AGNES MOOREHEAD in *Mrs. Parkington*, M-G-M.

DIRECTION

ALFRED HITCHCOCK for *Lifeboat*, 20th Century-Fox.
HENRY KING for *Wilson*, 20th Century-Fox.
★ LEO McCAREY for *Going My Way*, Paramount.
OTTO PREMINGER for *Laura*, 20th Century-Fox.
BILLY WILDER for *Double Indemnity*, Paramount.

WRITING

(Original Story)

★ GOING MY WAY, Paramount. Leo McCarey.
A GUY NAMED JOE, M-G-M. David Boehm and Chandler Sprague.
LIFEBOAT, 20th Century-Fox. John Steinbeck.
NONE SHALL ESCAPE, Columbia. Alfred Neumann and Joseph Than.
THE SULLIVANS, 20th Century-Fox. Edward Doherty and Jules Schermer.

(Original Screenplay)

HAIL THE CONQUERING HERO, Paramount. Preston Sturges.
THE MIRACLE OF MORGAN'S CREEK, Paramount. Preston Sturges.
TWO GIRLS AND A SAILOR, M-G-M. Richard Connell and Gladys Lehman.
★ WILSON, 20th Century-Fox. Lamar Trotti.
WING AND A PRAYER, 20th Century-Fox. Jerome Cady.

(Screenplay)

DOUBLE INDEMNITY, Paramount. Raymond Chandler and Billy Wilder.
GASLIGHT, M-G-M. John L. Balderston, Walter Reisch and John Van Druten.
★ GOING MY WAY, Paramount. Frank Butler and Frank Cavett.
LAURA, 20th Century-Fox. Jay Dratler, Samuel Hoffenstein and Betty Reinhardt.
MEET ME IN ST. LOUIS, M-G-M. Irving Brecher and Fred F. Finkelhoffe.

CINEMATOGRAPHY

(Black-and-White)

DOUBLE INDEMNITY, Paramount. John Seitz.
DRAGON SEED, M-G-M. Sidney Wagner.
GASLIGHT, M-G-M. Joseph Ruttenberg.
GOING MY WAY, Paramount. Lionel Lindon.
★ LAURA, 20th Century-Fox. Joseph LaShelle.
LIFEBOAT, 20th Century-Fox. Glen MacWilliams.

SINCE YOU WENT AWAY, Selznick, UA. Stanley Cortez and Lee Garmes.
THIRTY SECONDS OVER TOKYO, M-G-M. Robert Surtees and Harold Rosson.
THE UNINVITED, Paramount. Charles Lang.
THE WHITE CLIFFS OF DOVER, M-G-M. George Folsey.

(Color)

COVER GIRL, Columbia. Rudy Mate and Allen M. Davey.
HOME IN INDIANA, 20th Century-Fox. Edward Cronjager.
KISMET, M-G-M. Charles Rosher.
LADY IN THE DARK, Paramount. Ray Rennahan.
MEET ME IN ST. LOUIS, M-G-M. George Folsey.
★ WILSON, 20th Century-Fox. Leon Shamroy.

ART DIRECTION-INTERIOR DECORATION

(Black-and-White)

ADDRESS UNKNOWN, Columbia. Lionel Banks and Walter Holscher; Joseph Kish.
THE ADVENTURES OF MARK TWAIN, Warner Bros. John J. Hughes; Fred MacLean.
CASANOVA BROWN, International, RKO Radio. Perry Ferguson; Julia Heron.
★ GASLIGHT, M-G-M. Cedric Gibbons and William Ferrari; Edwin B. Willis and Paul Huldschinsky.
LAURA, 20th Century-Fox. Lyle Wheeler and Leland Fuller; Thomas Little.
NO TIME FOR LOVE, Paramount. Hans Dreier and Robert Usher; Sam Comer.
SINCE YOU WENT AWAY, Selznick, UA. Mark-Lee Kirk; Victor A. Gangelin.
STEP LIVELY, RKO Radio. Albert S. D'Agostino and Carroll Clark; Darrell Silvera and Claude Carpenter.

(Color)

THE CLIMAX, Universal. John B. Goodman and Alexander Golitzen; Russell A. Gausman and Ira S. Webb.
COVER GIRL, Columbia. Lionel Banks and Cary Odell; Fay Babcock.
THE DESERT SONG, Warner Bros. Charles Novi; Jack McConaghy.
KISMET, M-G-M. Cedric Gibbons and Daniel B. Cathcart; Edwin B. Willis and Richard Pefferle.
LADY IN THE DARK, Paramount. Hans Dreier and Raoul Pene du Bois; Ray Moyer.
THE PRINCESS AND THE PIRATE, Goldwyn, RKO Radio. Ernst Fegte; Howard Bristol.
★ WILSON, 20th Century-Fox. Wiard Ihnen; Thomas Little.

FILM EDITING

GOING MY WAY, Paramount. Leroy Stone.
JANIE, Warner Bros. Owen Marks.
NONE BUT THE LONELY HEART, RKO Radio. Roland Gross.

SINCE YOU WENT AWAY, Selznick, UA. Hal C. Kern and James E. Newcom.
★ WILSON, 20th Century-Fox. Barbara McLean.

SPECIAL EFFECTS

THE ADVENTURES OF MARK TWAIN, Warner Bros. Paul Detlefsen, John Crouse and Nathan Levinson.
DAYS OF GLORY, Robinson, RKO Radio. Vernon L. Walker, James G. Stewart and Roy Granville.
SECRET COMMAND, Columbia. David Allen, Ray Cory, Robert Wright, Russell Malmgren and Harry Kusnick.
SINCE YOU WENT AWAY, Selznick, UA. John R. Cosgrove and Arthur Johns.
THE STORY OF DR. WASSELL, DeMille, Paramount. Farciot Edouart, Gordon Jennings and George Dutton.
★ THIRTY SECONDS OVER TOKYO, M-G-M. A. Arnold Gillespie, Donald Jahraus, Warren Newcombe and Douglas Shearer.
WILSON, 20th Century-Fox. Fred Sersen and Roger Heman.

SOUND RECORDING

BRAZIL, Republic. Daniel J. Bloomberg.
CASANOVA BROWN, International RKO Radio. Thomas T. Moulton, Goldwyn Sound Department.
COVER GIRL, Columbia. John Livadary.
DOUBLE INDEMNITY, Paramount. Loren Ryder.
HIS BUTLER'S SISTER, Universal. Bernard B. Brown.
HOLLYWOOD CANTEEN, Warner Bros. Nathan Levinson.
IT HAPPENED TOMORROW, Arnold, UA. Jack Whitney, Sound Service Inc.
KISMET, M-G-M. Douglas Shearer.
MUSIC IN MANHATTAN, RKO Radio. Stephen Dunn.
VOICE IN THE WIND, Ripley-Monter, UA. W.M. Dalgleish, RCA Sound.
★ WILSON, 20th Century-Fox. E.H. Hansen.

MUSIC

(Song)

I COULDN'T SLEEP A WINK LAST NIGHT (*Higher and Higher*, RKO Radio); Music by Jimmy McHugh. Lyrics by Harold Adamson.
I'LL WALK ALONE (*Follow the Boys*, Feldman, Universal); Music by Jule Styne. Lyrics by Sammy Cahn.
I'M MAKING BELIEVE (*Sweet and Lowdown*, 20th Century-Fox); Music by James V. Monaco. Lyrics by Mack Gordon.
LONG AGO AND FAR AWAY (*Cover Girl*, Columbia); Music by Jerome Kern. Lyrics by Ira Gershwin.
NOW I KNOW (*Up in Arms*, RKO Radio); Music by Harold Arlen. Lyrics by Ted Koehler.

Special Award: Margaret O'Brien (above with Judy Garland in *Meet Me in St. Louis*) as "the outstanding child actress of 1944." The Academy first presented miniature Oscar statuettes to pint-sized performers in 1934 when Shirley Temple was honored; since then, other juveniles similarly singled out have been Deanna Durbin and Mickey Rooney (1938), Judy Garland (1939), Peggy Ann Garner (1945), Claude Jarman, Jr. (1946), Ivan Jandl (1948), Bobby Driscoll (1949), Jon Whitely and Vincent Winter (1954) and Hayley Mills (1960).

Wilson (20th Century-Fox; directed by Henry King) was a spectacular, flag-waving Darryl F. Zanuck production which nurtured the patriotism of wartime America just as emphatically as *Going My Way* touched the country's spiritual needs. *Wilson* traced the life of the 28th President of the United States (played by Alexander Knox, below with Geraldine Fitzgerald) from his days at Princeton through his two terms in the White House (1913-21), and it won Academy Awards for Original Screenplay, Color Cinematography, Color Art Direction, Sound Recording and Film Editing.

REMEMBER ME TO CAROLINA (*Minstrel Man,* PRC); Music by Harry Revel. Lyrics by Paul Webster.
RIO DE JANEIRO (*Brazil,* Republic); Music by Ary Barroso. Lyrics by Ned Washington.
SILVER SHADOWS AND GOLDEN DREAMS (*Lady Let's Dance,* Monogram); Music by Lew Pollack. Lyrics by Charles Newman.
SWEET DREAMS SWEETHEART (*Hollywood Canteen,* Warner Bros.); Music by M.K. Jerome. Lyrics by Ted Koehler.
★ SWINGING ON A STAR (*Going My Way,* Paramount); Music by James Van Heusen. Lyrics by Johnny Burke.
TOO MUCH IN LOVE (*Song of the Open Road,* Rogers, UA); Music by Walter Kent. Lyrics by Kim Gannon.
THE TROLLEY SONG (*Meet Me in St. Louis,* M-G-M); Music and Lyrics by Ralph Blane and Hugh Martin.

(Scoring of a Dramatic or Comedy Picture)
ADDRESS UNKNOWN, Columbia. Morris Stoloff and Ernst Toch.
THE ADVENTURES OF MARK TWAIN, Warner Bros. Max Steiner.
THE BRIDGE OF SAN LUIS REY, Bogeaus, UA. Dimitri Tiomkin.
CASANOVA BROWN, International, RKO Radio. Arthur Lange.
CHRISTMAS HOLIDAY, Universal. H.J. Salter.
DOUBLE INDEMNITY, Paramount. Miklos Rozsa.
THE FIGHTING SEABEES, Republic. Walter Scharf and Roy Webb.
THE HAIRY APE, Levey, UA. Michel Michelet and Edward Paul.
IT HAPPENED TOMORROW, Arnold, UA. Robert Stolz.
JACK LONDON, Bronston, UA. Frederic E. Rich.
KISMET, M-G-M. Herbert Stothart.
NONE BUT THE LONELY HEART, RKO Radio. C. Bakaleinikoff and Hanns Eisler.
THE PRINCESS AND THE PIRATE, Goldwyn, RKO Radio. David Rose.
★ SINCE YOU WENT AWAY, Selznick, UA. Max Steiner.
SUMMER STORM, Angelus, UA. Karl Hajos.
THREE RUSSIAN GIRLS, R & F Prods., UA. Franke Harling.
UP IN MABEL'S ROOM, Small, UA. Edward Paul.
VOICE IN THE WIND, Ripley-Monter, UA. Michel Michelet.
WILSON, 20th Century-Fox. Alfred Newman.
WOMAN OF THE TOWN, Sherman, UA. Miklos Rozsa.

(Scoring of a Musical Picture)
BRAZIL, Republic. Walter Scharf.
★ COVER GIRL, Columbia. Carmen Dragon and Morris Stoloff.
HIGHER AND HIGHER, RKO Radio. C. Bakaleinikoff.
HOLLYWOOD CANTEEN, Warner Bros. Ray Heindorf.
IRISH EYES ARE SMILING, 20th Century-Fox. Alfred Newman.
KNICKERBOCKER HOLIDAY, RCA, UA. Werner R. Heymann and Kurt Weill.
LADY IN THE DARK, Paramount. Robert Emmett Dolan.
LADY LET'S DANCE, Monogram. Edward Kay.
MEET ME IN ST. LOUIS, M-G-M. Georgie Stoll.
THE MERRY MONAHANS, Universal. H.J. Salter.
MINSTREL MAN, PRC. Leo Erdody and Ferdie Grofe.
SENSATIONS OF 1945, Stone, UA. Mahlon Merrick.
SONG OF THE OPEN ROAD, Rogers, UA. Charles Previn.
UP IN ARMS, Avalon, RKO Radio. Louis Forbes and Ray Heindorf.

SHORT SUBJECTS

(Cartoons)
AND TO THINK I SAW IT ON MULBERRY STREET, Paramount. (Puppetoon). George Pal, producer.
THE DOG, CAT AND CANARY, Columbia. (Screen Gems).
FISH FRY, Universal. Walter Lantz, producer.
HOW TO PLAY FOOTBALL, Disney, RKO Radio. Walt Disney, producer.
★ MOUSE TROUBLE, M-G-M. Frederick C. Quimby, producer.
MY BOY, JOHNNY, 20th Century-Fox. Paul Terry, producer.
SWOONER CROONER, Warner Bros.

(One-reel)
BLUE GRASS GENTLEMEN, 20th Century-Fox. (Sports Review). Edmund Reek, producer.
JAMMIN' THE BLUES, Warner Bros. (Melody Master Bands). Gordon Hollingshead, producer.
MOVIE PESTS, M-G-M. (Pete Smith Specialty). Pete Smith, producer.
50TH ANNIVERSARY OF MOTION PICTURES, Columbia. (Screen Snapshots). Ralph Staub, producer.
★ WHO'S WHO IN ANIMAL LAND, Paramount. (Speaking of Animals). Jerry Fairbanks, producer.

(Two-reel)
BOMBALERA, Paramount. (Musical Parade). Louis Harris, producer.
★ I WON'T PLAY, Warner Bros. (Featurette). Gordon Hollingshead, producer.
MAIN STREET TODAY, M-G-M. (Two-reel Special). Jerry Bresler, producer.

DOCUMENTARY

(Short Subjects)
ARTURO TOSCANINI, Motion Picture Bureau, Overseas Branch, Office of War Information.
NEW AMERICANS, This Is America Series, RKO Radio.
★ WITH THE MARINES AT TARAWA, U.S. Marine Corps.

(Features)
★ THE FIGHTING LADY, 20th Century-Fox and U.S. Navy.
RESISTING ENEMY INTERROGATION, U.S. Army Air Force.

SPECIAL AWARDS

TO MARGARET O'BRIEN, outstanding child actress of 1944. (miniature statuette)
TO BOB HOPE, for his many services to the Academy, a Life Membership in the Academy of Motion Picture Arts and Sciences.

1944 IRVING G. THALBERG MEMORIAL AWARD

TO DARRYL F. ZANUCK

SCIENTIFIC OR TECHNICAL

CLASS I (statuette)
None.

CLASS II (plaque)
STEPHEN DUNN and the RKO RADIO STUDIO SOUND DEPARTMENT and RADIO CORPORATION OF AMERICA for the design and development of the electronic compressor-limiter.

CLASS III (citation)
LINWOOD DUNN, CECIL LOVE and ACME TOOL MANUFACTURING CO.;
GROVER LAUBE and the 20TH CENTURY-FOX STUDIO CAMERA DEPARTMENT;
WESTERN ELECTRIC CO.;
RUSSELL BROWN, RAY HINSDALE and JOSEPH E. ROBBINS;
GORDON JENNINGS;
RADIO CORPORATION OF AMERICA and the RKO RADIO STUDIO SOUND DEPARTMENT;
DANIEL J. BLOOMBERG and the REPUBLIC STUDIO SOUND DEPARTMENT;
BERNARD B. BROWN and JOHN P. LIVADARY;
PAUL ZELL, S.J. TWINING and GEORGE SEID;
PAUL LERPAE.

★ INDICATES WINNER

Best Actress: Joan Crawford as Mildred Pierce Baragon in *Mildred Pierce* (Warner Bros.; directed by Michael Curtiz). Bette Davis, Barbara Stanwyck and Ann Sheridan all turned down the role of James M. Cain's middle-class housewife who works as a waitress, becomes a wealthy business woman and ultimately tries to take the blame for a murder committed by her over-indulged daughter. But Joan Crawford grabbed the part because her career was at a low ebb, and she'd been off the screen two years attempting to find a solid role to reestablish her reputation in Hollywood circles. *Mildred Pierce* did the trick, brought Joan Crawford back to the front ranks of stardom and made her an Academy Award winner.

1945 The Eighteenth Year

The year 1945 had been good for movies (critically, as well as at the box office) and a historic one for the world: President Roosevelt had died in office, World War II had ended, the first atom bomb was exploded on Hiroshima, the United Nations was founded in San Francisco and everyone began readjusting to peace. When it came time to salute 1945 with Oscars on March 7, 1946, at Grauman's Chinese Theatre, Hollywood again dressed up in tuxedos and finery as it had in those pre-war days, and the Hollywood staple—searchlights—again beamed over the city.

Most-nominated pictures of the year were *The Bells of St. Mary's,* a sequel to the previous years' Oscar-winning *Going My Way,* competing in eight categories, and *The Lost Weekend* with seven nominations. *Weekend* ultimately won four: Best Picture, Best Actor (Ray Milland), Best Director (Billy Wilder) and Best Screenplay (Charles Brackett and Wilder). Anne Revere was named Best Supporting Actress for *National Velvet,* and James Dunn was chosen Best Supporting Actor for *A Tree Grows in Brooklyn.* Biggest newsmaker of the evening, however, was Joan Crawford, named Best Actress for *Mildred Pierce.* A durable Hollywood headliner for twenty years, she was a first-time nominee for Oscar honors and in the midst of a major career comeback after several years of indifferent screen roles. Ill at her Brentwood home with the flu, she was unable to attend the ceremony and her Award was accepted in her behalf by her director Michael Curtiz. But, she said later, "It was the greatest moment of my life."

Bob Hope and James Stewart were co-hosts of the Awards program and additional Oscars were rather evenly distributed among a variety of fine films, including *The True Glory, Anchors Aweigh, Spellbound, State Fair, The Picture of Dorian Gray, Leave Her to Heaven, Marie-Louise, The House on 92nd Street* and *Frenchman's Creek.* For the last time, there were a myriad of nominees in the categories of Sound Recording (twelve) Song (fourteen), Scoring of a Drama or Comedy (twenty-one), and Scoring of a Musical (twelve); hereafter, there would be no more than five nominees in those divisions.

Outgoing Academy President Walter Wanger received a special plaque for his six-year term as head of the Academy, and Peggy Ann Garner of 1945's *A Tree Grows in Brooklyn, Junior Miss* and *Nob Hill* received a miniature statuette as the year's outstanding child actress. Perhaps the most significant Award of the night was the Special Oscar awarded to *The House I Live In,* a ten-minute short subject distributed by RKO and involving the talents of bobbysox idol Frank Sinatra, Frank Ross, Mervyn LeRoy and Albert Maltz. The film made a plea for racial tolerance, a growing concern now that the problems of a world war had been solved—at least temporarily.

Best Picture: The Lost Weekend
(Paramount; produced by Charles
Brackett), **Best Director: Billy Wilder** and
(above, right) **Best Actor: Ray Milland**
as Don Birnam in *The Lost Weekend*.
Decidedly off the beaten track among 1945
screen fare, it followed Milland as a
would-be writer on a booze-filled weekend
in New York City, trying to hock his
typewriter for set-ups, attempting to beg
drinks and suffering the D.T.s, as
audiences were let loose inside an
alcoholic's psyche. Producer Brackett and
director Wilder also won Oscars for the
Lost screenplay. Milland got his
Oscar-winning role when the first choice to
play Birnam, Broadway actor Jose Ferrer,
was unavailable.

Best Supporting Actress: Anne Revere as
Mrs. Brown (seated, with Donald Crisp and
Elizabeth Taylor) in *National Velvet*
(M-G-M; directed by Clarence Brown). A
long-time veteran of playing gentle,
understanding mums with strong values,
Anne Revere this time played the mother of
a horse-loving girl who wants to race her
horse in England's Grand National
Steeplechase. Previously nominated as
Jennifer Jones' mother in *The Song of
Bernadette* in 1943, she was again an Oscar
contender in 1947 as Gregory Peck's
mother in *Gentleman's Agreement*.

Best Supporting Actor: James Dunn as Johnny Nolan (above, with Dorothy McGuire) in *A Tree Grows in Brooklyn* (20th Century-Fox; directed by Elia Kazan). Like Ray Milland, James Dunn won his Oscar for playing a man fond of the spirits; like Joan Crawford, he was in the midst of a comeback to screen prominence after several years of secondary roles. *Brooklyn's* young Peggy Ann Garner also received a Special Award as the outstanding screen juvenile of the year.

Nominations 1945

PICTURE

ANCHORS AWEIGH, M-G-M. Produced by Joe Pasternak.
THE BELLS OF ST. MARY'S, Rainbow, RKO Radio. Produced by Leo McCarey.
* THE LOST WEEKEND, Paramount. Produced by Charles Brackett.
MILDRED PIERCE, Warner Bros. Produced by Jerry Wald.
SPELLBOUND, Selznick, UA. Produced by David O. Selznick.

ACTOR

BING CROSBY in *The Bells of St. Mary's*, Rainbow, RKO Radio.
GENE KELLY in *Anchors Aweigh*, M-G-M.
* RAY MILLAND in *The Lost Weekend*, Paramount.
GREGORY PECK in *The Keys of the Kingdom*, 20th Century-Fox.
CORNEL WILDE in *A Song to Remember*, Columbia.

ACTRESS

INGRID BERGMAN in *The Bells of St. Mary's*, Rainbow, RKO Radio.
* JOAN CRAWFORD in *Mildred Pierce*, Warner Bros.
GREER GARSON in *The Valley of Decision*, M-G-M.
JENNIFER JONES in *Love Letters*, Wallis, Paramount.
GENE TIERNEY in *Leave Her to Heaven*, 20th Century-Fox.

SUPPORTING ACTOR

MICHAEL CHEKHOV in *Spellbound*, Selznick, UA.
JOHN DALL in *The Corn Is Green*, Warner Bros.
* JAMES DUNN in *A Tree Grows in Brooklyn*, 20th Century-Fox.
ROBERT MITCHUM in *The Story of G.I. Joe*, Cowan, UA.
J. CARROL NAISH in *A Medal for Benny*, Paramount.

SUPPORTING ACTRESS

EVE ARDEN in *Mildred Pierce*, Warner Bros.
ANN BLYTH in *Mildred Pierce*, Warner Bros.
ANGELA LANSBURY in *The Picture of Dorian Gray*, M-G-M.
JOAN LORRING in *The Corn Is Green*, Warner Bros.
* ANNE REVERE in *National Velvet*, M-G-M.

DIRECTION

CLARENCE BROWN for *National Velvet*, M-G-M.
ALFRED HITCHCOCK for *Spellbound*, Selznick, UA.
LEO McCAREY for *The Bells of St. Mary's*, Rainbow, RKO Radio.
JEAN RENOIR for *The Southerner*, Loew-Hakim, UA.
* BILLY WILDER for *The Lost Weekend*, Paramount.

WRITING

(Original Story)

THE AFFAIRS OF SUSAN, Wallis, Paramount. Laszlo Gorog and Thomas Monroe.
* THE HOUSE ON 92ND STREET, 20th Century-Fox. Charles G. Booth.
A MEDAL FOR BENNY, Paramount. John Steinbeck and Jack Wagner.
OBJECTIVE, BURMA, Warner Bros. Alvah Bessie.
A SONG TO REMEMBER, Columbia. Ernst Marischka.

(Original Screenplay)

DILLINGER, Monogram. Philip Yordan.
* MARIE-LOUISE, Praesens Films (Swiss). Richard Schweizer.
MUSIC FOR MILLIONS, M-G-M. Myles Connolly.
SALTY O'ROURKE, Paramount. Milton Holmes.
WHAT NEXT, CORPORAL HARGROVE? M-G-M. Harry Kurnitz.

(Screenplay)

THE STORY OF G.I. JOE, Cowan, UA. Leopold Atlas, Guy Endore and Philip Stevenson.
* THE LOST WEEKEND, Paramount. Charles Brackett and Billy Wilder.
MILDRED PIERCE, Warner Bros. Ranald MacDougall.
PRIDE OF THE MARINES, Warner Bros. Albert Maltz.
A TREE GROWS IN BROOKLYN, 20th Century-Fox. Frank Davis and Tess Slesinger.

CINEMATOGRAPHY

(Black-and-White)

THE KEYS OF THE KINGDOM, 20th Century-Fox. Arthur Miller.
THE LOST WEEKEND, Paramount. John F. Seitz.
MILDRED PIERCE, Warner Bros. Ernest Haller.
* THE PICTURE OF DORIAN GRAY, M-G-M. Harry Stradling.
SPELLBOUND, Selznick, UA. George Barnes.

(Color)

ANCHORS AWEIGH, M-G-M. Robert Planck and Charles Boyle.
* LEAVE HER TO HEAVEN, 20th Century-Fox. Leon Shamroy.
NATIONAL VELVET, M-G-M. Leonard Smith.
A SONG TO REMEMBER, Columbia. Tony Gaudio and Allen M. Davey.
THE SPANISH MAIN, RKO Radio. George Barnes.

ART DIRECTION-INTERIOR DECORATION

(Black-and-White)

* BLOOD ON THE SUN, Cagney, UA. Wiard Ihnen; A. Roland Fields.
EXPERIMENT PERILOUS, RKO Radio. Albert S. D'Agostino and Jack Okey; Darrell Silvera and Claude Carpenter.
THE KEYS OF THE KINGDOM, 20th Century-Fox. James Basevi and William Darling; Thomas Little and Frank E. Hughes.
LOVE LETTERS, Wallis, Paramount. Hans Dreier and Roland Anderson; Sam Comer and Ray Moyer.
THE PICTURE OF DORIAN GRAY, M-G-M. Cedric Gibbons and Hans Peters; Edwin B. Willis, John Bonar and Hugh Hunt.

(Color)

* FRENCHMAN'S CREEK, Paramount. Hans Dreier and Ernst Fegte; Sam Comer.
LEAVE HER TO HEAVEN, 20th Century-Fox. Lyle Wheeler and Maurice Ransford; Thomas Little.
NATIONAL VELVET, M-G-M. Cedric Gibbons and Urie McCleary; Edwin B. Willis and Mildred Griffiths.
SAN ANTONIO, Warner Bros. Ted Smith; Jack McConaghy.
A THOUSAND AND ONE NIGHTS, Columbia. Stephen Goosson and Rudolph Sternad; Frank Tuttle.

SOUND RECORDING

* THE BELLS OF ST. MARY'S, Rainbow, RKO Radio. Stephen Dunn.
THE FLAME OF THE BARBARY COAST, Republic. Daniel J. Bloomberg.
LADY ON A TRAIN, Universal. Bernard B. Brown.
LEAVE HER TO HEAVEN, 20th Century-Fox. Thomas T. Moulton.
RHAPSODY IN BLUE, Warner Bros. Nathan Levinson.
A SONG TO REMEMBER, Columbia. John Livadary.
THE SOUTHERNER, Loew-Hakim, UA. Jack Whitney, General Service.
THEY WERE EXPENDABLE, M-G-M. Douglas Shearer.
THE THREE CABALLEROS, Disney, RKO Radio. C.O. Slyfield.
THREE IS A FAMILY, Master Productions, UA. W.V. Wolfe, RCA Sound.
THE UNSEEN, Paramount. Loren L. Ryder.
WONDER MAN, Goldwyn, RKO Radio. Gordon Sawyer.

FILM EDITING

THE BELLS OF ST. MARY'S, Rainbow, RKO Radio. Harry Marker.
THE LOST WEEKEND, Paramount. Doane Harrison.
* NATIONAL VELVET, M-G-M. Robert J. Kern.
OBJECTIVE—BURMA, Warner Bros. George Amy.
A SONG TO REMEMBER, Columbia. Charles Nelson.

SPECIAL EFFECTS

CAPTAIN EDDIE, 20th Century-Fox. Fred Sersen, Sol Halprin, Roger Heman and Harry Leonard.
SPELLBOUND, Selznick, UA. Jack Cosgrove.
THEY WERE EXPENDABLE, M-G-M. A. Arnold Gillespie, Donald Jahraus, R.A. MacDonald and Michael Steinore.
A THOUSAND AND ONE NIGHTS, Columbia. L.W. Butler and Ray Bomba.
* WONDER MAN, Goldwyn, RKO Radio. John Fulton and A.W. Johns.

MUSIC

(Song)

ACCENTUATE THE POSITIVE (*Here Come the Waves*, Paramount); Music by Harold Arlen. Lyrics by Johnny Mercer.
ANYWHERE (*Tonight and Every Night*, Columbia); Music by Jule Styne. Lyrics by Sammy Cahn.
AREN'T YOU GLAD YOU'RE YOU (*The Bells of St. Mary's*, Rainbow, RKO Radio); Music by James Van Heusen. Lyrics by Johnny Burke.
THE CAT AND THE CANARY (*Why Girls Leave Home*, PRC); Music by Jay Livingston. Lyrics by Ray Evans.
ENDLESSLY (*Earl Carroll Vanities*, Republic); Music by Walter Kent. Lyrics by Kim Gannon.
I FALL IN LOVE TOO EASILY (*Anchors Aweigh*, M-G-M); Music by Jule Styne. Lyrics by Sammy Cahn.
I'LL BUY THAT DREAM (*Sing Your Way Home*, RKO Radio); Music by Allie Wrubel. Lyrics by Herb Magidson.
* IT MIGHT AS WELL BE SPRING (*State Fair*, 20th Century-Fox); Music by Richard Rodgers. Lyrics by Oscar Hammerstein II.

(below) **The Picture of Dorian Gray** (M-G-M); produced by Pandro S. Berman) featured Hurd Hatfield as Oscar Wilde's famous young sinner who stayed young while his portrait grew old, and won Harry Stradling an Academy Award for his moody and effective cinematography. Until the 1970s, only a few cinematographers were known outside industry circles, but the Academy has been honoring them since the first 1927-28 Awards ceremony. In the first fifty years of the Oscars, the two most-honored recipients in that category, with four Awards each, were Joseph Ruttenberg (1938, 1942, 1956, 1958) and Leon Shamroy (1942, 1944, 1945, 1963). Stradling won again in 1964 for his color cinematography of *My Fair Lady*.

LINDA (*The Story Of G.I. Joe*, Cowan, UA); Music and Lyrics by Ann Ronell.
LOVE LETTERS (*Love Letters*, Wallis, Paramount); Music by Victor Young. Lyrics by Edward Heyman.
MORE AND MORE (*Can't Help Singing*, Universal); Music by Jerome Kern. Lyrics by E.Y. Harburg.
SLEIGHRIDE IN JULY (*Belle of the Yukon*, International, RKO Radio); Music by James Van Heusen. Lyrics by Johnny Burke.
SO IN LOVE (*Wonder Man*, Beverly Prods., RKO Radio); Music by David Rose. Lyrics by Leo Robin.
SOME SUNDAY MORNING (*San Antonio*, Warner Bros.); Music by Ray Heindorf and M.K. Jerome. Lyrics by Ted Koehler.

(Scoring of a Dramatic or Comedy Picture)

THE BELLS OF ST. MARY'S, Rainbow, RKO Radio. Robert Emmet Dolan.
BREWSTER'S MILLIONS, Small, UA. Lou Forbes.
CAPTAIN KIDD, Bogeaus, UA. Werner Janssen.
ENCHANTED COTTAGE, RKO Radio. Roy Webb.
FLAME OF THE BARBARY COAST, Republic. Dale Butts and Morton Scott.
G.I. HONEYMOON, Monogram. Edward J. Kay.
GUEST IN THE HOUSE, Guest in the House, Inc., UA. Werner Janssen.
GUEST WIFE, Green Tree, Prods., UA. Daniele Amfitheatrof.
THE KEYS OF THE KINGDOM, 20th Century-Fox. Alfred Newman.
THE LOST WEEKEND, Paramount. Miklos Rozsa.
LOVE LETTERS, Wallis, Paramount. Victor Young.
THE MAN WHO WALKED ALONE, PRC. Karl Hajos.
OBJECTIVE—BURMA, Warner Bros. Franz Waxman.
PARIS—UNDERGROUND, Bennett, UA. Alexander Tansman.
A SONG TO REMEMBER, Columbia. Miklos Rozsa and Morris Stoloff.
THE SOUTHERNER, Loew-Hakim, UA. Werner Janssen.
★ SPELLBOUND, Selznick, UA. Miklos Rozsa.
THE STORY OF G.I. JOE, Cowan, UA. Louis Applebaum and Ann Ronell.
THIS LOVE OF OURS, Universal, H.J. Salter.
THE VALLEY OF DECISION, M-G-M. Herbert Stothart.
THE WOMAN IN THE WINDOW, International, RKO Radio. Hugo Friedhofer and Arthur Lange.

(Scoring of a Musical Picture)

★ ANCHORS AWEIGH, M-G-M. Georgie Stoll.
BELLE OF THE YUKON, International, RKO Radio. Arthur Lange.
CAN'T HELP SINGING, Universal. Jerome Kern and H.J. Salter.
HITCHHIKE TO HAPPINESS, Republic. Morton Scott.
INCENDIARY BLONDE, Paramount. Robert Emmett Dolan.
RHAPSODY IN BLUE, Warner Bros. Ray Heindorf and Max Steiner.
STATE FAIR, 20th Century-Fox. Charles Henderson and Alfred Newman.
SUNBONNET SUE, Monogram. Edward J. Kay.
THE THREE CABALLEROS, Disney, RKO Radio, Edward Plumb, Paul J. Smith and Charles Wolcott.
TONIGHT AND EVERY NIGHT, Columbia. Marlin Skiles and Morris Stoloff.
WHY GIRLS LEAVE HOME, PRC. Walter Greene.
WONDER MAN, Goldwyn, RKO Radio. Lou Forbes and Ray Heindorf.

SHORT SUBJECTS

(Cartoons)

DONALD'S CRIME, Disney, RKO Radio. (Donald Duck). Walt Disney, producer.
JASPER AND THE BEANSTALK, Paramount. (Jasper Puppetoon). George Pal, producer.
LIFE WITH FEATHERS, Warner Bros. (Merrie Melodies). Eddie Selzer, producer.
MIGHTY MOUSE IN GYPSY LIFE, 20th Century-Fox. (Terrytoon). Paul Terry, producer.
POET AND PEASANT, Universal. (Lantz Cartune). Walter Lantz, producer.
★ QUIET PLEASE, M-G-M. (Tom & Jerry Series). Frederick Quimby, producer.
RIPPLING ROMANCE, Columbia. (Color Rhapsodies).

(One-reel)

ALONG THE RAINBOW TRAIL, 20th Century-Fox. (Movietone Adventure). Edmund Reek, producer.
SCREEN SNAPSHOTS 25TH ANNIVERSARY, Columbia. (Screen Snapshots). Ralph Staub, producer.
★ STAIRWAY TO LIGHT, M-G-M. (John Nesbitt Passing Parade). Herbert Moulton, producer.
STORY OF A DOG, Warner Bros. (Vitaphone Varieties). Gordon Hollingshead, producer.
WHITE RHAPSODY, Paramount. (Sportlights). Grantland Rice, producer.
YOUR NATIONAL GALLERY, Universal. (Variety Views). Joseph O'Brien and Thomas Mead, producers.

(Two-reel)

A GUN IN HIS HAND, M-G-M. (Crime Does Not Pay). Chester Franklin, producer.
THE JURY GOES ROUND 'N' ROUND, Columbia. (All Star Comedies). Jules White, producer.
THE LITTLE WITCH, Paramount. (Musical Parade). George Templeton, producer.
★ STAR IN THE NIGHT, Warner Bros. (Broadway Brevities). Gordon Hollingshead, producer.

DOCUMENTARY

(Short Subjects)

HITLER LIVES?, Warner Bros.
LIBRARY OF CONGRESS, Overseas Motion Picture Bureau, Office of War Information.
TO THE SHORES OF IWO JIMA, U.S. Marine Corps.

(Features)

THE LAST BOMB, U.S. Army Air Force.
★ THE TRUE GLORY, Governments of Great Britain and USA.

SPECIAL AWARDS

TO WALTER WANGER for his six years service as President of the Academy of Motion Picture Arts and Sciences. (special plaque)
TO PEGGY ANN GARNER, outstanding child actress of 1945. (miniature statuette)
TO THE HOUSE I LIVE IN, tolerance short subject; produced by Frank Ross and Mervyn LeRoy; directed by Mervyn LeRoy; screenplay by Albert Maltz; song *The House I Live In*, music by Earl Robinson, lyrics by Lewis Allen; starring Frank Sinatra; released by RKO Radio. (statuette)
TO REPUBLIC STUDIO, DANIEL J. BLOOMBERG and the REPUBLIC SOUND DEPARTMENT for the building of an outstanding musical scoring auditorium which provides optimum recording conditions and combines all elements of acoustic and engineering design. (certificates)

1945 IRVING G. THALBERG MEMORIAL AWARD

None given this year.

SCIENTIFIC OR TECHNICAL

CLASS I (statuette)

None.

CLASS II (plaque)

None.

CLASS III (citation)

LOREN L. RYDER, CHARLES R. DAILY and the PARAMOUNT STUDIO SOUND DEPARTMENT;
MICHAEL S. LESHING, BENJAMIN C. ROBINSON, ARTHUR B. CHATELAIN and ROBERT C. STEVENS of 20th Century-Fox Studio and JOHN G. CAPSTAFF of Eastman Kodak Co.

★ INDICATES WINNER

1946 The Nineteenth Year

The Academy made a major change in its voting rules for the 1946 Awards year. Instead of having nearly 10,000 members of the film community select the nominees and final Academy Award winners as they had during the past nine years, the rules were altered so the final decision would be made solely by bona fide Academy members. Not surprisingly, the announcement caused Academy membership rolls to swell from its 700 to a new high of 1,675. The new voting policy created a more reliable set of judges for the Academy, since votes would now be more specifically in the hands of craftsmen actually involved in picture making. Some say the new ruling also helped stimulate something the Academy has always abhored: active campaigning for voter attention in trade publications.

There were other significant changes, as well. After three years of presenting the Oscars at Grauman's Chinese Theatre, the Academy moved its setting to the mammoth Shrine Auditorium with a seating capacity of 6,700 seats, five hundred more than the Radio City Music Hall in New York. Because of the extra capacity, the general public for the first time was allowed to buy tickets and attend, side by side with industry members. The program on March 13, 1947, was produced for the Academy by Mervyn LeRoy and hosted by Jack Benny.

Samuel Goldwyn's distinctly American *The Best Years of Our Lives* received seven of the 1946 Awards, including those for Best Picture, Best Actor (Fredric March), Best Director (William Wyler) and Best Supporting Actor (Harold Russell). It was the second time both March and Wyler were honored by the Academy. Olivia de Havilland was named the year's Best Actress for *To Each His Own,* and Anne Baxter was named Best Supporting Actress for *The Razor's Edge.*

Two other films dealing with aspects of Americana—*The Yearling* and *The Jolson Story*—each won two Awards, but in some ways Americana took a back seat to European films. It had not happened before in an Oscar competition, but films from overseas were almost as prominent as American products, with six English-made movies (*Henry V, Brief Encounter, Caesar and Cleopatra, Vacation from Marriage, The Seventh Veil* and *Blithe Spirit*) winning eleven of the year's nominations, and three of the final Awards. Both France (with *Children of Paradise*) and Italy (via *Open City*) were also represented. It was a sign of things to come and, beginning the next Awards year, the Academy began to specifically acknowledge the vibrant postwar contributions of the European cinema.

Best Picture: The Best Years of Our Lives (RKO Radio; produced by Samuel Goldwyn), **Best Director: William Wyler, Best Actor: Fredric March** as Al Stephenson and **Best Supporting Actor: Harold Russell** as Homer Parrish. Some speculated that 1946 audiences wouldn't want to be reminded of the recent World War II and the complexities of returning to civilian life, but William Wyler and his company examined the problem so artfully in *The Best Years of Our Lives,* it became the picture of the year, and a genuine classic. Based on a blank-verse essay by Mackinlay Kantor titled *Glory for Me,* it examined the problems faced by three veterans (Harold Russell, Dana Andrews and Fredric March, above) when returning home after the war and readjusting to the lives they left behind. It brought March his second Oscar (the first: for 1931-32's *Dr. Jekyll and Mr. Hyde*); he played a devoted family man who suddenly finds his old bank job oddly unsatisfying. Russell, a nonprofessional and real-life arm amputee, won two Academy Awards as a sailor returning with his hands replaced by hooks. One was the Supporting Actor Award, the second was a Special Award for "bringing hope and courage to his fellow veterans." The expert *Best Years* cast also included Myrna Loy, Teresa Wright, Virginia Mayo, Hoagy Carmichael, Gladys George, Cathy O'Donnell and Steve Cochran.

Best Actress: Olivia de Havilland as Jody Norris (left, with Griff Barnett) in *To Each His Own* (Paramount; directed by Mitchell Leisen). The year 1946 marked an important screen comeback for Olivia de Havilland, important because she'd been unable to work for two years, waging a court battle against her home studio, Warner Bros., over an unenforced California law which limited to seven years the period any employer could enforce a contract against an employee, something Warner Bros. disputed. She won the case (officially on the books as The de Havilland Decision) and new freedom for all actors thereafter. When she returned to work, she had immediate success in two important dramas, *The Dark Mirror* and *To Each His Own,* and won the Academy Award for the latter. In it, she played an unwed mother who loses custody of her son, and becomes his "Aunt Jody" when he is adopted by another family. Spanning two wars and covering a 27-year period, the film required her to age from a fresh-faced young girl to a brusque, no-nonsense business woman and, after previous Academy nominations in 1939 and 1941, she became an Oscar winner.

The Yearling (M-G-M; produced by Sidney Franklin) starred Jane Wyman, Claude Jarman, Jr. and Gregory Peck (above) as the embodiment of the Baxter family, from Marjorie Kinnan Rawling's magnificent novel about life—and growing up—in the backwoods of Florida. One of the year's best-liked films, it won Academy Awards for Color Cinematography and Color Art Direction, plus a Special Award to Jarman as the outstanding child actor of 1946.

Special Award: Laurence Olivier (below) for "his outstanding achievements as actor, producer and director in bringing Henry V to the screen." Olivier made Henry in England during the war and despite limitations of money and production materials, and other adversities, it became the first successful Olivier adaptation of Shakespeare on the screen, although he'd appeared in celluloid Shakespeare before (1936's As You Like It), then solely as a performer.

Nominations 1946

PICTURE

* **THE BEST YEARS OF OUR LIVES,** Goldwyn, RKO Radio. Produced by Samuel Goldwyn.
  HENRY V, Rank-Two Cities, UA (British). Produced by Laurence Olivier.
  IT'S A WONDERFUL LIFE, Liberty, RKO Radio. Produced by Frank Capra.
  THE RAZOR'S EDGE, 20th Century-Fox. Produced by Darryl F. Zanuck.
  THE YEARLING, M-G-M. Produced by Sidney Franklin.

ACTOR

* **FREDRIC MARCH** in *The Best Years of Our Lives,* Goldwyn, RKO Radio.
  LAURENCE OLIVIER in *Henry V,* Rank-Two Cities, UA (British).
  LARRY PARKS in *The Jolson Story,* Columbia.
  GREGORY PECK in *The Yearling,* M-G-M.
  JAMES STEWART in *It's a Wonderful Life,* Liberty Films, RKO Radio.

ACTRESS

* **OLIVIA DE HAVILLAND** in *To Each His Own,* Paramount.
  CELIA JOHNSON in *Brief Encounter,* Rank, U-I (British).
  JENNIFER JONES in *Duel in the Sun,* Selznick International.
  ROSALIND RUSSELL in *Sister Kenny,* RKO Radio.
  JANE WYMAN in *The Yearling,* M-G-M.

SUPPORTING ACTOR

CHARLES COBURN in *The Green Years,* M-G-M.
WILLIAM DEMAREST in *The Jolson Story,* Columbia.
CLAUDE RAINS in *Notorious,* RKO Radio.
* **HAROLD RUSSELL** in *The Best Years of Our Lives,* Goldwyn, RKO Radio.
  CLIFTON WEBB in *The Razor's Edge,* 20th Century-Fox.

SUPPORTING ACTRESS

ETHEL BARRYMORE in *The Spiral Staircase,* RKO Radio.
* **ANNE BAXTER** in *The Razor's Edge,* 20th Century-Fox.
  LILLIAN GISH in *Duel in the Sun,* Selznick International.
  FLORA ROBSON in *Saratoga Trunk,* Warner Bros.
  GALE SONDERGAARD in *Anna and the King of Siam,* 20th Century-Fox.

DIRECTION

CLARENCE BROWN for *The Yearling,* M-G-M.
FRANK CAPRA for *It's a Wonderful Life,* Liberty, RKO Radio.
DAVID LEAN for *Brief Encounter,* Rank, U-I (British).
ROBERT SIODMAK for *The Killers,* Hellinger, Universal.
* **WILLIAM WYLER** for *The Best Years of our Lives,* Goldwyn, RKO Radio.

Best Supporting Actress: Anne Baxter
as Sophie MacDonald (above, with John Payne) in *The Razor's Edge* (20th Century-Fox; directed by Edmund Goulding). Created in a novel by Somerset Maugham, and acted by Anne Baxter, Sophie MacDonald was one of the screen's memorable characters of the 1940s: a gentle young mother who loses her husband and child in an automobile accident, then becomes a tragic and alcoholic wanton in Paris whom an old friend (played by Tyrone Power) unsuccessfully attempts to rehabilitate. By a paradox, Anne Baxter was not the first choice for her Oscar-winning role; producer Darryl F. Zanuck originally had assigned it to Betty Grable. The final *Razor*'s cast also included Gene Tierney, Clifton Webb, Herbert Marshall, Frank Latimore (as Sophie's husband) and Lucile Watson.

WRITING

(Original Story)
THE DARK MIRROR, U-I, Vladimir Pozner.
THE STRANGE LOVE OF MARTHA IVERS, Wallis, Paramount. Jack Patrick.
THE STRANGER, International, RKO Radio. Victor Trivas.
TO EACH HIS OWN, Paramount. Charles Brackett.
★ VACATION FROM MARRIAGE, London Films, M-G-M (British). Clemence Dane.

(Original Screenplay)
THE BLUE DAHLIA, Paramount. Raymond Chandler.
CHILDREN OF PARADISE, (French). Jacques Prevert.
NOTORIOUS, RKO Radio. Ben Hecht.
THE ROAD TO UTOPIA, Paramount. Norman Panama and Melvin Frank.
★ THE SEVENTH VEIL, Rank, Universal (British). Muriel Box and Sydney Box.

(Screenplay)
ANNA AND THE KING OF SIAM, 20th Century-Fox. Sally Benson and Talbot Jennings.
★ THE BEST YEARS OF OUR LIVES, Goldwyn, RKO Radio. Robert E. Sherwood.
BRIEF ENCOUNTER, Rank, U-I (British). Anthony Havelock-Allan, David Lean and Ronald Neame.
THE KILLERS, Hellinger, Universal. Anthony Veiller.
OPEN CITY, (Italian). Sergio Amidei and F. Fellini.

CINEMATOGRAPHY

(Black-and-White)
★ ANNA AND THE KING OF SIAM, 20th Century-Fox. Arthur Miller.
THE GREEN YEARS, M-G-M. George Folsey.

(Color)
THE JOLSON STORY, Columbia. Joseph Walker.
★ THE YEARLING, M-G-M. Charles Rosher, Leonard Smith and Arthur Arling.

ART DIRECTION-INTERIOR DECORATION

(Black-and-White)
★ ANNA AND THE KING OF SIAM, 20th Century-Fox. Lyle Wheeler and William Darling; Thomas Little and Frank E. Hughes.
KITTY, Paramount. Hans Dreier and Walter Tyler; Sam Comer and Ray Moyer.
THE RAZOR'S EDGE, 20th Century-Fox. Richard Day and Nathan Juran; Thomas Little and Paul S. Fox.

(Color)
CAESAR AND CLEOPATRA, Pascal, UA (British). John Bryan.
HENRY V, Rank-Two Cities, UA (British). Paul Sheriff and Carmen Dillon.
★ THE YEARLING, M-G-M. Cedric Gibbons and Paul Groesse; Edwin B. Willis.

SOUND RECORDING

THE BEST YEARS OF OUR LIVES, Goldwyn, RKO Radio. Gordon Sawyer.
IT'S A WONDERFUL LIFE, Liberty, RKO Radio. John Aalberg.
★ THE JOLSON STORY, Columbia. John Livadary.

FILM EDITING

★ THE BEST YEARS OF OUR LIVES, Goldwyn, RKO Radio. Daniel Mandell.
IT'S A WONDERFUL LIFE, Liberty, RKO Radio. William Hornbeck.
THE JOLSON STORY, Columbia. William Lyon.
THE KILLERS, Hellinger, Universal. Arthur Hilton.
THE YEARLING, M-G-M. Harold Kress.

SPECIAL EFFECTS

★ BLITHE SPIRIT, Rank-Two Cities, UA (British). Thomas Howard.
A STOLEN LIFE, Warner Bros. William McGann and Nathan Levinson.

MUSIC

(Song)
ALL THROUGH THE DAY (*Centennial Summer*, 20th Century-Fox); Music by Jerome Kern. Lyrics by Oscar Hammerstein II.
I CAN'T BEGIN TO TELL YOU (*The Dolly Sisters*, 20th Century-Fox); Music by James Monaco. Lyrics by Mack Gordon.
OLE BUTTERMILK SKY (*Canyon Passage*, Wanger, Universal); Music by Hoagy Carmichael. Lyrics by Jack Brooks.
★ ON THE ATCHISON, TOPEKA AND SANTA FE (*The Harvey Girls*, M-G-M); Music by Harry Warren. Lyrics by Johnny Mercer.
YOU KEEP COMING BACK LIKE A SONG (*Blue Skies*, Paramount); Music and Lyrics by Irving Berlin.

(Scoring of a Dramatic or Comedy Picture)
ANNA AND THE KING OF SIAM, 20th Century-Fox. Bernard Herrmann.
★ THE BEST YEARS OF OUR LIVES, Goldwyn, RKO Radio. Hugo Friedhofer.
HENRY V, Rank-Two Cities, UA (British). William Walton.
HUMORESQUE, Warner Bros. Franz Waxman.
THE KILLERS, Hellinger, Universal. Miklos Rozsa.

(Scoring of a Musical Picture)
BLUE SKIES, Paramount. Robert Emmett Dolan.
CENTENNIAL SUMMER, 20th Century-Fox. Alfred Newman.
THE HARVEY GIRLS, M-G-M. Lennie Hayton.
★ THE JOLSON STORY, Columbia. Morris Stoloff.
NIGHT AND DAY, Warner Bros. Ray Heindorf and Max Steiner.·

SHORT SUBJECTS

(Cartoons)
★ THE CAT CONCERTO, M-G-M. (Tom & Jerry). Frederick Quimby, producer.
CHOPIN'S MUSICAL MOMENTS, Universal. (Musical Miniatures). Walter Lantz, producer.

JOHN HENRY AND THE INKY POO, Paramount. (Puppetoon). George Pal, producer.
SQUATTER'S RIGHTS, Disney, RKO Radio. (Mickey Mouse). Walt Disney, producer.
WALKY TALKY HAWKY, Warner Bros. (Merrie Melodies). Edward Selzer, producer.

(One-reel)
DIVE-HI CHAMPS, Paramount. (Sportlights). Jack Eaton, producer.
★ FACING YOUR DANGER, Warner Bros. (Sports Parade). Gordon Hollingshead, producer.
GOLDEN HORSES, 20th Century-Fox. (Movietone Sports Review). Edmund Reek, producer.
SMART AS A FOX, Warner Bros. (Varieties). Gordon Hollingshead, producer.
SURE CURES, M-G-M. (Pete Smith Specialty). Pete Smith, producer.

(Two-reel)
★ A BOY AND HIS DOG, Warner Bros. (Featurettes). Gordon Hollingshead, producer.
COLLEGE QUEEN, Paramount. (Musical Parade). George Templeton, producer.
HISS AND YELL, Columbia. (All Star Comedies). Jules White, producer.
THE LUCKIEST GUY IN THE WORLD, M-G-M. (Two-reel Special). Jerry Bresler, producer.

DOCUMENTARY

(Short Subjects)
ATOMIC POWER, 20th Century-Fox.
LIFE AT THE ZOO, Artkino.
PARAMOUNT NEWS ISSUE #37, Paramount.
★ SEEDS OF DESTINY, U.S. War Department.
TRAFFIC WITH THE DEVIL, M-G-M.

(Features)
None nominated this year.

SPECIAL AWARDS

TO LAURENCE OLIVIER for his outstanding achievement as actor, producer and director in bringing *Henry V* to the screen. (statuette)
TO HAROLD RUSSELL for bringing hope and courage to his fellow veterans through his appearance in *The Best Years of Our Lives*. (statuette)
TO ERNST LUBITSCH for his distinguished contributions to the art of the motion picture. (scroll)
TO CLAUDE JARMAN, JR., outstanding child actor of 1946. (miniature statuette)

1946 IRVING G. THALBERG MEMORIAL AWARD

TO SAMUEL GOLDWYN

SCIENTIFIC OR TECHNICAL

CLASS I (statuette)
None.

CLASS II (plaque)
None.

CLASS III (citation)
HARLAN L. BAUMBACH and the PARAMOUNT WEST COAST LABORATORY;
HERBERT E. BRITT;
BURTON F. MILLER and the WARNER BROS. STUDIO SOUND and ELECTRICAL DEPARTMENTS;
CARL FAULKNER of the 20th Century-Fox Studio Sound Department;
MOLE-RICHARDSON CO.;
ARTHUR F. BLINN, ROBERT O. COOK, C.O. SLYFIELD and the WALT DISNEY STUDIO SOUND DEPARTMENT;
BURTON F. MILLER and the WARNER BROS. STUDIO SOUND DEPARTMENT;
MARTY MARTIN and HAL ADKINS of the RKO Radio Studio Miniature Department;
HAROLD NYE and the WARNER BROS. STUDIO ELECTRICAL DEPARTMENT.

★ INDICATES WINNER

1947 The Twentieth Year

It was the year of *Gentleman's Agreement* and *Life With Father* and *Forever Amber* and *The Egg and I,* but many people best remember the Academy's twentieth birthday party as the year of a wildly incorrect straw poll taken by a Hollywood trade publication. As was the custom, *Daily Variety* took a pre-show sampling of numerous Academy members asking how each voted in various Awards categories, then published the results—and predictions—on Oscar day. On March 20, 1948, the paper bannered that night's winners for 1947 would probably be *Gentleman's Agreement* as Best Picture, Ronald Colman in *A Double Life* as Best Actor (in a narrow margin over Gregory Peck of *Gentleman's*) and Edmund Gwenn (in *Miracle on 34th Street*) and Celeste Holm (in *Gentleman's*) winning in the Supporting divisions.

Among the nominees for Best Actress, the prediction was a "sure thing" for Rosalind Russell in *Mourning Becomes Electra* with her runners-up listed, in order, as Dorothy McGuire, Joan Crawford, Susan Hayward, and in the final spot, Loretta Young. By the end of the evening, most of the guesses were correct, but in the case of Best Actress they could not have been more wrong. Not only did the anticipated "sure thing" fail to happen, but the winner was the trailing "dark horse," Loretta Young in *The Farmer's Daughter.* It was the last time such a poll was regularly published; thereafter, the Academy requested its members keep mum on how ballots were marked.

Basically, the 1947 Awards were quite evenly distributed, with *Gentleman's Agreement* winning three (including Elia Kazan's as Best Director), *Miracle on 34th Street* receiving three, *A Double Life, Great Expectations* and *Black Narcissus* each winning two, and six other achievements winning one: *Body and Soul, Green Dolphin Street, Mother Wore Tights, The Bachelor and the Bobbysoxer, Song of the South,* and *The Bishop's Wife.* For the first time, the Academy specifically honored a foreign-language film, Italy's *Shoe-Shine,* as part of its Special Awards category; not until the 1956 Awards year were they saluted in a category of their own, with nominations. Also honored with a Special Oscar statuette was James Baskett, the endearing Uncle Remus of Walt Disney's *Song of the South.* A Special Award plaque went to another delight for the younger audiences, Ken Murray's *Bill and Coo,* the story of a humanized life style as enacted by birds. The Academy saluted it because "artistry and patience blended in a novel and entertaining use of the medium of motion pictures."

Best Actor: Ronald Colman as Anthony John in *A Double Life* (Universal-International; directed by George Cukor). Ronald Colman won his first recognition in the movies' silent era opposite Lillian Gish in *The White Sister* (1923) and received ever-wider popularity when the screen learned to speak, due to his unique, resonant voice. On the celebration of his 25th year as a star, he had one of his most demanding roles, as an actor so immersed in playing *Othello* that his stage character begins to take possession of his off-screen personality. *A Double Life* was written by Ruth Gordon and Garson Kanin, co-starred Signe Hasso and Edmond O'Brien and gave Shelley Winters her first important screen role as a waitress murdered by the actor. Shakespearean veteran Walter Hampden coached Colman for the slices of *Othello* incorporated into the film. At left, Colman as the actor in performance.

Best Picture: Gentleman's Agreement (20th Century-Fox; produced by Darryl F. Zanuck), **Best Director: Elia Kazan** and **Best Supporting Actress: Celeste Holm** as Anne Dettrey (above, with Gregory Peck, John Garfield, Robert Karnes and Gene Nelson) in *Gentleman's Agreement.* In 1947, Hollywood used the screen to take microscopic looks at minority groups and prejudice running rampant in the United States; one of the most successful was *Gentleman's Agreement,* based on Laura Z. Hobson's powerful novel about a writer who poses as a Jew for six months in order to research a series of articles he intends to write on anti-Semitism. The cast included Dorothy McGuire, Anne Revere, Albert Dekker, June Havoc, Jane Wyatt, Dean Stockwell and Sam Jaffe. Celeste Holm, in her third screen role, won the Academy Award as a compassionate friend of the writer; she was later nominated for Academy Awards again in 1949 (for *Come to the Stable*) and in 1950 (for *All About Eve*).

Best Actress: Loretta Young as Katie Holstrom (right, with Keith Andes, James Arness and Lex Barker) in *The Farmer's Daughter* (RKO Radio; directed by H.C. Potter). Loretta Young, like Ronald Colman, was a long-time screen veteran when she won her Oscar. After early days as a child extra, she played her first role at age 14 in 1927's *Naughty But Nice* with Colleen Moore, then became the personification of an elegant leading lady—charming, well-groomed, classy—in frothy comedies, major spectacles and romantic dramas. *The Farmer's Daughter* had originally been planned for Ingrid Bergman, but it fit the Young talents perfectly: with a Swedish accent and blonde hair, she was a Minnesota farm girl who begins as the household maid of a Congressman (Joseph Cotten) and ultimately is elected to Congress herself.

Nominations 1947

PICTURE

THE BISHOP'S WIFE, Goldwyn, RKO Radio. Produced by Samuel Goldwyn.
CROSSFIRE, RKO Radio. Produced by Adrian Scott.
★ GENTLEMAN'S AGREEMENT, 20th Century-Fox. Produced by Darryl F. Zanuck.
GREAT EXPECTATIONS, Rank-Cineguild, U-I (British). Produced by Ronald Neame.
MIRACLE ON 34TH STREET, 20th Century-Fox. Produced by William Perlberg.

ACTOR

★ RONALD COLMAN in A Double Life, Kanin, U-I.
JOHN GARFIELD in Body and Soul, Enterprise, UA.
GREGORY PECK in Gentleman's Agreement, 20th Century-Fox.
WILLIAM POWELL in Life With Father, Warner Bros.
MICHAEL REDGRAVE in Mourning Becomes Electra, RKO Radio.

ACTRESS

JOAN CRAWFORD in Possessed, Warner Bros.
SUSAN HAYWARD in Smash Up—The Story of a Woman, Wanger, U-I.
DOROTHY McGUIRE in Gentleman's Agreement, 20th Century-Fox.
ROSALIND RUSSELL in Mourning Becomes Electra, RKO Radio.
★ LORETTA YOUNG in The Farmer's Daughter, RKO Radio.

SUPPORTING ACTOR

CHARLES BICKFORD in The Farmer's Daughter, RKO Radio.
THOMAS GOMEZ in Ride the Pink Horse, U-I.
★ EDMUND GWENN in Miracle on 34th Street, 20th Century-Fox.
ROBERT RYAN in Crossfire, RKO Radio.
RICHARD WIDMARK in Kiss of Death, 20th Century-Fox.

SUPPORTING ACTRESS

ETHEL BARRYMORE in The Paradine Case, Selznick Releasing Organization.
GLORIA GRAHAME in Crossfire, RKO Radio.
★ CELESTE HOLM in Gentleman's Agreement, 20th Century-Fox.
MARJORIE MAIN in The Egg and I, U-I.
ANNE REVERE in Gentleman's Agreement, 20th Century-Fox.

DIRECTION

GEORGE CUKOR for A Double Life, Kanin, U-I.
EDWARD DMYTRYK for Crossfire, RKO Radio.
★ ELIA KAZAN for Gentleman's Agreement, 20th Century-Fox.
HENRY KOSTER for The Bishop's Wife, Goldwyn, RKO Radio.
DAVID LEAN for Great Expectations, Rank-Cineguild, U-I (British).

WRITING

(Original Story)

A CAGE OF NIGHTINGALES, Lopert Films (French). Georges Chaperot and Rene Wheeler.
IT HAPPENED ON FIFTH AVENUE, Del Ruth, Allied Artists. Herbert Clyde Lewis and Frederick Stephani.
KISS OF DEATH, 20th.Century-Fox. Eleazar Lipsky.
★ MIRACLE ON 34TH STREET, 20th Century-Fox. Valentine Davies.
SMASH-UP—THE STORY OF A WOMAN, Wanger, U-I. Dorothy Parker and Frank Cavett.

(Original Screenplay)

★ THE BACHELOR AND THE BOBBY-SOXER, RKO Radio. Sidney Sheldon.
BODY AND SOUL, Enterprise, UA. Abraham Polonsky.
A DOUBLE LIFE, Kanin, U-I. Ruth Gordon and Garson Kanin.
MONSIEUR VERDOUX, Chaplin, UA. Charles Chaplin.
SHOE-SHINE, Lopert Films (Italian). Sergio Amidei, Adolfo Franci, C.G. Viola and Cesare Zavattini.

(Screenplay)

BOOMERANG!, 20th Century-Fox. Richard Murphy.
CROSSFIRE, RKO Radio. John Paxton.
GENTLEMAN'S AGREEMENT, 20th Century-Fox. Moss Hart.
GREAT EXPECTATIONS, Rank-Cineguild, U-I (British). David Lean, Ronald Neame and Anthony Havelock-Allan.
★ MIRACLE ON 34TH STREET, 20th Century-Fox. George Seaton.

CINEMATOGRAPHY

(Black-and-White)

THE GHOST AND MRS. MUIR, 20th Century-Fox. Charles Lang, Jr.
★ GREAT EXPECTATIONS, Rank-Cineguild, U-I (British). Guy Green.
GREEN DOLPHIN STREET, M-G-M. George Folsey.

(Color)

★ BLACK NARCISSUS, Rank-Archer, U-I (British). Jack Cardiff.
LIFE WITH FATHER, Warner Bros. Peverell Marley and William V. Skall.
MOTHER WORE TIGHTS, 20th Century-Fox. Harry Jackson.

ART DIRECTION-SET DECORATION

(New classification)
(Winning art directors given statuettes; set decorator of the winning film given Academy plaque until 1955)

(Black-and-White)

THE FOXES OF HARROW, 20th Century-Fox. Lyle Wheeler and Maurice Ransford; Thomas Little and Paul S. Fox.
★ GREAT EXPECTATIONS, Rank-Cineguild, U-I (British). John Bryan; Wilfred Shingleton.

(Color)

★ BLACK NARCISSUS, Rank-Archers, U-I (British). Alfred Junge.
LIFE WITH FATHER, Warner Bros. Robert M. Haas; George James Hopkins.

SOUND RECORDING

★ THE BISHOP'S WIFE, Goldwyn, RKO Radio. Goldwyn Sound Department.
GREEN DOLPHIN STREET, M-G-M. M-G-M Sound Department.
T-MEN, Reliance Pictures, Eagle-Lion. Sound Services, Inc.

FILM EDITING

THE BISHOP'S WIFE, Goldwyn, RKO Radio. Monica Collingwood.
★ BODY AND SOUL, Enterprise, UA. Francis Lyon and Robert Parrish.
GENTLEMAN'S AGREEMENT, 20th Century-Fox. Harmon Jones.
GREEN DOLPHIN STREET, M-G-M. George White.
ODD MAN OUT, Rank-Two Cities, U-I (British). Fergus McDonnell.

SPECIAL EFFECTS

★ GREEN DOLPHIN STREET, M-G-M. A. Arnold Gillespie, Warren Newcombe, Douglas Shearer and Michael Steinore.
UNCONQUERED, DeMille, Paramount. Farciot Edouart, Devereux Jennings, Gordon Jennings, Wallace Kelley, Paul Lerpae and George Dutton.

Great Expectations (Universal-International; produced by Ronald Neame) won Academy Awards for Guy Green's Black-and-White Cinematography and John Bryan's Black-and-White Art Direction (with set decoration by Wilfred Shingleton) and helped give a noticeable impetus to the popularity of British-made films in America's general movie market. At the time, most films from England only found acceptance in specialized art-houses. It was based on the adventurous Charles Dickens novel and featured John Mills, Valerie Hobson, Alec Guinness and (above) Jean Simmons, Martita Hunt, Anthony Wager.

Black Narcissus (Universal-International; produced by Michael Powell and Emeric Pressburger). Pictorially stunning, this English-made morality drama was a study of five missionary nuns attempting to establish a convent-school and hospital in the remote Palace of Mopu, high in the Himalayas. It starred Deborah Kerr and Flora Robson (below), Jean Simmons, Sabu and David Farrar and won Academy Awards for Color Cinematography by Jack Cardiff and Color Art Direction by Alfred Junge.

Best Supporting Actor: Edmund Gwenn
as Kris Kringle (above, with Natalie Wood)
in *Miracle on 34th Street* (20th Century-Fox;
directed by George Seaton). Is he or isn't
he? In Valentine Davies' fresh and original
screenplay, the man hired to be Macy's
Santa Claus claims to be the real thing, and
even gets sent as far as the Supreme Court
on the question of his sanity. Edmund
Gwenn won the Academy Award for his
portrayal of Mr. Claus, alias Mr. Kringle,
aided and abetted by Maureen O'Hara,
John Payne and Thelma Ritter, among
others. Mr. Davies also won an Oscar
for his words.

Special Award: Shoe-Shine from Italy
(Lopert Films; produced in Italy by Paolo
W. Tamburella) received an Academy Award
from the Board of Governors because "the
high quality of this Italian-made motion
picture, brought to eloquent life in a
country scarred by war, is proof to the
world that the creative spirit can triumph
over adversity." Directed by Vittorio DeSica,
it was peopled with a cast of
nonprofessional children and mirrored
the struggle of two hungry, homeless boys
(Rinaldo Smordoni and Franco Interlenghi,
below) to survive on the streets after
the fall of Fascism in modern-day Italy.

MUSIC

(Song)
A GAL IN CALICO (*The Time, Place and the Girl,* Warner Bros.); Music by Arthur Schwartz. Lyrics by Leo Robin.
I WISH I DIDN'T LOVE YOU SO (*The Perils of Pauline,* Paramount); Music and Lyrics by Frank Loesser.
PASS THAT PEACE PIPE (*Good News,* M-G-M); Music and Lyrics by Ralph Blane, Hugh Martin and Roger Edens.
YOU DO (*Mother Wore Tights,* 20th Century-Fox); Music by Josef Myrow. Lyrics by Mack Gordon.
★ **ZIP-A-DEE-DOO-DAH** (*Song of the South,* Disney, RKO Radio); Music by Allie Wrubel. Lyrics by Ray Gilbert.

(Scoring of a Dramatic or Comedy Picture)
THE BISHOP'S WIFE, Goldwyn, RKO Radio. Hugo Freidhofer.
CAPTAIN FROM CASTILE, 20th Century-Fox. Alfred Newman.
★ **A DOUBLE LIFE,** Kanin, U-I. Miklos Rozsa.
FOREVER AMBER, 20th Century-Fox. David Raksin.
LIFE WITH FATHER, Warner Bros. Max Steiner.

(Scoring of a Musical Picture)
FIESTA, M-G-M. Johnny Green.
★ **MOTHER WORE TIGHTS,** 20th Century-Fox. Alfred Newman.
MY WILD IRISH ROSE, Warner Bros. Ray Heindorf and Max Steiner.
ROAD TO RIO, Paramount. Robert Emmett Dolan.
SONG OF THE SOUTH, Disney, RKO Radio. Daniele Amfitheatrof, Paul J. Smith and Charles Wolcott.

SHORT SUBJECTS

(Cartoons)
CHIP AN' DALE, Disney, RKO Radio. (Donald Duck). Walt Disney, producer.
DR. JEKYLL AND MR. MOUSE, M-G-M. (Tom & Jerry). Frederick Quimby, producer.
PLUTO'S BLUE NOTE, Disney, RKO Radio. (Pluto). Walt Disney, producer.
TUBBY THE TUBA, Paramount. (Puppetoon). George Pal, producer.
★ **TWEETIE PIE,** Warner Bros. (Merrie Melodies). Edward Selzer, producer.

(One-reel)
BROOKLYN, U.S.A., Universal-International. (Variety Series). Thomas Mead, producer.
★ **GOODBYE MISS TURLOCK,** M-G-M. (John Nesbitt Passing Parade). Herbert Moulton, producer.
MOON ROCKETS, Paramount. (Popular Science). Jerry Fairbanks, producer.
NOW YOU SEE IT, M-G-M. (Pete Smith Specialty). Pete Smith, producer.
SO YOU WANT TO BE IN PICTURES, Warner Bros. (Joe McDoakes). Gordon Hollingshead, producer.

(Two-reel)
CHAMPAGNE FOR TWO, Paramount. (Musical Parade Featurette). Harry Grey, producer.
★ **CLIMBING THE MATTERHORN,** Monogram. (Special). Irving Allen, producer.
FIGHT OF THE WILD STALLIONS, U-I. (Special). Thomas Mead, producer.
GIVE US THE EARTH, M-G-M. (Special). Herbert Morgan, producer.
A VOICE IS BORN, Columbia. (Musical Featurette). Ben Blake, producer.

DOCUMENTARY

(Short Subjects)
★ **FIRST STEPS,** United Nations Division of Films and Visual Education.
PASSPORT TO NOWHERE, RKO Radio (This Is America Series). Frederic Ullman, Jr., producer.
SCHOOL IN THE MAILBOX, Australian News and Information Bureau.

(Features)
★ **DESIGN FOR DEATH,** RKO Radio. Sid Rogell, executive producer; Theron Warth and Richard O. Fleischer, producers.
JOURNEY INTO MEDICINE, U.S. Department of State, Office of Information and Educational Exchange.
THE WORLD IS RICH, British Information Services. Paul Rotha, producer.

SPECIAL AWARDS

TO JAMES BASKETT for his able and heart-warming characterization of Uncle Remus, friend and story teller to the children of the world, in Walt Disney's *Song of the South.* (statuette)
TO BILL AND COO, in which artistry and patience blended in a novel and entertaining use of the medium of motion pictures. (plaque)
TO SHOE-SHINE—the high quality of this Italian-made motion picture, brought to eloquent life in a country scarred by war, is proof to the world that the creative spirit can triumph over adversity. (statuette)
TO COLONEL WILLIAM N. SELIG, ALBERT E. SMITH, THOMAS ARMAT and **GEORGE K. SPOOR** (one of) the small group of pioneers whose belief in a new medium, and whose contributions to its development, blazed the trail along which the motion picture has progressed, in their lifetime, from obscurity to world-wide acclaim. (statuettes)

1947 IRVING G. THALBERG MEMORIAL AWARD

None given this year.

SCIENTIFIC OR TECHNICAL

CLASS I (statuette)
None.

CLASS II (plaque)
C.C. DAVIS and **ELECTRICAL RESEARCH PRODUCTS, DIVISION OF WESTERN ELECTRIC CO.,** for the development and application of an improved film drive filter mechanism.
C.R. DAILY and the **PARAMOUNT STUDIO FILM LABORATORY, STILL** and **ENGINEERING DEPARTMENTS** for the development and first practical application to motion picture and still photography of a method of increasing film speed as first suggested to the industry by E.I. duPont de Nemours & Co.

CLASS III (citation)
NATHAN LEVINSON and the **WARNER BROS. STUDIO SOUND DEPARTMENT;**
FARCIOT EDOUART, C.R. DAILY, HAL CORL, H.G. CARTWRIGHT and the **PARAMOUNT STUDIO TRANSPARENCY** and **ENGINEERING DEPARTMENTS;**
FRED PONEDEL of Warner Bros. Studio;
KURT SINGER and the **RCA-VICTOR DIVISION** of the **RADIO CORPORATION OF AMERICA;**
JAMES GIBBONS of Warner Bros. Studio.

★ INDICATES WINNER

The Academy's Third Decade

ELIA KAZAN

" *I resigned from the Academy because I don't believe in lists, ten bests, awards and so on. The contrary fact remains that I sure as hell enjoyed getting my two Oscars. I wish the organization would become not less, but more active, actually do more about the Motion Picture Arts and Sciences. Or does it and I don't know about it?*

Academy means Academy. The only thing I know about the organization is the show it puts on once a year, which I watch with the rest of the movie fans and gossip hounds. It's sometimes fun, sometimes silly and every once in a while grand. I don't think the Academy is serious enough. At least whatever it has tried to do of more worth has never filtered down to me. Why hasn't it? **"**

Elia Kazan
Best Director, 1947; 1954

CLAIRE TREVOR

" *There are many jokes—like what to say if you win. Bogart's advice to me was 'Tell 'em you don't owe anybody anything —you did it all by yourself.' This was a few days before the awards when I won it for Key Largo. He was playing it cool in his usual 'screw you' Bogart character.*

So you try to play it cool and not care too much. You go to the theater and you see almost everyone you ever worked with—everyone you've always admired— and you're thrilled and nervous.

Then it narrows down to your category. There are years between the announcement of each nominee, and then—the winner's name.

There's sort of an explosion which makes you half dead and blind. Somehow you find yourself on the stage and you begin to hear the applause—and it doesn't stop! The proof is there, with every clap of the hand, that these are my people, whom I've worked with and loved all my life and they seem to love me back!

It's hard to say anything—it's hard not to cry. All the dues paid are overwhelmingly worthwhile. It's pure glory.

That's what it meant to 'tough guy' Bogart too when he won for African Queen. I know because I had presented an award and was one of the first to see him when he came backstage clutching his Oscar, beaming—full of glory! **"**

Claire Trevor
Best Supporting Actress, 1948

The war years (1942-1945) had been a period of prosperity for the motion picture industry. Movie attendance soared to 85 million paid admissions per week, the best financial news for filmmakers since the introduction of sound in the late 1920s. However, when the war ended, a multiplicity of problems hit Hollywood which forced a complete revolution in the production and distribution of films. The effect on the industry, naturally, had a corresponding effect on the Academy.

For many years, major studios had either owned, been owned by or been connected to vast theater chains, insuring outlets for their constant supply of product. It was an unquestioned way of life for the companies, as was block-booking, in which films were rented to theaters in multiple numbers, sold by blocks, offering a guarantee of playdates for weaker films when packaged in a block with several strong ones. After the war, independent theater owners filed an antitrust suit against the studios, which resulted in companies like Metro-Goldwyn-Mayer (connected to Loew's), RKO Radio, Warner Bros. and 20th Century-Fox having to divest themselves of their theater-chain affiliations, and block-booking was similarly declared illegal, both of which cut off guaranteed incomes for the studios at a time when production costs were rising dramatically. Increasing taxes on personal income also forced actors, writers and

Walter Huston, Claire Trevor, John Huston

James Stewart, Olivia de Havilland, Broderick Crawford, Jane Wyman

Judy Holliday, Jose Ferrer, Gloria Swanson, George Cukor

JOHN GREEN

❝From November 16, 1944, the date on which the Academy of Motion Picture Arts and Sciences invited me to regular membership in its music branch, through today, March 17, 1978, the Academy and I have been 'going steady,' having an affair, a liaison, a constant assignation—call it what you will. Like any intense romance, it has had its ups, its downs, its highs, its lows, its tears and laughter (much more of the latter than the former), its awful problems with happy resolutions to most of them, its violent lovers' quarrels with equally violent kiss-and-make-up fests.

Don't ever sell Oscar short. Carpers, critics, detractors and out-and-out slanderers come and go, but Oscar sails on as the number one, most respected, most prestigious award of its kind world-wide. For me, no doorstop, no closet item he! My fourteen nominations and my five Oscars are on unashamedly proud, conspicuous and constant display in my home and office.

Ten times I have been music director and conductor of the Awards show. Having been present at several of the shows prior to my first time on the podium, and having been appalled at the number of missed or delayed music cues, endless repetition of the same meaningless fanfare, no real connection between the music in the pit and the achievements being honored, I am the one who dreamed up the actually simple device by which the right music for the specific achievement hits instantaneously with the last syllable of the announcement of the winner—and this despite the fact that the conductor and his players have absolutely no advance inkling of any kind as to who the winner will be. The double whammy of this has been that, while being regarded as some sort of a miracle of precision, the device has been used as alleged evidence that the secrecy of the Awards is a myth and that 'of course, the conductor and the orchestra know in advance.' Year after year I have been interviewed by every branch of the media (local, national and international) about this item. As of only about a year ago, I have had the impression that the proper and showmanly catching of music cues is finally being recognized for its true colors and is no longer being regarded as a piece of crafty chicanery. ❞

John Green
Music (Scoring of a Musical Picture),
1948; 1951; 1961
Producer (One-reel Short Subject), 1953
Music (Scoring of a Musical Picture:
Original or Adaptation), 1968

directors to forego studio contracts for certain advantages offered by personal incorporation. Others were dropped by studios which no longer felt financially able to pay weekly salaries except to those artists who were currently at work on a production. There was confusion and upheaval everywhere because now, for the first time, in order to obtain top talent, film companies had to offer substantial salaries and percentages of pictures on a regular basis—rather than as an occasional enticement—which upped the cost of production budgets even higher.

The sudden popularity of television also exploded during the Academy's third decade, although it had been a dark cloud hovering over the industry as early as 1939. Wartime restrictions had limited the development of television and thus forestalled development of the formidable competition for a time. However, once the postwar manufacturing of sets resumed and programming improved—plus television was *free* to viewers once the initial investment in a receiver was made—attendance in movie theaters dropped sharply. It would have been advantageous for the studios to have controlled the new medium, but they were thwarted by FCC regulations in their attempts to gain a foothold.

Competition between the two giant mass media appeared for a while to be a standoff. In order to block television from gaining any more ground, studios refused to permit their stars to appear on any programs, barred the use of film clips on the air waves and stood guard over their most precious asset: the valuable backlog of feature films accumulating in the vaults since the movies began. The deadlock was finally ended

JANE WYMAN

" On your twenty-first birthday, it was my great privilege to bring you to my home, having been honored by you for my performance in Johnny Belinda.

Your artistic excellence and love have lived on through the years only because of the integrity, challenge and respect you command among our peers.

My best of good wishes on your fiftieth anniversary, and I hope you continue to bring as much joy to others as you did to me. "

Jane Wyman
Best Actress, 1948

FRED ASTAIRE

" I am of course delighted to have received my Honorary Academy Award given to me in 1949. Also to have been nominated for Best Supporting Actor in 1975.

In my opinion the whole Oscar thing is an exciting and inspiring experience for both the public and the performers. "

Fred Astaire
Special Award, 1949

MERCEDES McCAMBRIDGE

" Some women have a sable,
Some women have a yacht,
But my lovely golden Oscar
Not many women have got—
And I am ever grateful. "

Mercedes McCambridge
Best Supporting Actress, 1949

ERNEST BORGNINE

" It was one bet I hoped I'd lose. I had wagered a grand total of $1.98 with Jerry Lewis, who was the host of that year's show, that I wouldn't win. If you have an opportunity to look at an old film clip of that evening, you will notice that right after Grace Kelly opened the envelope and said, 'And the winner is Ernest Borgnine,' I rushed on stage and handed Jerry something. What I handed him was 198 pennies wrapped in a red sock belonging to my daughter. Two weeks later, when my life was starting to return to normal, a telegram arrived from Jerry saying, 'I saved the money, but spent the sock!' "

Ernest Borgnine
Best Actor, 1955

Laurence Olivier congratulates Vivien Leigh

when the studios, desperate for production funds and feeling the pinch at the box office, allowed stars still under contract to appear on certain television projects. They also began to use the new medium as a publicity tool for promoting new motion pictures made for theatrical showing. Soon they began releasing older blocks of their feature films to television and the once-distinct lines drawn between the two media began disappearing. Probably no single thing made this fact more apparent than the twenty-fifth Academy Awards presentation on March 19, 1953, when Hollywood's Oscar ceremony was broadcast for the first time on television. Movie attendance across the country hit a new low, but the show collected the largest single audience in television's five-year commercial history, and the Academy helped to underscore dramatically the fact the two media could work together for everyone's mutual benefit.

Thanks to that first televised Awards gala, the public not only had its initial opportunity to watch an Oscar ceremony in progress, but saw more major stars and Hollywood creators on their television screens than they ever had before. Many celebrities made their live television debuts that evening and the collection of names either participating or attending was noteworthy, including the first two ladies to win Academy Awards, Janet Gaynor and Mary Pickford, in addition to Loretta Young,

Karl Malden, Bette Davis, Humphrey Bogart, Greer Garson, Ronald Colman

March 19, 1953: Shirley Booth and the first Oscar telecast

Greer Garson, Olivia de Havilland, Joan Fontaine, Cecil B. DeMille, Gloria Swanson, Harold Lloyd, Victor McLaglen, Luise Rainer, Paul Muni, James Stewart, Ginger Rogers, Jane Darwell, Donald Crisp, Teresa Wright, Charles Coburn, Joan Crawford, Ray Milland, Fredric March, Anne Baxter, Ronald Colman, Celeste Holm, Edmund Gwenn, Jane Wyman, Claire Trevor, Broderick Crawford, Dean Jagger, Kim Hunter, Darryl F. Zanuck, Walt Disney, Frank Capra, Jean Hersholt, Dimitri Tiomkin, Piper Laurie, Tex Ritter, John Wayne, Shirley Booth, Gloria Grahame, Bob Hope and others. It set a precedent which became an Academy tradition: one television show, above all others, on which even stars who usually shied from the TV medium would willingly take part, without payment, in order to support their industry.

Marlene Dietrich, Italian Consul Mario Ungaro

GENE KELLY

❝ My relations with Oscar were always distant but remain quite warm in my memory. Let me explain: When I was nominated in 1945 for Anchors Aweigh, I was away with the U.S. Naval Air Force. When I was actually presented with a Special Oscar in 1952, 'in appreciation of his versatility as an actor, singer, director and dancer, and specifically for his brilliant achievements in the art of choreography on film,' I was making a picture in Europe for M-G-M, and was told the good news over the long-distance telephone. That explains the distance factor, but the warmth, of course, remains with me forever.❞

Gene Kelly
Honorary Award, 1951

HOAGY CARMICHAEL

❝ Naturally, I was overjoyed at receiving my Oscar for the song 'In The Cool, Cool, Cool Of The Evening.' I'm not sure that my lyricist, Johnny Mercer, was as overjoyed as I because he already had a vulgar display of three Oscars at his home from former years.

Possibly we didn't deserve it because we both forgot to thank Jane Wyman and Danny Kaye for singing it the night of the Oscar show, and I'm not too sure we thanked Jane and Bing for making it a hit in the picture. On this occasion Johnny and I were pulling together, but once we were worlds apart when his song 'On the Atchison, Topeka and Santa Fe' beat out my 'Ole Buttermilk Sky.' ❞

Hoagy Carmichael
Music (Song), 1951

DEAN JAGGER

❝ They said I would have to spend money advertising. I didn't spend two cents . . . and when I won . . . it was beautiful! ❞

Dean Jagger
Best Supporting Actor, 1949

KIM HUNTER

❝ As thrilled as I was to win my Oscar, I question the possibility of choosing 'Bests' in any artistic field. I sincerely congratulate the Academy on its 50th Anniversary, and all the past nominees and winners for their accomplishments. But this occasion shouldn't go by without also cheering for the countless individuals who've contributed as much or more to the excellence of motion pictures without receiving the Academy's glamorous, 'official' accolade. ❞

Kim Hunter
Best Supporting Actress, 1951

FRED ZINNEMANN

" *Everything went blank when I heard my name being called as the Oscar winner for directing* From Here To Eternity. *There seemed to be lots of applause coming from far away throughout the Pantages Theatre, and a blinding light shone on my head. I only came to when I felt someone thump my back and shout 'Congratulations.' It was a friend and fellow nominee, George Stevens, who was seated directly behind me. From then on, everything became a golden blur.* "

Fred Zinnemann
Best Director, 1953; 1966

Judy Garland, Greer Garson, Jane Wyman at first (and only) telecast of Oscar nominations, February 12, 1955

IRENE SHARAFF

" *It is joy to congratulate the Academy on its Golden Anniversary and to celebrate its achievements in encouraging excellence in motion pictures and promoting various cultural and educational activities. Many, many happy returns!*

I, of course, appreciate very much indeed the nominations and Oscars awarded me by the Academy and am glad for this opportunity to thank warmly the members of the Academy for noticing my work. It is recognition also of the many people in the costume departments and workrooms who worked with me to produce the results on film. Many, many happy returns to all of them, too! "

Irene Sharaff
Costume Design (Color),
1951; 1956; 1961; 1963
Costume Design (Black-and-white), 1966

KARL MALDEN

" *To achieve within yourself the definition and understanding of a specific role is a challenge that, when successfully met, brings a glowing personal satisfaction.*

To have that achievement recognized by the craftsmen and actors of the motion picture industry is an unrivalled thrill.

I received an Academy Award for a supporting role in A Streetcar Named Desire *when Oscar was only twenty-four years old. That was twenty-six years ago. I have not forgotten it. I never will!* "

Karl Malden
Best Supporting Actor, 1951

The Academy also had another brush with political involvement as its third decade came to an end, brought about by investigations which began in 1947 of Communist infiltration into the motion picture industry, conducted by the Committee on Un-American Activities of the House of Representatives in Washington, D.C. At these hearings, nineteen members of the motion picture industry were called as witnesses, and ten of them questioned the committee's right to interrogate, after which they became known as the "Unfriendly Ten." They were blacklisted from employment within the motion picture industry and, in June of 1950, received jail sentences of up to one year. Though the Academy stayed clear of the blacklisting controversy, either directly or implied, it became involved later when certain scripts by writers involved in the so-called Un-American investigations became eligible for Oscar consideration although their authors were denied screen credit. This was based on a 1952 agreement between individual studios and the Screen

Marlon Brando, Bette Davis

Grace Kelly, William Holden and the press

Writers Guild. To avoid further confusion, at a meeting on February 6, 1957, the Academy revised a bylaw which stated:

> "Any person who, before any duly constituted Federal legislative committee or body, shall have admitted that he is a member of the Communist party (and has not since publicly renounced the party), or who shall have refused to answer whether or not he is, or was, a member of the Communist party, or shall have refused to respond to a subpoena to appear before such a committee or body, shall not be eligible for an Academy Award so long as he persists in such a refusal."

It was an innocent gesture, made in a spirit of patriotic goodwill to inspire faith in the moral well-being of the industry, but it proved to be something of an embarrassment almost at once. The following year, several Academy members, including Academy President George Seaton, urged the repeal of the rule and, on January 12, 1959, it was revoked by the Academy's Board of Governors. The Board issued an official statement calling the rule "unworkable and impractical to administer and enforce." The statement brought an official end to Hollywood's mystery-shrouded "blacklist" era.

As the third decade drew to a close, something new was also initiated. At the 1957 Academy Awards ceremony, for the first time, the motion picture industry itself—instead of commercial sponsors—began financing the annual Oscar telecasts, and continued to do so for the telecasts honoring 1958 and 1959 achievements.

ACADEMY PRESIDENTS, THE THIRD DECADE

May 1947-May 1948	JEAN HERSHOLT
May 1948-May 1949	JEAN HERSHOLT
May 1949-May 1950	CHARLES BRACKETT
May 1950-May 1951	CHARLES BRACKETT
May 1951-May 1952	CHARLES BRACKETT
May 1952-May 1953	CHARLES BRACKETT
May 1953-May 1954	CHARLES BRACKETT
May 1954-May 1955	CHARLES BRACKETT
June 1955-May 1956	GEORGE SEATON
June 1956-May 1957	GEORGE SEATON

DIMITRI TIOMKIN

❝ The fiftieth anniversary of the Academy of Motion Picture Arts and Sciences brings back to me unforgettable memories of my life and work in the motion picture business. I emphasize the word 'unforgettable' with a deep sense of nostalgia because I remember so vividly the fun, the excitement, the hopes and the natural disappointments leading to the final days of Academy Award presentations.

By nature I have always been a 'sucker' for awards and recognition. I like them both. They help me to forget the necessary daily routine (or process of trying to make money!). The motion picture Academy developed in its members a sense of trial and responsibility, and a desire to better themselves. Now, in my old age, I would like to express my thanks that providence gave me the chance to participate, for so many years, in the excitements, triumphs, and sorrows connected with the results of that great night of Academy Award decisions.

I would like to wish the Academy a further fifty years of continued success.

God bless you all. Be happy, healthy, stubborn and reasonable. ❞

Dimitri Tiomkin
Music (Scoring of a Dramatic or Comedy Picture), 1952; 1954; 1958
Music (Song), 1952

ALAN JAY LERNER

❝ I have won three Oscars. The first was for the original screenplay for An American in Paris in 1951, and I was not present because of an illness in the family. When I was nominated for the screenplay and song for Gigi in 1959, I was in the arena. I was more astonished and more incredulous when I was not there than when I was there, due, I suppose, to the fact that I am ill at ease in the hot lights. I remember feeling that no one knew how I felt—but, alas, today I do not remember how I felt. But it must have been lovely. ❞

Alan Jay Lerner
Writing (Story and Screenplay), 1951
Writing (Screenplay, Adapted), 1958
Music (Best Song/Lyrics), 1958

GLORIA GRAHAME

❝ My deepest feeling about the Oscar is that the people with whom I worked liked what I did. ❞

Gloria Grahame
Best Supporting Actress, 1952

EDMOND O'BRIEN

" If an actor does not have the right words, he'll never win anything.

I was lucky enough in The Barefoot Contessa to have my words written, produced and directed by one of the great talents of our time, Mr. Joseph Mankiewicz. He also wrote All About Eve, etc., etc.

One year before The Barefoot Contessa, Joe Mankiewicz had directed me in his production of Shakespeare's Julius Caesar.

Joe Mankiewicz actually wrote the part in Contessa with me in mind. He sent me the script from Connecticut. I read it, called him and said, 'Yes!'

It takes great writing and directing to win an Academy Award. I had them both, thanks to Joe Mankiewicz.

For me, an award from the Academy of Motion Picture Arts and Sciences is the most meaningful award in the film world. I have won other awards but the Academy Award is the one I treasure most. "

Edmond O'Brien
Best Supporting Actor, 1954

GRACE KELLY

" Being nominated for an Academy Award by your fellow actors is quite an honor; winning one is a special honor and a fantastic, though numbing, experience.

After the nominations are announced, speculation begins and the fever mounts. This period of waiting seems to bring out the best and worst in everyone connected with the business. No one nominated escapes the jaundiced eye of criticism as to this one's worth and that one's talent. Even the Academy takes it on the nose. Why all this fuss? Is it really worthwhile? How important is an Oscar anyway? So-and-so never won an award and it didn't hurt her career, etc. Besides, who needs it?

Well, I suppose no one really needs it; but, believe me, it is awfully nice to have. When my turn came, I was longing to win, and wanted to so badly that I was afraid that I would stand up no matter which name was read out. I said to Don Hartman of Paramount, who was next to me, 'Hold me down, if it isn't my name.' And when it was, I kept asking him, 'Are you sure, are you sure?' Then, all I could think was, 'Just try to get up there, Grace, without tripping.' Well, I managed to make it without tripping on my dress or the steps, but didn't do so well on the speech. "

Grace Kelly
Best Actress, 1954

Robert Burke, Claudette Colbert

Anna Magnani

SIDNEY SHELDON

❝ In show business, where even the biggest names go through up and down periods of being 'hot' and 'cold,' there is one name that for the past fifty years has always been 'hot'—Oscar. Everybody wants him. Comes each January, studios spend millions of dollars in trade advertising, trying to coax Oscar onto their trophy shelves. It is rumored that certain stars would kill to get him. Myths and rumors surround Oscar: If you win him, you'll never want again; if you win him, you'll never work again. It's all politics. Oscar can be bought. Oscar night is a glamorous, rigged spectacle. The nominees know in advance who's going to win. The myths are exactly that. Myths.

It is true Oscar winners do go through dry spells sometimes, but then, so do the losers. You can't advertise your way to an Oscar, nor is he for sale. He is awarded solely by the vote of one's peers.

As for knowing in advance who the winners are, I can refute that from my own experience. When a screenplay I wrote was nominated I was so sure I would not win that I did not even bother to think about an acceptance speech. When my name was called, I was in a state of shock. I mumbled some ridiculous acceptance speech, grabbed Oscar and fled. No, the winners don't know in advance. The suspense of the evening is legitimate.

Over the years, since the evening I received my Oscar, I have been working on the acceptance speech I would like to have given. It is witty and warm, touching and modest, yet filled with sincerity. It begins, 'Ladies and gentlemen . . .' ❞

Sidney Sheldon
Writing (Original Screenplay), 1947

ALEC GUINNESS

❝ With the proliferation of awards in the cinema there is only one that everyone knows about and that is the Oscar, and it is the most highly prized of all. ❞

Alec Guinness
Best Actor, 1957

SAMMY CAHN

❝ I really believe that I have lost more Oscars than I have won (four, count them, four) and mainly because the membership thinks I have won so many. I actually lost thirteen straight times and was starting to feel like the eternal loser when I won for the first time with Jule Styne for 'Three Coins in the Fountain.' But the 'losers' are my favorite songs and stories. I would like to ask the Board of Governors not to seat the contestants in the same category together; it really makes for over-politeness and lousy acting. One year there we were seated behind our nemesis (or is it nemesi?) the talented team of Livingston & Evans. They were nominated for 'Buttons and Bows' and Nicholas Brodszky and I for 'Be My Love.' Now the contents of the Academy Awards envelopes are the best-kept secrets of all award shows, and I always felt that if I really was the winner someone would whisper in my ear, 'Relax, it is you!' No one ever does. So you devise little tricks of trying to catch a hint of the result. That year I watched the lips of the presenter after he had opened the envelope, and sure enough his lips formed the letter 'B' so Brodszky and I started to rise when he said, 'Buttons and Bows.' Of course we slunk back in our seats, Brodszky snarling in my ear, 'It's a fix!' I smiled my customary loser's smile and said, 'If it were a fix, we would be up there!' The last time we thought we had a winner was the night when the genius James Van Heusen and I were nominated for 'Thoroughly Modern Millie,' and the songs against us were the formidable David and Bacharach smash 'The Look of Love' and an ingenious song called 'Talk to the Animals.' Well—there we were, all the contestants seated together. Bacharach turned to me and said, 'Looks like it's you again.' I, half-lying because I did think it could be me again, said, 'No way, you and Hal have never won and this has to be your year!' And so it went, 'No it's you!' and 'No it's you!' until they announced the winner for the best scoring of a musical, Elmer Bernstein! That could only mean that Van Heusen and I had to win for "Millie" because there just wasn't that much scoring to the film. By now I am half meaning it when I say to Hal and Burt, 'You two are a cinch!' I am sure you know that the winner was 'Talk to the Animals' ! Finally let me say there is no thrill quite like the thrill of hearing the man say 'and the winner is' and walking to the stage and being handed the Oscar. My 'cahn-tempt' is total for those who refuse it and for those who use it as a doorstop! Some doorstop! Mine are proudly displayed in my home, and I carry the miniature 'Oscars' in my pocket; they are the most marvelous 'worry-beads,' and I am never without them! ❞

Sammy Cahn
Music (Song), 1954; 1957; 1959; 1963

DANIEL TARADASH

❝ I am grateful indeed to the Academy for two of the most thrilling moments in my life. Each was connected with an 'Oscar,' one that I won, one that I presented. The winner was for the Best Screenplay (adaptation from another medium) for From Here To Eternity. I can't say I was surprised because the film already had won extraordinary critical acclaim and commercial success, in part because it was based on a bold book which, in 1953, just 'couldn't be made.' Still, among the other screenplays nominated in my category were those for Roman Holiday and Shane, and these were certainly magnificent works of writing. So I was on tenterhooks until Kirk Douglas announced my name. And that moment, as I'm sure every 'Oscar' winner will testify, is one you never forget.

The second 'Oscar' delight came in 1972 when, as President of the Academy, I presented a Special Honorary Academy Award (an 'Oscar' statuette) to Charlie Chaplin. To be part of the climactic moment which included the return of Chaplin to Hollywood and the Academy taking him to its heart was a thrill which is still alive in my mind and will always continue to be. ❞

Daniel Taradash
Writing (Screenplay), 1953

FRANK SINATRA

" I've been up and down in my life more often than a roller coaster on the Fourth of July. At thirty-eight years old, I was a has-been. Sitting by a phone that wouldn't ring. Wondering what happened to all the friends who grew invisible when the music stopped. Finding out fast how tough it is to borrow money when you're all washed up.

Yes, when 1953 slid down the pole in Times Square, my only collateral was a dream. A dream to end my nightmare. And what a dream it was.

It began when I dozed off after finishing an absolutely fascinating book written by a giant, James Jones. More than a book, it was a portrait of people I knew, understood and could feel, and in it I saw myself as clearly as I see myself every morning when I shave. I was Maggio. No matter who said what, I was Maggio, and Maggio was I. And I would prove it, up there on the big screen. I would prove it no matter how many tests I was asked to make, nor what the money. I was going to become Maggio if it was the last thing I ever did in life.

It was that gifted actress Mercedes McCambridge who woke me out of the dream. She stood there on the stage of the old RKO Pantages with half the world watching. I was never in better company than on that night of March 25, 1954. Eddie Albert had been brilliant in Roman Holiday. In Shane, Brandon DeWilde and Jack Palance had more than proven they were winners. And Bob Strauss had pulled off a tour de force in Stalag 17.

But God chose to smile on me that night. Mercedes, my dear, I don't know what was written on that slip of paper, but I'll thank you eternally for saying: 'And the winner is Frank Sinatra for From Here to Eternity.'

It's quite a dream. I still have it three nights a week. I'd have it seven nights a week, but I don't go to bed four nights a week.

Talk about being 'born again.' It's the one time in my life when I had such happiness I couldn't even share it with another human being. I ducked the party, lost the crowds and took a walk. Just me and Oscar. I think I relived my entire lifetime that night as I walked up and down the streets of Beverly Hills.

Even when the cop stopped me, he couldn't bring me down to earth. He was very nice about it, although I did have to wait till his partner got out of the cruiser to assure him I was who I said I was and that I hadn't stolen the statue I was carrying.

Since that night, the roller coaster

Frank Sinatra, Mercedes McCambridge, Donna Reed, Walter Brennan

evened out and every day is the Fourth of July.

Yes, I started out the third decade of the Academy of Motion Picture Arts and Sciences as the 'man least likely' and closed it out as a grateful human being, given a second shot at life.

As far as my thoughts are now in retrospect, I recall presenting a Special Oscar to Cary Grant on behalf of the Academy in 1969. In his gracious acceptance, Cary began by saying, 'Ours is a collaborative business.' True. Very true. We all help each other.

Just as armies of grips and boom men, lighting men and extras helped me on the set of Eternity in 1953, so too, now on motion picture sets all over the world, people in our industry are helping other people in our industry. Just as Burt Lancaster, Monty Clift, Deborah Kerr, Donna Reed, Ernie Borgnine and so many other warm people pushed me up on that stage of the Pantages by pushing me harder on the set in Hawaii, other artists continue in the Fraternity of Helpers which has long been the motion picture industry.

God bless you all. "

Frank Sinatra
Best Supporting Actor, 1953

DOROTHY MALONE

" CARRY ON!

At times when things seem perfect all
　about us,
And Lady Luck grants us a lucky star,
We must try to keep these memories
　forever,
For things cannot remain just as they are.

There are times when all our universe
　seems hopeless,
And all our hopes and dreams are
　smashed to bits.
It is then we have to keep our wits
　about us,
And strive against all odds to keep those
　wits!

For if all our happy moments were
　unending,
We wouldn't know the heartbreak when
　they're gone,
And learn to grit our teeth at
　disappointment—
To hold our head up high and carry on! "

Dorothy Malone
Best Supporting Actress, 1956

Dorothy Malone, Anthony Quinn, Anna Magnani, Yul Brynner

YUL BRYNNER

❝My advice:

1. Be content to be just nominated.

2. When your name is called out, make sure you don't stumble on the way to the stage, which would entitle you only to a cheap laugh.

3. Never prepare an acceptance speech until you have your hands firmly on the Oscar, otherwise it will be haunting you in the years to come as an unfulfilled dream.❞

Yul Brynner
Best Actor, 1956

RED BUTTONS

❝I am proud to own an Oscar. Some of the greatest people in the history of the world never got an Oscar.

Adam—who said in the Garden of Eden, 'I've got more ribs, have you got more girls?' —never got an Oscar.

Moses—who said at the Red Sea, 'Surf's up!' —never got an Oscar.

King Solomon—who said to his thousand wives, 'For better service, take a number' —never got an Oscar.

Amelia Earhart—who said, 'Stop looking for me; see if you can find my luggage' —never got an Oscar.

I repeat: I am proud to own an Oscar.❞

Red Buttons
Best Supporting Actor, 1957

JACK LEMMON

❝With whatever problems one faces in trying to decide which of five different performances is the best, there is still no question that the fortunate winner is receiving a very high honor indeed.

But there are many who may justifiably feel that the nomination itself is an equal honor.

Though the craft of acting is basically geared to a general audience acceptance, there is still the understandable and special pride that the actor feels when his peers deem his efforts to be worthy of an Oscar.

Long may that joy persist.❞

Jack Lemmon
Best Supporting Actor, 1955
Best Actor, 1973

EVA MARIE SAINT

❝I received the Oscar and one day later gave birth to Darrell. Both fellows have been a joy in my life.❞

Eva Marie Saint
Best Supporting Actress, 1954

JO VAN FLEET

❝I have very vivid and warm feelings about that eventful night that I won the Oscar for East of Eden. I believe the voting was somewhat different at that time. I know I was competing against myself for the nomination for I'll Cry Tomorrow and East of Eden.

I was working at Paramount at the time on Gunfight at the O.K. Corral. Edith Head kindly helped me get an evening gown, stole, gloves, etc. I was given a hair dryer in my dressing room, where I made myself up, did my own hair and dressed. I was picked up by Helen Rose's limousine and was escorted to the Awards ceremony by Sydney Guilleroff. The nominees for Best Supporting Actress were seated near the rear of the theater. When my name was called as having won, I simply did not hear it! Mr. Guilleroff said, poking me in the ribs, 'Go on. You won!' And I ran all the way down the aisle and up the steps. I was presented the Oscar by Edmond O'Brien, who was crying, and that almost made me cry too. (I did later.)

As I said, it was totally unexpected— my winning that night—and I took great pride in the fact that I did not put an advertisement in the trade papers, though I recall being asked to by some reporters who warned me that if I didn't advertise I had no chance of winning!!

Later, Jerry Lewis kindly gave me a film clip of my part of the ceremony, which I still have in my possession.

It was a great night, a beautiful experience and one I shall never forget.❞

Jo Van Fleet
Best Supporting Actress, 1955

DELBERT MANN

❝I am sure I was in a state of shock. I guess I couldn't believe it was all real. I know that I lurched into the wings without a word of thanks or appreciation to anyone.

So I appreciate the opportunity to say thanks to Paddy, to Harold Hecht, who believed in Marty so completely, to Ernie Borgnine, Betsy Blair, Joe Mantell and the rest of that beautiful company of actors, to a truly supportive staff—Paul Helmick, Joe La Shelle, Ted Haworth and all the others—and most of all to my mentor and teacher Fred Coe, who launched me and guided me and made my whole career possible.

I wish I had pulled myself together enough to say it then. I'm glad to say it now!❞

Delbert Mann
Best Director, 1955

Best Actress: Jane Wyman as Belinda
McDonald (above) in *Johnny Belinda*
(Warner Bros.; directed by Jean Negulesco).
As a stage play, *Johnny Belinda* had not
been a success, but the movie adaptation
produced by Henry Blanke was one of 1948's
most popular tickets, primarily due to
Jane Wyman's pivotal performance as a
deaf-mute farm girl in rural Nova Scotia who
is befriended by a country doctor
(Lew Ayres), and helped through the birth of
an illegitimate son whom she names
Johnny. Throughout the film's 103-minute
running time, she didn't speak a word
and, later in receiving her Oscar, and said,
"I accept this very gratefully for keeping
my mouth shut. I think I'll do it again . . ."

1948 The Twenty-First Year

After two Oscar presentations at the Shrine Auditorium, the 1948 Awards party on March 24, 1949, was given at the Academy's own theater, a 985-seat house. The primary reason for the change of locales (and the loss of some 5,750 extra seats at the Shrine) was because the major Hollywood studios—M-G-M, 20th Century-Fox, Warner Bros., Paramount and RKO Radio—had withdrawn their financial support of the Awards in order to remove rumors that they had been trying to exert their influence on voters. The new, shrunken seating capacity made it impossible to accommodate more than a fraction of those who hoped to attend, and that last-minute withdrawal of studio support had left no time for Academy officials to raise the needed funds to rent a larger location.

But the show went on, produced for the Academy by William Dozier, with Johnny Green as musical director and Robert Montgomery as master of ceremonies; presenters included the previous year's winners (Ronald Colman, Loretta Young, Edmund Gwenn, Celeste Holm) plus new screen beauties like Ava Gardner, Elizabeth Taylor and Arlene Dahl. Warner Bros. dominated the year's nominations, with three of its films—*Johnny Belinda, The Treasure of the Sierra Madre* and *Key Largo* —pulling in a total of fifteen nominations.

But England clearly dominated Oscar itself. Two British-made imports, *Hamlet* and *The Red Shoes,* won six of the night's Awards, including Oscars to *Hamlet* as Best Picture and to Laurence Olivier as Best Actor. Douglas Fairbanks, Jr. accepted the award for Olivier, who was in England.

Warner Bros. ultimately won five awards: Jane Wyman in *Johnny Belinda* as Best Actress; Claire Trevor in *Key Largo* as Best Supporting Actress; and three awards for *Treasure,* including two for John Huston (for Best Director and for writing the Best Screenplay) and one for his father, Walter Huston, as Best Supporting Actor. Said the elder Huston in his acceptance speech: "Many, many years ago, I raised a son and I said to him, 'If you ever become a writer or director, please find a good part for your old man.' " Said Miss Trevor: "May my three sons grow up to give their old lady a part . . ."

In their constant attempt to clarify Awards categories, and extend honors where justified, Academy officials decided in 1948 to—at last— honor the field of motion picture costume design, an area long neglected by Oscar. Nominees were separately classified between color films and those in black-and-white, and the first winners were Roger K. Furse for *Hamlet* (Black-and-white Costume Design) and Dorothy Jeakins and Karinska for *Joan of Arc* (Color Costume Design).

Best Picture: Hamlet (Rank-Two Cities/Universal-International release; produced and directed by Laurence Olivier) and **Best Actor: Laurence Olivier** as the Prince of Denmark (above, with Felix Aylmer) in *Hamlet.* Not until the dynamic Olivier came along did the movie medium seem a very advantageous place for Shakespeare's plays, although over 66 motion pictures had been based on his works since *Macbeth* in the silent days of 1905. Olivier seemed to have the key: he used the Bard as the basis for a movie that *moved,* and turned his *Hamlet* not only into a first-rate suspense thriller but also into the first film from a foreign land to win the Academy's Best Picture award.

(right) **The Treasure of the Sierra Madre** (Warner Bros.; produced by Henry Blanke) won Oscars for **Best Director: John Huston** and (pictured with Humphrey Bogart and Tim Holt) **Best Supporting Actor: Walter Huston** as Howard, a grizzly old-time prospector on an ill-fated expedition for gold into the treacherous Sierra Madre terrain in Mexico. Never before had a father-son team been similarly honored by the Academy; son John also received an Oscar for *Treasure's* Best Screenplay.

Nominations 1948

PICTURE

* HAMLET, Rank-Two Cities, U-I (British). Produced by Laurence Olivier.
JOHNNY BELINDA, Warner Bros. Produced by Jerry Wald.
THE RED SHOES, Rank-Archers, Eagle-Lion (British). Produced by Michael Powell and Eric Pressburger.
THE SNAKE PIT, 20th Century-Fox. Produced by Anatole Litvak and Robert Bassler.
THE TREASURE OF THE SIERRA MADRE, Warner Bros. Produced by Henry Blanke.

ACTOR

LEW AYRES in Johnny Belinda, Warner Bros.
MONTGOMERY CLIFT in The Search, Praesens Films, M-G-M (Swiss).
DAN DAILEY in When My Baby Smiles at Me, 20th Century-Fox.
* LAURENCE OLIVIER in Hamlet, Rank-Two Cities, U-I (British).
CLIFTON WEBB in Sitting Pretty, 20th Century-Fox.

ACTRESS

INGRID BERGMAN in Joan of Arc, Wanger-Sierra, RKO Radio.
OLIVIA DE HAVILLAND in The Snake Pit, 20th Century-Fox.
IRENE DUNNE in I Remember Mama, RKO Radio.
BARBARA STANWYCK in Sorry, Wrong Number, Wallis, Paramount.
* JANE WYMAN in Johnny Belinda, Warner Bros.

SUPPORTING ACTOR

CHARLES BICKFORD in Johnny Belinda, Warner Bros.
JOSE FERRER in Joan of Arc, Sierra, RKO Radio.
OSCAR HOMOLKA in I Remember Mama, RKO Radio.
* WALTER HUSTON in The Treasure of the Sierra Madre, Warner Bros.
CECIL KELLAWAY in The Luck of the Irish, 20th Century-Fox.

SUPPORTING ACTRESS

BARBARA BEL GEDDES in I Remember Mama, RKO Radio.
ELLEN CORBY in I Remember Mama, RKO Radio.
AGNES MOOREHEAD in Johnny Belinda, Warner Bros.
JEAN SIMMONS in Hamlet, Rank-Two Cities, U-I (British).
* CLAIRE TREVOR in Key Largo, Warner Bros.

DIRECTION

* JOHN HUSTON for The Treasure of the Sierra Madre, Warner Bros.
ANATOLE LITVAK for The Snake Pit, 20th Century-Fox.
JEAN NEGULESCO for Johnny Belinda, Warner Bros.
LAURENCE OLIVIER for Hamlet, Rank-Two Cities, U-I (British).
FRED ZINNEMANN for The Search, M-G-M (Swiss).

CINEMATOGRAPHY

(Black-and-White)

A FOREIGN AFFAIR, Paramount. Charles B. Lang, Jr.
I REMEMBER MAMA, RKO Radio. Nicholas Musuraca.
JOHNNY BELINDA, Warner Bros. Ted McCord.
* THE NAKED CITY, Hellinger, U-I. William Daniels.
PORTRAIT OF JENNIE, Selznick Releasing Organization. Joseph August.

(Color)

GREEN GRASS OF WYOMING, 20th Century-Fox. Charles G. Clarke.
* JOAN OF ARC, Wanger-Sierra, RKO Radio. Joseph Valentine, William V. Skall and Winton Hoch.
THE LOVES OF CARMEN, Beckworth, Columbia. William Snyder.
THE THREE MUSKETEERS, M-G-M. Robert Planck.

WRITING
—New classifications—

(Motion Picture Story)

THE LOUISIANA STORY, Robert Flaherty, Lopert. Frances Flaherty and Robert Flaherty.
THE NAKED CITY, Hellinger, U-I. Malvin Wald.
RED RIVER, Hawks-Monterey, UA. Borden Chase.
THE RED SHOES, Rank-Archers, Eagle-Lion (British). Emeric Pressburger.
* THE SEARCH, M-G-M (Swiss). Richard Schweizer and David Wechsler.

(Screenplay)

A FOREIGN AFFAIR, Paramount. Charles Brackett, Billy Wilder and Richard L. Breen.
JOHNNY BELINDA, Warner Bros. Irmgard Von Cube and Allen Vincent.
THE SEARCH, M-G-M (Swiss). Richard Schweizer and David Wechsler.
THE SNAKE PIT, 20th Century-Fox. Frank Partos and Millen Brand.
* THE TREASURE OF THE SIERRA MADRE, Warner Bros. John Huston.

ART DIRECTION-
SET DECORATION

(Black-and-White)

* HAMLET, Rank-Two Cities, U-I (British). Roger K. Furse; Carmen Dillon.
JOHNNY BELINDA, Warner Bros. Robert Haas; William Wallace.

(Color)

JOAN OF ARC, Wanger-Sierra, RKO Radio. Richard Day; Edwin Casey Roberts and Joseph Kish.
* THE RED SHOES, Rank-Archers, Eagle-Lion (British). Hein Heckroth, Arthur Lawson.

COSTUME DESIGN
(New category)

(Black-and-White)

B.F.'S DAUGHTER, M-G-M. Irene.
* HAMLET, Rank-Two Cities, U-I (British). Roger K. Furse.

(Color)

THE EMPEROR WALTZ, Paramount. Edith Head and Gile Steele.
* JOAN OF ARC, Wanger-Sierra, RKO Radio. Dorothy Jeakins and Karinska.

SOUND RECORDING

JOHNNY BELINDA, Warner Bros. Warner Bros. Sound Department.
MOONRISE, Republic. Republic Sound Department.
* THE SNAKE PIT, 20th Century-Fox. 20th Century-Fox Sound Department.

FILM EDITING

JOAN OF ARC, Wanger-Sierra, RKO Radio. Frank Sullivan.
JOHNNY BELINDA, Warner Bros. David Weisbart.
* THE NAKED CITY, Hellinger, U-I. Paul Weatherwax.
RED RIVER, Hawks-Monterey, UA. Christian Nyby.
THE RED SHOES, Rank-Archers, Eagle-Lion (British). Reginald Mills.

SPECIAL EFFECTS

DEEP WATERS, 20th Century-Fox. Ralph Hammeras, Fred Sersen, Edward Snyder and Roger Heman.
* PORTRAIT OF JENNIE, Selznick Releasing Organization. Paul Eagler, J. McMillan Johnson, Russell Shearman, Clarence Slifer, Charles Freeman and James G. Stewart.

SHORT SUBJECTS

(Cartoons)

* THE LITTLE ORPHAN, M-G-M. (Tom & Jerry). Fred Quimby, producer.
MICKEY AND THE SEAL, Disney, RKO Radio. (Pluto). Walt Disney, producer.
MOUSE WRECKERS, Warner Bros. (Looney Tunes). Edward Selzer, producer.

Joan of Arc (RKO Radio; produced by Walter Wanger) was the first film to win an Oscar for Color Costume Design; prior to 1948, the field of costume design had not been honored by the Academy. *Joan of Arc* also received a Special Award for producer Wanger, and an Academy Award for Color Cinematography; it starred Ingrid Bergman as the Maid of Orleans who effected the coronation of Charles VII in 1429 amid court intrigue and conspiracy.

The Red Shoes (Rank-Archers, released by Eagle-Lion; produced and directed by Michael Powell and Emeric Pressburger) starred Moira Shearer (above, dancing *The Red Shoes Ballet* with Robert Helpmann) and won Oscars for Color Art Direction and Best Score of a Dramatic or Comedy Picture. Like *Hamlet,* it was a British-made stunner which elevated the movies' postwar image and found great favor with audiences and with Hollywood's Academy membership.

Best Supporting Actress: Claire Trevor as Gaye Dawn in *Key Largo* (Warner Bros.; directed by John Huston). Long a Hollywood workhorse, and always a favorite with moviegoers, Claire Trevor won her Award playing the whiskey-soaked mistress of a cruel gangster (Edward G. Robinson, below) on a rampage in Florida. She was also nominated for *Dead End* in 1939, and in 1954 for *The High and the Mighty.*

ROBIN HOODLUM, UPA, Columbia. (Fox & Crow). United Productions of America, producer.
TEA FOR TWO HUNDRED, Disney, RKO Radio. (Donald Duck). Walt Disney, producer.

(One-reel)
ANNIE WAS A WONDER, M-G-M. (John Nesbitt Passing Parade). Herbert Moulton, producer.
CINDERELLA HORSE, Warner Bros. (Sports Parade). Gordon Hollingshead, producer.
SO YOU WANT TO BE ON THE RADIO, Warner Bros. (Joe McDoakes). Gordon Hollingshead, producer.
* SYMPHONY OF A CITY, 20th Century-Fox. (Movietone Specialty). Edmund H. Reek, producer.
YOU CAN'T WIN, M-G-M. (Pete Smith Specialty). Pete Smith, producer.

(Two-reel)
CALGARY STAMPEDE, Warner Bros. (Technicolor Special). Gordon Hollingshead, producer.
GOING TO BLAZES, M-G-M. (Special). Herbert Morgan, producer.
SAMBA-MANIA, Paramount. (Musical Parade). Harry Grey, producer.
* SEAL ISLAND, Disney, RKO Radio. (True-Life Adventure). Walt Disney, producer.
SNOW CAPERS, U-I. (Special Series). Thomas Mead, producer.

DOCUMENTARY

(Short Subjects)
HEART TO HEART, Fact Film Organization. Herbert Morgan, producer.
OPERATION VITTLES, U.S. Army Air Force.
* TOWARD INDEPENDENCE, U.S. Army.

(Features)
THE QUIET ONE, Mayer-Burstyn. Janice Loeb, producer.
* THE SECRET LAND, U.S. Navy, M-G-M. O.O. Dull, producer.

MUSIC

(Song)
* BUTTONS AND BOWS (*The Paleface,* Paramount); Music and Lyrics by Jay Livingston and Ray Evans.
FOR EVERY MAN THERE'S A WOMAN (*Casbah,* Marston, U-I); Music by Harold Arlen. Lyrics by Leo Robin.
IT'S MAGIC (*Romance on the High Seas,* Warner Bros.); Music by Jule Styne. Lyrics by Sammy Cahn.
THIS IS THE MOMENT (*That Lady In Ermine,* 20th Century-Fox); Music by Frederick Hollander. Lyrics by Leo Robin.
THE WOODY WOODPECKER SONG (*Wet Blanket Policy,* Lantz, UA Cartoon); Music and Lyrics by Ramey Idriss and George Tibbles.

(Scoring of a Dramatic or Comedy Picture)
HAMLET, Rank-Two Cities, U-I (British). William Walton.
JOAN OF ARC, Wanger-Sierra, RKO Radio. Hugo Friedhofer.
JOHNNY BELINDA, Warner Bros. Max Steiner.
* THE RED SHOES, Rank-Archers, Eagle-Lion (British). Brian Easdale.
THE SNAKE PIT, 20th Century-Fox. Alfred Newman.

(Scoring of a Musical Picture)
* EASTER PARADE, M-G-M. Johnny Green and Roger Edens.
THE EMPEROR WALTZ, Paramount. Victor Young.
THE PIRATE, M-G-M. Lennie Hayton.
ROMANCE ON THE HIGH SEAS, Warner Bros. Ray Heindorf.
WHEN MY BABY SMILES AT ME, 20th Century-Fox. Alfred Newman.

SPECIAL AWARDS

TO MONSIEUR VINCENT (French)— voted by the Academy Board of Governors as the most outstanding foreign language film released in the United States during 1948. (statuette)
TO IVAN JANDL, for the outstanding juvenile performance of 1948 in *The Search.* (miniature statuette)
TO SID GRAUMAN, master showman, who raised the standard of exhibition of motion pictures. (statuette)
TO ADOLPH ZUKOR, a man who has been called the father of the feature film in America, for his services to the industry over a period of forty years. (statuette)
TO WALTER WANGER for distinguished service to the industry in adding to its moral stature in the world community by his production of the picture *Joan of Arc.* (statuette)

1948 IRVING G. THALBERG MEMORIAL AWARD

TO JERRY WALD

SCIENTIFIC OR TECHNICAL

CLASS I (statuette)
None.

CLASS II (plaque)
VICTOR CACCIALANZA, MAURICE AYERS and the PARAMOUNT STUDIO SET CONSTRUCTION DEPARTMENT for the development and application of "Paralite," a new lightweight plaster process for set construction.

NICK KALTEN, LOUIS J. WITTI and the 20TH CENTURY-FOX STUDIO MECHANICAL EFFECTS DEPARTMENT for a process of preserving and flame-proofing foliage.

CLASS III (citation)
MARTY MARTIN, JACK LANNON, RUSSELL SHEARMAN and the RKO RADIO STUDIO SPECIAL EFFECTS DEPARTMENT;
A.J. MORAN and the WARNER BROS. STUDIO ELECTRICAL DEPARTMENT.

* INDICATES WINNER

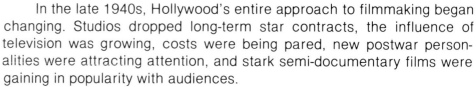

1949

The Twenty-Second Year

In the late 1940s, Hollywood's entire approach to filmmaking began changing. Studios dropped long-term star contracts, the influence of television was growing, costs were being pared, new postwar personalities were attracting attention, and stark semi-documentary films were gaining in popularity with audiences.

One thing didn't change: the Academy's appreciation of quality films. On March 23, 1950, at the 1949 Academy Awards presentation, the most honored picture of the year was Paramount's *The Heiress* with four awards, including one to Olivia de Havilland as Best Actress, the second time she had been so honored in three years. Columbia's stark, powerful *All the King's Men* received three awards (Best Picture, Broderick Crawford as Best Actor, newcomer Mercedes McCambridge as Best Supporting Actress) and *A Letter to Three Wives* won two, both of them for Joseph L. Mankiewicz (as Best Director, and author of Best Screenplay).

Best Supporting Actor was Dean Jagger in *12 O'Clock High,* a film also honored for its Sound Recording. The booming war story *Battleground* won two Awards: one for Robert Pirosh's Story and Screenplay, and one for Paul Vogel's Black-and-white Cinematography.

The site for the Awards was moved again, for the third time in four years, this time to the 2,812-seat RKO Pantages Theatre, the biggest motion picture house in Hollywood. The ceremony remained there for the next eleven years. Paul Douglas, a long-time stage veteran but new Hollywood name via Mankiewicz' *A Letter to Three Wives,* was the evening's M.C., and Johnny Green turned over his musical baton to Robert Emmett Dolan and was sole producer of the Academy show.

Two other Special Awards provided the evening with sizeable impact, primarily because they went to a pair of screen innovators who had never been honored before, both of whom were helpful in keeping the public on the big screen and away from that (supposedly) threatening television box. One went to Fred Astaire; it was presented by Ginger Rogers, with whom he had been reunited after a ten-year absence in 1949's *The Barkley's of Broadway.* The other Special Award went to Cecil B. DeMille for his 37 years of screen showmanship; *Samson and Delilah,* his first new film in two years, had not been released in Los Angeles in time for 1949 Awards eligibility, but it was helpful in bringing public focus to a grand old filmmaker.

Best Picture: All the King's Men (Columbia; produced and directed by Robert Rossen) and **Best Actor: Broderick Crawford** as Willie Stark and **Best Supporting Actress: Mercedes McCambridge** as Sadie Burke in *All the King's Men.* A bold and blunt drama based on Robert Penn Warren's Pulitzer Prize novel about a corrupt political boss who bore a close resemblance to Louisiana's powerful Huey Long, stopped by an assassin's bullet in 1935. It was a first film for Mercedes McCambridge, a veteran radio actress, and a bellringer for Crawford, who'd made three dozen films before but never had such a meaty role to play. The cast included Joanne Dru, John Ireland, John Derek and Shepperd Strudwick; Rossen also wrote the screenplay.

The Adventures of Don Juan (Warner Bros.; produced by Jerry Wald) was a sumptuous swashbuckling epic in the Errol Flynn tradition, on the drawing boards since 1945 but finally filmed and especially notable for its magnificent costumes which won the Color Costume Design Academy Award for designers Leah Rhodes, Travilla and Marjorie Best. Viveca Lindfors played Queen Margaret of 17th-century Spain and Flynn—in his last big budget actioner at Warner Bros.—played the frisky Don.

Best Actress: Olivia de Havilland as Catherine Sloper (right, with Ralph Richardson) in *The Heiress* (Paramount; directed by William Wyler). *The Heiress* was derived via a Broadway play from Henry James' novel *Washington Square,* about an awkward girl of the 1850s dominated by her wealthy father and bitterly disillusioned by a handsome fortune hunter, on whom she finally gets sweet revenge. Olivia de Havilland brilliantly played the multi-faceted woman and won the second Academy Award of her career; the picture itself also won more Oscars than any other 1949 film, including ones for Art Direction (Black-and-White), Costume Design (Black-and-White) and Music Score.

Nominations 1949

PICTURE

* **ALL THE KING'S MEN,** Rossen, Columbia. Produced by Robert Rossen.
BATTLEGROUND, M-G-M. Produced by Dore Schary.
THE HEIRESS, Paramount. Produced by William Wyler.
A LETTER TO THREE WIVES, 20th Century-Fox. Produced by Sol C. Siegel.
12 O'CLOCK HIGH, 20th Century-Fox. Produced by Darryl F. Zanuck.

ACTOR

* **BRODERICK CRAWFORD** in *All the King's Men,* Rossen, Columbia.
KIRK DOUGLAS in *Champion,* Kramer, UA.
GREGORY PECK in *12 O'Clock High,* 20th Century-Fox.
RICHARD TODD in *The Hasty Heart,* Warner Bros.
JOHN WAYNE in *Sands of Iwo Jima,* Republic.

ACTRESS

JEANNE CRAIN in *Pinky,* 20th Century-Fox.
* **OLIVIA DE HAVILLAND** in *The Heiress,* Paramount.
SUSAN HAYWARD in *My Foolish Heart,* Goldwyn, RKO Radio.
DEBORAH KERR in *Edward, My Son,* M-G-M.
LORETTA YOUNG in *Come to the Stable,* 20th Century-Fox

SUPPORTING ACTOR

JOHN IRELAND in *All the King's Men,* Rossen, Columbia.
* **DEAN JAGGER** in *12 O'Clock High,* 20th Century-Fox.
ARTHUR KENNEDY in *Champion,* Kramer, UA.
RALPH RICHARDSON in *The Heiress,* Paramount.
JAMES WHITMORE in *Battleground,* M-G-M.

SUPPORTING ACTRESS

ETHEL BARRYMORE in *Pinky,* 20th Century-Fox.

CELESTE HOLM in *Come to the Stable,* 20th Century-Fox.
ELSA LANCHESTER in *Come to the Stable,* 20th Century-Fox.
* **MERCEDES McCAMBRIDGE** in *All the King's Men,* Rossen, Columbia.
ETHEL WATERS in *Pinky,* 20th Century-Fox.

DIRECTION

* **JOSEPH L. MANKIEWICA** for *A Letter to Three Wives,* 20th Century-Fox.
CAROL REED for *The Fallen Idol,* London Films, SRO (British).
ROBERT ROSSEN for *All the King's Men,* Rossen, Columbia.
WILLIAM A. WELLMAN for *Battleground,* M-G-M.
WILLIAM WYLER for *The Heiress,* Paramount.

ART DIRECTION-SET DECORATION

(Black-and-White)

COME TO THE STABLE, 20th Century-Fox. Lyle Wheeler and Joseph C. Wright; Thomas Little and Paul S. Fox.
* **THE HEIRESS,** Paramount. John Meehan and Harry Horner; Emile Kuri.
MADAME BOVARY, M-G-M. Cedric Gibbons and Jack Martin Smith; Edwin B. Willis and Richard A. Pefferle.

(Color)

ADVENTURES OF DON JUAN, Warner Bros. Edward Carrere; Lyle Reifsnider.
* **LITTLE WOMEN,** M-G-M. Cedric Gibbons and Paul Groesse; Edwin B. Willis and Jack D. Moore.
SARABAND, Rank-Ealing, Eagle-Lion (British). Jim Morahan, William Kellner and Michael Relph.

WRITING

—New classification—

(Motion Picture Story)

COME TO THE STABLE, 20th Century-Fox. Clare Booth Luce.
IT HAPPENS EVERY SPRING, 20th Century-Fox. Shirley W. Smith and Valentine Davies.
SANDS OF IWO JIMA, Republic. Harry Brown.

* **THE STRATTON STORY,** M-G-M. Douglas Morrow.
WHITE HEAT, Warner Bros. Virginia Kellogg.

(Screenplay)

ALL THE KING'S MEN, Rossen, Columbia. Robert Rossen.
THE BICYCLE THIEF, De Sica, Mayer-Burstyn (Italian). Cesare Zavattini.
CHAMPION, Kramer, UA. Carl Foreman.
THE FALLEN IDOL, London Films, SRO (British). Graham Greene.
* **A LETTER TO THREE WIVES,** 20th Century-Fox. Joseph L. Mankiewicz.

(Story and Screenplay)

* **BATTLEGROUND,** M-G-M. Robert Pirosh.
JOLSON SINGS AGAIN, Columbia. Sidney Buchman.
PAISAN, Rossellini, Mayer-Burstyn (Italian). Alfred Hayes, Federico Fellini, Sergio Amidei, Marcello Pagliero and Roberto Rossellini.
PASSPORT TO PIMLICO, Rank-Ealing, Eagle-Lion (British). T.E.B. Clarke.
THE QUIET ONE, Film Documents, Mayer-Burstyn. Helen Levitt, Janice Loeb and Sidney Meyers.

CINEMATOGRAPHY

(Black-and-White)

* **BATTLEGROUND,** M-G-M. Paul C. Vogel.
CHAMPION, Kramer, UA. Frank Planer.
COME TO THE STABLE, 20th Century-Fox. Joseph LaShelle.
THE HEIRESS, Paramount. Leo Tover.
PRINCE OF FOXES, 20th Century-Fox. Leon Shamroy.

(Color)

THE BARKLEYS OF BROADWAY, M-G-M. Harry Stradling.
JOLSON SINGS AGAIN, Columbia. William Snyder.
LITTLE WOMEN, M-G-M. Robert Planck and Charles Schoenbaum.
SAND, 20th Century-Fox. Charles G. Clarke.
* **SHE WORE A YELLOW RIBBON,** Argosy, RKO Radio. Winton Hoch.

SOUND RECORDING

ONCE MORE, MY DARLING, U-I. Universal-International Sound Department.
SANDS OF IWO JIMA, Republic. Republic Sound Department.
* **12 O'CLOCK HIGH,** 20th Century-Fox. 20th Century-Fox Sound Department.

FILM EDITING

ALL THE KING'S MEN, Rossen, Columbia. Robert Parrish and Al Clark.
BATTLEGROUND, M-G-M. John Dunning.
* **CHAMPION,** Kramer, UA. Harry Gerstad.
SANDS OF IWO JIMA, Republic. Richard L. Van Enger.
THE WINDOW, RKO Radio. Frederic Knudtson.

SPECIAL EFFECTS

* **MIGHTY JOE YOUNG,** Cooper, RKO Radio.
TULSA, Wanger, Eagle-Lion.

MUSIC

(Song)

* **BABY, IT'S COLD OUTSIDE** (*Neptune's Daughter,* M-G-M.); Music and Lyrics by Frank Loesser.
IT'S A GREAT FEELING (*It's A Great Feeling,* Warner Bros.); Music by Jule Styne. Lyrics by Sammy Cahn.
LAVENDER BLUE (*So Dear To My Heart,* Disney, RKO Radio); Music by Eliot Daniel. Lyrics by Larry Morey.
MY FOOLISH HEART (*My Foolish Heart,* Goldwyn, RKO Radio); Music by Victor Young. Lyrics by Ned Washington.
THROUGH A LONG AND SLEEPLESS NIGHT (*Come To The Stable,* 20th Century-Fox); Music by Alfred Newman. Lyrics by Mack Gordon.

(Scoring of a Dramatic or Comedy Picture)

BEYOND THE FOREST, Warner Bros. Max Steiner.
CHAMPION, Kramer, UA. Dimitri Tiomkin.
* **THE HEIRESS,** Paramount. Aaron Copland.

(Scoring of a Musical Picture)

JOLSON SINGS AGAIN, Columbia. Morris Stoloff and George Duning.
LOOK FOR THE SILVER LINING, Warner Bros. Ray Heindorf.
* **ON THE TOWN,** M-G-M. Roger Edens and Lennie Hayton.

SHORT SUBJECTS

(Cartoons)

* **FOR SCENT-IMENTAL REASONS,** Warner Bros. (Looney Tunes). Edward Selzer, producer.
HATCH UP YOUR TROUBLES, M-G-M. (Tom & Jerry). Fred Quimby, producer.
MAGIC FLUKE, UPA, Columbia. (Fox & Crow). Stephen Bosustow, producer.
TOY TINKERS, Disney, RKO Radio. Walt Disney, producer.

She Wore a Yellow Ribbon (RKO Radio; directed by John Ford) was a big-boned and Technicolored western with John Wayne as a United States Cavalry captain heading troops across silhouetted plains and through dangerous Indian territory. It won Winton Hoch the Oscar for Color Cinematography, and remains one of the best-liked films in the Ford-Wayne list of collaborations.

1848, A.F. Films, Inc. French Cinema General Cooperative, producer.
THE RISING TIDE, National Film Board of Canada. St. Francis-Xavier University (Nova Scotia), producer.
* SO MUCH FOR SO LITTLE, Warner Bros. Edward Selzer, producer.

(Features)
* DAYBREAK IN UDI, British Information Services. Crown Film Unit, producer.
KENJI COMES HOME, A Protestant Film Commission Prod. Paul F. Heard, producer.

(One-reel)
* AQUATIC HOUSE-PARTY, Paramount. (Grantland Rice Sportlights). Jack Eaton, producer.
ROLLER DERBY GIRL, Paramount. (Pacemaker). Justin Herman, producer.
SO YOU THINK YOU'RE NOT GUILTY, Warner Bros. (Joe McDoakes). Gordon Hollingshead, producer.
SPILLS AND CHILLS, Warner Bros. (Sports Review). Walton C. Ament, producer.
WATER TRIX, M-G-M. (Pete Smith Specialty). Pete Smith, producer.

(Two-reel)
BOY AND THE EAGLE, RKO Radio. William Lasky, producer.
CHASE OF DEATH, Irving Allen Productions. Irving Allen, producer.
THE GRASS IS ALWAYS GREENER, Warner Bros. Gordon Hollingshead, producer.
SNOW CARNIVAL, Warner Bros. Gordon Hollingshead, producer.
* VAN GOGH, Canton-Weiner. Gaston Diehl and Robert Haessens, producers.

COSTUME DESIGN

(Black-and-White)
* THE HEIRESS, Paramount. Edith Head and Gile Steele.
PRINCE OF FOXES, 20th Century-Fox. Vittorio Nino Novarese.

(Color)
* ADVENTURES OF DON JUAN, Warner Bros. Leah Rhodes, Travilla and Marjorie Best.
MOTHER IS A FRESHMAN, 20th Century-Fox. Kay Nelson.

DOCUMENTARY

(Short Subjects)
* A CHANCE TO LIVE, March of Time, 20th Century-Fox. Richard de Rochemont, producer.

SPECIAL AWARDS

TO THE BICYCLE THIEF (Italian)—voted by the Academy Board of Governors as the most outstanding foreign language film released in the United States during 1949. (statuette)
TO BOBBY DRISCOLL, as the outstanding juvenile actor of 1949. (miniature statuette)
TO FRED ASTAIRE for his unique artistry and his contributions to the technique of musical pictures. (statuette)
TO CECIL B. DeMILLE, distinguished motion picture pioneer, for 37 years of brilliant showmanship. (statuette)
TO JEAN HERSHOLT, for distinguished service to the motion picture industry. (statuette)

1949 IRVING G. THALBERG MEMORIAL AWARD

None given this year.

SCIENTIFIC OR TECHNICAL

CLASS I (statuette)
EASTMAN KODAK CO. for the development and introduction of an improved safety base motion picture film.

CLASS II (plaque)
None.

CLASS III (citation)
LOREN L. RYDER, BRUCE H. DENNEY, ROBERT CARR and the PARAMOUNT STUDIO SOUND DEPARTMENT;
M.B. PAUL;
HERBERT BRITT;
ANDRE COUTANT and JACQUES MATHOT;
CHARLES R. DAILY, STEVE CSILLAG and the PARAMOUNT STUDIO ENGINEERING, EDITORIAL and MUSIC DEPARTMENTS;
INTERNATIONAL PROJECTOR CORP.;
ALEXANDER VELCOFF.

★ INDICATES WINNER

Best Supporting Actor: Dean Jagger as Major Stovall (above, with Gregory Peck) in *12 O'Clock High* (20th Century-Fox; directed by Henry King). A personal production of Darryl F. Zanuck, *12 O'Clock High* was a psychological drama of World War II, dealing with problems inside an American bomber base in England; Jagger was a middle-aged major assigned to the base which Peck—as a young general—turns into an inspired, forceful unit.

Best Director: Joseph L. Mankiewicz for *A Letter to Three Wives* (20th Century-Fox; produced by Sol Siegel) presented Linda Darnell, Ann Sothern and Jeanne Crain (right) as three wives who receive a letter from a local friend informing them she has just run off with the husband of one. But which one? An intriguing premise, artfully handled, *A Letter* also won a second 1949 Academy Award for Mankiewicz: as author of the year's Best Screenplay. The following year, with 1950's *All About Eve,* he again won in the same two Oscar categories.

Best Picture: All About Eve (20th Century-Fox; produced by Darryl F. Zanuck), **Best Director: Joseph L. Mankiewicz** and (left, with Anne Baxter, Bette Davis and Marilyn Monroe) **Best Supporting Actor: George Sanders** as Addison DeWitt in *All About Eve*. Mankiewicz used a Mary Orr short story, "The Wisdom of Eve," as a foundation for his stingingly comic examination of the New York theatrical jungle and came up with a creative and original zinger ultimately nominated for a record fourteen Academy Awards, winning six of them. *All About Eve* followed the intermingled lives of an aging Broadway actress, a young director, a dedicated playwright and his nonprofessional wife as they are affected by a dangerously ambitious young actress. Sanders won his Oscar as a cynical critic who takes the girl under his wing. Everyone involved was meticulously cast, including Celeste Holm, Hugh Marlowe, Gary Merrill, Thelma Ritter and Gregory Ratoff.

Sunset Boulevard (Paramount; produced by Charles Brackett) gave Hollywood the same kind of naked examination *All About Eve* gave to Broadway, with Gloria Swanson (right) as a past-tense movie queen unable to make a transition into private life as a human being. It was directed by Billy Wilder, co-starred William Holden, Erich Von Stroheim and Nancy Olson, and won three Oscars, including writing statuettes for Wilder, Brackett and D.M. Marshman, Jr. *Sunset Boulevard* also helped make moviegoing decidedly worthwhile in the days when television was beginning to grab a foothold on the affection—and the pocketbooks—of audiences.

1950

The Twenty-Third Year

Hollywood took some sharp jabs at the world of the legitimate theater in 1950's *All About Eve,* then told some equally painful truths about itself in *Sunset Boulevard,* easily two of the best films of the year. Between them, they were nominated for twenty-five Academy Awards. *Eve,* in fact, became Oscar's most-nominated film ever, with fourteen acknowledgments, competing with itself in categories such as the Best Actress (Bette Davis and Anne Baxter) and the Best Supporting Actress (Celeste Holm and Thelma Ritter) divisions. There was an abundance of other good work, too: *Born Yesterday* (four nominations), *Samson and Delilah* (five), *The Third Man* (three), *Father of the Bride* (three), *The Asphalt Jungle* (four), *Annie Get Your Gun* (four), *King Solomon's Mines* (three), *Adam's Rib* (one), among others.

When awards were handed out, March 29, 1951, at the RKO Pantages Theatre in Hollywood, *Eve* and *Sunset* still held center stage with the biggest Oscar totals for the year. *All About Eve* was honored with six awards, including Best Picture, Best Director (Joseph L. Mankiewicz) and Best Supporting Actor (George Sanders). Mankiewicz also won for Best Screenplay, making the second year in a row he had won in both the Director-Screenplay categories. *Sunset Boulevard* received three awards: Best Story and Screenplay, Best Art Direction and Best Dramatic Score.

The world of the theater was also evident in the evening's other acting Awards. Judy Holliday was named Best Actress for *Born Yesterday,* a role she had played extensively on the Broadway stage. Jose Ferrer was chosen Best Actor for *Cyrano de Bergerac,* which he had also played before on the boards. The same is true of Josephine Hull, named Best Supporting Actress for *Harvey.* Louis B. Mayer, outgoing head of the M-G-M Studio empire, was voted an Honorary Oscar for his distinguished service to the motion picture industry, and the Franco-Italian *The Walls of Malapaga* received an Honorary Award as the year's outstanding foreign language film.

The ceremony itself was produced by Richard L. Breen and hosted by Fred Astaire, but most of the winners (and several nominees) who were currently in New York plays held their own party at the La Zambra cafe there, listening to the results on an ABC radio broadcast. Back in Hollywood, Marlene Dietrich wore a dress that exposed the famous Dietrich legs to the knee and stole the show as she climbed the stairs to the stage to present an Award. The evening was blessed with showmanship, just as 1950 had been brightened by some superior films.

Best Actor: Jose Ferrer as Cyrano (at right) in *Cyrano de Bergerac* (United Artists; directed by Michael Gordon). *Cyrano,* produced by Stanley Kramer, was an adaptation of Edmond Rostand's famous love story about a poetic, swaggering swordsman in 17th-century Paris who possessed an oversized nose and a secret passion for a damsel named Roxanne; in the title role Ferrer gave a robustly appealing performance, wearing a lengthy 2¾-inch beak which was created by Josef and Gustaf Norin. Earlier, Pierre Magnier had played Cyrano in a silent 1925 movie version, and Ferrer again played him in a 1964 French film, *Cyrano and D'Artagnan.*

Best Actress: Judy Holliday as Billie Dawn in *Born Yesterday* (Columbia; directed by George Cukor). Judy Holliday played Billie Dawn on the Broadway stage for three years and 1,200 performances to enormous success but almost didn't get the movie role; Columbia studio boss Harry Cohn bought the property for Rita Hayworth, then spent two years testing and considering every other young actress in Hollywood. When she did play it on film, she was an instant success as the dumb blonde mistress of a corrupt tycoon (Broderick Crawford) who is tutored by a magazine writer (William Holden) while visiting Washington, D.C., and learns to think for herself.

Nominations 1950

PICTURE

★ **ALL ABOUT EVE**, 20th Century-Fox. Produced by Darryl F. Zanuck.
BORN YESTERDAY, Columbia. Produced by S. Sylvan Simon.
FATHER OF THE BRIDE, M-G-M. Produced by Pandro S. Berman.
KING SOLOMON'S MINES, M-G-M. Produced by Sam Zimbalist.
SUNSET BOULEVARD, Paramount. Produced by Charles Brackett.

ACTOR

LOUIS CALHERN in *The Magnificent Yankee*, M-G-M.
★ **JOSE FERRER** in *Cyrano de Bergerac*, Kramer, UA.
WILLIAM HOLDEN in *Sunset Boulevard*, Paramount.
JAMES STEWART in *Harvey*, U-I.
SPENCER TRACY in *Father of the Bride*, M-G-M.

ACTRESS

ANNE BAXTER in *All About Eve*, 20th Century-Fox.
BETTE DAVIS in *All About Eve*, 20th Century-Fox.
★ **JUDY HOLLIDAY** in *Born Yesterday*, Columbia.
ELEANOR PARKER in *Caged*, Warner Bros.
GLORIA SWANSON in *Sunset Boulevard*, Paramount.

SUPPORTING ACTOR

JEFF CHANDLER in *Broken Arrow*, 20th Century-Fox.
EDMUND GWENN in *Mister 880*, 20th Century-Fox.
SAM JAFFE in *The Asphalt Jungle*, M-G-M.
★ **GEORGE SANDERS** in *All About Eve*, 20th Century-Fox.
ERICH VON STROHEIM in *Sunset Boulevard*, Paramount.

SUPPORTING ACTRESS

HOPE EMERSON in *Caged*, Warner Bros.
CELESTE HOLM in *All About Eve*, 20th Century-Fox.
★ **JOSEPHINE HULL** in *Harvey*, U-I.

NANCY OLSON in *Sunset Boulevard*, Paramount.
THELMA RITTER in *All About Eve*, 20th Century-Fox.

DIRECTION

GEORGE CUKOR for *Born Yesterday*, Columbia.
JOHN HUSTON for *The Asphalt Jungle*, M-G-M.
★ **JOSEPH L. MANKIEWICZ** for *All About Eve*, 20th Century-Fox.
CAROL REED for *The Third Man*, Selznick-London Films, SRO (British).
BILLY WILDER for *Sunset Boulevard*, Paramount.

WRITING

(Motion Picture Story)
BITTER RICE, Lux Films (Italian). Giuseppe De Santis and Carlo Lizzani.
THE GUNFIGHTER, 20th Century-Fox. William Bowers and Andre de Tóth.
MYSTERY STREET, M-G-M. Leonard Spigelgass.
★ **PANIC IN THE STREETS**, 20th Century-Fox. Edna Anhalt and Edward Anhalt.
WHEN WILLIE COMES MARCHING HOME, 20th Century-Fox. Sy Gomberg.

(Screenplay)
★ **ALL ABOUT EVE**, 20th Century-Fox. Joseph L. Mankiewicz.
THE ASPHALT JUNGLE, M-G-M. Ben Maddow and John Huston.
BORN YESTERDAY, Columbia. Albert Mannheimer.
BROKEN ARROW, 20th Century-Fox. Michael Blankfort.
FATHER OF THE BRIDE, M-G-M. Frances Goodrich and Albert Hackett.

(Story and Screenplay)
ADAM'S RIB, M-G-M. Ruth Gordon and Garson Kanin.
CAGED, Warner Bros. Virginia Kellogg and Bernard C. Schoenfeld.
THE MEN, Kramer, UA. Carl Foreman.
NO WAY OUT, 20th Century-Fox. Joseph L. Mankiewicz and Lesser Samuels.
★ **SUNSET BOULEVARD**, Paramount. Charles Brackett, Billy Wilder and D.M. Marshman, Jr.

CINEMATOGRAPHY

(Black-and-White)
ALL ABOUT EVE, 20th Century-Fox. Milton Krasner.
THE ASPHALT JUNGLE, M-G-M. Harold Rosson.
THE FURIES, Wallis, Paramount. Victor Milner.
SUNSET BOULEVARD, Paramount. John F. Seitz.
★ **THE THIRD MAN**, Selznick-London Films, SRO (British). Robert Krasker.

(Color)
ANNIE GET YOUR GUN, M-G-M. Charles Rosher.
BROKEN ARROW, 20th Century-Fox. Ernest Palmer.
THE FLAME AND THE ARROW, Norma, Warner Bros. Ernest Haller.
★ **KING SOLOMON'S MINES**, M-G-M. Robert Surtees.
SAMSON AND DELILAH, DeMille, Paramount. George Barnes.

ART DIRECTION-SET DECORATION

(Black-and-White)
ALL ABOUT EVE, 20th Century-Fox. Lyle Wheeler and George Davis; Thomas Little and Walter M. Scott.
THE RED DANUBE, M-G-M. Cedric Gibbons and Hans Peters; Edwin B. Willis and Hugh Hunt.
★ **SUNSET BOULEVARD**, Paramount. Hans Dreier and John Meehan; Sam Comer and Ray Moyer.

(Color)
ANNIE GET YOUR GUN, M-G-M. Cedric Gibbons and Paul Groesse; Edwin B. Willis and Richard A. Pefferle.
DESTINATION MOON, Pal, Eagle-Lion. Ernst Fegte; George Sawley.
★ **SAMSON AND DELILAH**, DeMille, Paramount. Hans Dreier and Walter Tyler; Sam Comer and Ray Moyer.

COSTUME DESIGN

(Black-and-White)
★ **ALL ABOUT EVE**, 20th Century-Fox. Edith Head and Charles LeMaire.
BORN YESTERDAY, Columbia. Jean Louis.
THE MAGNIFICENT YANKEE, M-G-M. Walter Plunkett.

(Color)
THE BLACK ROSE, 20th Century-Fox. Michael Whittaker.

★ **SAMSON AND DELILAH**, DeMille, Paramount. Edith Head, Dorothy Jeakins, Elois Jenssen, Gile Steele and Gwen Wakeling.
THAT FORSYTE WOMAN, M-G-M. Walter Plunkett and Valles.

SOUND RECORDING

★ **ALL ABOUT EVE**, 20th Century-Fox. 20th Century-Fox Sound department.
CINDERELLA, Disney, RKO Radio. Disney Sound Department.
LOUISA, U-I. Universal-International Sound Department.
OUR VERY OWN, Goldwyn, RKO Radio. Goldwyn Sound Department.
TRIO, Rank-Sydney Box, Paramount (British).

FILM EDITING

ALL ABOUT EVE, 20th Century-Fox. Barbara McLean.
ANNIE GET YOUR GUN, M-G-M. James E. Newcom.
★ **KING SOLOMON'S MINES**, M-G-M. Ralph E. Winters and Conrad A. Nervig.
SUNSET BOULEVARD, Paramount. Arthur Schmidt and Doane Harrison.
THE THIRD MAN, Selznick-London Films, SRO (British). Oswald Hafenrichter.

SPECIAL EFFECTS

★ **DESTINATION MOON**, Pal, Eagle-Lion.
SAMSON AND DELILAH, DeMille, Paramount.

MUSIC

(Song)
BE MY LOVE (*The Toast of New Orleans*, M-G-M); Music by Nicholas Brodszky. Lyrics by Sammy Cahn.
BIBBIDY-BOBBIDI-BOO (*Cinderella*, Disney, RKO Radio); Music and Lyrics by Mack David, Al Hoffman and Jerry Livingston.
★ **MONA LISA** (*Captain Carey, USA*, Paramount); Music and Lyrics by Ray Evans and Jay Livingston.
MULE TRAIN (*Singing Guns*, Republic); Music and Lyrics by Fred Glickman, Hy Heath and Johnny Lange.
WILHELMINA (*Wabash Avenue*, 20th Century-Fox); Music by Josef Myrow. Lyrics by Mack Gordon.

(Scoring of a Dramatic or Comedy Picture)
ALL ABOUT EVE, 20th Century-Fox. Alfred Newman.
THE FLAME AND THE ARROW, Norma, Warner Bros. Max Steiner.

(left) **King Solomon's Mines** (M-G-M; produced by Sam Zimbalist). M-G-M actually took cast and crew to Africa to shoot the major portions of this remake of H. Rider Haggard's adventure classic about a safari into unchartered areas of the continent, searching for a lost explorer who had gone hunting for the legendary diamond mine. It starred Stewart Granger, Deborah Kerr and Richard Carlson, featured dozens of Watutsi natives and won Oscars for Color Cinematography by Robert Surtees and the Film Editing of Ralph E. Winters and Conrad A. Nervig.

(right) **Best Supporting Actress: Josephine Hull** as Veda Louise Simmons in *Harvey* (Universal-International; directed by Henry Koster). Josephine Hull had an extremely abbreviated screen career—only three movies in the sound era—but two of those appearances preserved on film a pair of her most famous stage roles: the sweet little poison-serving aunt in *Arsenic and Old Lace,* and (at right, with James Stewart) in *Harvey* as the daffy, long-suffering sister of a man who chums around with an invisible rabbit, for which she won an Academy Award. Her third and final film, in 1951, was called *The Lady from Texas.*

The Third Man (Selznick Releasing Organization; directed by Carol Reed) won an Oscar for Robert Krasker's Cinematography (Black-and-White), most of it done on Vienna's cobbled and starkly colorful streets. Orson Welles (below) starred as a mystery man named Harry Lime, involved in postwar black marketeering, while eerie zither music hummed *The Third Man Theme* in the background. Graham Greene wrote the screenplay from his own novel.

NO SAD SONGS FOR ME, Columbia. George Duning.
SAMSON AND DELILAH, Paramount. Victor Young.
* SUNSET BOULEVARD, Paramount. Franz Waxman.

(Scoring of a Musical Picture)
* ANNIE GET YOUR GUN, M-G-M. Adolph Deutsch and Roger Edens.
CINDERELLA, Disney, RKO Radio. Oliver Wallace and Paul J. Smith.
I'LL GET BY, 20th Century-Fox. Lionel Newman.
THREE LITTLE WORDS, M-G-M. Andre Previn.
THE WEST POINT STORY, Warner Bros. Ray Heindorf.

SHORT SUBJECTS

(Cartoons)
* GERALD McBOING-BOING, UPA, Columbia. (Jolly Frolics Series). Stephen Bosustow, executive producer.
JERRY'S COUSIN, M-G-M. (Tom & Jerry). Fred Quimby, producer.
TROUBLE INDEMNITY, UPA, Columbia. (Mr. Magoo Series). Stephen Bosustow, executive producer.

(One-reel)
BLAZE BUSTERS, Warner Bros. (Vitaphone Novelties). Robert Youngson, producer.
* GRANDAD OF RACES, Warner Bros. (Sports Parade). Gordon Hollingshead, producer.
WRONG WAY BUTCH, M-G-M. (Pete Smith Specialty). Pete Smith, producer.

(Two-reel)
* BEAVER VALLEY, Disney, RKO Radio. (True-Life Adventure). Walt Disney, producer.
GRANDMA MOSES, Falcon Films, Inc., A.F. Films. Falcon Films, Inc., producer.
MY COUNTRY 'TIS OF THEE, Warner Bros. (Featurette Series). Gordon Hollingshead, producer.

DOCUMENTARY

(Short Subjects)
THE FIGHT: SCIENCE AGAINST CANCER, National Film Board of Canada in cooperation with the Medical Film Institute of the Association of American Medical Colleges.

THE STAIRS, Film Documents, Inc.
* WHY KOREA?, 20th Century-Fox Movietone. Edmund Reek, producer.

(Features)
* THE TITAN: STORY OF MICHELANGELO, Michelangelo Co., Classics Pictures, Inc. Robert Snyder, producer.
WITH THESE HANDS, Promotional Films Co., Inc. Jack Arnold and Lee Goodman, producers.

HONORARY AND OTHER AWARDS
(New classification)

TO GEORGE MURPHY for his services in interpreting the film industry to the country at large. (statuette)
TO LOUIS B. MAYER for distinguished service to the motion picture industry. (statuette)
TO THE WALLS OF MALAPAGA (Franco-Italian)—voted by the Board of Governors as the most outstanding foreign language film released in the United States in 1950. (statuette)

1950 IRVING G. THALBERG MEMORIAL AWARD

TO DARRYL F. ZANUCK

SCIENTIFIC OR TECHNICAL

CLASS I (statuette)
None.

CLASS II (plaque)
JAMES B. GORDON and the 20TH CENTURY-FOX STUDIO CAMERA DEPARTMENT for the design and development of a multiple image film viewer.
JOHN PAUL LIVADARY, FLOYD CAMPBELL, L.W. RUSSELL and the COLUMBIA STUDIO SOUND DEPARTMENT for the development of a multi-track magnetic re-recording system.
LOREN L. RYDER and the PARAMOUNT STUDIO SOUND DEPARTMENT for the first studio-wide application of magnetic sound recording to motion picture production.

CLASS III (citation)
None.

★ INDICATES WINNER

1951 The Twenty-Fourth Year

Humphrey Bogart won his one and only Academy Award at the 1951 Awards ceremony, held March 20, 1952, at the RKO Pantages Theatre in Hollywood. It obviously rattled the famous tough guy, who had gone to the ceremony, he told friends, expecting Marlon Brando to win. But the unexpected has always been a fascinating ingredient of the Academy Awards story. No matter what fortunetellers, Ouija boards and the crystal ball may predict, every year seems to produce a lively upset or two to make Oscar-watching especially interesting. Said Bogart when he received the Best Actor Award for *The African Queen*, ''It's a long way from the Belgian Congo to the Pantages Theatre, but I'd rather be here than there.''

Another major surprise occurred in 1951 when Ronald Colman opened the sealed envelope and announced the musical *An American in Paris* as the year's Best Picture; only twice before had a musical been voted the Academy's highest accolade (*The Broadway Melody* in 1928-29, *The Great Ziegfeld* in 1936). Most Awards-watchers predicted one of two heavy dramas—either *A Streetcar Named Desire* or *A Place in the Sun*—would be honored. Even M-G-M, producers of the winning film, were caught off guard, and ran a whimsical trade advertisement afterwards which had a caricature of the studio's Leo the Lion trademark, looking modestly at an Oscar statue, saying with some embarrassment, ''Honestly, I was just standing *in the Sun* waiting for *A Streetcar*.''

Danny Kaye was M.C. for the program; it was produced by Arthur Freed, with Johnny Green as musical director (and a set designed by Mitchell Leisen). *A Streetcar Named Desire* became the first motion picture to win three awards for acting: Vivien Leigh was named the year's Best Actress, Karl Malden was chosen Best Supporting Actor and Kim Hunter was announced as Best Supporting Actress. Miss Leigh was in New York, co-starring with husband Laurence Olivier in a stage production of *Antony and Cleopatra* and heard the news via radio.

Special Oscars were voted to Japan's *Rashomon* as the outstanding foreign language film, and to Gene Kelly on behalf of his screen versatility and choreographic contributions to *An American in Paris. Paris* and *A Place in the Sun* tied for the most wins of the night, with six each. No one knew it at the time, but something else unexpected was about to happen: after this year, television cameras would be a permanent part of the Academy Awards story.

Best Picture: American in Paris (M-G-M; produced by Arthur Freed). Exhuberant moviemaking at its do-re-mi best, *An American in Paris* proved—if proof was needed—that nobody could make a musical quite like Hollywood, especially those artists in the prolific Arthur Freed unit at M-G-M. Vincente Minnelli directed, the score was wall-to-wall Gershwin, and Gene Kelly starred with 19-year-old Leslie Caron from the Ballet des Champs Elysses in Paris (above, in a portion of a 17½-minute ballet sequence which climaxed the film). The cast included Oscar Levant, Nina Foch and Georges Guetary; the finale featured 120 dancers working in settings and styles patterned after paintings of Paris by Utrillo, Toulouse-Lautrec, Dufy, Renoir, Rousseau and van Gogh.

Best Actor: Humphrey Bogart as Charlie Allnut (with Katharine Hepburn) in *The African Queen* (United Artists; directed by John Huston). Bogart played a scruffy, gin-loving vagabond aboard a 30-foot river steamboat and heading down a thousand miles of unchartered, risky rivers in German East African during World War I, battling the elements on one hand and, on the other, a chatty spinster who is accompanying him. Bogart was also nominated for Oscars in 1943 for *Casablanca* and in 1954 for *The Caine Mutiny*, but made no secret of the fact he was not generally in favor of awards for actors. "The only true test would be to have every actor play *Hamlet* and decide who is best," he said.

(below and right) **A Streetcar Named Desire**
(Warner Bros.; directed by Elia Kazan) was
based on the powerful play by Tennessee
Williams and became the first motion
picture to win three Academy Awards for
acting, for (pictured at right) **Best Actress:
Vivien Leigh** as Blanche du Bois and **Best
Supporting Actor: Karl Malden** as Harold
Miller, and (below, with Marlon Brando)
Best Supporting Actress: Kim Hunter as
Stella Kowalski. It marked the second
Oscar for Vivien Leigh, this time as a
desperate, faded beauty who hides her
sexual maladjustments beneath a
coquettish and ladylike surface, then
tragically clashes with the animal honesty
of her brother-in-law. Kim Hunter played
her sister; Malden, a would-be suitor.

Best Director: for *A Place in the Sun* (Paramount; also produced by Stevens) with Elizabeth Taylor and Montgomery Clift, an adaptation of Theodore Dreiser's classic *An American Tragedy*, which had earlier been filmed in 1931 by Paramount. The dramatic *A Place in the Sun* gave enormous career boosts to the popularity of Taylor and Clift, plus started Shelley Winters on a new career of essaying young character roles. It also won Oscars for Screenplay (by Michael Wilson and Harry Brown), Cinematography (by William C. Mellor), Dramatic Music Score (by Franz Waxman), Film Editing (by William Hornbeck) and Costume Design (by Edith Head).

Nominations 1951

PICTURE

* **AN AMERICAN IN PARIS**, M-G-M. Produced by Arthur Freed.
  DECISION BEFORE DAWN, 20th Century-Fox. Produced by Anatole Litvak and Frank McCarthy.
  A PLACE IN THE SUN, Paramount. Produced by George Stevens.
  QUO VADIS, M-G-M. Produced by Sam Zimbalist.
  A STREETCAR NAMED DESIRE, Feldman, Warner Bros. Produced by Charles K. Feldman.

ACTOR

* **HUMPHREY BOGART** in *The African Queen*, Horizon, UA.
  MARLON BRANDO in *A Streetcar Named Desire*, Charles K. Feldman, Warner Bros.
  MONTGOMERY CLIFT in *A Place in the Sun*, Paramount.
  ARTHUR KENNEDY in *Bright Victory*, U-I.
  FREDRIC MARCH in *Death of a Salesman*, Stanley Kramer, Columbia.

ACTRESS

  KATHARINE HEPBURN in *The African Queen*, Horizon, UA.
* **VIVIEN LEIGH** in *A Streetcar Named Desire*, Charles K. Feldman, Warner Bros.
  ELEANOR PARKER in *Detective Story*, Paramount.
  SHELLEY WINTERS in *A Place in the Sun*, Paramount.
  JANE WYMAN in *The Blue Veil*, Wald-Krasna, RKO Radio.

SUPPORTING ACTOR

  LEO GENN in *Quo Vadis*, M-G-M.
* **KARL MALDEN** in *A Streetcar Named Desire*, Charles K. Feldman, Warner Bros.
  KEVIN McCARTHY in *Death of a Salesman*, Kramer, Columbia.
  PETER USTINOV in *Quo Vadis*, M-G-M.
  GIG YOUNG in *Come Fill the Cup*, Warner Bros.

SUPPORTING ACTRESS

  JOAN BLONDELL in *The Blue Veil*, Wald-Krasna, RKO Radio.
  MILDRED DUNNOCK in *Death of a Salesman*, Kramer, Columbia.
  LEE GRANT in *Detective Story*, Paramount.
* **KIM HUNTER** in *A Streetcar Named Desire*, Charles K. Feldman, Warner Bros.
  THELMA RITTER in *The Mating Season*, Paramount.

DIRECTION

  JOHN HUSTON for *The African Queen*, Horizon-Romulus, UA.
  ELIA KAZAN for *A Streetcar Named Desire*, Feldman, Warner Bros.
  VINCENTE MINNELLI for *An American In Paris*, M-G-M.
* **GEORGE STEVENS** for *A Place in the Sun*, Paramount.
  WILLIAM WYLER for *Detective Story*, Paramount.

WRITING

(Motion Picture Story)

  BULLFIGHTER AND THE LADY, Republic. Budd Boetticher and Ray Nazarro.
  THE FROGMEN, 20th Century-Fox. Oscar Millard.
  HERE COMES THE GROOM, Paramount. Robert Riskin and Liam O'Brien.
* **SEVEN DAYS TO NOON**, Boulting Bros., Mayer-Kingsley (British). Paul Dehn and James Bernard.
  TERESA, M-G-M. Alfred Hayes and Stewart Stern.

(Screenplay)

  THE AFRICAN QUEEN, Horizon-Romulus, UA. James Agee and John Huston.
  DETECTIVE STORY, Paramount. Philip Yordan and Robert Wyler.
  LA RONDE, Commercial Pictures (French). Jacques Natanson and Max Ophuls.
* **A PLACE IN THE SUN**, Paramount. Michael Wilson and Harry Brown.
  A STREETCAR NAMED DESIRE, Feldman, Warner Bros. Tennessee Williams.

(Story and Screenplay)

* **AN AMERICAN IN PARIS**, M-G-M. Alan Jay Lerner.
  THE BIG CARNIVAL, Paramount. Billy Wilder, Lesser Samuels and Walter Newman.
  DAVID AND BATHSHEBA, 20th Century-Fox. Philip Dunne.
  GO FOR BROKE!, M-G-M. Robert Pirosh.
  THE WELL, Popkin, UA. Clarence Greene and Russell Rouse.

CINEMATOGRAPHY

(Black-and-White)

  DEATH OF A SALESMAN, Kramer, Columbia. Frank Planer.
  THE FROGMEN, 20th Century-Fox. Norbert Brodine.
* **A PLACE IN THE SUN**, Paramount. William C. Mellor.
  STRANGERS ON A TRAIN, Warner Bros. Robert Burks.
  A STREETCAR NAMED DESIRE, Feldman, Warner Bros. Harry Stradling.

(Color)

* **AN AMERICAN IN PARIS**, M-G-M. Alfred Gilks and John Alton.
  DAVID AND BATHSHEBA, 20th Century-Fox. Leon Shamroy.
  QUO VADIS, M-G-M. Robert Surtees and William V. Skall.
  SHOW BOAT, M-G-M. Charles Rosher.
  WHEN WORLDS COLLIDE, Pal, Paramount. John F. Seitz and W. Howard Greene.

ART DIRECTION-SET DECORATION

(Black-and-White)

  FOURTEEN HOURS, 20th Century-Fox. Lyle Wheeler and Leland Fuller; Thomas Little and Fred J. Rode.
  HOUSE ON TELEGRAPH HILL, 20th Century-Fox. Lyle Wheeler and John DeCuir; Thomas Little and Paul S. Fox.
  LA RONDE, Commercial Pictures (French). D'Eaubonne.
* **A STREETCAR NAMED DESIRE**, Feldman, Warner Bros. Richard Day; George James Hopkins.
  TOO YOUNG TO KISS, M-G-M. Cedric Gibbons and Paul Groesse; Edwin B. Willis and Jack D. Moore.

(Color)

* **AN AMERICAN IN PARIS**, M-G-M. Cedric Gibbons and Preston Ames; Edwin B. Willis and Keogh Gleason.
  DAVID AND BATHSHEBA, 20th Century-Fox. Lyle Wheeler and George Davis; Thomas Little and Paul S. Fox.
  ON THE RIVIERA, 20th Century-Fox. Lyle Wheeler and Leland Fuller; Joseph C. Wright, Thomas Little and Walter M. Scott.
  QUO VADIS, M-G-M. William A. Horning, Cedric Gibbons and Edward Carfagno; Hugh Hunt.
  TALES OF HOFFMANN, Powell-Pressburger, Lopert (British). Hein Heckroth.

Special Award: Rashomon (Japanese; produced by Jingo Minoura) received an Oscar statuette from the Board of Governors as the outstanding foreign language film released during 1951. It starred Toshiro Mifune and Machiko Kyo and told the story of a bandit attack and rape from three individual viewpoints. In 1964, director Martin Ritt used *Rashomon* as the basis for *The Outrage* with Paul Newman and Claire Bloom.

SHORT SUBJECTS

(Cartoons)
LAMBERT, THE SHEEPISH LION, Disney, RKO Radio. (Special). Walt Disney, producer.
ROOTY TOOT TOOT, UPA, Columbia (Jolly Frolics). Stephen Bosustow, executive producer.
★ **TWO MOUSEKETEERS,** M-G-M. (Tom & Jerry). Fred Quimby, producer.

(One-reel)
RIDIN' THE RAILS, Paramount. (Sportlights). Jack Eaton, producer.
THE STORY OF TIME, A Signal Films Production by Robert G. Leffingwell, Cornell Film Company (British).
★ **WORLD OF KIDS,** Warner Bros. (Vitaphone Novelties). Robert Youngson, producer.

(Two-reel)
BALZAC, Les Films Du Compass, A.F. Films, Inc. (French). Les Films Du Compass, producer.
DANGER UNDER THE SEA, U-I. Tom Mead, producer.
★ **NATURE'S HALF ACRE,** Disney, RKO Radio. (True-Life Adventure). Walt Disney, producer.

DOCUMENTARY

(Short Subjects)
★ **BENJY,** Made by Fred Zinnemann with the cooperation of Paramount Pictures Corp. for the Los Angeles Orthopaedic Hospital.
ONE WHO CAME BACK, Owen Crump, producer. (Film sponsored by the Disabled American Veterans, in co-operation with the United States Department of Defense and the Association of Motion Picture Producers.)
THE SEEING EYE, Warner Bros. Gordon Hollingshead, producer.

(Features)
I WAS A COMMUNIST FOR THE F.B.I., Warner Bros. Bryan Foy, producer.
★ **KON-TIKI,** Artfilm Prod., RKO Radio (Norwegian). Olle Nordemar, producer.

SPECIAL EFFECTS

NOTE: 1951 through 1953, Special Effects classified as an "other" award (not necessarily given each year); hence, no nominations.

★ **WHEN WORLDS COLLIDE,** Pal, Paramount.

MUSIC

(Song)
★ **IN THE COOL, COOL, COOL OF THE EVENING** (*Here Comes the Groom,* Paramount); Music by Hoagy Carmichael. Lyrics by Johnny Mercer.
A KISS TO BUILD A DREAM ON (*The Strip,* M-G-M); Music and Lyrics by Bert Kalmar, Harry Ruby and Oscar Hammerstein, II.
NEVER (*Golden Girl,* 20th Century-Fox); Music by Lionel Newman. Lyrics by Eliot Daniel.
TOO LATE NOW (*Royal Wedding,* M-G-M); Music by Burton Lane. Lyrics by Alan Jay Lerner.
WONDER WHY (*Rich, Young and Pretty,* M-G-M); Music by Nicholas Brodsky. Lyrics by Sammy Cahn.

(Scoring of a Dramatic or Comedy Picture)
DAVID AND BATHSHEBA, 20th Century-Fox. Alfred Newman.
DEATH OF A SALESMAN, Kramer, Columbia. Alex North.
★ **A PLACE IN THE SUN,** Paramount. Franz Waxman.
QUO VADIS, M-G-M. Miklos Rozsa.
A STREETCAR NAMED DESIRE, Feldman, Warner Bros. Alex North.

(Scoring of a Musical Picture)
ALICE IN WONDERLAND, Disney, RKO Radio. Oliver Wallace.
★ **AN AMERICAN IN PARIS,** M-G-M. Johnny Green and Saul Chaplin.
THE GREAT CARUSO, M-G-M. Peter Herman Adler and Johnny Green.
ON THE RIVIERA, 20th Century-Fox. Alfred Newman.
SHOW BOAT, M-G-M. Adolph Deutsch and Conrad Salinger.

COSTUME DESIGN

(Black-and-White)
KIND LADY, M-G-M. Walter Plunkett and Gile Steele.
THE MODEL AND THE MARRIAGE BROKER, 20th Century-Fox. Charles LeMaire and Renie.
THE MUDLARK, 20th Century-Fox. Edward Stevenson and Margaret Furse.
★ **A PLACE IN THE SUN,** Paramount. Edith Head.
A STREETCAR NAMED DESIRE, Feldman, Warner Bros. Lucinda Ballard.

(Color)
★ **AN AMERICAN IN PARIS,** M-G-M. Orry-Kelly, Walter Plunkett and Irene Sharaff.
DAVID AND BATHSHEBA, 20th Century-Fox. Charles LeMaire and Edward Stevenson.
THE GREAT CARUSO, M-G-M. Helen Rose and Gile Steele.
QUO VADIS, M-G-M. Herschel McCoy.
TALES OF HOFFMANN, Powell-Pressburger, Lopert (British). Hein Heckroth.

SOUND RECORDING

BRIGHT VICTORY, U-I. Leslie I. Carey, sound director.
★ **THE GREAT CARUSO,** M-G-M. Douglas Shearer, sound director.
I WANT YOU, Goldwyn, RKO Radio. Gordon Sawyer, sound director.
A STREETCAR NAMED DESIRE, Feldman, Warner Bros. Col. Nathan Levinson, sound director.
TWO TICKETS TO BROADWAY, RKO Radio. John O. Aalberg, sound director.

FILM EDITING

AN AMERICAN IN PARIS, M-G-M. Adrienne Fazan.
DECISION BEFORE DAWN, 20th Century-Fox. Dorothy Spencer.
★ **A PLACE IN THE SUN,** Paramount. William Hornbeck.
QUO VADIS, M-G-M. Ralph E. Winters.
THE WELL, Popkin, UA. Chester Schaeffer.

HONORARY AND OTHER AWARDS

TO GENE KELLY in appreciation of his versatility as an actor, singer, director and dancer, and specifically for his brilliant achievements in the art of choreography on film. (statuette)
TO RASHOMON (Japanese)—voted by the Board of Governors as the most outstanding foreign language film released in the United States during 1951. (statuette)

1951 IRVING G. THALBERG MEMORIAL AWARD

TO ARTHUR FREED

SCIENTIFIC OR TECHNICAL

CLASS I (statuette)
None.

CLASS II (plaque)
GORDON JENNINGS, S.L. STANCLIFFE and the **PARAMOUNT STUDIO SPECIAL PHOTOGRAPHIC** and **ENGINEERING DEPARTMENTS** for the design, construction and application of a servo-operated recording and repeating device.
OLIN L. DUPY of M-G-M Studio for the design, construction and application of a motion picture reproducing system.
RADIO CORPORATION OF AMERICA, VICTOR DIVISION, for pioneering direct positive recording with anticipatory noise reduction.

CLASS III (citation)
RICHARD M. HAFF, FRANK P. HERRNFELD, GARLAND C. MISENER and the **ANSCO FILM DIVISION OF GENERAL ANILINE AND FILM CORP.;**
FRED PONEDEL, RALPH AYRES and **GEORGE BROWN** of Warner Bros. Studio;
GLEN ROBINSON and the **METRO-GOLDWYN-MAYER STUDIO CONSTRUCTION DEPARTMENT;**
JACK GAYLORD and the **METRO-GOLDWYN-MAYER STUDIO CONSTRUCTION DEPARTMENT;**
CARLOS RIVAS of **METRO-GOLDWYN-MAYER STUDIO.**

★ INDICATES WINNER

When Worlds Collide (Paramount; produced by George Pal) showed the havoc that happened—at least in the imagination of original authors Edwin Balmer and Philip Wylie—when another planet collided with Earth. It was voted an Oscar for Special Effects under a new 1951 Academy ruling which specified such an award would be presented only at such times there was an outstanding achievement deserving to be honored.

1952 The Twenty-Fifth Year

Television loomed as a frightening ogre to most motion picture makers in the early 1950s. Hollywood studio bosses were justifiably concerned with the new medium's seemingly insatiable appetite, and rightfully worried about the public's growing interest in it as an entertainment source. Most studios went so far as to forbid their contractees to work for the competition, but sooner or later it was inevitable the walls would come tumbling down. It finally happened on March 19, 1953; television cameras covered the twenty-fifth Academy Awards presentation, and they have been an integral part of the Oscar story every year since.

It happened partly by default. The Academy had consistently turned down requests from the networks to buy the rights for TV coverage of the annual show, mainly to help protect the interests of the industry it represented. However, close to the time for the 1952 Oscar show to take form, several major film companies (Warner Bros., Columbia, Universal-International and Republic) refused to come up with their usual share of expenses to help underwrite the ceremony. The timing seemed right. Had NBC-RCA not made a $100,000 bid for radio and TV rights at that moment, there would have been no Oscar ceremony that year.

The show itself worked remarkably well for a first-timer. The presentation originated in Hollywood at the RKO Pantages Theatre with Bob Hope as M.C. A companion show took place in New York at the International Theatre, hosted by Conrad Nagel. Cameras switched back and forth from the two coasts, depending on which city held the presenter, or the winner. Johnny Green produced for the Academy, with Adolph Deutsch as musical director. Robert L. Welch produced for NBC-TV, and William A. Bennington directed for the network. The show was a refreshing novelty for home viewers, unaccustomed to seeing such a large collection of famous names, and it received the largest single audience to that date in television's five-year commercial history.

The Bad and the Beautiful won the most Oscars of the night, a total of five, including the Best Supporting Actress Award to Gloria Grahame. Gary Cooper (in *High Noon*) won the Best Actor Award for the second time in his career, and Anthony Quinn was chosen Best Supporting Actor (for *Viva Zapata!*); both men were working together on location in Mexico and absent from the festivities in Hollywood. Shirley Booth, in New York appearing on stage in *Time of the Cuckoo,* was named Best Actress for *Come Back, Little Sheba* and came close to taking a public pratfall when she rushed on stage to accept her award, and momentarily stumbled. John Ford was named Best Director for the fourth time in his career (this one for *The Quiet Man*) and, also for the fourth time, was not present to accept his statuette. Once again, there was also a major surprise when the Best Picture winner was announced. Decidedly a dark horse, Cecil B. DeMille's *The Greatest Show on Earth* was chosen, the first DeMille movie so honored by Oscar. The Award was appropriately presented by another motion picture pioneer, Mary Pickford.

Best Picture: The Greatest Show on Earth (Paramount; produced and directed by Cecil B. DeMille) starred Cornel Wilde and Betty Hutton (airborne above) as rival aerialists in a 2-hour, 31-minute spectacle-drama using the Ringling Bros.-Barnum & Bailey Circus as a backdrop—and as a focal point. Other co-stars included Charlton Heston (as a manager struggling to keep the Big Top in business), James Stewart (as a clown hiding from police), Dorothy Lamour, Gloria Grahame, Henry Wilcoxon and a tent full of others. Rousing entertainment, the film also won an Academy Award for Motion Picture Story, while DeMille himself —Hollywood's old Master Showman— received the 1952 Irving G. Thalberg Memorial Award.

Best Actress: Shirley Booth as Lola Delaney (left, with Burt Lancaster) in *Come Back, Little Sheba* (Paramount; directed by Daniel Mann). In the 1950s, juicy stage roles didn't often go to their original Broadway creators, even when they'd had as much critical success as Shirley Booth did playing Lola Delaney, a slovenly but good-hearted housewife who endlessly waddles around her home, munching chocolates, listening to radio soap operas, mourning her lost pup Sheba and inadvertently driving her husband to drink. When Hal Wallis transferred *Sheba* to film, however, he cast it with an eye more to interpretation than to box office and got both—a brilliant performance by Miss Booth in her first film role, and a successful moneymaker as well.

Best Actor: Gary Cooper as Will Kane (below, in battle) in *High Noon* (United Artists; directed by Fred Zinnemann). Cooper played a small-town ex-marshal of the 1870s, struggling to round up a posse that might help him deal with four desperadoes arriving on a noon train to kill him; deserted by former friends and misunderstood by his new bride, he is forced to meet the gunmen singlehandedly. On the soundtrack, an unseen Tex Ritter sang a plaintive lament, in the manner of a Greek chorus, and *High Noon* became one of the year's genuine triumphs. It brought Cooper his second Academy Award (after 1941's *Sergeant York*) and also received Awards for Film Editing, Song and Music Scoring of a Drama.

Best Supporting Actress: Gloria Grahame as Rosemary Bartlow (above, with Dick Powell) in *The Bad and the Beautiful* (M-G-M; directed by Vincente Minnelli). It was a productive year for the actress with strong roles in four well-seen, well-liked releases: *The Greatest Show on Earth, Sudden Fear, Macao* and *The Bad and the Beautiful*. For the latter, playing the coquettish Southern-belle wife of a novelist-turned-screenwriter, she officially won her Academy Award. *The Bad* was also the year's most-honored film by the Academy, winning four additional awards.

Best Director: John Ford for *The Quiet Man* (Argosy, Republic; produced by Ford and Merian C. Cooper) starred John Wayne (below, with Barry Fitzgerald) as an ex-prizefighter from Pittsburgh who returns to his Irish birthplace seeking peace and quiet and, instead, finds rough-and-tumble problems with a marriageable spitfire (Maureen O'Hara) and her ill-tempered brother (Victor McLaglen). It was peopled with familiar Ford players (including Ward Bond, Mildred Natwick, Arthur Shields and Frances Ford), filmed in Ireland in Technicolor, and acclaimed as one of the year's most robust delights. It also won Ford his fourth Oscar for direction, the largest total won by any individual in that category during Oscar's first 50 years.

Nominations 1952

PICTURE

* **THE GREATEST SHOW ON EARTH,** DeMille, Paramount. Produced by Cecil B. DeMille.
  HIGH NOON, Kramer, UA. Produced by Stanley Kramer.
  IVANHOE, M-G-M. Produced by Pandro S. Berman.
  MOULIN ROUGE, Romulus, UA. Produced by John Huston.
  THE QUIET MAN, Argosy, Republic. Produced by John Ford and Merian C. Cooper.

ACTOR

  MARLON BRANDO in *Viva Zapata!,* 20th Century-Fox.
* **GARY COOPER** in *High Noon,* Kramer, UA.
  KIRK DOUGLAS in *The Bad and the Beautiful,* M-G-M.
  JOSE FERRER in *Moulin Rouge,* Romulus, UA.
  ALEC GUINNESS in *The Lavender Hill Mob,* Rank-Ealing, U-I (British).

ACTRESS

* **SHIRLEY BOOTH** in *Come Back, Little Sheba,* Wallis, Paramount.
  JOAN CRAWFORD in *Sudden Fear,* Kaufman, RKO Radio.
  BETTE DAVIS in *The Star,* Friedlob, 20th Century-Fox.
  JULIE HARRIS in *The Member of the Wedding,* Kramer, Columbia.
  SUSAN HAYWARD in *With a Song in My Heart,* 20th Century-Fox.

SUPPORTING ACTOR

  RICHARD BURTON in *My Cousin Rachel,* 20th Century-Fox.
  ARTHUR HUNNICUTT in *The Big Sky,* Winchester, RKO Radio.
  VICTOR McLAGLEN in *The Quiet Man,* Argosy, Republic.
  JACK PALANCE in *Sudden Fear,* Kaufman, RKO Radio.
* **ANTHONY QUINN** in *Viva Zapata!,* 20th Century-Fox.

SUPPORTING ACTRESS

* **GLORIA GRAHAME** in *The Bad and the Beautiful,* M-G-M.
  JEAN HAGEN in *Singin' in the Rain,* M-G-M.
  COLETTE MARCHAND in *Moulin Rouge,* Romulus, UA.
  TERRY MOORE in *Come Back, Little Sheba,* Wallis, Paramount.
  THELMA RITTER in *With a Song in My Heart,* 20th Century-Fox.

DIRECTION

  CECIL B. DeMILLE for *The Greatest Show on Earth,* DeMille, Paramount.
* **JOHN FORD** for *The Quiet Man,* Argosy, Republic.
  JOHN HUSTON for *Moulin Rouge,* Romulus, UA.
  JOSEPH L. MANKIEWICZ for *Five Fingers,* 20th Century-Fox.
  FRED ZINNEMANN for *High Noon,* Stanley Kramer, UA.

WRITING

(Motion Picture Story)

* **THE GREATEST SHOW ON EARTH,** DeMille, Paramount. Frederick M. Frank, Theodore St. John and Frank Cavett.
  MY SON JOHN, Rainbow, Paramount. Leo McCarey.
  THE NARROW MARGIN, RKO Radio. Martin Goldsmith and Jack Leonard.
  THE PRIDE OF ST. LOUIS, 20th Century-Fox. Guy Trosper.
  THE SNIPER, Kramer, Columbia. Edna Anhalt and Edward Anhalt.

(Screenplay)

* **THE BAD AND THE BEAUTIFUL,** M-G-M. Charles Schnee.
  FIVE FINGERS, 20th Century-Fox. Michael Wilson.

  HIGH NOON, Kramer, UA. Carl Foreman.
  THE MAN IN THE WHITE SUIT, Rank-Ealing, U-I (British). Roger MacDougall, John Dighton and Alexander Mackendrick.
  THE QUIET MAN, Argosy, Republic. Frank S. Nugent.

(Story and Screenplay)

  THE ATOMIC CITY, Paramount. Sydney Boehm.
  BREAKING THE SOUND BARRIER, London Films, UA (British). Terence Rattigan.
* **THE LAVENDER HILL MOB,** Rank-Ealing, U-I (British). T.E.B. Clarke.
  PAT AND MIKE, M-G-M. Ruth Gordon and Garson Kanin.
  VIVA ZAPATA!, 20th Century-Fox. John Steinbeck.

CINEMATOGRAPHY

(Black-and-White)

* **THE BAD AND THE BEAUTIFUL,** M-G-M. Robert Surtees.
  THE BIG SKY, Winchester, RKO Radio. Russell Harlan.
  MY COUSIN RACHEL, 20th Century-Fox. Joseph LaShelle.
  NAVAJO, Bartlett-Foster, Lippert. Virgil E. Miller.
  SUDDEN FEAR, Kaufman, RKO Radio. Charles B. Lang, Jr.

(Color)

  HANS CHRISTIAN ANDERSEN, Goldwyn, RKO Radio. Harry Stradling.
  IVANHOE, M-G-M. F.A. Young.
  MILLION DOLLAR MERMAID, M-G-M. George J. Folsey.
* **THE QUIET MAN,** Argosy, Republic. Winton C. Hoch and Archie Stout.
  THE SNOWS OF KILIMANJARO, 20th Century-Fox. Leon Shamroy.

ART DIRECTION-
SET DECORATION

(Black-and-White)

* **THE BAD AND THE BEAUTIFUL,** M-G-M. Cedric Gibbons and Edward Carfagno; Edwin B. Willis and Keogh Gleason.
  CARRIE, Paramount. Hal Pereira and Roland Anderson; Emile Kuri.
  MY COUSIN RACHEL, 20th Century-Fox. Lyle Wheeler and John DeCuir; Walter M. Scott.
  RASHO-MON, RKO Radio (Japanese). Matsuyama; H. Motsumoto.
  VIVA ZAPATA!, 20th Century-Fox. Lyle Wheeler and Leland Fuller; Thomas Little and Claude Carpenter.

(Color)

  HANS CHRISTIAN ANDERSEN, Goldwyn, RKO Radio. Richard Day and Clave; Howard Bristol.
  THE MERRY WIDOW, M-G-M. Cedric Gibbons and Paul Groesse; Edwin B. Willis and Arthur Krams.
* **MOULIN ROUGE,** Romulus, UA. Paul Sheriff; Marcel Vertes.
  THE QUIET MAN, Argosy, Republic. Frank Hotaling; John McCarthy, Jr. and Charles Thompson.
  THE SNOWS OF KILIMANJARO, 20th Century-Fox. Lyle Wheeler and John DeCuir; Thomas Little and Paul S. Fox.

COSTUME DESIGN

(Black-and-White)

  AFFAIR IN TRINIDAD, Beckworth, Columbia. Jean Louis.
* **THE BAD AND THE BEAUTIFUL,** M-G-M. Helen Rose.
  CARRIE, Paramount. Edith Head.
  MY COUSIN RACHEL, 20th Century-Fox. Charles LeMaire and Dorothy Jeakins.
  SUDDEN FEAR, Kaufman, RKO Radio. Sheila O'Brien.

(Color)

  THE GREATEST SHOW ON EARTH, DeMille, Paramount. Edith Head, Dorothy Jeakins and Miles White.
  HANS CHRISTIAN ANDERSEN, Goldwyn, RKO Radio. Clave, Mary Wills and Madame Karinska.

THE MERRY WIDOW, M-G-M. Helen Rose and Gile Steele.
* MOULIN ROUGE, Romulus, UA. Marcel Vertes.
WITH A SONG IN MY HEART, 20th Century-Fox. Charles LeMaire.

SOUND RECORDING

* BREAKING THE SOUND BARRIER, London Films, UA (British). London Film Sound Department.
HANS CHRISTIAN ANDERSEN, Goldwyn, RKO Radio. Goldwyn Sound Department; Gordon Sawyer, sound director.
THE PROMOTER, Rank-Neame, U-I (British). Pinewood Studios Sound Department.
THE QUIET MAN, Argosy, Republic. Republic Sound Department; Daniel J. Bloomberg, sound director.
WITH A SONG IN MY HEART, 20th Century-Fox. 20th Century-Fox Sound Department; Thomas T. Moulton, sound director.

FILM EDITING

COME BACK, LITTLE SHEBA, Wallis, Paramount. Warren Low.
FLAT TOP, Monogram. William Austin.
THE GREATEST SHOW ON EARTH, DeMille, Paramount. Anne Bauchens.
* HIGH NOON, Kramer, UA. Elmo Williams and Harry Gerstad.
MOULIN ROUGE, Romulus, UA. Ralph Kemplen.

SPECIAL EFFECTS

NOTE: 1951 through 1953, Special Effects classified as an ''other'' award (not necessarily given each year); hence, no nominations.
* PLYMOUTH ADVENTURE, M-G-M.

MUSIC

(Song)
AM I IN LOVE (Son of Paleface, Paramount); Music and Lyrics by Jack Brooks.

BECAUSE YOU'RE MINE (Because You're Mine, M-G-M); Music by Nicholas Brodszky. Lyrics by Sammy Cahn.
* HIGH NOON (DO NOT FORSAKE ME, OH MY DARLIN') (High Noon, Kramer, UA); Music by Dimitri Tiomkin. Lyrics by Ned Washington.
THUMBELINA (Hans Christian Andersen, Goldwyn, RKO Radio); Music and Lyrics by Frank Loesser.
ZING A LITTLE ZONG (Just for You, Paramount); Music by Harry Warren. Lyrics by Leo Robin.

(Scoring of a Dramatic or Comedy Picture)
* HIGH NOON, Kramer, UA. Dimitri Tiomkin.
IVANHOE, M-G-M. Miklos Rozsa.
THE MIRACLE OF FATIMA, Foy, Warner Bros. Max Steiner.
THE THIEF, Popkin, UA. Herschel Burke Gilbert.
VIVA ZAPATA!, 20th Century-Fox. Alex North.

(Scoring of a Musical Picture)
HANS CHRISTIAN ANDERSEN, Goldwyn, RKO Radio. Walter Scharf.
THE JAZZ SINGER, Warner Bros. Ray Heindorf and Max Steiner.
THE MEDIUM, Transfilm-Lopert (Italian). Gian-Carlo Menotti.
SINGIN' IN THE RAIN, M-G-M. Lennie Hayton.
* WITH A SONG IN MY HEART, 20th Century-Fox. Alfred Newman.

SHORT SUBJECTS

(Cartoons)
* JOHANN MOUSE, M-G-M. (Tom & Jerry). Fred Quimby, producer.
LITTLE JOHNNY JET, M-G-M. (M-G-M Series). Fred Quimby, producer.
MADELINE, UPA, Columbia. (Jolly Frolics). Stephen Bosustow, executive producer.
PINK AND BLUE BLUES, UPA, Columbia. (Mister Magoo). Stephen Bosustow, executive producer.
ROMANCE OF TRANSPORTATION, National Film Board of Canada. (Canadian). Tom Daly, producer.

(One-reel)
ATHLETES OF THE SADDLE, Paramount. (Sportlights Series). Jack Eaton, producer.
DESERT KILLER, Warner Bros. (Sports Parade). Gordon Hollingshead, producer.
* LIGHT IN THE WINDOW, Art Films Prods., 20th Century-Fox. (Art Series). Boris Vermont, producer.
NEIGHBOURS, National Film Board of Canada (Canadian). Norman McLaren, producer.
ROYAL SCOTLAND, Crown Film Unit, British Information Services (British).

(Two-reel)
BRIDGE OF TIME, London Film Prod., British Information Services (British).
DEVIL TAKE US, Theatre of Life Prod. (Theatre of Life Series). Herbert Morgan, producer.
THAR SHE BLOWS!, Warner Bros. (Technicolor Special). Gordon Hollingshead, producer.
* WATER BIRDS, Disney, RKO Radio. (True-Life Adventure). Walt Disney, producer.

DOCUMENTARY

(Short Subjects)
DEVIL TAKE US, Theatre of Life Prod. Herbert Morgan, producer.
THE GARDEN SPIDER (EPEIRA DIADEMA), Cristallo Films, I.F.E. Releasing Corp. (Italian). Alberto Ancilotto, producer.
MAN ALIVE!, UPA for the American Cancer Society. Stephen Bosustow, executive producer.
* NEIGHBOURS, National Film Board of Canada, Mayer-Kingsley, Inc. (Canadian). Norman McLaren, producer.

(Features)
THE HOAXTERS, M-G-M. Dore Schary, producer.
NAVAJO, Bartlett-Foster Prod., Lippert Pictures, Inc. Hall Bartlett, producer.
* THE SEA AROUND US, RKO Radio. Irwin Allen, producer.

HONORARY AND OTHER AWARDS

TO GEORGE ALFRED MITCHELL for the design and development of the camera which bears his name and for his continued and dominant presence in the field of cinematography. (statuette)
TO JOSEPH M. SCHENCK for long and distinguished service to the motion picture industry. (statuette)
TO MERIAN C. COOPER for his many innovations and contributions to the art of motion pictures. (statuette)
TO HAROLD LLOYD, master comedian and good citizen. (statuette)
TO BOB HOPE for his contribution to the laughter of the world, his service to the motion picture industry, and his devotion to the American premise. (statuette)
TO FORBIDDEN GAMES (French)—Best Foreign Language Film first released in the United States during 1952. (statuette)

1952 IRVING G. THALBERG MEMORIAL AWARD

TO CECIL B. DeMILLE

SCIENTIFIC OR TECHNICAL

CLASS I (statuette)
EASTMAN KODAK CO. for the introduction of Eastman color negative and Eastman color print film.
ANSCO DIVISION, GENERAL ANILINE AND FILM CORP., for the introduction of Ansco color negative and Ansco color print film.

CLASS II (plaque)
TECHNICOLOR MOTION PICTURE CORP. for an improved method of color motion picture photography under incandescent light.

CLASS III (citation)
PROJECTION, STILL PHOTOGRAPHIC and DEVELOPMENT ENGINEERING DEPARTMENTS of METRO-GOLDWYN-MAYER STUDIO;
JOHN G. FRAYNE and R.R. SCOVILLE and WESTREX CORP.;
PHOTO RESEARCH CORP.;
GUSTAV JIROUCH;
CARLOS RIVAS of Metro-Goldwyn-Mayer Studio.

★ INDICATES WINNER

Best Supporting Actor: Anthony Quinn as Eufemio Zapata (left, with Marlon Brando) in *Viva Zapata!* (20th Century-Fox; directed by Elia Kazan). Quinn made his motion picture debut in 1936's *Parole* and spent the next sixteen years supporting everyone from Anna May Wong to Bing Crosby in lucrative but lackluster roles; as the wild, dissolute brother of Mexican rebel leader Emiliano Zapata, he won his first Academy Award and marked the beginning of a prolific career.

Best Picture: From Here to Eternity
(Columbia; produced by Buddy Adler) and
Best Director: Fred Zinnemann for *From
Here to Eternity*. James Jones' novel about
Army life at the Scofield Barracks in
Hawaii just prior to the 1941 Japanese
attack was originally considered too salty
for ideal film material, but it became a
powerful and tasteful blockbuster, acted
by a meticulously chosen cast including
(above) Burt Lancaster and Deborah Kerr,
and won eight Academy Awards, more than
any film since *Gone With the Wind* of 1939.

Best Supporting Actress: Donna Reed as
Lorene (below) in *From Here to Eternity*.
One reason for the *Eternity* impact was the
casting of first-class players in off-beat
roles, among them Donna Reed as a
somewhat embittered play-for-pay hostess
who falls in love with soldier Montgomery
Clift, a far cry from the sweet and
unspoiled ingenues she'd played at
M-G-M, Paramount and Columbia for the
preceeding twelve years. She received the
Oscar, and deservedly.

Best Supporting Actor: Frank Sinatra
as Angelo Maggio (above, with Montgomery
Clift) in *From Here to Eternity*. At first,
no one but Frank Sinatra envisioned Frank
Sinatra as *Eternity*'s hard-luck Maggio,
the feisty little Italian soldier who
tragically locks horns with a sadistic
stockade supervisor. Sinatra campaigned for
the nonstarring role, won it and
delivered a performance which sparked one
of the genuinely impressive comebacks
in Hollywood's scrapbook. He won
the Academy Award, then two years later
was nominated as 1955's Best Actor for *The
Man with the Golden Arm,* and in 1971
received the Jean Hersholt Humanitarian
Award. And since *Eternity,* his career has
never been less than first-string.

1953 The Twenty-Sixth Year

The year 1953 had been one of great Hollywood revitalization and enthusiasm, most of it connected to a wide-screen boom of Techni-colored CinemaScope projection methods and 3-D gimmicks which were heavily promoted to lure audiences away from their television sets at home. Curiously, however, the big Oscar winners of the year—*From Here to Eternity, Roman Holiday* and *Stalag 17*—were all filmed in black-and-white, in standard-sized ratios, sans gimmicks of any kind. Once again, voters had obviously opted for quality, first and foremost.

On March 25, 1954, the night Hollywood recognized screen achievements for 1953 movies, Frank Sinatra was named Best Supporting Actor for his work in *From Here to Eternity* and put the final stroke on a show business comeback of sizeable proportions. *Eternity* itself was named Best Picture, the first film to come along and tie the long-standing record of eight Academy Awards set by *Gone With the Wind* fourteen years before. Other winners for *Eternity* included Donna Reed (Best Supporting Actress) and Fred Zinnemann (Best Director). Next most-honored film was *Roman Holiday,* with three awards, including one for Audrey Hepburn as Best Actress of the year. William Holden was named Best Actor for *Stalag 17.*

An estimated 43,000,000 television viewers watched the 1953 Awards show which was again telecast over NBC-TV, with cut-ins from New York (when Audrey Hepburn won) and Philadelphia (where Shirley Booth presented the award to Holden by long distance). Donald O'Connor was master of ceremonies from the Pantages Theatre base in Hollywood; Fredric March was the M.C. in New York at the Century Theater. Audrey Hepburn was appearing on Broadway at the time in *Ondine* and, after her final curtain, was rushed by police motorcycle escort to the Century Theater just in time to hear her name announced. The show itself was given a two-hour running time by NBC and ran late, necessitating William Holden to cut his acceptance speech to a "thank you" before exiting into the wings. Mitchell Leisen produced for the Academy, Andre Previn was musical director and William A. Bennington (in Hollywood) and Gray Lockwood (in New York) shared directorial duties for NBC.

Most conspicuous man of the night, next to Oscar himself, was Walt Disney. During the course of the evening, he was called to the stage four times to accept awards for *The Alaskan Eskimo* (Documentary Short Subject), *The Living Desert* (Documentary Feature), *Toot, Whistle, Plunk and Boom* (Cartoon Short) and *Bear Country* (Two-Reel Short). No person—male or female—had personally collected so many Oscars in one session.

Best Actor: William Holden as Sefton in *Stalag 17* (Paramount; directed by Billy Wilder). John Ericson created the role of *Stalag*'s Sefton on Broadway; on film, Holden played the hero-heel, a cynical World War II prisoner in a German POW barracks who is suspected by his fellow inmates of being an informer. Previously, Holden had been nominated in 1950 for *Sunset Boulevard* (also directed by Billy Wilder) and was again nominated in 1976 for *Network.*

The Robe (20th Century-Fox; produced by Frank Ross) was the first motion picture photographed and released in CinemaScope, a new wide-screen process requiring an anamorphic lens (and more horizontal screen) for projection. It was based on Lloyd C. Douglas' best-seller, starred Jean Simmons and Richard Burton (left, with Jay Robinson as Emperor Caligula) and won Academy Awards for Color Art Direction and Color Costume Design. 20th Century-Fox was also awarded a special statuette "in recognition of their imagination, showmanship and foresight in introducing the revolutionary process known as CinemaScope."

Nominations 1953

PICTURE

★ FROM HERE TO ETERNITY, Columbia. Produced by Buddy Adler.
JULIUS CAESAR, M-G-M. Produced by John Houseman.
THE ROBE, 20th Century-Fox. Produced by Frank Ross.
ROMAN HOLIDAY, Paramount. Produced by William Wyler.
SHANE, Paramount. Produced by George Stevens.

ACTOR

MARLON BRANDO in Julius Caesar, M-G-M.
RICHARD BURTON in The Robe, 20th Century-Fox.
MONTGOMERY CLIFT in From Here to Eternity, Columbia.
★ WILLIAM HOLDEN in Stalag 17, Paramount.
BURT LANCASTER in From Here to Eternity, Columbia.

ACTRESS

LESLIE CARON in Lili, M-G-M.
AVA GARDNER in Mogambo, M-G-M.
★ AUDREY HEPBURN in Roman Holiday, Paramount.
DEBORAH KERR in From Here to Eternity, Columbia.
MAGGIE McNAMARA in The Moon Is Blue, Preminger-Herbert, UA.

SUPPORTING ACTOR

EDDIE ALBERT in Roman Holiday, Paramount.
BRANDON DE WILDE in Shane, Paramount.
JACK PALANCE in Shane, Paramount.
★ FRANK SINATRA in From Here to Eternity, Columbia.
ROBERT STRAUSS in Stalag 17, Paramount.

SUPPORTING ACTRESS

GRACE KELLY in Mogambo, M-G-M.
GERALDINE PAGE in Hondo, Wayne-Fellows, Warner Bros.
MARJORIE RAMBEAU in Torch Song, M-G-M.

★ DONNA REED in From Here to Eternity, Columbia.
THELMA RITTER in Pickup on South Street, 20th Century-Fox.

DIRECTION

GEORGE STEVENS for Shane, Paramount.
CHARLES WALTERS for Lili, M-G-M.
BILLY WILDER for Stalag 17, Paramount.
WILLIAM WYLER for Roman Holiday, Paramount.
★ FRED ZINNEMANN for From Here to Eternity, Columbia.

WRITING

(Motion Picture Story)
ABOVE AND BEYOND, M-G-M. Beirne Lay, Jr.
THE CAPTAIN'S PARADISE, London Films, Lopert-UA (British). Alec Coppel.
LITTLE FUGITIVE, Burstyn Releasing. Ray Ashley, Morris Engel and Ruth Orkin.
★ ROMAN HOLIDAY, Paramount. Ian McLellan Hunter.

(Screenplay)
THE CRUEL SEA, Rank-Ealing, U-I (British). Eric Ambler.
★ FROM HERE TO ETERNITY, Columbia. Daniel Taradash.
LILI, M-G-M. Helen Deutsch.
ROMAN HOLIDAY, Paramount. Ian McLellan Hunter and John Dighton.
SHANE, Paramount. A.B. Guthrie, Jr.

(Story and Screenplay)
THE BAND WAGON, M-G-M. Betty Comden and Adolph Green.
THE DESERT RATS, 20th Century-Fox. Richard Murphy.
THE NAKED SPUR, M-G-M. Sam Rolfe and Harold Jack Bloom.
TAKE THE HIGH GROUND, M-G-M. Millard Kaufman.
★ TITANIC, 20th Century-Fox. Charles Brackett, Walter Reisch and Richard Breen.

CINEMATOGRAPHY

(Black-and-White)
THE FOUR POSTER, Kramer, Columbia. Hal Mohr.
★ FROM HERE TO ETERNITY, Columbia. Burnett Guffey.

JULIUS CAESAR, M-G-M. Joseph Ruttenberg.
MARTIN LUTHER, de Rochemont Assocs. Joseph C. Brun.
ROMAN HOLIDAY, Paramount. Frank Planer and Henry Alekan.

(Color)
ALL THE BROTHERS WERE VALIANT, M-G-M. George Folsey.
BENEATH THE 12 MILE REEF, 20th Century-Fox. Edward Cronjager.
LILI, M-G-M. Robert Planck.
THE ROBE, 20th Century-Fox. Leon Shamroy.
★ SHANE, Paramount. Loyal Griggs.

ART DIRECTION-SET DECORATION

(Black-and-White)
★ JULIUS CAESAR, M-G-M. Cedric Gibbons and Edward Carfagno; Edwin B. Willis and Hugh Hunt.
MARTIN LUTHER, de Rochemont Assocs. Fritz Maurischat and Paul Markwitz.
THE PRESIDENT'S LADY, 20th Century-Fox. Lyle Wheeler and Leland Fuller; Paul S. Fox.
ROMAN HOLIDAY, Paramount. Hal Pereira and Walter Tyler.
TITANIC, 20th Century-Fox. Lyle Wheeler and Maurice Ransford; Stuart Reiss.

(Color)
KNIGHTS OF THE ROUND TABLE, M-G-M. Alfred Junge and Hans Peters; John Jarvis.
LILI, M-G-M. Cedric Gibbons and Paul Groesse; Edwin B. Willis and Arthur Krams.
★ THE ROBE, 20th Century-Fox. Lyle Wheeler and George W. Davis; Walter M. Scott and Paul S. Fox.
THE STORY OF THREE LOVES, M-G-M. Cedric Gibbons, Preston Ames, Edward Carfagno and Gabriel Scognamillo; Edwin B. Willis, Keogh Gleason, Arthur Krams and Jack D. Moore.
YOUNG BESS, M-G-M. Cedric Gibbons and Urie McCleary; Edwin B. Willis and Jack D. Moore.

COSTUME DESIGN

(Black-and-White)
THE ACTRESS, M-G-M. Walter Plunkett.

Shane (Paramount; produced by George Stevens) starred Alan Ladd (below, with Brandon De Wilde), Jean Arthur and Van Heflin in a Technicolor outdoor drama filmed near the Grand Tetons in Wyoming. A classic of its kind, it won an Oscar for Color Cinematography, and its producer-director, George Stevens, received 1953's Irving G. Thalberg Memorial Award for "consistently high quality of production."

Best Actress: Audrey Hepburn as Princess Anne (above) in *Roman Holiday* (Paramount; directed by William Wyler). Audrey Hepburn made her initial impact in 1951 on Broadway in *Gigi*, then two years later had the same effect on moviegoers when she played the princess who sneaks away from her royal duties while on a visit to Rome, and investigates the Eternal City—incognito—with a reporter (Gregory Peck) and a photographer (Eddie Albert). It was a genuinely delightful performance, and won her the Oscar; since then, she has also been nominated for *Sabrina* (1954), *The Nun's Story* (1959), *Breakfast at Tiffany's* (1961) and *Wait Until Dark* (1967).

DREAM WIFE, M-G-M. Helen Rose and Herschel McCoy.
FROM HERE TO ETERNITY, Columbia. Jean Louis.
THE PRESIDENT'S LADY, 20th Century-Fox. Charles LeMaire and Renie.
★ ROMAN HOLIDAY, Paramount. Edith Head.

(Color)
THE BAND WAGON, M-G-M. Mary Ann Nyberg.
CALL ME MADAM, 20th Century-Fox. Irene Sharaff.
HOW TO MARRY A MILLIONAIRE, 20th Century-Fox. Charles LeMaire and Travilla.
★ THE ROBE, 20th Century-Fox. Charles LeMaire and Emile Santiago.
YOUNG BESS, M-G-M. Walter Plunkett.

SOUND RECORDING

CALAMITY JANE, Warner Bros. Warner Bros. Sound Department; William A. Mueller, sound director.
★ FROM HERE TO ETERNITY, Columbia. Columbia Sound Department; John P. Livadary, sound director.
KNIGHTS OF THE ROUND TABLE, M-G-M. M-G-M Sound Department; A.W. Watkins, sound director.
THE MISSISSIPPI GAMBLER, U-I. Universal-International Sound Department; Leslie I. Carey, sound director.
THE WAR OF THE WORLDS, Pal, Paramount. Paramount Sound Department; Loren L. Ryder, sound director.

FILM EDITING

CRAZYLEGS, Bartlett, Republic. Irvine (Cotton) Warburton.
★ FROM HERE TO ETERNITY, Columbia. William Lyon.
THE MOON IS BLUE, Preminger-Herbert, UA. Otto Ludwig.
ROMAN HOLIDAY, Paramount. Robert Swink.

THE WAR OF THE WORLDS, Pal, Paramount. Everett Douglas.

SPECIAL EFFECTS

NOTE: 1951 through 1953, Special Effects classified as an "other" award (not necessarily given each year); hence, no nominations.
★ THE WAR OF THE WORLDS, Pal, Paramount.

MUSIC

(Song)
THE MOON IS BLUE (*The Moon Is Blue*, Preminger-Herbert, UA); Music by Herschel Burke Gilbert. Lyrics by Sylvia Fine.
MY FLAMING HEART (*Small Town Girl*, M-G-M); Music by Nicholas Brodszky. Lyrics by Leo Robin.
SADIE THOMPSON'S SONG (BLUE PACIFIC BLUES) (*Miss Sadie Thompson*, Beckworth, Columbia); Music by Lester Lee. Lyrics by Ned Washington.
★ SECRET LOVE (*Calamity Jane*, Warner Bros.); Music by Sammy Fain. Lyrics by Paul Francis Webster.
THAT'S AMORE (*The Caddy*, Paramount); Music by Harry Warren. Lyrics by Jack Brooks.

(Scoring of a Dramatic or Comedy Picture)
ABOVE AND BEYOND, M-G-M. Hugo Friedhofer.
FROM HERE TO ETERNITY, Columbia. Morris Stoloff and George Duning.
JULIUS CAESAR, M-G-M. Miklos Rozsa.
★ LILI, M-G-M. Bronislau Kaper.
THIS IS CINERAMA, Cinerama Corp. Louis Forbes.

(Scoring of a Musical Picture)
THE BAND WAGON, M-G-M. Adloph Deutsch.
CALAMITY JANE, Warner Bros. Ray Heindorf.

★ CALL ME MADAM, 20th Century-Fox. Alfred Newman.
5,000 FINGERS OF DR. T., Kramer, Columbia. Frederick Hollander and Morris Stoloff.
KISS ME KATE, M-G-M. Andre Previn and Saul Chaplin.

SHORT SUBJECTS

(Cartoons)
CHRISTOPHER CRUMPET, UPA, Columbia. (Jolly Frolics). Stephen Bosustow, producer.
FROM A TO Z-Z-Z-Z, Warner Bros. (Looney Tunes). Edward Selzer, producer.
RUGGED BEAR, Disney, RKO Radio. (Donald Duck). Walt Disney, producer.
THE TELL TALE HEART, UPA, Columbia. (Cartoon Special). Stephen Bosustow, producer.
★ TOOT, WHISTLE, PLUNK AND BOOM, Disney, Buena Vista. (Special Music Series). Walt Disney, producer.

(One-reel)
CHRIST AMONG THE PRIMITIVES, IFE Releasing Corp. (Italian). Vincenzo Lucci-Chiarissi, producer.
HERRING HUNT, National Film Board of Canada, RKO Pathe, Inc. (Canadian). (Canada Carries On Series).
JOY OF LIVING, Art Film Prods., 20th Century-Fox. (Art Film Series). Boris Vermont, producer.
★ THE MERRY WIVES OF WINDSOR OVERTURE, M-G-M. (Overture Series). Johnny Green, producer.
WEE WATER WONDERS, Paramount. (Grantland Rice Sportlights Series). Jack Eaton, producer.

(Two-reel)
★ BEAR COUNTRY, Disney, RKO Radio. (True-Life Adventure). Walt Disney, producer.
BEN AND ME, Disney, Buena Vista. (Cartoon Special Series). Walt Disney, producer.
RETURN TO GLENNASCAUL, Dublin Gate Theatre Prod., Mayer-Kingsley Inc.
VESUVIUS EXPRESS, 20th Century-Fox. (CinemaScope Shorts Series). Otto Lang, producer.
WINTER PARADISE, Warner Bros. (Technicolor Special). Cedric Francis, producer.

DOCUMENTARY

(Short Subjects)
★ THE ALASKAN ESKIMO, Disney, RKO Radio. Walt Disney, producer.
THE LIVING CITY, Encyclopaedia Britannica Films, Inc. John Barnes, producer.
OPERATION BLUE JAY, U.S. Army Signal Corps.

THEY PLANTED A STONE, World Wide Pictures, British Information Services (British). James Carr, producer.
THE WORD, 20th Century-Fox. John Healy and John Adams, producers.

(Features)
THE CONQUEST OF EVEREST, Countryman Films, Group 3 Ltd., UA (British). John Taylor, Leon Clore and Grahame Tharp, producers.
★ THE LIVING DESERT, Disney, Buena Vista. Walt Disney, producer.
A QUEEN IS CROWNED, J. Arthur Rank, U-I (British). Castleton Knight, producer.

HONORARY AND OTHER AWARDS

TO PETE SMITH for his witty and pungent observations on the American scene in his series of "Pete Smith Specialties." (statuette)
TO 20TH CENTURY-FOX FILM CORPORATION in recognition of their imagination, showmanship and foresight in introducing the revolutionary process known as CinemaScope. (statuette)
TO JOSEPH I. BREEN for his conscientious, open-minded and dignified management of the Motion Picture Production Code. (statuette)
TO BELL AND HOWELL COMPANY for their pioneering and basic achievements in the advancement of the motion picture industry. (statuette)

1953 IRVING G. THALBERG MEMORIAL AWARD

TO GEORGE STEVENS

SCIENTIFIC OR TECHNICAL

CLASS I (statuette)
PROFESSOR HENRI CHRETIEN and EARL SPONABLE, SOL HALPRIN, LORIN GRIGNON, HERBERT BRAGG and CARL FAULKNER of 20th Century-Fox Studios for creating, developing and engineering the equipment, processes and techniques known as CinemaScope.
FRED WALLER for designing and developing the multiple photographic and projection systems which culminated in Cinerama.

CLASS II (plaque)
REEVES SOUNDCRAFT CORP. for their development of a process of applying stripes of magnetic oxide to motion picture film for sound recording and reproduction.

CLASS III (citation)
WESTREX CORP.

★ INDICATES WINNER

1954
The Twenty-Seventh Year

Greta Garbo, retired from motion pictures for thirteen years and never an Academy Award winner during her active screen career, was voted an Honorary Academy Award statuette at the 1954 Awards, held March 30, 1955, and telecast both from Hollywood (with Bob Hope as M.C.) and from New York (with Thelma Ritter as hostess). Earlier in the year, Garbo had been the subject of a biographical series in *Life Magazine,* sparking a renewed interest in revivals of her films with the Oscar Award paying tribute to her timeless career. The elusive Garbo, of course, did not attend the ceremony; the award was accepted for her by Nancy Kelly.

Another major actress, this one a nominee, was also absent. Judy Garland, nominated for *A Star Is Born,* was a patient in Cedars of Lebanon Hospital, the mother of a day-old-son. NBC-TV, anticipating a possible Garland victory as Best Actress, had television equipment set up outside her hospital room window, balanced on a special scaffolding, ready for on-the-spot coverage, just in case. However, Grace Kelly, present at the Pantages Theatre in Hollywood, was ultimately announced as the year's Best Actress for *The Country Girl,* and quickly switched the focus away from Cedars. Biggest winner of the night was *On the Waterfront* with eight awards, including Best Picture, Best Actor (Marlon Brando), Best Supporting Actress (Eva Marie Saint) and Best Director (Elia Kazan). With its total, it tied the all-time Oscar record set by *Gone With the Wind* in 1939, and equalled by 1953's *From Here to Eternity.* Edmond O'Brien was chosen Best Supporting Actor for *The Barefoot Contessa.*

Danny Kaye received an Honorary Oscar for his unique talents and services to the Academy, the industry and the American people; and Japan's *Gate of Hell* was voted an Honorary statuette as the year's finest foreign language film released in the United States. Dimitri Tiomkin, winner of the Best Music Score Award for *The High and the Mighty,* accepted his Oscar by thanking a few helpers by name: "Brahms, Bach, Beethoven, Richard Strauss and Johann Strauss . . ."

Two months earlier, on February 12, 1955, the announcement of nominees was made on a live telecast aired over NBC-TV and beamed from Romanoff's restaurant in Hollywood, Ciro's nightclub on the Sunset Strip, the Cocoanut Grove near downtown Los Angeles and the NBC-TV studios in Burbank. It was not considered a success and the experiment was never repeated.

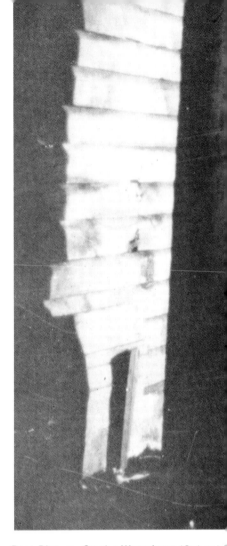

Best Picture: On the Waterfront (Columbi produced by Sam Spiegel), **Best Director: Elia Kazan,** and (above) **Best Actor: Marlon Brando** as Terry Malloy and **Best Supporting Actress: Eva Marie Saint** as Edie Doyle in *On the Waterfront.* Produce on a small budget ($820,000) in an era whe most picture makers were concentrating on new wide-screen processes and CinemaScopic subjects, it stemmed from series of crusading newspaper articles by Malcolm Johnson, fashioned into a taut script by Budd Schulberg and told about brutality and corruption on New York's shipping docks. Brando played a longshoreman who awakens to the fact it morally wrong to be enslaved by a crooke politician boss; Eva Marie Saint played his sensitive girlfriend who encourages th longshoreman's better instincts. Told in semi-documentary style, it was strong, powerful screen fare, and 1954's most-honored film with 12 nominations for Awards and, ultimately, eight Oscars to its credit.

Best Actress: Grace Kelly as Georgie Elgin (left, with William Holden) in *The Country Girl* (Paramount; directed by George Seaton). Uta Hagen created the role on Broadway; Jennifer Jones was originally set to star in the film version with William Holden and Bing Crosby but had to withdraw because of pregnancy. Grace Kelly, relatively new to the film scene, then got the part and—against type—played the plain, embittered wife of an aging and alcoholic matinee idol who tries to cover up for her husband's weaknesses but is misunderstood in her motives. The preceding year, she had also been a part of the Oscar story, nominated for her supporting performance in *Mogambo* (1953).

20,000 Leagues Under the Sea (Buena Vista; produced by Walt Disney) was honored for Color Art Direction and for Special Effects. Kirk Douglas, James Mason, Paul Lukas and Peter Lorre starred in the undersea adventure, based on the tales by Jules Verne, in which—among other perils—the men of the submarine Nautilus battle a giant squid.

Best Supporting Actor: Edmond O'Brien as Oscar Muldoon in *The Barefoot Contessa* (United Artists; directed by Joseph L. Mankiewicz). Humphrey Bogart, Ava Gardner and Rossano Brazzi were the stars of this brittle but glamorous assessment of the tragedy behind a beautiful actress-sex symbol's rise and death; Edmond O'Brien (below, with Maruis Goring) won the Academy's highest honor as a sweating, harassed and overbearing press agent involved in their lives.

PICTURE

THE CAINE MUTINY, Kramer, Columbia. Produced by Stanley Kramer.
THE COUNTRY GIRL, Perlberg-Seaton, Paramount. Produced by William Perlberg.
* **ON THE WATERFRONT**, Horizon-American, Columbia. Produced by Sam Spiegel.
SEVEN BRIDES FOR SEVEN BROTHERS, M-G-M. Produced by Jack Cummings.
THREE COINS IN THE FOUNTAIN, 20th Century-Fox. Produced by Sol C. Siegel.

ACTOR

HUMPHREY BOGART in·*The Caine Mutiny*, Kramer, Columbia.
* **MARLON BRANDO** in *On the Waterfront*, Horizon-American. Columbia.
BING CROSBY in *The Country Girl*, Perlberg-Seaton, Paramount.
JAMES MASON in *A Star Is Born*, Transcona, Warner Bros.
DAN O'HERLIHY in *Adventures of Robinson Crusoe*, Dancigers-Ehrlich, UA.

ACTRESS

DOROTHY DANDRIDGE in *Carmen Jones*, Preminger, 20th Century-Fox.
JUDY GARLAND in *A Star Is Born*, Transcona, Warner Bros.
AUDREY HEPBURN in *Sabrina*, Paramount.
* **GRACE KELLY** in *The Country Girl*, Perlberg-Seaton, Paramount.
JANE WYMAN in *The Magnificent Obsession*, Universal-International.

Nominations 1954

SUPPORTING ACTOR

LEE J. COBB in *On the Waterfront*, Horizon-American, Columbia.
KARL MALDEN in *On the Waterfront*, Horizon-American, Columbia.
* **EDMOND O'BRIEN** in *The Barefoot Contessa*, Figaro, UA.
ROD STEIGER in *On the Waterfront*, Horizon-American, Columbia.
TOM TULLY in *The Caine Mutiny*, Kramer, Columbia.

SUPPORTING ACTRESS

NINA FOCH in *Executive Suite*, M-G-M.
KATY JURADO in *Broken Lance*, 20th Century-Fox.
* **EVA MARIE SAINT** in *On the Waterfront*, Horizon-American, Columbia.
JAN STERLING in *The High and the Mighty*, Wayne-Fellows, Warner Bros.
CLAIRE TREVOR in *The High and the Mighty*, Wayne-Fellows, Warner Bros.

DIRECTION

ALFRED HITCHCOCK for *Rear Window*, Hitchcock, Paramount.
* **ELIA KAZAN** for *On the Waterfront*, Horizon, Columbia.
GEORGE SEATON for *The Country Girl*, Perlberg-Seaton, Paramount.
WILLIAM WELLMAN for *The High and the Mighty*, Wayne-Fellows, Warner Bros.
BILLY WILDER for *Sabrina*, Paramount.

WRITING

(Motion Picture Story)
BREAD, LOVE AND DREAMS, Titanus, I.F.E. Releasing (Italian). Ettore Margadonna.
* **BROKEN LANCE**, 20th Century-Fox. Philip Yordan.
FORBIDDEN GAMES, Times Film Corp. (French). Francois Boyer.
NIGHT PEOPLE, 20th Century-Fox. Jed Harris and Tom Reed.
THERE'S NO BUSINESS LIKE SHOW BUSINESS, 20th Century-Fox. Lamar Trotti.

(Screenplay)
THE CAINE MUTINY, Kramer, Columbia. Stanley Roberts.
* **THE COUNTRY GIRL**, Perlberg-Seaton, Paramount. George Seaton.
REAR WINDOW, Hitchcock, Paramount. John Michael Hayes.
SABRINA, Paramount. Billy Wilder. Samuel Taylor and Ernest Lehman.
SEVEN BRIDES FOR SEVEN BROTHERS, M-G-M. Albert Hackett, Frances Goodrich and Dorothy Kingsley.

(Story and Screenplay)
THE BAREFOOT CONTESSA, Figaro, UA. Joseph Mankiewicz.
GENEVIEVE, Rank-Sirius, U-I (British). William Rose.
THE GLENN MILLER STORY, U-I. Valentine Davies and Oscar Brodney.
KNOCK ON WOOD, Dena, Paramount. Norman Panama and Melvin Frank.
* **ON THE WATERFRONT**, Horizon, Columbia. Budd Schulberg.

Special Award: Greta Garbo. Greta Garbo had been nominated for Academy Awards in 1929-30 (for *Anna Christie* and *Romance*), in 1937 (for *Camille*) and in 1939 (for *Ninotchka*) but had never been voted the final Oscar statuette. To make up for the oversight and, at last, to honor one of the industry's finest artists, the Board of Governors voted her a Special 1954 Academy Award for "her unforgettable screen performances."

CINEMATOGRAPHY

(Black-and-White)
THE COUNTRY GIRL, Perlberg-Seaton, Paramount. John F. Warren.
EXECUTIVE SUITE, M-G-M. George Folsey.
★ ON THE WATERFRONT, Horizon, Columbia. Boris Kaufman.
ROGUE COP, M-G-M. John Seitz.
SABRINA, Paramount. Charles Lang, Jr.

(Color)
THE EGYPTIAN, 20th Century-Fox. Leon Shamroy.
REAR WINDOW, Hitchcock, Paramount. Robert Burks.
SEVEN BRIDES FOR SEVEN BROTHERS, M-G-M. George Folsey.
THE SILVER CHALICE, Saville, Warner Bros. William V. Skall.
★ THREE COINS IN THE FOUNTAIN, 20th Century-Fox. Milton Krasner.

ART DIRECTION-SET DECORATION

(Black-and-White)
THE COUNTRY GIRL, Perlberg-Seaton, Paramount. Hal Pereira and Roland Anderson; Sam Comer and Grace Gregory.
EXECUTIVE SUITE, M-G-M. Cedric Gibbons and Edward Carfagno; Edwin B. Willis and Emile Kuri.
LE PLAISIR, Meyer-Kingsley (French). Max Ophuls.
★ ON THE WATERFRONT, Horizon, Columbia. Richard Day.
SABRINA, Paramount. Hal Pereira and Walter Tyler; Sam Comer and Ray Moyer.

(Color)
BRIGADOON, M-G-M. Cedric Gibbons and Preston Ames; Edwin B. Willis and Keogh Gleason.
DESIREE, 20th Century-Fox. Lyle Wheeler and Leland Fuller; Walter M. Scott and Paul S. Fox.
RED GARTERS, Paramount. Hal Pereira and Roland Anderson; Sam Comer and Ray Moyer.
A STAR IS BORN, Transcona, Warner Bros. Malcolm Bert, Gene Allen and Irene Sharaff; George James Hopkins.
★ 20,000 LEAGUES UNDER THE SEA, Disney, Buena Vista. John Meehan; Emile Kuri.

COSTUME DESIGN

(Black-and-White)
THE EARRINGS OF MADAME DE . . ., Arlan Pictures (French). Georges Annenkov and Rosine Delamare.
EXECUTIVE SUITE, M-G-M. Helen Rose.
INDISCRETION OF AN AMERICAN WIFE, DeSica, Columbia. Christian Dior.
IT SHOULD HAPPEN TO YOU, Columbia. Jean Louis.
★ SABRINA, Paramount. Edith Head.

(Color)
BRIGADOON, M-G-M. Irene Sharaff.
DESIREE, 20th Century-Fox. Charles LeMaire and Rene Hubert.
★ GATE OF HELL, Daiei, Edward Harrison (Japanese). Sanzo Wada.
A STAR IS BORN, Transcona, Warner Bros. Jean Louis, Mary Ann Nyberg and Irene Sharaff.
THERE'S NO BUSINESS LIKE SHOW BUSINESS, 20th Century-Fox. Charles LeMaire, Travilla and Miles White.

SOUND RECORDING

BRIGADOON, M-G-M. Wesley C. Miller, sound director.
THE CAINE MUTINY, Columbia. John P. Livadary, sound director.
★ THE GLENN MILLER STORY, U-I. Leslie I. Carey, sound director.
REAR WINDOW, Hitchcock, Paramount. Loren L. Ryder, sound director.
SUSAN SLEPT HERE, RKO Radio. John O. Aalberg, sound director.

FILM EDITING

THE CAINE MUTINY, Kramer, Columbia. William A. Lyon and Henry Batista.
THE HIGH AND THE MIGHTY, Wayne-Fellows, Warner Bros. Ralph Dawson.
★ ON THE WATERFRONT, Horizon, Columbia. Gene Milford.
SEVEN BRIDES FOR SEVEN BROTHERS, M-G-M. Ralph E. Winters.
20,000 LEAGUES UNDER THE SEA, Disney, Buena Vista. Elmo Williams.

SPECIAL EFFECTS

(A regular Award category for the first time since 1950)
HELL AND HIGH WATER, 20th Century-Fox.
THEM!, Warner Bros.
★ 20,000 LEAGUES UNDER THE SEA, Walt Disney Studios.

MUSIC

(Song)
COUNT YOUR BLESSINGS INSTEAD OF SHEEP (*White Christmas*, Paramount); Music and Lyrics by Irving Berlin.
THE HIGH AND THE MIGHTY (*The High and the Mighty*, Wayne-Fellows, Warner Bros.); Music by Dimitri Tiomkin. Lyrics by Ned Washington.
HOLD MY HAND (*Susan Slept Here*, RKO Radio); Music and Lyrics by Jack Lawrence and Richard Myers.
THE MAN THAT GOT AWAY (*A Star Is Born*, Transcona, Warner Bros.); Music by Harold Arlen. Lyrics by Ira Gershwin.
★ THREE COINS IN THE FOUNTAIN (*Three Coins in the Fountain*, 20th Century-Fox); Music by Jule Styne. Lyrics by Sammy Cahn.

(Scoring of a Dramatic or Comedy Picture)
THE CAINE MUTINY, Kramer, Columbia. Max Steiner.
GENEVIEVE, Rank-Sirius, U-I (British). Muir Mathieson.
★ THE HIGH AND THE MIGHTY, Wayne-Fellows, Warner Bros. Dimitri Tiomkin.
ON THE WATERFRONT, Horizon, Columbia. Leonard Bernstein.
THE SILVER CHALICE, Saville, Warner Bros. Franz Waxman.

(Scoring of a Musical Picture)
CARMEN JONES, Preminger, 20th Century-Fox. Herschel Burke Gilbert.
THE GLENN MILLER STORY, U-I. Joseph Gershenson and Henry Mancini.
★ SEVEN BRIDES FOR SEVEN BROTHERS, M-G-M. Adolph Deutsch and Saul Chaplin.
A STAR IS BORN, Transcona, Warner Bros. Ray Heindorf.
THERE'S NO BUSINESS LIKE SHOW BUSINESS, 20th Century-Fox. Alfred Newman and Lionel Newman.

SHORT SUBJECTS

(Cartoons)
CRAZY MIXED UP PUP, Lantz, U-I. Walter Lantz, producer.
PIGS IS PIGS, Disney, RKO Radio. Walt Disney, producer.
SANDY CLAWS, Warner Bros. Edward Selzer, producer.
TOUCHE, PUSSY CAT, M-G-M. Fred Quimby, producer.
★ WHEN MAGOO FLEW, UPA, Columbia. Stephen Bosustow, producer.

(One-reel)
THE FIRST PIANO QUARTETTE, 20th Century-Fox. Otto Lang, producer.
THE STRAUSS FANTASY, M-G-M. Johnny Green, producer.
★ THIS MECHANICAL AGE, Warner Bros. Robert Youngson, producer.

(Two-reel)
BEAUTY AND THE BULL, Warner Bros. Cedric Francis, producer.
JET CARRIER, 20th Century-Fox. Otto Lang, producer.
SIAM, Disney, Buena Vista. Walt Disney, producer.
★ A TIME OUT OF WAR, Carnival Prods., Denis and Terry Sanders, producers.

DOCUMENTARY

(Short Subjects)
JET CARRIER, 20th Century-Fox. Otto Lang, producer.
REMBRANDT: A SELF-PORTRAIT, Distributors Corp. of America. Morrie Roizman, producer.

★ THURSDAY'S CHILDREN, British Information Services (British). World Wide Pictures and Morse Films, producers.

(Features)
THE STRATFORD ADVENTURE, National Film Board of Canada, Continental (Canadian). Guy Glover, producer.
★ THE VANISHING PRAIRIE, Disney, Buena Vista. Walt Disney, producer.

HONORARY AND OTHER AWARDS

TO BAUSCH & LOMB OPTICAL COMPANY for their contributions to the advancement of the motion picture industry. (statuette)
TO KEMP R. NIVER for the development of the Renovare Process which has made possible the restoration of the Library of Congress Paper Film Collection. (statuette)
TO GRETA GARBO for her unforgettable screen performances. (statuette)
TO DANNY KAYE for his unique talents, his service to the Academy, the motion picture industry, and the American people. (statuette)
TO JON WHITELEY for his outstanding juvenile performance in *The Little Kidnappers*. (miniature statuette)
TO VINCENT WINTER for his outstanding performance in *The Little Kidnappers*. (miniature statuette)
TO GATE OF HELL (Japanese)—Best Foreign Language Film first released in the United States during 1954. (statuette)

1954 IRVING G. THALBERG MEMORIAL AWARD

None given this year.

SCIENTIFIC OR TECHNICAL

CLASS I (statuette)
PARAMOUNT PICTURES, INC., LOREN L. RYDER, JOHN R. BISHOP and all the members of the technical and engineering staff for developing a method of producing and exhibiting motion pictures known as VistaVision.

CLASS II (plaque)
None.

CLASS III (citation)
DAVID S. HORSLEY and the UNIVERSAL-INTERNATIONAL STUDIO SPECIAL PHOTOGRAPHIC DEPARTMENT;
KARL FREUND and FRANK CRANDELL of Photo Research Corp.;
WESLEY C. MILLER, J.W. STAFFORD, K.M. FRIERSON and the METRO-GOLDWYN-MAYER STUDIO SOUND DEPARTMENT;
JOHN P. LIVADARY, LLOYD RUSSELL and the COLUMBIA STUDIO SOUND DEPARTMENT;
ROLAND MILLER and MAX GOEPPINGER of Magnascope Corp.;
CARLOS RIVAS, G.M. SPRAGUE and the METRO-GOLDWYN-MAYER STUDIO SOUND DEPARTMENT;
FRED WILSON of the Samuel Goldwyn Studio Sound Department;
P.C. YOUNG of the M-G-M Studio Projection Department;
FRED KNOTH and ORIEN ERNEST of the Universal-International Studio Technical Department.

★ INDICATES WINNER

1955
The Twenty-Eighth Year

Before 1955, Oscars had been given to numerous revamped Broadway shows, novels and short stories, but at the twenty-eighth session, March 21, 1956, Academy members voted their top prize to a motion pictured based on a *television* play. Never before had the film industry been so complimentary to the TV world. It was an omen of things to come.

Marty, in its transition from tube to big screen, received four of the 1955 Awards including Best Picture, Best Actor (Ernest Borgnine) and Best Director (Delbert Mann), plus a Screenplay Award to the man who created it all, Paddy Chayefsky. Among the actors nominated alongside Borgnine was James Dean, who had been killed in an auto accident six months before, the first actor posthumously nominated for an Academy Award. The next year, he would again be nominated, for *Giant,* completed just prior to his death. Italy's vibrant Anna Magnani was named Best Actress for *The Rose Tattoo,* her first Hollywood-made movie; she was asleep at home in Rome when she received the news in a transatlantic telephone call.

Jack Lemmon was chosen Best Supporting Actor for *Mister Roberts* and Jo Van Fleet was named Best Supporting Actress for *East of Eden* (she had also been prominent in two other 1955-nominated films, *The Rose Tattoo* with Magnani, and *I'll Cry Tomorrow* with Susan Hayward). *Samurai* was voted an Honorary Award as the outstanding foreign language film, the second Japanese film in two years so recognized.

The Academy Award ceremony itself was again telecast on NBC-TV as a two-coast affair, with Jerry Lewis handling M.C. responsibilities in Hollywood, and Claudette Colbert sharing similar duties with Joseph L. Mankiewicz (for whom she almost made *All About Eve* six years before) in New York's Century Theater.

Robert Emmett Dolan and George Seaton co-produced for the Academy, and William A. Bennington again directed for the network. Most of the Awards were presented by the year's acting nominees, or the previous year's winners. Main thrust of attention on this Academy Award night fell on Grace Kelly, on hand to present the year's Best Actor Award. Three months before, she announced her engagement to Prince Rainier of Monaco and announced her screen retirement. The 1955 Academy Award show was her last public appearance before heading to New York days later, then on to Monaco for the wedding.

Best Picture: Marty (United Artists; produced by Harold Hecht), **Best Director: Delbert Mann** and **Best Actor: Ernest Borgnine** as Marty in *Marty.* Written by Paddy Chayefsky and originally done as a television play with Rod Steiger and Nancy Marchand, *Marty* became the first born-in-TV drama to win the Academy's Best Picture Award. Made for a slim $343,000, it told the simple, poignant story of two lonely, plain-looking people (Ernest Borgnine and Betsy Blair) who find each other; Borgnine turned the role of the ordinary, fattish Brooklyn butcher into a star-making part and the picture additionally won the Academy's Screenplay Award to the man who started it all, author Chayefsky.

Best Actress: Anna Magnani as Serafina Delle Rose (above, battling with Burt Lancaster) in *The Rose Tattoo* (Paramount; directed by Daniel Mann). Tennessee Williams originally wrote *The Rose Tattoo* for Italy's Anna to play on Broadway, but she rejected the offer because of her difficulty at the time with the English language; by the time Hal Wallis was ready to roll movie cameras on *Tattoo,* however, she was ready, and she delivered a blistering performance as the seamstress who neurotically worships the memory of a deceased (and unfaithful) husband.

Best Supporting Actor: Jack Lemmon as Ensign Pulver (left, with nurses) in *Mister Roberts* (Warner Bros.; directed by John Ford and Mervyn LeRoy). The Thomas Heggen-Joshua Logan play of 1948 was perfect and robust screen material, one of the year's most popular pictures and allowed newcomer Lemmon, in his fourth film, to underscore his growing reputation as an ace new comedian. He played *Roberts'* wily and mischievous Pulver aboard the ship *Reluctant* during World War II, among a crew that included Henry Fonda, James Cagney and William Powell.

Honorary Award: Samurai (Fine Arts Films; produced in Japan by Kazuo Takimura) starred Toshiro Mifune (below) as a 16th-century villager who wants to become a samurai warrior, joins a losing war and ultimately ends his days as a missionary. The Academy honored *Samurai* as the Best Foreign Language Film released in the United States during 1955, as chosen by the Board of Governors. Hereafter, beginning with the 1956 Awards, foreign films were honored in their own regular Award category, with nominations, rather than as Special or Honorary Awards.

Nominations 1955

PICTURE

LOVE IS A MANY-SPLENDORED THING, 20th Century-Fox. Produced by Buddy Adler.
* **MARTY,** Hecht-Lancaster, UA. Produced by Harold Hecht.
MISTER ROBERTS, Orange, Warner Bros. Produced by Leland Hayward.
PICNIC, Columbia. Produced by Fred Kohlmar.
THE ROSE TATTOO, Wallis, Paramount. Produced by Hal Wallis.

ACTOR

* **ERNEST BORGNINE** in *Marty*, Hecht-Lancaster, UA.
JAMES CAGNEY in *Love Me or Leave Me*, M-G-M.
JAMES DEAN in *East of Eden*, Warner Bros.
FRANK SINATRA in *The Man With the Golden Arm*, Preminger, UA.
SPENCER TRACY in *Bad Day at Black Rock*, M-G-M.

ACTRESS

SUSAN HAYWARD in *I'll Cry Tomorrow*, M-G-M.
KATHARINE HEPBURN in *Summertime*, Lopert-Lean, UA (Anglo-American).
JENNIFER JONES in *Love Is a Many-Splendored Thing*, 20th Century-Fox.
* **ANNA MAGNANI** in *The Rose Tattoo*, Wallis, Paramount.
ELEANOR PARKER in *Interrupted Melody*, M-G-M.

SUPPORTING ACTOR

ARTHUR KENNEDY in *Trial*, M-G-M.
* **JACK LEMMON** in *Mister Roberts*, Orange, Warner Bros.

JOE MANTELL in *Marty*, Hecht-Lancaster, UA.
SAL MINEO in *Rebel Without a Cause*, Warner Bros.
ARTHUR O'CONNELL in *Picnic*, Columbia.

SUPPORTING ACTRESS

BETSY BLAIR in *Marty*, Hecht-Lancaster, UA.
PEGGY LEE in *Pete Kelly's Blues*, Mark VII, Warner Bros.
MARISA PAVAN in *The Rose Tattoo*, Wallis, Paramount.
* **JO VAN FLEET** in *East of Eden*, Warner Bros.
NATALIE WOOD in *Rebel Without a Cause*, Warner Bros.

DIRECTION

ELIA KAZAN for *East of Eden*, Warner Bros.
DAVID LEAN for *Summertime*, Lopert, UA (Anglo-American).
JOSHUA LOGAN for *Picnic*, Columbia.
* **DELBERT MANN** for *Marty*, Hecht-Lancaster, UA.
JOHN STURGES for *Bad Day at Black Rock*, M-G-M.

WRITING

(Motion Picture Story)
* **LOVE ME OR LEAVE ME**, M-G-M. Daniel Fuchs.
THE PRIVATE WAR OF MAJOR BENSON, U-I. Joe Connelly and Bob Mosher.
REBEL WITHOUT A CAUSE, Warner Bros. Nicholas Ray.
THE SHEEP HAS 5 LEGS, U.M.P.O. (French). Jean Marsan, Henry Troyat, Jacques Perret, Henri Verneuil and Raoul Ploquin.
STRATEGIC AIR COMMAND, Paramount. Beirne Lay, Jr.

(Screenplay)
BAD DAY AT BLACK ROCK, M-G-M. Millard Kaufman.
BLACKBOARD JUNGLE, M-G-M. Richard Brooks.
EAST OF EDEN, Warner Bros. Paul Osborn.
LOVE ME OR LEAVE ME, M-G-M. Daniel Fuchs and Isobel Lennart.
* **MARTY**, Hecht-Lancaster, UA. Paddy Chayefsky.

(Story and Screenplay)
THE COURT-MARTIAL OF BILLY MITCHELL, United States Pictures, Warner Bros. Milton Sperling and Emmet Lavery.
* **INTERRUPTED MELODY**, M-G-M. William Ludwig and Sonya Levien.
IT'S ALWAYS FAIR WEATHER, M-G-M. Betty Comden and Adolph Green.
MR. HULOT'S HOLIDAY, GBD International Releasing (French). Jacques Tati and Henri Marquet.
THE SEVEN LITTLE FOYS, Paramount. Melville Shavelson and Jack Rose.

CINEMATOGRAPHY

(Black-and-White)
BLACKBOARD JUNGLE, M-G-M. Russell Harlan.
I'LL CRY TOMORROW, M-G-M. Arthur E. Arling.
MARTY, Hecht-Lancaster, UA. Joseph LaShelle.
QUEEN BEE, Columbia. Charles Lang.
* **THE ROSE TATTOO**, Wallis, Paramount. James Wong Howe.

(Color)
GUYS AND DOLLS, Goldwyn, M-G-M. Harry Stradling.
LOVE IS A MANY-SPLENDORED THING, 20th Century-Fox. Leon Shamroy.

Best Supporting Actress: Jo Van Fleet as Kate (right, with James Dean) in *East of Eden* (Warner Bros.; directed by Elia Kazan). Jo Van Fleet had three strong film roles in 1955: as Susan Hayward's ambitious mother in *I'll Cry Tomorrow,* as Anna Magnani's visitor in *The Rose Tattoo* and as the mysterious madam-mother of James Dean and Richard Davalos in *East of Eden.* For the latter, based on the book by John Steinbeck, she won the Academy Award; it was her first film appearance, and an auspicious debut for the New York-based actress.

A MAN CALLED PETER, 20th Century-Fox. Harold Lipstein.
OKLAHOMA!, Hornblow, Magna Corp. Robert Surtees.
★ TO CATCH A THIEF, Hitchcock, Paramount. Robert Burks.

ART DIRECTION-SET DECORATION

(For the first time, set decorators as well as art directors of winning film received a full-size Academy statuette, instead of certificate or plaque)

(Black-and-White)
BLACKBOARD JUNGLE, M-G-M. Cedric Gibbons and Randall Duell; Edwin B. Willis and Henry Grace.
I'LL CRY TOMORROW, M-G-M. Cedric Gibbons and Malcolm Brown; Edwin B. Willis and Hugh B. Hunt.
THE MAN WITH THE GOLDEN ARM, Preminger, UA. Joseph C. Wright; Darrell Silvera.
MARTY, Hecht-Lancaster, UA. Edward S. Haworth and Walter Simonds; Robert Priestly.
★ THE ROSE TATTOO, Wallis, Paramount. Hal Pereira and Tambi Larsen; Sam Comer and Arthur Krams.

(Color)
DADDY LONG LEGS, 20th Century-Fox. Lyle Wheeler and John DeCuir; Walter M. Scott and Paul S. Fox.
GUYS AND DOLLS, Goldwyn, M-G-M. Oliver Smith and Joseph C. Wright; Howard Bristol.
LOVE IS A MANY-SPLENDORED THING, 20th Century-Fox. Lyle Wheeler and George W. Davis; Walter M. Scott and Jack Stubbs.
★ PICNIC, Columbia, William Flannery and Jo Mielziner; Robert Priestley.
TO CATCH A THIEF, Hitchcock, Paramount. Hal Pereira and Joseph McMillan Johnson; Sam Comer and Arthur Krams.

COSTUME DESIGN

(Black-and-White)
★ I'LL CRY TOMORROW, M-G-M. Helen Rose.
THE PICKWICK PAPERS, Renown, Kingsley International (British). Beatrice Dawson.
QUEEN BEE, Columbia. Jean Louis.
THE ROSE TATTOO, Wallis, Paramount. Edith Head.
UGETSU, Daiei, Edward Harrison Releasing (Japanese). Tadaoto Kainoscho.

(Color)
GUYS AND DOLLS, Goldwyn, M-G-M. Irene Sharaff.
INTERRUPTED MELODY, M-G-M. Helen Rose.
★ LOVE IS A MANY-SPLENDORED THING, 20th Century-Fox. Charles LeMaire.
TO CATCH A THIEF, Hitchcock, Paramount. Edith Head.
THE VIRGIN QUEEN, 20th Century-Fox. Charles LeMaire and Mary Wills.

SOUND RECORDING

LOVE IS A MANY-SPLENDORED THING, 20th Century-Fox. Carl W. Faulkner, sound director.
LOVE ME OR LEAVE ME, M-G-M. Wesley C. Miller, sound director.
MISTER ROBERTS, Warner Bros. William A. Mueller, sound director.
NOT AS A STRANGER, Kramer, UA. RCA Sound Department; Watson Jones, sound director.
★ OKLAHOMA!, Hornblow, Magna. Todd-AO Sound Department; Fred Hynes, sound director.

FILM EDITING

BLACKBOARD JUNGLE, M-G-M. Ferris Webster.
THE BRIDGES AT TOKO-RI, Perlberg-Seaton, Paramount. Alma Macrorie.
OKLAHOMA!, Hornblow, Magna Corp. Gene Ruggiero and George Boemler.
★ PICNIC, Columbia. Charles Nelson and William A. Lyon.
THE ROSE TATTOO, Wallis, Paramount. Warren Low.

SPECIAL EFFECTS

★ THE BRIDGES AT TOKO-RI, Paramount.
THE DAM BUSTERS, Associated British, Warner Bros (British).
THE RAINS OF RANCHIPUR, 20th Century-Fox.

MUSIC

(Song)
I'LL NEVER STOP LOVING YOU (*Love Me or Leave Me,* M-G-M); Music by Nicholas Brodszky. Lyrics by Sammy Cahn.
★ LOVE IS A MANY-SPLENDORED THING (*Love Is a Many-Splendored Thing,* 20th Century-Fox); Music by Sammy Fain. Lyrics by Paul Francis Webster.
SOMETHING'S GOTTA GIVE (*Daddy Long Legs,* 20th Century-Fox); Music and Lyrics by Johnny Mercer.
(LOVE IS) THE TENDER TRAP (*The Tender Trap,* M-G-M); Music by James Van Heusen. Lyrics by Sammy Cahn.

UNCHAINED MELODY (*Unchained,* Bartlett, Warner Bros.); Music by Alex North. Lyrics by Hy Zaret.

(Scoring of a Dramatic or Comedy Picture)
BATTLE CRY, Warner Bros. Max Steiner.
★ LOVE IS A MANY-SPLENDORED THING, 20th Century-Fox. Alfred Newman.
THE MAN WITH THE GOLDEN ARM, Preminger, UA. Elmer Bernstein.
PICNIC, Columbia. George Duning.
THE ROSE TATTOO, Wallis, Paramount. Alex North.

(Scoring of a Musical Picture)
DADDY LONG LEGS, 20th Century-Fox. Alfred Newman.
GUYS AND DOLLS, Goldwyn, M-G-M. Jay Blackton and Cyril J. Mockridge.
IT'S ALWAYS FAIR WEATHER, M-G-M. Andre Previn.
LOVE ME OR LEAVE ME, M-G-M. Percy Faith and George Stoll.
★ OKLAHOMA!, Hornblow, Magna Corp. Robert Russell Bennett, Jay Blackton and Adolph Deutsch.

SHORT SUBJECTS

(Cartoons)
GOOD WILL TO MEN, M-G-M. Fred Quimby, William Hanna and Joseph Barbera, producers.
THE LEGEND OF ROCK-A-BYE-POINT, Lantz, U-I. Walter Lantz, producer.
NO HUNTING, Disney, RKO Radio. Walt Disney, producer.
★ SPEEDY GONZALES, Warner Bros. Edward Selzer, producer.

(One-reel)
GADGETS GALORE, Warner Bros. Robert Youngson, producer.
★ SURVIVAL CITY, 20th Century-Fox. Edmund Reek, producer.
3RD AVE. EL, Davidson Prods., Ardee Films. Carson Davidson, producer.
THREE KISSES, Paramount. Justin Herman, producer.

(Two-reel)
THE BATTLE OF GETTYSBURG, M-G-M. Dore Schary, producer.
★ THE FACE OF LINCOLN, University of Southern California, Cavalcade Pictures. Wilbur T. Blume, producer.
ON THE TWELFTH DAY . . ., Go Pictures, George Brest & Assocs. George K. Arthur, producer.
SWITZERLAND, Disney, Buena Vista. Walt Disney, producer.
24 HOUR ALERT, Warner Bros. Cedric Francis, producer.

DOCUMENTARY

(Short Subjects)
THE BATTLE OF GETTYSBURG, M-G-M. Dore Schary, producer.
THE FACE OF LINCOLN, University of Southern California, Cavalcade Pictures. Wilbur T. Blume, producer.
★ MEN AGAINST THE ARCTIC, Disney, Buena Vista. Walt Disney, producer.

(Features)
HEARTBREAK RIDGE, Rene Risacher Prod., Tudor Pictures (French). Rene Risacher, producer.
★ HELEN KELLER IN HER STORY, Nancy Hamilton Presentation. Nancy Hamilton, producer.

HONORARY AND OTHER AWARDS

TO SAMURAI, The Legend of Musashi, (Japanese)—Best Foreign Language Film first released in the United States during 1955. (statuette)

1955 IRVING G. THALBERG MEMORIAL AWARD

None given this year.

SCIENTIFIC OR TECHNICAL

CLASS I (statuette)
NATIONAL CARBON CO. for the development and production of a high efficiency yellow flame carbon for motion picture color photography.

CLASS II (plaque)
EASTMAN KODAK CO. for Eastman Tri-X panchromatic negative film.

FARCIOT EDOUART, HAL CORL and the PARAMOUNT STUDIO TRANSPARENCY DEPT. for the engineering and development of a double-frame, triple-head background projector.

CLASS III (citation)
20TH CENTURY-FOX STUDIO and BAUSCH & LOMB CO.;
WALTER JOLLEY, MAURICE LARSON and R.H. SPIES of 20th Century-Fox Studio;
STEVE KRILANOVICH;
DAVE ANDERSON of 20th Century-Fox Studio;
LOREN L. RYDER, CHARLES WEST, HENRY FRACKER and PARAMOUNT STUDIO;
FARCIOT EDOUART, HAL CORL and the PARAMOUNT STUDIO TRANSPARENCY DEPARTMENT.

★ INDICATES WINNER

1956 The Twenty-Ninth Year

Ingrid Bergman received a rousing welcome back to the Hollywood (and international) movie scene on March 27, 1957, when she was announced as the Academy's Best Actress winner of 1956 for *Anastasia.* For the preceding six years, the star had worked exclusively in Italian-made films, most of them directed by her husband, Roberto Rossellini, none of them as commercially successful as her earlier work in Holly-wood under the management of David O. Selznick. At the time of the Oscar announcement, she was in Paris, appearing on stage in *Tea and Sympathy,* and her Award was accepted by former co-star Cary Grant.

Controversy erupted in the Academy's writing category. Early in 1956, the name of screenwriter Michael Wilson had been deleted from the credits of *Friendly Persuasion* by Allied Artists, the film's distributor, based on a 1952 agreement between the Screen Writers Guild and various production companies. That agreement gave studios the right to omit from the screen the name of any individual who had failed to clear himself before a duly constituted legislative committee of Congress if accused of Communist affiliations, as was the case with Wilson at the time. The Academy, in the awkward position of possibly conferring its highest honor on someone whose name had been omitted from screen credit, revised its bylaws at a special February 6, 1957, meeting. That revision, in essence, allowed that in such cases, the achievement itself could be eligible for nomination, but the specific writer would be ineligible. (The bylaw was repealed by the Academy as "unworkable" on January 12, 1959.)

Also, when nominations were announced, Edward Bernds and Elwood Ullman, the authors of a Bowery Boys quickie titled *High Society,* were among the contenders but respectfully withdrew their own names, aware that voters had probably mistaken their *High Society* with a 1956 release of the same title which was written by John Patrick and starred Bing Crosby, Grace Kelly and Frank Sinatra. There was further confusion when the final winners were announced (at the Pantages Theatre in Hollywood, plus New York's Century Theater, telecast by NBC) and the Best Motion Picture Story winner was *The Brave One,* credited to Robert Rich. The Rich name was later acknowledged as a pseudonym, with exact writer credit not officially established for several years until Dalton Trumbo was confirmed as the author; in 1956, he had been unable to work under his own name because of the earlier House Un-American Activities investigations into the motion picture industry. Shortly before Trumbo's death, Academy President Walter Mirisch presented the screenwriter his Oscar.

Most-honored films of the year were *Around the World in 80 Days* (five Awards, including Best Picture) and *The King and I* (five Awards, including Best Actor Yul Brynner). Anthony Quinn, Dorothy Malone and director George Stevens were also honored and, for the first year, foreign language films were classified in a separate category, nominated and voted along with other Awards instead of being presented as an Honorary Award with no nominations. M.C. of the Oscar night show itself was Jerry Lewis in Hollywood, with Celeste Holm handling hostess duties on the New York sister-show.

Best Actress: Ingrid Bergman as the Woman (above) in *Anastasia* (20th Century-Fox; directed by Anatole Litvak). Filmed entirely in Europe, Ingrid Bergman played a Paris derelict, saved from suicide by a trio of White Russians who train her to pose as the missing daughter of Czar Nicholas II of Russia, who had supposedly escaped death in the 1918 assassination of the Royal Family; plagued by self fears of insanity and with only vague recollections of her own past, the woman wins recognition from the Dowager Empress (Helen Hayes) and even gives evidence she might be the real Anastasia. Originally a Broadway success with Viveca Lindfors in the title role, *Anastasia* brought Ingrid Bergman back into the front-line of the motion picture world after a six-year absence and earned her a second Oscar. A third one came 18 years later, for *Murder on the Orient Express.*

Best Picture: Around the World in 80 Days (United Artists; produced by Michael Todd). Broadway showman Michael Todd had never made a motion picture before, and he didn't tip-toe in with his first one, based on Jules Verne's lampoon of Victorian manners in which a proper Britisher of 1872 sets out to win a wager that he can circle the globe in precisely 80 days. Todd turned it into a 178-minute movie carnival—and an exceptionally super film —featuring (above) Robert Newton, Cantinflas, Shirley MacLaine and David Niven. He also coined a new show business phrase, "cameo role," to cover major stars he'd enticed into playing bit roles, including Frank Sinatra, Marlene Dietrich, Jose Greco, Ronald Colman, Noel Coward, Beatrice Lillie, Red Skelton, Victor McLaglen, Buster Keaton and others who did unexpected walk-ons. Michael Anderson directed.

Best Actor: Yul Brynner as the King of Siam (left) in *The King and I* (20th Century-Fox; directed by Walter Lang). Yul Brynner had appeared on screen only once before (in 1949's minor *Port of New York*) but in 1956 he made an imposing screen impression in three of the year's most conspicuous films: *The King and I, The Ten Commandments* and *Anastasia.* He won the Academy Award for the first, as the virile Siamese tyrant of the 1800s whose desire to be a cultivated and educated man clashes with his traditional, royal arrogance and with an imported governess, played by Deborah Kerr. Brynner had played the King before, on Broadway opposite Gertrude Lawrence, when the story was first set to Rodgers and Hammerstein music in 1951. The King had also been in the movies before, portrayed by Rex Harrison in a 1946 nonmusical version, *Anna and the King of Siam.*

Best Director: George Stevens (above, with James Dean) for *Giant* (Warner Bros.; also produced by Stevens, with Henry Ginsberg). Based on the Edna Ferber novel, *Giant* was a mammoth (198 minutes) and sprawling epic focusing on the Benedict clan (headed by Rock Hudson with Elizabeth Taylor) of Texas. Stevens had previously won the Academy Award for 1951's *A Place in the Sun*, also with Elizabeth Taylor, and was additionally nominated in 1943 (for *The More the Merrier*), 1953 (for *Shane*) and 1959 (for *The Diary of Anne Frank*). He also received the 1953 Irving G. Thalberg Memorial Award.

Best Supporting Actress: Dorothy Malone as Marylee Hadley (below, with Rock Hudson) in *Written on the Wind* (Universal-International; directed by Douglas Sirk). After a long career (14 years, 39 films) of work-horse roles, the majority of them in B-budget projects, Dorothy Malone had an actress's field day playing a sexually maladjusted, poor-little-rich-girl sister of Robert Stack, out to conquer family friend Rock Hudson. She won the Oscar, but not Hudson.

Nominations 1956

PICTURE

* ★ **AROUND THE WORLD IN 80 DAYS,** Todd, UA. Produced by Michael Todd.
* **FRIENDLY PERSUASION,** Allied Artists. Produced by William Wyler.
* **GIANT,** Warner Bros. Produced by George Stevens and Henry Ginsberg.
* **THE KING AND I,** 20th Century-Fox. Produced by Charles Brackett.
* **THE TEN COMMANDMENTS,** DeMille, Paramount. Produced by Cecil B. DeMille.

ACTOR

* ★ **YUL BRYNNER** in *The King and I*, 20th Century-Fox.
* **JAMES DEAN** in *Giant*, Warner Bros.
* **KIRK DOUGLAS** in *Lust for Life*, M-G-M.
* **ROCK HUDSON** in *Giant*, Warner Bros.
* **SIR LAURENCE OLIVIER** in *Richard III*, Olivier, Lopert Films (British).

ACTRESS

* **CARROLL BAKER** in *Baby Doll*, Newtown, Warner Bros.
* ★ **INGRID BERGMAN** in *Anastasia*, 20th Century-Fox.
* **KATHARINE HEPBURN** in *The Rainmaker*, Wallis, Paramount.
* **NANCY KELLY** in *The Bad Seed*, Warner Bros.
* **DEBORAH KERR** in *The King and I*, 20th Century-Fox.

SUPPORTING ACTOR

* **DON MURRAY** in *Bus Stop*, 20th Century-Fox.
* **ANTHONY PERKINS** in *Friendly Persuasion*, Allied Artists.
* ★ **ANTHONY QUINN** in *Lust for Life*, M-G-M.
* **MICKEY ROONEY** in *The Bold and the Brave*, Filmakers Releasing, RKO Radio.
* **ROBERT STACK** in *Written on the Wind, U-I*.

SUPPORTING ACTRESS

* **MILDRED DUNNOCK** in *Baby Doll*, Newtown, Warner Bros.
* **EILEEN HECKART** in *The Bad Seed*, Warner Bros.
* **MERCEDES McCAMBRIDGE** in *Giant*, Warner Bros.
* **PATTY McCORMACK** in *The Bad Seed*, Warner Bros.
* ★ **DOROTHY MALONE** IN *Written on the Wind*, U-I.

DIRECTION

* **MICHAEL ANDERSON** for *Around the World in 80 Days*, Todd, UA.
* **WALTER LANG** for *The King and I*, 20th Century-Fox.
* ★ **GEORGE STEVENS** for *Giant*, Warner Bros.
* **KING VIDOR** for *War and Peace*, Ponti-De Laurentiis, Paramount (Italo-American).
* **WILLIAM WYLER** for *Friendly Persuasion*, Allied Artists.

WRITING

(Motion Picture Story)

* ★ **THE BRAVE ONE,** King Bros., RKO Radio. Dalton Trumbo (aka Robert Rich).
* **THE EDDY DUCHIN STORY,** Columbia. Leo Katcher.
* **HIGH SOCIETY,** Allied Artists. Edward Bernds and Elwood Ullman. (Withdrawn from final ballot.)
* **THE PROUD AND THE BEAUTIFUL,** Kingsley International (French). Jean Paul Sartre.
* **UMBERTO D.,** Harrison & Davidson Releasing (Italian). Ceasare Zavattini.

(Best Screenplay—adapted)

* ★ **AROUND THE WORLD IN 80 DAYS,** Todd, UA. James Poe, John Farrow and S.J. Perelman.
* **BABY DOLL,** Newtown, Warner Bros. Tennessee Williams.
* **GIANT,** Warner Bros. Fred Guiol and Ivan Moffat.

LUST FOR LIFE, M-G-M. Norman Corwin.
FRIENDLY PERSUASION, Allied Artists. (Writer Michael Wilson ineligible for nomination under Academy bylaws.)

(Best Screenplay—original)

* **THE BOLD AND THE BRAVE,** Filmakers, RKO Radio. Robert Lewin.
* **JULIE,** Arwin, M-G-M. Andrew L. Stone.
* **LA STRADA,** Ponti-De Laurentiis, Trans-Lux Dist. Corp. (Italian). Federico Fellini and Tullio Pinelli.
* **THE LADY KILLERS,** Ealing, Continental Dist. (British). William Rose.
* ★ **THE RED BALLOON,** Lopert Films (French). Albert Lamorisse.

CINEMATOGRAPHY

(Black-and-White)

* **BABY DOLL,** Newtown, Warner Bros. Boris Kaufman.
* **THE BAD SEED,** Warner Bros. Hal Rosson.
* **THE HARDER THEY FALL,** Columbia. Burnett Guffey.
* ★ **SOMEBODY UP THERE LIKES ME,** M-G-M. Joseph Ruttenberg.
* **STAGECOACH TO FURY,** Regal Films, 20th Century-Fox. Walter Strenge.

(Color)

* ★ **AROUND THE WORLD IN 80 DAYS,** Todd, UA. Lionel Lindon.
* **THE EDDY DUCHIN STORY,** Columbia. Harry Stradling.
* **THE KING AND I,** 20th Century-Fox. Leon Shamroy.
* **THE TEN COMMANDMENTS,** DeMille, Paramount. Loyal Griggs.
* **WAR AND PEACE,** Ponti-De Laurentiis, Paramount (Italo-American). Jack Cardiff.

ART DIRECTION-SET DECORATION

(Black-and-White)

* **THE MAGNIFICENT SEVEN,** Toho, Kingsley International (Japanese). Takashi Matsuyama.
* **THE PROUD AND THE PROFANE,** Perlberg-Seaton, Paramount. Hal Pereira and A. Earl Hedrick; Samuel M. Comer and Frank R. McKelvy.
* **THE SOLID GOLD CADILLAC,** Columbia. Ross Bellah; William R. Kiernan and Louis Diage.
* ★ **SOMEBODY UP THERE LIKES ME,** M-G-M. Cedric Gibbons and Malcolm F. Brown; Edwin B. Willis and F. Keogh Gleason.
* **TEENAGE REBEL,** 20th Century-Fox. Lyle R. Wheeler and Jack Martin Smith; Walter M. Scott and Stuart A. Reiss.

(Color)

* **AROUND THE WORLD IN 80 DAYS,** Todd, UA. James W. Sullivan and Ken Adams; Ross J. Dowd.
* **GIANT,** Warner Bros. Boris Leven; Ralph S. Hurst.
* ★ **THE KING AND I,** 20th Century-Fox. Lyle R. Wheeler and John DeCuir; Walter M. Scott and Paul S. Fox.
* **LUST FOR LIFE,** M-G-M. Cedric Gibbons, Hans Peters and Preston Ames; Edwin B. Willis and F. Keogh Gleason.
* **THE TEN COMMANDMENTS,** DeMille, Paramount. Hal Pereira, Walter H. Tyler and Albert Nozaki; Sam M. Comer and Ray Moyer.

COSTUME DESIGN

(Black-and-White)

* **THE MAGNIFICENT SEVEN,** Toho, Kingsley International (Japanese). Kohei Ezaki.
* **THE POWER AND THE PRIZE,** M-G-M. Helen Rose.
* **THE PROUD AND THE PROFANE,** Perlberg-Seaton, Paramount. Edith Head.
* ★ **THE SOLID GOLD CADILLAC,** Columbia. Jean Louis.
* **TEENAGE REBEL,** 20th Century-Fox. Charles LeMaire and Mary Wills.

(Color)

* **AROUND THE WORLD IN 80 DAYS,** Todd, UA. Miles White.

GIANT, Warner Bros. Moss Mabry and Marjorie Best.
* THE KING AND I, 20th Century-Fox. Irene Sharaff.
THE TEN COMMANDMENTS, DeMille, Paramount. Edith Head, Ralph Jester, John Jensen, Dorothy Jeakins and Arnold Friberg.
WAR AND PEACE, Ponti-De Laurentiis, Paramount (Italo-American). Marie De Matteis.

SOUND RECORDING

THE BRAVE ONE, King Bros., RKO Radio. John Myers, sound director.
THE EDDY DUCHIN STORY, Columbia. Columbia Studio Sound Department; John Livadary, sound director.
FRIENDLY PERSUASION, Allied Artists. Westrex Sound Services, Inc.; Gordon R. Glennan, sound director, and Samuel Goldwyn Studio Sound Department; Gordon Sawyer, sound director.
* THE KING AND I, 20th Century-Fox. 20th Century-Fox Studio Sound Department; Carl Faulkner, sound director.
THE TEN COMMANDMENTS, DeMille, Paramount. Paramount Studio Sound Department; Loren L. Ryder, sound director.

FILM EDITING

* AROUND THE WORLD IN 80 DAYS, Todd, UA. Gene Ruggiero and Paul Weatherwax.
THE BRAVE ONE, King Bros., RKO Radio. Merrill G. White.
GIANT, Warner Bros. William Hornbeck, Philip W. Anderson and Fred Bohanan.
SOMEBODY UP THERE LIKES ME, M-G-M. Albert Akst.
THE TEN COMMANDMENTS, DeMille, Paramount. Anne Bauchens.

SPECIAL EFFECTS

FORBIDDEN PLANET, M-G-M. A. Arnold Gillespie, Irving Ries and Wesley C. Miller.
* THE TEN COMMANDMENTS, DeMille, Paramount. John Fulton.

MUSIC

(Song)
FRIENDLY PERSUASION (THEE I LOVE) (Friendly Persuasion, Allied Artists); Music by Dimitri Tiomkin. Lyrics by Paul Francis Webster.
JULIE (Julie, Arwin, M-G-M); Music by Leith Stevens. Lyrics by Tom Adair.
TRUE LOVE (High Society, Siegel, M-G-M); Music and Lyrics by Cole Porter.
* WHATEVER WILL BE, WILL BE (QUE SERA, SERA) (The Man Who Knew Too Much, Hitchcock, Paramount); Music and Lyrics by Jay Livingston and Ray Evans.
WRITTEN ON THE WIND (Written on the Wind, U-I); Music by Victor Young. Lyrics by Sammy Cahn.

(Scoring of a Dramatic or Comedy Picture)
ANASTASIA, 20th Century-Fox. Alfred Newman.
* AROUND THE WORLD IN 80 DAYS, Todd, UA. Victor Young.
BETWEEN HEAVEN AND HELL, 20th Century-Fox. Hugo Friedhofer.
GIANT, Warner Bros. Dimitri Tiomkin.
THE RAINMAKER, Wallis, Paramount. Alex North.

(Scoring of a Musical Picture)
THE BEST THINGS IN LIFE ARE FREE, 20th Century-Fox. Lionel Newman.
THE EDDY DUCHIN STORY, Columbia. Morris Stoloff and George Duning.
HIGH SOCIETY, Siegel, M-G-M. Johnny Green and Saul Chaplin.
* THE KING AND I, 20th Century-Fox. Alfred Newman and Ken Darby.
MEET ME IN LAS VEGAS, M-G-M. George Stoll and Johnny Green.

SHORT SUBJECTS

(Cartoons)
GERALD McBOING-BOING ON PLANET MOO, UPA, Columbia. Stephen Bosustow, producer.

THE JAYWALKER, UPA, Columbia. Stephen Bosustow, producer.
* MISTER MAGOO'S PUDDLE JUMPER, UPA, Columbia. Stephen Bosustow, producer.

(One-reel)
* CRASHING THE WATER BARRIER, Warner Bros. Konstantin Kalser, producer.
I NEVER FORGET A FACE, Warner Bros. Robert Youngson, producer.
TIME STOOD STILL, Warner Bros. Cedric Francis, producer.

(Two-reel)
* THE BESPOKE OVERCOAT, Romulus Films, George K. Arthur, producer.
COW DOG, Disney, Buena Vista. Larry Lansburgh, producer.
THE DARK WAVE, 20th Century-Fox. John Healy, producer.
SAMOA, Disney, Buena Vista. Walt Disney, producer.

DOCUMENTARY

(Short Subjects)
A CITY DECIDES, Charles Guggenheim & Assocs.
THE DARK WAVE, 20th Century-Fox. John Healy, producer.
THE HOUSE WITHOUT A NAME, U-I. Valentine Davies, producer.
MAN IN SPACE, Disney, Buena Vista. Ward Kimball, producer.
* THE TRUE STORY OF THE CIVIL WAR, Camera Eye Pictures. Louis Clyde Stoumen, producer.

(Features)
THE NAKED EYE, Camera Eye Pictures. Louis Clyde Stoumen, producer.
* THE SILENT WORLD, Filmad-F.S.J.Y.C., Columbia (French). Jacques-Yves Cousteau, producer.
WHERE MOUNTAINS FLOAT, Brandon Films (Danish). The Government Film Committee of Denmark, producer.

FOREIGN LANGUAGE FILM

(First year of nominations; previously honored in the Special Award division)

THE CAPTAIN OF KOPENICK, (Germany).
GERVAISE, (France).
HARP OF BURMA, (Japan).
* LA STRADA, (Italy).
QIVITOQ, (Denmark).

HONORARY AND OTHER AWARDS

TO EDDIE CANTOR for distinguished service to the film industry. (statuette)

1956 IRVING G. THALBERG MEMORIAL AWARD

TO BUDDY ADLER

1956 JEAN HERSHOLT HUMANITARIAN AWARD
(New category)

TO Y. FRANK FREEMAN

SCIENTIFIC OR TECHNICAL

CLASS I (statuette)
None.

CLASS II (plaque)
None.

CLASS III (citation)
RICHARD H. RANGER of Rangertone Inc.;
TED HIRSCH, CARL HAUGE and EDWARD REICHARD of Consolidated Film Industries;
THE TECHNICAL DEPARTMENTS of PARAMOUNT PICTURES CORP.;
ROY C. STEWART AND SONS of Stewart-Trans Lux Corp., DR. C.R. DAILY and the TRANSPARENCY DEPARTMENT of PARAMOUNT PICTURES CORP.;
THE CONSTRUCTION DEPARTMENT of METRO-GOLDWYN-MAYER STUDIO;
DANIEL J. BLOOMBERG, JOHN POND, WILLIAM WADE and the ENGINEERING and CAMERA DEPARTMENTS of REPUBLIC STUDIO.

★ INDICATES WINNER

Best Supporting Actor: Anthony Quinn as Paul Gauguin (above, with Kirk Douglas) in *Lust for Life* (M-G-M; directed by Vincente Minnelli). Quinn won his second Supporting Actor Oscar as the real-life Gauguin, ego-ridden painter and housemate of the tormented Vincent van Gogh. He played the role with vitality and dark humor, and it was one of the shortest performances ever to win an Academy Award, constituting only a matter of minutes of total screen time, a supporting performance in the best sense of the word.

The Brave One (RKO Radio; produced by Maurice King and Frank King) featured Michel Ray (below) as a young Mexican boy who attempts to save his pet bull from being sent into the bullring. The film received an Oscar for Motion Picture Story and unintentionally spawned confusion: the name of the writer credited with authorship, Robert Rich, turned out to be an alias. Two decades later, the mystery was officially solved and the Academy statuette went to its rightful owner, screenwriter Dalton Trumbo, blacklisted in 1956 by the industry for political affiliations.

Best Actress: Joanne Woodward as Eve White (above, with Lee J. Cobb) in *The Three Faces of Eve* (20th Century-Fox; directed by Nunnally Johnson). First offered to Judy Garland and Carroll Baker, among others, *Eve* was based on an actual split-personality case, recorded by two Georgia psychiatrists, in which a drab housewife suffered severe headaches and during subsequent blackouts underwent a striking personality change (to Eve 'Black'), then under psychiatric treatment gave way to a third personality ('Jane'). It was a plump and showy role, finally entrusted to newcomer Joanne Woodward, and she gave it her own indelible mark. *Eve* won her the Academy Award, and made her a major star.

1957 The Thirtieth Year

In newspaper parlance, 30 means "the end," but when the Academy turned thirty with the 1957 Awards ceremony, March 26, 1958, it was the start of something new: for the first time in the six years Oscar shows had been televised, the show itself was TV-sponsored solely by the motion picture industry, financed by the major studios, independent producers and theater owners, who used the telecast to promote new film products instead of unallied commercial products, as had been the case. It was an auspicious idea and continued for three television years, but ultimately proved too much of an organizational and financial burden.

Voting rules were also drastically altered. Since 1946, the final voting decision on Oscars had been made by the Academy's approximately 2,000 members, but yearly nominations for Awards had been chosen by more than 12,000 individuals, members of the Academy, industry guilds and unions; beginning with the 1957 Awards, both the nominations *and* final selections were left strictly in the hands of the Academy members. The number of categories, which had swelled to thirty-one in the previous year, was also streamlined down to twenty-three.

Because the NBC telecast was wholly an industry affair, it was especially crowded with major box office names, several of whom—like Clark Gable and Jennifer Jones—had never appeared on television before. It was produced for the Academy by Jerry Wald. Five people shared master of ceremonies duties (James Stewart, David Niven, Jack Lemmon, Rosalind Russell, Bob Hope) with some animated help from Donald Duck, who hosted a seven-minute combined live-action and cartoon history of the movies. The entire show came from the Pantages Theatre in Hollywood, with no New York cut-in, another first for Oscar's television career. Among the entertainment highlights of the evening was the opening number: a medley of previous Oscar-winning songs, done by Betty Grable and Harry James, Mae West and Rock Hudson, Marge and Gower Champion, Bob Hope and Rhonda Fleming, Shirley MacLaine and others.

The Bridge on the River Kwai dominated the evening's Awards, winning seven, including Best Picture, Best Actor (Alec Guinness) and Best Director (David Lean). *Sayonara* was runner-up with four Oscars, including those for Best Supporting Actor (Red Buttons) and Best Supporting Actress (Miyoshi Umeki). Best Actress was 28-year-old Joanne Woodward in *The Three Faces of Eve,* and Italy's *The Nights of Cabiria* was selected as Best Foreign Language Film. All the acting winners were on hand at the Pantages, except winner Guinness, who was in England filming *The Horse's Mouth.* His Award was accepted by Jean Simmons.

Best Picture: The Bridge on the River Kwai (Columbia; produced by Sam Spiegel) and (right) **Best Actor: Alec Guinness** as Colonel Nicholson in *The Bridge on the River Kwai.* It took a hot and uncomfortable three-and-a-half months in the Ceylon jungle to film Pierre Boulle's grim novel about the folly of men unwittingly involved in the useless game of war, but it paid off with the most realistic antiwar movie since *All Quiet on the Western Front* 27 years before. It won seven Academy Awards, including an Oscar (and new international fame) for Alec Guinness as a British colonel held captive with his men in a World War II Japanese prisoner-of-war camp. A strict disciplinarian, the colonel has a rigid conflict of wills with his Japanese captors over military protocol, and later supervises the building of a railway bridge for the Japanese without regard for the aid it gives the enemy, obsessed instead with proving his battalion is superior to his enemy. Guinness' fellow players included William Holden, Jack Hawkins, Sessue Hayakawa and Geoffrey Horne.

Best Director: David Lean (above, with Alec Guinness) for *The Bridge on the River Kwai.* England's David Lean first became a part of the Academy Awards story in 1946 when he was twice nominated for *Brief Encounter* (as director and for co-writing the screenplay); the following year, he was again nominated in the same two divisions, for *Great Expectations,* and in 1955 for directing *Summertime.* He won his first Oscar for 1957's *Bridge* and a second for directing *Lawrence of Arabia* in 1962. In 1965, he was again nominated as director, for *Doctor Zhivago.* A remarkable record, not only because of his Academy tally but because of his versatility in subject matter.

Nominations 1957

PICTURE

* **THE BRIDGE ON THE RIVER KWAI,** Horizon, Columbia. Produced by Sam Spiegel.
  PEYTON PLACE, Wald, 20th Century-Fox. Produced by Jerry Wald.
  SAYONARA, Goetz, Warner Bros. Produced by William Goetz.
  12 ANGRY MEN, Orion-Nova, UA. Produced by Henry Fonda and Reginald Rose.
  WITNESS FOR THE PROSECUTION, Small-Hornblow, UA. Produced by Arthur Hornblow, Jr.

ACTOR

MARLON BRANDO in *Sayonara,* Goetz, Warner Bros.
ANTHONY FRANCIOSA in *A Hatful of Rain,* 20th Century-Fox.
* **ALEC GUINNESS** in *The Bridge on the River Kwai,* Horizon, Columbia.
CHARLES LAUGHTON in *Witness for the Prosecution,* Small-Hornblow, UA.
ANTHONY QUINN in *Wild Is the Wind,* Wallis, Paramount.

ACTRESS

DEBORAH KERR in *Heaven Knows Mr. Allison,* 20th Century-Fox.
ANNA MAGNANI in *Wild Is the Wind,* Wallis, Paramount.
ELIZABETH TAYLOR in *Raintree County,* M-G-M.
LANE TURNER in *Peyton Place,* Wald, 20th Century-Fox.
* **JOANNE WOODWARD** in *The Three Faces of Eve,* 20th Century-Fox.

SUPPORTING ACTOR

* **RED BUTTONS** in *Sayonara,* Goetz, Warner Bros.
VITTORIO DE SICA in *A Farewell to Arms,* Selznick, 20th Century-Fox.
SESSUE HAYAKAWA in *The Bridge on the River Kwai,* Horizon, Columbia.
ARTHUR KENNEDY in *Peyton Place,* Wald, 20th Century-Fox.
RUSS TAMBLYN in *Peyton Place,* Wald, 20th Century-Fox.

SUPPORTING ACTRESS

CAROLYN JONES in *The Bachelor Party,* Norma, UA.
ELSA LANCHESTER in *Witness for the Prosecution,* Small-Hornblow, UA.
HOPE LANGE in *Peyton Place,* Wald, 20th Century-Fox.
* **MIYOSHI UMEKI** in *Sayonara,* Goetz, Warner Bros.
DIANE VARSI in *Peyton Place,* Wald, 20th Century-Fox.

DIRECTION

* **DAVID LEAN** for *The Bridge on the River Kwai,* Horizon, Columbia.
JOSHUA LOGAN for *Sayonara,* Goetz, Warner Bros.
SIDNEY LUMET for *12 Angry Men,* Orion-Nova Prod., UA.
MARK ROBSON for *Peyton Place,* Wald, 20th Century-Fox.
BILLY WILDER for *Witness for the Prosecution,* Small-Hornblow, UA.

WRITING

(New classifications; two awards for writing instead of three as previously given since 1940)

(Screenplay—based on material from another medium)
* **THE BRIDGE ON THE RIVER KWAI,** Horizon, Columbia. Pierre Boulle.
HEAVEN KNOWS, MR. ALLISON, 20th Century-Fox. John Lee Mahin and John Huston.
PEYTON PLACE, Wald, 20th Century-Fox. John Michael Hayes.
SAYONARA, Goetz, Warner Bros. Paul Osborn.
12 ANGRY MEN, Orion-Nova Prod., UA. Reginald Rose.

(Story and Screenplay—written directly for the screen)
* **DESIGNING WOMAN,** M-G-M. George Wells.
FUNNY FACE, Paramount. Leonard Gershe.
MAN OF A THOUSAND FACES, U-I. Ralph Wheelright, R. Wright Campbell, Ivan Goff and Ben Roberts.
THE TIN STAR, Perlberg-Seaton, Paramount. Barney Slater, Joel Kane and Dudley Nichols.
VITELLONI, API-Janus (Italian). Federico Fellini, Ennio Flaiano, and Tullio Pinelli.

CINEMATOGRAPHY

(New classification; one award instead of separate awards for black-and-white and color films, for the first year since 1938)

AN AFFAIR TO REMEMBER, Wald, 20th Century-Fox. Milton Krasner.
* **THE BRIDGE ON THE RIVER KWAI,** Horizon, Columbia. Jack Hildyard.
FUNNY FACE, Paramount, Ray June.
PEYTON PLACE, Wald, 20th Century-Fox. William Mellor.
SAYONARA, Goetz, Warner Bros. Ellsworth Fredericks.

ART DIRECTION-SET DECORATION

(New classification; one award instead of separate awards for black-and-white and color films, for the first year since 1939)

FUNNY FACE, Paramount. Hal Pereira and George W. Davis; Sam Comer and Ray Moyer.
LES GIRLS, Siegel, M-G-M. William A. Horning and Gene Allen; Edwin B. Willis and Richard Pefferle.
PAL JOEY, Essex-Sidney, Columbia. Walter Holscher; William Kiernan and Louis Diage.
RAINTREE COUNTY, M-G-M. William A. Horning and Urie McCleary; Edwin B. Willis and Hugh Hunt.
* **SAYONARA,** Goetz, Warner Bros. Ted Haworth; Robert Priestley.

COSTUME DESIGN

(New classification; one award instead of separate awards for black-and-white and color films, for first time in this category)

AN AFFAIR TO REMEMBER, Wald, 20th Century-Fox. Charles LeMaire.
FUNNY FACE, Paramount. Edith Head and Hubert de Givenchy.
* **LES GIRLS,** Siegel, M-G-M. Orry-Kelly.
PAL JOEY, Essex-Sidney, Columbia. Jean Louis.
RAINTREE COUNTY, M-G-M. Walter Plunkett.

SOUND RECORDING

GUNFIGHT AT THE O.K. CORRAL, Wallis, Paramount. Paramount Studio Sound Department; George Dutton, sound director.

LES GIRLS, Siegel, M-G-M. M-G-M Studio Sound Department; Dr. Wesley C. Miller, sound director.

PAL JOEY, Essex-Sidney, Columbia. Columbia Studio Sound Dept.; John P. Livadary, sound director.

★ SAYONARA, Goetz, Warner Bros. Warner Bros. Studio Sound Dept.; George Groves, sound director.

WITNESS FOR THE PROSECUTION, Small-Hornblow, UA. Samuel Goldwyn Studio Sound Department; Gordon Sawyer, sound director.

FILM EDITING

★ THE BRIDGE ON THE RIVER KWAI, Horizon, Columbia. Peter Taylor.

GUNFIGHT AT THE O.K. CORRAL, Wallis, Paramount. Warren Low.

PAL JOEY, Essex-Sidney, Columbia. Viola Lawrence and Jerome Thoms.

SAYONARA, Goetz, Warner Bros. Arthur P. Schmidt and Philip W. Anderson.

WITNESS FOR THE PROSECUTION, Small-Hornblow, UA. Daniel Mandell.

SPECIAL EFFECTS

★ THE ENEMY BELOW, 20th Century-Fox. Walter Rossi.

THE SPIRIT OF ST. LOUIS, Hayward-Wilder, Warner Bros. Louis Lichtenfield.

MUSIC

(Song)

AN AFFAIR TO REMEMBER (*An Affair to Remember,* Wald, 20th Century-Fox); Music by Harry Warren. Lyrics by Harold Adamson and Leo McCarey.

★ ALL THE WAY (*The Joker Is Wild,* Paramount); Music by James Van Heusen. Lyrics by Sammy Cahn.

APRIL LOVE (*April Love,* 20th Century-Fox); Music by Sammy Fain. Lyrics by Paul Francis Webster.

TAMMY (*Tammy and the Bachelor,* U-I); Music and Lyrics by Ray Evans and Jay Livingston.

WILD IS THE WIND (*Wild Is the Wind,* Wallis, Paramount); Music by Dimitri Tiomkin. Lyrics by Ned Washington.

(Music Scoring)

(New classification; one award for Music Scoring instead of two, for first year since 1937)

AN AFFAIR TO REMEMBER, Wald, 20th Century-Fox. Hugo Friedhofer.

BOY ON A DOLPHIN, 20th Century-Fox. Hugo Friedhofer.

★ THE BRIDGE ON THE RIVER KWAI, Horizon, Columbia. Malcolm Arnold.

PERRI, Disney, Buena Vista. Paul Smith.

RAINTREE COUNTY, M-G-M. Johnny Green.

SHORT SUBJECTS

(New rules: two categories for short subjects, instead of three as previously given.)

(Cartoons)

★ BIRDS ANONYMOUS, Warner Bros. Edward Selzer, producer.

ONE DROOPY KNIGHT, M-G-M. William Hanna and Joseph Barbera, producers.

TABASCO ROAD, Warner Bros. Edward Selzer, producer.

TREES AND JAMAICA DADDY, UPA, Columbia. Stephen Bosustow, producer.

THE TRUTH ABOUT MOTHER GOOSE, Disney, Buena Vista. Walt Disney, producer.

(Live Action Subjects)

A CHAIRY TALE, National Film Board of Canada, Kingsley International. Norman McLaren, producer.

CITY OF GOLD, National Film Board of Canada, Kingsley International. Tom Daly, producer.

FOOTHOLD ON ANTARCTICA, World Wide Pictures, Schoenfeld Films. James Carr, producer.

PORTUGAL, Disney, Buena Vista. Ben Sharpsteen, producer.

★ THE WETBACK HOUND, Disney, Buena Vista. Larry Lansburgh, producer.

DOCUMENTARY

(Short Subjects)

No nominations or award this year

(Features)

★ ALBERT SCHWEITZER, Hill and Anderson Prod., Louis de Rochemont Assocs. Jerome Hill, producer.

ON THE BOWERY, Rogosin, Film Representations, Inc. Lionel Rogosin, producer.

TORERO!, Producciones Barbachano Ponce, Columbia (Mexican). Manuel Barbachano Ponce, producer.

FOREIGN LANGUAGE FILM

THE DEVIL CAME AT NIGHT, (Germany).

GATES OF PARIS, (France).

MOTHER INDIA, (India).

★ THE NIGHTS OF CABIRIA, (Italy).

NINE LIVES, (Norway).

HONORARY AND OTHER AWARDS

TO CHARLES BRACKETT for outstanding service to the Academy. (statuette)

TO B.B. KAHANE for distinguished service to the motion picture industry. (statuette)

TO GILBERT M. ("Broncho Billy") ANDERSON, motion picture pioneer, for his contributions to the development of motion pictures as entertainment. (statuette)

TO THE SOCIETY OF MOTION PICTURE AND TELEVISION ENGINEERS for their contributions to the advancement of the motion picture industry. (statuette)

1957 IRVING G. THALBERG MEMORIAL AWARD

None given this year.

1957 JEAN HERSHOLT HUMANITARIAN AWARD

TO SAMUEL GOLDWYN

SCIENTIFIC OR TECHNICAL

CLASS I (statuette)

TODD-AO CORP. and WESTREX CORP. for developing a method of producing and exhibiting wide-film motion pictures known as the Todd-AO System.

MOTION PICTURE RESEARCH COUNCIL for the design and development of a high efficiency projection screen for drive-in theatres.

CLASS II (plaque)

SOCIETE D'OPTIQUE ET DE MECANIQUE DE HAUTE PRECISION for the development of a high speed varifocal photographic lens.

HARLAN L. BAUMBACH, LORAND WARGO, HOWARD M. LITTLE and the UNICORN ENGINEERING CORP. for the development of an automatic printer light selector.

CLASS III (citation)

CHARLES E. SUTTER, WILLIAM B. SMITH, PARAMOUNT PICTURES CORP. and GENERAL CABLE CORP.

★ INDICATES WINNER

Best Supporting Actress: Miyoshi Umeki as Katsumi and **Best Supporting Actor: Red Buttons** as Sgt. Joe Kelly in *Sayonara* (Warner Bros.; directed by Joshua Logan). As an ill-fated married couple hounded by prejudice—and military red tape—stacked against mixed marriages in postwar Japan, Miyoshi Umeki and Red Buttons gave poignant, touching performances in this sumptuous and romantic version of James A. Michener's novel, and each received Academy Awards. Marlon Brando played an Air Force major who championed their cause before it tragically ends in a double suicide pact.

The Academy's Fourth Decade

1958-1967

WENDY HILLER

"The first Oscar I ever saw was on Mr. Shaw's mantelshelf in his home at Ayot St. Lawrence. My first thought on hearing that I had got one was that if the great G.B.S. thought it was respectable then who was I to worry?"

Wendy Hiller
Best Supporting Actress, 1958

VINCENTE MINNELLI

"I was nominated for An American in Paris *but something happened. That 'something' was George Stevens for directing* A Place In The Sun.

So when I was nominated again for Gigi *and was leaving very early the next morning on location to direct the drama* Home From The Hill *with Robert Mitchum, I almost didn't attend the ceremony, thinking 'they'll never give an Oscar to a musical.'*

Then I heard my name called; it was a miraculous, glorious, earth-shattering feeling and one I shall treasure always."

Vincente Minnelli
Best Director, 1958

DAVID NIVEN

"Many think I am the first self-confessed drunk to win the Oscar. When my name was read out, and the odds are always four to one against this happening, I thought I had better get up on that stage before everybody changed their minds. I rushed down to the front of the theater, my coattail flapping, and fell headlong up the steps onto the stage. Not having prepared an acceptance speech for fear of attracting bad luck, I grabbed the proffered Oscar and the microphone and tried to explain my rather peculiar arrival. 'The reason I just fell over,' I said, and I intended to continue, 'was because I was so loaded with good luck charms that I was top heavy.' Unfortunately, I made an idiot pause after the word 'loaded.' This brought down the house, and knowing I could never top that I tottered off the stage with my prize."

David Niven
Best Actor, 1958

Unlike the preceding years, which had seen the Academy of Motion Picture Arts and Sciences actively, but often inadvertently, involved in studio-labor disputes, political controversies and other weighty industry problems, the organization's fourth decade was one of relative serenity. Conversely, the film industry itself spent most of those ten years in a state of turmoil and confusion, caused by the ever-changing tastes of moviegoers and the tumultuous times through which everyone was living. There seemed to be one blow after another: the Vietnam war, the Cuban missile crisis, equal rights demonstrations, the assassinations of President John F. Kennedy and Martin Luther King, Jr., and social changes such as the beginning of the drug culture. On the more positive side were advances in space exploration, medicine and technology.

The Academy, still housed in its Melrose Avenue headquarters, continued to expand, rapidly making a future move to larger quarters and, hopefully, a new Academy building of its own—a distinct possibility. The library acquired more and more material for its research files, including clippings, still photographs, periodicals, press books and memorabilia. There was barely room to house the numerous scrapbooks and private collections of valuable materials donated to the Academy by individuals and organizations related to the motion picture industry.

Other Academy activities also continued: private screenings for members of new and older films in the downstairs Academy Award

William Wyler, Charlton Heston

Burl Ives, Susan Hayward, David Niven

Theater, as well as publication three times each year of both the *Academy Players Directory* and the *Screen Achievement Records Bulletin*. In 1965, the Academy also began sponsoring a scholarship program for film students (which, beginning in 1973, would also include official Student Film Awards presented by the Academy). In cooperation with the American Film Institute and the Society of Motion Picture and Television Engineers, an internship program for young filmmakers was also inaugurated.

Also, with spectacular results, the Academy Awards presentations continued to thrive and capture the interest and the imagination of the world's public and press. Since March 23, 1950, the annual ceremony had been held at the RKO Pantages Theatre in the heart of Hollywood, a few doors east of the intersection of Hollywood and Vine. Beginning April 17, 1961, the night the thirty-third Awards were distributed, Oscar

Edmond O'Brien, Shelley Winters

CHARLTON HESTON

" *There are many awards given to filmmakers, perhaps too many. It seems to me the reason the Academy Award remains the most highly prized is clear: it represents the opinion of your peers. When you receive an Academy nomination, it means that the people who do the work you do thought you did it well. Each of us would rather have that approval than any other.* **"**

Charlton Heston
Best Actor, 1959
Jean Hersholt Humanitarian Award, 1977

MAURICE JARRE

" *You are a kid in Lyon, France, living under the Nazi occupation. Not much to eat, not much to smile about. But one dream to hold on to: 'I am going to be a COMPOSER some day.'*

Fade out.

Paris radio announces that you have been nominated for an Academy Award for the music of a film called Lawrence of Arabia.

The excitement you feel is somewhat dampened when you hear the lugubrious voice of the producer telling you, 'Baby you haven't got a chance. The competition is ferocious.'

Okay.

So you go to bed like Harry Truman and the next thing you hear is the Paris radio announcing: 'You have WON!'

Maybe this gives a glimpse of the giddy pleasure of the event.

Wresting my Oscar from the reluctant grip of the producer was perhaps the most difficult task of all. So I was determined to be present when I was in the running again for Dr. Zhivago. This time I literally hurled myself onto the stage, took a firm hold on my gold statue and haltingly said the words that had been filling my heart: 'To be chosen by your fellow composers for a nomination is already the achievement. With my deep respect I say for these thrilling moments of my life, thank you, thank you all.' **"**

Maurice Jarre
Music Score (Substantially Original),
1962; 1965

BILL THOMAS

" *Winning an 'Oscar' was the culmination of an exciting career in this exciting business of ours—and knowing that Oscar will show himself every year makes each new assignment even more of a challenge, hoping that the Academy might again see a possibility for a mate for Oscar Number One.* **"**

Bill Thomas
Costume Design (Color), 1960

ELIZABETH TAYLOR

" The Oscar is the highest award in motion picture history given to you by your peers; therefore, I feel to every actor it's the most important one. I've known the disappointment of losing. I've known the amazing feeling of excitement of winning two Oscars. I will never forget the night I won my first one for Butterfield 8. I had been nominated before and lost, so I had become almost superstitious about having any acceptance speech even remotely in mind.

A great friend of mine, Yul Brynner, who had won the year before, was presenting the woman's award, and he teased me over dinner the previous evening that if my name was in the envelope he was going to milk it.

On that evening there were five of us sitting on the aisle. I watched Yul open the envelope, take the longest pause in the history of my memory, case every actress in the house and finally settle his eyes on me; then beat, beat, beat, his mischievous smile lit up and he said, 'the winner is' —and vaguely from somewhere I heard my name, somebody poking me in the ribs, somebody else telling me to stand up and walk down the aisle—that I had won.

I have no recollection at all of what I said except thank you—I still say thank you. "

Elizabeth Taylor
Best Actress, 1960; 1966

SHIRLEY JONES

"The funny thing about Oscar is that you actually plan your whole life to get one, from childhood on. And the little kid dream never ends, even after the little kid does. It only grows more vivid as reality brings you into some proximity. You plan further— with every picture, every script, every idea —'maybe this one,' 'maybe this one.' Then, a good roll of the dice—one of them gets near the winner's circle, and the dream is close. You plan the night, you plan the dress, and you plan the speech. And there you are—the envelope open— my God, it's me. The music, the cheers, the mike, and all the world awaiting the simple words you've been planning for twenty years. AND YOU'RE A ZOMBIE; A BABBLING, GIGGLING, SLOBBERING ZOMBIE—without a two-cent string of intelligible sounds to save your soul— and nothing left but twenty years to look back and 'plan' the way it SHOULD have gone!!!

Ah, Oscar, you can WIN one, but you CAN'T WIN!!! "

Shirley Jones
Best Supporting Actress, 1960

Stage full of stars: 31st Awards Show, April 6, 1959

moved to a new location, the Santa Monica Civic Auditorium, miles away from the nearest film studio, in Santa Monica, California, and returned there annually for eight years. Also during the decade, the Academy ceremony was telecast in color for the first time (April 18, 1966) and two new records were set: 1959's *Ben-Hur* became the most honored of all Academy Award-winning films, winning eleven awards, and 1961's *West Side Story* became a close runner-up, winning ten awards plus a Special Award voted by the Board of Governors to Jerome Robbins for his choreography on the film. Eligibility rules, especially those for judging the Best Foreign Language Film Award continued to change from year to year as the Academy Board attempted to make rules for Awards judging as fair as possible. If anything, that was still the most rigid thing about the Academy: its determination to remain flexible.

Peter Ustinov, Shirley Jones, Elizabeth Taylor, Burt Lancaster

From time to time, as before, there was speculation that pressures from certain studios might be responsible for the outcome of Academy members' voting, or that some members of the film community were attempting to "buy" Academy attention by purchasing full-page ads in the trade papers and Los Angeles newspapers to bring attention to a specific accomplishment. No one was more disapproving of industry pressures—if they really did exist—or the extravagant use of blatant advertising for votes—which was considerable—than the Academy itself. The association issued a statement in the 1960s denouncing the practice, something they have had to do almost annually since, with only limited success at correcting the problem, which still proves to be an embarrassment.

Preparations for the yearly Awards show, as might be expected, require Herculean efforts on the part of the Academy's own staff. In a

Jack L. Warner, Audrey Hepburn, Rex Harrison, George Cukor

EDITH HEAD

" When I received my first award—The Heiress, in 1950—I was so terrified I merely mumbled 'Thank you' and scurried off.

When I received my eighth award—The Sting, in 1974—I don't actually remember what I said, but at least people laughed and applauded.

People who work in the motion picture industry have stimulating lives, but nothing will ever compare with the actual receiving of the Oscar. "

Edith Head
Costume Design (Black-and-white)
1949; 1950; 1951; 1953; 1954; 1960
Costume Design (Color), 1950
Costume Design, 1973

MARTIN BALSAM

" Aside from remembering the precise moment of my name being called, I remember feeling as if someone put a sky hook in my collar and yanked me from my chair and put me on stage to receive my Oscar.

My memories of that night include someone saying, 'Don't scratch it. There may be chocolate underneath.' There wasn't. It was sturdy and solid, but sweet.

Looking at it, or it looking at me, still gives me the pleasure of a treasured moment. "

Martin Balsam
Best Supporting Actor, 1965

FREDDIE YOUNG

" Three of the highlights in my life were winning my three Oscars. Whatever anybody might say to the contrary, to win an Oscar is a very special thing.

To be nominated is very exciting, but to actually win an Oscar! Well, you just have to be lucky. "

Freddie Young
Cinematography (Color), 1962; 1965
Cinematography, 1970

LILA KEDROVA

" To win the Oscar for Best Supporting Actress was not only a great honor, but was, without question, the most exciting and moving moment in my career. It opened up a new life to me, and has given me the great joy and opportunity to play in many, many countries around the world. I will always be deeply grateful to the members of the Academy who opened their hearts to 'Bouboulina!' "

Lila Kedrova
Best Supporting Actress, 1964

Joan Crawford, Patty Duke

special section devoted to the Awards in 1962, the *Hollywood Citizen-News* paper reported:

"Unsung heroes of the Awards presentations are the staff members of the Academy of Motion Picture Arts and Sciences. The 30-odd employees have literally led a dog's life during the past six weeks while 'doggedly' toiling to make the affair a success.

"This 'dogged' existence hit its stride the day the nominations (for the 34th Awards presentations) were announced on February 26 at the Academy Award Theater. Many of them were 'imprisoned' there from 2 am until the announcements were made at 10 am. This is a precautionary measure taken each year to ensure secrecy of the nominations.

"Some of the staff had to come to work at 2 am to begin assembling photographs and biographies of the nominees as soon as the list was delivered in an armored car from the auditing firm which tabulated

Anthony Quinn, Lila Kedrova

the secret ballots. They weren't allowed to leave the library area of the Theater or use telephones until the announcement, together with the photos and biographies, were released to almost 100 members of the press.

"However, that was only the forerunner of the countless hours of leg work which had to be done from then until the grand finale last night. 'Our work is just beginning now,' said Mrs. Joseph Segar, secretary to Sam Brown, assistant executive director of the Academy, following the announcements. As a ten-year employee of the Academy, she knew whereof she spoke. She explained that between then and the grand finale last night, the staff would have to contact all the nominees and work out all the details for them or their representatives to be present, plus handling the myriad other details connected with the arrangements for the show.

"One of the female staffers' observations last night as she stood backstage watching the proceedings on a television set reflected the employees' point-of-view on the affair: 'Do you know that I wore out three typewriter ribbons, and wore an inch-long callus on my dialing finger trying to get a simple answer from that actress as to whether she was going to be here tonight, or send someone else?'

"She was referring to a blonde smiling broadly at one of emcee Bob Hope's barbs, and explained that the actress had been moving around on movie locations in Europe for the past several months. The staffer then sighed resignedly while massaging her callused finger and said, 'And just think of all the thank-you notes we're going to have to write after all this is over for everybody else!'"

During the decade, Bob Hope continued to be Oscar's most conspicuous host, acting as master of ceremonies (at least partially) at eight of the ten Awards shows, missing only the 1962 Awards and the 1963 Awards due to a conflict of interests between the sponsors of the Academy show and Hope's own television shows. There were also several provocative and newsworthy incidents that occurred during those Academy Awards nights. As a co-host of the 1958 affair, Jerry Lewis found himself faced with the problem having to fill twenty extra minutes of air time after all the Awards had been distributed more quickly than had been anticipated. In order to make the best of an

Sidney Poitier

MIKE NICHOLS

❝ I was so out of it when I received the 'Oscar' that I've often wished I could go back and do it again. This time I would really enjoy it. **❞**

Mike Nichols
Best Director, 1967

RICHARD M. SHERMAN & ROBERT B. SHERMAN

❝ Ever since that incredible night thirteen years ago, when we each won two Oscars (Mary Poppins Score; Best Song 'Chim Chim Cher-ee') we have worn with pride the designation, 'Academy Award winners.' Now, each time we begin a new film-musical, those Golden Gentlemen are there to remind us that all it will take for us to achieve something excellent is hard work, a shipload of good luck and an army of talented people all doing their thing on the same project with us. **❞**

Richard M. Sherman
Robert B. Sherman
Music Score (Substantially Original), 1964
Music (Song), 1964

ROBERT WISE

❝ In early 1962, I was assured that meeting and appearing before the Queen of England at the Command Performance of West Side Story in London would be a memorable evening—and it was.

However, the evening was definitely overshadowed a few weeks later by the Academy Awards and by being called to the stage twice for Oscars for my part in West Side Story. Few experiences can match the excitement and reward of approval by one's peers. **❞**

Robert Wise
Best Director, 1961
Irving G. Thalberg Memorial Award, 1966

CLAUDE LELOUCH

❝ Nothing is more suspect than an award . . . and nothing is more delightful to receive. **❞**

Claude Lelouch
Writing (Best Story and Screenplay written directly for the screen), 1966

WALTER MATTHAU

" *The night I won my Academy Award I was still in a state of shock from an accident the day before. I had fallen off a bicycle on the Pacific Coast Highway. I was speeding and hit a bump in the road and flew through the air and landed heavily on my left elbow, breaking it in sixteen places and getting about three pounds of gravel into my ears, eyes, nose and throat. And so when my name was announced as the winner of the Academy Award, I thought it was still part of the accident. I thought it was some sort of aftershock. But it seemed strange to me that an accident could be so thrilling.* "

Walter Matthau
Best Supporting Actor, 1966

WALTER MIRISCH

" *I recall sitting in the end seat of a row at the Academy Awards presentation in 1968. Sitting in front of me and behind me were the producers of* Bonnie and Clyde, The Graduate, Guess Who's Coming To Dinner *and* Doctor Doolittle.

I had by then pretty well insulated myself against the disappointment of losing by the traditional method: namely, convincing myself that another film was practically a foregone certainty to win. Of course, under that method one still leaves just a tiny glimmer of hope to remain until that very last second.

As Julie Andrews began to name the Best Picture nominees, that tiny glimmer of hope suddenly rose to mountainous proportions. When she read In The Heat Of The Night *and my name, the surging hope reached an unbelievable climax, and I rose almost mechanically to walk to the podium. I accepted the award from Julie and I began to speak bits and pieces of things I had sorted out—just in case. In essence, 'Thank you to all.' I then walked to the wings. Sidney Poitier and Rod Steiger both came out to greet me. I threw my arms around Sidney and kissed him.* "

Walter Mirisch
Best Picture, 1967
Irving G. Thalberg Memorial Award, 1977

HENRY MANCINI

" *I would like to take my space here to thank the Academy for two marvelous nights shared with my huckleberry friend, Johnny Mercer.* "

Henry Mancini
Music (Scoring of Dramatic or
Comedy Picture), 1961
Music (Song), 1961; 1962

ill-timed situation, Lewis took a baton, briefly conducted the orchestra, and clowned, while a stage full of stars began dancing (including Cary Grant, Ingrid Bergman, Laurence Olivier, Sophia Loren, Bette Davis, James Cagney, Gary Cooper, Irene Dunne, John Wayne, Joan Fontaine, Rock Hudson, Elizabeth Taylor, David Niven, Susan Hayward and June Allyson) until the program finally came to an end.

At the 1961 Awards ceremony, on April 9, 1962, a professional gate-crasher somehow got past an army of uniformed police guards, sprinted on stage of the Santa Monica Civic Auditorium during the program and presented a small, hand-made Oscar to a briefly startled Hope. "Who needs Price Waterhouse? What we need is a doorman," smiled the comedian. He was equally surprised four years later when he was presented the Academy's first Gold Medal, for "unique and distinguished service to the motion picture industry and the Academy," voted by the Board of Governors. Hope had previously been presented a special silver Academy plaque at the 1940 ceremony "in recognition of his unselfish services to the motion picture industry," a life membership in the Academy at the 1944 ceremony "for his many services to the Academy" a Special Award Oscar statuette in 1952 for "his contribution to the laughter of the world, his service to the motion picture industry, and his devotion to the American premise," and an Oscar statuette as winner of the 1959 Jean Hersholt Humanitarian Award.

The 1967 Awards ceremony in 1968 was postponed two days due to the assassination of Martin Luther King, Jr. The annual Board of Governors' Ball following the presentation of Awards was canceled altogether. The year before, the Oscar TV show itself was almost canceled, due to a lingering strike by the theatrical union governing live telecasts. The American Federation of Television and Radio Artists (AFTRA), but three hours before the ceremony was to begin the strike was settled, allowing telecast coverage after all.

Music also played an unusually striking part in the Academy's fourth decade of existence. At the 34th Awards show on April 9, 1962, one of the nominees as Best Song of 1961, "Bachelor in Paradise," was sung by a little-known performer named Ann-Margret, delivered in an unabashed style that literally launched her motion picture career; Ann-Margret was never "unknown" again, and later became a two-time nominee for acting honors. Angela Lansbury, Joan Collins and Dana Wynter in 1959 did a special-material number, "It's Bully Not to Be Nominated," a parody of a number done the previous year, "It's Great

Julie Christie

Walter Matthau

PAUL SCOFIELD

❝ I am very proud to be one of the recipients of the Oscar. It was a great joy to me when I was awarded it for my performance in A Man For All Seasons, and I hope that the occasion of its fiftieth year will be a happy and successful one for the Academy of Motion Picture Arts and Sciences.

I am most gratefully and sincerely yours, ❞

Paul Scofield
Best Actor, 1966

GEORGE CUKOR

❝ The great, the unique thing about the Academy Awards is that it's on the level —absolutely on the level.

I've been around a long time, and never in my experience has anyone offered me a bribe, or tried in any way to influence me in how I voted. Even friendship doesn't count for much. You may think in advance that you will vote for a good pal, but when the chips are down, and you are alone with your God and your ballot, you find yourself voting for what you really think. It is sometimes said, disparagingly, that an Oscar is just a reward for popularity. Ina Claire told me that when she was a young star on the stage she was introduced to Sarah Bernhardt as a 'great American actress.' She modestly said, 'Oh no, I happen to be a popular actress.' Bernhardt, then at the end of her long and distinguished career, replied, 'Very well, very well, first come popular, then come great. The public is never wrong.' Old Sarah was absolutely right. True popularity means something; it cannot be faked. If you look back over the history of the Awards, in a curious way the truth does come out; the choices of the Academy withstand the test of time.

I am not one of those who think prizes are ignoble. But some are obviously more valuable than others. The Academy Award is most valuable because it is dearly won. It is an expert, professional judgment, at once the most merciless and, sometimes, the most amazingly generous.

It is good for the soul, if not very pleasant, to sit there with your nomination and be turned down in front of a hundred million people. But when you do get it, it is a glory. Mine seemed to be an inordinately long time coming, but when at last I got it, it meant more to me than any other award I have ever received. ❞

George Cukor
Best Director, 1964

Not to Be Nominated,'' performed by Burt Lancaster and Kirk Douglas as a humorous ''sour grapes'' ballad giving tongue-in-cheek reasons they weren't in the competition for acting awards. Mitzi Gaynor had a spectacular moment on the 1966 Awards show performing a mod musical interpretation of ''Georgy Girl'' with four male partners, as did Angela Lansbury as she Charlestoned with her partners to ''Thoroughly Modern Millie'' on the 1967 Awards program.

But if music and the awarding of film excellence and the myriad of other activities was an on-going fact of life to the Academy itself as the decade drew to a conclusion, so was the unavoidable problem of space —or the lack of it. The Academy had once again outgrown its home base and, in the decade ahead, would make a final, long-awaited move.

ACADEMY PRESIDENTS, THE FOURTH DECADE

June 1957-May 1958	GEORGE SEATON
June 1958-May 1959	GEORGE STEVENS
June 1959-May 1960	B.B. KAHANE
June 1960-September 1960	B.B. KAHANE*
September 1960-May 1961	VALENTINE DAVIES
May 1961-July 1961	VALENTINE DAVIES**
August 1961-May 1962	WENDELL COREY
May 1962-May 1963	WENDELL COREY
June 1963-May 1964	ARTHUR FREED
June 1964-May 1965	ARTHUR FREED
June 1965-May 1966	ARTHUR FREED
June 1966-May 1967	ARTHUR FREED
June 1966-May 1967	ARTHUR FREED

*Died during second term
**Died during second term

1958 The Thirty-First Year

A new decade, and a new record! On April 6, 1959, the start of Oscar's fourth decade, M-G-M's gilded *Gigi* set a new, all-time Academy record to date, with nine Oscar Awards for 1958 achievement; the previous record holders had been *Gone With the Wind* (1939), *From Here to Eternity* (1953) and *On the Waterfront* (1954), with eight Awards each. The *Gigi* total included Awards for Best Picture, Best Director (Vincente Minnelli), Best Costume Design (Cecil Beaton) and Best Song ("Gigi" by Alan Jay Lerner and Frederick Loewe), and it was additionally responsible for an Honorary Award to Maurice Chevalier, specifically noted for his contributions to the entertainment world for over a half century. *Gigi* didn't hold its record long (it would be broken the next year), but it was in interesting Oscar paradox on two levels: it was one of the few films to win all Awards for which it had been nominated, and it was one of only seven Best Picture winners in the Academy's fifty-year history to not receive a single acting nomination for any of its cast members. The others: *Wings* (1927-28), *All Quiet on the Western Front* (1929-30), *Grand Hotel* (1932-33), *An American in Paris* (1951), *The Greatest Show on Earth* (1952) and *Around the World in 80 Days* (1956).

For the second year, NBC's telecast of the ceremony was fully sponsored by the motion picture industry itself, produced by Jerry Wald for the Academy; it was produced and directed for NBC by Alan Handley from the Pantages Theatre in Hollywood. Once again, six personalities shared hosting duties, in turn: Bob Hope, David Niven, Tony Randall, Mort Sahl, Sir Laurence Olivier and Jerry Lewis. As the final M.C. of the night, Jerry Lewis found himself in the awkward position of having to stretch out the show when all business at hand was completed. With twenty minutes of a scheduled two hours of air time still to be filled, NBC finally switched its cameras to a sports review filler.

Susan Hayward, on her fifth nomination as Best Actress, won for *I Want to Live!;* David Niven, on his first, won as Best Actor for *Separate Tables.* Supporting Awards went to Wendy Hiller (for *Separate Tables*) and Burl Ives (for *The Big Country*), and France's comedy *My Uncle* was chosen Best Foreign Language Film. It was also a big night for the durable Bugs Bunny. After a long life on the Hollywood drawing boards, he won his very first Oscar when Warner Bros.' *Knighty Knight Bugs* won the statuette as Best Cartoon.

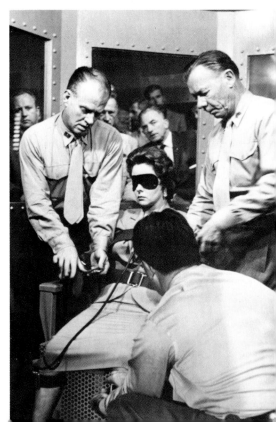

Best Actress: Susan Hayward as Barbara Graham in *I Want to Live!* (United Artists; directed by Robert Wise). The story was based on fact: a California woman named Barbara Graham was executed in the San Quentin gas chamber on June 3, 1955, for allegedly joining two men in the murder of a Burbank widow during an attempted robbery. As a movie produced by Walter Wanger, the first half of the film swiftly tells how Miss Graham was caught; part two chronicles her final, agonizing days on death row, enduring stays of execution, last-minute postponements and the final walk to the gas chamber. As Barbara, Susan Hayward gave a tour de force performance, and won the Academy Award which had elusively passed her by four times previously, when she was nominated in 1947 for *Smash Up—The Story of a Woman,* in 1949 for *My Foolish Heart,* in 1952 for *With a Song in My Heart* and in 1955 for *I'll Cry Tomorrow.*

Best Picture: Gigi (M-G-M; produced by Arthur Freed) and **Best Director: Vincente Minnelli** for *Gigi. Gigi* was Hollywood's answer to Broadway's *My Fair Lady,* which had opened in New York in 1956 and also featured a captivating musical score by Alan Jay Lerner and Frederick Loewe, and awesome costumes by Cecil Beaton. Basis for the new project was a 60-page novelette by French writer Colette, which became a French play, later a French movie, finally a Broadway play with Audrey Hepburn. This latest reincarnation had a blithe spirit and a French sense of humor: in Paris of 1900, a teenage girl is trained by a wealthy aunt to be a courtesan in the tradition of her family, only to eventually upset the plan by putting marriage first. The cast included (left) Hermione Gingold, Louis Jourdan and Leslie Caron, plus Maurice Chevalier, Isabel Jeans, Eva Gabor and Jacques Bergerac. It set a new Academy record with nine Awards and by virtue of that earlier French film (made in 1950 with Daniele Delorme but without music), it also became the first "remake" to win an Oscar for Best Picture.

Best Actor: David Niven as Major Pollock in *Separate Tables* (United Artists; directed by Delbert Mann). When originally presented on stage, Terence Rattigan's story, set in a small English hotel on the south coast of Britain, was written as two single-act plays, with Eric Portman and Margaret Leighton each playing dual roles. The screenplay united the plays and had four starring roles instead of two, with Niven as a phony major who covers up his basic fears and frustrations with boring lies about desert campaigns during World War II. He is finally exposed as a fake when arrested for molesting a woman in a theater, but is defended by a shy, mousy resident at the hotel (Deborah Kerr, right, with Niven) he had earlier befriended. After 23 years and 52 films, Niven won his first Academy nomination —and his first Academy Award.

Best Supporting Actress: Wendy Hiller as Miss Cooper (above, with Rita Hayworth) in *Separate Tables* (United Artists; directed by Delbert Mann). Previously nominated in 1938 as Best Actress for *Pygmalion*, Wendy Hiller won her award an an efficient but lonely hotel manager in a British seaside boarding house; ultimately she loses the one interesting man in her life because of the unexpected arrival at the hotel of his ex-wife. Miss Hiller was again nominated in 1966 for *A Man for All Seasons*.

Nominations 1958

PICTURE

AUNTIE MAME, Warner Bros. Jack L. Warner, studio head.
CAT ON A HOT TIN ROOF, Avon, M-G-M. Produced by Lawrence Weingarten.
THE DEFIANT ONES, Kramer, UA. Produced by Stanley Kramer.
★ **GIGI,** Freed, M-G-M. Produced by Arthur Freed.
SEPARATE TABLES, Hecht-Hill-Lancaster, UA. Produced by Harold Hecht.

ACTOR

TONY CURTIS in *The Defiant Ones*, Kramer, UA.
PAUL NEWMAN in *Cat on a Hot Tin Roof*, Avon, M-G-M.
★ **DAVID NIVEN** in *Separate Tables*, Hecht-Hill-Lancaster, UA.
SIDNEY POITIER in *The Defiant Ones*, Kramer, UA.
SPENCER TRACY in *The Old Man and the Sea*, Hayward, Warner Bros.

ACTRESS

★ **SUSAN HAYWARD** in *I Want to Live!*, Figaro, UA.
DEBORAH KERR in *Separate Tables*, Hecht-Hill-Lancaster, UA.
SHIRLEY MacLAINE in *Some Came Running*, Siegel, M-G-M.
ROSALIND RUSSELL in *Auntie Mame*, Warner Bros.
ELIZABETH TAYLOR in *Cat on a Hot Tin Roof*, Avon, M-G-M.

SUPPORTING ACTOR

THEODORE BIKEL in *The Defiant Ones*, Kramer, UA.
LEE J. COBB in *The Brothers Karamazov*, Avon, M-G-M.
★ **BURL IVES** in *The Big Country*, Anthony-Worldwide, UA.
ARTHUR KENNEDY in *Some Came Running*, Siegel, M-G-M.
GIG YOUNG in *Teacher's Pet*, Perlberg-Seaton, Paramount.

SUPPORTING ACTRESS

PEGGY CASS in *Auntie Mame*, Warner Bros.
★ **WENDY HILLER** in *Separate Tables*, Hecht-Hill-Lancaster, UA.
MARTHA HYER in *Some Came Running*, Siegel, M-G-M.
MAUREEN STAPLETON in *Lonelyhearts*, Schary, UA.
CARA WILLIAMS in *The Defiant Ones*, Kramer, UA.

DIRECTION

RICHARD BROOKS for *Cat on a Hot Tin Roof*, Avon, M-G-M.
STANLEY KRAMER for *The Defiant Onces*, Kramer, UA.
★ **VINCENTE MINNELLI** for *Gigi*, Freed, M-G-M.
MARK ROBSON for *The Inn of the Sixth Happiness*, 20th Century-Fox.
ROBERT WISE for *I Want to Live!*, Wanger-Figaro, UA.

WRITING

(Screenplay—based on material from another medium)
CAT ON A HOT TIN ROOF, Avon, M-G-M. Richard Brooks and James Poe.
★ **GIGI,** Freed, M-G-M. Alan Jay Lerner.
THE HORSE'S MOUTH, Lopert-UA (British). Alec Guinness.
I WANT TO LIVE!, Wanger-Figaro, UA. Nelson Gidding and Don Mankiewicz.
SEPARATE TABLES, Hecht-Hill-Lancaster, UA. Terence Rattigan and John Gay.

(Story and Screenplay—written directly for the screen)
★ **THE DEFIANT ONES,** Kramer, UA. Nathan E. Douglas and Harold Jacob Smith.

THE GODDESS, Perlman, Columbia. Paddy Chayefsky.
HOUSEBOAT, Paramount. Melville Shavelson and Jack Rose.
THE SHEEPMAN, M-G-M. Story by James Edward Grant. Screenplay by William Bowers and James Edward Grant.
TEACHER'S PET, Perlberg-Seaton. Paramount. Fay and Michael Kanin.

CINEMATOGRAPHY

(After a one-year change in 1957, two awards again given for cinematography achievement)

(Black-and-White)
★ **THE DEFIANT ONES,** Kramer, UA. Sam Leavitt.
DESIRE UNDER THE ELMS, Hartman, Paramount. Daniel L. Fapp.
I WANT TO LIVE!, Wanger-Figaro, Inc., UA. Lionel Lindon.
SEPARATE TABLES, Hecht-Hill-Lancaster, UA. Charles Lang, Jr.
THE YOUNG LIONS, 20th Century-Fox. Joe MacDonald.

(Color)
AUNTIE MAME, Warner Bros. Harry Stradling, Sr.
CAT ON A HOT TIN ROOF, Avon, M-G-M. William Daniels.
★ **GIGI,** Freed, M-G-M. Joseph Ruttenberg.
THE OLD MAN AND THE SEA, Hayward, Warner Bros. James Wong Howe.
SOUTH PACIFIC, Magna Corp., 20th Century-Fox. Leon Shamroy.

ART DIRECTION-SET DECORATION

(Black-and-White or Color)
AUNTIE MAME, Warner Bros. Malcolm Bert; George James Hopkins.
BELL, BOOK AND CANDLE, Phoenix, Columbia. Cary Odell; Louis Diage.
A CERTAIN SMILE, 20th Century-Fox. Lyle R. Wheeler and John DeCuir; Walter M. Scott and Paul S. Fox.
★ **GIGI,** Freed, M-G-M. William A. Horning and Preston Ames; Henry Grace and Keogh Gleason.
VERTIGO, Hitchcock, Paramount. Hal Pereira and Henry Bumstead; Sam Comer and Frank McKelvy.

Best Supporting Actor: Burl Ives as Rufus Hannassey (above, with Charles Bickford) in *The Big Country* (United Artists; directed by William Wyler). Best known as a folksinger and balladeer, Burl Ives co-starred in three important 1958 dramas without singing a note: *Desire Under the Elms, Cat on a Hot Tin Roof* and *The Big Country.* He won his Academy Award for the latter, an impressive 2-hour, 46-minute western epic in which he played a tough cattle baron at war over water rights with another strong-willed rancher.

The Defiant Ones (United Artists; directed by Stanley Kramer) was a powerful preachment about racial intolerance and brotherhood, with (below) Sidney Poitier and Tony Curtis as convicts shackled together— a Negro and a white man attempting to escape prison, and each other. It won Oscars for Story and Screenplay (Nathan E. Douglas and Harold Jacob Smith) and for Black-and-White Cinematography (Sam Leavitt).

COSTUME DESIGN
(Black-and-White or Color)
BELL, BOOK AND CANDLE, Phoenix, Columbia. Jean Louis.
THE BUCCANEER, DeMille, Paramount. Ralph Jester, Edith Head and John Jensen.
A CERTAIN SMILE, 20th Century-Fox. Charles LeMaire and Mary Wills.
★ GIGI, Freed, M-G-M. Cecil Beaton.
SOME CAME RUNNING, Siegel, M-G-M. Walter Plunkett.

SOUND
(No longer categorized as 'Sound Recording')
I WANT TO LIVE!, Wanger-Figaro, UA. Samuel Goldwyn Studio Sound Department; Gordon E. Sawyer, sound director.
★ SOUTH PACIFIC, Magna Corp., 20th Century-Fox. Todd-AO Sound Department. Fred Hynes, sound director.
A TIME TO LOVE AND A TIME TO DIE, U-I. Universal-International Studio Sound Department; Leslie I. Carey, sound director.
VERTIGO, Hitchcock, Paramount. Paramount Studio Sound Department; George Dutton, sound director.
THE YOUNG LIONS, 20th Century-Fox. 20th Century-Fox Studio Sound Department; Carl Faulkner, sound director.

FILM EDITING
AUNTIE MAME, Warner Bros. William Ziegler.
COWBOY, Phoenix, Columbia. William A. Lyon and Al Clark.
THE DEFIANT ONES, Kramer, UA. Frederic Knudtson.
★ GIGI, Freed, M-G-M. Adrienne Fazan.
I WANT TO LIVE!, Wanger-Figaro, UA. William Hornbeck.

SPECIAL EFFECTS
★ TOM THUMB, Pal, M-G-M. Tom Howard.
TORPEDO RUN, M-G-M. A Arnold Gillespie and Harold Humbrock.

MUSIC
(Song)
ALMOST IN YOUR ARMS (Love Song from *Houseboat*) (*Houseboat,* Paramount); Music and Lyrics by Jay Livingston and Ray Evans.
A CERTAIN SMILE (*A Certain Smile,* 20th Century-Fox); Music by Sammy Fain. Lyrics by Paul Francis Webster.
★ GIGI (*Gigi,* Freed, M-G-M); Music by Frederick Loewe. Lyrics by Alan Jay Lerner.
TO LOVE AND BE LOVED (*Some Came Running,* Siegel, M-G-M); Music by James Van Heusen. Lyrics by Sammy Cahn.
A VERY PRECIOUS LOVE (*Marjorie Morningstar,* Sperling, Warner Bros.); Music by Sammy Fain. Lyrics by Paul Francis Webster.

(NOTE: After a one-year change in 1957, two awards again given for achievement in Music Scoring)

(Scoring of a Dramatic or Comedy Picture)
THE BIG COUNTRY, Anthony-Worldwide, UA. Jerome Moross.
★ THE OLD MAN AND THE SEA, Hayward, Warner Bros. Dimitri Tiomkin.
SEPARATE TABLES, Hecht-Hill-Lancaster, UA. David Raksin.
WHITE WILDERNESS, Disney, Buena Vista. Oliver Wallace.
THE YOUNG LIONS, 20th Century-Fox. Hugo Friedhofer.

(Scoring of a Musical Picture)
THE BOLSHOI BALLET, Czinner-Maxwell, Rank Releasing (British). Yuri Faier and G. Rozhdestvensky.
DAMN YANKEES, Warner Bros. Ray Heindorf.
★ GIGI, Freed, M-G-M. Andre Previn.
MARDI GRAS, Wald, 20th Century-Fox. Lionel Newman.
SOUTH PACIFIC, Magna Corp., 20th Century-Fox. Alfred Newman and Ken Darby.

SHORT SUBJECTS
(Cartoons)
★ KNIGHTY KNIGHT BUGS, Warner Bros. John W. Burton, producer.
PAUL BUNYAN, Walt Disney Prods., Buena Vista Film Distribution. Walt Disney, producer.
SIDNEY'S FAMILY TREE, Terrytoons, 20th Century-Fox. William M. Weiss, producer.

(Live Action Subjects)
★ GRAND CANYON, Walt Disney Prods., Buena Vista. Walt Disney, producer.
JOURNEY INTO SPRING, British Transport Films, Lester A. Schoenfeld Films. Ian Ferguson, producer.
THE KISS, Cohay Prods., Continental Distributing, Inc. John Patrick Hayes, producer.
SNOWS OF AORANGI, New Zealand Screen Board, George Brest Assocs.
T IS FOR TUMBLEWEED, Continental Distributing, Inc. James A. Lebenthal, producer.

DOCUMENTARY
(Short Subjects)
★ AMA GIRLS, Disney Prods., Buena Vista. Ben Sharpsteen, producer.
EMPLOYEES ONLY, Hughes Aircraft Co. Kenneth G. Brown, producer.
JOURNEY INTO SPRING, British Transport Films, Lester A. Schoenfeld Films. Ian Ferguson, producer.
THE LIVING STONE, National Film Board of Canada. Tom Daly, producer.
OVERTURE, United Nations Film Service. Thorold Dickinson, producer.

(Features)
ANTARCTIC CROSSING, World Wide Pictures, Lester A. Schoenfeld Films. James Carr, producer.
THE HIDDEN WORLD, Small World Co. Robert Snyder, producer.
PSYCHIATRIC NURSING, Dynamic Films, Inc. Nathan Zucker, producer.
★ WHITE WILDERNESS, Disney Prods., Buena Vista. Ben Sharpsteen, producer.

FOREIGN LANGUAGE FILM
ARMS AND THE MAN, (Germany).
LA VENGANZA, (Spain).
★ MY UNCLE, (France).
THE ROAD A YEAR LONG, (Yugoslavia).
THE USUAL UNIDENTIFIED THIEVES, (Italy).

HONORARY AND OTHER AWARDS
TO MAURICE CHEVALIER for his contributions to the world of entertainment for more than half a century. (statuette)

1958 IRVING G. THALBERG MEMORIAL AWARD
TO JACK L. WARNER

1958 JEAN HERSHOLT HUMANITARIAN AWARD
None given this year.

SCIENTIFIC OR TECHNICAL
CLASS I (statuette)
None.

CLASS II (plaque)
DON W. PRIDEAUX, LEROY G. LEIGHTON and the LAMP DIVISION of GENERAL ELECTRIC CO. for the development and production of an improved 10 kilowatt lamp for motion picture set lighting.
PANAVISION, INC., for the design and development of the Auto Panatar anamorphic photographic lens for 35mm CinemaScope photography.

CLASS III (citation)
WILLY BORBERG of the GENERAL PRECISION LABORATORY, INC.;
FRED PONEDEL, GEORGE BROWN and CONRAD BOYE of the WARNER BROS. SPECIAL EFFECTS DEPT.

1959

The Thirty-Second Year

Best Picture: Ben-Hur (M-G-M; produced by Sam Zimbalist), **Best Director: William Wyler** (below) and **Best Actor: Charlton Heston** as Judah Ben-Hur (at right) in *Ben-Hur.* M-G-M's decision to make a second version of Gen. Lew Wallace's *Ben-Hur* was risky: at the time, the studio was teetering on financial bankruptcy, and yet the decision was made to pour $15 million into the single do-or-die project. But *Ben* turned out to be a great critical success, and a box office bonanza, saving—at least temporarily—Culver City's Lion for more roars in the future. The most awesome sequence in *Ben-Hur* was a mind-blowing chariot race which ran 11 minutes of the film's 3-hour, 32-minutes running time, and Charlton Heston was equally impressive as a wealthy Jew sentenced to life as a galley slave by his once-best friend. Director Wyler also deservedly received great praise for *Ben-Hur;* he proved conclusively it was possible to make a rousing spectacle in which audiences could also care about the people involved.

For the second year in a row, M-G-M was the noise and the news at the Academy Awards ceremony. Held April 4, 1960, at the Pantages Theatre in Hollywood, and telecast by NBC, the studio's *Ben-Hur,* nominated for twelve Academy Awards, won eleven of them, a new Oscar record, topping the previous high of nine awards won by M-G-M's *Gigi* in the preceding year. The *Ben-Hur* awards included Best Picture, Best Actor (Charlton Heston), Best Supporting Actor (Hugh Griffith) and Best Director (William Wyler, his third Oscar in that category). The only area where *Ben-Hur* was nominated and bested was in the Best Screenplay division, where Neil Paterson received the award for *Room at the Top,* a British-made drama. *Ben-Hur* was also the second remake of an earlier film to win a Best Picture statuette (the first: 1958's *Gigi*).

Next to *Ben-Hur,* the evening had a distinctly French flavor. France's Simone Signoret, who had never appeared in a Hollywood-made motion picture, won the Best Actress Award (for *Room at the Top*) and became the first actress to win the Academy Award for a performance in a British or foreign-made film (the first actor was Charles Laughton in 1932-33). France's *Black Orpheus* was chosen Best Foreign Language Film; Miss Signoret's husband Yves Montand entertained at the Awards show; and two-time Oscar winner Olivia de Havilland, a resident of Paris, returned to her native Hollywood to present one of the evening's awards.

Other Award winners included Shelley Winters as Best Supporting Actress for *The Diary of Anne Frank,* which, next to *Ben-Hur,* won the most awards of the evening with a total of three, including Black-and-White Cinematography, and Black-and-White Art Direction. Buster Keaton received an Honorary Oscar for his comedic talents. This award was not presented on the Awards show but at the post-award Board of Governors Ball at the Beverly Hilton in Beverly Hills.

The telecast itself was again hosted by Bob Hope, who was also the recipient of the evening's Jean Hersholt Humanitarian Award. It was the last time, at least during Oscar's first fifty years, the motion picture industry sponsored the Academy ceremony. The financial burden had become too steep, and—due to one-studio sweeps such as *Gigi* and *Ben-Hur*—it had become increasingly difficult to get studios to pay for an expensive telecast which might spotlight a rival's product. But it had been worth the try.

Nominations 1959

PICTURE

ANATOMY OF A MURDER, Preminger, Columbia. Produced by Otto Preminger.
★ **BEN-HUR**, M-G-M. Produced by Sam Zimbalist.
THE DIARY OF ANNE FRANK, 20th Century-Fox. Produced by George Stevens.
THE NUN'S STORY, Warner Bros. Produced by Henry Blanke.
ROOM AT THE TOP, Romulus, Continental (British). Produced by John and James Woolf.

ACTOR

LAURENCE HARVEY in *Room at the Top*, Romulus, Continental (British).
★ **CHARLTON HESTON** in *Ben-Hur*, M-G-M.
JACK LEMMON in *Some Like It Hot*, Ashton-Mirisch, UA.
PAUL MUNI in *The Last Angry Man*, Kohlmar, Columbia.
JAMES STEWART in *Anatomy of a Murder*, Preminger, Columbia.

ACTRESS

DORIS DAY in *Pillow Talk*, Arwin, U-I.
AUDREY HEPBURN in *The Nun's Story*, Warner Bros.
KATHARINE HEPBURN in *Suddenly, Last Summer*, Horizon, Columbia.
★ **SIMONE SIGNORET** in *Room at the Top*, Romulus, Continental (British).
ELIZABETH TAYLOR in *Suddenly, Last Summer*, Horizon, Columbia.

SUPPORTING ACTOR

★ **HUGH GRIFFITH** in *Ben-Hur*, M-G-M.
ARTHUR O'CONNELL in *Anatomy of a Murder*, Preminger, Columbia.
GEORGE C. SCOTT in *Anatomy of a Murder*, Preminger, Columbia.
ROBERT VAUGHN in *The Young Philadelphians*, Warner Bros.
ED WYNN in *The Diary of Anne Frank*, 20th Century-Fox.

SUPPORTING ACTRESS

HERMIONE BADDELEY in *Room at the Top*, Romulus, Continental (British).
SUSAN KOHNER in *Imitation of Life*, U-I.
JUANITA MOORE in *Imitation of Life*, U-I.
THELMA RITTER in *Pillow Talk*, Arwin, U-I.
★ **SHELLEY WINTERS** in *The Diary of Anne Frank*, 20th Century-Fox.

DIRECTION

JACK CLAYTON for *Room at the Top*, Romulus, Continental (British).
GEORGE STEVENS for *The Diary of Anne Frank*, 20th Century-Fox.
BILLY WILDER for *Some Like It Hot*, Mirisch-Ashton, UA.
★ **WILLIAM WYLER** for *Ben-Hur*, M-G-M.
FRED ZINNEMANN for *The Nun's Story*, Warner Bros.

WRITING

(Screenplay—based on material from another medium)
ANATOMY OF A MURDER, Preminger, Columbia. Wendell Mayes.
BEN-HUR, M-G-M. Karl Tunberg.
THE NUN'S STORY, Warner Bros. Robert Anderson.
★ **ROOM AT THE TOP**, Romulus. Continental (British). Neil Paterson.
SOME LIKE IT HOT, Mirisch-Ashton, UA. Billy Wilder and I.A.L. Diamond.

(Story and Screenplay—written directly for the screen)

THE 400 BLOWS, Zenith International (French). Francois Truffaut and Marcel Moussy.
NORTH BY NORTHWEST, Hitchcock, M-G-M. Ernest Lehman.
OPERATION PETTICOAT, Granart, U-I. Paul King, Joseph Stone, Stanley Shapiro and Maurice Richlin.
★ **PILLOW TALK**, Arwin, U-I. Russell Rouse, Clarence Greene, Stanley Shapiro and Maurice Richlin.
WILD STRAWBERRIES, Janus Films (Swedish) Ingmar Bergman.

CINEMATOGRAPHY

(Black-and-White)
ANATOMY OF A MURDER, Preminger, Columbia. Sam Leavitt.
CAREER, Wallis, Paramount. Joseph LaShelle.
★ **THE DIARY OF ANNE FRANK**, 20th Century-Fox. William C. Mellor.
SOME LIKE IT HOT, Mirisch-Ashton, UA. Charles Lang, Jr.
THE YOUNG PHILADELPHIANS, Warner Bros. Harry Stradling, Sr.

(Color)
★ **BEN-HUR**, M-G-M. Robert L. Surtees.
THE BIG FISHERMAN, Rowland V. Lee, Buena Vista. Lee Garmes.
THE FIVE PENNIES, Dena, Paramount. Daniel L. Fapp.
THE NUN'S STORY, Warner Bros. Franz Planer.
PORGY AND BESS, Goldwyn, Columbia. Leon Shamroy.

ART DIRECTION-SET DECORATION

(After a change in 1957-1958, two awards again given for achievements in this category)

(Black-and-White)
CAREER, Wallis, Paramount. Hal Pereira and Walter Tyler; Sam Comer and Arthur Krams.
★ **THE DIARY OF ANNE FRANK**, 20th Century-Fox. Lyle R. Wheeler and George W. Davis; Walter M. Scott and Stuart A. Reiss.
THE LAST ANGRY MAN, Kohlmar, Columbia. Carl Anderson; William Kiernan.
SOME LIKE IT HOT, Mirisch-Ashton, UA. Ted Haworth; Edward G. Boyle.
SUDDENLY, LAST SUMMER, Horizon, Columbia. Oliver Messel and William Kellner; Scot Slimon.

(Color)
★ **BEN-HUR**, M-G-M. William A. Horning and Edward Carfagno; Hugh Hunt.
THE BIG FISHERMAN, Rowland V. Lee, Buena Vista. John DeCuir; Julia Heron.
JOURNEY TO THE CENTER OF THE EARTH, 20th Century-Fox. Lyle R. Wheeler, Franz Bachelin and Herman A. Blumenthal; Walter M. Scott and Joseph Kish.
NORTH BY NORTHWEST, Hitchcock, M-G-M. William A. Horning, Robert Boyle and Merrill Pye; Henry Grace and Frank McKelvy.
PILLOW TALK, Arwin, U-I. Richard H. Riedel; Russell A. Gausman and Ruby R. Levitt.

COSTUME DESIGN

(After a change in 1957-1958, two awards again given for costume design achievements)

(Black-and-White)
CAREER, Wallis, Paramount. Edith Head.
THE DIARY OF ANNE FRANK, 20th Century-Fox. Charles LeMaire and Mary Wills.

Best Supporting Actor: Hugh Griffith as Sheik Ilderim in *Ben-Hur*. In his Oscar-winning performance, England's prolific scene-stealer played the man who befriends Judah Ben-Hur (Charlton Heston) and helps him into a mammoth Roman chariot race. Griffith was also a nominee in 1963 as the daffy squire in *Tom Jones* and in one of only a handful of performers who have appeared in three Oscar-winning Best Pictures (*Ben-Hur*, *Tom Jones* and 1968's *Oliver!*).

Best Supporting Actress: Shelley Winters as Mrs. Van Daan in *The Diary of Anne Frank* (20th Century-Fox; directed by George Stevens). She spent the first phase of her career playing svelte glamor girls, but Shelley Winters found her niche in films as a character actress—and a superb one. As Mrs. Van Daan, she was one of eight Jews attempting to survive in Nazi-occupied Amsterdam by hiding in a cramped attic for two years. She won the Academy Award, and a second one in 1965 for *A Patch of Blue*.

Best Actress: Simone Signoret as Alice Aisgill (above, with Laurence Harvey) in *Room at the Top* (Continental Distributing; directed by Jack Clayton). "When we made the film, we thought it would be a picture we would like and some of our friends would like," said Simone Signoret. "Its success came as a great surprise." Made in England, the film was about an ambitious young schemer in a Yorkshire mill town who has an affair with an unhappily married woman, 10 years his senior, played by Miss Signoret; when he discards her to marry a mill owner's young daughter who can help his career, the older woman tragically dies in an automobile accident. Sultry, plumpish and frankly 40, the German-born Signoret was a new kind of leading lady to American audiences, and an immediate success. In 1965 she received a second Oscar nomination, for *Ship of Fools.*

THE GAZEBO, Avon, M-G-M. Helen Rose.
★ SOME LIKE IT HOT, Mirisch-Ashton, UA. Orry-Kelly.
THE YOUNG PHILADELPHIANS, Warner Bros. Howard Shoup.

(Color)

★ BEN-HUR, M-G-M. Elizabeth Haffenden.
THE BEST OF EVERYTHING, Wald, 20th Century-Fox. Adele Palmer.
THE BIG FISHERMAN, Rowland V. Lee, Buena Vista. Renie.
THE FIVE PENNIES, Dena, Paramount. Edith Head.
PORGY AND BESS, Goldwyn, Columbia. Irene Sharaff.

SOUND

★ BEN-HUR, M-G-M. Metro-Goldwyn-Mayer Studio Sound Department; Franklin E. Milton, sound director.
JOURNEY TO THE CENTER OF THE EARTH, 20th Century-Fox. 20th Century-Fox Sound Dept.; Carl Faulkner, sound director.
LIBEL!, M-G-M (British). Metro-Goldwyn-Mayer London Sound Dept.; A.W. Watkins, sound director.
THE NUN'S STORY, Warner Bros. Warner Bros. Studio Sound Dept.; George R. Groves, sound director.

PORGY AND BESS, Goldwyn, Columbia. Samuel Goldwyn Studio Sound Dept.; Gordon E. Sawyer, sound director; and Todd-AO Sound Dept., Fred Hynes, sound director.

FILM EDITING

ANATOMY OF A MURDER, Preminger, Columbia. Louis R. Loeffler.
★ BEN-HUR, M-G-M. Ralph E. Winters and John D. Dunning.
NORTH BY NORTHWEST, Hitchcock, M-G-M. George Tomasini.
THE NUN'S STORY, Warner Bros. Walter Thompson.
ON THE BEACH, Kramer, UA. Frederic Knudtson.

SPECIAL EFFECTS

★ BEN-HUR, M-G-M. A. Arnold Gillespie, Robert MacDonald and Milo Lory.
JOURNEY TO THE CENTER OF THE EARTH, 20th Century-Fox. L.B. Abbott, James B. Gordon and Carl Faulkner.

MUSIC

(Song)

THE BEST OF EVERYTHING (*The Best of Everything*, Wald, 20th Century-Fox); Music by Alfred Newman. Lyrics by Sammy Cahn.
THE FIVE PENNIES (*The Five Pennies*, Dena, Paramount); Music and Lyrics by Sylvia Fine.
THE HANGING TREE (*The Hanging Tree*, Warner Bros.); Music by Jerry Livingston. Lyrics by Mack David.
★ HIGH HOPES (*A Hole in the Head*, Sincap, UA); Music by James Van Heusen. Lyrics by Sammy Cahn.
STRANGE ARE THE WAYS OF LOVE (*The Young Land*, C.V. Whitney, Columbia); Music by Dimitri Tiomkin. Lyrics by Ned Washington.

(Scoring of a Dramatic or Comedy Picture)

★ BEN-HUR, M-G-M. Miklos Rozsa.
THE DIARY OF ANNE FRANK, 20th Century-Fox. Alfred Newman.
THE NUN'S STORY, Warner Bros. Franz Waxman.
ON THE BEACH, Kramer, UA. Ernest Gold.
PILLOW TALK, Arwin, U-I. Frank DeVol.

(Scoring of a Musical Picture)

THE FIVE PENNIES, Dena, Paramount. Leith Stevens.
LI'L ABNER, Panama and Frank, Paramount. Nelson Riddle and Joseph J. Lilley.

PORGY AND BESS, Goldwyn, Columbia. Andre Previn and Ken Darby.
SAY ONE FOR ME, Crosby, 20th Century-Fox. Lionel Newman.
SLEEPING BEAUTY, Disney, Buena Vista. George Bruns.

SHORT SUBJECTS

(Cartoons)

MEXICALI SHMOES, Warner Bros. John W. Burton, producer.
★ MOONBIRD, Storyboard-Harrison. John Hubley, producer.
NOAH'S ARK, Disney, Buena Vista. Walt Disney, producer.
THE VIOLINIST, Pintoff Prods., Kingsley International. Ernest Pintoff, producer.

(Live Action Subjects)

BETWEEN THE TIDES, British Transport Films, Schoenfeld Films (British). Ian Ferguson, producer.
★ THE GOLDEN FISH, Les Requins Associes, Columbia (French). Jacques-Yves Cousteau, producer.
MYSTERIES OF THE DEEP, Disney, Buena Vista. Walt Disney, producer.
THE RUNNING, JUMPING AND STANDING-STILL FILM, Lion International, Kingsley-Union Films (British). Peter Sellers, producer.
SKYSCRAPER, Burstyn Film Enterprises. Shirley Clarke, Willard Van Dyke and Irving Jacoby, producers.

DOCUMENTARY

(Short Subjects)

DONALD IN MATHMAGIC LAND, Disney, Buena Vista. Walt Disney, producer.
FROM GENERATION TO GENERATION, Cullen Assocs., Maternity Center Assoc. Edward F. Cullen, producer.
★ GLASS, Netherlands Government, George K. Arthur-Go Pictures (The Netherlands). Bert Haanstra, producer.

(Features)

THE RACE FOR SPACE, Wolper, Inc. David L. Wolper, producer.
★ SERENGETI SHALL NOT DIE, Okapia-Film Prods., Transocean Film (German). Bernhard Grzimek, producer.

FOREIGN LANGUAGE FILM

★ BLACK ORPHEUS, (France).
THE BRIDGE, (Germany).
THE GREAT WAR, (Italy).
PAW, (Denmark).
THE VILLAGE ON THE RIVER, (The Netherlands.)

HONORARY AND OTHER AWARDS

TO LEE DE FOREST for his pioneering inventions which brought sound to the motion picture. (statuette)
TO BUSTER KEATON for his unique talents which brought immortal comedies to the screen. (statuette)

1959 IRVING G. THALBERG MEMORIAL AWARD

None given this year.

1959 JEAN HERSHOLT HUMANITARIAN AWARD

TO BOB HOPE

SCIENTIFIC OR TECHNICAL

CLASS I (statuette)

None.

CLASS II (plaque)

DOUGLAS G. SHEARER of M-G-M, Inc., and ROBERT E. GOTTSCHALK and JOHN R. MOORE of Panavision, Inc., for the development of a system of producing and exhibiting wide-film motion pictures known as Camera 65.
WADSWORTH E. POHL, WILLIAM EVANS, WERNER HOPF, S.E. HOWSE, THOMAS P. DIXON, STANFORD RESEARCH INSTITUTE and TECHNICOLOR CORP. for the design and development of the Technicolor electronic printing timer.
WADSWORTH E. POHL, JACK ALFORD, HENRY IMUS, JOSEPH SCHMIT, PAUL FASSNACHT, AL LOFQUIST and TECHNICOLOR CORP. for the development and practical application of equipment for wet printing.
DR. HOWARD S. COLEMAN, DR. A. FRANCIS TURNER, HAROLD H. SCHROEDER, JAMES R. BENFORD and HAROLD E. ROSENBERGER of the Bausch & Lomb Optical Co. for the design and development of the Balcold projection mirror.
ROBERT P. GUTTERMAN of General Kinetics, Inc., and the LIPSNER-SMITH CORP. for the design and development of the CF-2 Ultra-sonic Film Cleaner.

CLASS III (citation)

UB IWERKS of Walt Disney Prods.;
E.L. STONES, GLEN ROBINSON, WINFIELD HUBBARD and LUTHER NEWMAN of the M-G-M Studio Construction Dept.

★ INDICATES WINNER

Best Supporting Actress: Shirley Jones
as Lulu Bains and **Best Actor: Burt Lancaster**
as Elmer in *Elmer Gantry* (United Artists;
directed by Richard Brooks). It was a sharp
change of pace for Shirley Jones, playing
a tough-talking, hardened prostitute who
blows the whistle on a hypocritical
do-gooder; in her previous five films, she
had played soft ingenues, usually singing
Rodgers and Hammerstein songs to
Gordon MacRae. For Burt Lancaster, *Elmer
Gantry* offered a definitive role, marvelously
suited to his unique vitality and
mannerisms. Both won Academy Awards
for the film, based on the first half of a
33-year-old novel by Sinclair Lewis about
a traveling salesman and con man who
becomes a successful revivalist-preacher,
sells salvation and ultimately crashes
to a downfall. Jean Simmons, Dean Jagger,
Arthur Kennedy and Patti Page were also
in the cast; director Brooks also received an
Oscar for writing *Elmer*'s screenplay.

1960 The Thirty-Third Year

For the 1960 Academy Awards presentations, Oscar moved to a new setting: the Santa Monica Civic Auditorium, sixteen and one-half miles away from the Hollywood-Los Angeles area which had played host for the previous thirty-two years. There were several reasons for the move. Interest in Oscar and the awards continued to grow, requiring more seating space for nominees, guests and supporters. Simultaneously, the audience capacity at the Pantages Theatre in Hollywood had been reduced in order to install a larger screen for a roadshow presentation of *Spartacus;* and, after investigation, no other auditorium in the area was found by the Academy to be either big enough or available on the dates required. So, on April 17, 1961, Hollywood's finest drove away from the cinema hub into Santa Monica to attend the festivities. That location remained Oscar's home for the next nine Awards presentations.

Also for the first time, the ceremony itself was telecast over the ABC-TV network, under a newly signed five-year contract with the Academy for exclusive television and radio rights. Richard Dunlap produced and directed for the network, while Arthur Freed produced and Vincente Minnelli directed for the Academy. Andre Previn was the evening's musical director and Bob Hope was again master of ceremonies while an estimated seventy million viewers watched. Of added interest was Elizabeth Taylor, one of the nominees (and eventual winner) as Best Actress for *Butterfield 8;* she was making her first public appearance since surviving a much-headlined bout with pneumonia. Other acting winners included Burt Lancaster (Best Actor for *Elmer Gantry*) and Peter Ustinov (Best Supporting Actor in *Spartacus*).

The Apartment was the biggest winner of the evening, with five awards, including Oscars for Best Picture, Best Director (Billy Wilder) and Best Story and Screenplay (Wilder and I.A.L. Diamond). Sweden's *The Virgin Spring* was honored as Best Foreign Language Film, and—another first-time occurrence—a song from a foreign-made film was named winner in that music category (Manos Hadjidakis' "Never on Sunday").

Honorary Awards went to Hayley Mills, Stan Laurel and Gary Cooper and—next to the drama surrounding Elizabeth Taylor's appearance—the Cooper award caused the major talk of the night. Unable to attend, his statuette was accepted by friend James Stewart, the man who had presented Cooper with his 1941 Oscar for *Sergeant York,* and caused speculation the actor was terminally ill. He was, and died one month later, on May 13, 1961.

Best Actress: Elizabeth Taylor as Gloria Wandrous (above) in *Butterfield 8* (M-G-M; directed by Daniel Mann). Elizabeth Taylor never cared for the *Butterfield 8* script, from John O'Hara's novel about a New York model and part-time call girl who tragically falls in love with a wealthy, disillusioned married man. But she made it, primarily to complete contractual ties to M-G-M, so she could be free to accept an unprecedented offer of $1 million from 20th Century-Fox to do a film about Cleopatra. *Butterfield* turned out to be her Oscar charm; after three previous nominations in a row, she won the Academy Award, her first. A second one arrived six years later, for 1966's *Who's Afraid of Virginia Woolf?*.

Best Picture: The Apartment (United Artists; produced by Billy Wilder) and **Best Director: Billy Wilder** for *The Apartment.* Swinging like a pendulum between farce and near-tragic drama, *The Apartment* was about a struggling insurance clerk (played by Jack Lemmon, (left, with Jack Kruschen and Shirley MacLaine) who lends his Manhattan apartment to company executives for their extra-curricular activities, in return for promotions. The film was the pick of 1960's films with Academy voters, and it won five awards, including three to the man behind the whole sly idea: Billy Wilder, as producer of the year's Best Picture, as director and as co-author, with I.A.L. Diamond.

Best Supporting Actor: Peter Ustinov as Batiatus (right, with Jean Simmons) in *Spartacus* (Universal-International; directed by Stanley Kubrick). The big-scale *Spartacus* was a saga of Roman gladiators, emperors and intrigues, and received four Academy Awards, one for Ustinov as a clownish slave in B.C. Rome, plus additional ones for Color Cinematography, for Color Art Direction and for Color Costume Design. *Spartacus* was based on a novel by Howard Fast and featured a distinguished cast including Kirk Douglas, Laurence Olivier, Charles Laughton, John Gavin, Tony Curtis, Nina Foch and John Dall. Ustinov was also prominent during 1960 in Fred Zinnemann's superb *The Sundowners*, and he won a second Oscar four years later, for *Topkapi*.

Nominations 1960

PICTURE

THE ALAMO, Batjac, UA. Produced by John Wayne.
* THE APARTMENT, Mirisch, UA. Produced by Billy Wilder.
ELMER GANTRY, Lancaster-Brooks, UA. Produced by Bernard Smith.
SONS AND LOVERS, Wald, 20th Century-Fox. Produced by Jerry Wald.
THE SUNDOWNERS, Warner Bros. Produced by Fred Zinnemann.

ACTOR

TREVOR HOWARD in *Sons and Lovers*, Wald, 20th Century-Fox.
* BURT LANCASTER in *Elmer Gantry*, Lancaster-Brooks, UA.
JACK LEMMON in *The Apartment*, Mirisch, UA.
LAURENCE OLIVIER in *The Entertainer*, Woodfall, Continental (British).
SPENCER TRACY in *Inherit the Wind*, Kramer, UA.

ACTRESS

GREER GARSON in *Sunrise at Campobello*, Schary, Warner Bros.
DEBORAH KERR in *The Sundowners*, Warner Bros.
SHIRLEY MacLAINE in *The Apartment*, Mirisch, UA.
MELINA MERCOURI in *Never on Sunday*, Melinafilm, Lopert Pictures (Greek).
* ELIZABETH TAYLOR in *Butterfield 8*, Afton-Linebrook, M-G-M.

SUPPORTING ACTOR

PETER FALK in *Murder, Inc.*, 20th Century-Fox.
JACK KRUSCHEN in *The Apartment*, Mirisch, UA.
SAL MINEO in *Exodus*, Preminger, UA.
* PETER USTINOV in *Spartacus*, Bryna, U-I.
CHILL WILLS in *The Alamo*, Batjac, UA.

SUPPORTING ACTRESS

GLYNIS JOHNS in *The Sundowners*, Warner Bros.
* SHIRLEY JONES in *Elmer Gantry*, Lancaster-Brooks, UA.
SHIRLEY KNIGHT in *The Dark at the Top of the Stairs*, Warner Bros.

JANET LEIGH in *Psycho*, Hitchcock, Paramount.
MARY URE in *Sons and Lovers*, Wald, 20th Century-Fox.

DIRECTION

JACK CARDIFF for *Sons and Lovers*, Wald, 20th Century-Fox.
JULES DASSIN for *Never on Sunday*, Melinafilm, Lopert Pictures (Greek).
ALFRED HITCHCOCK for *Psycho*, Hitchcock, Paramount.
* BILLY WILDER for *The Apartment*, Mirisch, UA.
FRED ZINNEMANN for *The Sundowners*, Warner Bros.

WRITING

(Screenplay—based on material from another medium)
* ELMER GANTRY, Lancaster-Brooks, UA. Richard Brooks.
INHERIT THE WIND, Kramer, UA. Nathan E. Douglas and Harold Jacob Smith.
SONS AND LOVERS, Wald, 20th Century-Fox. Gavin Lambert and T.E.B. Clarke.
THE SUNDOWNERS, Warner Bros. Isobel Lennart.
TUNES OF GLORY, Lopert Pictures (British). James Kennaway.

(Story and Screenplay—written directly for the screen)
THE ANGRY SILENCE, Beaver Films, Lion International (British). Richard Gregson, Michael Craig and Bryan Forbes.
* THE APARTMENT, Mirisch, UA. Billy Wilder and I.A.L. Diamond.
THE FACTS OF LIFE, Panama and Frank, UA. Norman Panama and Melvin Frank.
HIROSHIMA, MON AMOUR, Zenith International (French-Japanese). Marguerite Duras.
NEVER ON SUNDAY, Melinafilm, Lopert Pictures (Greek). Jules Dassin.

CINEMATOGRAPHY

(Black-and-White)
THE APARTMENT, Mirisch, UA. Joseph LaShelle.
THE FACTS OF LIFE, Panama and Frank Prod., UA. Charles B. Lang, Jr.

INHERIT THE WIND, Kramer, UA. Ernest Laszlo.
PSYCHO, Hitchcock, Paramount. John L. Russell.
* SONS AND LOVERS, Wald, 20th Century-Fox. Freddie Francis.

(Color)
THE ALAMO, Batjac, UA. William H. Clothier.
BUTTERFIELD 8, Afton-Linebrook, M-G-M. Joseph Ruttenberg and Charles Harten.
EXODUS, Preminger, UA. Sam Leavitt.
PEPE, Sidney, Columbia. Joe MacDonald.
* SPARTACUS, Bryna, U-I. Russell Metty.

ART DIRECTION-SET DECORATION

(Black-and-White)
* THE APARTMENT, Mirisch, UA. Alexander Trauner; Edward G. Boyle.
THE FACTS OF LIFE, Panama and Frank, UA. Joseph McMillan Johnson and Kenneth A. Reid; Ross Dowd.
PSYCHO, Hitchcock, Paramount. Joseph Hurley and Robert Clatworthy; George Milo.
SONS AND LOVERS, Wald, 20th Century-Fox. Tom Morahan; Lionel Couch.
VISIT TO A SMALL PLANET, Wallis, Paramount. Hal Pereira and Walter Tyler; Sam Comer and Arthur Krams.

(Color)
CIMARRON, M-G-M. George W. Davis and Addison Hehr; Henry Grace, Hugh Hunt and Otto Siegel.
IT STARTED IN NAPLES, Paramount. Hal Pereira and Roland Anderson; Sam Comer and Arrigo Breschi.
PEPE, Sidney, Columbia. Ted Haworth; William Kiernan.
* SPARTACUS, Bryna, U-I. Alexander Golitzen and Eric Orbom; Russell A. Gausman and Julia Heron.
SUNRISE AT CAMPOBELLO, Schary, Warner Bros. Edward Carrere; George James Hopkins.

COSTUME DESIGN

(Black-and-White)
* THE FACTS OF LIFE, Panama and Frank Prod., UA. Edith Head and Edward Stevenson.

Best Foreign Language Film: The Virgin Spring from Sweden (Janus Films; directed by Ingmar Bergman). Birgitta Pettersson (below) was featured as an innocent Swedish maiden who is raped and murdered by two goatherds in the Middle Ages, a story based on a 13th-century Swedish legend about revenge and repentance. Academy voters chose it as the year's outstanding foreign film, the first Ingmar Bergman film so honored. In its country of origin, it was called *Jung Fru Kallan*; with Max von Sydow, Birgitta Valberg and Gunnel Lindblom were also in the cast.

Sons and Lovers (20th Century-Fox; produced by Jerry Wald) was made in England and based on D.H. Lawrence's classic 1913 novel about the strong relationship between a mother and son in a bleak coal town. One of the year's outstanding dramas (and a co-winner with *The Apartment* of the New York Film Critics' Best Picture award); it won an Oscar for the Cinematography (Black-and-White) of Freddie Francis and was directed by Jack Cardiff, himself an Academy Award winner as a cinematographer. The leading players were Dean Stockwell and Wendy Hiller (above, under the umbrella), Trevor Howard, Mary Ure and Heather Sears.

Honorary Award: Hayley Mills (below, in *Pollyanna*) for "the outstanding juvenile performance during 1960." The daughter of England's acting family headed by John Mills, she was the twelfth juvenile performer (and, to date, the last) to receive an honorary miniature Oscar, voted by the Academy's Board of Governors. Her statuette was presented at the Awards ceremony by the first talented tot to win one, Shirley Temple.

NEVER ON SUNDAY, Melinafilm, Lopert Pictures (Greek). Denny Vachlioti.
THE RISE AND FALL OF LEGS DIAMOND, United States Prod., Bros. Howard Shoup.
SEVEN THIEVES, 20th Century-Fox. Bill Thomas.
THE VIRGIN SPRING, Janus Films (Swedish). Marik Vos.

(Color)
CAN-CAN, Suffolk-Cummings, 20th Century-Fox. Irene Sharaff.
MIDNIGHT LACE, Hunter-Arwin, U-I. Irene.
PEPE, Sidney, Columbia. Edith Head.
★ SPARTACUS, Bryna, U-I. Valles and Bill Thomas.
SUNRISE AT CAMPOBELLO, Schary, Warner Bros. Marjorie Best.

SOUND
★ THE ALAMO, Batjac, UA. Samuel Goldwyn Studio Sound Dept., Gordon E. Sawyer, sound director; and Todd-AO Sound Dept., Fred Hynes, sound director.
THE APARTMENT, Mirisch, UA. Samuel Goldwyn Studio Sound Dept.; Gordon E. Sawyer, sound director.
CIMARRON, M-G-M. Metro-Goldwyn-Mayer Studio Sound Dept.; Franklin E. Milton, sound director.
PEPE, Sidney, Columbia. Columbia Studio Sound Dept.; Charles Rice, sound director.
SUNRISE AT CAMPOBELLO, Schary, Warner Bros. Warner Bros. Studio Sound Dept.; George R. Groves, sound director.

FILM EDITING
THE ALAMO, Batjac, UA. Stuart Gilmore.
★ THE APARTMENT, Mirisch, UA. Daniel Mandell.
INHERIT THE WIND, Kramer, UA. Frederic Knudtson.
PEPE, Sidney, Columbia. Viola Lawrence and Al Clark.
SPARTACUS, Bryna, U-I. Robert Lawrence.

SPECIAL EFFECTS
THE LAST VOYAGE, Stone, M-G-M. A.J. Lohman.
★ THE TIME MACHINE, Pal, M-G-M. Gene Warren and Tim Baar.

MUSIC
(Song)
THE FACTS OF LIFE (*The Facts of Life,* Panama and Frank, UA); Music and Lyrics by Johnny Mercer.
FARAWAY PART OF TOWN (*Pepe,* Sidney, Columbia); Music by Andre Previn. Lyrics by Dory Langdon.
THE GREEN LEAVES OF SUMMER (*The Alamo,* Batjac, UA); Music by Dimitri Tiomkin. Lyrics by Paul Francis Webster.
★ NEVER ON SUNDAY (*Never on Sunday,* Melinafilm, Lopert Pictures; Greek); Music and Lyrics by Manos Hadjidakis.
THE SECOND TIME AROUND (*High Time,* Crosby, 20th Century-Fox); Music by James Van Heusen. Lyrics by Sammy Cahn.

(Scoring of a Dramatic or Comedy Picture)
THE ALAMO, Batjac, UA. Dimitri Tiomkin.
ELMER GANTRY, Lancaster-Brooks, UA. Andre Previn.
★ EXODUS, Preminger, UA. Ernest Gold.
THE MAGNIFICENT SEVEN, Mirisch-Alpha, UA. Elmer Bernstein.
SPARTACUS, Bryna, U-I. Alex North.

(Scoring of a Musical Picture)
BELLS ARE RINGING, Freed, M-G-M. Andre Previn.
CAN-CAN, Suffolk-Cummings, 20th Century-Fox. Nelson Riddle.
LET'S MAKE LOVE, Wald, 20th Century-Fox. Lionel Newman and Earle H. Hagen.
PEPE, Sidney, Columbia. Johnny Green.
★ SONG WITHOUT END, Goetz, Columbia. Morris Stoloff and Harry Sukman.

SHORT SUBJECTS
(Cartoons)
GOLIATH II, Disney, Buena Vista. Walt Disney, producer.
HIGH NOTE, Warner Bros.
MOUSE AND GARDEN, Warner Bros.
★ MUNRO, Rembrandt Films, Film Representations. William L. Snyder, producer.
A PLACE IN THE SUN, George K. Arthur-Go Pictures (Czechoslovakian). Frantisek Vystrecil, producer.

(Live Action Subjects)
THE CREATION OF WOMAN, Trident Films, Sterling World Distributors (Indian). Charles F. Schwep and Ismail Merchant, producers.
★ DAY OF THE PAINTER, Little Movies, Kingsley-Union Films. Ezra R. Baker, producer.
ISLANDS OF THE SEA, Disney, Buena Vista. Walt Disney, producer.
A SPORT IS BORN, Paramount. Leslie Winik, producer.

DOCUMENTARY
(Short Subjects)
BEYOND SILENCE, U.S. Information Agency.
A CITY CALLED COPENHAGEN, Statens Filmcentral, Danish Film Office (Danish).
GEORGE GROSZ' INTERREGNUM, Educational Communications Corp. Charles and Altina Carey, producers.
★ GIUSEPPINA, Schoenfeld Films (British). James Hill, producer.
UNIVERSE, National Film Board of Canada, Schoenfeld Films (Canadian). Colin Low, producer.

(Features)
★ THE HORSE WITH THE FLYING TAIL, Disney, Buena Vista. Larry Lansburgh, producer.
REBEL IN PARADISE, Tiare Co. Robert D. Fraser, producer.

FOREIGN LANGUAGE FILM
KAPO, (Italy).
LA VERITE, (France).
MACARIO, (Mexico).
THE NINTH CIRCLE, (Yugoslavia).
★ THE VIRGIN SPRING, (Sweden).

HONORARY AND OTHER AWARDS
TO GARY COOPER for his many memorable screen performances and the international recognition he, as an individual, has gained for the motion picture industry. (statuette)
TO STAN LAUREL for his creative pioneering in the field of cinema comedy. (statuette)
TO HAYLEY MILLS for *Pollyanna,* the most outstanding juvenile performance during 1960. (miniature statuette)

1960 IRVING G. THALBERG MEMORIAL AWARD
None given this year.

1960 JEAN HERSHOLT HUMANITARIAN AWARD
TO SOL LESSER

SCIENTIFIC OR TECHNICAL
CLASS I (statuette)
None.

CLASS II (plaque)
AMPEX PROFESSIONAL PRODUCTS CO. for the production of a well-engineered multi-purpose sound system combining high standards of quality with convenience of control, dependable operation and simplified emergency provisions.

CLASS III (citation)
ARTHUR HOLCOMB, PETRO VLAHOS and COLUMBIA STUDIO CAMERA DEPT.;
ANTHONY PAGLIA and the 20TH CENTURY-FOX STUDIO MECHANICAL EFFECTS DEPT.;
CARL HAUGE, ROBERT GRUBEL and EDWARD REICHARD of Consolidated Film Industries.

★ INDICATES WINNER

Best Picture: West Side Story (United Artists; produced by Robert Wise), **Best Directors: Robert Wise and Jerome Robbins** and (above) **Best Supporting Actor: George Chakiris** as Bernardo and **Best Supporting Actress: Rita Moreno** as Anita in *West Side Story*.
On the Broadway stage, *West Side Story* opened Sept. 25, 1957, and was a spellbinder; four years later, it became a 153-minute motion picture, with its qualities enhanced even further by the ability of the film medium to give limitless elbow room to its vitality. It was also *Romeo and Juliet* set to music (by Elmer Bernstein and Stephen Sondheim), with the Capulet-Montague friction in Verona translated into a Puerto Rican-American gang rivalry on the streets of Manhattan's upper West Side. Natalie Wood, beginning her adult screen career, and Richard Beymer were the star-crossed lovers and, among the cast, George Chakiris and Rita Moreno made particularly striking impressions—and won Oscars—as the leader of the Puerto Rican "Shark" gang and his fiery girl friend. Considerable attention was given to the fact Marni Nixon was the off-camera singing voice for Wood; Beymer was musically dubbed by Jim Bryant. Ultimately, and rightfully, *West Side Story* won a near-record 10 Academy Awards, including those for Color Cinematography, Color Art Direction, Color Costume Design, Sound, Scoring of a Musical, Film Editing, plus a Special Award to Robbins for his choreography.

1961 The Thirty-Fourth Year

Blatant advertising for Academy votes in Hollywood trade publications had become a major embarrassment to the Academy by the early 1960s, causing the Board of Governors to issue a statement of policy on the subject. "We feel it has now become necessary to state our position in regard to all potential nominees," it read, "and we are mindful that throughout the years the great majority of those nominated, or seeking nominations, have exercised restraint in reminding the voting members of the Academy of their achievements. Regrettably, however, last year a few resorted to outright, excessive and vulgar solicitation of votes. This became a serious embarrassment to the Academy and our industry. We are hesitant to set down specific rules governing advertising (and) leave the decision for this year to the good conscience of the nominees."

The statement further requested a cooperative effort to eliminate those advertising practices "which are irrelevant to the honest evaluation of artistic and technical accomplishments and violate the principles under which the Academy was established. Any honorary organization such as the Academy can command respect only as long as its members and the nominees take unto themselves the responsibility of dignified conduct." The statement concluded: "We are hopeful this reminder will be sufficient." Unfortunately, similar admonishments have had to be made in succeeding years.

The Awards for 1961 were presented April 9, 1962, again at the Santa Monica Civic Auditorium. Sophia Loren, winner as Best Actress for *Two Women,* wasn't on hand to accept her statuette (Greer Garson did stand-in duty for Sophia); she was at home in Rome awaiting the outcome. She was the first performer in a foreign language film to be nominated for an Academy Award, and so became Oscar's initial subtitled acting winner. It was an evening for Oscar "firsts." Maximilian Schell, chosen Best Actor for *Judgment at Nuremberg,* became the first performer to win an Academy Award for re-creating on screen a role he had originally done on television. Also for the initial time, two directors won in the Best Director category: Jerome Robbins and Robert Wise of *West Side Story. West Side Story* was the big winner of the year with ten awards, including ones for Best Picture, Supporting Actor (George Chakiris), Supporting Actress (Rita Moreno), plus a Special Oscar to Robbins for his *West Side Story* choreography.

Earlier, there had been another first. Shortly after the nominations were announced, George C. Scott informed Academy officials he wished to decline his nomination in the Supporting Actor category; his name, however, remained on the ballot.

ABC-TV again carried the telecast, with Richard Dunlap producing-directing for the network, and Arthur Freed producing for the Academy. Johnny Green was musical director, Bob Hope was master of ceremonies, and Ann-Margret, a relative newcomer to movie circles, attracted major attention when she delivered a version of "Bachelor in Paradise," one of the year's nominees as Best Song. There was also an unabashed (and uninvited) visitor on stage: Stan Berman, a professional gate crasher, bypassed 125 uniformed police guards during the evening and went on stage to hand a home-made Oscar to a surprised Bob Hope.

Best Actor: Maximilian Schell as Hans Rolfe in *Judgment at Nuremberg* (United Artists; directed by Stanley Kramer). Maximilian Schell first played Hans Rolfe in an April 1959 CBS-TV version of *Judgment at Nuremberg,* directed by George Roy Hill; when Stanley Kramer expanded the story into a 3-hour, 15-minute movie, Schell was the only actor chosen to repeat his role, and he was the least-known face among the film's powerhouse cast which included Spencer Tracy, Burt Lancaster, Richard Widmark, Montgomery Clift, Marlene Dietrich and Judy Garland. Schell played a German lawyer in the 1948 war crimes trial held in Nuremberg, Germany, defending four Nazis on trial for their part in supporting Hitler's precepts during World War II. His argument: in wartime, it was their duty—not a choice— to accept the orders of their leader and follow them. Ultimately, Hans Rolfe lost the case, but actor Schell won the Academy Award. During Oscar's first 50 years, he was again nominated as Best Actor in 1975 for *The Man in the Glass Booth* and as Best Supporting Actor in 1977 for *Julia.* He also co-produced and directed *First Love,* a 1970 Academy nominee as Best Foreign Language Film.

Best Actress: Sophia Loren as Cesira (right) in *Two Women* (Embassy; directed by Vittorio DeSica). The role—volcanic, lusty and warm—was originally designed for Anna Magnani; in the hands of Sophia Loren, it became the first performance delivered in a foreign language film to win an Academy Award. Sophia played a passionate Italian widow, unable to face 1943 wartime dangers in Rome, who leaves the city with her 13-year-old daughter (Eleanora Brown) in order to sit out the war in her mountainside birthplace, miles away; on their journey, both are raped in a gutted church by Moroccan soldiers, and the resultant trauma threatens to wreck the daughter's life and the mother-daughter relationship. Filmed in Italy, in Italian, *Two Women* co-starred Jean-Paul Belmondo and Raf Vallone and was one of the first subtitled foreign language films to find a wide popular acceptance by the public in the United States; it also proved Sophia, then most famous as a movie sex symbol, could hold her own with anyone as an actress.

Nominations 1961

PICTURE

FANNY, Mansfield, Warner Bros. Produced by Joshua Logan.
THE GUNS OF NAVARONE, Foreman, Columbia. Produced by Carl Foreman.
THE HUSTLER, Rossen, 20th Century-Fox. Produced by Robert Rossen.
JUDGMENT AT NUREMBERG, Kramer, UA. Produced by Stanley Kramer.
★ WEST SIDE STORY, Mirisch-B&P Enterprises, UA. Produced by Robert Wise.

ACTOR

CHARLES BOYER in *Fanny*, Mansfield, Warner Bros.
PAUL NEWMAN in *The Hustler*, Rossen, 20th Century-Fox.
★ MAXIMILIAN SCHELL in *Judgment at Nuremberg*, Kramer, UA.
SPENCER TRACY in *Judgment at Nuremberg*, Kramer, UA.
STUART WHITMAN in *The Mark*, Buchman-Stross, Continental (British).

ACTRESS

AUDREY HEPBURN in *Breakfast at Tiffany's*, Jurow-Shepherd, Paramount.
PIPER LAURIE in *The Hustler*, Rossen, 20th Century-Fox.
★ SOPHIA LOREN in *Two Women*, Ponti, Embassy (Italian).
GERALDINE PAGE in *Summer and Smoke*, Wallis, Paramount.
NATALIE WOOD in *Splendor in the Grass*, Kazan, Warner Bros.

SUPPORTING ACTOR

★ GEORGE CHAKIRIS in *West Side Story*, Mirisch-B&P Enterprises, UA.
MONTGOMERY CLIFT in *Judgment at Nuremberg*, Kramer, UA.
PETER FALK in *Pocketful Of Miracles*, Franton, UA.
JACKIE GLEASON in *The Hustler*, Rossen, 20th Century-Fox.
GEORGE C. SCOTT in *The Hustler*, Rossen, 20th Century-Fox.

SUPPORTING ACTRESS

FAY BAINTER in *The Children's Hour*, Mirisch-Worldwide, UA.
JUDY GARLAND in *Judgment at Nuremberg*, Kramer, UA.
LOTTE LENYA in *The Roman Spring of Mrs. Stone*, Seven Arts, Warner Bros.
UNA MERKEL in *Summer and Smoke*, Wallis, Paramount.
★ RITA MORENO in *West Side Story*, Mirisch-B&P Enterprises, UA.

DIRECTION

FEDERICO FELLINI for *La Dolce Vita*, Astor Pictures (Italian).
STANLEY KRAMER for *Judgment at Nuremberg*, Kramer, UA.
ROBERT ROSSEN for *The Hustler*, Rossen, 20th Century-Fox.
J. LEE THOMPSON for *The Guns of Navarone*, Foreman, Columbia.
★ ROBERT WISE and JEROME ROBBINS for *West Side Story*, Mirisch-Seven Arts, UA.

WRITING

(Screenplay—based on material from another medium)
BREAKFAST AT TIFFANY'S, Jurow-Shepherd, Paramount. George Axelrod.
THE GUNS OF NAVARONE, Foreman, Columbia. Carl Foreman.
THE HUSTLER, Rossen, 20th Century-Fox. Sidney Carroll and Robert Rossen.
★ JUDGMENT AT NUREMBERG, Kramer, UA. Abby Mann.
WEST SIDE STORY, Mirisch-Seven Arts, UA. Ernest Lehman.

(Story and Screenplay—written directly for the screen)
BALLAD OF A SOLDIER, Kingsley International-M.J.P. (Russian). Valentin Yoshov and Grigori Chukhrai.
GENERAL DELLA ROVERE, Continental Distributing (Italian). Sergio Amidei, Diego Fabbri and Indro Montanelli.
LA DOLCE VITA, Astor Pictures (Italian). Federico Fellini, Tullio Pinelli, Ennio Flaiano and Brunello Rondi.
LOVER COME BACK, Shapiro-Arwin, U-I. Stanley Shapiro and Paul Henning.
★ SPLENDOR IN THE GRASS, Kazan, Warner Bros. William Inge.

CINEMATOGRAPHY

(Black-and-White)
THE ABSENT MINDED PROFESSOR, Disney, Buena Vista. Edward Colman.
THE CHILDREN'S HOUR, Mirisch-Worldwide, UA. Franz F. Planer.
★ THE HUSTLER, Rossen, 20th Century-Fox. Eugen Shuftan.
JUDGMENT AT NUREMBERG, Kramer, UA. Ernest Laszlo.
ONE, TWO, THREE, Mirisch-Pyramid, UA. Daniel L. Fapp.

(Color)
FANNY, Logan, Warner Bros. Jack Cardiff.
FLOWER DRUM SONG, Hunter, U-I. Russell Metty.
A MAJORITY OF ONE, Warner Bros. Harry Stradling, Sr.
ONE-EYED JACKS, Pennebaker, Paramount. Charles Lang, Jr.
★ WEST SIDE STORY, Mirisch-Seven Arts, UA. Daniel L. Fapp.

ART DIRECTION-SET DECORATION

(Black-and-White)
THE ABSENT MINDED PROFESSOR, Disney, Buena Vista. Carroll Clark; Emile Kuri and Hal Gausman.
THE CHILDREN'S HOUR, Mirisch-Worldwide, UA. Fernando Carrere; Edward G. Boyle.
★ THE HUSTLER, Rossen, 20th Century-Fox. Harry Horner; Gene Callahan.
JUDGMENT AT NUREMBERG, Kramer, UA. Rudolph Sternad; George Milo.
LA DOLCE VITA, Astor Pictures (Italian); Piero Gherardi.

(Color)
BREAKFAST AT TIFFANY'S, Jurow-Shepherd, Paramount. Hal Pereira and Roland Anderson; Sam Comer and Ray Moyer.
EL CID, Bronston, Allied Artists. Veniero Colasanti and John Moore.
FLOWER DRUM SONG, Hunter, U-I. Alexander Golitzen and Joseph Wright; Howard Bristol.
SUMMER AND SMOKE, Wallis, Paramount. Hal Pereira and Walter Tyler; Sam Comer and Arthur Krams.
★ WEST SIDE STORY, Mirisch-Seven Arts, UA. Boris Leven; Victor A. Gangelin.

COSTUME DESIGN

(Black-and-White)
THE CHILDREN'S HOUR, Mirisch-Worldwide, UA. Dorothy Jeakins.
CLAUDELLE INGLISH, Warner Bros. Howard Shoup.
JUDGMENT AT NUREMBERG, Kramer, UA. Jean Louis.
★ LA DOLCE VITA, Astor Pictures (Italian). Piero Gherardi.
YOJIMBO, Toho Company (Japanese). Yoshiro Muraki.

(Color)
BABES IN TOYLAND, Disney, Buena Vista. Bill Thomas.
BACK STREET, Hunter, U-I. Jean Louis.
FLOWER DRUM SONG, Hunter, U-I. Irene Sharaff.
POCKETFUL OF MIRACLES, Franton, UA. Edith Head and Walter Plunkett.
★ WEST SIDE STORY, Mirisch-Seven Arts, UA. Irene Sharaff.

SOUND

THE CHILDREN'S HOUR, Mirisch-Worldwide, UA. Samuel Goldwyn Studio Sound Dept.; Gordon E. Sawyer, sound director.
FLOWER DRUM SONG, Hunter, U-I. Revue Studio Sound Dept.; Waldon O. Watson, sound director.
THE GUNS OF NAVARONE, Foreman, Columbia. Shepperton Studio Sound Dept.; John Cox, sound director.
THE PARENT TRAP, Disney, Buena Vista. Walt Disney Studio Sound Dept.; Robert O. Cook, sound director.
★ WEST SIDE STORY, Mirisch-Seven Arts, UA. Todd-AO Sound Dept., Fred Hynes, sound director, and Samuel Goldwyn Studio Sound Dept.; Gordon E. Sawyer, sound director.

FILM EDITING

FANNY, Logan, Warner Bros. William H. Reynolds.
THE GUNS OF NAVARONE, Foreman, Columbia. Alan Osbiston.
JUDGMENT AT NUREMBERG, Kramer, UA. Frederic Knudtson.
THE PARENT TRAP, Disney, Buena Vista. Philip W. Anderson.
★ WEST SIDE STORY, Mirisch-Seven Arts, UA. Thomas Stanford.

SPECIAL EFFECTS

THE ABSENT MINDED PROFESSOR, Disney, Buena Vista. Robert A. Mattey and Eustace Lycett.
★ THE GUNS OF NAVARONE, Foreman, Columbia. Bill Warrington and Vivian C. Greenham.

MUSIC

(Song)
BACHELOR IN PARADISE (*Bachelor in Paradise*, Richmond, M-G-M); Music by Henry Mancini. Lyrics by Mack David.
LOVE THEME FROM EL CID (*El Cid*, Bronston, Allied Artists); Music by Miklos Rozsa. Lyrics by Paul Francis Webster.
★ MOON RIVER (*Breakfast at Tiffany's*, Jurow-Shepherd, Paramount); Music by Henry Mancini. Lyrics by Johnny Mercer.
POCKETFUL OF MIRACLES (*Pocketful of Miracles*, Franton, UA); Music by James Van Heusen. Lyrics by Sammy Cahn.
TOWN WITHOUT PITY (*Town Without Pity*, Mirisch-Gloria, UA); Music by Dimitri Tiomkin. Lyrics by Ned Washington.

(Scoring of a Dramatic or Comedy Picture)
★ BREAKFAST AT TIFFANY'S, Jurow-Shepherd, Paramount. Henry Mancini.
EL CID, Bronston, Allied Artists. Miklos Rozsa.
FANNY, Logan, Warner Bros. Morris Stoloff and Harry Sukman.
THE GUNS OF NAVARONE, Foreman, Columbia. Dimitri Tiomkin.
SUMMER AND SMOKE, Wallis, Paramount. Elmer Bernstein.

(Scoring of a Musical Picture)
BABES IN TOYLAND, Disney, Buena Vista. George Bruns.
FLOWER DRUM SONG, Hunter, U-I. Alfred Newman and Ken Darby.
KHOVANSHCHINA, Artkino (Russian). Dimitri Shostakovich.
PARIS BLUES, Pennebaker, UA. Duke Ellington.
★ WEST SIDE STORY, Mirisch-Seven Arts, UA. Saul Chaplin, Johnny Green, Sid Ramin and Irwin Kostal.

SHORT SUBJECTS

(Cartoons)
AQUAMANIA, Disney, Buena Vista. Walt Disney, producer.
BEEP PREPARED, Warner Bros. Chuck Jones, producer.
★ ERSATZ (The Substitute), Zagreb Film, Herts-Lion International Corp.
NELLY'S FOLLY, Warner Bros. Chuck Jones, producer.
PIED PIPER OF GUADALUPE, Warner Bros. Friz Freleng, producer.

(Live Action Subjects)
BALLON VOLE (Play Ball!), Ciné. Documents, Kingsley International.
THE FACE OF JESUS, Jennings-Stern, Inc. Dr. John D. Jennings, producer.
ROOFTOPS OF NEW YORK, McCarty-Rush-Gaffney. Columbia.
★ SEAWARDS THE GREAT SHIPS, Templar Film Studios, Schoenfeld Films.
VERY NICE, VERY NICE, National Film Board of Canada, Kingsley International.

DOCUMENTARY

(Short Subjects)
BREAKING THE LANGUAGE BARRIER, U.S. Air Force.
CRADLE OF GENIUS, Plough Prods., Lesser Films (Irish). Jim O'Connor and Tom Hayes, producers.
KAHL, Dido-Film-GmbH., AEG-Filmdienst (German).
L'UOMO IN GRIGIO (The Man In Gray), (Italian). Benedetto Benedetti, producer.
★ PROJECT HOPE, Klaeger Films. Frank P. Bibas, producer.

(Features)
LA GRANDE OLIMPIADE (Olympic Games 1960), Cineriz (Italian).
★ LE CIEL ET LA BOUE (Sky Above And Mud Beneath), Rank Films (French). Arthur Cohn and René Lafuite, producers.

FOREIGN LANGUAGE FILM

HARRY AND THE BUTLER, (Denmark).
IMMORTAL LOVE, (Japan).
THE IMPORTANT MAN, (Mexico).
PLACIDO, (Spain).
★ THROUGH A GLASS DARKLY, (Sweden).

HONORARY AND OTHER AWARDS

TO WILLIAM L. HENDRICKS for his outstanding patriotic service in the conception, writing and production of the Marine Corps film, *A Force in Readiness*, which has brought honor to the Academy and the motion picture industry. (statuette)
TO FRED L. METZLER for his dedication and outstanding service to the Academy of Motion Picture Arts and Sciences. (statuette)
TO JEROME ROBBINS for his brilliant achievements in the art of choreography on film. (statuette)

1961 IRVING G. THALBERG MEMORIAL AWARD

TO STANLEY KRAMER

1961 JEAN HERSHOLT HUMANITARIAN AWARD

TO GEORGE SEATON

SCIENTIFIC OR TECHNICAL

CLASS I (statuette)
None.

CLASS II (plaque)
SYLVANIA ELECTRIC PRODUCTS, INC., for the development of a hand held high-power photographic lighting unit known as the Sun Gun Professional.
JAMES DALE, S. WILSON, H.E. RICE, JOHN RUDE, LAURIE ATKIN, WADSWORTH E. POHL, H. PEASGOOD and TECHNICOLOR CORP. for a process of automatic selective printing.
20TH CENTURY-FOX RESEARCH DEPT., under the direction of E.I. SPONABLE and HERBERT E. BRAGG, and DELUXE LABORATORIES, INC., with the assistance of F.D. LESLIE, R.D. WHITMORE, A.A. ALDEN, ENDEL POOL and JAMES B. GORDON for a system of decompressing and re-composing CinemaScope pictures for conventional aspect ratios.

CLASS III (citation)
HURLETRON, INC., ELECTRIC EYE DIVISION;
WADSWORTH E. POHL and TECHNICOLOR CORP.

★ INDICATES WINNER

1962 The Thirty-Fifth Year

Frank Sinatra made his first appearance as an Academy Awards host on April 8, 1963—the night 1962 film achievements were honored —but he almost missed the show. Running late, he forgot to apply the proper sticker to his car and was refused admittance to the Santa Monica Civic Auditorium arrival area. He had to park his car himself, then rush on foot to the stage area. Bob Hope, usually in charge, had to sit this one out because of a product conflict between the sponsors of the Academy telecast and his own television specials.

The thirty-fifth Academy ceremony was telecast on ABC-TV, produced for the Academy for the fifth time by Arthur Freed, with Alfred Newman as musical director. Richard Dunlap produced and directed for the network.

Lawrence of Arabia, a prize example of the kind of international moviemaking becoming more prevalent in the industry, received a total of seven awards (including ones for Best Picture and David Lean as Best Director); Gregory Peck, on his fifth nomination as Best Actor, won for *To Kill a Mockingbird,* and told reporters, "I hate to give it (the statuette) back to the Academy, even if it's only to have my name engraved on it!" Anne Bancroft, appearing on stage in New York in *Mother Courage,* was named Best Actress in *The Miracle Worker;* her award was accepted in her absence by Joan Crawford.

Sixteen-year-old Patty Duke, Best Supporting Actress in *The Miracle Worker,* was the first under 18 performer to win a competitive Academy Award; for the preceding twenty-eight years, child actors had been honored by the Academy only in the Special Award division. One of her fellow nominees, Mary Badham of *To Kill a Mockingbird,* was even younger; she was nine at the time. Veteran character actor Ed Begley won as the year's Best Supporting Actor (for *Sweet Bird of Youth*) and France's *Sundays and Cybele* was chosen Best Foreign Language Film, the sixth French film similarly honored.

A slight pre-show controversy surrounded the planned entertainment portions of the 1962 telecast. Since Ethel Merman had been asked to sing a medley of Irving Berlin songs, and Eddie Fisher had also agreed to do a medley of eleven past Oscar-winning tunes, program planners announced the five Best Song nominees would not be performed during the program, an Oscar tradition. That decision struck a negative response from members in the Academy's Music Branch, so the songs were quickly reinstated. But with a slight alteration. This year, for the first time, they were not sung individually, but as a medley. Robert Goulet did the honors.

Best Actor: Gregory Peck as Atticus Finch (lower right, talking to James Anderson) in *To Kill a Mockingbird* (Universal-International; directed by Robert Mulligan). Atticus was the mainspring of Harper Lee's best-selling novel, a wise and gentle small town Alabama lawyer of 1932, rearing his motherless offspring and defending a Negro falsely accused of rape. Under the soft-spoken guidance of Atticus, his youngsters emerge from the world of childhood fantasy towards maturity, but in the courtroom, Southern prejudice defeats his case because the man he defends is colored. Gregory Peck's performance won him his first Academy Award after four previous nominations in 1945, 1946, 1947 and 1949; in 1967, he was voted the Jean Hersholt Humanitarian Award by the Academy's Board of Governors. He also served as Academy president for three terms, 1967-1970.

Best Picture: Lawrence of Arabia
(Columbia; produced by Sam Spiegel) and
Best Director: David Lean (left, with
Peter O'Toole) for *Lawrence of Arabia.* For
their first reteaming after their highly
successful *The Bridge on the River Kwai*
in 1957, Sam Spiegel and David Lean first
toyed with the idea of filming the life of
Mahatma Gandhi, then discarded it when
Spiegel was able to purchase the rights to
Thomas Edward Lawrence's *Seven Pillars of
Wisdom.* Marlon Brando was the first
choice to play Lawrence but he was filming
Mutiny on the Bounty and unable to accept,
so the role went to 28-year-old Peter
O'Toole, relatively unknown in film circles.
Location filming went on for many months
in raw temperatures, but the hardships
ultimately added to the authenticity and
grandeur of the finished film, a visually
stunning epic which concentrated on the
guerilla desert campaigns of Lawrence at
the time of World War I, leading Arab raids
against the Turks; at times, it also
pondered the man's mysterious nature and
his occasional streaks of sadism. *Lawrence*
co-starred Alec Guinness, Anthony Quinn,
Jack Hawkins, Jose Ferrer, Omar Sharif,
Claude Rains, Arthur Kennedy, Anthony
Quayle and won a total of seven Academy
Awards for its excellence.

Best Supporting Actor: Ed Begley as Boss Finley in *Sweet Bird of Youth* (M-G-M; directed by Richard Brooks). Tennessee Williams wrote it, Sidney Blackmer originated the character on Broadway, and Ed Begley played Boss Finley on film, a corrupt and powerful Florida political boss determined to keep his daughter (Shirley Knight) away from an aging beachboy-hustler (Paul Newman) who loves her. Geraldine Page co-starred as a has-been movie star on a lost weekend in the town Boss Finley controls.

Nominations 1962

PICTURE

* **LAWRENCE OF ARABIA**, Horizon-Spiegel-Lean, Columbia. Produced by Sam Spiegel.
THE LONGEST DAY, Zanuck, 20th Century-Fox. Produced by Darryl F. Zanuck.
THE MUSIC MAN, Warner Bros. Produced by Morton Da Costa.
MUTINY ON THE BOUNTY, Arcola, M-G-M. Produced by Aaron Rosenberg.
TO KILL A MOCKINGBIRD, Pakula-Mulligan-Brentwood, U-I. Produced by Alan J. Pakula.

ACTOR

BURT LANCASTER in *Bird Man of Alcatraz*, Hecht, UA.
JACK LEMMON in *Days of Wine and Roses*, Manulis-Jalem, Warner Bros.
MARCELLO MASTROIANNI in *Divorce—Italian Style*, Embassy (Italian).
PETER O'TOOLE in *Lawrence of Arabia*, Horizon-Spiegel-Lean, Columbia.
* **GREGORY PECK** in *To Kill a Mockingbird*, Pakula-Mulligan-Brentwood, U-I.

ACTRESS

* **ANNE BANCROFT** in *The Miracle Worker*, Playfilms, UA.
BETTE DAVIS in *What Ever Happened to Baby Jane?*, Seven Arts-Associates & Aldrich, Warner Bros.
KATHARINE HEPBURN in *Long Day's Journey Into Night*, Landau, Embassy.
GERALDINE PAGE in *Sweet Bird of Youth*, Roxbury, M-G-M.
LEE REMICK in *Days of Wine and Roses*, Manulis-Jalem, Warner Bros.

SUPPORTING ACTOR

* **ED BEGLEY** in *Sweet Bird of Youth*, Roxbury, M-G-M.
VICTOR BUONO in *What Ever Happened to Baby Jane?*, Seven Arts-Associates & Aldrich, Warner Bros.
TELLY SAVALAS in *Bird Man of Alcatraz*, Hecht, UA.
OMAR SHARIF in *Lawrence of Arabia*, Horizon-Spiegel-Lean, Columbia.
TERENCE STAMP IN *Billy Dugg*, Harvest, Allied Artists.

SUPPORTING ACTRESS

MARY BADHAM in *Too Kill a Mockingbird*, Pakula-Mulligan-Brentwood, U-I.
* **PATTY DUKE** in *The Miracle Worker*, Playfilms, UA.
SHIRLEY KNIGHT in *Sweet Bird of Youth*, Roxbury, M-G-M.

ANGELA LANSBURY in *The Manchurian Candidate*, M.C. Prod., UA.
THELMA RITTER in *Bird Man of Alcatraz*, Hecht, UA.

DIRECTION

PIETRO GERMI for *Divorce—Italian Style*, Embassy Pictures (Italian).
* **DAVID LEAN** for *Lawrence of Arabia*, Horizon, Columbia.
ROBERT MULLIGAN for *To Kill a Mockingbird*, Pakula-Mulligan, U-I.
ARTHUR PENN for *The Miracle Worker*, Playfilms, UA.
FRANK PERRY for *David and Lisa*, Heller-Perry, Continental.

WRITING

(Screenplay—based on material from another medium)
DAVID AND LISA, Heller-Perry, Continental. Eleanor Perry.
LAWRENCE OF ARABIA, Horizon, Columbia. Robert Bolt.
LOLITA, Seven Arts, M-G-M. Vladimir Nabokov.
THE MIRACLE WORKER, Playfilms, UA. William Gibson.
* **TO KILL A MOCKINGBIRD**, Pakula-Mulligan, U-I. Horton Foote.

(Story and Screenplay—written directly for the screen)
* **DIVORCE—ITALIAN STYLE**, Embassy Pictures (Italian). Ennio de Concini, Alfredo Giannetti and Pietro Germi.
FREUD, Huston, U-I. Charles Kaufman and Wolfgang Reinhardt.
LAST YEAR AT MARIENBAD, Astor Pictures (French). Alain Robbe-Grillet.
THAT TOUCH OF MINK, Granley-Arwin-Shapiro, U-I. Stanley Shapiro and Nate Monaster.
THROUGH A GLASS DARKLY, Janus Films (Swedish). Ingmar Bergman.

CINEMATOGRAPHY

(Black-and-White)
BIRD MAN OF ALCATRAZ, Hecht, UA. Burnett Guffey.
* **THE LONGEST DAY**, Zanuck, 20th Century-Fox. Jean Bourgoin and Walter Wottitz.
TO KILL A MOCKINGBIRD, Pakula-Mulligan, U-I. Russell Harlan.
TWO FOR THE SEESAW, Mirisch-Argyle-Talbot-Seven Arts, UA. Ted McCord.
WHAT EVER HAPPENED TO BABY JANE?, Seven Arts-Aldrich, Warner Bros. Ernest Haller.

(Color)
GYPSY, Warner Bros. Harry Stradling, Sr.
HATARI!, Hawks, Paramount. Russell Harlan.
* **LAWRENCE OF ARABIA**, Horizon, Columbia. Fred A. Young.
MUTINY ON THE BOUNTY, Arcola, M-G-M. Robert L. Surtees.
THE WONDERFUL WORLD OF THE BROTHERS GRIMM, M-G-M and Cinerama. Paul C. Vogel.

MUSIC

(Song)
* **DAYS OF WINE AND ROSES** (*Days of Wine and Roses*, Manulis-Jalen, Warner Bros.); Music by Henry Mancini. Lyrics by Johnny Mercer.
LOVE SONG FROM MUTINY ON THE BOUNTY (Follow Me) (*Mutiny on the Bounty*, Arcola, M-G-M); Music by Bronislau Kaper. Lyrics by Paul Francis Webster.
SONG FROM TWO FOR THE SEESAW (Second Chance) (*Two for the Seesaw*, Mirisch-Argyle-Talbot-Seven Arts, UA); Music by Andre Previn. Lyrics by Dory Langdon.
TENDER IS THE NIGHT (*Tender Is the Night*, 20th Century-Fox); Music by Sammy Fain. Lyrics by Paul Francis Webster.
WALK ON THE WILD SIDE (*Walk on the Wild Side*, Feldman-Famous Artists, Columbia); Music by Elmer Bernstein. Lyrics by Mack David.

(Music Score—substantially original)
(New classification)
FREUD, Huston, U-I. Jerry Goldsmith.
* **LAWRENCE OF ARABIA**, Horizon, Columbia. Maurice Jarre.
MUTINY ON THE BOUNTY, Arcola, M-G-M. Bronislau Kaper.
TARAS BULBA, Hecht, UA. Franz Waxman.
TO KILL A MOCKINGBIRD, Pakula-Mulligan, U-I. Elmer Bernstein.

(Scoring of Music—adaptation or treatment)
(New classification)

What Ever Happened to Baby Jane? (Warner Bros.; produced by Robert Aldrich) gave rousing screen roles to Joan Crawford and Bette Davis (below) and was voted the Academy Award for Norma Koch's Black-and-White Costume Designs. The actresses played former celebrities, living like recluses in a decaying Hollywood mansion; one is an apparent cripple, the other a grotesque misfit who can't forget she was once a child star in vaudeville. Robert Aldrich directed it.

Best Actress: Anne Bancroft as Anne Sullivan and **Best Supporting Actress: Patty Duke** as Helen Keller in *The Miracle Worker* (United Artists; directed by Arthur Penn). *The Miracle Worker* first appeared as a 1957 television play with Teresa Wright and Patty McCormack, then became a 1959 Broadway play with Anne Bancroft and Patty Duke and, finally, a 1962 motion picture, again with Bancroft and Duke (above). The story followed real-life Anne Sullivan, half-blind from a childhood illness, as she attempts to teach deaf-and-blind young Helen how to speak through the sense of touch, concurrently having to battle the girl's animal-like stubbornness. It became one of 1962's most-admired, and best-acted, dramas.

BILLY ROSE'S JUMBO, Euterpe-Arwin, M-G-M. George Stoll.
GIGOT, Seven Arts, 20th Century-Fox. Michel Magne.
GYPSY, Warner Bros. Frank Perkins.
★ THE MUSIC MAN, Warner Bros. Ray Heindorf.
THE WONDERFUL WORLD OF THE BROTHERS GRIMM, M-G-M and Cinerama. Leigh Harline.

ART DIRECTION-SET DECORATION

(Black-and-White)
DAYS OF WINE AND ROSES, Manulis-Jalem, Warner Bros. Joseph Wright; George James Hopkins.
THE LONGEST DAY, Zanuck, 20th Century-Fox. Ted Haworth, Leon Barsacq and Vincent Korda; Gabriel Bechir.
PERIOD OF ADJUSTMENT, Marten, M-G-M. George W. Davis and Edward Carfagno; Henry Grace and Dick Pefferle.
THE PIGEON THAT TOOK ROME, Llenroc, Paramount. Hal Pereira and Roland Anderson; Sam Comer and Frank R. McKelvy.
★ TO KILL A MOCKINGBIRD, Pakula-Mulligan, U-I. Alexander Golitzen and Henry Bumstead; Oliver Emert.

(Color)
★ LAWRENCE OF ARABIA, Horizon, Columbia. John Box and John Stoll; Dario Simoni.
THE MUSIC MAN, Warner Bros. Paul Groesse; George James Hopkins.
MUTINY ON THE BOUNTY, Arcola, M-G-M. George W. Davis and J. McMillan Johnson; Henry Grace and Hugh Hunt.
THAT TOUCH OF MINK, Granley-Arwin-Shapiro, U-I. Alexander Golitzen and Robert Clatworthy; George Milo.

THE WONDERFUL WORLD OF THE BROTHERS GRIMM, M-G-M and Cinerama. George W. Davis and Edward Carfagno; Henry Grace and Dick Pefferle.

COSTUME DESIGN

(Black-and-White)
DAYS OF WINE AND ROSES, Manulis-Jalem, Warner Bros. Don Feld.
THE MAN WHO SHOT LIBERTY VALANCE, Ford, Paramount. Edith Head.
THE MIRACLE WORKER, Playfilms, UA. Ruth Morley.
PHAEDRA, Dassin-Melinafilm, Lopert Pictures, Denny Vachlioti.
★ WHAT EVER HAPPENED TO BABY JANE?, Seven Arts-Aldrich, Warner Bros. Norma Koch.

(Color)
BON VOYAGE, Disney, Buena Vista. Bill Thomas.
GYPSY, Warner Bros. Orry-Kelly.
THE MUSIC MAN, Warner Bros. Dorothy Jeakins.
MY GEISHA, Sachiko, Paramount. Edith Head.
★ THE WONDERFUL WORLD OF THE BROTHERS GRIMM, M-G-M and Cinerama. Mary Wills.

SOUND

BON VOYAGE, Disney, Buena Vista. Walt Disney Studio Sound Dept.; Robert O. Cook, sound director.
★ LAWRENCE OF ARABIA, Horizon, Columbia. Shepperton Studio Sound Dept.; John Cox, sound director.
THE MUSIC MAN, Warner Bros. Warner Bros. Studio Sound Dept.; George R. Groves, sound director.
THAT TOUCH OF MINK, Granley-Arwin-Shapiro, U-I. Universal City Studio Sound Dept.; Waldon O. Watson, sound director.

WHAT EVER HAPPENED TO BABY JANE?, Seven Arts-Warner Bros. Glen Glenn Sound Dept.; Joseph Kelly, sound director.

FILM EDITING

★ LAWRENCE OF ARABIA, Horizon, Columbia. Anne Coates.
THE LONGEST DAY, Zanuck, 20th Century-Fox. Samuel E. Beetley.
THE MANCHURIAN CANDIDATE, Axelrod-Frankenheimer, UA. Ferris Webster.
THE MUSIC MAN, Warner Bros. William Ziegler.
MUTINY ON THE BOUNTY, Arcola, M-G-M. John McSweeney, Jr.

SPECIAL EFFECTS

★ THE LONGEST DAY, Zanuck, 20th Century-Fox. Robert MacDonald and Jacques Maumont.
MUTINY ON THE BOUNTY, Arcola, M-G-M. A. Arnold Gillespie and Milo Lory.

SHORT SUBJECTS

(Cartoons)
★ THE HOLE, Storyboard Inc., Brandon Films. John and Faith Hubley, producers.
ICARUS MONTGOLFIER WRIGHT, Format Films, UA. Jules Engel, producer.
NOW HEAR THIS, Warner Bros.
SELF DEFENSE—FOR COWARDS, Rembrandt Films, Film Representations. William L. Snyder, producer.
SYMPOSIUM ON POPULAR SONGS, Disney, Buena Vista. Walt Disney, producer.

(Live Action Subjects)
BIG CITY BLUES, Mayfair Pictures. Martina and Charles Huguenot van der Linden, producers.
THE CADILLAC, United Producers Releasing. Robert Clouse, producer.
THE CLIFF DWELLERS, (a.k.a. *One Plus One*), Group II Film Prods., Schoenfeld Films. Hayward Anderson, producer.
★ HEUREUX ANNIVERSAIRE (Happy Anniversary), Atlantic Pictures (French). Pierre Etaix and J.C. Carriere, producers.
PAN, Mayfair Pictures. Herman van der Horst, producer.

DOCUMENTARY

(Short Subjects)
★ DYLAN THOMAS, TWW Ltd., Janus Films (Welsh). Jack Howells, producer.

THE JOHN GLENN STORY, Department of the Navy, Warner Bros. William L. Hendricks, producer.
THE ROAD TO THE WALL, CBS Films, Department of Defense. Robert Saudek, producer.

(Features)
ALVORADA (Brazil's Changing Face), MW Filmproduktion (German). Hugo Niebeling, producer.
★ BLACK FOX, Image Prods., Heritage Films. Louis Clyde Stoumen, producer.

FOREIGN LANGUAGE FILM

ELECTRA, (Greece).
THE FOUR DAYS OF NAPLES, (Italy).
KEEPER OF PROMISES (The Given Word), (Brazil).
★ SUNDAYS AND CYBELE, (France).
TLAYUCAN, (Mexico).

HONORARY AND OTHER AWARDS

None given this year.

1962 IRVING G. THALBERG MEMORIAL AWARD

None given this year.

1962 JEAN HERSHOLT HUMANITARIAN AWARD

None given this year.

SCIENTIFIC OR TECHNICAL

CLASS I (statuette)
None.

CLASS II (plaque)
RALPH CHAPMAN for the design and development of an advanced motion picture camera crane.
ALBERT S. PRATT, JAMES L. WASSELL and HANS C. WOHLRAB of the Professional Division, Bell & Howell Co., for the design and development of a new and improved automatic motion picture additive color printer.
NORTH AMERICAN PHILIPS CO., INC., for the design and engineering of the Norelco Universal 70/35mm motion picture projector.
CHARLES E. SUTTER, WILLIAM BRYSON SMITH and LOUIS C. KENNELL of Paramount Pictures Corp. for the engineering and application to motion picture production of a new system of electric power distribution.

CLASS III (citation)
ELECTRO-VOICE, INC.;
LOUIS G. MacKENZIE.

★ INDICATES WINNER

1963 The Thirty-Sixth Year

This was a serious year, with political questions relating to Vietnam becoming more difficult, strong actions in the civil rights corner and the assassination of President John F. Kennedy. If laughter was ever needed this was the time and, almost on cue, came a ribald, scampish British laugh-inducer named *Tom Jones*. It won great favor with audiences and Academy voters, and was honored with four Oscars, including Best Picture and Best Director (Tony Richardson). It was only the second time in Academy annals a British-made film had won the Best Picture statuette, the first occasion being *Hamlet's* 1948 Oscar.

Cleopatra, probably the most publicized motion picture of the decade, also won four Academy Awards: Best Color Cinematography, Best Color Art Direction, Best Costume Design and Best Special Effects. Other multiple winners included *Hud* (three Awards, including Best Actress Patricia Neal and Best Supporting Actor Melvyn Douglas), *How the West Was Won* (three awards) and *Federico Fellini's 8½* from Italy with two awards, including Best Foreign Language Film. Sidney Poitier was named Best Actor for *Lilies of the Field* and became the first Black to win one of the Academy's two major acting awards. England's Margaret Rutherford was named Best Supporting Actress for *The V.I.P.s.*

Oscar night—April 13, 1964—showed the strong influence of English talents on the 1963 movie world: ten of the twenty acting nominees were either British-born or cited for their work in British films.

The Awards were presented at the Santa Monica Civic Auditorium, Jack Lemmon was the evening's M.C. and George Sidney produced the program for the Academy. Richard Dunlap again produced and directed for the ABC network.

Among the acting winners, only Poitier was present to receive his award. Annabella accepted for Patricia Neal, who was in England, Peter Ustinov accepted for Margaret Rutherford, also in England, and Brandon de Wilde did stand-in duty for Melvyn Douglas, who was working in Spain.

Sammy Davis, Jr. provided the biggest off-the-cuff laugh of the evening. When he was handed the incorrect envelope to announce the music awards, he quipped, "Wait until the NAACP hears about this . . ."

Best Actress: Patricia Neal as Alma (left) in *Hud* (Paramount; directed by Martin Ritt). "I thought that the days when I would be offered a part like Alma were over," said Patricia Neal. Alma was a brief role but a strong one: she's the wise but slatternly housekeeper for the Bannon household in modern Texas, which consists of an honest, cattleman father (Melvyn Douglas), his ruthless, virile son (Paul Newman) and a 17-year-old nephew (Brandon de Wilde) who's still in his formative and impressionable years. Alma cooks and cleans for the clan, mockingly aware of the son's corruption; after he attempts to rape her, she boards a bus and leaves town, well aware she's too fascinated by him to stay. Unlike most Oscar-winning roles, Alma had no high, dramatic soliloquies or moments and was played mostly in the background to the other characters, all the more credit to Patricia Neal's superb abilities as an actress to make it so memorable.

Best Actor: Sidney Poitier as Homer Smith (left, with Lilia Skala) in *Lilies of the Field* (United Artists; directed by Ralph Nelson). It was a little film and a labor of love, modestly budgeted at $450,000 and based on a 92-page novelette by W.E. Barrett. Sidney Poitier charmingly played a footloose handyman and ex-G.I., traveling the Arizona countryside in a station wagon, who stops to repair a farmhouse roof for five refugee German nuns; the nuns are convinced he is the answer to prayers for a helper, so they cajole him into helping them build a chapel on some desolate desert land bequeathed to them. *Lilies* helped established a precedent for Black actors in American films, spotlighting the Poitier character as an individual rather than as a colored man, and was free of racial preachments or violence. When Academy Awards were voted, Poitier was a popular choice for his performance as handyman Homer.

Best Picture: Tom Jones (United Artists; produced in England by Tony Richardson) and **Best Director: Tony Richardson** for *Tom Jones*. Boisterous and bawdy, it was derived from the Henry Fielding classic about a bastard baby boy, born in mysterious circumstances and raised as the son of an English squire, who is later banished from his home, pegged as a thief and almost hung on the gallows before he is left with his rightful inheritance. Albert Finney (right, with Susannah York) starred as the lusty Tom, and director Richardson infected the picture with a frenetic pace, wild fist fights, an eye-boggling fox hunt (with cross-cuts between a hand-held camera and helicopter views), even occasional asides by the actors to the camera. Audiences loved it; Academy voters did, too. Besides being a fine film, it was probably the least stuffy costume picture ever put on celluloid.

Best Supporting Actress: Margaret Rutherford as the Duchess of Brighton in *The V.I.P.s* (M-G-M; directed by Anthony Asquith). In the style of *Grand Hotel*, with an all-star cast of unrelated characters in a common environment, *The V.I.P.s* was written by Terence Rattigan and took place in London's bustling airport, involving travelers such as Elizabeth Taylor, Richard Burton, Louis Jourdan, Orson Welles and Maggie Smith. The tweedy Miss Rutherford was at her quivering best as a confused and eccentric dowager traveling tourist class to Florida, grounded at the terminal by fog. On hearing she'd won an Oscar, the 72-year-old actress told newsmen in England, "I'm absolutely thrilled. This may sound presumptuous at my age, but I like to feel that this will be the starting point of a new little phase for me in films."

Nominations 1963

PICTURE

AMERICA, AMERICA, Athena, Warner Bros. Produced by Elia Kazan.
CLEOPATRA, 20th Century-Fox. Produced by Walter Wanger.
HOW THE WEST WAS WON, M-G-M. Cinerama. Produced by Bernard Smith.
LILIES OF THE FIELD, Rainbow, UA. Produced by Ralph Nelson.
* TOM JONES, Woodfall, UA-Lopert (British). Produced by Tony Richardson.

ACTOR

ALBERT FINNEY in *Tom Jones*, Woodfall, UA-Lopert (British).
RICHARD HARRIS in *This Sporting Life*, Wintle-Parkyn, Reade-Sterling-Continental (British).
REX HARRISON in *Cleopatra*, 20th Century-Fox.
PAUL NEWMAN in *Hud*, Salem-Dover, Paramount.
* SIDNEY POITIER in *Lilies of the Field*, Rainbow, UA.

ACTRESS

LESLIE CARON in *The L-Shaped Room*, Romulus, Columbia (British).
SHIRLEY MacLAINE in *Irma La Douce*, Mirisch-Phalanx, UA.
* PATRICIA NEAL in *Hud*, Salem-Dover, Paramount.
RACHEL ROBERTS in *This Sporting Life*, Wintle-Parkyn, Reade-Sterling-Continental (British).
NATALIE WOOD in *Love With the Proper Stranger*, Boardwalk-Rona, Paramount.

SUPPORTING ACTOR

NICK ADAMS in *Twilight of Honor*, Perlberg-Seaton, M-G-M.
BOBBY DARIN in *Captain Newman, M.D.*, Brentwood-Reynard, Universal.
* MELVYN DOUGLAS in *Hud*, Salem-Dover, Parmount.
HUGH GRIFFITH in *Tom Jones*, Woodfall, UA-Lopert (British).
JOHN HUSTON in *The Cardinal*, Preminger, Columbia.

SUPPORTING ACTRESS

DIANE CILENTO in *Tom Jones*, Woodfall, UA-Lopert (British).
DAME EDITH EVANS in *Tom Jones*, Woodfall, UA-Lopert (British).
JOYCE REDMAN in *Tom Jones*, Woodfall, UA-Lopert (British).
* MARGARET RUTHERFORD in *The V.I.P.s*, M-G-M.
LILIA SKALA in *Lilies of the Field*, Rainbow, UA.

DIRECTION

FEDERICO FELLINI for *Federico Fellini's 8½*, Embassy Pictures (Italian).
ELIA KAZAN for *America America*, Kazan, Warner Bros.
OTTO PREMINGER for *The Cardinal*, Preminger, Columbia.
* TONY RICHARDSON for *Tom Jones*, Woodfall, UA-Lopert (British).
MARTIN RITT for *Hud*, Salem-Dover, Paramount.

WRITING

(Screenplay—based on material from another medium)
CAPTAIN NEWMAN, M.D., Brentwood-Reynard, Universal. Richard L. Breen, Phoebe and Henry Ephron.
HUD, Salem-Dover, Paramount. Irving Ravetch and Harriet Frank, Jr.
LILIES OF THE FIELD, Rainbow, UA. James Poe.
SUNDAYS AND CYBELE, Columbia (French). Serge Bourguignon and Antoine Tudal.
* TOM JONES, Woodfall, UA-Lopert (British). John Osborne.

(Story and Screenplay—written directly for the screen)
AMERICA AMERICA, Kazan, Warner Bros. Elia Kazan.
FEDERICO FELLINI'S 8½, Embassy Pictures (Italian). Federico Fellini, Ennio Flaiano, Tullio Pinelli and Brunello Rondi.
THE FOUR DAYS OF NAPLES, Titanus, M-G-M (Italian). Pasquale Festa Campanile, Massino Franciosa, Nanni Loy, Vasco Pratolini and Carlo Bernari.

* HOW THE WEST WAS WON, M-G-M and Cinerama. James R. Webb.
LOVE WITH THE PROPER STRANGER, Pakula-Mulligan, Paramount. Arnold Schulman.

CINEMATOGRAPHY

(Black-and-White)
THE BALCONY, Allen-Hodgdon, Reade-Sterling-Continental Dist. George Folsey.
THE CARETAKERS, Bartlett, UA. Lucien Ballard.
* HUD, Salem-Dover, Paramount. James Wong Howe.
LILIES OF THE FIELD, Rainbow, UA. Ernest Haller.
LOVE WITH THE PROPER STRANGER, Pakula-Mulligan, Paramount. Milton Krasner.

(Color)
THE CARDINAL, Preminger, Columbia. Leon Shamroy.
* CLEOPATRA, Wanger, 20th Century-Fox. Leon Shamroy.
HOW THE WEST WAS WON, M-G-M and Cinerama. William H. Daniels, Milton Krasner, Charles Lang, Jr. and Joseph LaShelle.
IRMA LA DOUCE, Mirisch-Alperson, UA. Joseph LaShelle.
IT'S A MAD, MAD, MAD, MAD WORLD, Kramer, UA. Ernest Laszlo.

ART DIRECTION-SET DECORATION

(Black-and-White)
* AMERICA AMERICA, Kazan, Warner Bros. Gene Callahan.
FEDERICO FELLINI'S 8½, Embassy Pictures (Italian). Piero Gherardi.
HUD, Salem-Dover, Paramount. Hal Pereira and Tambi Larsen; Sam Comer and Robert Benton.
LOVE WITH THE PROPER STRANGER, Pakula-Mulligan, Paramount. Hal Pereira and Roland Anderson; Sam Comer and Grace Gregory.

TWILIGHT OF HONOR, Perlberg-Seaton, M-G-M. George W. Davis and Paul Groesse; Henry Grace and Hugh Hunt.

(Color)
THE CARDINAL, Preminger, Columbia. Lyle Wheeler; Gene Callahan.
* CLEOPATRA, Wanger, 20th Century-Fox. John DeCuir, Jack Martin Smith, Hilyard Brown, Herman Blumenthal, Elven Webb, Maurice Pelling and Boris Juraga; Walter M. Scott, Paul S. Fox and Ray Moyer.
COME BLOW YOUR HORN, Essex-Tandem, Paramount. Hal Pereira and Roland Anderson; Sam Comer and James Payne.
HOW THE WEST WAS WON, M-G-M and Cinerama. George W. Davis, William Ferrari and Addison Hehr; Henry Grace, Don Greenwood, Jr. and Jack Mills.
TOM JONES, Woodfall, UA-Lopert (British). Ralph Brinton, Ted Marshall and Jocelyn Herbert; Josie MacAvin.

COSTUME DESIGN

(Black-and-White)
* FEDERICO FELLINI'S 8½, Embassy Pictures (Italian). Piero Gherardi.
LOVE WITH THE PROPER STRANGER, Pakula-Mulligan, Paramount. Edith Head.
THE STRIPPER, Wald, 20th Century-Fox. Travilla.
TOYS IN THE ATTIC, Mirisch-Claude, UA. Bill Thomas.
WIVES AND LOVERS, Wallis, Paramount. Edith Head.

(Color)
THE CARDINAL, Preminger, Columbia. Donald Brooks.
* CLEOPATRA, Wanger, 20th Century-Fox. Irene Sharaff, Vittorio Nino Novarese and Renie.
HOW THE WEST WAS WON, M-G-M and Cinerama. Walter Plunkett.
THE LEOPARD, Titanus, 20th Century-Fox. Piero Tosi.
A NEW KIND OF LOVE, Llenroc, Paramount. Edith Head.

Best Supporting Actor: Melvyn Douglas as Homer Bannon (below, with Paul Newman) in *Hud* (Paramount; directed by Martin Ritt). Melvyn Douglas first established himself in movies as a suave, aristocratic leading man to actresses like Greta Garbo, Marlene Dietrich, Katharine Hepburn and Merle Oberon, then he concentrated his talents on the legitimate theater in the 1950s. After an 11-year absence, he returned to movie making in 1962's *Billy Budd,* then the following year he made *Hud,* playing an aging cattle rancher with old-fashioned, idealistic principles, a man in sharp contrast to a greedy, insensitive son (played by Newman). *Hud* also won an Academy Award for James Wong Howe's magnificent Black-and-White Cinematography.

SOUND

BYE BYE BIRDIE, Kohlmar-Sidney, Columbia. Columbia Studio Sound Dept. Charles Rice, sound director.
CAPTAIN NEWMAN, M.D., Brentwood-Reynard, Universal, Universal City Studio Sound Dept.; Waldon O. Watson, sound director.
CLEOPATRA, Wanger, 20th Century-Fox. 20th Century-Fox Studio Sound Dept.; James P. Corcoran, sound director; and Todd A-O Sound Dept., Fred Hynes, sound director.
★ **HOW THE WEST WAS WON,** M-G-M and Cinerama. M-G-M Studio Sound Dept.; Franklin E. Milton, sound director.
IT'S A MAD, MAD, MAD, MAD WORLD, Kramer, UA. Samuel Goldwyn Studio Sound Dept.; Gordon E. Sawyer, sound director.

FILM EDITING

THE CARDINAL, Preminger, Columbia. Louis R. Loeffler.
CLEOPATRA, Wanger, 20th Century-Fox. Dorothy Spencer.
THE GREAT ESCAPE, Mirisch-Alpha, UA. Ferris Webster.
★ **HOW THE WEST WAS WON,** M-G-M and Cinerama. Harold F. Kress.
IT'S A MAD, MAD, MAD, MAD WORLD, Kramer, UA. Frederic Knudtson, Robert C. Jones and Gene Fowler, Jr.

SPECIAL VISUAL EFFECTS
(New classification)

THE BIRDS, Hitchcock, Universal, Ub Iwerks.
★ **CLEOPATRA,** Wanger, 20th Century-Fox. Emil Kosa, Jr.

SOUND EFFECTS
(New classification)

A GATHERING OF EAGLES, Universal. Robert L. Bratton.
★ **IT'S A MAD, MAD, MAD, MAD WORLD,** Kramer, UA. Walter G. Elliott.

MUSIC
(Song)

★ **CALL ME IRRESPONSIBLE** (*Papa's Delicate Condition,* Amro, Paramount); Music by James Van Heusen. Lyrics by Sammy Cahn.
CHARADE (*Charade,* Donen, Universal); Music by Henry Mancini. Lyrics by Johnny Mercer.
IT'S A MAD, MAD, MAD, MAD WORLD (*It's a Mad, Mad, Mad, Mad World,* Kramer, UA); Music by Ernest Gold. Lyrics by Mack David.
MORE (*Mondo Cane,* Cineriz Prods., Times Film); Music by Riz Ortolani and Nino Oliviero. Lyrics by Norman Newell.
SO LITTLE TIME (*55 Days at Peking,* Bronston, Allied Artists); Music by Dimitri Tiomkin. Lyrics by Paul Francis Webster.

(Music Score—substantially original)

CLEOPATRA, Wanger, 20th Century-Fox. Alex North.
55 DAYS AT PEKING, Bronston, Allied Artists. Dimitri Tiomkin.
HOW THE WEST WAS WON, M-G-M and Cinerama. Alfred Newman and Ken Darby.
IT'S A MAD, MAD, MAD, MAD WORLD, Kramer, UA. Ernest Gold.
★ **TOM JONES,** Woodfall, UA-Lopert (British). John Addison.

(Scoring of Music—adaptation or treatment)

BYE BYE BIRDIE, Kohlmar-Sidney, Columbia. John Green.
★ **IRMA LA DOUCE,** Mirisch-Alperson, UA. Andre Previn.
A NEW KIND OF LOVE, Llenroc, Paramount. Leith Stevens.
SUNDAYS AND CYBELE, Columbia (French) Maurice Jarre.
THE SWORD IN THE STONE, Disney, Buena Vista. George Bruns.

SHORT SUBJECTS
(Cartoons)

AUTOMANIA 2000, Pathe Contemporary Films. John Halas, producer.
★ **THE CRITIC,** Pintoff-Crossbow Prods., Columbia. Ernest Pintoff, producer.
THE GAME (Ingra), Rembrandt Films-Film Representations. Dusan Vukotic, producer.
MY FINANCIAL CAREER, National Film Board of Canada, Walter Reade-Sterling-Continental Distributing. Colin Low and Tom Daly, producers.
PIANISSIMO, Cinema 16. Carmen D'Avino, producer.

(Live Action Subjects)

THE CONCERT, King Corp., George K. Arthur-Go Pictures. Ezra Baker, producer.
HOME-MADE CAR, Schoenfeld Films. James Hill, producer.
★ **AN OCCURRENCE AT OWL CREEK BRIDGE,** Janus Films. Paul de Roubaix and Marcel Ichac, producers.
SIX-SIDED TRIANGLE, Lion International. Christopher Miles, producer.
THAT'S ME, Pathe Contemporary Films. Walker Stuart, producer.

DOCUMENTARY
(Short Subjects)

★ **CHAGALL,** Auerbach-Flag Films. Simon Schiffrin, producer.
THE FIVE CITIES OF JUNE, US Information Agency. George Stevens, Jr., producer.
THE SPIRIT OF AMERICA, Spotlite News. Algernon G. Walker, producer.
THIRTY MILLION LETTERS, British Transport Films. Edgar Anstey, producer.
TO LIVE AGAIN, Wilding Inc. Mel London, producer.

(Features)

LE MAILLON ET LA CHAINE (The Link And The Chain), Films Du Centaure-Filmartic (French). Paul de Roubaix, producer.
★ **ROBERT FROST: A LOVER'S QUARREL WITH THE WORLD,** WGBH Educational Foundation. Robert Hughes, producer.
THE YANKS ARE COMING, David L. Wolper Prods. Marshall Flaum, producer.

FOREIGN LANGUAGE FILM

★ **FEDERICO FELLINI'S 8½,** (Italy).
KNIFE IN THE WATER, (Poland).
LOS TARANTOS, (Spain).
THE RED LANTERNS, (Greece).
TWIN SISTERS OF KYOTO, (Japan).

HONORARY AND OTHER AWARDS

None given this year.

1963 IRVING G. THALBERG MEMORIAL AWARD

TO SAM SPIEGEL

1963 JEAN HERSHOLT HUMANITARIAN AWARD

None given this year.

SCIENTIFIC OR TECHNICAL

CLASS I (statuette)
None.

CLASS II (plaque)
None.

CLASS III (citation)
DOUGLAS G. SHEARER and **A. ARNOLD GILLESPIE** of M-G-M. Studios.

★ **INDICATES WINNER**

1964

The Thirty-Seventh Year

Two musical ladies—*Mary Poppins* and *My Fair Lady*—shared the Academy Awards spotlight on April 5, 1965, when awards for 1964 achievements were announced at the Santa Monica Civic Auditorium. *Poppins* was nominated for thirteen awards, *My Fair Lady* was nominated for twelve and they had something more in common: Julie Andrews, star of the *Poppins* movie, had earlier created the *My Fair Lady* Eliza Doolittle role on the stage. When the final tally was in, *My Fair Lady* received eight awards, including Best Picture, Best Actor (Rex Harrison) and Best Director (George Cukor), and *Mary Poppins* received five, including Julie Andrews as Best Actress. For director Cukor, it was his first Oscar in a distinguished thirty-five year career, during which he had directed five actors into Academy wins (James Stewart, Ingrid Bergman, Ronald Colman, Judy Holliday and Harrison) and some fourteen others to nominations.

Peter Ustinov received his second Academy Award as Best Supporting Actor, this one for *Topkapi,* and Lila Kedrova was chosen Best Supporting Actress for *Zorba the Greek.* Italy's *Yesterday, Today and Tomorrow* was named Best Foreign Language Film, and makeup expert William Tuttle was given an Honorary Award for his achievement on *7 Faces of Dr. Lao,* the first time the area of makeup had been singled out by the Academy's Board of Governors.

Joe Pasternak produced the presentation show for the Academy, telecast over ABC-TV, and Bob Hope was master of ceremonies. Among the presenters, Martha Raye and Jimmy Durante created an Oscar highlight when they got tongue-tied reading the names of a few foreign-born nominees. Two popular television doctors, Dr. Kildare (Richard Chamberlain) and Dr. Ben Casey (Vince Edwards), appeared together for the first time, Judy Garland sang a special medley of Cole Porter songs, and Peter Gennaro danced to Gershwin's "I Got Rhythm." It was also the last year home viewers would see an Academy Awards ceremony telecast only in black-and-white.

Best Actress: Julie Andrews as Mary Poppins (left) in *Mary Poppins* (Buena Vista; directed by Robert Stevenson). Julie Andrews had made a major success on stage in the original *My Fair Lady* opposite Rex Harrison. She was bypassed for the film version, but made her movie debut the same year for Walt Disney in his musical version of P.L. Travers' *Mary Poppins* books, as a 1910 English nanny who travels through the air via an open umbrella, and takes charge of two unruly children and an unsettled household, helped by liberal doses of magic. The movie won Miss Andrews the Academy Award, and received others for Song ("Chim Chim Cher-ee"), Original Music Score, Film Editing and Visual Effects, the latter a new Awards category classification.

Best Picture: My Fair Lady (Warner Bros.; produced by Jack L. Warner) and **Best Actor: Rex Harrison** as Professor Henry Higgins (left) in *My Fair Lady*. The story of a Cockney flower girl named Eliza Doolittle who blooms from a weed into an orchid under the tutelage of a crusty English professor, *My Fair Lady* was a musical version of George Bernard Shaw's *Pygmalion* and had become the longest-running musical in American theater history when Warner Bros. outbid all competitors for the screen rights in 1962. On screen, it became as much of a classic as it had been on stage, with Audrey Hepburn as the movie Eliza (with her singing dubbed by Marni Nixon) and Rex Harrison—full of rascally charm and likeable brashness—playing Higgins for the 1007th time since he'd created the singing 'enry 'iggins on stage. *My Fair Lady*, in all, won eight Academy Awards.

Best Director: George Cukor (right) for *My Fair Lady*. Not all of the great talents of the motion picture business become Academy Award winners, and many conspicuous contributors have been inexplicably overlooked for years. George Cukor was nominated four times (for 1932-33's *Little Women,* 1940's *The Philadelphia Story,* 1947's *A Double Life* and 1950's *Born Yesterday*) and had directed numerous performers toward Oscars and/or nominations, without receiving an Award himself. Then along came *My Fair Lady* and, at long last, Mr. Cukor got his due.

Becket (Paramount; produced by Hal Wallis) won an Academy Award for Edward Anhalt's screenplay, which was based on Jean Anouilh's powerful drama about King Henry II and Thomas Becket, former friends who battled when Becket became Archbishop of Canterbury. Nominated for 11 other awards, the eloquent film starred (right) Peter O'Toole and Richard Burton, and was directed by Peter Glenville.

Nominations 1964

PICTURE

BECKET, Wallis, Paramount. Produced by Hal Wallis.
DR. STRANGELOVE OR: HOW I LEARNED TO STOP WORRYING AND LOVE THE BOMB, Hawk Films, Columbia. Produced by Stanley Kramer.
MARY POPPINS, Disney, Buena Vista. Produced by Walt Disney and Bill Walsh.
* MY FAIR LADY, Warner Bros. Produced by Jack L. Warner.
ZORBA THE GREEK, Rochley, 20th Century-Fox/International Classics. Produced by Michael Cacoyannis.

ACTOR

RICHARD BURTON in Becket, Wallis, Paramount.
* REX HARRISON in My Fair Lady, Warner Bros.
PETER O'TOOLE in Becket, Wallis, Paramount.
ANTHONY QUINN in Zorba the Green, Rochley, 20th Century-Fox/International Classics.
PETER SELLERS in Dr. Strangelove or: How I Learned to Stop Worrying and Love the Bomb, Hawk Films, Columbia.

ACTRESS

* JULIE ANDREWS in Mary Poppins, Disney, Buena Vista.
ANNE BANCROFT in The Pumpkin Eater, Romulus, Royal Films International/Columbia (British).
SOPHIA LOREN in Marriage Italian Style, Champion-Concordia, Embassy (Italian).
DEBBIE REYNOLDS in The Unsinkable Molly Brown, Marten, M-G-M.
KIM STANLEY in Seance on a Wet Afternoon, Attenborough-Forbes Artixo (British).

SUPPORTING ACTOR

JOHN GIELGUD in Becket, Wallis, Paramount.
STANLEY HOLLOWAY in My Fair Lady, Warner Bros.
EDMOND O'BRIEN in Seven Days in May, Joel, Paramount.
LEE TRACY in The Best Man, Millar-Turman, UA.
* PETER USTINOV in Topkapi, Filmways, UA.

SUPPORTING ACTRESS

GLADYS COOPER in My Fair Lady, Warner Bros.
DAME EDITH EVANS in The Chalk Garden, Hunter, Universal.
GRAYSON HALL in The Night of the Iguana, Seven Arts, M-G-M.
* LILA KEDROVA in Zorba the Greek, Rochley, 20th Century-Fox/International Classics.
AGNES MOOREHEAD in Hush . . . Hush, Sweet Charlotte, Associates & Aldrich, 20th Century-Fox.

DIRECTION

MICHAEL CACOYANNIS for Zorba the Greek, Rochley, International Classics/20th Century-Fox.
* GEORGE CUKOR for My Fair Lady, Warner Bros.
PETER GLENVILLE for Becket, Wallis, Paramount.
STANLEY KUBRICK for Dr. Strangelove or: How I Learned to Stop Worrying and Love the Bomb, Kubrick, Columbia.
ROBERT STEVENSON for Mary Poppins, Disney, Buena Vista.

WRITING

(Screenplay—based on material from another medium)
* BECKET, Wallis, Paramount. Edward Anhalt.
DR. STRANGELOVE OR: HOW I LEARNED TO STOP WORRYING AND LOVE THE BOMB, Kubrick, Columbia. Stanley Kubrick, Peter George and Terry Southern.
MARY POPPINS, Disney, Buena Vista. Bill Walsh and Don DaGradi.
MY FAIR LADY, Warner Bros. Alan Jay Lerner.
ZORBA THE GREEK, Rochley, International Classics/20th Century-Fox. Michael Cacoyannis.

(Story and Screenplay—written directly for the screen)
* FATHER GOOSE, Granox, Universal. S.H. Barnett, Peter Stone and Frank Tarloff.
A HARD DAY'S NIGHT, Shenson-UA (British). Alun Owen.
ONE POTATO, TWO POTATO, Cinema V. Orville H. Hampton and Raphael Hayes.

THE ORGANIZER, Reade-Sterling-Continental (Italian). Age, Scarpelli and Mario Monicelli.
THAT MAN FROM RIO, Lopert (French). Jean-Paul Rappeneau, Ariane Mnouchkine, Daniel Boulanger and Philippe De Broca.

CINEMATOGRAPHY

(Black-and-White)
THE AMERICANIZATION OF EMILY, Ransohoff, M-G-M. Philip H. Lathrop.
FATE IS THE HUNTER, Arcola, 20th Century-Fox. Milton Krasner.
HUSH . . . HUSH, SWEET CHARLOTTE, Aldrich, 20th Century-Fox. Joseph Biroc.
THE NIGHT OF THE IGUANA, Seven Arts, M-G-M. Gabriel Figueroa.
* ZORBA THE GREEK, Rochley, International Classics/20th Century-Fox. Walter Lassally.

(Color)
BECKET, Wallis, Paramount. Geoffrey Unsworth.
CHEYENNE AUTUMN, Ford-Smith, Warner Bros. William H. Clothier.
MARY POPPINS, Disney, Buena Vista. Edward Colman.
* MY FAIR LADY, Warner Bros. Harry Stradling.
THE UNSINKABLE MOLLY BROWN, Marten, M-G-M. Daniel L. Fapp.

ART DIRECTION-SET DECORATION

(Black-and-White)
THE AMERICANIZATION OF EMILY, Ransohoff, M-G-M. George W. Davis, Hans Peters and Elliot Scott; Henry Grace and Robert R. Benton.
HUSH . . . HUSH, SWEET CHARLOTTE, Aldrich, 20th Century-Fox. William Glasgow; Raphael Bretton.
THE NIGHT OF THE IGUANA, Seven Arts, M-G-M. Stephen Grimes.
SEVEN DAYS IN MAY, Joel, Paramount. Cary Odell; Edward G. Boyle.
* ZORBA THE GREEK, Rochley, International Classics, 20th Century-Fox. Vassilis Fotopoulos.

(Color)
BECKET, Wallis, Paramount. John Bryan and Maurice Carter; Patrick McLoughlin and Robert Cartwright.
MARY POPPINS, Disney, Buena Vista. Carroll Clark and William H. Tuntke; Emile Kuri and Hal Gausman.

* MY FAIR LADY, Warner Bros. Gene Allen and Cecil Beaton; George James Hopkins.
THE UNSINKABLE MOLLY BROWN, Marten, M-G-M. George W. Davis and Preston Ames; Henry Grace and Hugh Hunt.
WHAT A WAY TO GO, Apjac-Orchard, 20th Century-Fox. Jack Martin Smith and Ted Haworth; Walter M. Scott and Stuart A. Reiss.

COSTUME DESIGN

(Black-and-White)
A HOUSE IS NOT A HOME, Greene-Rouse, Embassy Pictures. Edith Head.
HUSH . . . HUSH, SWEET CHARLOTTE, Aldrich, 20th Century-Fox. Norma Koch.
KISSES FOR MY PRESIDENT, Pearlayne, Warner Bros. Howard Shoup.
* THE NIGHT OF THE IGUANA, Seven Arts, M-G-M. Dorothy Jeakins.
THE VISIT, DeRode, 20th Century-Fox. Rene Hubert.

(Color)
BECKET, Wallis, Paramount. Margaret Furse.
MARY POPPINS, Disney, Buena Vista. Tony Walton.
* MY FAIR LADY, Warner Bros. Cecil Beaton.
THE UNSINKABLE MOLLY BROWN, Marten, M-G-M. Morton Haack.
WHAT A WAY TO GO, Apjac-Orchard, 20th Century-Fox. Edith Head and Moss Mabry.

SOUND

BECKET, Wallis, Paramount. Shepperton Studio Sound Dept.; John Cox, sound director.
FATHER GOOSE, Granox, Universal. Universal City Studio Sound Dept.; Waldon O. Watson, sound director.
MARY POPPINS, Disney, Buena Vista. Walt Disney Studio Sound Dept.; Robert O. Cook, sound director.
* MY FAIR LADY, Warner Bros. Warner Bros. Studio Sound Dept.; George R. Groves, sound director.
THE UNSINKABLE MOLLY BROWN, Marten, M-G-M. M-G-M Studio Sound Dept.; Franklin E. Milton, sound director.

Best Supporting Actress: Lila Kedrova as Madame Hortense (right, with Anthony Quinn) in *Zorba the Greek* (20th Century-Fox; directed by Michael Cacoyannis). Born in Leningrad and well known as a European stage actress, she played an eccentric, aging courtesan briefly involved with a lusty and vibrant Greek, played by Quinn. Simone Signoret had begun filming the role, then withdrew, and Miss Kedrova replaced her, and won the Academy Award.

Best Supporting Actor: Peter Ustinov as Arthur Simpson (below) in *Topkapi* (United Artists; directed by Jules Dassin). Ustinov won his second Oscar (the first one came in 1960) as a small-time con man and tourist-guide in a Greek seaport town, mixed up in an attempt to steal an emerald-studded dagger from a museum in Istanbul. Ustinov was again an Academy Award nominee in 1968, as co-author of the story and screenplay of *Hot Millions*.

FILM EDITING

BECKET, Wallis, Paramount. Anne Coates.
FATHER GOOSE, Granox, Universal. Ted J. Kent.
HUSH . . . HUSH, SWEET CHARLOTTE, Aldrich, 20th Century-Fox. Michael Luciano.
* MARY POPPINS, Disney, Buena Vista. Cotton Warburton.
MY FAIR LADY, Warner Bros. William Ziegler.

SPECIAL VISUAL EFFECTS

* MARY POPPINS, Disney, Buena Vista. Peter Ellenshaw, Hamilton Luske and Eustace Lycett.
7 FACES OF DR. LAO, Pal, M-G-M. Jim Danforth.

SOUND EFFECTS

* GOLDFINGER, Broccoli-Saltzman-Eon, UA (British). Norman Wanstall.
THE LIVELY SET, Universal. Robert L. Bratton.

MUSIC

(Song)
* CHIM CHIM CHER-EE (*Mary Poppins*, Disney, Buena Vista); Music and Lyrics by Richard M. Sherman and Robert B. Sherman.
DEAR HEART (*Dear Heart*, Warner Bros.); Music by Henry Mancini. Lyrics by Jay Livingston and Ray Evans.
HUSH . . . HUSH, SWEET CHARLOTTE (*Hush . . . Hush, Sweet Charlotte*, Aldrich, 20th Century-Fox); Music by Frank DeVol. Lyrics by Mack David.
MY KIND OF TOWN (*Robin and the 7 Hoods,* Warner Bros.); Music by James Van Heusen. Lyrics by Sammy Cahn.
WHERE LOVE HAS GONE (*Where Love Has Gone*, Embassy, Paramount); Music by James Van Heusen. Lyrics by Sammy Cahn.

(Music Score—substantially original)
BECKET, Wallis, Paramount. Laurence Rosenthal.
THE FALL OF THE ROMAN EMPIRE, Bronston, Paramount. Dimitri Tiomkin.
HUSH . . . HUSH, SWEET CHARLOTTE, Aldrich, 20th Century-Fox. Frank DeVol.
* MARY POPPINS, Disney, Buena Vista. Richard M. Sherman and Robert B. Sherman.
THE PINK PANTHER, Mirisch, UA. Henry Mancini.

(Scoring of Music—adaptation or treatment)
A HARD DAY'S NIGHT, Shenson, UA (British). George Martin.

MARY POPPINS, Disney, Buena Vista. Irwin Kostal.
* MY FAIR LADY, Warner Bros. Andre Previn.
ROBIN AND THE 7 HOODS, Warner Bros. Nelson Riddle.
THE UNSINKABLE MOLLY BROWN, Marten, M-G-M. Robert Armbruster, Leo Arnaud, Jack Elliott, Jack Hayes, Calvin Jackson and Leo Shuken.

SHORT SUBJECTS

(Cartoons)
CHRISTMAS CRACKER, National Film Board of Canada, Favorite Films of California.
HOW TO AVOID FRIENDSHIP, Rembrandt Films, Film Representations. William L. Snyder, producer.
NUDNIK #2, Rembrandt Films, Film Representations. William L. Snyder, producer.
* THE PINK PHINK, Mirisch-Geoffrey, UA. David H. DePatie and Fritz Freleng, producers.

(Live Action Subjects)
* CASALS CONDUCTS: 1964, Thalia Films, Beckman Film Corp. Edward Schreiber, producer.
HELP! MY SNOWMAN'S BURNING DOWN, Pathe Contemporary Films. Carson Davidson, producer.
THE LEGEND OF JIMMY BLUE EYES, Topaz Film Corp. Robert Clouse, producer.

DOCUMENTARY

(Short Subjects)
BREAKING THE HABIT, American Cancer Society, Modern Talking Picture Service. Henry Jacobs and John Korty, producers.
CHILDREN WITHOUT, National Education Association, Guggenheim Productions.
KENOJUAK, National Film Board of Canada.
* NINE FROM LITTLE ROCK, US Information Agency, Guggenheim Productions.
140 DAYS UNDER THE WORLD, New Zealand National Film Unit, Rank Films. Geoffrey Scott and Oxley Hughan, producers.

(Features)
THE FINEST HOURS, Le Vien Films, Columbia. Jack Le Vien, producer.
FOUR DAYS IN NOVEMBER, David L. Wolper Prods., UA. Mel Stuart, producer.
THE HUMAN DUTCH, Haanstra Filmproductie. Bert Haanstra, producer.
* JACQUES-YVES COUSTEAU'S WORLD WITHOUT SUN, Columbia. Jacques-Yves Cousteau, producer.

OVER THERE, 1914-18, Zodiac Prods., Pathe Contemporary Films. Jean Aurel, producer.

FOREIGN LANGUAGE FILM

RAVEN'S END, (Sweden).
SALLAH, (Israel).
THE UMBRELLAS OF CHERBOURG, (France).
WOMAN IN THE DUNES, (Japan).
* YESTERDAY, TODAY AND TOMORROW, (Italy).

HONORARY AND OTHER AWARDS

TO WILLIAM TUTTLE for his outstanding make-up achievement for *7 Faces of Dr. Lao.* (statuette)

1964 IRVING G. THALBERG MEMORIAL AWARD

None given this year.

1964 JEAN HERSHOLT HUMANITARIAN AWARD

None given this year.

SCIENTIFIC OR TECHNICAL

CLASS I (statuette)
PETRO VLAHOS, WADSWORTH E. POHL and UB IWERKS for the conception and perfection of techniques for Color Traveling Matte Composite Cinematography.

CLASS II (plaque)
SIDNEY P. SOLOW, EDWARD H. REICHARD, CARL W. HAUGE and JOB SANDERSON of Consolidated Film Industries for the design and development of a versatile Automatic 35mm Composite Color Printer.
PIERRE ANGENIEUX for the development of a ten-to-one Zoom Lens for cinematography.

CLASS III (citation)
MILTON FORMAN, RICHARD B. GLICKMAN and DANIEL J. PEARLMAN of ColorTran Industries;
STEWART FILMSCREEN CORPORATION;
ANTHONY PAGLIA and the 20TH CENTURY-FOX STUDIO MECHANICAL EFFECTS DEPT.;
EDWARD H. REICHARD (2 citations) and CARL W. HAUGE (2 citations) and LEONARD L. SOKOLOW of Consolidated Film Industries;
NELSON TYLER.

★ INDICATES WINNER

1965 The Thirty-Eighth Year

The first telecast of an Academy Awards ceremony in *color* took place April 18, 1966, when Awards for 1965 were announced on ABC-TV, produced and directed for the network by Richard Dunlap, and produced for the Academy by Joe Pasternak. To heighten the impact given Oscar by color hues, art directors Alexander Golitzen and William Morris designed an unusually spectacular setting as a backdrop which employed forty-two fountains spraying water. Bob Hope was again M.C., and as in the preceding year, a musical—*The Sound of Music*—was named Best Picture.

Both *The Sound of Music* and *Doctor Zhivago* were nominated for ten awards, and both won five of them, the two most honored films of the year. Lee Marvin in *Cat Ballou* was named Best Actor, Julie Christie in *Darling* was chosen Best Actress, and Martin Balsam in *A Thousand Clowns* was awarded the Best Supporting Actor Oscar. Shelley Winters was named Best Supporting Actress in *A Patch of Blue* and became the first actress to win two Oscars in that category. Robert Wise (for *The Sound of Music*) received the Best Director statuette, Czechoslovakia's *The Shop on Main Street* was chosen Best Foreign Language Film and Bob Hope was presented an Honorary Award in the form of a gold medal for his services to the Academy and the motion picture industry.

Nominated songs were sung by, among others, Liza Minnelli, Robert Goulet and Michel Legrand, and Cyd Charisse joined James Mitchell in a dance specialty to music by George Gershwin and Leonard Bernstein. An added highlight was the showing of film clips in which past Oscar winners discussed how it felt to win. It was a big and colorful evening for Oscar, but the biggest single star attraction of the night was someone not affiliated with the motion picture industry: Lynda Bird Johnson, daughter of the president of the United States was in Hollywood to attend her first Academy Awards presentation, escorted by actor George Hamilton.

Best Picture: The Sound of Music (20th Century-Fox; produced by Robert Wise) and **Best Director: Robert Wise** for *The Sound of Music*. It was a rare thing: a movie everyone agreed was an improvement over its stage original. By doing extensive location filming in Salzburg, Austria, Robert Wise and his troupe (including Julie Andrews, below, with kids) were able to open up the vistas that *The Sound of Music*'s real-life story required; audiences liked it as much as Oscar did, and it immediately became one of the movies' all-time best-loved entertainments. The story followed the adventures of Maria Trapp, first as a music-loving postulant in Austria's Nonnberg Abbey, then as a governess to seven children, later as the wife of widower Capt. von Trapp (Christopher Plummer), a strong-willed opposer to the Nazi annexation of Austria in 1938. Eleanor Parker, Richard Haydn, Peggy Wood and Anna Lee were also in the cast; the music—a major asset—was by Richard Rodgers and Oscar Hammerstein II.

Best Actor: Lee Marvin as Kid Shelleen and as Tin Strawn in *Cat Ballou* (Columbia; directed by Elliot Silverstein). A western spoof starring Jane Fonda and set in Wyoming, circa 1894, *Cat Ballou* was filmed in a fast 32 days, partially on location in Colorado, and became the year's most talked-about "sleeper." It also gave Lee Marvin a chance to have an actor's field day, playing two outrageous roles: one as a seedy, booze-soaked gunman who's been hired to battle a desperado even though he can barely stand; the other as the gunman's cool, evil brother who wears an artificial silver nose because "the real one was bit off in a fight." It was a daffy, beautifully conceived performance, in sharp contrast to Marvin's dramatic role in 1965's *Ship of Fools,* and Academy voters chose him as Best Actor of the year. Receiving his Award, he said: "I think half of this belongs to a horse somewhere out in the Valley."

Best Actress: Julie Christie as Diana Scott in *Darling* (Embassy; directed by John Schlesinger). Told in flashback, *Darling* opens as an English beauty named Diana—now the Princess della Romita—narrates her life story, in a somewhat misleading manner, to a woman's magazine; in reality, she bounces from one affair to another, progresses from a fun-loving model to an international swinger and ends up as the bored wife of an aging Italian prince, a victim of the very world she set out to conquer. Julie Christie, previously unknown to most film audiences, won the Academy Award as the restless Diana; during the year, she also sealed her reputation as a bright new actress in *Young Cassidy* and *Doctor Zhivago.* Dirk Bogarde and Laurence Harvey were her *Darling* co-stars.

Doctor Zhivago (M-G-M; produced by Carlo Ponti) tied with *The Sound of Music* as the most honored film of 1965, with five awards: for Screenplay (Robert Bolt), Color Cinematography (Freddie Young), Color Art Direction (John Box and Terry Marsh, with set decoration by Dario Simoni), Music Score (Maurice Jarre) and Color Costume Design (Phyllis Dalton). *Zhivago* was based on Boris Pasternak's novel of life in Russia in the early 1900s, and starred Julie Christie (above), Omar Sharif, Rod Steiger, Geraldine Chaplin, Alec Guinness, Ralph Richardson and Tom Courtenay.

Best Supporting Actor: Martin Balsam as Arnold Burns in *A Thousand Clowns* (United Artists; directed by Fred Coe). A veteran of television's early days of live drama, Balsam was honored by the Academy for his performance as the conventional brother of a decidedly off-beat New Yorker (Jason Robards), the latter a cheery rebel determined to remain a nonconformist. The screenplay was by Herb Gardner, based on his original Broadway comedy.

Nominations 1965

PICTURE

DARLING, Anglo-Amalgamated, Embassy (British). Produced by Joseph Janni.
DOCTOR ZHIVAGO, Sostar, S.A., M-G-M. Produced by Carlo Ponti.
SHIP OF FOOLS, Kramer, Columbia. Produced by Stanley Kramer.
* THE SOUND OF MUSIC, Argyle, 20th Century-Fox. Produced by Robert Wise.
A THOUSAND CLOWNS, Harrell, UA. Produced by Fred Coe.

ACTOR

RICHARD BURTON in *The Spy Who Came in from the Cold,* Salem, Paramount.
* LEE MARVIN in *Cat Ballou,* Hecht, Columbia.
LAURENCE OLIVIER in *Othello,* B.H.E., Warner Bros. (British).
ROD STEIGER in *The Pawnbroker,* Ely Landau, American International.
OSKAR WERNER in *Ship of Fools,* Kramer, Columbia.

ACTRESS

JULIE ANDREWS in *The Sound of Music,* Argyle, 20th Century-Fox.
* JULIE CHRISTIE in *Darling,* Anglo-Amalgamated, Embassy (British).
SAMANTHA EGGAR in *The Collector,* Columbia.
ELIZABETH HARTMAN in *A Patch of Blue,* Berman-Green, M-G-M.
SIMONE SIGNORET in *Ship of Fools,* Kramer, Columbia.

SUPPORTING ACTOR

* MARTIN BALSAM in *A Thousand Clowns,* Harrell, UA.
IAN BANNEN in *The Flight of the Phoenix,* Associates & Aldrich, 20th Century-Fox.
TOM COURTENAY in *Doctor Zhivago,* Sostar, S.A., M-G-M.
MICHAEL DUNN in *Ship of Fools,* Kramer, Columbia.
FRANK FINLAY in *Othello,* B.H.E., Warner Bros. (British).

SUPPORTING ACTRESS

RUTH GORDON in *Inside Daisy Clover,* Park Place, Warner Bros.
JOYCE REDMAN in *Othello,* B.H.E., Warner Bros. (British).
MAGGIE SMITH in *Othello,* B.H.E., Warner Bros. (British).
* SHELLEY WINTERS in *A Patch of Blue,* Berman-Green, M-G-M.
PEGGY WOOD in *The Sound of Music,* Argyle, 20th Century-Fox.

DIRECTION

DAVID LEAN for *Doctor Zhivago,* Ponti, M-G-M.
JOHN SCHLESINGER for *Darling,* Embassy (British).
HIROSHI TESHIGAHARA for *Woman in the Dunes,* Pathe Contemporary Films (Japanese).
* ROBERT WISE for *The Sound of Music,* 20th Century-Fox.
WILLIAM WYLER for *The Collector,* Columbia.

WRITING

(Screenplay—based on material from another medium)
CAT BALLOU, Hecht, Columbia. Walter Newman and Frank R. Pierson.
THE COLLECTOR, Columbia. Stanley Mann and John Kohn.
* DOCTOR ZHIVAGO, Ponti, M-G-M. Robert Bolt.
SHIP OF FOOLS, Kramer, Columbia. Abby Mann.
A THOUSAND CLOWNS, Harrell, UA. Herb Gardner.

(Story and Screenplay—written directly for the screen)
CASANOVA '70, Embassy (Italian). Age, Scarpelli, Mario Monicelli, Tonino Guerra, Giorgio Salvioni and Suso Cecchi D'Amico.
* DARLING, Embassy (British). Frederic Raphael.

THOSE MAGNIFICENT MEN IN THEIR FLYING MACHINES, 20th Century-Fox. Jack Davies and Ken Annakin.
THE TRAIN, Les Prods., UA. Franklin Coen and Frank Davis.
THE UMBRELLAS OF CHERBOURG, Landau Releasing (French). Jacques Demy.

CINEMATOGRAPHY

(Black-and-White)
IN HARM'S WAY, Preminger, Paramount. Loyal Griggs.
KING RAT, Coleytown, Columbia. Burnett Guffey.
MORITURI, Arcola-Colony, 20th Century-Fox. Conrad Hall.
A PATCH OF BLUE, Berman-Green, M-G-M. Robert Burks.
* SHIP OF FOOLS, Kramer, Columbia. Ernest Laszlo.

(Color)
THE AGONY AND THE ECSTASY, 20th Century-Fox. Leon Shamroy.
* DOCTOR ZHIVAGO, Ponti, M-G-M. Freddie Young.
THE GREAT RACE, Patricia-Jalem-Reynard, Warner Bros. Russell Harlan.
THE GREATEST STORY EVER TOLD, Stevens, UA. William C. Mellor and Loyal Griggs.
THE SOUND OF MUSIC, 20th Century-Fox. Ted McCord.

ART DIRECTION-SET DECORATION

(Black-and-White)
KING RAT, Coleytown, Columbia. Robert Emmet Smith; Frank Tuttle.
A PATCH OF BLUE, Berman-Green, M-G-M. George W. Davis and Urie McCleary; Henry Grace and Charles S. Thompson.
* SHIP OF FOOLS, Kramer, Columbia. Robert Clatworthy; Joseph Kish.
THE SLENDER THREAD, Paramount. Hal Pereira and Jack Poplin; Robert Benton and Joseph Kish.
THE SPY WHO CAME IN FROM THE COLD, Salem, Paramount. Hal Pereira, Tambi Larsen and Edward Marshall; Josie MacAvin.

(Color)
THE AGONY AND THE ECSTASY, 20th Century-Fox. John DeCuir and Jack Martin Smith; Dario Simoni.
* DOCTOR ZHIVAGO, Ponti, M-G-M. John Box and Terry Marsh; Dario Simoni.
THE GREATEST STORY EVER TOLD, Stevens, UA. Richard Day, William Creber and David Hall; Ray Moyer, Fred MacLean and Norman Rockett.
INSIDE DAISY CLOVER, Pakula-Mulligan, Warner Bros. Robert Clatworthy; George James Hopkins.
THE SOUND OF MUSIC, 20th Century-Fox. Boris Leven; Walter M. Scott and Ruby Levitt.

COSTUME DESIGN

(Black-and-White)
* DARLING, Embassy (British). Julie Harris.
MORITURI, Arcola-Colony, 20th Century-Fox. Moss Mabry.
A RAGE TO LIVE, Mirisch-Araho, UA. Howard Shoup.
SHIP OF FOOLS, Kramer, Columbia. Bill Thomas and Jean Louis.
THE SLENDER THREAD, Paramount. Edith Head.

(Color)
THE AGONY AND THE ECSTASY, 20th Century-Fox. Vittorio Nino Novarese.
* DOCTOR ZHIVAGO, Ponti, M-G-M. Phyllis Dalton.
THE GREATEST STORY EVER TOLD, Stevens, UA. Vittorio Nino Novarese and Marjorie Best.
INSIDE DAISY CLOVER, Pakula-Mulligan, Warner Bros. Edith Head and Bill Thomas.
THE SOUND OF MUSIC, 20th Century-Fox. Dorothy Jeakins.

Ship of Fools Columbia; produced by Stanley Kramer) received Oscars for Black-and-White Cinematography (by Ernest Laszlo) and for Black-and-White Art Direction (by Robert Clatworthy, with set decoration by Joseph Kish). It was based on the novel by Katherine Anne Porter, with screenplay by Abby Mann, and took place aboard a German passenger vessel in 1933, traveling from Mexico to the Rhineland. Among the passengers: Vivien Leigh as an aging divorcee and Lee Marvin as a lanky Texan (above), Simone Signoret, Oskar Werner, Jose Ferrer, Jose Greco and George Segal.

Best Supporting Actress: Shelley Winters as Rose-Ann D'Arcy (below, painting toenails) in *A Patch of Blue* (M-G-M; directed by Guy Green). Shelley Winters, a previous Supporting Actress winner in 1959 for *The Diary of Anne Frank,* won her second statuette as the amoral, savage mother of a blind girl (Elizabeth Hartman) who was befriended by a gentle Negro, played by Sidney Poitier. She also received two other Academy nominations during Oscar's first 50 years: in 1951 as Best Actress for *A Place in the Sun* and in 1972 for her supporting role in *The Poseidon Adventure.*

SOUND

THE AGONY AND THE ECSTASY, 20th Century-Fox. 20th Century-Fox Studio Sound Dept.; James P. Corcoran, sound director.
DOCTOR ZHIVAGO, M-G-M. M-G-M British Studio Sound Dept., A.W. Watkins, sound director; and M-G-M Studio Sound Dept., Franklin E. Milton, sound director.
THE GREAT RACE, Patricia-Jalem-Reynard, Warner Bros. Warner Bros. Studio Sound Dept.; George R. Groves, sound director.
SHENANDOAH, Universal. Universal City Sound Dept.; Waldon O. Watson, sound director.
* THE SOUND OF MUSIC, 20th Century-Fox. 20th Century-Fox Studio Sound Dept., James P. Corcoran, sound director; and Todd A-O Sound Dept., Fred Hynes, sound director.

FILM EDITING

CAT BALLOU, Hecht, Columbia. Charles Nelson.
DOCTOR ZHIVAGO, Ponti, M-G-M. Norman Savage.
THE FLIGHT OF THE PHOENIX, Aldrich, 20th Century-Fox. Michael Luciano.
THE GREAT RACE, Patricia-Jalem-Reynard, Warner Bros. Ralph E. Winters.
* THE SOUND OF MUSIC, 20th Century-Fox. William Reynolds.

SPECIAL VISUAL EFFECTS

THE GREATEST STORY EVER TOLD, Stevens, UA. J. McMillan Johnson.
* THUNDERBALL, Broccoli-Saltzman-McClory, UA (British). John Stears.

SOUND EFFECTS

* THE GREAT RACE, Patricia-Jalem-Reynard, Warner Bros. Tregoweth Brown.
VON RYAN'S EXPRESS, 20th Century-Fox. Walter A. Rossi.

MUSIC

(Song)
THE BALLAD OF CAT BALLOU (*Cat Ballou,* Hecht, Columbia); Music by Jerry Livingston. Lyrics by Mack David.
I WILL WAIT FOR YOU (*The Umbrellas of Cherbourg,* Landau Releasing; French); Music by Michel Legrand. Lyrics by Jacques Demy.
* THE SHADOW OF YOUR SMILE (*The Sandpiper,* Filmways-Venice, M-G-M); Music by Johnny Mandel. Lyrics by Paul Francis Webster.
THE SWEETHEART TREE (*The Great Race,* Patricia-Jalem-Reynard, Warner Bros.); Music by Henry Mancini. Lyrics by Johnny Mercer.
WHAT'S NEW PUSSYCAT? (*What's New Pussycat?,* Famous Artists-Famartists, UA); Music by Burt Bacharach. Lyrics by Hal David.

(Music Score—substantially original)
THE AGONY AND THE ECSTASY, 20th Century-Fox. Alex North.
* DOCTOR ZHIVAGO, Ponti, M-G-M. Maurice Jarre.
THE GREATEST STORY EVER TOLD, Stevens, UA. Alfred Newman.
A PATCH OF BLUE, Berman-Green Prod., M-G-M. Jerry Goldsmith.
THE UMBRELLAS OF CHERBOURG, Landau Releasing (French). Michel Legrand and Jacques Demy.

(Scoring of Music—adaptation or treatment)
CAT BALLOU, Hecht, Columbia. DeVol.
THE PLEASURE SEEKERS, 20th Century-Fox. Lionel Newman and Alexander Courage.
* THE SOUND OF MUSIC, 20th Century-Fox. Irwin Kostal.
A THOUSAND CLOWNS, Harrell, UA. Don Walker.
THE UMBRELLAS OF CHERBOURG, Landau Releasing (French). Michel Legrand.

SHORT SUBJECTS

(Cartoons)
CLAY OR THE ORIGIN OF SPECIES, Harvard University, Pathe Contemporary Films. Eliot Noyes, Jr., producer.
* THE DOT AND THE LINE, M-G-M. Chuck Jones and Les Goldman, producers.
THE THIEVING MAGPIE (La Gazza Ladra), Allied Artists. Emanuele Luzzati, producer.

(Live Action Subjects)
* THE CHICKEN (Le Poulet), Pathe Contemporary Films (French). Claude Berri, producer.
FORTRESS OF PEACE, Farner-Looser Films, Cinerama. Lothar Wolff, producer.
SKATERDATER, Byway Prods., UA. Marshal Backlar and Noel Black, producers.
SNOW, Manson Distributing. Edgar Anstey, producer.
TIME PIECE, Muppets, Inc., Pathe Contemporary Films. Jim Henson, producer.

DOCUMENTARY

(Short Subjects)
MURAL ON OUR STREET, Henry Street Settlement, Pathe Contemporary Films. Kirk Smallman, producer.
OUVERTURE, Mafilm Prods., Hungarofilm-Pathe Contemporary Films.
POINT OF VIEW, Vision Associates Prod., National Tuberculosis Assoc.
* TO BE ALIVE!, Johnson Wax. Francis Thompson, Inc., producer.
YEATS COUNTRY, Aengus Films for the Dept. of External Affairs of Ireland. Patrick Carey and Joe Mendoza, producers.

(Features)
THE BATTLE OF THE BULGE . . . THE BRAVE RIFLES, Mascott Prods. Laurence E. Mascott, producer.
* THE ELEANOR ROOSEVELT STORY, American International. Sidney Glazier, producer.
THE FORTH ROAD BRIDGE, Random Film Prods., Shell-Mex and B.P. Film Library. Peter Mills, producer.
LET MY PEOPLE GO, David L. Wolper Prods. Marshall Flaum, producer.
TO DIE IN MADRID, Altura Films International. Frederic Rossif, producer.

FOREIGN LANGUAGE FILM

BLOOD ON THE LAND, (Greece).
* DEAR JOHN, (Sweden).
KWAIDAN, (Japan).
MARRIAGE ITALIAN STYLE, (Italy).
THE SHOP ON MAIN STREET, (Czechoslovakia).

HONORARY AND OTHER AWARDS

TO BOB HOPE for unique and distinguished service to our industry and the Academy. (gold medal)

1965 IRVING G. THALBERG MEMORIAL AWARD

TO WILLIAM WYLER

1965 JEAN HERSHOLT HUMANITARIAN AWARD

TO EDMOND L. DePATIE

SCIENTIFIC OR TECHNICAL

CLASS I (statuette)
None.

CLASS II (plaque)
ARTHUR J. HATCH of the Strong Electric Corporation, subsidiary of General Precision Equipment Corporation, for the design and development of an Air Blown Carbon Arc Projection Lamp.
STEFAN KUDELSKI for the design and development of the Nagra portable ¼″ tape recording system for motion picture sound recording.

CLASS III (citation)
None.

* INDICATES WINNER

1966 The Thirty-Ninth Year

The telecast of the 1966 Academy Awards Presentations came hairline close to being canceled on April 10, 1967, because of a strike involving the American Federation of Television and Radio Artists (AFTRA), the theatrical union governing live telecasts. The blackout of TV coverage would have meant a loss to the Academy of approximately $700,000 in revenue paid by the ABC network for rights, but the Academy was prepared to proceed with the Awards at the Santa Monica Civic Auditorium without the usual coverage. Happily, it was settled in movie serial fashion, just three hours before the ceremony was scheduled to begin.

Most nominated picture of the year was *Who's Afraid of Virginia Woolf?* with a near-record thirteen (and topped only by the fourteen nominations accorded *All About Eve* in 1950); it won five of them, including Awards to Elizabeth Taylor as Best Actress, and to Sandy Dennis as Best Supporting Actress. *A Man for All Seasons* won six Awards, including Best Picture, Best Actor (Paul Scofield) and Best Director (Fred Zinnemann). Best Supporting Actor was Walter Matthau in *The Fortune Cookie;* Matthau received his Award with a broken arm and bruised face, the result of a cycling accident. It was the first time in twenty-five years two sisters (Vanessa Redgrave and Lynn Redgrave) were both nominees in the Best Actress category. It had happened before in 1941 when Olivia de Havilland and Joan Fontaine were dually nominated.

The program, again telecast in color and produced for the Academy by Joe Pasternak with Bob Hope as M.C., was notable for Mitzi Gaynor's high-energy rendition of ''Georgy Girl,'' one of the year's nominees as Best Song, plus an impromptu dance by Fred Astaire and Ginger Rogers when they momentarily reteamed to present one of the evening's Awards. Patricia Neal, making her first Hollywood appearance since a near-fatal illness of two years before, received a standing ovation from the audience. Among the guests in the audience was California's Governor Ronald Reagan, a long-time Academy member and supporter.

Best Actress: Elizabeth Taylor as Martha (left, with Richard Burton) in *Who's Afraid of Virginia Woolf?* (Warner Bros.; directed by Mike Nichols). It was unlikely casting, and a shocker: Hollywood's 33-year-old personification of beauty as Edward Albee's middle-aged, venomous Martha, a woman engaged in a drunken, all-night battle with her husband. But Elizabeth Taylor astounded the doubters and won the critics with a bravura performance, winning her second Academy Award, and enjoying her finest hour to date as a motion picture actress. The picture itself, outspoken and sprinkled with graphic profanities, won five Oscars and was a bold step forward for those who wanted the screen to occasionally tackle stronger themes than previously had been allowed.

Best Picture: A Man for All Seasons
(Columbia; produced by Fred Zinnemann),
Best Director: Fred Zinnemann and **Best
Actor: Paul Scofield** as Sir Thomas More
(above) in *A Man for All Seasons.* It began as
a 1960 play by Robert Bolt, first on the
London stage, then later in New York, and it
told of the last seven years in the life of Sir
Thomas More, the respected 16th-century
English chancellor beheaded by King
Henry VIII. Scofield, a superb artist generally
unknown to 1966 moviegoers, re-created his
original stage role, and permanently
preserved on celluloid one of the
decade. The film itself won a total of six
awards.

Best Supporting Actor: Walter Matthau as
Willie Gingrich (right, with Jack Lemmon)
in *The Fortune Cookie* (United Artists;
directed by Billy Wilder). Matthau was
a comical but shady lawyer, of the
ambulance-chasing variety, who maneuvers
his brother-in-law into an elaborate
accident-insurance swindle. He was
later nominated as Best Actor in 1971 for *Kotch*
and, four years later, for 1975's *The
Sunshine Boys.*

Nominations 1966

Best Supporting Actress: Sandy Dennis as Honey in *Who's Afraid of Virginia Woolf?* (Warner Bros.; directed by Mike Nichols). It was Sandy Dennis' second movie (the first: Elia Kazan's *Splendor in the Grass,* 1961), and she'd made a recent success on Broadway in *Any Wednesday;* as Honey, she was the nervous and naive wife of a schoolteacher (George Segal), beyond her depth when they become the guests—and targets—at the home of a destructive and battling older couple.

PICTURE

ALFIE, Sheldrake, Paramount (British). Produced by Lewis Gilbert.

✶ **A MAN FOR ALL SEASONS**, Highland Films, Columbia. Produced by Fred Zinnemann.

THE RUSSIANS ARE COMING THE RUSSIANS ARE COMING, Mirisch, UA. Produced by Norman Jewison.

THE SAND PEBBLES, Argyle-Solar, 20th Century-Fox. Produced by Robert Wise.

WHO'S AFRAID OF VIRGINIA WOOLF? Chenault, Warner Bros. Produced by Ernest Lehman.

ACTOR

ALAN ARKIN in *The Russians Are Coming The Russians Are Coming,* Mirisch, UA.

RICHARD BURTON in *Who's Afraid of Virginia Woolf?,* Chenault, Warner Bros.

MICHAEL CAINE in *Alfie,* Sheldrake, Paramount (British).

STEVE McQUEEN in *The Sand Pebbles,* Argyle-Solar, 20th Century-Fox.

✶ **PAUL SCOFIELD** in *A Man for All Seasons,* Highland Films, Columbia.

ACTRESS

ANOUK AIMEE in *A Man and a Woman,* Allied Artists (French).

IDA KAMINSKA in *The Shop in Main Street,* Prominent Films (Czechoslovakia).

LYNN REDGRAVE in *Georgy Girl,* Everglades, Columbia (British).

VANESSA REDGRAVE in *Morgan!,* Quintra Films, Cinema V (British).

✶ **ELIZABETH TAYLOR** in *Who's Afraid of Virginia Woolf?,* Chenault, Warner Bros.

SUPPORTING ACTOR

MAKO in *The Sand Pebbles,* Argyle-Solar, 20th Century-Fox.

JAMES MASON in *Georgy Girl,* Everglades, Columbia (British).

✶ **WALTER MATTHAU** in *The Fortune Cookie,* Phalanx-Jalem-Mirisch, UA.

GEORGE SEGAL in *Who's Afraid of Virginia Woolf?,* Chenault, Warner Bros.

ROBERT SHAW in *A Man for All Seasons,* Highland Films, Columbia.

SUPPORTING ACTRESS

✶ **SANDY DENNIS** in *Who's Afraid of Virginia Woolf?,* Chenault, Warner Bros.

WENDY HILLER in *A Man for All Seasons,* Highland Films, Columbia.

JOCELYNE LAGARDE in *Hawaii,* Mirisch, UA.

VIVIEN MERCHANT in *Alfie,* Sheldrake, Paramount (British).

GERALDINE PAGE in *You're a Big Boy Now,* Seven Arts.

DIRECTION

MICHELANGELO ANTONIONI for *Blow-Up,* Ponti, Premier Productions (British).

RICHARD BROOKS for *The Professionals,* Brooks, Columbia.

CLAUDE LELOUCH for *A Man and a Woman,* Les Films 13, Allied Artists (French).

MIKE NICHOLS for *Who's Afraid of Virginia Woolf?,* Chenault, Warner Bros.

✶ **FRED ZINNEMANN** for *A Man for All Seasons,* Highland Films, Columbia.

WRITING

(Screenplay—based on material from another medium)

ALFIE, Paramount (British), Bill Naughton.

✶ **A MAN FOR ALL SEASONS**, Highland Films, Columbia. Robert Bolt.

THE PROFESSIONALS, Brooks, Columbia. Richard Brooks.

THE RUSSIANS ARE COMING THE RUSSIANS ARE COMING, Mirisch, UA. William Rose.

WHO'S AFRAID OF VIRGINIA WOOLF? Chenault, Warner Bros. Ernest Lehman.

(Story and Screenplay—written directly for the screen)

BLOW-UP, Ponti Premier Productions (British), Michelangelo Antonioni, Tonino Guerra and Edward Bond.

THE FORTUNE COOKIE, Phalanx-Jalem-Mirisch, UA. Billy Wilder and I.A.L. Diamond.

KHARTOUM, Blaustein, UA. Robert Ardrey.

✶ **A MAN AND A WOMAN**, Les Films 13, Allied Artists (French). Claude Lelouch and Pierre Uytterhoeven.

THE NAKED PREY, Theodora, Paramount. Clint Johnston and Don Peters.

CINEMATOGRAPHY

(Black-and-White)

THE FORTUNE COOKIE, Phalanx-Jalem-Mirisch, UA. Joseph LaShelle.

GEORGY GIRL, Columbia (British). Ken Higgins.

IS PARIS BURNING?, Transcontinenta Films-Marianne, Paramount. Marcel Grignon.

SECONDS, Paramount. James Wong Howe.

✶ **WHO'S AFRAID OF VIRGINIA WOOLF?**, Chenault, Warner Bros. Haskell Wexler.

(Color)

FANTASTIC VOYAGE, 20th Century-Fox. Ernest Laszlo.

HAWAII, Mirisch, UA. Russell Harlan.

✶ **A MAN FOR ALL SEASONS**, Highland Films, Columbia. Ted Moore.

THE PROFESSIONALS, Brooks, Columbia. Conrad Hall.

THE SAND PEBBLES, Argyle-Solar, 20th Century-Fox. Joseph MacDonald.

ART DIRECTION-
SET DECORATION

(Black-and-White)

THE FORTUNE COOKIE, Phalanx-Jalem-Mirisch, UA. Robert Luthardt. Edward G. Boyle.

THE GOSPEL ACCORDING TO ST. MATTHEW, Walter Reade-Continental (Italian). Luigi Scaccianoce.

IS PARIS BURNING?, Transcontinental Films-Marianne, Paramount. Willy Holt; Marc Frederix and Pierre Guffroy.

MISTER BUDDWING, M-G-M. George W. Davis and Paul Groesse; Henry Grace and Hugh Hunt.

✶ **WHO'S AFRAID OF VIRGINIA WOOLF?**, Chenault, Warner Bros. Richard Sylbert; George James Hopkins.

(Color)

✶ **FANTASTIC VOYAGE**, 20th Century-Fox. Jack Martin Smith and Dale Hennesy; Walter M. Scott and Stuart A. Reiss.

GAMBIT, Universal. Alexander Golitzen and George C. Webb; John McCarthy and John Austin.

JULIET OF THE SPIRITS, Rizzoli Films (Italian). Piero Gherardi.

THE OSCAR, Greene-Rouse, Embassy. Hal Pereira and Arthur Lonergan; Robert Benton and James Payne.

THE SAND PEBBLES, Argyle-Solar, 20th Century-Fox. Boris Leven; Walter M. Scott, John Sturtevant and William Kiernan.

COSTUME DESIGN

(Black-and-White)

THE GOSPEL ACCORDING TO ST. MATTHEW, Walter Reade-Continental (Italian). Danilo Donati.

MANDRAGOLA, (Italian). Danilo Donati.

MISTER BUDDWING, DDD-Cherokee, M-G-M. Helen Rose.

MORGAN!, (British), Cinema V. Jocelyn Rickards.

✶ **WHO'S AFRAID OF VIRGINIA WOOLF?**, Chenault, Warner Bros. Irene Sharaff.

(Color)

GAMBIT, Universal. Jean Louis.

HAWAII, Mirisch, UA. Dorothy Jeakins.

JULIET OF THE SPIRITS, Rizzoli Films (Italian). Piero Gherardi.

✶ **A MAN FOR ALL SEASONS**, Highland Films, Columbia. Elizabeth Haffenden and Joan Bridge.

THE OSCAR, Greene-Rouse, Embassy. Edith Head.

Fantastic Voyage (20th Century-Fox; produced by Saul David) was a superb example of Hollywood's ability to conjure up wild visual magic; the Academy honored it in the categories of Art Direction and Special Visual Effects. Directed by Richard Fleischer and starring Stephen Boyd, Raquel Welch, Edmond O'Brien and Donald Pleasence, it had a unique premise, even for imaginative science-fiction films: a group of scientists, shrunken to minute proportions, are injected into the bloodstream of an injured man, and take an eye-boggling trip through his body.

SOUND

GAMBIT, Universal. Universal City Studio Sound Dept.; Waldon O. Watson, sound director.

★ GRAND PRIX, Lewis-Frankenheimer-Cherokee, M-G-M. M-G-M Studio Sound Dept.; Franklin E. Milton, sound director.

HAWAII, Mirisch, UA. Samuel Goldwyn Studio Sound Dept.; Gordon E. Sawyer, sound director.

THE SAND PEBBLES, Argyle-Solar, 20th Century-Fox. 20th Century-Fox Studio Sound Dept.; James P. Corcoran, sound director.

WHO'S AFRAID OF VIRGINIA WOOLF?, Chenault, Warner Bros. Warner Bros. Studio Sound Dept.; George R. Groves, sound director.

FILM EDITING

FANTASTIC VOYAGE, 20th Century-Fox. William B. Murphy.

★ GRAND PRIX, Lewis-Frankenheimer-Cherokee, M-G-M. Fredric Steinkamp, Henry Berman, Stewart Linder and Frank Santillo.

THE RUSSIANS ARE COMING THE RUSSIANS ARE COMING, Mirisch, UA. Hal Ashby and J. Terry Williams.

THE SAND PEBBLES, Argyle-Solar, 20th Century-Fox. William Reynolds.

WHO'S AFRAID OF VIRGINIA WOOLF?, Chenault, Warner Bros. Sam O'Steen.

SPECIAL VISUAL EFFECTS

★ FANTASTIC VOYAGE, 20th Century-Fox. Art Cruickshank.

HAWAII, Mirisch, UA. Linwood G. Dunn.

SOUND EFFECTS

FANTASTIC VOYAGE, 20th Century-Fox. Walter Rossi.

★ GRAND PRIX, Lewis-Frankenheimer-Cherokee, M-G-M. Gordon Daniel.

MUSIC

(Song)

ALFIE (Alfie, Paramount; British); Music by Burt Bacharach. Lyrics by Hal David.

★ BORN FREE (Born Free, Open Road-Atlas Films, Columbia; British); Music by John Barry. Lyrics by Don Black.

GEORGY GIRL (Georgy Girl, Columbia; British); Music by Tom Springfield. Lyrics by Jim Dale.

MY WISHING DOLL (Hawaii, Mirisch, UA); Music by Elmer Bernstein. Lyrics by Mack David.

A TIME FOR LOVE (An American Dream, Warner Bros.); Music by Johnny Mandel. Lyrics by Paul Francis Webster.

(Original Music Score)

THE BIBLE, DeLaurentiis-Seven Arts, 20th Century-Fox. Toshiro Mayuzumi.

★ BORN FREE, Open Road-Atlas Films, Columbia (British). John Barry.

HAWAII, Mirisch, UA. Elmer Bernstein.

THE SAND PEBBLES, Argyle-Solar, 20th Century-Fox. Jerry Goldsmith.

WHO'S AFRAID OF VIRGINIA WOOLF?, Chenault, Warner Bros. Alex North.

(Scoring of Music—adaptation or treatment)

★ A FUNNY THING HAPPENED ON THE WAY TO THE FORUM, Frank, UA. Ken Thorne.

THE GOSPEL ACCORDING TO ST. MATTHEW, Walter Reade-Continental (Italian). Luis Enrique Bacalov.

RETURN OF THE SEVEN, Mirisch, UA. Elmer Bernstein.

THE SINGING NUN, M-G-M. Harry Sukman.

STOP THE WORLD—I WANT TO GET OFF, Warner Bros. Al Ham.

SHORT SUBJECTS

(Cartoons)

THE DRAG, National Film Board of Canada, Favorite Films. Wolf Koenig and Robert Verrall, producers.

★ HERB ALPERT AND THE TIJUANA BRASS DOUBLE FEATURE, Paramount. John and Faith Hubley, producers.

THE PINK BLUEPRINT, Mirisch-Geoffrey-DePatie-Freleng, UA. David H. DePatie and Friz Freleng, producers.

(Live Action Subjects)

TURKEY THE BRIDGE, Samaritan Prods., Schoenfeld Films. Derek Williams, producer.

★ WILD WINGS, British Transport Films, Manson Distributing. Edgar Anstey, producer.

THE WINNING STRAIN, Winik Films, Paramount. Leslie Winik, producer.

DOCUMENTARY

(Short Subjects)

ADOLESCENCE, M.K. Prods. Marin Karmitz and Vladimir Forgency, producers.

COWBOY, U.S. Information Agency. Michael Ahnemann and Gary Schlosser, producers.

THE ODDS AGAINST, Vision Associates Prod. for The American Foundation Institute of Corrections. Lee R. Bobker and Helen Kristt Radin, producers.

SAINT MATTHEW PASSION, Mafilm Studio, Hungarofilm.

★ A YEAR TOWARD TOMORROW, Sun Dial Films for Office of Economic Opportunity. Edmond A. Levy, producer.

(Features)

THE FACE OF GENIUS, WBZ-TV, Group W, Boston. Alfred R. Kelman, producer.

HELICOPTER CANADA, Centennial Commission, National Film Board of Canada. Peter Jones and Tom Daly, producers.

LE VOLCAN INTERDIT (The Forbidden Volcano). Cine Documents Tazieff, Athos Films. Haroun Tazieff, producer.

THE REALLY BIG FAMILY, David L. Wolper Prod. Alex Grasshoff, producer.

★ THE WAR GAME, BBC Prod. for the British Film Institute, Pathe Contemporary Films. Peter Watkins, producer.

FOREIGN LANGUAGE FILM

THE BATTLE OF ALGIERS, (Italy).

LOVES OF A BLONDE, (Czechoslovakia).

★ A MAN AND A WOMAN, (France).

PHARAOH, (Poland).

THREE, (Yugoslavia).

HONORARY AND OTHER AWARDS

TO Y. FRANK FREEMAN for unusual and outstanding service to the Academy during this thirty years in Hollywood. (statuette)

TO YAKIMA CANUTT for achievements as a stunt man and for developing safety devices to protect stunt men everywhere. (statuette)

1966 IRVING G. THALBERG MEMORIAL AWARD

TO ROBERT WISE

1966 JEAN HERSHOLT HUMANITARIAN AWARD

TO GEORGE BAGNALL

SCIENTIFIC OR TECHNICAL

CLASS I (statuette)

None.

CLASS II (plaque)

MITCHELL CAMERA CORPORATION for the design and development of the Mitchell Mark II 35mm Portable Motion Picture Reflex Camera.

ARNOLD & RICHTER KG for the design and development of the Arriflex 35mm Portable Motion Picture Reflex Camera.

CLASS III (citation)

PANAVISION INCORPORATED; CARROLL KNUDSON; RUBY RAKSIN.

★ INDICATES WINNER

1967

The Fortieth Year

"I am enormously touched," Katharine Hepburn told a reporter in Nice when informed she had won the 1967 Academy Award as Best Actress for *Guess Who's Coming to Dinner.* "They don't usually give these things to the old girls, you know." Miss Hepburn later cabled an official reply to the Academy, saying, "It was delightful, a total surprise. I feel I have received a big, affectionate hug from my fellow workers." The awards were presented April 10, 1968, at the Santa Monica Civic Auditorium, postponed two days because of the assassination of Civil Rights leader Dr. Martin Luther King, Jr.

In the Heat of the Night received the most awards of the evening, a total of five including Best Picture and Best Actor (Rod Steiger); it was the first film in the detective genre so honored by Academy voters through the years. Mike Nichols was named Best Director for *The Graduate,* George Kennedy was chosen Best Supporting Actor in *Cool Hand Luke* and Estelle Parsons was Best Supporting Actress for *Bonnie and Clyde.* Next to *In the Heat of the Night,* the most honored film of the year was *Camelot* with three awards.

For the fourteenth year, Bob Hope handled M.C. duties and it was Oscar's eighth visit to the Santa Monica Civic Auditorium. Arthur Freed produced for the Academy, and Richard Dunlap produced and directed for the ABC network. Due to an all-out push by the Academy's president, Gregory Peck, eighteen of the twenty acting nominees were present at the ceremony; only Miss Hepburn, filming *The Madwoman of Chaillot* in France, and the late Spencer Tracy, nominated posthumously, were missing. Alfred Hitchcock received the Irving G. Thalberg Memorial Award, Peck was presented the Jean Hersholt Humanitarian Award and the Board of Governors voted an Honorary Oscar to Arthur Freed.

Color, now an integral part of Academy Awards telecasts, had also begun to dominate the motion picture screen so completely, with black-and-white films so rare, it was decided to restructure the Art Direction, Cinematography and Costume Design categories to one award per division rather than continue separate awards for black-and-white and color achievements.

Best Picture: In the Heat of the Night (United Artists; produced by Walter Mirisch) and **Best Actor: Rod Steiger** as Bill Gillespie in *In the Heat of the Night.* It was the first detective story to win Oscar's Best Picture honors, and centered on a fictional Negro detective named Virgil Tibbs from Philadelphia (played by Sidney Poitier) who is called into a sleepy little Mississippi town to solve a murder (right), much to the irritation of the local police chief, who's slow-moving, bigoted and white. Directed by Norman Jewison, Rod Steiger (above) won the Academy Award as the drawling sheriff, and the success of the film inspired two later sequels, *They Call Me Mister Tibbs!* (1970) and *The Organization* (1971). John Ball authored the original novel, and *In the Heat of the Night* won additional Awards for Screenplay, Sound and Film Editing.

Best Actress: Katharine Hepburn as Christina Drayton (left, with Spencer Tracy) in *Guess Who's Coming to Dinner* (Columbia; directed by Stanley Kramer). Katharine Hepburn had been totally absent from the screen for five years when she made *Guess Who's Coming to Dinner,* playing a socially prominent, liberal-thinking parent whose daughter suddenly informs the family she plans to marry a distinguished Negro scientist. It was one of the less demanding roles of her career, but she was enormously fond of it; it also marked the first time in her enduring career Katharine Hepburn had ever played a happily married wife and mother. It was her ninth and last film opposite Spencer Tracy, and—35 years after her first Oscar victory— she was again voted the year's Best Actress.

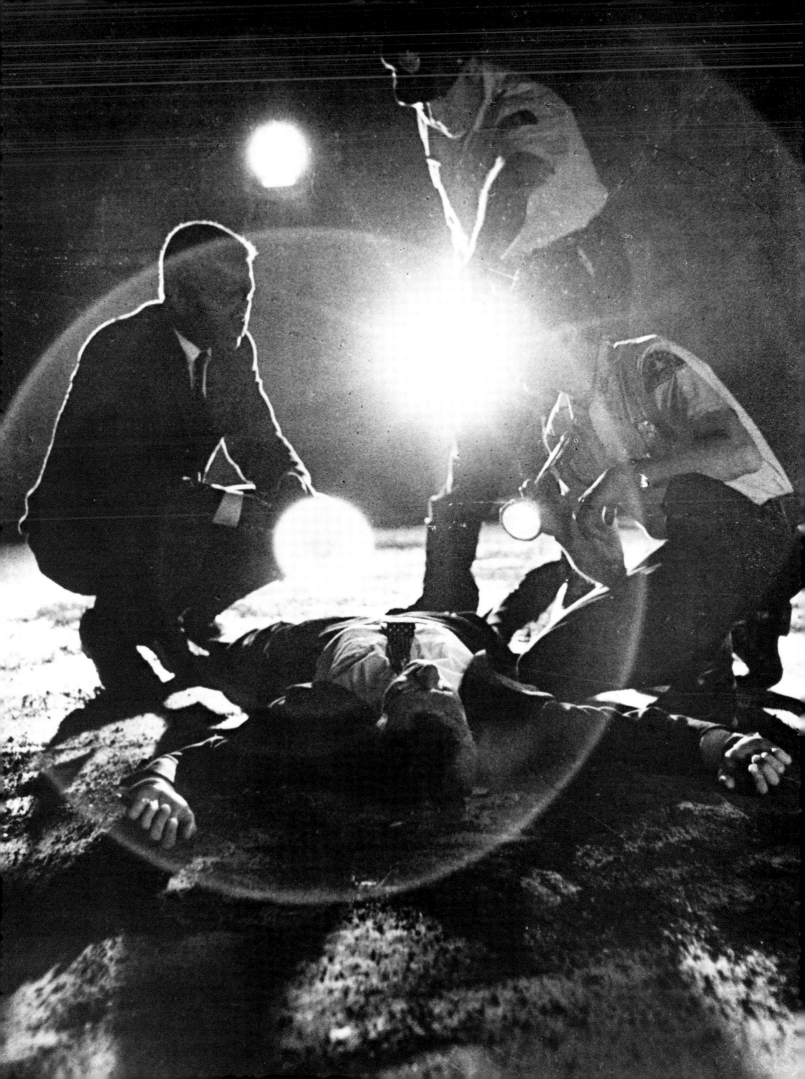

Nominations 1967

PICTURE

BONNIE AND CLYDE, Tatira-Hiller, Warner Bros.-Seven Arts. Produced by Warren Beatty.
DOCTOR DOLITTLE, Apjac, 20th Century-Fox. Produced by Arthur P. Jacobs.
THE GRADUATE, Nichols-Turman, Embassy. Produced by Lawrence Turman.
GUESS WHO'S COMING TO DINNER, Kramer, Columbia. Produced by Stanley Kramer.
★ **IN THE HEAT OF THE NIGHT**, Mirisch, UA. Produced by Walter Mirisch.

ACTOR

WARREN BEATTY in *Bonnie and Clyde*, Tatira-Hiller, Warner Bros.-Seven Arts.
DUSTIN HOFFMAN in *The Graduate*, Nichols-Turman, Embassy.
PAUL NEWMAN in *Cool Hand Luke*, Jalem, Warner Bros.-Seven Arts.
★ **ROD STEIGER** in *In the Heat of the Night*, Mirisch, UA.
SPENCER TRACY in *Guess Who's Coming to Dinner*, Kramer Columbia.

ACTRESS

ANNE BANCROFT in *The Graduate*, Nichols-Turman, Embassy.
FAYE DUNAWAY in *Bonnie and Clyde*, Tatira-Hiller, Warner Bros.-Seven Arts.
DAME EDITH EVANS in *The Whisperers*, Seven Pines, UA/Lopert (British).
AUDREY HEPBURN in *Wait Until Dark*, Warner Bros.-Seven Arts.
★ **KATHARINE HEPBURN** in *Guess Who's Coming to Dinner*, Kramer, Columbia.

SUPPORTING ACTOR

JOHN CASSAVETES in *The Dirty Dozen*, Aldrich, M-G-M.
GENE HACKMAN in *Bonnie and Clyde*, Tatira-Hiller, Warner Bros.-Seven Arts.
CECIL KELLAWAY in *Guess Who's Coming to Dinner*, Kramer, Columbia.
★ **GEORGE KENNEDY** in *Cool Hand Luke*, Jalem, Warner Bros.-Seven Arts.
MICHAEL J. POLLARD in *Bonnie and Clyde*, Tatira-Hiller, Warner Bros.-Seven Arts.

SUPPORTING ACTRESS

CAROL CHANNING in *Thoroughly Modern Millie*, Hunter, Universal.
MILDRED NATWICK in *Barefoot in the Park*, Wallis, Paramount.
★ **ESTELLE PARSONS** in *Bonnie and Clyde*, Tatira-Hiller, Warner Bros.-Seven Arts.
BEAH RICHARDS in *Guess Who's Coming to Dinner*, Kramer, Columbia.
KATHARINE ROSS in *The Graduate*, Nichols-Turman, Embassy.

DIRECTION

RICHARD BROOKS for *In Cold Blood*, Brooks, Columbia.
NORMAN JEWISON for *In the Heat of the Night*, Mirisch, UA.
STANELY KRAMER for *Guess Who's Coming to Dinner*, Kramer, Columbia.
★ **MIKE NICHOLS** for *The Graduate*, Nichols-Turman, Embassy.
ARTHUR PENN for *Bonnie and Clyde*, Tatira-Hiller, Warner Bros.-Seven Arts.

WRITING

(Screenplay—based on material from another medium)
COOL HAND LUKE, Jalem, Warner Bros.-Seven Arts. Donn Pearce and Frank R. Pierson.
THE GRADUATE, Nichols-Turman, Embassy. Calder Willingham and Buck Henry.
IN COLD BLOOD, Brooks, Columbia. Richard Brooks.
★ **IN THE HEAT OF THE NIGHT**, Mirisch, UA. Stirling Silliphant.
ULYSSES, Walter Reade-Continental Distributing. Joseph Strick and Fred Haines.

(Story and Screenplay—written directly for the screen)
BONNIE AND CLYDE, Tatira-Hiller, Warner Bros.-Seven Arts. David Newman and Robert Benton.
DIVORCE AMERICAN STYLE, Tandem-National General, Columbia. Robert Kaufman and Norman Lear.
★ **GUESS WHO'S COMING TO DINNER**, Kramer, Columbia. William Rose.
LA GUERRE EST FINIE, Sofracima-Europa, Brandon Films (French). Jorge Semprun.
TWO FOR THE ROAD, Donen, 20th Century-Fox. Frederic Raphael.

CINEMATOGRAPHY

(New classification; one award instead of separate awards for Black-and-Whte and Color achievements)
★ **BONNIE AND CLYDE**, Tatira-Hiller, Warner Bros.-Seven Arts. Burnett Guffey.
CAMELOT, Warner Bros.-Seven Arts. Richard H. Kline.
DOCTOR DOLITTLE, Apjac, 20th Century-Fox. Robert Surtees.
THE GRADUATE, Nichols-Turman, Embassy. Robert Surtees.
IN COLD BLOOD, Brooks, Columbia. Conrad Hall.

ART DIRECTION-SET DECORATION

(New classification: one award instead of separate awards for Black-and-White and Color achievements)
★ **CAMELOT**, Warner Bros.-Seven Arts. John Truscott and Edward Carrere; John W. Brown.
DOCTOR DOLITTLE, Apjac, 20th Century-Fox. Mario Chiari, Jack Martin Smith and Ed Graves; Walter M. Scott and Stuart A. Reiss.
GUESS WHO'S COMING TO DINNER, Kramer, Columbia. Robert Clatworthy; Frank Tuttle.
THE TAMING OF THE SHREW, Royal Films International, Columbia. Renzo Mongiardino, John DeCuir, Elven Webb and Giuseppe Mariani; Dario Simoni and Luigi Gervasi.
THOROUGHLY MODERN MILLIE, Hunter, Universal. Alexander Golitzen and George C. Webb; Howard Bristol.

COSTUME DESIGN

(New classification: one award instead of separate awards for Black-and-White and Color achievements)

Best Supporting Actress: Estelle Parsons as Blanche Barrow in *Bonnie and Clyde* (Warner Bros.; directed by Arthur Penn). Produced by Warren Beatty, *Bonnie and Clyde* made waves and caused talk; there was considerable controversy whether or not it glamorized violence, but no argument whatsoever about its brilliance as a well-made motion picture or about Estelle Parsons' performance as the noisy wife of Buck Barrow (Gene Hackman) and sister-in-law of Clyde Barrow (Warren Beatty), a team of real-life bank robbers and killers in Texas and Oklahoma, just after the depression.

Best Foreign Language Film: Closely Watched Trains, from Czechoslovakia (right). It was the second film in three years from that country to be honored by the Academy voters, following 1965's *The Shop on Main Street,* and it told the story of patriotism during the Second World War and the attempt of citizens to stop German munitions trains passing with priority through their occupied country. Jiri Menzel directed.

Best Director: Mike Nichols for *The Graduate* (Embassy; produced by Lawrence Turman). One of the year's most intensely liked, and best-made, successes, *The Graduate* made a star of movie newcomer Dustin Hoffman, playing a bewildered and comical grad who is seduced by the wife of his father's law partner, then falls in love with the lady's beautiful daughter. Anne Bancroft and Katharine Ross co-starred, and *The Graduate* won the Academy Award for the man behind the camera who made it all happen: Mike Nichols.

BONNIE AND CLYDE, Tatira-Hiller, Warner Bros.-Seven Arts. Theadora Van Runkle.
★ CAMELOT, Warner Bros.-Seven Arts. John Truscott.
THE HAPPIEST MILLIONAIRE, Disney, Buena Vista. Bill Thomas.
THE TAMING OF THE SHREW, Royal Films International, Columbia. Irene Sharaff and Danilo Donati.
THOROUGHLY MODERN MILLIE, Hunter, Universal. Jean Louis.

SOUND

CAMELOT, Warner Bros.-Seven Arts. Warner Bros.-Seven Arts Studio Sound Dept.
THE DIRTY DOZEN, Aldrich, M-G-M. M-G-M. Studio Sound Dept.
DOCTOR DOLITTLE, Apjac, 20th Century-Fox. 20th Century-Fox Studio Sound Dept.
★ IN THE HEAT OF THE NIGHT, Mirisch, UA. Samuel Goldwyn Studio Sound Dept.
THOROUGHLY MODERN MILLIE, Hunter, Universal. Universal City Studio Sound Dept.

FILM EDITING

BEACH RED, Theadora, UA. Frank P. Keller.
THE DIRTY DOZEN, Aldrich, M-G-M. Michael Luciano.
DOCTOR DOLITTLE, Apjac, 20th Century-Fox. Samuel E. Beetley and Marjorie Fowler.
GUESS WHO'S COMING TO DINNER, Kramer, Columbia. Robert C. Jones.
★ IN THE HEAT OF THE NIGHT, Mirisch, UA. Hal Ashby.

SPECIAL VISUAL EFFECTS

★ DOCTOR DOLITTLE, Apjac, 20th Century-Fox. L.B. Abbott.
TOBRUK, Gibraltar-Corman, Universal. Howard A. Anderson, Jr. and Albert Whitlock.

SOUND EFFECTS
(Not given after this year)

★ THE DIRTY DOZEN, Aldrich, M-G-M. John Poyner.
IN THE HEAT OF THE NIGHT, Mirisch, UA. James A. Richard.

MUSIC
(Song)

THE BARE NECESSITIES (*The Jungle Book*, Disney, Buena Vista); Music and Lyrics by Terry Gilkyson.
THE EYES OF LOVE (*Banning*, Universal); Music by Quincy Jones. Lyrics by Bob Russell.
THE LOOK OF LOVE (*Casino Royale*, Famous Artists, Columbia); Music by Burt Bacharach. Lyrics by Hal David.
★ TALK TO THE ANIMALS (*Doctor Dolittle*, Apjac, 20th Century-Fox); Music and Lyrics by Leslie Bricusse.
THOROUGHLY MODERN MILLIE (*Thoroughly Modern Millie*, Hunter, Universal); Music and Lyrics by James Van Heusen and Sammy Cahn.

(Original Music Score)

COOL HAND LUKE, Jalem, Warner Bros.-Seven Arts. Lalo Schifrin.
DOCTOR DOLITTLE, Apjac, 20th Century-Fox. Leslie Bricusse.
FAR FROM THE MADDING CROWD, Appia, M-G-M. Richard Rodney Bennett.
IN COLD BLOOD, Brooks, Columbia. Quincy Jones.
★ THOROUGHLY MODERN MILLIE, Hunter, Universal. Elmer Bernstein.

(Scoring of Music—adaptation or treatment)

★ CAMELOT, Warner Bros.-Seven Arts. Alfred Newman and Ken Darby.
DOCTOR DOLITTLE, Apjac, 20th Century-Fox. Lionel Newman and Alexander Courage.
GUESS WHO'S COMING TO DINNER, Kramer, Columbia. DeVol.
THOROUGHLY MODERN MILLIE, Hunter, Universal. Andre Previn and Joseph Gershenson.
VALLEY OF THE DOLLS, Red Lion, 20th Century-Fox. John Williams.

SHORT SUBJECTS
(Cartoons)

★ THE BOX, Brandon Films. Fred Wolf, producer.
HYPOTHESE BETA, Films Orzeaux, Pathe Contemporary Films. Jean-Charles Meunier, producer.
WHAT ON EARTH!, National Film Board of Canada, Columbia. Robert Verrall and Wolf Koenig, producers.

(Live Action Subjects)

PADDLE TO THE SEA, National Film Board of Canada, Favorite Films, Julian Biggs, producer.
★ A PLACE TO STAND, T.D.F. Prod. for Ontario Dept. of Economics and Development, Columbia. Christopher Chapman, producer.
SKY OVER HOLLAND, Ferno Prod. for The Netherlands, Seneca International. John Ferno, producer.
STOP, LOOK AND LISTEN, M-G-M. Len Janson and Chuck Menville, producers.

DOCUMENTARY
(Short Subjects)

MONUMENT TO THE DREAM, Guggenheim Prods. Charles E. Guggenheim, producer.
A PLACE TO STAND, T.D.F. Prod. for The Ontario Department of Economics and Development. Christopher Chapman, producer.
★ THE REDWOODS, King Screen Prods. Mark Harris and Trevor Greenwood, producers.
SEE YOU AT THE PILLAR, Associated British-Pathe Prod. Robert Fitchett, producer.
WHILE I RUN THIS RACE, Sun Dial Films for VISTA. Carl V. Ragsdale, producer.

(Features)

★ THE ANDERSON PLATOON, French Broadcasting System. Pierre Schoendoerffer, producer.
FESTIVAL, Patchke Prods. Murray Lerner, producer.

HARVEST, U.S. Information Agency. Carroll Ballard, producer.
A KING'S STORY, Jack Le Vien Prod. Jack Le Vien, producer.
A TIME FOR BURNING, Quest Prods. for Lutheran Film Associates. William C. Jersey, producer.

FOREIGN LANGUAGE FILM

★ CLOSELY WATCHED TRAINS, (Czechoslovakia).
EL AMOR BRUJO, (Spain).
I EVEN MET HAPPY GYPSIES, (Yugoslavia).
LIVE FOR LIFE, (France).
PORTRAIT OF CHIEKO, (Japan).

HONORARY AND OTHER AWARDS

TO ARTHUR FREED for distinguished service to the Academy and the production of six top-rated Awards telecasts. (statuette)

1967 IRVING G. THALBERG MEMORIAL AWARD

TO ALFRED HITCHCOCK

1967 JEAN HERSHOLT HUMANITARIAN AWARD

TO GREGORY PECK

SCIENTIFIC OR TECHNICAL

CLASS I (statuette)
None.

CLASS II (plaque)
None.

CLASS III (citation)
ELECTRO-OPTICAL DIVISION of the KOLLMORGEN CORPORATION; PANAVISION INCORPORATED; FRED R. WILSON of the SAMUEL GOLDWYN STUDIO SOUND DEPT.; WALDON O. WATSON and the UNIVERSAL CITY STUDIO SOUND DEPT.

★ INDICATES WINNER

Best Supporting Actor: George Kennedy as Dragline (left, with Paul Newman) in *Cool Hand Luke* (Warner Bros.; directed by Stuart Rosenberg). The movie was a strong essay on individuality, a pertinent and a well-liked theme in the late 1960s, and Kennedy won his Academy Award as a chain-gang convict in a Southern state who battles Luke (played by Newman) for leadership of the gang, then ends up his friend and would-be protector.

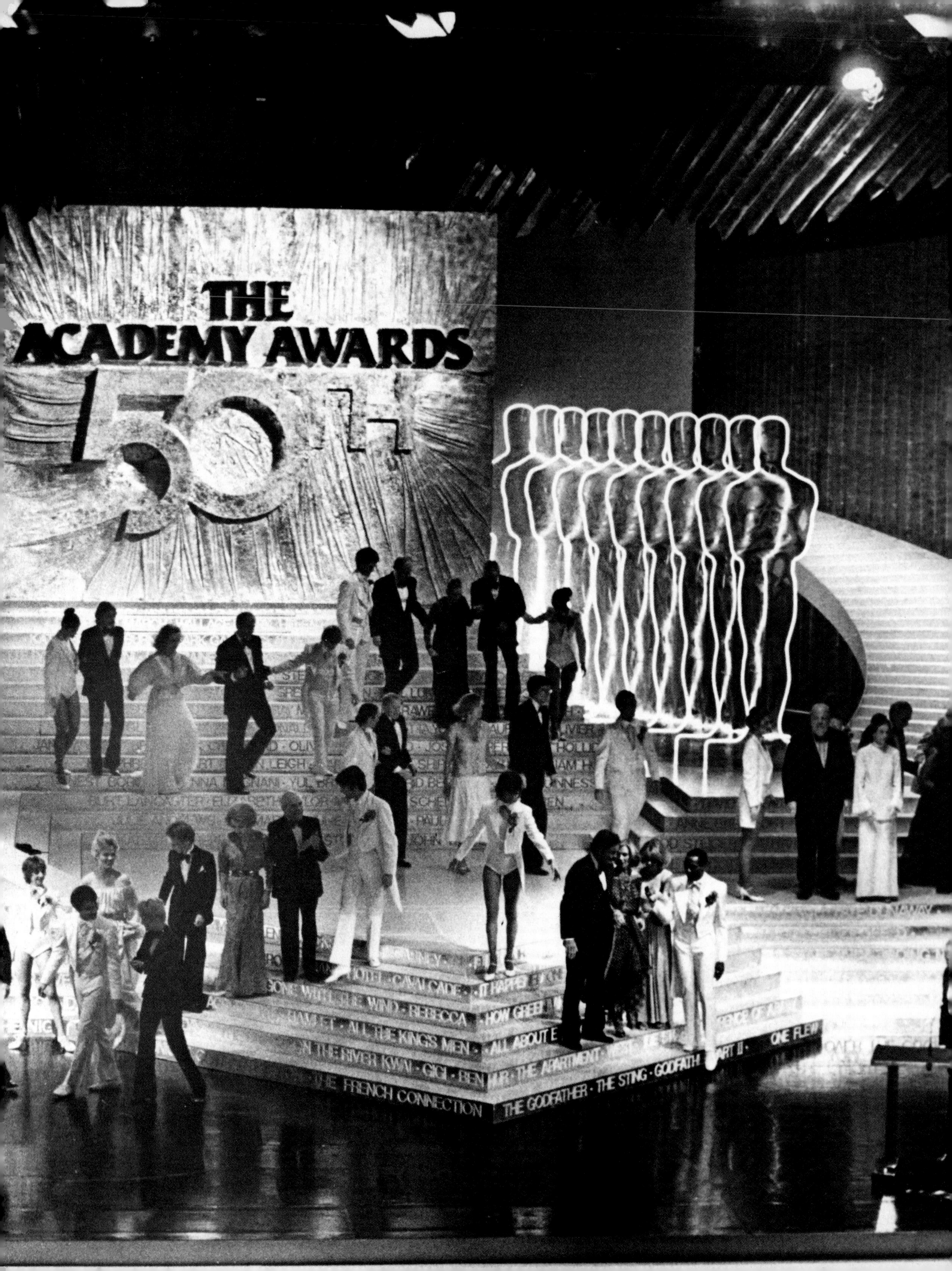

The Academy's Fifth Decade

1968-1977

The Academy's fifth decade saw the fulfillment of that dream which had been in the making for almost fifty years: a new, specially designed headquarters for the organization, and for the first time all of the Academy's many facilities would be located under one roof. At last Oscar would have a home of its own.

Academy of Motion Picture Arts and Sciences building, dedicated in December 1975, Beverly Hills, Calif.

The Academy's Margaret Herrick Library,
a central source of information on all
facets of motion pictures.

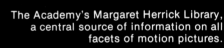

The new building, located at 8949 Wilshire Boulevard in Beverly Hills, was designed by Maxwell Starkman and built by the Buckeye Construction Company of Los Angeles. The Academy's activities are organized into the seven floors as follows:

Ground floor: grand lobby, patio, building foyer, theater manager's office, caterers' workroom;

Second floor: Samuel Goldwyn Theater (1111 seats), lobby display of one-sheet posters of past Academy Award-winning films;

Third floor: special screening room (80 seats), projection booth, editing room, film storage area;

Fourth floor: Margaret Herrick Research Library;

Fifth floor: library storage area;

Sixth floor: Academy membership office, Academy Players Directory office, Scientific and Technical Awards office, Theater operations office, Administrative office;

Seventh floor: executive offices for the Academy president, executive director, Board of Governors' conference room.

Groundbreaking for the site took place on September 18, 1973, and the official dedication ceremony was held nearly two years later, on December 8, 1975. At that time the Academy hosted a series of grand

A capacity audience filled the Samuel Goldwyn Theater (above) for the Fifth Annual Student Film Awards Presentations, in May, 1978. The Academy's theater, which meets or exceeds every world standard for cinemas, is dedicated to motion picture pioneer Samuel Goldwyn (lower right).

opening parties in the lobby of the new complex for Academy members, press, civic leaders and industry friends. Among those attending the first evening were sixteen performers who had won Academy Awards during preceding years: Red Buttons, Patty Duke Astin, Ben Johnson, Jack Lemmon, Karl Malden, Walter Matthau, Laurence Olivier, Sidney Poitier, Ginger Rogers, Harold Russell, Eva Marie Saint, Maximilian Schell, Rod Steiger, Claire Trevor, Peter Ustinov, and Shelley Winters. In addition to organized tours of the building, guests were invited into the Samuel Goldwyn Theater for a special screening of sequences from all the past Academy Award-winning Best Pictures, beginning with *Wings,* the 1927-28 winner.

The whole decade was an active one for the Academy. In 1969, it received one of its most extensive donations to date, from Paramount Pictures. The collection encompasses stills, scripts and press material from more than 2,200 Paramount releases, dating to the earliest silent film days. The opening of the new Academy building provided the space for the proper filing and storage of such collections donated to the Academy, which now include the valuable RKO Radio Studios still

Mayor Tom Bradley presents commendation from the City of Los Angeles recognizing the Academy's contribution to the community.

The Golden Anniversary luncheon celebration May 11, 1977, in the Crystal Ballroom of the Los Angeles Biltmore Hotel—exactly 50 years to the day from the Academy's original organizational meeting held in the same ballroom.

Cary Grant

(Cary Grant requested that his acceptance speech for the Honorary Award he received at the 42nd Annual Academy Awards be reproduced as his contribution to this publication.)

CARY GRANT

" I'm very grateful to the Academy's Board for this happy tribute, and to Frank for coming here especially to give it to me, and to all the fellows who worked so hard in finding and assembling those film clips . . .

You know, I may never look at this without remembering the quiet patience of the directors who were so kind to me, who were kind enough to put up with me more than once—some of them even three or four times. There were Howard Hawks, Alfred Hitchcock, the late Leo McCarey, George Stevens, George Cukor and Stanley Donen. And all the writers . . . There were Philip Barry, Dore Schary, Bob Sherwood, Ben Hecht, dear Clifford Odets, Sidney Sheldon and more recently Stanley Shapiro and Peter Stone. Well, I trust they and all the other directors, writers and producers, and leading women, have all forgiven me what I didn't know.

I realize it's conventional and usual to praise one's fellow workers on these occasions . . . but why not? Ours is a collaborative medium; we all need each other! And what better opportunity is there to publicly express one's appreciation and admiration and affection for all those who contribute so much to each of our welfare?

You know, I've never been a joiner or a member of any—oh, particular—social set, but I've been privileged to be a part of Hollywood's most glorious era. And yet, tonight, thinking of all the empty screens that are waiting to be filled with marvelous images, ideologies, points of view— whatever—and considering all the students who are studying film techniques in the universities throughout the world, and the astonishing young talents that are coming up in our midsts, I think there's an even more glorious era right around the corner.

So, before I leave you, I want to thank you very much for signifying your approval of this. I shall cherish it until I die . . . because probably no greater honor can come to any man than the respect of his colleagues.

Thank you. "

Cary Grant
Honorary Award, 1969

photos collection, the papers of writer-director Lamont Johnson, the Cecil B. DeMille still photograph books, the Howard Estabrook papers, the William Wright collection, the Technicolor Film Continuity Sheets, the Ivan Kahn collection, the Mack Sennett collection, the Lever Brothers-Lux Radio Theater collection, among others. The Margaret Herrick Library, named for the Academy's first librarian and later its executive director who retired in 1970 after forty years of service, also established a new collection of its own: the Black American Film History collection, to recognize and preserve important contributions made by Blacks in the film industry.

In 1970, the Academy joined with the Writers Guild to jointly publish an extensive directory of screenwriting credits called *Who Wrote the Movie (and What Else Did He Write?)*, covering the years 1936 through 1969, filling a research need that had been lacking for years. Two years later, in 1972, another attempt was made in the area of publishing an on-going magazine, called *Academy Leader*, offering news, reviews and photographs about the motion picture industry. This was planned as a quarterly publication, but it only existed for three issues. A comprehensive book, *Introduction to the Photoplay*, was

JOHN WAYNE

❝For us in the industry the Oscar is the highest and most cherished award. It is a goal for which all of us instinctively strive. It is our most coveted honor, because it means recognition from our peers.

It is also the only way we who work in front of the camera have to publicly thank those wonderful craftsmen, technicians and artists whose invention, skill and imagination make us who paint our faces popular, interesting, or at least palatable to the public taste. To these people I will be forever grateful.

I have spent nearly fifty years chasing this elusive fellow with good performances and bad, so I was extremely delighted when he was handed to me by Barbra Streisand.❞

John Wayne
Best Actor, 1969

LIZA MINNELLI

❝It was wonderful to be even nominated, and then receiving the Oscar knowing that my peers had voted for me was totally thrilling and an honor I will cherish always. ❞

Liza Minnelli
Best Actress, 1972

John Wayne

Eileen Heckart, Joel Grey, Liza Minnelli

JOEL GREY

❝The night I won my Oscar for Cabaret, I went to the ceremonies all but convinced I wouldn't win so, when Diana Ross opened the envelope and the name she announced was mine, it was like this incredible shot of electricity or adrenalin swept through me and the moment seemed to stand still in time. All I remember was kissing my wife, and then I guess 'my feet did their stuff' because the next thing I knew, I was no longer in my seat but up on stage warming in the affection and approval of my peers and finally saying, 'Don't let anybody tell you this isn't terrific.' ❞

Joel Grey
Best Supporting Actor, 1972

MARTHA RAYE

❝One of the proudest moments of my life was receiving the Oscar for the Jean Hersholt Humanitarian Award.

Ever grateful,❞,

Martha Raye
Jean Hersholt Humanitarian Award, 1968

published in 1978 as a limited edition by the National Film Society, with the Academy's involvement and cooperation. The book is based on previously unpublished works compiled from fifteen lectures delivered back in 1929 at the University of Southern California by leading film professionals, including Irving Thalberg, William Cameron Menzies, William C. deMille, Conrad Nagel and Benjamin Glazer.

Both the *Academy Players Directory* and the *Screen Achievement Records Bulletin* continued to flourish throughout the decade. The *Directory*, more and more considered an invaluable aid for casting purposes, had grown to include in excess of ten thousand individual players. More than fifteen hundred copies per issue are distributed.

David Niven and 1974's unexpected streaker

The *Bulletin* had become equally indispensable, as the only regularly published reference book which compiles current individual screen credits.

The Student Film Awards program was inaugurated in 1973 as a program of the Academy, the Academy Foundation and later co-sponsored by the American Telephone and Telegraph Company to recognize and encourage excellence in college filmmaking. Since the annual program began, over four hundred students per year from across the United States have taken part in the competition, vying for awards and cash grants, with their student films judged in four specific categories: dramatic, animated, documentary and experimental films.

LIONEL NEWMAN

One of the odd sensations with respect to winning an Oscar is that the 'magic moment' and the 'Cinderella evening' inevitably have to end. Actually, upon hearing one's name called, one doesn't care about himself, but is concerned that his wife, children and friends are proud of him—to say nothing of his peers.

So many people make it all possible. I have been nominated twelve times and finally received the Oscar for Hello Dolly. *I'm damned proud to display it where it can be seen. No bullshit about a 'doorstop' or using it as a 'paperweight.'*

I love our industry and am very grateful to be a small part of it . . . To the next fifty years!

Lionel Newman
Scoring of a Musical Picture
(Original or Adaptation), 1969

ONNA WHITE

Dear Oscar,
Congratulations on your fiftieth anniversary. It is with great pleasure that I have been made a part of your association by being named the first female choreographer for a Special Oscar. Thank you.

Onna White
Honorary Award, 1968

CLIFF ROBERTSON

Charly was not an easy delivery . . . seven years. I am indebted to all attendants. I am in debt to all who believed.

Cliff Robertson
Best Actor, 1968

GOLDIE HAWN

I was in London when I first heard the news that I won the Award. I was so sure that I was not going to get it, that when I received the call at six in the morning, I had no idea who could be calling me at that hour. After the hysterics and tears were over, I then wished so hard that I could have been there to accept my Oscar. Receiving an Academy Award for my first motion picture was, I realized, a great achievement, but it didn't carry the impact for me as it would have, had I done other pictures prior to winning and thereby been more aware of how difficult it is to earn an Oscar.

But I am forever grateful.

Goldie Hawn
Best Supporting Actress, 1969

BURT BACHARACH

" When I was nominated three years in a row, it was a tremendously exciting thing, but the night that I won two Oscars has to just about qualify as one of the greatest nights in my life. "

Burt Bacharach
Music (Original Score), 1969
Music (Song), 1969

JOHN SCHLESINGER

" I was in England shooting Sunday Bloody Sunday when the Academy Awards were to be announced for the previous year, and Midnight Cowboy was one of the nominations. Obviously, we had all prepared ourselves not to win, and although United Artists said they would stop shooting and pay for me to fly over for the occasion, I thought there would be nothing worse than the possibility of my returning empty handed to my unit, who might have been hanging around for three days waiting for a jet-lagged director.

At 5:15 English time on the morning of the Awards, the telephone rang, and my secretary from Midnight Cowboy (who was by now working for the Academy Awards show) was backstage, and they were just coming up to the writer awards. She certainly had a sense of timing. Everyone in my house grabbed extension phones, and we listened to the distant sounds of the Academy Awards night over the trans-Atlantic phone connected backstage, where my ex-secretary screamed with delight every time Cowboy won another award.

In many ways it was the best way to hear the news. There was not much work done on the set that day—too many interruptions and celebratory drinks, but I was happy to share the occasion with my unit and cast. After all, the pleasure of winning an Academy Award is that it is an accolade from one's colleagues and peers. "

John Schlesinger
Best Director, 1969

SIR JOHN MILLS, C.B.E.

" Expressing my thoughts on receiving the Oscar proves rather difficult, as on that particular evening, my mind was almost a complete blank, but I do know that it was one of the most exciting things that has ever happened to me. In fact, I have barely recovered from the shock yet.

I send my very best wishes to the Academy. "

Sir John Mills, C.B.E.
Best Supporting Actor, 1970

Lillian Gish, Melvyn Douglas

Honorary Awards have also been given to films of exceptional merit, which have not otherwise been recognized in the competition. Winners are flown to Los Angeles and honored at an annual Awards banquet, where they meet with Hollywood professionals.

The Marvin Borowsky Lectureship on Screenwriting was established in 1974 by Mr. Borowsky's widow Maxine, and overseen by the Academy as a lecture-seminar series in which noted screenwriters lecture on their craft, then answer questions posed by Academy members, students of screenwriting and professionals in attendance.

Throughout the decade, the Academy also continued to extend Hollywood beyond its own borders, with an extensive Visiting Artists Program, providing distinguished members of the film industry for speaking engagements on college and university campuses throughout the United States. This extremely successful program has been an attempt to bridge the gap between the classroom and the world of professional filmmakers, and traveling participants have included such Academy members as Frank Capra, King Vidor, Robert Towne, Rouben Mamoulian, Lee Garmes, Thomas Stanford, Verna Fields, Paul Schrader and Linwood Dunn. Realizing the great value of the program, members have waived any fees offered for their speaking services and the Academy accepts no compensation for administering the program.

Goldie Hawn announcing "It's George C. Scott!"

Roger Moore, Liv Ullmann, Sacheen Littlefeather

GEORGE ROY HILL

❝Awards for any of the arts have always struck me as unavoidably capricious and, more often than not, given for reasons other than for genuine artistic achievement. Time is going to be the final judge of merit regardless of what the contemporary awards say. But knowing this somehow did not diminish one whit my delight in receiving it. It was a hell of a thrill.❞

George Roy Hill
Best Director, 1973

BEN JOHNSON

❝I will always be grateful to the Academy for the fair and impartial way in which it conducts the Oscar Awards.

For an Oklahoma cowboy-turned-actor to win a major award, without a campaign or war-chest, proved to me beyond a shadow of doubt that the Academy always deals from the top of the deck. And as I said when I received the Award, 'It couldn't have happened to a nicer feller!'❞

Ben Johnson
Best Supporting Actor, 1971

CLORIS LEACHMAN

❝ The American ethic is to be the best. From the Nobel Prize to Queen for a Day, from the Olympics to the best apple pie. At worst it is merchandising our business. It creates jobs and opportunities for everyone, and in the tradition of great American competition the Oscar reflects that.

We take turns being the catalyst for other professionals. We actors, producers, directors, writers, etc., all motivate each other. My mother always said there is plenty of room at the top. That to me means excellence. With all the ramifications of the Academy Awards, excellence encourages excellence. It nourishes each of us.

I was astonished and literally swept off my feet by the response that night I was honored. Suddenly it was no longer a committee or a faceless group, it was everybody cheering YEAH!! for you, and I can pass that on. I felt that night that it wasn't necessary at that point in my career but I certainly felt loved, and it was terrific!❞

Cloris Leachman
Best Supporting Actress, 1971

GENE HACKMAN

" *The Academy Award did one thing for me. It made me far more patient of those sometimes protracted thank you speeches of acceptance. Standing there, feeling the weight of the statue for the first time, you suddenly are overwhelmed with the thought of thirty years of people to be thanked and how to squeeze it into thirty seconds. The Oscar meant two other things to me, two of the films I take a certain pride in having worked on. I've been told by the people who made them that the glow of that Oscar had something to do with the opportunity to get* Scarecrow *and Francis Coppola's* The Conversation *made. It's hard for me to believe that the power of the scripts and the talent-value of the creators involved wouldn't have made the films inevitable. But Hollywood is filled with that kind of contradiction. If my Oscar was put into the realization of two worthwhile films, chalk another two up for Oscar.* "

Gene Hackman
Best Actor, 1971

EILEEN HECKART

" *All the people who have touched your life win with you. You suddenly even hear from that freckle-faced boy who sat behind you in psychology class in 1942.* "

Eileen Heckart
Best Supporting Actress, 1972

JOEL HIRSCHHORN

" *As a youngster I used to race to the Kingsbridge Theatre in the Bronx and sit through all the popular musicals, fantasizing about the day I could be a part of Hollywood. My favorite was* An American in Paris, *which I saw at least twenty times. You can imagine, then, my sense of joy and fulfillment when I won as Oscar, and the further excitement I felt being presented the award by Gene Kelly.* "

Joel Hirschhorn
Music (Song), 1972; 1974

LEE GRANT

" *The 'Oscar' has endured because of our yearning for excellence. Getting one is like being appointed valedictorian from the bottom of the class. The 'outs' like me, get their moment to be 'in,' for as long as it lasts.* "

Lee Grant
Best Supporting Actress, 1975

Lawrence Weingarten, Katharine Hepburn

Paul Williams, Barbra Streisand

One of the projects of the Academy Foundation (established in 1944) is the annual disbursement of grants, fellowships and internships to individuals and/or organizations, to support and encourage a wide spectrum of film-related projects. The Academy Internship Program, administered by the American Film Institute, has proved valuable, allowing film students and professionals to study the making of motion pictures from inception through completion, working side by side with distinguished directors. There have also been scholarship grants to students majoring in the film sciences, selected with the cooperation of the Society of Motion Picture and Television Engineers, and financial assistance to several scholarly projects involved in such fields as animation and set design.

Charlie Chaplin comes home

Louise Fletcher

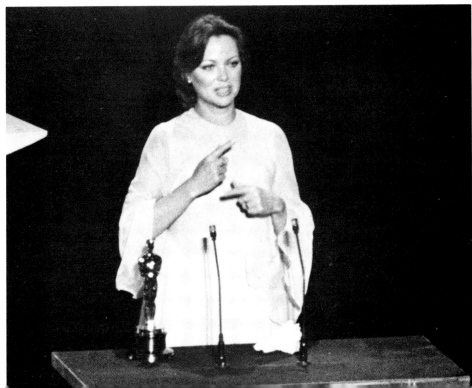

MILOS FORMAN

"I was sitting in the auditorium at the Academy Awards with my two twelve-year-old sons. They had arrived the night before from Czechoslovakia. It was their first time in America and I hadn't seen them in five years. We were strangers to each other that evening. They didn't speak English, but they had learned the name of my film: Cuksunext.

The film was mentioned as a nominee for Best Supporting Actor. The boys got very excited, and when George Burns won in this category for Sunshine Boys, *my boys gave me a standing ovation.*

'Cut it,' I said. 'You are making fools of yourselves. We lost.'

They looked at me like I was making a very bad joke. After we lost four nominations in a row, Petr fell asleep and Matej started concentrating on his bubble gum. I realized that if I didn't win, the boys would never understand what they had come for.

Finally, I won. I was filled with pride and self confidence as a father. 'Tell me anything in the world you want,' I said generously. 'I'll get it for you.'

'Anything?' They looked at each other. 'Anything.'

Without hesitation, they replied, "We want to meet that Columbo guy Peter Falk, and then we want to see Jaws!'"

Milos Forman
Best Director, 1975

FAYE DUNAWAY

"All my years of work as an actress seemed to come together the night I won the Oscar for Network, *and for a brief moment I felt that I had reached the pinnacle. That kind of elation lasts only for a few hours, but it's something I'll always remember.*

In this business you go on to the next film, or play, or whatever, and it's almost like starting from scratch every time. Winning an Oscar doesn't mean you can rest on your laurels, and it certainly shouldn't become a bench mark for measuring subsequent performances because you have to approach each new role as a totally separate entity if you're going to maintain your integrity as an artist. If you dwell too long in past achievements, you're in trouble.

Success is a relative quotient, and fame can be ephemeral. An Oscar is something that becomes a part of your record, a tangible acknowledgement that your efforts have made a difference."

Faye Dunaway
Best Actress, 1976

CARMINE COPPOLA

"*As I get older, I realize how much more I need to learn; how different it is than when I was a young composer, out to dazzle everyone. I knew everything.*

When I received the Oscar for Best Music Score I finally realized, not only a great prize and honor, but also that possibly I had started to learn something about music and in a little while longer could learn even more. My years with Juilliard, Toscanini and Joseph Schellinger in composition served me well."

Carmine Coppola
Music (Original Dramatic Score), 1974

INGRID BERGMAN

"*I belong to the group of people who like the tradition of the Academy Award under the friendly name of Oscar. I am aware that many people find that too many artists have been overlooked. Too many people have been given awards, as they used to say, for sentimental reasons. In other words, after several nominations and losing the award, you would get it for a picture less worthy. Well, I am not against the sentimentality of these awards. I am sad that people like Greta Garbo and Ernst Lubitsch were overlooked. That people like Charles Chaplin and Jean Renoir were given Special Awards so late in their creative careers. Despite its shortcomings, it is still the most valuable award in the film industry of the entire world, and no one can deny the excitement felt by the people present at the award-giving ceremony or those watching it at home on television. I look with pride on my three and feel immensely happy and proud to have received them.*"

Ingrid Bergman
Best Actress, 1944; 1956
Best Supporting Actress, 1974

BEATRICE STRAIGHT

"*Next to my marriage and the birth of my children, winning the Oscar was one of the most exciting and happy moments of my life—full of deep gratitude to my fellow actors and partners in work, and the joy of being an artist. I was also fully aware that I was only one of many, but had been lucky enough to be in the right part at the right time.*"

Beatrice Straight
Best Supporting Actress, 1976

But the decade wasn't all confined to scholarly endeavors. On May 11, 1977, fifty years to the day after the initial Academy of Motion Picture Arts and Sciences' organization meeting in the Crystal Ballroom of the Los Angeles Biltmore Hotel, a year-long celebration of Oscar's Fiftieth Anniversary officially began in the same room, filled with a towering birthday cake, attended by Academy leaders, film industry executives, civic officials and friends, and emceed by Bob Hope.

Proclamations honoring the Academy and its contributions were presented by the City of Los Angeles, the State of California, the United States Senate and the House of Representatives, and President Jimmy Carter. Life memberships were presented to sixteen film professionals who were admitted to the Academy during its first year, and a twenty-two minute film called *Oscar's First Fifty Years*, hosted by Jack Lemmon was shown. It marked the first time the Academy had described its own broad range of activities on film, and the featurette was later made available to schools, museums, service clubs and other organizations for showing. A special seven-minute version was also made available to hundreds of theaters across the country, prior to the Fiftieth Academy Awards presentation, to further enhance interest in Oscar's golden anniversary.

While the Academy itself began a retrospective series of showings of all past Oscar-winning Best Picture selections, in the Samuel Goldwyn

Ingrid Bergman

George Burns, Ben Johnson, Linda Blair

Theater for Academy members, the organization also participated in a series of television specials aired on the ABC-TV network. They included "Oscar's Best Music" (telecast November 25, 1975), "Oscar's Best Movies" (February 13, 1977), "Oscar Presents the War Movies and John Wayne" (November 22, 1977) and "Oscar's Best Actors" (aired May 23, 1978). All the activities culminated, with an appropriate serving of spectacle, at the actual Fiftieth Academy Awards presentation, April 3, 1978, and telecast on the ABC-TV network. It set a new record for television viewership: more than seventy million American TV viewers watched the show, eclipsing Oscar's previous total audience record of 68.5 million, set in 1976. Additionally, more than three hundred million persons in over fifty countries also saw the telecast.

It was a far, far cry from those beginning days when only a handful of interested pioneers started it all. At the conclusion of the decade, the Academy was stronger than ever, a survivor of wars, depressions, prosperity, political unrest, criticisms, revolutionary inventions, changing styles, even a gate-crasher and a streaker. Equally important, it had remained flexible to its times and formats, and ambitiously dedicated to represent, encourage and preserve the very best aspects of the motion picture world.

ACADEMY PRESIDENTS, THE FIFTH DECADE
June 1967-May 1968	GREGORY PECK
June 1968-May 1969	GREGORY PECK
June 1969-May 1970	GREGORY PECK
June 1970-May 1971	DANIEL TARADASH
June 1971-May 1972	DANIEL TARADASH
June 1972-May 1973	DANIEL TARADASH
June 1973-May 1974	WALTER MIRISCH
June 1974-May 1975	WALTER MIRISCH
June 1975-May 1976	WALTER MIRISCH
June 1976-May 1977	WALTER MIRISCH
June 1977-May 1978	HOWARD W. KOCH

AL KASHA

❝ My father was a barber and I lived over a store in Brooklyn. The possibility of winning an award like this seemed an impossible dream. It was an overwhelming feeling that night when my name was announced. I remembered the days over that store and said to myself, 'This can't be happening to Al Kasha!' ❞

Al Kasha
Music (Song), 1972; 1974

RICHARD DREYFUSS

❝ The night was a complete fuzz out. At the time, it seemed highly rational that I was being considered for an Academy Award. It was only later I realized that my God, I won the Best Actor Award of 1977.

I wanted to be in control so that when I turned to the audience I could appreciate the experience moment by moment, but my mind turned to Jello and all I could do was guffaw into the microphone.

We've all participated in two rituals: one is the watching of the Academy Awards and the other is the putting down of the Academy Awards. Both are very sacred and traditional American events. I always vowed that I would never go to an Academy Award presentation that I was involved in. (This was in my days of chutzpah and cockiness.) But as the reality became closer and closer and I saw myself in a vision: driving Pacific Coast Highway alone in my car listening to the Academy Awards presentation on the radio, and hearing my name and saying to myself "Schmuck . . . what are you doing here?' So, I decided I would go to the Oscars.

It is extraordinary, but the most relevant part of the experience to me is not from that night, but from what I have been carrying with me ever since. And that is this: I would have to work very hard to deny my success now. I would have to expend an enormous amount of effort to say that I'm not doing well in this business. The accolade, the acceptance, the acknowledgement that this award has given me, to my surprise, more whiffs of personal happiness in my soul than I ever expected it to do. Usually once every two or three days, for periods of two or three minutes at a time, an enormous giggle of happiness comes over me . . . not only that I won, that I am the winner, but that I'm here and I'm me and I can enjoy it and it's all wonderful. ❞

Richard Dreyfuss
Best Actor, 1977

Bob Hope, Walter Mirisch and Oscar's 50th birthday cake

ROGER CHRISTIAN

❝It was an honor to be thanked by members of my own profession.❞

Roger Christian
Set Direction, 1977

RICHARD F. CHEW

❝My memories of Oscar night, of That Magic Moment: I was prepared. I sensed we would win because everything else in my life had gone to pieces in the preceding twenty-four hours. However, at the moment when our names were announced, my heart jumped to my mouth and I to my feel involuntarily—both from exhilaration and in surprise.❞

Richard F. Chew
Film Editing, 1977

LES DILLEY

❝It was nerve-racking and probably the most exciting moment in my film career.❞

Les Dilley
Art Direction, 1977

BEN BURTT

❝My achievement award was announced publicly a few weeks before the Oscar ceremony. I was stunned when I found out, and I leaped on my bike and rode home to tell my wife.

It was a tremendous honor to be recognized by the Academy, and I experienced a month of anxiety knowing I had to appear on the television show.❞

Ben Burtt
Special Achievement Award, 1977

JOHN MOLLO

❝Prior to the nominations, I was working with a recent winner who advised me, if I were nominated, to move heaven and earth to attend the ceremony— 'the experience of a lifetime,' he said, 'and not to be missed on any account.' So I went forewarned to some extent, but the reality, in particular the friendliness of everyone concerned, far surpassed the telling.❞

John Mollo
Costume Design, 1977

GEORGE BURNS

❝I was thrilled when I was nominated, but it was very, very exciting to win an Oscar. Imagine, winning an Oscar when you're eighty years old. I've been in show business all my life, and I've always played myself, George Burns. Here I make one movie, The Sunshine Boys, where for the first time I didn't play myself. I played a character 'Al Lewis' and won an Oscar. I guess that could mean I've been doing the wrong thing for the last eighty years. It's a good thing I found out before it's too late.

Happy birthday and best wishes.❞

George Burns
Best Supporting Actor, 1975

NORMAN REYNOLDS

❝I was thrilled beyond all measure.❞

Norman Reynolds
Art Direction, 1977

ELLEN BURSTYN

" When I was awarded my Oscar, I couldn't be there to receive it in person because I was working in a play in New York. Two nights later, Jack Lemmon and Walter Matthau delivered my ''gold statue'' to the theater in New York, then took me out to dinner with a few friends afterwards. During dinner Oscar sat on the floor in a little felt bag between Walter and me. Over coffee, I turned to Walter and said, 'What is that down there in the bag, Walter? What is an Oscar? What does it mean?' And Walter said, 'Let's put it this way, Ellen. When you die, the newspapers will say, ''The Academy Award-winning actress Ellen Burstyn died today.'' '

'Oh,' said the Academy Award-winning actress, and finished her coffee, silent and informed. "

Ellen Burstyn
Best Actress, 1974

TATUM O'NEAL

" That night was like a shining light which never goes out. I sat with most of my beloved family and suddenly my name was called—I was lifted up into another world, leaving many childish things behind, but happily.

It was only four years ago. I was ten years old and now I'm fourteen and stretching myself from fourteen to eighteen in International Velvet.

I love my profession. It is important and noble. "

Tatum O'Neal
Best Supporting Actress, 1973

VERNA FIELDS

" Winning the Oscar is for anyone in our industry the ultimate accolade from one's peers. It is an honor to receive and a feeling of great personal pride to feel one has accomplished something to deserve it. As I glance up and see my Oscar, it reminds me of the many years it took to learn what I needed to know to achieve that honor. "

Verna Fields
Film Editing, 1975

BILL GOLDMAN

" I understand the voting is secret, the specific results never announced; and that is as it should be. But why couldn't we have a listing of the order of the five candidates? Or, if you feel that would be embarrassing, why not make some kind of note when the voting was particularly close? (Say, for example, when the second place winner was within a certain percentage of winning.)

I think this is valid for one reason and one reason only. We all know—those of us who work in the movie business—that is an industry award. And only occasionally do we sense the mood of the industry clearly. Example: I don't think there's any doubt in most people's minds that Taylor won Best Actress in 1960, not for Butterfield 8, but because she had pneumonia and came back, and the industry properly loves survivors. Also, Taylor had not won for either Cat on a Hot Tin Roof or, most particularly, the year before in Suddenly, Last Summer.

Personally, I don't believe that movies are 'good' or 'bad' when they are released. They either 'work' or 'don't work.' I think the former terms are something only to be used when time has had a chance to operate. But the awards, as they should be, are about movies that work or don't work for the public. Has a flop ever won anything? Doubtful.

Okay, to try and sum up: if we knew who was close to winning, or the order of the five, or at least the runner-up, we would have a wonderful way of trying to gauge the sentiment and thoughts of the industry at a particular point in time. "

Bill Goldman
Writing (Story and Screenplay
written directly for the screen), 1969
Writing (Screenplay based on material
from another medium), 1976

ALAN AND MARILYN BERGMAN

" About winning the Oscar? It's all been said—and all of it is true.

But if you want to recall that feeling up there, our advise is: win two.

Our first (for 'Windmills of Your Mind') was dazzling—a thrill—but, alas, a blur. The second was sweeter simply because we remember 'The Way We Were'! "

Alan and Marilyn Bergman
Music (Song), 1968; 1973

DONALD W. MacDOUGALL

" 'And the winner is,' . . . the sound of silence that follows those words is deafening. In that brief instant, you relive all the torturous hours spent in personal anguish breathing life into an image on the screen.

When Star Wars won Best Sound for 1977, I was immediately filled with an overwhelming sense of accomplishment and pride for my colleagues, for our work, for having made a journey filled with great adventure. "

Donald W. MacDougall
Sound, 1977

JOHN BARRY

" It was without doubt the high point of my career as a designer. The number of foreign technicians who have been honored in this way illustrates the generosity of the Academy and the truly international nature of the industry. "

John Barry
Art Direction, 1977

ROBERT BLALACK

" The release of Star Wars became a phenomena in America and the world rivalled perhaps only by the Hula Hoop. My surprise at its instant success was only surpassed by my astonishment that we might win an Oscar for the visual effects. I was completely uncertain whether Close Encounters would win, and I felt that as their effects might be seen as more 'traditional,' we might well not be the Oscar recipients.

I was focused on the part of the event which was the Visual Effects Oscar, and when they started to list the contenders, I felt like I was walking a tightrope across a significant divide. 'The envelope please' statement made me want to freeze time and suspend it there: I didn't want to know the results. As Joan Fontaine started to read our names, I felt transformed, completely acknowledged, and elated. We all ran up to the stage, hugging each other and laughing uncontrollably.

I had prepared a speech in case we won, and I had been careful in it to say that the award was possible only because of the past effects workers, and the optical effects crew. I wanted to be clear that this is our Oscar.

Having received it, I am now much more credible to filmmakers and producers, and I do not have to explain or justify what I did on Star Wars.

The little fellow carries a great deal of weight. "

Robert Blalack
Best Achievement in Visual Effects, 1977

For the second time in Academy Awards history, two performers tied in a single acting category. **Best Actress: Katharine Hepburn** as Eleanor of Aquitaine (above) in *The Lion in Winter* (Avco Embassy; directed by Anthony Harvey) and **Best Actress: Barbra Streisand** as Fannie Brice (below) in *Funny Girl* (Columbia; directed by William Wyler). For Miss Hepburn, it was her 36th film and her third Oscar for acting, a new record, as the estranged wife of aging King Henry II; for Miss Streisand, it was her first film, a recreation and extension of her 1964 Broadway success as Ziegfeld's great musical comedienne.

1968 The Forty-First Year

It almost required a certified public accountant to keep tabs on the records set during the 1968 Oscar Awards, held April 14, 1969. Katharine Hepburn became the first person to win three Academy Awards in either the Best Actor or Best Actress categories (Walter Brennan had earlier won three in the Supporting classification), this time for *The Lion in Winter*. Having also won the preceding year, she became the third individual (following Luise Rainer and Spencer Tracy) to win the honor in consecutive years. Her eleven acting nominations were also a new industry record. Further, Miss Hepburn won the latest award in a tie with Barbra Streisand (for *Funny Girl*), the second time in history two performers had tied for a single Oscar honor.

This tie, however, was precedent setting. In 1931-32, when Fredric March and Wallace Beery were announced as co-winners as Best Actor, a tie was officially declared. The policy then was to award a tie when any runner-up came within three votes of a winner; Beery, it was announced, had come within one vote of March's total. To share the honor under 1968 rules, both Miss Hepburn and Miss Streisand had to receive the exact same number of votes from the Academy's 3,030 voting members.

For the first time in years, the Oscar show also changed residences, moving to the 3,400-seat Dorothy Chandler Pavilion of the Los Angeles Music Center for the Awards presentation. Gower Champion produced, directed and choreographed the program for the Academy, while Richard Dunlap produced and directed for ABC. There was no single M.C.; instead, awards were handed out by a rotating group of ten Friends of Oscar, including Ingrid Bergman, Rosalind Russell, Frank Sinatra, Burt Lancaster, Sidney Poitier, Walter Matthau, Jane Fonda, Natalie Wood, Diahann Carroll and Tony Curtis.

Oliver! received five awards including Best Picture and Best Director (Carol Reed), the biggest total of the evening. Cliff Robertson in *Charly* was named Best Actor, Jack Albertson in *The Subject Was Roses* was Best Supporting Actor and Ruth Gordon in *Rosemary's Baby* was Best Supporting Actress. Russia's mammoth *War and Peace* was chosen Best Foreign Language Film.

Bob Hope, in a brief appearance, received an ovation from the industry audience as did one of his former co-stars, Martha Raye. She was presented the Jean Hersholt Humanitarian Award, the first woman so honored. For the first time in forty years, the actual ceremony was not carried on any radio station, but it was telecast worldwide in thirty-seven countries, in a fifty-six minute capsule version, bringing Oscar and the Awards to an estimated international audience of somewhere between two hundred fifty million and six hundred million people.

Best Actor: Cliff Robertson as Charly Gordon in *Charly* (Cinerama Releasing; directed by Ralph Nelson). Robertson had played Charly on television, as a 1961 U.S. Steel Hour drama, then bought the property and helped bring it to the screen. He played a mentally retarded adult of thirty who undergoes an experimental brain operation and briefly becomes a man of superior intellect before tragically regressing to his former condition. Filming was done in Boston, and Claire Bloom co-starred as a therapist with whom he has a romantic attachment.

Best Picture: Oliver! (Columbia; produced by John Woolf) and **Best Director: Carol Reed** for *Oliver!* Charles Dickens' 130-year-old story *Oliver Twist,* following the adventures of a nine-year-old runaway orphan in 19th-century London, had been filmed eight times as a straight Dickens drama, then was streamlined as a London stage musical in 1960 with music, lyrics and book by Lionel Bart, then became an Academy Award-winning picture. It marked a distinct change of pace for director Carol Reed, best known for mystery-dramas such as those which had won him earlier Oscar nominations, 1949's *The Fallen Idol* and 1950's *The Third Man.* The lively cast included Ron Moody, Oliver Reed, Shani Wallis, Hugh Griffith, Mark Lester and Jack Wild, and *Oliver!* won five Awards, plus a Special Award to Onna White for her choreography.

Nominations 1968

PICTURE

FUNNY GIRL, Rastar, Columbia. Produced by Ray Stark.

THE LION IN WINTER, Haworth, Avco Embassy. Produced by Martin Poll.

★ **OLIVER!**, Romulus, Columbia. Produced by John Woolf.

RACHEL, RACHEL, Kayos, Warner Bros.-Seven Arts. Produced by Paul Newman.

ROMEO AND JULIET, B.H.E.-Verona-De Laurentiis, Paramount. Produced by Anthony Havelock-Allan and John Brabourne.

ACTOR

ALAN ARKIN in *The Heart Is a Lonely Hunter*, Warner Bros.-Seven Arts.

ALAN BATES in *The Fixer*, Frankenheimer-Lewis, M-G-M.

RON MOODY in *Oliver!*, Romulus, Columbia.

PETER O'TOOLE in *The Lion in Winter*, Haworth, Avco Embassy.

★ **CLIFF ROBERTSON** in *Charly*, ABC-Selmur, Cinerama.

ACTRESS

★ **KATHARINE HEPBURN** in *The Lion in Winter*, Haworth, Avco Embassy.

PATRICIA NEAL in *The Subject Was Roses*, M-G-M.

VANESSA REDGRAVE in *Isadora*, Hakim, Universal.

★ **BARBRA STREISAND** in *Funny Girl*, Rastar, Columbia.

JOANNE WOODWARD in *Rachel, Rachel*, Kayos, Warner Bros.-Seven Arts.

SUPPORTING ACTOR

★ **JACK ALBERTSON** in *The Subject Was Roses*, M-G-M.

SEYMOUR CASSEL in *Faces*, Cassavetes, Reade-Continental.

DANIEL MASSEY in *Star!*, Wise, 20th Century-Fox.

JACK WILD in *Oliver!*, Romulus, Columbia.

GENE WILDER in *The Producers*, Glazier, Avco Embassy.

SUPPORTING ACTRESS

LYNN CARLIN in *Faces*, Cassavetes, Reade-Continental.

★ **RUTH GORDON** in *Rosemary's Baby*, Castle, Paramount.

SONDRA LOCKE in *The Heart Is a Lonely Hunter*, Warner Bros.-Seven Arts.

KAY MEDFORD in *Funny Girl*, Rastar, Columbia.

ESTELLE PARSONS in *Rachel, Rachel*, Kayos, Warner Bros.-Seven Arts.

DIRECTION

ANTHONY HARVEY for *The Lion in Winter*, Haworth, Avco Embassy.

STANLEY KUBRICK for *2001: A Space Odyssey*, Polaris, M-G-M.

GILLO PONTECORVO for *The Battle of Algiers*, Igor-Casbah, Allied Artists (Italian).

★ **CAROL REED** for *Oliver!*, Romulus, Columbia.

FRANCO ZEFFIRELLI for *Romeo and Juliet*, B.H.E.-Verona-De Laurentiis, Paramount.

WRITING

(Screenplay—based on material from another medium)

★ **THE LION IN WINTER**, Haworth, Avco Embassy. James Goldman.

THE ODD COUPLE, Koch, Paramount. Neil Simon.

OLIVER!, Romulus, Columbia. Vernon Harris.

RACHEL, RACHEL, Kayos, Warner Bros.-Seven Arts. Stewart Stern.

ROSEMARY'S BABY, Castle, Paramount. Roman Polanski.

(Story and Screenplay—written directly for the screen)

THE BATTLE OF ALGIERS, Igor-Casbah, Allied Artists (Italian). Franco Solinas and Gillo Pontecorvo.

FACES, Cassavetes, Walter Reade-Continental. John Cassavetes.

HOT MILLIONS, Alberg, M-G-M. Ira Wallach and Peter Ustinov.

★ **THE PRODUCERS**, Glazier, Avco Embassy. Mel Brooks.

2001: A SPACE ODYSSEY, Polaris, M-G-M. Stanley Kubrick and Arthur C. Clarke.

CINEMATOGRAPHY

FUNNY GIRL, Rastar, Columbia. Harry Stradling.

ICE STATION ZEBRA, Filmways, M-G-M. Daniel L. Fapp.

OLIVER!, Romulus, Columbia. Oswald Morris.

★ **ROMEO AND JULIET**, B.H.E.-Verona-DeLaurentiis, Paramount. Pasqualino De Santis.

STAR!, Wise, 20th Century-Fox. Ernest Laszlo.

ART DIRECTION-SET DECORATION

★ **OLIVER!**, Romulus, Columbia. John Box and Terence Marsh; Vernon Dixon and Ken Muggleston.

THE SHOES OF THE FISHERMAN, Englund, M-G-M. George W. Davis and Edward Carfagno.

STAR!, Wise, 20th Century-Fox. Boris Leven; Walter M. Scott and Howard Bristol.

2001: A SPACE ODYSSEY, Polaris, M-G-M. Tony Masters, Harry Lange and Ernie Archer.

WAR AND PEACE, Mosfilm, Walter Reade-Continental (Russian). Mikhail Bogdanov and Gennady Myasnikov; G. Koshelev and V. Uvarov.

COSTUME DESIGN

THE LION IN WINTER, Haworth, Avco Embassy. Margaret Furse.

OLIVER!, Romulus, Columbia. Phyllis Dalton.

PLANET OF THE APES, Apjac, 20th Century-Fox. Morton Haack.

★ **ROMEO AND JULIET**, B.H.E.-Verona-DeLaurentiis, Paramount. Danilo Donati.

STAR!, Wise, 20th Century-Fox. Donald Brooks.

SOUND

BULLITT, Solar, Warner Bros.-Seven Arts. Warner Bros.-Seven Arts Studio Sound Dept.

FINIAN'S RAINBOW, Warner Bros.-Seven Arts. Warner Bros.-Seven Arts Studio Sound Dept.

FUNNY GIRL, Rastar, Columbia. Columbia Studio Sound Dept.

★ **OLIVER!**, Romulus, Columbia. Shepperton Studio Sound Dept.

STAR!, Wise, 20th Century-Fox. 20th Century-Fox Studio Sound Dept.

FILM EDITING

★ **BULLITT**, Solar, Warner Bros.-Seven Arts. Frank P. Keller.

FUNNY GIRL, Rastar, Columbia. Robert Swink, Maury Winetrobe and William Sands.

THE ODD COUPLE, Koch, Paramount. Frank Bracht.

OLIVER!, Romulus, Columbia. Ralph Kemplen.

WILD IN THE STREETS, American International. Fred Feitshans and Eve Newman.

SPECIAL VISUAL EFFECTS

ICE STATION ZEBRA, Filmways, M-G-M. Hal Millar and J. McMillan Johnson.

★ **2001: A SPACE ODYSSEY**, Polaris, M-G-M. Stanley Kubrick.

Best Supporting Actor: Jack Albertson as Jack Cleary in *The Subject Was Roses* (M-G-M; directed by Ulu Grosbard). Author Jack Gilroy refused to sell the rights to his Pulitzer Prize-winning play unless it was agreed Jack Albertson would replay his original role in the screen version. Gilroy got his way, and Albertson got an Oscar for his exacting performance as the hostile husband of Patricia Neal, and the vitriolic father of Martin Sheen, living out their damaged lives in a Bronx apartment.

Best Supporting Actress: Ruth Gordon as Minnie Castevet (below, with Mia Farrow) in *Rosemary's Baby* (Paramount; directed by Roman Polanski). Ruth Gordon was no stranger to the Academy's honor rolls when she won her Oscar as a mysterious neighbor (and witch) in Ira Levin's chiller story about dark powers in modern day Manhattan. Earlier nominated as a performer for 1965's *Inside Daisy Clover*, she also has been nominated three times for her screenwriting: for 1947's *A Double Life*, 1949's *Adam's Rib* and and 1952's *Pat and Mike*.

Best Foreign Language Film: War and Peace from Russia (above). It was a truly monumental undertaking, an adaptation of Leo Tolstoy's epic novel, directed by Sergei Bondarchuk, which took five years to film, at a reported cost of $100 million, and ran 7 hours and 14 minutes in its original form (but was cut to 6 hours, 13 minutes for United States distribution). Filled with awesome scenes of a magnitude rarely (if ever) captured on film before, *War and Peace* set a new standard for the grandiose film, and became the first Russian-made film honored by the Academy in its Foreign Language Film Award category. Sergei Bondarchuk directed and co-starred (as Pierre), with Ludmila Savelyeva (as Natasha) and Vyacheslav Tihonov (as Andrei).

MUSIC

(Song)
CHITTY CHITTY BANG BANG (*Chitty Chitty Bang Bang*, Warfield, UA); Music and Lyrics by Richard M. Sherman and Robert B. Sherman.
FOR LOVE OF IVY (*For Love of Ivy*, ABC-Palomar, Cinerama); Music by Quincy Jones, Lyrics by Bob Russell.
FUNNY GIRL (*Funny Girl*, Rastar, Columbia); Music by Jule Styne. Lyrics by Bob Merrill.
STAR! (*Star!*, Wise, 20th Century-Fox); Music by Jimmy Van Heusen. Lyrics by Sammy Cahn.
★ THE WINDMILLS OF YOUR MIND (*The Thomas Crown Affair*, Mirisch-Simkoe-Solar, UA); Music by Michel Legrand. Lyrics by Alan and Marilyn Bergman.

(Original Score—for a motion picture [not a musical])
THE FOX, Stross, Claridge Pictures. Lalo Schifrin.
★ THE LION IN WINTER, Haworth, Avco Embassy. John Barry.
PLANET OF THE APES, Apjac, 20th Century-Fox. Jerry Goldsmith.
THE SHOES OF THE FISHERMAN, Englund, M-G-M. Alex North.
THE THOMAS CROWN AFFAIR, Mirisch-Simkoe-Solar, UA. Michel Legrand.

(Score of a Musical Picture—[original or adaptation])
FINIAN'S RAINBOW, Warner Bros.-Seven Arts. Ray Heindorf.
FUNNY GIRL, Rastar, Columbia. Walter Scharf.
★ OLIVER!, Romulus, Columbia. John Green.
STAR!, Wise, 20th Century-Fox. Lennie Hayton.
THE YOUNG GIRLS OF ROCHEFORT, Warner Bros.- Seven Arts (French). Michel Legrand and Jacques Demy.

SHORT SUBJECTS

(Cartoons)
THE HOUSE THAT JACK BUILT, National Film Board of Canada, Columbia.
Wolf Koenig and Jim MacKay, producers.
THE MAGIC PEAR TREE, Bing Crosby Prods. Jimmy Murakami, producer.
WINDY DAY, Hubley Studios, Paramount. John and Faith Hubley, producers.
★ WINNIE THE POOH AND THE BLUSTERY DAY, Disney, Buena Vista. Walt Disney, producer.

(Live Action Subjects)
THE DOVE, Coe-Davis, Schoenfeld Films. George Coe, Sidney Davis and Anthony Lover, producers.
DUO, National Film Board of Canada, Columbia.
PRELUDE, Prelude Company, Excelsior Dist. John Astin, producer.
★ ROBERT KENNEDY REMEMBERED, Guggenheim Prods., National General. Charles Guggenheim, producer.

DOCUMENTARY

(Short Subjects)
THE HOUSE THAT ANANDA BUILT, Films Division, Government of India. Fali Bilimoria, producer.
THE REVOLVING DOOR, Vision Associates for American Foundation Institute of Corrections. Lee R. Bobker, producer.
A SPACE TO GROW, Office of Economic Opportunity for Project Upward Bound. Thomas P. Kelly, Jr. producer.
A WAY OUT OF THE WILDERNESS, John Sutherland Prods. Dan E. Weisburd, producer.
★ WHY MAN CREATES, Saul Bass & Associates. Saul Bass, producer.

(Features)
A FEW NOTES ON OUR FOOD PROBLEM, U.S. Information Agency. James Blue, producer.
★ JOURNEY INTO SELF, Western Behavioral Sciences Institute. Bill McGaw, producer.
THE LEGENDARY CHAMPIONS, Turn Of The Century Fights. William Cayton, producer.

OTHER VOICES, DHS Films. David H. Sawyer, producer.
YOUNG AMERICANS, The Young Americans Prod. Robert Cohn and Alex Grasshoff, producers.

Note: YOUNG AMERICANS was originally voted the award but later (on May 7, 1969) was declared ineligible after it was learned picture was first shown in a theater in October 1967 and therefore not eligible for a 1968 Award. **JOURNEY INTO SELF**, first runner-up, was announced as the official winner on May 8, 1969.

FOREIGN LANGUAGE FILM

THE BOYS OF PAUL STREET, (Hungary).
THE FIREMEN'S BALL, (Czechoslovakia).
THE GIRL WITH THE PISTOL, (Italy).
STOLEN KISSES, (France).
★ WAR AND PEACE, (Russia).

HONORARY AND OTHER AWARDS

TO JOHN CHAMBERS for his outstanding make-up achievement for *Planet Of The Apes*. (statuette)
TO ONNA WHITE for her outstanding choreography achievement for *Oliver!*. (statuette)

1968 IRVING G. THALBERG MEMORIAL AWARD

None given this year.

1968 JEAN HERSHOLT HUMANITARIAN AWARD

TO MARTHA RAYE

SCIENTIFIC OR TECHNICAL

CLASS I (statuette)
PHILIP V. PALMQUIST of MINNESOTA MINING AND MANUFACTURING CO., to DR. HERBERT MEYER of the MOTION PICTURE AND TELEVISION RESEARCH CENTER, and to CHARLES D. STAFFELL of the RANK ORGANISATION for the development of a successful embodiment of the relfex background projection system for composite cinematography.
EASTMAN KODAK COMPANY for the development and introduction of a color reversal intermediate film for motion pictures.

CLASS II (plaque)
DONALD W. NORWOOD for the design and development of the Norwood Photographic Exposure Meters.
EASTMAN KODAK COMPANY and PRODUCERS SERVICE COMPANY for the development of a new high-speed step-optical reduction printer.
EDMUND M. DiGIULIO, NIELS G. PETERSEN and NORMAN S. HUGHES of the CINEMA PRODUCT DEVELOPMENT COMPANY for the design and application of a conversion which makes available the reflex viewing system for motion picture cameras.
OPTICAL COATING LABORATORIES, INC., for the development of an improved anti-reflection coating for photographic and projection lens systems.
EASTMAN KODAK COMPANY for the introduction of a new high speed motion picture color negative film.
PANAVISION INCORPORATED for the conception, design and introduction of a 65mm hand-held motion picture camera.
TODD-AO COMPANY and the MITCHELL CAMERA COMPANY for the design and engineering of the Todd-AO hand-held motion picture camera.

CLASS III (citation)
CARL W. HAUGE and EDWARD H. REICHARD of CONSOLIDATED FILM INDUSTRIES and E. MICHAEL MEAHL and ROY J. RIDENOUR of RAMTRONICS;
EASTMAN KODAK COMPANY and CONSOLIDATED FILM INDUSTRIES.

★ INDICATES WINNER

1969

The Forty-Second Year

The 1969 Academy Awards had a distinctly western flavor. *Butch Cassidy and the Sundance Kid,* a blockbuster about two turn-of-the-century gunmen, received the most Oscars for the year—four, including two statuettes to composer Burt Bacharach for his music. *Midnight Cowboy,* a stark contemporary drama about a different sort of western 'hero,' won three awards, including Best Picture and Best Director (John Schlesinger). And the most durable cowboy of all, John Wayne, was named Best Actor for *True Grit,* playing a paunchy U.S. marshal.

The Awards were presented April 7, 1970, again at the Dorothy Chandler Pavilion of the Los Angeles Music Center, produced by M.J. Frankovich and directed by Jack Haley, Jr., with Richard Dunlap producing and directing for the ABC-TV network. For the second year, there was no official master of ceremonies, but awards presented by "Friends of Oscar," this time seventeen of them: Bob Hope, John Wayne, Barbra Streisand, Fred Astaire, Jon Voight, Myrna Loy, Clint Eastwood, Raquel Welch, Candice Bergen, James Earl Jones, Katharine Ross, Cliff Robertson, Ali MacGraw, Barbara McNair, Elliott Gould, Claudia Cardinale and —wearing a much-publicized $1.5 million diamond—Elizabeth Taylor.

The year's Best Actress Award went to England's Maggie Smith for *The Prime of Miss Jean Brodie,* Goldie Hawn was named Best Supporting Actress for *Cactus Flower* and Gig Young was chosen Best Supporting Actor for *They Shoot Horses, Don't They?. Z,* nominated in the Best Picture category, was honored as the Best Foreign Language Film, possible under 1969 qualification rules, which were later changed.

Possibly the most popular award of the evening was the Honorary statuette presented to Cary Grant, a durable screen contributor who had never been honored previously by Academy voters. He received a standing ovation after a montage of film clips from his thirty-four-year screen career was shown. Frank Sinatra made the presentation.

Best Actor: John Wayne as Rooster Cogburn (right) in *True Grit* (Paramount; directed by Henry Hathaway). Hollywood's durable Duke, at age 62, celebrated his 40th year in the film business with a towering role and performance, as a hard-drinking, one-eyed old U.S. marshal who helps a young girl (Kim Darby) and a Texas ranger (Glen Campbell) avenge a murder in 1880 Arkansas. Wayne had also been an Academy Award nominee in 1949 for *Sands of Iwo Jima* and again played crusty Rooster in a 1975 sequel, *Rooster Cogburn,* with Katharine Hepburn.

Best Actress: Maggie Smith as Jean Brodie (left) in *The Prime of Miss Jean Brodie* (20th Century-Fox; directed by Ronald Neame). Miss Brodie, an odd and spinsterish Edinburgh schoolteacher with a flair for unconsciously imparting dangerous misinformation to her students, was created on the London stage by Vanessa Redgrave and on Broadway by Zoe Caldwell; in her screen incarnation, she was played by Maggie Smith—and played brilliantly. Earlier, Maggie had been a Supporting Actress nominee for *Othello* (1965), and she was nominated again in 1972 for *Travels with My Aunt.*

Best Picture: Midnight Cowboy (United Artists; produced by Jerome Hellman) and **Best Director: John Schlesinger** for *Midnight Cowboy.* At the time, *Midnight Cowboy* had been given an X-rating by the Motion Picture Association of America, making it the first film with that rating to win the Academy's highest Award; in later years, however, it was re-classified to an R (for Restricted). Tough and hard-hitting, it took a compassionate look at some humanity encased at the bottom of the world, and starred (below) Dustin Hoffman as a sickly con man and Jon Voight as a would-be male hustler, attempting to survive together. It also won an Oscar for Waldo Salt's Screenplay.

Nominations 1969

PICTURE

ANNE OF THE THOUSAND DAYS, Wallis, Universal. Produced by Hal Wallis.

BUTCH CASSIDY AND THE SUNDANCE KID, Hill-Monash, 20th Century-Fox. Produced by John Foreman.

HELLO, DOLLY! Chenault, 20th Century-Fox. Produced by Ernest Lehman.

★ **MIDNIGHT COWBOY,** Hellman-Schlesinger, UA. Produced by Jerome Hellman.

Z, Reggane Films-O.N.C.I.C., Cinema V (Algerian). Produced by Jacques Perrin and Hamed Rachedi.

ACTOR

RICHARD BURTON in *Anne of the Thousand Days,* Wallis, Universal.

DUSTIN HOFFMAN in *Midnight Cowboy,* Hellman-Schlesigner, UA.

PETER O'TOOLE in *Goodbye, Mr. Chips,* Apjac, M-G-M.

JON VOIGHT in *Midnight Cowboy,* Hellman-Schlesigner, UA.

★ **JOHN WAYNE** in *True Grit,* Wallis, Paramount.

ACTRESS

GENEVIEVE BUJOLD in *Anne of the Thousand Days,* Wallis, Universal.

JANE FONDA in *They Shoot Horses, Don't They?,* Chartoff-Winkler-Pollack, ABC Pictures, Cinerama.

LIZA MINNELLI in *The Sterile Cuckoo,* Boardwalk, Paramount.

JEAN SIMMONS in *The Happy Ending,* Pax Films.

★ **MAGGIE SMITH** in *The Prime of Miss Jean Brodie,* 20th Century-Fox.

SUPPORTING ACTOR

RUPERT CROSSE in *The Reivers,* Ravetch-Kramer-Solar, Cinema Center/National General.

ELLIOTT GOULD in *Bob & Carol & Ted & Alice,* Frankovich, Columbia.

JACK NICHOLSON in *Easy Rider,* Pando-Raybert, Columbia.

ANTHONY QUAYLE in *Anne of the Thousand Days,* Wallis, Universal.

★ **GIG YOUNG** in *They Shoot Horses, Don't They?,* Chartoff-Winkler-Pollack/ABC Pictures, Cinerama.

SUPPORTING ACTRESS

CATHERINE BURNS in *Last Summer,* Perry-Alsid, Allied Artists.

DYAN CANNON in *Bob & Carol & Ted & Alice,* Frankovich, Columbia.

★ **GOLDIE HAWN** in *Cactus Flower,* Frankovich, Columbia.

SYLVIA MILES in *Midnight Cowboy,* Hellman-Schlesigner, UA.

SUSANNAH YORK in *They Shoot Horses, Don't They?,* Chartoff-Winkler-Pollack/ABC Pictures, Cinerama.

DIRECTION

COSTA-GAVRAS for *Z,* Reggane Films-O.N.C.I.C., Cinema V (Algerian).

GEORGE ROY HILL for *Butch Cassidy and the Sundance Kid,* Hill-Monash, 20th Century-Fox.

ARTHUR PENN for *Alice's Restaurant,* Florin Prod., UA.

SYDNEY POLLACK for *They Shoot Horses, Don't They?,* Chartoff-Winkler-Pollack, ABC Pictures, Cinerama.

★ **JOHN SCHLESINGER** for *Midnight Cowboy,* Hellman-Schlesinger, UA.

WRITING

(Screenplay—based on material from another medium)

ANNE OF THE THOUSAND DAYS, Wallis, Universal. John Hale, Bridget Boland and Richard Sokolove.

GOODBYE, COLUMBUS, Willow Tree, Paramount. Arnold Schulman.

★ **MIDNIGHT COWBOY,** Hellman-Schlesinger, UA. Waldo Salt.

THEY SHOOT HORSES, DON'T THEY?, Chartoff-Winkler-Pollack, ABC Pictures, Cinerama. James Poe and Robert E. Thompson.

Z, Reggane Films-O.N.C.I.C., Cinema V (Algerian). Jorge Semprun and Costa-Gavras.

(Story and Screenplay—based on material not previously published or produced)

BOB & CAROL & TED & ALICE, Frankovich, Columbia. Paul Mazursky and Larry Tucker.

★ **BUTCH CASSIDY AND THE SUNDANCE KID,** Hill-Monash, 20th Century-Fox. William Goldman.

THE DAMNED, Pegaso-Praesidens, Warner Bros. Nicola Badalucco, Enrico Medioli and Luchino Visconti.

EASY RIDER, Pando-Raybert, Columbia. Peter Fonda, Dennis Hopper and Terry Southern.

THE WILD BUNCH, Feldman, Warner Bros. Walon Green, Roy N. Sickner and Sam Peckinpah.

CINEMATOGRAPHY

ANNE OF THE THOUSAND DAYS, Wallis, Universal. Arthur Ibbetson.

BOB & CAROL & TED & ALICE, Frankovich, Columbia. Charles B. Lang.

★ **BUTCH CASSIDY AND THE SUNDANCE KID,** Hill-Monash, 20th Century-Fox. Conrad Hall.

HELLO, DOLLY! Chenault, 20th Century-Fox. Harry Stradling.

MAROONED, Frankovich-Sturges, Columbia. Daniel Fapp.

ART DIRECTION-SET DECORATION

ANNE OF THE THOUSAND DAYS, Wallis, Universal. Maurice Carter and Lionel Couch; Patrick McLoughlin.

GAILY, GAILY, Mirisch-Cartier, UA. Robert Boyle and George B. Chan; Edward Boyle and Carl Biddiscombe.

★ **HELLO, DOLLY!,** Chenault, 20th Century-Fox. John DeCuir, Jack Martin Smith and Herman Blumenthal; Walter M. Scott, George Hopkins and Raphael Bretton.

SWEET CHARITY, Universal. Alexander Golitzen and George C. Webb; Jack D. Moore.

THEY SHOOT HORSES, DON'T THEY?, Chartoff-Winkler-Pollack, ABC Pictures, Cinerama. Harry Horner; Frank McKelvey.

COSTUME DESIGN

★ **ANNE OF THE THOUSAND DAYS,** Wallis, Universal. Margaret Furse.

GAILY, GAILY, Mirisch-Cartier, UA. Ray Aghayan.

HELLO, DOLLY!, Chenault, 20th Century-Fox. Irene Sharaff.

SWEET CHARITY, Universal. Edith Head.

THEY SHOOT HORSES, DON'T THEY? Chartoff-Winkler-Pollack, ABC Pictures, Cinerama. Donfeld.

Butch Cassidy and the Sundance Kid (20th Century-Fox; produced by John Foreman) told the tongue-in-cheek exploits of two real-life, turn-of-the-century outlaws, played by Paul Newman and Robert Redford (above), was a genuine audience pleaser. It was also the year's most honored film by Academy voters, with four Awards: for Story and Screenplay (by William Goldman), Cinematography (Conrad Hall), Song ("Raindrops Keep Fallin' on My Head" by Burt Bacharach and Hal David) and Original Score of a Non-Musical (Burt Bacharach).

Best Supporting Actor: Gig Young as Rocky in *They Shoot Horses, Don't They?* (Cinerama Releasing; directed by Sydney Pollock). Nominated for Oscars in 1951 for *Come Fill the Cup* and in 1958 for *Teacher's Pet,* and best known as a light comedian, Gig Young won his Academy statuette as a jaded, puffy-eyed and dissipated dance marathon emcee of the Depression years in the drama based on a 1935 novel by Horace McCoy. The cast also included Jane Fonda, Michael Sarrazin, Susannah York, Red Buttons and Bruce Dern.

SOUND

ANNE OF THE THOUSAND DAYS, Wallis, Universal. John Aldred.
BUTCH CASSIDY AND THE SUNDANCE KID, Hill-Monash, 20th Century-Fox. William Edmundson and David Dockendorf.
GAILY, GAILY, Mirisch-Cartier, UA. Robert Martin and Clem Portman.
★ **HELLO, DOLLY!,** Chenault, 20th Century-Fox. Jack Solomon and Murray Spivack.
MAROONED, Frankovich-Sturges, Columbia. Les Fresholtz and Arthur Piantadosi.

FILM EDITING

HELLO, DOLLY!, Chenault, 20th Century-Fox. William Reynolds.
MIDNIGHT COWBOY, Hellman-Schlesinger, UA. Hugh A. Robertson.
THE SECRET OF SANTA VITTORIA, Kramer, UA. William Lyon and Earle Herdan.
THEY SHOOT HORSES, DON'T THEY?, Chartoff-Winkler-Pollack, ABC Pictures, Cinerama. Fredric Steinkamp.
★ **Z,** Reggane Films-O.N.C.I.C., Cinema V (Algerian). Francoise Bonnot.

SPECIAL VISUAL EFFECTS

KRAKATOA, EAST OF JAVA, ABC Pictures, Cinerama. Eugene Lourie and Alex Weldon.
★ **MAROONED,** Frankovich-Sturges, Columbia. Robbie Robertson.

MUSIC

(Song)
COME SATURDAY MORNING (*The Sterile Cuckoo,* Boardwalk, Paramount); Music by Fred Karlin. Lyrics by Dory Previn.
JEAN (*The Prime of Miss Jean Brodie,* 20th Century-Fox); Music and Lyrics by Rod McKuen.
★ **RAINDROPS KEEP FALLIN' ON MY HEAD** (*Butch Cassidy and the Sundance Kid,* Hill-Monash, 20th Century-Fox); Music by Burt Bacharach. Lyrics by Hal David.
TRUE GRIT (*True Grit,* Wallis, Paramount); Music by Elmer Bernstein. Lyrics by Don Black.
WHAT ARE YOU DOING THE REST OF YOUR LIFE? (*The Happy Ending,* Brooks, UA); Music by Michel Legrand. Lyrics by Alan and Marilyn Bergman.

(Original Score—for a motion picture [not a musical])
ANNE OF THE THOUSAND DAYS, Wallis, Universal. Georges Delerue.
★ **BUTCH CASSIDY AND THE SUNDANCE KID,** Hill-Monash, 20th Century-Fox. Burt Bacharach.
THE REIVERS, Ravetch-Kramer-Solar, Cinema Center Films, National General. John Williams.
THE SECRET OF SANTA VITTORIA, Kramer, UA. Ernest Gold.
THE WILD BUNCH, Feldman, Warner Bros. Jerry Fielding.

(Score of a Musical Picture—[original or adaptation])
GOODBYE, MR. CHIPS, Apjac, M-G-M. Leslie Bricusse and John Williams.
★ **HELLO, DOLLY!,** Chenault, 20th Century-Fox. Lennie Hayton and Lionel Newman.
PAINT YOUR WAGON, Lerner, Paramount. Nelson Riddle.
SWEET CHARITY, Universal. Cy Coleman.
THEY SHOOT HORSES, DON'T THEY?, Chartoff-Winkler-Pollack, ABC Pictures, Cinerama. John Green and Albert Woodbury.

SHORT SUBJECTS

(Cartoons)
★ **IT'S TOUGH TO BE A BIRD,** Disney, Buena Vista. Ward Kimball, producer.
OF MEN AND DEMONS, Hubley Studios, Paramount. John and Faith Hubley, producers.

WALKING, National Film Board of Canada, Columbia. Ryan Larkin, producer.

(Live Action Subjects)
BLAKE, National Film Board of Canada, Vaudeo Inc. Doug Jackson, producer.
★ **THE MAGIC MACHINES,** Fly-By-Night Prods., Manson Distributing. Joan Keller Stern, producer.
PEOPLE SOUP, Pangloss Prods., Columbia. Marc Merson, producer.

DOCUMENTARY

(Short Subjects)
★ **CZECHOSLOVAKIA 1968,** Sanders-Fresco Film Makers for U.S. Information Agency. Denis Sanders and Robert M. Fresco, producers.
AN IMPRESSION OF JOHN STEINBECK: WRITER, Donald Wrye Prods. for U.S. Information Agency. Donald Wrye, producer.
JENNY IS A GOOD THING, A.C.I. Prod. for Project Head Start. Joan Horvath, producer.
LEO BEUERMAN, Centron Prod. Arthur H. Wolf and Russell A. Mosser, producers.
THE MAGIC MACHINES, Fly-By-Night Prods., Manson Distributing. Joan Keller Stern, producer.

(Features)
★ **ARTHUR RUBINSTEIN—THE LOVE OF LIFE,** Midem, Prod. Bernard Chevry, producer.
BEFORE THE MOUNTAIN WAS MOVED, Robert K. Sharpe Prods. for The Office of Economic Opportunity. Robert K. Sharpe, producer.
IN THE YEAR OF THE PIG, Emile de Antonio Prod. Emile de Antonio, producer.
THE OLYMPICS IN MEXICO, Film Section of the Organizing Committee for the XIX Olympic Games.
THE WOLF MEN, M-G-M. Irwin Rosten, producer.

FOREIGN LANGUAGE FILM

ADALEN '31, (Sweden).
THE BATTLE OF NERETVA, (Yugoslavia).
THE BROTHERS KARAMAZOV, (U.S.S.R.)
MY NIGHT WITH MAUD, (France).
★ **Z,** (Algeria).

HONORARY AND OTHER AWARDS

TO CARY GRANT for his unique mastery of the art of screen acting with the respect and affection of his colleagues. (statuette)

1969 IRVING G. THALBERG MEMORIAL AWARD

None given this year.

1969 JEAN HERSHOLT HUMANITARIAN AWARD

TO GEORGE JESSEL

SCIENTIFIC OR TECHNICAL

CLASS I (statuette)
None.

CLASS II (plaque)
HAZELTINE CORPORATION for the design and development of the Hazeltine Color Film Analyzer.
FOUAD SAID for the design and introduction of the Cinemobile series of equipment trucks for location motion picture production.
JUAN DE LA CIERVA and **DYNA-SCIENCES CORPORATION** for the design and development of the Dynalens optical image motion compensator.

CLASS III (citation)
OTTO POPELKA of Magna-Tech Electronics Co., Inc.;
FENTON HAMILTON of M-G-M Studios;
PANAVISION INCORPORATED;
ROBERT M. FLYNN and **RUSSELL HESSY** of Universal City Studios, Inc.

★ INDICATES WINNER

Best Supporting Actress: Goldie Hawn as Toni Simmons (below, with Rick Lenz) in *Cactus Flower* (Columbia; directed by Gene Saks). Goldie came to the movies from TV's successful *Laugh-In* series and won the Academy Award for her first post-*Laugh-In* performance, as a kookie Greenwich Village girl pursued by a middle-aged dentist (Walter Matthau) who pretends to be married to an "unfaithful" wife (Ingrid Bergman), who is in reality his dental assistant.

1970 The Forty-Third Year

In a movie year dominated by escalating admission prices at the box office, a widespread invasion of pornographic movies and extensive unemployment among film craftsmen, 20th Century-Fox's *Patton* dominated the 1970 Academy Awards, presented April 15, 1971, at the Dorothy Chandler Pavilion of the Los Angeles Music Center. *Patton* won seven Awards, including Best Picture, Best Actor (George C. Scott), Best Director (Franklin J. Schaffner) and Best Story and Screenplay (Francis Ford Coppola and Edmund H. North).

Scott chose to decline the nomination and the Award, but it remained an Academy Award fact. As explained by then-President of the Academy Daniel Taradash, "Nominations and Awards are voted for achievements as they appear on the screen, therefore a person responsible for the achievement cannot decline the nomination after it is voted. Actually, Mr. Scott is not involved. It is his performance in *Patton* which is involved."

Except for *Patton,* the only other 1970 release to win more than one Award was *Ryan's Daughter,* with two, Best Supporting Actor (John Mills) and Best Cinematography (Freddie Young). The rest of the year's honors were evenly distributed over ten other films, including *Love Story, M*A*S*H, Woodstock, Tora! Tora! Tora!, Cromwell* and Italy's *Investigation of a Citizen Under Suspicion.* Glenda Jackson was named Best Actress for *Women in Love,* and Helen Hayes was named Best Supporting Actress for *Airport.* Miss Hayes, a Best Actress Oscar winner in 1931-32, became the first actor or actress to receive Academy Awards in the two categories honoring performers. The Beatles also became Academy Award winners, for their Best Original Song Score for *Let It Be.*

The telecast was produced for the Academy by Robert E. Wise, and aired over NBC-TV for the first time in eleven years, produced and directed for the network by Richard Dunlap. Award presentation and hosting duties were handled by thirty-two different "Friends of Oscar," including Merle Oberon, Steve McQueen, Jeanne Moreau, Bob Hope, Maggie Smith, Walter Matthau, Joan Blondell and the first Oscar winner, Janet Gaynor. Ingmar Bergman was voted the 1970 Irving G. Thalberg Memorial Award, Frank Sinatra received the Jean Hersholt Humanitarian Award and Honorary Oscars went to two motion picture legends "for their superlative and distinguished service in the making of motion pictures": Lillian Gish and Orson Welles.

Best Picture: Patton (20th Century-Fox; produced by Frank McCarthy); **Best Director: Franklin J. Schaffner** and **Best Actor: George C. Scott** as Gen. George S. Patton, Jr. (right) in *Patton.* Producer McCarthy began in 1951 trying to ignite interest in a screen biography of World War II's flamboyant General Patton, but the project generated no interest for eighteen years, until it received the green light from 20th Century-Fox. In its final form, it turned out to be a brilliant film and a riveting examination of a controversial soldier in wartime, following Patton from 1943 in North Africa when he assumed command of the Second Army, to 1945, just before he died in an auto accident. George C. Scott dominated the film as the complex man—dedicated but disobedient, merciless but compassionate, persevering and swaggering—and *Patton* ultimately received seven Academy Awards, including ones for Story and Screenplay, Art Direction, Sound and Film Editing.

Best Actress: Glenda Jackson as Gudrun Brangwen in *Women in Love* (United Artists; directed by Ken Russell). Glenda Jackson was a powerful, fascinating newcomer to film audiences when she first appeared as D.H. Lawrence's ill-fated Gudrun, at once vulnerable, domineering, confident, brutal and always memorable, caught in a tragic affair with a gruff, earthy coal-mining executive (Oliver Reed). She created her own unique niche as a screen actress, won the Academy Award and, three years later, won a second one for 1973's *A Touch of Class.* She also received nominations in 1971 for *Sunday Bloody Sunday* and in 1975 for *Hedda.*

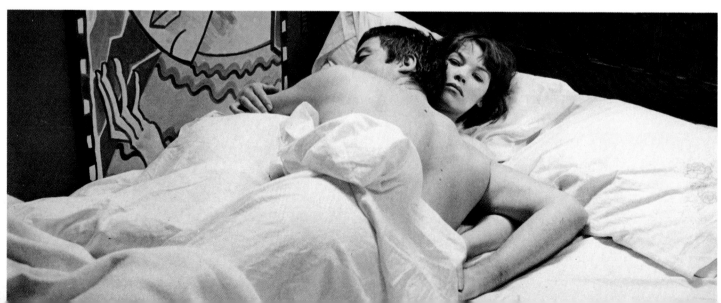

Best Supporting Actor: John Mills as Michael in *Ryan's Daughter* (M-G-M; directed by David Lean). Mills played a gentle but misshapen village mute in David Lean's epic drama, set during the 1916 Irish Revolution and filmed in Ireland and Africa. It was Mills' fifth performance under Lean's direction, and he became the second member of his acting family honored by the Academy; daughter Hayley had won an Honorary Award as a juvenile performer in 1960.

Nominations 1970

PICTURE

AIRPORT, Hunter, Universal. Produced by Ross Hunter.
FIVE EASY PIECES, BBS Productions, Columbia. Produced by Bob Rafelson and Richard Wechsler.
LOVE STORY, Paramount. Produced by Howard G. Minsky.
M*A*S*H, Aspen, 20th Century-Fox. Produced by Ingo Preminger.
★ PATTON, 20th Century-Fox. Produced by Frank McCarthy.

ACTOR

MELVYN DOUGLAS in *I Never Sang for My Father*, Jamel, Columbia.
JAMES EARL JONES in *The Great White Hope*, Turman, 20th Century-Fox.
JACK NICHOLSON in *Five Easy Pieces*, BBS Productions, Columbia.
RYAN O'NEAL in *Love Story*, Paramount.
★ GEORGE C. SCOTT in *Patton*, 20th Century-Fox.

ACTRESS

JANE ALEXANDER in *The Great White Hope*, Turman, 20th Century-Fox.
★ GLENDA JACKSON in *Women in Love*, Kramer-Rosen, UA.
ALI MacGRAW in *Love Story*, Paramount.
SARAH MILES in *Ryan's Daughter*, Faraway, M-G-M.
CARRIE SNODGRESS in *Diary of a Mad Housewife*, Perry, Universal.

SUPPORTING ACTOR

RICHARD CASTELLANO in *Lovers and Other Strangers*, ABC Pictures, Cinerama.
CHIEF DAN GEORGE in *Little Big Man*, Hiller-Stockbridge, Cinema Center Films/National General.
GENE HACKMAN in *I Never Sang for My Father*, Jamel, Columbia.
JOHN MARLEY in *Love Story*, Paramount.
★ JOHN MILLS in *Ryan's Daughter*, Faraway, M-G-M.

SUPPORTING ACTRESS

KAREN BLACK in *Five Easy Pieces*, BBS Productions, Columbia.
LEE GRANT in *The Landlord*, Mirisch-Cartier, UA.
★ HELEN HAYES in *Airport*, Hunter, Universal.
SALLY KELLERMAN in *M*A*S*H*, Aspen, 20th Century-Fox.
MAUREEN STAPLETON in *Airport*, Hunter, Universal.

DIRECTION

ROBERT ALTMAN for *M*A*S*H*, Aspen, 20th Century-Fox.
FEDERICO FELLINI for *Fellini Satyricon*, Grimaldi, UA (Italian).
ARTHUR HILLER for *Love Story*, Paramount.
KEN RUSSELL for *Women in Love*, Kramer-Rosen, UA.
★ FRANKLIN J. SCHAFFNER for *Patton*, 20th Century-Fox.

WRITING

(Screenplay—based on material from another medium)
AIRPORT, Hunter, Universal. George Seaton.
I NEVER SANG FOR MY FATHER, Jamel, Columbia. Robert Anderson.
LOVERS AND OTHER STRANGERS, ABC Pictures, Cinerama. Renee Taylor, Joseph Bologna and David Zelag Goodman.
★ M*A*S*H, Aspen, 20th Century-Fox. Ring Lardner, Jr.
WOMEN IN LOVE, Kramer-Rosen, UA. Larry Kramer.

(Story and Screenplay—based on factual material or material not previously published or produced)
FIVE EASY PIECES, BBS Prods., Columbia. Bob Rafelson and Adrien Joyce.
JOE, Cannon Group, Cannon Releasing. Norman Wexler.
LOVE STORY, Paramount, Erich Segal.
MY NIGHT AT MAUD'S (aka My Night With Maud), Pathe Contemporary (French). Eric Rohmer.
★ PATTON, 20th Century-Fox. Francis Ford Coppola and Edmund H. North.

CINEMATOGRAPHY

AIRPORT, Hunter, Universal. Ernest Laszlo.
PATTON, 20th Century-Fox. Fred Koenekamp.
★ RYAN'S DAUGHTER, Faraway Prods., M-G-M. Freddie Young.
TORA! TORA! TORA!, 20th Century-Fox. Charles F. Wheeler, Osami Furuya, Sinsaku Himeda and Masamichi Satoh.
WOMEN IN LOVE, Kramer-Rosen, UA. Billy Williams.

ART DIRECTION-SET DECORATION

AIRPORT, Hunter, Universal. Alexander Golitzen and E. Preston Ames; Jack D. Moore and Mickey S. Michaels.

THE MOLLY MAGUIRES, Tamm Prods., Paramount. Tambi Larsen; Darrell Silvera.
★ PATTON, 20th Century-Fox. Urie McCleary and Gil Parrondo; Antonio Mateos and Pierre-Louis Thevenet.
SCROOGE, Waterbury Films, Cinema Center Films, National General. Terry Marsh and Bob Cartwright; Pamela Cornell.
TORA! TORA! TORA!, 20th Century-Fox. Jack Martin Smith, Yoshiro Muraki, Richard Day and Taizoh Kawashima; Walter M. Scott, Norman Rockett and Carl Biddiscombe.

COSTUME DESIGN

AIRPORT, Hunter, Universal. Edith Head.
★ CROMWELL, Irving Allen, Columbia. Nino Novarese.
DARLING LILI, Geoffrey Prods., Paramount. Donald Brooks and Jack Bear.
THE HAWAIIANS, Mirisch, UA. Bill Thomas.
SCROOGE, Waterbury Films, Cinema Center Films, National General. Margaret Furse.

SOUND

AIRPORT, Hunter, Universal. Ronald Pierce and David Moriarty.
★ PATTON, 20th Century-Fox. Douglas Williams and Don Bassman.
RYAN'S DAUGHTER, Faraway Prods., M-G-M. Gordon K. McCallum and John Bramall.
TORA! TORA! TORA!, 20th Century-Fox. Murray Spivack and Herman Lewis.
WOODSTOCK, Wadleigh-Maurice, Warner Bros. Dan Wallin and Larry Johnson.

FILM EDITING

AIRPORT, Hunter, Universal. Stuart Gilmore.
M*A*S*H, Aspen, 20th Century-Fox. Danford B. Greene.
★ PATTON, 20th Century-Fox. Hugh S. Fowler.
TORA! TORA! TORA!, 20th Century-Fox. James E. Newcom, Pembroke J. Herring and Inoue Chikaya.
WOODSTOCK, Wadleigh-Maurice, Warner Bros. Thelma Schoonmaker.

SPECIAL VISUAL EFFECTS

PATTON, 20th Century-Fox. Alex Weldon.
★ TORA! TORA! TORA!, 20th Century-Fox. A.D. Flowers and L.B. Abbott.

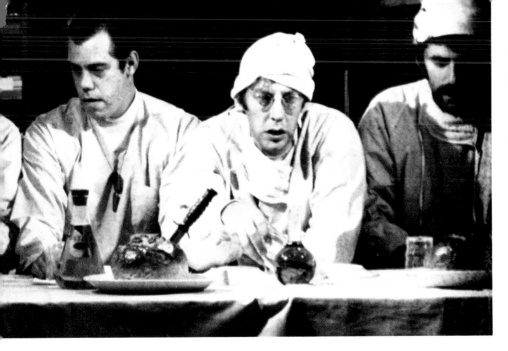

M*A*S*H (20th Century-Fox; produced by Ingo Preminger) was made by director Robert Altman in a snappy 42 days and was a series of adventures and pranks unraveling around a Military Army Surgical Hospital behind the battle lines in Korea. The cast included Donald Sutherland, Elliott Gould, Sally Kellerman, Robert Duvall, Michael Murphy, Gary Burghoff and Bud Cort and it won the Academy Award for Ring Lardner Jr.'s Screenplay. Later, it also became the basis for a successful television series.

Best Supporting Actress: Helen Hayes as Ada Quonsett in *Airport* (Universal; directed by George Seaton). Helen Hayes hadn't made a film in the 14 years since 1956's *Anastasia* when she signed on as the elderly stowaway in *Airport,* inadvertently on a jet flight with a psychopathic bomber among its passengers. A previous Academy winner as Best Actress of 1931-32, she became the first performer to win Oscars in both the leading and the supporting acting categories.

MUSIC

(Song)
* **FOR ALL WE KNOW** (*Lovers and Other Strangers*, ABC Pictures, Cinerama); Music by Fred Karlin. Lyrics by Robb Royer and James Griffin aka Robb Wilson and Arthur James.
PIECES OF DREAMS (*Pieces of Dreams*, RFB Enterprises, UA); Music by Michel Legrand. Lyrics by Alan and Marilyn Bergman.
THANK YOU VERY MUCH (*Scrooge*, Waterbury Films, Cinema Center Films, National General); Music and Lyrics by Leslie Bricusse.
TILL LOVE TOUCHES YOUR LIFE (*Madron*, Four Star-Excelsior Releasing); Music by Riz Ortolani. Lyrics by Arthur Hamilton.
WHISTLING AWAY THE DARK (*Darling Lili*, Geoffrey Prods., Paramount); Music by Henry Mancini. Lyrics by Johnny Mercer.

(Original Score)
AIRPORT, Hunter, Universal. Alfred Newman.
CROMWELL, Irving Allen, Columbia. Frank Cordell.
* LOVE STORY, Paramount. Francis Lai.
PATTON, 20th Century-Fox. Jerry Goldsmith.
SUNFLOWER, Sostar Prod., Avco Embassy. Henry Mancini.

(Original Song Score)
THE BABY MAKER, Robert Wise Prod., National General. Fred Karlin and Tylwyth Kymry.
A BOY NAMED CHARLIE BROWN, Mendelson-Melendez, Cinema Center Films, National General. Rod McKuen, John Scott Trotter, Bill Melendez, Al Shean and Vince Guaraldi.
DARLING LILI, Geoffrey Prods., Paramount. Henry Mancini and Johnny Mercer.
* LET IT BE, Beatles-Apple Prods., UA. The Beatles.
SCROOGE, Waterbury Films, Cinema Center Films, National General. Leslie Bricusse, Ian Fraser and Herbert W. Spencer.

SHORT SUBJECTS

(Cartoons)
THE FURTHER ADVENTURES OF UNCLE SAM: PART TWO, Haboush Company, Goldstone Films. Robert Mitchell and Dale Case, producers.
* IS IT ALWAYS RIGHT TO BE RIGHT?, Stephen Bosustow Prods., Schoenfeld Films. Nick Bosustow, producer.
THE SHEPHERD, Cameron Guess and Associates, Brandon Films. Cameron Guess, producer.

(Live Action Subjects)
* THE RESURRECTION OF BRONCHO BILLY, University of Southern California, Dept. of Cinema, Universal. John Longenecker, producer.
SHUT UP . . . I'M CRYING, Robert Siegler Prods., Schoenfeld Films. Robert Siegler, producer.
STICKY MY FINGERS . . . FLEET MY FEET, American Film Institute, Schoenfeld Films. John Hancock, producer.

DOCUMENTARY

(Short Subjects)
THE GIFTS, Richter-McBride Prods. for The Water Quality Office of the Environmental Protection Agency. Robert McBride, producer.
* INTERVIEWS WITH MY LAI VETERANS, Laser Film Corp. Joseph Strick, producer.
A LONG WAY FROM NOWHERE, Robert Aller Prods. Bob Aller, producer.
OISIN, An Aengus Film. Vivien and Patrick Carey, producers.
TIME IS RUNNING OUT, Gesellschaft fur bildende Filme. Horst Dallmayr and Robert Menegoz, producers.

(Features)
CHARIOTS OF THE GODS, Terra-Filmkumst GmbH. Dr. Harald Reinl, producer.
JACK JOHNSON, The Big Fights. Jim Jacobs, producer.
KING: A FILMED RECORD . . . MONTGOMERY TO MEMPHIS, Commonwealth United Prod. Ely Landau, producer.

SAY GOODBYE, A Wolper Prod. David H. Vowell, producer.
* WOODSTOCK, Wadleigh-Maurice. Warner Bros. Bob Maurice, producer.

FOREIGN LANGUAGE FILM

FIRST LOVE, (Switzerland).
HOA-BINH, (France).
* INVESTIGATION OF A CITIZEN ABOVE SUSPICION, (Italy).
PAIX SUR LES CHAMPS, (Belgium).
TRISTANA, (Spain).

HONORARY AND OTHER AWARDS

TO LILLIAN GISH for superlative artistry and for distinguished contribution to the progress of motion pictures. (statuette)
TO ORSON WELLES for superlative artistry and versatility in the creation of motion pictures. (statuette)

1970 IRVING G. THALBERG MEMORIAL AWARD

TO INGMAR BERGMAN

1970 JEAN HERSHOLT HUMANITARIAN AWARD

TO FRANK SINATRA

SCIENTIFIC OR TECHNICAL

CLASS I (statuette)
None.

CLASS II (plaque)
LEONARD SOKOLOW and EDWARD H. REICHARD of Consolidated Film Industries for the concept and engineering of the Color Proofing Printer for motion pictures.

CLASS III (citation)
SYLVANIA ELECTRIC PRODUCTS, INC.;
B.J. LOSMANDY;
EASTMAN KODAK COMPANY and PHOTO ELECTRONICS CORPORATION;
ELECTRO SOUND INCORPORATED.

* **INDICATES WINNER**

1971 The Forty-Fourth Year

Charles Chaplin, just a week away from his eighty-third birthday, returned to Hollywood for the first time in twenty years to receive the Academy's Honorary Oscar, officially for "the incalculable effect he has had in making motion pictures the art form of the century." Out of respect, no other Special Awards were voted for 1971, and the presentation to Chaplin by Jack Lemmon was the evening's last order of business on April 10, 1972, at the Dorothy Chandler Pavilion of the Los Angeles Music Center. Chaplin had received a Special Academy Award at the very first Oscar ceremony (for achievement during 1927-28) but had not been honored subsequently for his work. It was undeniably a high point of the evening, and brought unusually heavy international attention to the Academy and the Oscars.

The French Connection received the most Academy Awards of any 1971 film, winning five, including Best Picture, Best Actor (Gene Hackman) and Best Director (William Friedkin). Fiddler on the Roof won three awards, The Last Picture Show garnered two (for Best Supporting Actor Ben Johnson and Best Supporting Actress Cloris Leachman), Nicholas and Alexandra received two, and seven others won one each. Jane Fonda was chosen the year's Best Actress for her performance in Klute, and Italy's The Garden of the Finzi-Continis was named Best Foreign Language Film. Isaac Hayes' "Theme from Shaft" was the Oscar winner for Best Song, and was the subject of spectacular staging by Ron Field during the night's telecast on NBC-TV.

Howard W. Koch produced the telecast for the Academy, Robert Finkel was the executive producer for the network, and Marty Pasetta directed the telecast. Helen Hayes, Alan King, Sammy Davis, Jr. and Jack Lemmon shared master of ceremony turns, and presenters included Frank Capra, Tennessee Williams, Raquel Welch, Betty Grable and Dick Haymes.

Among the highlights of the night, in addition to Hollywood's welcome back to the legendary Chaplin, was a knockout opening number called "Lights, Camera, Action." It was choreographed by Ron Field, written by Billy Barnes, interpreted by Joel Grey and took a swooping musical look at Hollywood's past.

Best Picture: The French Connection and **Best Actor: Gene Hackman** as Detective Jimmy Doyle in The French Connection (20th Century-Fox; produced by Philip D'Antoni). From the best-selling book by Robin Moore, based on experiences of two real-life detectives (Eddie "Popeye" Egan and Sonny Grosso) who stumbled onto a case in 1962 which involved the seizure of $32 million in heroin smuggled into New York from Marseilles, this was action moviemaking at its best. Also among the best: Hackman's performance as the colorful Egan (here renamed Doyle). The film's giant success inspired a 1975 sequel, French Connection II, again starring Hackman.

Best Director: William Friedkin for The French Connection. Friedkin (right) was new to motion picture circles when he made Connection; he had, in fact, made only four previous films (1967's Good Times, 1968's The Birthday Party and The Night They Raided Minsky's, 1970's The Boys in the Band) but had a solid background as a television director of commercials, dramatic shows and documentaries. Later, in 1977, he produced the Academy's own annual Oscar telecast.

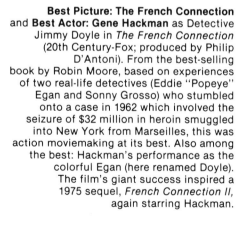

Best Supporting Actor: Ben Johnson as Sam the Lion in *The Last Picture Show* (Columbia; directed by Peter Bogdanovich). Johnson, a 30-year veteran of cinematic sagebrush wars, had his finest film role to date as a graying old cowboy in a decaying Texas town, circa 1951, who owned the local pool hall, cafe and movie theater, and befriended teenagers Sonny (Timothy Bottoms) and Duane (Jeff Bridges). Said Bogdanovich: "Having Ben Johnson in the picture was having the real thing."

Best Actress: Jane Fonda as Bree in *Klute* (Warner Bros.; directed by Alan Pakula). Previously nominated in 1969 as Best Actress for *They Shoot Horses, Don't They?*, actress Fonda won for her skillful portrait of a worn-but-wise Manhattan call girl threatened by an unknown, would-be killer. Donald Sutherland played the title role of Klute, the detective who helped Bree set a trap for her shadowy assailant.

Best Supporting Actress: Cloris Leachman as Ruth Popper in *The Last Picture Show* (Columbia; directed by Peter Bogdanovich). In her Oscar-winning role, she played the lonely, sexually deprived wife of a small town coach who stumbles into an affair with one of her husband's high school students (Timothy Bottoms) and is eventually deserted by him. Says the actress: "I based my characterization on some Ruth Poppers I knew when I was growing up in Des Moines."

Nicholas and Alexandra (Columbia; produced by Sam Spiegel) was based on the mammoth historical novel by Robert K. Massie and starred (at right) Michael Jayston and Janet Suzman as the ill-fated Russian royalty whose family was executed on July 16, 1918. Sumptuously produced and tastefully made, it won two Academy Awards, for Art Direction/Set Decoration and for Costume Design.

Nominations 1971

PICTURE

A CLOCKWORK ORANGE, Hawk Films, Warner Bros. Produced by Stanley Kubrick.
FIDDLER ON THE ROOF, Mirisch-Cartier, UA. Produced by Norman Jewison.
★ THE FRENCH CONNECTION, D'Antoni-Schine-Moore, 20th Century-Fox. Produced by Philip D'Antoni.
THE LAST PICTURE SHOW, BBS Productions, Columbia. Produced by Stephen J. Friedman.
NICHOLAS AND ALEXANDRA, Horizon, Columbia. Produced by Sam Spiegel.

ACTOR

PETER FINCH in Sunday Bloody Sunday, Janni, UA.
★ GENE HACKMAN in The French Connection, D'Antoni-Schine-Moore, 20th Century-Fox.
WALTER MATTHAU in Kotch, ABC Pictures, Cinerama.
GEORGE C. SCOTT in The Hospital, Gottfried-Chayefsky-Hiller, UA.
TOPOL in Fiddler on the Roof, Mirisch-Cartier, UA.

ACTRESS

JULIE CHRISTIE in McCabe & Mrs. Miller, Altman-Foster, Warner Bros.
★ JANE FONDA in Klute, Gus, Warner Bros.
GLENDA JACKSON in Sunday Bloody Sunday, Janni, UA.
VANESSA REDGRAVE in Mary, Queen of Scots, Wallis, Universal.
JANET SUZMAN in Nicholas and Alexandra, Horizon, Columbia.

SUPPORTING ACTOR

JEFF BRIDGES in The Last Picture Show, BBS Productions, Columbia.
LEONARD FREY in Fiddler on the Roof, Mirisch-Cartier, UA.
RICHARD JAECKEL in Sometimes a Great Notion, Newman-Foreman, Universal.
★ BEN JOHNSON in The Last Picture Show, BBS Productions, Columbia.
ROY SCHEIDER in The French Connection, D'Antoni-Schine-Moore, 20th Century-Fox.

SUPPORTING ACTRESS

ELLEN BURSTYN in The Last Picture Show, BBS Productions, Columbia.
BARBARA HARRIS in Who is Harry Kellerman and Why Is He Saying Those Terrible Things About Me?, Cinema Center Films/National General.
★ CLORIS LEACHMAN in The Last Picture Show, BBS Productions, Columbia.
MARGARET LEIGHTON in The Go-Between, World Film Services, Columbia.
ANN-MARGRET in Carnal Knowledge, Icarus, Avco Embassy.

DIRECTION

PETER BOGDANOVICH for The Last Picture Show, BBS Prods., Columbia.
★ WILLIAM FRIEDKIN for The French Connection, 20th Century-Fox.
NORMAN JEWISON for Fiddler on the Roof, Mirisch-Cartier, UA.
STANLEY KUBRICK for A Clockwork Orange, Hawks Films, Warner Bros.
JOHN SCHLESINGER for Sunday Bloody Sunday, Janni, UA.

WRITING

(Screenplay—based on material from another medium)
A CLOCKWORK ORANGE, Hawks Films, Warner Bros. Stanley Kubrick.
THE CONFORMIST, Paramount (Italian). Bernardo Bertolucci.
★ THE FRENCH CONNECTION, 20th Century-Fox. Ernest Tidyman.
THE GARDEN OF THE FINZI-CONTINIS, Cinema V (Italian). Ugo Pirro and Vittorio Bonicelli.
THE LAST PICTURE SHOW, BBS Prods., Columbia. Larry McMurtry and Peter Bogdanovich.

(Story and Screenplay—based on factual material or material not previously published or produced)
★ THE HOSPITAL, Gottfried-Chayefsky-Hiller, UA. Paddy Chayefsky.
INVESTIGATION OF A CITIZEN ABOVE SUSPICION, Columbia (Italian). Elio Petri and Ugo Pirro.
KLUTE, Gus Prod., Warner Bros. Andy and Dave Lewis.

SUMMER OF '42, Mulligan-Roth, Warner Bros. Herman Raucher.
SUNDAY BLOODY SUNDAY, Janni, UA. Penelope Gilliatt.

ART DIRECTION-SET DECORATION

THE ANDROMEDA STRAIN, Robert Wise Prods., Universal. Boris Leven and William Tuntke; Ruby Levitt.
BEDKNOBS AND BROOMSTICKS, Disney, Buena Vista. John B. Mansbridge and Peter Ellenshaw; Emile Kuri and Hal Gausman.
FIDDLER ON THE ROOF, Mirisch-Cartier, UA. Robert Boyle and Michael Stringer; Peter Lamont.
MARY, QUEEN OF SCOTS, Wallis, Universal. Terence Marsh and Robert Cartwright; Peter Howitt.
★ NICHOLAS AND ALEXANDRA, Horizon, Columbia. John Box, Ernest Archer, Jack Maxsted and Gil Parrondo; Vernon Dixon.

COSTUME DESIGN

BEDKNOBS AND BROOMSTICKS, Disney, Buena Vista. Bill Thomas.
DEATH IN VENICE, Alfa Cinematografica-P.E.C.F., Warner Bros. Piero Tosi.
MARY, QUEEN OF SCOTS, Wallis, Universal. Margaret Furse.
★ NICHOLAS AND ALEXANDRA, Horizon, Columbia. Yvonne Blake and Antonio Castillo.
WHAT'S THE MATTER WITH HELEN? Filmways-Raymax, UA. Morton Haack.

SOUND

DIAMONDS ARE FOREVER, Broccoli-Saltzman, UA. Gordon K. McCallum, John Mitchell and Alfred J. Overton.
★ FIDDLER ON THE ROOF, Mirisch-Cartier, UA. Gordon K. McCallum and David Hildyard.
THE FRENCH CONNECTION, 20th Century-Fox. Theodore Soderberg and Christopher Newman.
KOTCH, ABC Pictures, Cinerama. Richard Portman and Jack Solomon.
MARY, QUEEN OF SCOTS, Wallis, Universal. Bob Jones and John Aldred.

FILM EDITING

THE ANDROMEDA STRAIN, Robert Wise Prod., Universal. Stuart Gilmore and John W. Holmes.
A CLOCKWORK ORANGE, Hawks Films, Warner Bros. Bill Butler.
★ THE FRENCH CONNECTION, 20th Century-Fox. Jerry Greenberg.
KOTCH, ABC Pictures, Cinerama. Ralph E. Winters.
SUMMER OF '42, Mulligan-Roth, Warner Bros. Folmar Blangsted.

CINEMATOGRAPHY

★ FIDDLER ON THE ROOF, Mirisch-Cartier, UA. Oswald Morris.
THE FRENCH CONNECTION, 20th Century-Fox. Owen Roizman.
THE LAST PICTURE SHOW, BBS Prods., Columbia. Robert Surtees.
NICHOLAS AND ALEXANDRA, Horizon, Columbia. Freddie Young.
SUMMER OF '42, Mulligan-Roth, Warner Bros. Robert Surtees.

SHORT SUBJECTS

(New classification: designation of first category changed from 'cartoons' to 'animated films')

(Animated Films)
★ THE CRUNCH BIRD, Maxwell-Petok-Petrovich Prods., Regency Films. Ted Petok, producer.
EVOLUTION, National Film Board of Canada. Columbia. Michael Mills, producer.
THE SELFISH GIANT, Potterton Prods., Pyramid Films. Peter Sander and Murray Shostak, producers.

(Live Action Films)
GOOD MORNING, E/G Films, Seymour Borde & Associates. Denny Evans and Ken Greenwald, producers.
THE REHEARSAL, Cinema Verona Prod., Schoenfeld Films. Stephen F. Verona, producer.
★ SENTINELS OF SILENCE, Producciones Concord, Paramount. Manuel Arango and Robert Amram, producers.

Fiddler on the Roof (United Artists; produced by Norman Jewison) won three Oscars: for Cinematography, Music Scoring and Sound. At the time it was put on film, *Fiddler* had become Broadway's all-time longest-running stage play; on film, Topol (right) played the likeable milkman named Tevye who had his hands full with five marriageable daughters, a sharp-tongued wife, and a lame horse.

Special Honorary Award to **Charles Chaplin** (above). On the eve of his 83rd birthday, he was born April 16, 1889), the movies' legendary Charlie-the-Tramp returned to the town he helped create in order to receive an Honorary Oscar from the Academy's Board of Governors. He received a standing ovation from the in-theater audience of 3,200 and, repressing tears, said simply, "Words seem, oh, so futile, so feeble. This is a very emotional moment for me. You are wonderful . . . sweet people." Then, once more, he donned the Tramp's bowler hat.

MUSIC

(Song)

THE AGE OF NOT BELIEVING (*Bedknobs and Broomsticks*, Disney, Buena Vista); Music and Lyrics by Richard M. Sherman and Robert B. Sherman.
ALL HIS CHILDREN (*Sometimes a Great Notion*, Newman-Foreman, Universal); Music by Henry Mancini. Lyrics by Alan and Marilyn Bergman.
BLESS THE BEASTS & CHILDREN (*Bless the Beasts & Children*, Columbia); Music and Lyrics by Barry DeVorzon and Perry Botkin, Jr.
LIFE IS WHAT YOU MAKE IT (*Kotch*, ABC Pictures, Cinerama); Music by Marvin Hamlisch. Lyrics by Johnny Mercer.
★ **THEME FROM SHAFT** (*Shaft*, M-G-M); Music and Lyrics by Isaac Hayes.

(Original Dramatic Score)

MARY, QUEEN OF SCOTS, Wallis, Universal. John Barry.
NICHOLAS AND ALEXANDRA, Horizon, Columbia. Richard Rodney Bennett.
SHAFT, M-G-M. Isaac Hayes.
STRAW DOGS, ABC Pictures, Cinerama. Jerry Fielding.
★ **SUMMER OF '42**, Mulligan-Roth, Warner Bros. Michel Legrand.

(Scoring: Adaptation and Original Song Score)

BEDKNOBS AND BROOMSTICKS, Disney, Buena Vista. Richard M. Sherman, Robert B. Sherman and Irwin Kostal.
THE BOY FRIEND, Russflix, M-G-M. Peter Maxwell Davies and Peter Greenwell.
★ **FIDDLER ON THE ROOF**, Mirisch-Cartier, UA. John Williams.
TCHAIKOVSKY, Dimitri Tiomkin-Mosfilm Studios (U.S.S.R.). Dimitri Tiomkin.
WILLY WONKA AND THE CHOCOLATE FACTORY, Wolper, Paramount. Leslie Bricusse, Anthony Newley and Walter Scharf.

SPECIAL VISUAL EFFECTS

(Not given as an annual Award after this year)

★ **BEDKNOBS AND BROOMSTICKS**, Disney, Buena Vista. Alan Maley, Eustace Lycett and Danny Lee.
WHEN DINOSAURS RULED THE EARTH, Hammer, Warner Bros. Jim Danforth and Roger Dicken.

DOCUMENTARY

(Short Subjects)

ADVENTURES IN PERCEPTION, Han van Gelder Filmproduktie for Netherlands Information Service. Han van Gelder, producer.
ART IS . . ., Henry Strauss Associates for Sears Roebuck Foundation. Julian Krainin and DeWitt L. Sage, Jr., producers.
THE NUMBERS START WITH THE RIVER, A WH Picture for U.S. Information Agency. Donald Wrye, producer.
★ **SENTINELS OF SILENCE**, Producciones Concord, Paramount. Manuel Arango and Robert Amram, producers.
SOMEBODY WAITING, Snider Prods., for University of California Medical Film Library. Hal Riney, Dick Snider and Sherwood Omens, producers.

(Features)

ALASKA WILDERNESS LAKE, Alan Landsburg Prods. Alan Landsburg, producer.
★ **THE HELLSTROM CHRONICLE**, David L. Wolper, Cinema V. Walon Green, producer.
ON ANY SUNDAY, Brown-Solar, Cinema V. Bruce Brown, producer.
THE RA EXPEDITIONS, Swedish Broadcasting Company, Interwest Film Corp. Lennart Ehrenborg and Thor Heyerdahl, producers.
THE SORROW AND THE PITY, Cinema V (French). Marcel Ophuls, producer.

FOREIGN LANGUAGE FILM

DODES'KA-DEN, (Japan)
THE EMIGRANTS, (Sweden)
★ **THE GARDEN OF THE FINZI-CONTINIS**, (Italy)
THE POLICEMAN, (Israel)
TCHAIKOVSKY, (U.S.S.R.)

HONORARY AND OTHER AWARDS

TO CHARLES CHAPLIN for the incalculable effect he has had in making motion pictures the art form of this century. (statuette)

1971 IRVING G. THALBERG MEMORIAL AWARD

None given this year.

1971 JEAN HERSHOLT HUMANITARIAN AWARD

None given this year.

SCIENTIFIC OR TECHNICAL

CLASS I (statuette)
None.

CLASS II (plaque)
JOHN N. WILKINSON of Optical Radiation Corporation for the development and engineering of a system of xenon arc lamphouses for motion picture projection.

CLASS III (citation)
THOMAS JEFFERSON HUTCHINSON, JAMES R. ROCHESTER and **FENTON HAMILTON**;
PHOTO RESEARCH, A Division of Kollmorgen Corporation;
ROBERT D. AUGUSTE and **CINEMA PRODUCTS CO.**;
PRODUCERS SERVICE CORPORATION and **CONSOLIDATED FILM INDUSTRIES**; and to **CINEMA RESEARCH CORPORATION** and **RESEARCH PRODUCTS, INC.**; **CINEMA PRODUCTS CO.**

★ **INDICATES WINNER**

1972 The Forty-Fifth Year

The Godfather and *Cabaret* dominated the 1972 Academy Awards presentations, March 27, 1973, held for the fifth year at the Dorothy Chandler Pavilion of the Los Angeles Music Center and telecast on NBC-TV. *Cabaret* won eight Awards, including Best Actress (Liza Minnelli), Best Director (Bob Fosse) and Best Supporting Actor (Joel Grey), more than any other picture in Academy history which didn't go on to also win the Best Picture statuette. That Award went to *The Godfather,* along with Awards for Best Actor (Marlon Brando) and Best Screenplay (Mario Puzo and Francis Ford Coppola). Brando rejected the Award—his second as Best Actor—and had his reasons read by a young Indian girl, Sacheen Littlefeather, later identified as an actress named Maria Cruz. His primary objections were to the industry's treatment of Indians in films, on TV and in movie reruns.

The Awards were produced by Howard W. Koch and directed by Marty Pasetta. M.C.s were Carol Burnett, Michael Caine, Charlton Heston and Rock Hudson; Heston fell victim to a flat tire on his way to the ceremony and arrived fifteen minutes after his first show entrance was scheduled, so Clint Eastwood briefly did stand-in duty.

Among the musical segments was an opulent opening, "Make a Little Magic," written by Billy Barnes, choreographed by Carl Jablonski and featuring Angela Lansbury, in the tradition of bygone Hollywood musical production numbers. A musical salute to Walt Disney Studios' fiftieth anniversary, featured, among others, the durable Mickey Mouse.

The Jean Hersholt Humanitarian Award went to Rosalind Russell, and other Honorary Awards went to the late Edward G. Robinson, industry veteran Charles Boren and to *The Poseidon Adventure* for its Special Visual Effects. Eileen Heckart was named Best Supporting Actress for *Butterflies Are Free,* France's *The Discreet Charm of the Bourgeoisie* was selected as Best Foreign Language Film. And, as in the preceding year, Charles Chaplin was once again an Academy Award winner. Along with the late Raymond Rasch and Larry Russell, he won the 1972 Best Original Dramatic Score Award for *Limelight,* a movie made in 1952. Its belated eligibility was due to the fact the film had never been shown in the Los Angeles until 1972, and only then qualified for Award consideration.

There was also a new rule in 1972 related to Short Subjects and Documentary eligibility. For the first time, Short Subjects which also qualified as Documentary Short Subjects could compete in either category, but not in both, as in previous years. The choice of area consideration was to be designated by the producers involved at the time the entry was submitted to the Academy for preliminary voting.

Best Picture: The Godfather (Paramount; produced by Albert Ruddy) and **Best Actor: Marlon Brando** as Don Vito Corleone in *The Godfather.* Mario Puzo's powerful and popular novel about organized crime made a bang-up movie, rich in detail and performances, as it inspected the fall of a powerful Cosa Nostra chieftan (Brando, above) and the concurrent rise to power of his son, a fresh-faced Ivy Leaguer who becomes a cool, lethal hood (played by Al Pacino). Brando, at age 46, was almost unrecognizable as the elderly Italian Don, and he dominated the film, which included in its cast Robert Duvall, Talia Shire, Morgana King, James Caan (all below, with Brando) plus Diane Keaton, Richard Conte, Sterling Hayden and others, directed by Francis Ford Coppola. Two years later, there was a sequel: *The Godfather Part II,* which also became an Academy Award-winning Best Picture of the Year.

Best Director: Bob Fosse, and (pictured, right) Best Actress: Liza Minnelli as Sally Bowles and Best Supporting Actor: Joel Grey as the master of ceremonies in *Cabaret* (ABC Pictures/Allied Artists; produced by Cy Feuer). *Cabaret* was the newest reincarnation of Christopher Isherwood's original *Berlin Stories* (earlier made into a 1951 play and a 1955 movie called *I Am a Camera*) and focused on five lives tangled together in pre-Hitler Germany of the 1930s. Liza Minnelli was the "divinely decadent" and available cabaret singer with green fingernails, saucer eyes and flexible morals; Joel Grey recreated his Broadway role of the white-faced, rouge-lipped M.C. of the Kit Kat Klub who symbolized the decay which helped the Nazi menace gain momentum, while no one really bothered to be concerned.

Best Supporting Actress: Eileen Heckart as Mrs. Baker in *Butterflies Are Free* (Columbia; directed by Milton Katselas). Re-creating her original 1969 Broadway role, she played a Hillsborough mother who has difficulty cutting the umbilical cord from a blind son (Edward Albert, left, with Miss Heckart) who wants to live in his own San Francisco apartment and attempt to make it without Mama. It was her second Academy nomination (the first one: 1956's *Bad Seed*), and her first win.

Nominations 1972

PICTURE

CABARET, ABC Pictures, Allied Artists. Produced by Cy Feuer.
DELIVERANCE, Warner Bros. Produced by John Boorman.
THE EMIGRANTS, Svensk Filmindustri, Warner Bros. (Swedish). Produced by Bengt Forslund.
✷ **THE GODFATHER,** Ruddy, Paramount. Produced by Albert S. Ruddy.
SOUNDER, Radnitz/Mattel, 20th Century-Fox. Produced by Robert B. Radnitz.

ACTOR

✷ **MARLON BRANDO** in *The Godfather*, Ruddy, Paramount.
MICHAEL CAINE in *Sleuth*, Palomar, 20th Century-Fox.
LAURENCE OLIVIER in *Sleuth*, Palomar, 20th Century-Fox.
PETER O'TOOLE in *The Ruling Class*, Keep Films, Avco Embassy.
PAUL WINFIELD in *Sounder*, Radnitz/Mattel, 20th Century-Fox.

ACTRESS

✷ **LIZA MINNELLI** in *Cabaret*, ABC Pictures, Allied Artists.
DIANA ROSS in *Lady Sings the Blues*, Motown-Weston-Furie, Paramount.
MAGGIE SMITH in *Travels With My Aunt*, Fryer, M-G-M.
CICELY TYSON in *Sounder*, Radnitz/Mattel, 20th Century-Fox.
LIV ULLMANN in *The Emigrants*, Svensk Filmindustri, Warner Bros. (Swedish).

SUPPORTING ACTOR

EDDIE ALBERT in *The Heartbreak Kid*, Palomar, 20th Century-Fox.
JAMES CAAN in *The Godfather*, Ruddy, Paramount.
ROBERT DUVALL in *The Godfather*, Ruddy, Paramount.
✷ **JOEL GREY** in *Cabaret*, ABC Pictures, Allied Artists.
AL PACINO in *The Godfather*, Ruddy, Paramount.

SUPPORTING ACTRESS

JEANNIE BERLIN in *The Heartbreak Kid*, Palomar, 20th Century-Fox.
✷ **EILEEN HECKART** in *Butterflies Are Free*, Frankovich, Columbia.
GERALDINE PAGE in *Pete 'N' Tillie*, Ritt-Epstein, Universal.

SUSAN TYRRELL in *Fat City*, Rastar, Columbia.
SHELLEY WINTERS in *The Poseidon Adventure*, Irwin Allen, 20th Century-Fox.

DIRECTION

JOHN BOORMAN for *Deliverance*, Warner Bros.
FRANCIS FORD COPPOLA for *The Godfather*, Ruddy, Paramount.
✷ **BOB FOSSE** for *Cabaret*, ABC Pictures, Allied Artists.
JOSEPH L. MANKIEWICZ for *Sleuth*, Palomar, 20th Century-Fox.
JAN TROELL for *The Emigrants*, Svensk Filmindustri, Warner Bros. (Swedish)

WRITING

(Screenplay—Based on Material From Another Medium)
CABARET, ABC Pictures, Allied Artists. Jay Allen.
THE EMIGRANTS, Svensk Filmindustri, Warner Bros. (Swedish). Jan Troell and Bengt Forslund.
✷ **THE GODFATHER,** Ruddy, Paramount. Mario Puzo and Francis Ford Coppola.
PETE 'N' TILLIE, Ritt-Epstein, Universal. Julius J. Epstein.
SOUNDER, Radnitz/Mattel, 20th Century-Fox. Lonne Elder, III.

(Story and Screenplay—based on factual material or material not previously published or produced)
✷ **THE CANDIDATE,** Redford-Ritchie, Warner Bros. Jeremy Larner.
THE DISCREET CHARM OF THE BOURGEOISIE, Silberman, 20th Century-Fox (French). Luis Bunuel and Jean-Claude Carriere.
LADY SINGS THE BLUES, Motown-Weston-Furie, Paramount. Terence McCloy, Chris Clark and Suzanne de Passe.
MURMUR OF THE HEART, Continental Distributing (French). Louis Malle.
YOUNG WINSTON, Open Road Films, Columbia. Carl Foreman.

CINEMATOGRAPHY

BUTTERFLIES ARE FREE, Frankovich, Columbia. Charles B. Lang.
✷ **CABARET,** ABC Pictures, Allied Artists. Geoffrey Unsworth.
THE POSEIDON ADVENTURE, Irwin Allen, 20th Century-Fox. Harold E. Stine.
"1776," Jack L. Warner, Columbia. Harry Stradling, Jr.
TRAVELS WITH MY AUNT, Fryer, M-G-M. Douglas Slocombe.

ART DIRECTION-SET DECORATION

✷ **CABARET,** ABC Pictures, Allied Artists. Rolf Zehetbauer and Jurgen Kiebach. Herbert Strabel.
LADY SINGS THE BLUES, Motown-Weston-Furie, Paramount. Carl Anderson; Reg Allen.
THE POSEIDON ADVENTURE, Irwin Allen, 20th Century-Fox. William Creber; Raphael Bretton.
TRAVELS WITH MY AUNT, Fryer, M-G-M. John Box, Gil Parrondo and Robert W. Laing.
YOUNG WINSTON, Open Road Films, Columbia. Don Ashton, Geoffrey Drake, John Graysmark and William Hutchinson; Peter James.

COSTUME DESIGN

THE GODFATHER, Ruddy, Paramount. Anna Hill Johnstone.
LADY SINGS THE BLUES, Motown-Weston-Furie, Paramount. Bob Mackie, Ray Aghayan and Norma Koch.
THE POSEIDON ADVENTURE, Irwin Allen, 20th Century-Fox. Paul Zastupnevich.
✷ **TRAVELS WITH MY AUNT,** Fryer, M-G-M. Anthony Powell.
YOUNG WINSTON, Open Road Films, Columbia. Anthony Mendleson.

SOUND

BUTTERFLIES ARE FREE, Frankovich, Columbia. Arthur Piantadosi and Charles Knight.
✷ **CABARET,** ABC Pictures, Allied Artists. Robert Knudson and David Hildyard.
THE CANDIDATE, Redford-Ritchie, Warner Bros. Richard Portman and Gene Cantamessa.
THE GODFATHER, Ruddy, Paramount. Bud Grenzbach, Richard Portman and Christopher Newman.
THE POSEIDON ADVENTURE, Irwin Allen, 20th Century-Fox. Theodore Soderberg and Herman Lewis.

FILM EDITING

✷ **CABARET,** ABC Pictures, Allied Artists. David Bretherton.
DELIVERANCE, Warner Bros. Tom Priestley.
THE GODFATHER, Ruddy, Paramount. William Reynolds and Peter Zinner.
THE HOT ROCK, Landers-Roberts, 20th Century-Fox. Frank P. Keller and Fred W. Berger.
THE POSEIDON ADVENTURE, Irwin Allen, 20th Century-Fox. Harold F. Kress.

The Poseidon Adventure (20th Century-Fox; produced by Irwin Allen) received a Special Achievement Award for the Visual Effects of A.D. Flowers and L.B. Abbott who, as a team, helped capsize in mid-ocean a fictional luxury liner named the Poseidon, necessitating its cast (including Gene Hackman, Shelley Winters, Ernest Borgnine, Jack Albertson and Red Buttons) to climb upward, through more special effects hazards, to safety. *Poseidon* also received another Oscar, for Al Kasha and Joel Hirschhorn's song, ''The Morning After.''

SHORT SUBJECTS

(Animated Films)
★ A CHRISTMAS CAROL, American Broadcasting Company Film Services. Richard Williams, producer.
KAMA SUTRA RIDES AGAIN, Lion International Films. Bob Godfrey, producer.
TUP TUP, Zagreb Film-Corona Cinematografica, Manson Distributing. Nedeljko Dragic, producer.

(Live Action Films)
FROG STORY, Gidron Productions, Schoenfeld Films. Ron Satlof and Ray Gideon, producers.
★ NORMAN ROCKWELL'S WORLD . . . AN AMERICAN DREAM, Concepts Unlimited, Columbia. Richard Barclay, producer.
SOLO, Pyramid Films, UA. David Adams, producer.

DOCUMENTARY

(Short Subjects)
HUNDERTWASSER'S RAINY DAY, Argos Films-Schamoni Film Prod. Peter Schamoni, producer.
K-Z, Nexus Films. Giorgio Treves, producer.
SELLING OUT, Unit Productions Films. Tadeusz Jaworski, producer.
★ THIS TINY WORLD, A Charles Huguenot van der Linden Production. Charles and Martina Huguenot van der Linden, producers.
THE TIDE OF TRAFFIC, BP-Greenpark. Humphrey Swingler, producer.

(Features)
APE AND SUPER-APE, Netherlands Ministry of Culture, Recreation and Social Welfare. Bert Haanstra, producer.
MALCOLM X, Warner Bros. Marvin Worth and Arnold Perl, producers.
MANSON, Merrick International. Robert Hendrickson and Laurence Merrick, producers.
★ MARJOE, Cinema X, Cinema 5, Ltd. Howard Smith and Sarah Kernochan, producers.
THE SILENT REVOLUTION, Leonaris Films. Eckehard Munck, producer.

FOREIGN LANGUAGE FILM

THE DAWNS HERE ARE QUIET, (U.S.S.R.).
★ THE DISCREET CHARM OF THE BOURGEOISIE, (France).
I LOVE YOU ROSA, (Israel).
MY DEAREST SENORITA, (Spain).
THE NEW LAND, (Sweden).

MUSIC

(Song)
BEN (*Ben,* Bing Crosby Prods., Cinerama); Music by Walter Scharf. Lyrics by Don Black.
COME FOLLOW, FOLLOW ME (*The Little Ark,* Radnitz, Cinema Center Films, National General); Music by Fred Karlin. Lyrics by Marsha Karlin.
MARMALADE, MOLASSES & HONEY (*The Life and Times of Judge Roy Bean,* First Artists, National General); Music by Maurice Jarre. Lyrics by Marilyn and Alan Bergman.
★ THE MORNING AFTER (*The Poseidon Adventure,* Irwin Allen, 20th Century-Fox); Music and Lyrics by Al Kasha and Joel Hirschhorn.

STRANGE ARE THE WAYS OF LOVE (*The Stepmother,* Crown International); Music by Sammy Fain. Lyrics by Paul Francis Webster.

(Original Dramatic Score)
IMAGES, Hemdale-Lion's Gate Films, Columbia. John Williams.
★ LIMELIGHT, Charles Chaplin, Columbia. Charles Chaplin, Raymond Rasch and Larry Russell.
NAPOLEON AND SAMANTHA, Disney, Buena Vista. Buddy Baker.
THE POSEIDON ADVENTURE, Irwin Allen, 20th Century-Fox. John Williams.
SLEUTH, Palomar Pictures, 20th Century-Fox. John Addison.
(Note: *The Godfather* score, composed by Nino Rota, was originally announced as one of the five official nominees, but was later declared ineligible and withdrawn when it was disclosed portions of the composition had previously been used in Rota's score for 1958 Italian film *Fortunella.* Additionally, *Limelight,* made in 1952, was belatedly eligible for 1972 consideration because it had not previously been shown in a Los Angeles theater as Academy rules require.)

(Scoring: Adaptation and Original Song Score)
★ CABARET, ABC Pictures, Allied Artists. Ralph Burns.
LADY SINGS THE BLUES, Motown-Weston-Furie, Paramount. Gil Askey.
MAN OF LA MANCHA, PEA Produzioni Europee Associate Prod., UA. Laurence Rosenthal.

SPECIAL ACHIEVEMENT AWARD
(New classification)
For Visual Effects: **L.B. ABBOTT** and **A.D. FLOWERS** for *The Poseidon Adventure,* Irwin Allen, 20th Century-Fox.

HONORARY AND OTHER AWARDS

TO CHARLES S. BOREN, Leader for 38 years of the industry's enlightened labor relations and architect of its policy of non-discrimination. With the respect and affection of all who work in films. (statuette)

TO EDWARD G. ROBINSON who achieved greatness as a player, a patron of the arts and a dedicated citizen . . . in sum, a Renaissance man. From his friends in the industry he loves. (statuette)

1972 IRVING G. THALBERG MEMORIAL AWARD
None given this year.

1972 JEAN HERSHOLT HUMANITARIAN AWARD
TO ROSALIND RUSSELL

SCIENTIFIC OR TECHNICAL

CLASS I (statuette)
None.

CLASS II (plaque)
JOSEPH E. BLUTH for research and development in the field of electronic photography and transfer of video tape to motion picture film.
EDWARD H. REICHARD and HOWARD T. LA ZARE of Consolidated Film Industries, and EDWARD EFRON of IBM for the engineering of a computerized light valve monitoring system for motion picture printing.
PANAVISION INCORPORATED for the development and engineering of the Panaflex motion picture camera.

CLASS III (citation)
PHOTO RESEARCH, a Division of Kollmorgen Corporation, and PCS TECHNOLOGY INC., Acme Products Division;
CARTER EQUIPMENT COMPANY, INC. and RAMTRONICS;
DAVID DEGENKOLB, HARRY LARSON, MANFRED MICHELSON and FRED SCOBEY of Deluxe General Inc.;
JIRO MUKAI and RYUSHO HIROSE of Canon, Inc. and WILTON R. HOLM of the AMPTP Motion Picture and Television Research Center;
PHILIP V. PALMQUIST and LEONARD L. OLSON of the 3M Company, and FRANK P. CLARK of the AMPTP Motion Picture and Television Research Center;
E.H. GEISSLER and G.M. BERGGREN of Wil-Kin Inc.

★ INDICATES WINNER

1973 The Forty-Sixth Year

"I'm the living proof someone can wait forty-one years to be unselfish," Katharine Hepburn told the Academy Awards audience April 2, 1974, gathered to honor 1973 motion picture achievements. Miss Hepburn had won three Academy Awards as Best Actress in the past—an Oscar record—but had never attended an Academy presentation before. She put aside her own dislike of public appearances to appear at the Dorothy Chandler Pavilion of the Los Angeles Music Center and present the Academy's Irving G. Thalberg Memorial Award to her friend producer Lawrence Weingarten. Wearing a black Mao-type pantsuit, she told the surprised, delighted audience, "I'm so glad no one called out, "It's about time!" Susan Hayward also made a rare public appearance which, unknown at the time, would be her final one.

The Sting won a total of seven 1973 Academy Awards, including Best Picture, Best Director (George Roy Hill), and Best Costume Design (Edith Head, her eighth Oscar, an industry record among women). Jack Lemmon was named Best Actor for *Save the Tiger;* it was his second Oscar, but his first in that category, having won previously as the Best Supporting Actor of 1955 in *Mister Roberts.* Glenda Jackson also became a two-time Academy Award winner, named Best Actress for *A Touch of Class,* after winning three years before in that same category. John Houseman, age seventy-one and best known as a distinguished producer, was chosen Best Supporting Actor in *The Paper Chase,* and Tatum O'Neal, age ten, became the youngest winner ever in a competitive Academy Awards category when she was named Best Supporting Actress in *Paper Moon.*

Marvin Hamlisch set a new Oscar record when he won all three of the year's music awards: Best Song (with Alan and Marilyn Bergman), Best Original Dramatic Score, and Best Scoring. Special Awards went to comedian Groucho Marx and French film curator Henri Langlois, and Lew Wasserman of Universal/MCA received the Jean Hersholt Humanitarian Award.

Jack Haley, Jr. produced the show, Marty Pasetta directed for NBC and hosting duties were handled by John Huston, Diana Ross, Burt Reynolds and David Niven. Liza Minnelli performed a vivacious opening number, "Oscar," written especially for the night by Fred Ebb and John Kanter, staged by Broadway's Ron Field.

Moments before David Niven announced Elizabeth Taylor as one of the evening's presenters, there was another Oscar first: a streaker, fully stripped, unexpectedly charged across the large Music Center stage. "Isn't it fascinating," quipped Niven, "to think that probably the only laugh that man will ever get in his life is by stripping off his clothes and showing his shortcomings."

Best Actor: Jack Lemmon as Harry Stoner (above) in *Save the Tiger* (Paramount; directed by John G. Avildsen). Lemmon had been a Supporting Oscar winner in 1955 for *Mister Roberts* and a nominee in 1959 (for *Some Like It Hot*), 1960 (for *The Apartment*) and 1962 (for *Days of Wine and Roses*). As *Tiger*'s Harry Stoner, he won his second Award, but his first as Best Actor, playing a middle-aged, disillusioned businessman living through a day of crisis in which he comes to grips with the realization his great American dream has gone far astray. The film was a pet project of producer-writer Steve Shagan and, said Lemmon, "I'm very proud of the film we finally got. I also believe very deeply in what it has to say."

Best Picture: The Sting (Universal; produced by Tony Bill, Michael and Julia Phillips) starred Robert Shaw and (left) Robert Redford, Paul Newman and was lightweight, impish and diverting; it was also a movie-movie that brilliantly accomplished exactly what it set out to do: entertain. *The Sting* not only possessed a soundtrack bouncing with ragtime tunes by the late Scott Joplin (adapted by Marvin Hamlisch) but contained enough plot twists, deceptions, counteractions and complications by screenwriter David S. Ward to fill a dozen films, as con men Redford and Newman get revenge on a racketeer (Shaw) by fleecing him in a phony off-track horse-betting ploy. Set in the Depression days, the film opened with Universal Studios' old trademark logo of that era, which hadn't been used in decades.

Best Actress: Glenda Jackson as Vicki Allessio (right) in *A Touch of Class* (Avco Embassy; directed by Melvin Frank). Three years after winning her first Academy Award (for 1970's dramatic *Women in Love*), Glenda Jackson was again a winner, this time in a comedy role, as a partially liberated, London-based business woman of the 1970s, laboriously trying to have a light love affair with an American fellow who's married (George Segal). "I gave both my Oscars to my mother in Cheshire," she said. "It's not that I don't treasure them, but if I display them in my own home, I'm afraid people will think I'm big-headed."

Nominations 1973

PICTURE

AMERICAN GRAFFITI, Universal-Lucasfilm, Ltd.- Coppola Co. Prod., Universal. Francis Ford Coppola, producer, Gary Kurtz, co-producer.
CRIES AND WHISPERS, Svenska Filminstitutet-Cinematograph AB Prod., New World Pictures. Ingmar Bergman, producer.
THE EXORCIST, Hoya Prods., Warner Bros. William Peter Blatty, producer.
★ **THE STING**, Universal-Bill/Phillips-George Roy Hill Film Prod., Zanuck/Brown Presentation, Universal. Tony Bill, Michael and Julia Phillips, producers.
A TOUCH OF CLASS, Brut Prods., Avco Embassy. Melvin Frank, producer.

ACTOR

MARLON BRANDO in *Last Tango in Paris*, UA.
★ **JACK LEMMON** in *Save the Tiger*, Filmways-Jalem-Cirandinha, Paramount.
JACK NICHOLSON in *The Last Detail*, Acrobat, Columbia.
AL PACINO in *Serpico*, De Laurentiis, Paramount.
ROBERT REDFORD in *The Sting*, Bill/Phillips-Hill, Zanuck/Brown, Universal.

ACTRESS

ELLEN BURSTYN in *The Exorcist*, Hoya, Warner Bros.
★ **GLENDA JACKSON** in *A Touch of Class*, Brut, Avco Embassy.
MARSHA MASON in *Cinderella Liberty*, Sanford, 20th Century-Fox.
BARBRA STREISAND in *The Way We Were*, Rastar, Columbia.
JOANNE WOODWARD in *Summer Wishes, Winter Dreams*, Rastar, Columbia.

SUPPORTING ACTOR

VINCENT GARDENIA in *Bang the Drum Slowly*, Rosenfield, Paramount.
JACK GILFORD in *Save the Tiger*, Filmways-Jalem-Cirandinha, Paramount.

★ **JOHN HOUSEMAN** in *The Paper Chase*, Thompson-Paul, 20th Century-Fox.
JASON MILLER in *The Exorcist*, Hoya, Warner Bros.
RANDY QUAID in *The Last Detail*, Acrobat, Columbia.

SUPPORTING ACTRESS

LINDA BLAIR in *The Exorcist*, Hoya, Warner Bros.
CANDY CLARK in *American Graffiti*, Lucasfilm-Coppola, Universal.
MADELINE KAHN in *Paper Moon*, Directors Company, Paramount.
★ **TATUM O'NEAL** in *Paper Moon*, Directors Company, Paramount.
SYLVIA SIDNEY in *Summer Wishes, Winter Dreams*, Rastar, Columbia.

DIRECTION

INGMAR BERGMAN for *Cries And Whispers*, New World Pictures (Swedish).
BERNARDO BERTOLUCCI for *Last Tango in Paris*, UA.
WILLIAM FRIEDKIN for *The Exorcist*, Hoya Prods., Warner Bros.
★ **GEORGE ROY HILL** for *The Sting*, Bill/Phillips-Hill-Zanuck/Brown, Universal.
GEORGE LUCAS for *American Graffiti*, Lucasfilm/Coppola Company, Universal.

WRITING

(Best Screenplay—based on material from another medium)
★ **THE EXORCIST**, Hoya Prods., Warner Bros. William Peter Blatty.
THE LAST DETAIL, Acrobat Films, Columbia. Robert Towne.
THE PAPER CHASE, Thompson-Paul Prods., 20th Century-Fox. James Bridges.
PAPER MOON, Directors Company, Paramount. Alvin Sargent.
SERPICO, De Laurentiis, Paramount. Waldo Salt and Norman Wexler.

(Best Story and Screenplay—based on factual material or material not previously published or produced)
AMERICAN GRAFFITI, Lucasfilm/Coppola Company, Universal. George Lucas, Gloria Katz and Willard Huyck.

CRIES AND WHISPERS, New World Pictures (Swedish). Ingmar Bergman.
SAVE THE TIGER, Filmways-Jalem-Cirandinha, Paramount. Steve Shagan.
★ **THE STING**, Bill/Phillips-Hill-Zanuck/Brown, Universal. David S. Ward.
A TOUCH OF CLASS, Brut, Avco Embassy. Melvin Frank and Jack Rose.

CINEMATOGRAPHY

★ **CRIES AND WHISPERS**, New World Pictures (Swedish). Sven Nykvist.
THE EXORCIST, Hoya Prods., Warner Bros. Owen Roizman.
JONATHAN LIVINGSTON SEAGULL, Bartlett, Paramount. Jack Couffer.
THE STING, Bill/Phillips-Hill-Zanuck/Brown, Universal. Robert Surtees.
THE WAY WE WERE, Rastar, Columbia. Harry Stradling, Jr.

ART DIRECTION-SET DECORATION

BROTHER SUN SISTER MOON, Euro International-Vic Film Ltd., Paramount. Lorenzo Mongiardino and Gianni Quaranta; Carmelo Patrono.
THE EXORCIST, Hoya Prods., Warner Bros. Bill Malley; Jerry Wunderlich.
★ **THE STING**, Bill/Phillips-Hill-Zanuck/Brown, Universal. Henry Bumstead; James Payne.
TOM SAWYER, Jacobs, Reader's Digest, UA. Philip Jefferies; Robert de Vestel.
THE WAY WE WERE, Rastar, Columbia. Stephen Grimes; William Kiernan.

COSTUME DESIGN

CRIES AND WHISPERS, New World Pictures (Swedish). Marik Vos.
LUDWIG, Mega Film S.p.A. Prod., M-G-M. Piero Tosi.
★ **THE STING**, Bill/Phillips-Hill-Zanuck/Brown, Universal. Edith Head.
TOM SAWYER, Jacobs, Reader's Digest, UA. Donfeld.
THE WAY WE WERE, Rastar, Columbia. Dorothy Jeakins and Moss Mabry.

SOUND

THE DAY OF THE DOLPHIN, Icarus, Avco Embassy. Richard Portman and Lawrence O. Jost.
★ **THE EXORCIST**, Hoya Prods., Warner Bros. Robert Knudson and Chris Newman.

Best Supporting Actress: Tatum O'Neal as Addie Pray (above) in *Paper Moon* (Paramount; directed by Peter Bogdanovich). Tatum, age 10 and a first-time performer, co-starred with her real-life father, Ryan O'Neal, as a street-wise, cigarette-puffing moppet in the Depression days of the 1930s who teams up with a dandy; together, they con their way into billfolds all across Kansas and Missouri, bilking without a blink. With her win, Tatum became the youngest recipient to date to be voted an Oscar in a regular Academy Awards category.

Best Supporting Actor: John Houseman as Professor Kingsford (left) in *The Paper Chase* (20th Century-Fox; directed by James Bridges). Houseman, age 71, had acted in only one previous film (1964's *Seven Days in May*) but between 1945-1962 he had produced 18 important features (including *The Bad and the Beautiful, Julius Caesar* and *Lust for Life*) and was also a stalwart contributor to the legitimate theater. He stepped into his *Paper Chase* role when previously-signed James Mason had to bow out, and then won the Oscar for his playing of an academic dictator in Harvard's law school, a man who looms over his students (including Timothy Bottoms, Edward Herrmann and James Naughton) like a quietly-arrogant Goliath.

Best Director: George Roy Hill (right, with Paul Newman and Robert Redford) for *The Sting.* Initially an actor and then a TV writer, Hill first received wide notice as a producer-director-writer during television's creative 1950s, and later moved on to Broadway as a director. Beginning in 1962, he shifted his talents to the films and in 1969 received his first Academy Awards nomination, for directing Newman and Redford in *Butch Cassidy and the Sundance Kid.* After that, everyone was on the lookout for an appropriate project to reteam the trio, and then came *The Sting.* And an Oscar for the multi-talented man who called its shots.

THE PAPER CHASE, Thompson-Paul Prods., 20th Century-Fox. Donald O. Mitchell and Lawrence O. Jost.
PAPER MOON, Directors Company, Paramount. Richard Portman and Les Fresholtz.
THE STING, Bill/Phillips-Hill-Zanuck/Brown, Universal. Ronald K. Pierce and Robert Bertrand.

FILM EDITING

AMERICAN GRAFFITI, Lucasfilm/Coppola Company, Universal. Verna Fields and Marcia Lucas.
THE DAY OF THE JACKAL, Warwick Films, Universal. Ralph Kemplen.
THE EXORCIST, Hoya Prods., Warner Bros. Jordan Leondopoulos, Bud Smith, Evan Lottman and Norman Gay.
JONATHAN LIVINGSTON SEAGULL, Bartlett, Paramount. Frank P. Keller and James Galloway.
* THE STING, Bill/Phillips-Hill-Zanuck/Brown, Universal. William Reynolds.

MUSIC

(Song)
ALL THAT LOVE WENT TO WASTE (*A Touch of Class,* Brut, Avco Embassy); Music by George Barrie. Lyrics by Sammy Cahn.
LIVE AND LET DIE (*Live and Let Die,* Eon, UA); Music and Lyrics by Paul and Linda McCartney.
LOVE (*Robin Hood,* Disney, Buena Vista); Music by George Bruns. Lyrics by Floyd Huddleston.
* THE WAY WE WERE (*The Way We Were,* Rastar, Columbia); Music by Marvin Hamlisch. Lyrics by Alan and Marilyn Bergman.
NICE TO BE AROUND (*Cinderella Liberty,* Sanford Prod., 20th Century-Fox); Music by John Williams. Lyrics by Paul Williams.

(Best Original Dramatic Score)
CINDERELLA LIBERTY, Sanford Prod., 20th Century-Fox. John Williams.

THE DAY OF THE DOLPHIN, Icarus Prods., Avco Embassy, Georges Delerue.
PAPILLON, Corona-General Productions, Allied Artists. Jerry Goldsmith.
A TOUCH OF CLASS, Brut, Avco Embassy. John Cameron.
* THE WAY WE WERE, Rastar, Columbia. Marvin Hamlisch.

(Best Scoring: Original Song Score and/or Adaptation)
JESUS CHRIST SUPERSTAR, Jewison-Stigwood, Universal. Andre Previn, Herbert Spencer and Andrew Lloyd Webber.
* THE STING, Bill/Phillips-Hill-Zanuck/Brown, Universal. Marvin Hamlisch.
TOM SAWYER, Jacobs, Reader's Digest, UA. Richard M. Sherman, Robert B. Sherman and John Williams.

SHORT SUBJECTS

(Animated Films)
* FRANK FILM, Frank Mouris Production, Frank Mouris, producer.
THE LEGEND OF JOHN HENRY, Bosustow-Pyramid Films. Nick Bosustow and David Adams, producers.
PULCINELLA, Luzzati-Gianini Prod. Emanuele Luzzati and Guilio Gianini, producers.

(Live Action Films)
* THE BOLERO, Allan Miller Production. Allan Miller and William Fertik, producers.
CLOCKMAKER, James Street Prods. Richard Gayer, producer.
LIFE TIMES NINE, Insight Prods. Pen Densham and John Watson, producers.

DOCUMENTARY

(Short Subjects)
BACKGROUND, D'Avino and Fucci-Stone Prods. Carmen D'Avino, producer.

CHILDREN AT WORK, (Paisti Ag Obair), Gael-Linn Films. Louis Marcus, producer.
CHRISTO'S VALLEY CURTAIN, Maysles Films. Albert and David Maysles, producers.
FOUR STONES FOR KANEMITSU, A Tamarind Prod. (producer credit is not established.)
* PRINCETON: A SEARCH FOR ANSWERS, Krainin-Sage Prods. Julian Krainin and DeWitt L. Sage, Jr., producers.

(Features)
ALWAYS A NEW BEGINNING, Goodell Motion Pictures. John D. Goodell, producer.
BATTLE OF BERLIN, Chronos Film. Bengt von zur Muehlen, producer.
* THE GREAT AMERICAN COWBOY, Merrill-Rodeo Film Prods. Kieth Merrill, producer.
JOURNEY TO THE OUTER LIMITS, National Geographic Society and Wolper Prods. Alex Grasshoff, producer.
WALLS OF FIRE, Mentor Prods. Gertrude Ross Marks and Edmund F. Penney, producers.

FOREIGN LANGUAGE FILM

* DAY FOR NIGHT, (France).
THE HOUSE ON CHELOUCHE STREET, (Israel).
L'INVITATION, (Switzerland).
THE PEDESTRIAN, (Federal Republic of West Germany).
TURKISH DELIGHT, (The Netherlands).

HONORARY AND OTHER AWARDS

TO HENRI LANGLOIS for his devotion to the art of film, his massive contributions in preserving its past and his unswerving faith in its future. (statuette)
TO GROUCHO MARX in recognition of his brilliant creativity and for the unequalled achievements of the Marx Brothers in the art of motion picture comedy. (statuette)

SPECIAL ACHIEVEMENT AWARD

None given this year.

1973 IRVING G. THALBERG MEMORIAL AWARD

TO LAWRENCE WEINGARTEN

1973 JEAN HERSHOLT HUMANITARIAN AWARD

TO LEW WASSERMAN

SCIENTIFIC OR TECHNICAL

CLASS I (statuette)
None.

CLASS II (plaque)
JOACHIM GERB and ERICH KASTNER of The Arnold and Richter Company for the development and engineering of the Arriflex 35BL motion-picture camera.
MAGNA-TECH ELECTRONIC CO., INC. for the engineering and development of a high-speed re-recording system for motion-picture production.
WILLIAM W. VALLIANT of PSC Technology Inc., HOWARD F. OTT of Eastman Kodak Company, and GERRY DIEBOLD of The Richmark Camera Service Inc. for the development of a liquid-gate system for motion picture printers.
HAROLD A. SCHEIB, CLIFFORD H. ELLIS and ROGER W. BANKS of Research Products Incorporated for the concept and engineering of the Model 2101 optical printer for motion-picture optical effects.

CLASS III (citation)
ROSCO LABORATORIES, INC.;
RICHARD H. VETTER of the Todd-AO Corporation.

* INDICATES WINNER

Best Actor: Art Carney as Harry in *Harry and Tonto* (20th Century-Fox; directed by Paul Mazursky). *Harry and Tonto* was a series of gentle vignettes with 55-year-old Art Carney as a 72-year-old widower who gets evicted from his New York apartment and decides to open up his shrinking world by traveling cross-country with his cat, Tonto; at the end of their journey, he loses Tonto to old age but has regained his own vitality and self-esteem. It was one of the year's most pleasant movie surprises with an unusual theme for the blood-and-thunder 1970s: life is available to anyone, at any age, who wants it.

1974 The Forty-Seventh Year

Motion picture showmanship was fully evident during 1974 via a number of so-called "disaster" epics (or, according to some, "survival" pictures), most of them laden with famous faces, spectacular special effects and a nerve-wracking premise which audiences could vicariously enjoy without leaving the safety of their theater seats. When 1974 Academy Awards for achievement were handed out, April 8, 1975, at the Dorothy Chandler Pavilion of the Los Angeles Music Center, two of the "disaster" genre were well represented: *The Towering Inferno* with three technical Awards, and *Earthquake* with two, including a Special Achievement Award for Special Effects.

The most conspicuous films of the night, however, had less to do with awesome effects than they did with powerhouse melodrama: *Chinatown* and *The Godfather Part II,* both from Paramount Studios, were each nominated for eleven Oscars. When the award totals were tallied, *Chinatown* won one (for Robert Towne's Best Original Screenplay), and *The Godfather Part II* received six, including Best Picture, Best Director (Francis Ford Coppola), Best Supporting Actor (Robert De Niro) and Best Adapted Screenplay (Coppola and Mario Puzo). It thus became the first motion picture sequel to win the Academy's Best Picture statuette, just as the original, *The Godfather,* had done two years before.

In other categories, Art Carney was named Best Actor (for *Harry and Tonto*), Ellen Burstyn was chosen Best Actress (for *Alice Doesn't Live Here Anymore*) and Ingrid Bergman won her third Academy Award, as Best Supporting Actress in *Murder on the Orient Express,* the first time she had been honored in that division (she had previously won as Best Actress in 1945 and in 1956). She also became the first Academy winner to devote an acceptance speech to praise the virtues of a competitor. After complimenting the performance of fellow nominee Valentina Cortese in *Day for Night,* she charmingly complained, "Now I'm her rival, and I don't like it at all. Please forgive me, Valentina. I didn't mean to (win) . . ." Special Awards went to directors Howard Hawks and Jean Renoir, and Italy's *Amarcord* was named Best Foreign Language Film.

The ceremony was again telecast on NBC, with a quartet of master of ceremonies in charge: Sammy Davis, Jr., Bob Hope, Shirley MacLaine and Frank Sinatra. Howard W. Koch produced the show, and Marty Pasetta directed.

During the program, there was some controversy over the political implications in a telegram read by producer Bert Schneider when he accepted an Oscar for his Best Documentary Feature *Hearts and Minds,* a film about the Vietnamese war; before the show ended, an impromptu disclaimer in the name of the Academy was read from the stage by Frank Sinatra. Since Article II of the Academy's bylaws specifically state that "The Academy is expressly prohibited from concerning itself with economic, political or labor issues," it was thought best to make the announcement, as Sinatra did, "The Academy is not responsible for any political references on this program, and we are sorry that they had to take place this evening."

Best Picture: The Godfather Part II (Paramount; produced by Francis Ford Coppola) and **Best Supporting Actor: Robert De Niro** as Vito Corleone (above) in *The Godfather Part II.* A mammoth and magnificent follow-up to 1972's Academy Award-winning *The Godfather,* it showed the rise to power of the young Vito Corleone, played by De Niro, and the decline of his son Michael (played by Al Pacino) a decade later, shifting back and forth in time between the two generations and forming a prologue and epilogue around the first *Godfather* feature. It became the first sequel to an Oscar-winning film to duplicate the Award success of its predecessor and, by virtue of De Niro's own Academy Award, it also marked the first time two different actors (De Niro, and Marlon Brando as Vito Corleone in the original *Godfather*) received Oscars for playing variations of the same role.

Best Actress: Ellen Burstyn as Alice Hyatt in *Alice Doesn't Live Here Anymore* (Warner Bros.; directed by Martin Scorsese). The script had been rejected by several producers and stars before Ellen Burstyn found it, and played the spunky new widow who works her way across the Southwest, with a 12-year-old son in tow, singing in dives and working in hash houses as she attempts to reconstruct her life. She had earlier been nominated for Academy Awards in 1971 as Supporting Actress in *The Last Picture Show* and in 1973 as Best Actress in *The Exorcist,* and *Alice* became the basis for a successful weekly television series starring Linda Lavin.

Nominations 1974

PICTURE

CHINATOWN, Evans, Paramount. Produced by Robert Evans.
THE CONVERSATION, Directors Company, Paramount. Produced by Francis Ford Coppola.
★ THE GODFATHER PART II, Coppola Company, Paramount. Produced by Francis Ford Coppola.
LENNY, Worth, UA. Produced by Marvin Worth.
THE TOWERING INFERNO, Irwin Allen, 20th Century-Fox/Warner Bros. Produced by Irwin Allen.

ACTOR

★ ART CARNEY in *Harry and Tonto*, 20th Century-Fox.
ALBERT FINNEY in *Murder on the Orient Express*, G.W. Films, Paramount.
DUSTIN HOFFMAN in *Lenny*, Worth, UA.
JACK NICHOLSON in *Chinatown*, Evans, Paramount.
AL PACINO in *The Godfather Part II*, Coppola Company, Paramount.

ACTRESS

★ ELLEN BURSTYN in *Alice Doesn't Live Here Anymore*, Warner Bros.
DIAHANN CARROLL in *Claudine*, Third World Cinema-Selznick-Pine, 20th Century-Fox.
FAYE DUNAWAY in *Chinatown*, Evans, Paramount.
VALERIE PERRINE in *Lenny*, Worth, UA.
GENA ROWLANDS in *A Woman Under the Influence*, Faces International.

SUPPORTING ACTOR

FRED ASTAIRE in *The Towering Inferno*, Irwin Allen, 20th Century-Fox/Warner Bros.
JEFF BRIDGES in *Thunderbolt and Lightfoot*, Malpaso, UA.
★ ROBERT DE NIRO in *The Godfather Part II*, Coppola Company, Paramount.
MICHAEL V. GAZZO in *The Godfather Part II*, Coppola Company, Paramount.
LEE STRASBERG in *The Godfather Part II*, Coppola Company, Paramount.

SUPPORTING ACTRESS

★ INGRID BERGMAN in *Murder on the Orient Express*, G.W. Films, Paramount.
VALENTINA CORTESE in *Day for Night* (French), Warner Bros.
MADELINE KAHN in *Blazing Saddles*, Warner Bros.
DIANE LADD in *Alice Doesn't Live Here Anymore*, Warner Bros.
TALIA SHIRE in *The Godfather Part II*, Coppola Company, Paramount.

DIRECTION

JOHN CASSAVETES for *A Woman Under the Influence*, Faces International.
★ FRANCIS FORD COPPOLA for *The Godfather Part II*, Coppola Company, Paramount.
BOB FOSSE for *Lenny*, Marvin Worth, UA.
ROMAN POLANSKI for *Chinatown*, Robert Evans, Paramount.
FRANCOIS TRUFFAUT for *Day for Night*, Warner Bros. (French).

WRITING

(New classifications)

(Original Screenplay)

ALICE DOESN'T LIVE HERE ANYMORE, Warner Bros. Robert Getchell.
★ CHINATOWN, Robert Evans, Paramount. Robert Towne.

THE CONVERSATION, Directors Company, Paramount. Francis Ford Coppola.
DAY FOR NIGHT, Warner Bros. (French). Francois Truffaut, Jean-Louis Richard, and Suzanne Schiffman.
HARRY AND TONTO, 20th Century-Fox. Paul Mazursky and Josh Greenfeld.

(Screenplay Adapted From Other Material)

THE APPRENTICESHIP OF DUDDY KRAVITZ, International Cinemedia Centre, Paramount. Mordecai Richler and Lionel Chetwynd.
★ THE GODFATHER PART II, Coppola Company, Paramount. Francis Ford Coppola and Mario Puzo.
LENNY, Marvin Worth, UA. Julian Barry.
MURDER ON THE ORIENT EXPRESS, G.W. Films, Ltd., Paramount. Paul Dehn.
YOUNG FRANKENSTEIN, Gruskoff/Venture Films-Crossbow-Jouer, 20th Century-Fox. Gene Wilder and Mel Brooks.

CINEMATOGRAPHY

CHINATOWN, Robert Evans, Paramount. John A. Alonzo.
EARTHQUAKE, Robson-Filmakers Group, Universal. Philip Lathrop.
LENNY, Marvin Worth, UA. Bruce Surtees.
MURDER ON THE ORIENT EXPRESS, G.W. Films, Ltd., Paramount. Geoffrey Unsworth.
★ THE TOWERING INFERNO, Irwin Allen, 20th Century-Fox/Warner Bros. Fred Koenekamp and Joseph Biroc.

ART DIRECTION-SET DECORATION

CHINATOWN, Robert Evans, Paramount. Richard Sylbert and W. Stewart Campbell; Ruby Levitt.
EARTHQUAKE, Robson-Filmakers Group, Universal. Alexander Golitzen and E. Preston Ames; Frank McKelvy.

THE CONVERSATION, Directors Company, Paramount. Francis Ford Coppola.
★ THE GODFATHER PART II, Coppola Company, Paramount. Dean Tavoularis and Angelo Graham; George R. Nelson.
THE ISLAND AT THE TOP OF THE WORLD, Disney, Buena Vista. Peter Ellenshaw, John B. Mansbridge, Walter Tyler and Al Roelofs; Hal Gausman.
THE TOWERING INFERNO, Irwin Allen, 20th Century-Fox/Warner Bros. William Creber and Ward Preston; Raphael Bretton.

COSTUME DESIGN

CHINATOWN, Robert Evans, Paramount. Anthea Sylbert.
DAISY MILLER, Directors Company, Paramount. John Furness.
THE GODFATHER PART II, Coppola Company, Paramount. Theadora Van Runkle.
★ THE GREAT GATSBY, David Merrick, Paramount. Theoni V. Aldredge.
MURDER ON THE ORIENT EXPRESS, G.W. Films, Ltd., Paramount. Tony Walton.

SOUND

CHINATOWN, Robert Evans, Paramount. Bud Grenzbach and Larry Jost.
THE CONVERSATION, Directors Company, Paramount. Walter Murch and Arthur Rochester.
★ EARTHQUAKE, Robson-Filmakers Group, Universal. Ronald Pierce and Melvin Metcalfe, Sr.
THE TOWERING INFERNO, Irwin Allen, 20th Century-Fox/Warner Bros. Theodore Soderberg and Herman Lewis.
YOUNG FRANKENSTEIN, Gruskoff/Venture Films-Crossbow-Jouer, 20th Century-Fox. Richard Portman and Gene Cantamessa.

FILM EDITING

BLAZING SADDLES, Warner Bros. John C. Howard and Danford Greene.

Best Director: Francis Ford Coppola for *The Godfather Part II*. Coppola won his first Academy Award at age 31, for co-writing the story and screenplay of 1970's *Patton;* two years later, he won another for co-writing the screenplay of *The Godfather* (1972), and he received an additional nomination as 1972's Best Director. In 1974, there was Coppola everywhere: he won three Academy Awards (as producer of the year's Best Picture, as Director, and as co-author of the screenplay of *The Godfather Part II* and was also nominated twice for *The Conversation* (as producer, and as sole author of its original screenplay). A busy year, a talented creator.

Best Supporting Actress: Ingrid Bergman
as Gretta Ohlsson (above) in *Murder on the Orient Express* (Paramount; directed by Sidney Lumet). Ingrid Bergman's contribution to the film was short, but a prime example of why the Academy instigated Supporting Awards categories in the first place, to properly honor well-played smaller roles and gem-like junior performances which add so immeasurably to motion pictures. As a mousy Swedish missionary on the Orient Express, she basically had but one lengthy scene, interrogated by detective Hercule Piorot (Albert Finney) about an unsolved murder in their midst. It was a true cameo performance, and it brought her a third Academy Award, her first in the Supporting division. Earlier, she won for *Gaslight* (1944) and *Anastasia* (1956).

CHINATOWN, Robert Evans, Paramount. Sam O'Steen.
EARTHQUAKE, Robson-Filmakers Group, Universal. Dorothy Spencer.
THE LONGEST YARD, Ruddy, Paramount. Michael Luciano.
★ THE TOWERING INFERNO, Irwin Allen, 20th Century-Fox/Warner Bros. Harold F. Kress and Carl Kress.

MUSIC

(Song)
BENJI'S THEME (I FEEL LOVE) (*Benji*, Mulberry Square); Music by Euel Box. Lyrics by Betty Box.
BLAZING SADDLES (*Blazing Saddles*, Warner Bros.); Music by John Morris. Lyrics by Mel Brooks.
LITTLE PRINCE (*The Little Prince*, Stanley Donen, Paramount); Music by Frederick Loewe. Lyrics by Alan Jay Lerner.
★ WE MAY NEVER LOVE LIKE THIS AGAIN (*The Towering Inferno*, Irwin Allen, 20th Century-Fox/Warner Bros.); Music and Lyrics by Al Kasha and Joel Hirschhorn.
WHEREVER LOVE TAKES ME (*Gold*, Avton, Allied Artists); Music by Elmer Bernstein. Lyrics by Don Black.

(Original Dramatic Score)
CHINATOWN, Robert Evans, Paramount. Jerry Goldsmith.
★ THE GODFATHER PART II, Coppola Company, Paramount. Nino Rota and Carmine Coppola.
MURDER ON THE ORIENT EXPRESS, G.W. Films, Ltd., Paramount. Richard Rodney Bennett.
SHANKS, William Castle, Paramount. Alex North.
THE TOWERING INFERNO, Irwin Allen, 20th Century-Fox/Warner Bros. John Williams.

(Scoring: Original Song Score and/or Adaptation)
★ THE GREAT GATSBY, David Merrick, Paramount. Nelson Riddle.
THE LITTLE PRINCE, Stanley Donen, Paramount. Alan Jay Lerner, Frederick Loewe; Angela Morley and Douglas Gamley.
PHANTOM OF THE PARADISE, Harbor Prods., 20th Century-Fox. Paul Williams and George Aliceson Tipton.

SHORT FILMS
(Previously listed as Short Subjects)

(Animated Films)
★ CLOSED MONDAYS, Lighthouse Productions. Will Vinton and Bob Gardiner, producers.
THE FAMILY THAT DWELT APART, National Film Board of Canada. Yvon Mallette and Robert Verrall, producers.
HUNGER, National Film Board of Canada. Peter Foldes and Rene Jodoin, producers.
VOYAGE TO NEXT, Hubley Studio. Faith and John Hubley, producers.
WINNIE THE POOH AND TIGGER TOO, Disney, Buena Vista. Wolfgang Reitherman, producer.

(Live Action Films)
CLIMB, Dewitt Jones Productions. Dewitt Jones, producer.
THE CONCERT, The Black And White Colour Film Company, Ltd. Julian and Claude Chagrin, producers.
★ ONE-EYED MEN ARE KINGS, C.A.P.A.C. Productions (Paris). Paul Claudon and Edmond Sechan, producers.
PLANET OCEAN, Graphic Films. George V. Casey, producer.
THE VIOLIN, Sincinkin, Ltd. Andrew Welsh and George Pastic, producers.

DOCUMENTARY
(Short Subjects)
CITY OUT OF WILDERNESS, Francis Thompson Inc. Francis Thompson, producer.
★ DON'T, R.A. Films. Robin Lehman, producer.
EXPLORATORIUM, Jon Boorstin Prod. Jan Boorstin, producer.
JOHN MUIR'S HIGH SIERRA, Dewitt Jones Prods. Dewitt Jones and Lesley Foster, producers.

NAKED YOGA, Filmshop Prod. Ronald S. Kass and Mervyn Lloyd, producers.

(Features)
ANTONIA: A PORTRAIT OF THE WOMAN, Rocky Mountain Prods. Judy Collins and Jill Godmilow, producers.
THE CHALLENGE . . . A TRIBUTE TO MODERN ART, World View. Herbert Kline, producer.
THE 81ST BLOW, Ghetto Fighters House. Jacquot Ehrlich, David Bergman and Haim Gouri, producers.
★ HEARTS AND MINDS, Touchstone-Audjeff-BBS Prod., Zuker/Jaglom-Rainbow Pictures. Peter Davis and Bert Schneider, producers.
THE WILD AND THE BRAVE, E.S.J.-Tomorrow Entertainment-Jones/ Howard Ltd. Natalie R. Jones and Eugene S. Jones, producers.

FOREIGN LANGUAGE FILM
★ AMARCORD, (Italy).
CATSPLAY, (Hungary).
THE DELUGE, (Poland).
LACOMBE, LUCIEN, (France).
THE TRUCE, (Argentina).

HONORARY AND OTHER AWARDS

TO HOWARD HAWKS—A master American filmmaker whose creative efforts hold a distinguished place in world cinema. (statuette)
TO JEAN RENOIR—a genius who, with grace, responsibility and enviable devotion through silent film, sound film, feature, documentary and television, has won the world's admiration. (statuette)

SPECIAL ACHIEVEMENT AWARDS

For Visual Effects: FRANK BRENDEL, GLEN ROBINSON and ALBERT WHITLOCK for *Earthquake*, a Universal-Mark Robson-Filmakers Group Production, Universal.

1974 IRVING G. THALBERG MEMORIAL AWARD

None given this year.

1974 JEAN HERSHOLT HUMANITARIAN AWARD
TO ARTHUR B. KRIM

SCIENTIFIC OR TECHNICAL

CLASS I (statuette)
None.

CLASS II (plaque)
JOSEPH D. KELLY of Glen Glenn Sound for the design of new audio control consoles which have advanced the state of the art of sound recording and rerecording for motion picture production.
THE BURBANK STUDIOS Sound Department for the design of new audio control consoles engineered and constructed by the Quad-Eight Sound Corporation.
SAMUEL GOLDWYN STUDIOS Sound Department for the design of a new audio control console engineered and constructed by the Quad-Eight Sound Corporation.
QUAD-EIGHT SOUND CORPORATION for the engineering and construction of new audio control consoles designed by The Burbank Studios Sound Department and by the Samuel Goldwyn Studios Sound Department.
WALDON O. WATSON, RICHARD J. STUMPF, ROBERT J. LEONARD and the UNIVERSAL CITY STUDIOS Sound Department for the development and engineering of the Sensurround System for motion picture presentation.

CLASS III (citation)
ELEMACK COMPANY of Rome, Italy; LOUIS AMI of the Universal City Studios.

★ INDICATES WINNER

Best Supporting Actress: Lee Grant as Felicia Karpf (above) in *Shampoo* (Columbia; directed by Hal Ashby). Previously nominated in 1959 for *Detective Story* and in 1970 for *The Landlord,* Lee Grant won her Academy Award as the frisky wife of a wealthy Los Angeles businessman (Jack Warden), a lady with an interest in her hairdresser (Warren Beatty) beyond his ability to comb curls. She was also nominated again in 1976 for *The Voyage of the Damned.*

1975 The Forty-Eighth Year

One Flew Over the Cuckoo's Nest, a project which took years to get off the Hollywood drawing boards, justified the tenacity of its backers by winning five major awards at the 1975 Academy Awards presentation, held March 29, 1976. *Cuckoo's Nest* won the awards for Best Picture, Best Actor (Jack Nicholson), Best Actress (Louise Fletcher), Best Director (Milos Forman) and Best Screenplay Adaptation (Lawrence Hauben and Bo Goldman). It was the first film to win all four of the Academy's most famous awards—Picture, Actor, Actress, Director—since *It Happened One Night* forty-two years earlier.

The Awards ceremony was held again at the Dorothy Chandler Pavilion of the Los Angeles Music Center and telecast over ABC for the first time in six years. Howard W. Koch produced for the Academy, Marty Pasetta directed for ABC, and co-hosts of the evening were Walter Matthau, Robert Shaw, George Segal, Goldie Hawn and Gene Kelly. Ray Bolger and 24 dancers opened the show with a special number, "Hollywood Honors Its Own," and Elizabeth Taylor closed it by leading a salute to the country's Bicentennial.

George Burns, age 80, was named Best Supporting Actor of the Year (for *The Sunshine Boys*), and thus became the oldest performer to win an Academy Award. Lee Grant was named Best Supporting Actress (for *Shampoo*). The Soviet Union's *Dersu Uzala* was picked as Best Foreign Language Film, Mervyn LeRoy received the Irving G. Thalberg Memorial Award and Dr. Jules Stein was honored with the Jean Hersholt Humanitarian Award.

Two ladies—one a Hollywood veteran, the other a newcomer—dominated the show. Mary Pickford, one of the industry's bona fide legends and a past Academy Award winner, received an Honorary Oscar from the Academy's Board of Governors, specifically "in recognition of her unique contributions to the film industry and the development of film as an artistic medium." She accepted the statuette from Academy President Walter Mirisch in a ceremony pre-taped at her Pickfair estate. Later, Best Actress winner Louise Fletcher gave her acceptance speech partially in sign language to her deaf parents watching at home in Birmingham, Alabama, which rated as one of the most moving Oscar moments on record. "I want to say thank you . . . for teaching me to have a dream," she told them. "You are seeing . . . my dream come true."

Best Supporting Actor: George Burns as Al Lewis (right, with Walter Matthau) in *The Sunshine Boys* (M-G-M/United Artists; directed by Herbert Ross). The role was created on Broadway by Sam Levene and, for Burns, was his first role in a motion picture in thirty-six years (since 1939's *Honolulu*). He played a long-retired vaudevillian in the midst of making a one-shot comeback on television with a former partner with whom he's been on the outs for years. Said Burns, age 80: "This is all so exciting, I've decided to keep making one movie every thirty-six years."

Best Picture: One Flew Over the Cuckoo's Nest (United Artists; produced by Saul Zaentz and Michael Douglas), **Best Director: Milos Forman,** and (above) **Best Actress: Louise Fletcher** as Nurse Ratched and **Best Actor: Jack Nicholson** as Randle P. McMurphy in *One Flew Over the Cuckoo's Nest.* It took 13 years to get Ken Kesey's powerful anti-establishment novel on the screen, but the result hit the jackpot, with five of 1975's top Academy Awards honors. Filmed at the Oregon State Hospital in Salem, Oregon, it was the story of a non-conforming con man (played by Nicholson) who feigns insanity to avoid prison work, and is sent to a mental hospital where he is ultimately destroyed when he tries to go against "the system"—and a poisonous nurse, played by Miss Fletcher.

Honorary Award: Mary Pickford (right, with Academy President Walter Mirisch). No star ever held quite such a grasp on the world of movies, or its audiences, as Mary Pickford, and the Academy Board of Governors saluted her in appreciation of her numerous accomplishments and contributions to the industry. One of the original founders of the Academy, she was also a winner in 1928-29 for her performance in *Coquette.*

Nominations 1975

PICTURE

BARRY LYNDON, Hawk Films, Warner Bros. Produced by Stanley Kubrick.
DOG DAY AFTERNOON, Warner Bros. Produced by Martin Bregman and Martin Elfand.
JAWS, Zanuck/Brown, Universal. Produced by Richard D. Zanuck and David Brown.
NASHVILLE, ABC Entertainment-Weintraub-Altman, Paramount. Produced by Robert Altman.
★ **ONE FLEW OVER THE CUKOO'S NEST**, Fantasy Films, UA. Produced by Saul Zaentz and Michael Douglas.

ACTOR

WALTER MATTHAU in *The Sunshine Boys*, Stark, M-G-M.
★ **JACK NICHOLSON** in *One Flew over the Cuckoo's Nest*, Fantasy Films, UA.
AL PACINO in *Dog Day Afternoon*, Warner Bros.
MAXIMILIAN SCHELL in *The Man in the Glass Booth*, Landau, AFT Distributing.
JAMES WHITMORE in *Give 'em Hell, Harry!*, Theatrovision, Avco Embassy.

ACTRESS

ISABELLE ADJANI in *The Story of Adele H.*, New World Pictures (French).
ANN-MARGRET in *Tommy*, Stigwood, Columbia.
★ **LOUISE FLETCHER** in *One Flew over the Cuckoo's Nest*, Fantasy Films, UA.
GLENDA JACKSON in *Hedda*, Royal Shakespeare-Barrie/Enders, Brut Productions.
CAROL KANE in *Hester Street*, Midwest Films.

SUPPORTING ACTOR

★ **GEORGE BURNS** in *The Sunshine Boys*, M-G-M.
BRAD DOURIF in *One Flew over the Cuckoo's Nest*, Fantasy Films, UA.
BURGESS MEREDITH in *The Day of the Locust*, Hellman, Paramount.
CHRIS SARANDON in *Dog Day Afternoon*, Warner Bros.
JACK WARDEN in *Shampoo*, Rubeeker, Columbia.

SUPPORTING ACTRESS

RONEE BLAKLEY in *Nashville*, ABC Entertainment-Weintraub-Altman, Paramount.
★ **LEE GRANT** in *Shampoo*, Rubeeker, Columbia.
SYLVIA MILES in *Farewell, My Lovely*, Kastner-ITC, Avco Embassy.
LILY TOMLIN in *Nashville*, ABC Entertainment-Weintraub-Altman, Paramount.
BRENDA VACCARO in *Jacqueline Susann's Once Is Not Enough*, Koch, Paramount.

DIRECTION

ROBERT ALTMAN for *Nashville*, ABC Entertainment-Weintraub-Altman, Paramount.
FEDERICO FELLINI for *Amarcord*, New World Pictures (Italian).
★ **MILOS FORMAN** for *One Flew over the Cuckoo's Nest*, Fantasy Films, UA.
STANLEY KUBRICK for *Barry Lyndon*, Hawk Films, Warner Bros.
SIDNEY LUMET for *Dog Day Afternoon*, Warner Bros.

WRITING

(Original Screenplay)
AMARCORD, New World Pictures (Italian). Federico Fellini and Tonino Guerra.
AND NOW MY LOVE, Avco Embassy (French). Claude Lelouch and Pierre Uytterhoeven.
★ **DOG DAY AFTERNOON**, Warner Bros. Frank Pierson.
LIES MY FATHER TOLD ME, Pentimento-Pentacle VIII, Columbia. Ted Allan.
SHAMPOO, Rubeeker, Columbia. Robert Towne and Warren Beatty.

(Screenplay Adapted From Other Material)
BARRY LYNDON, Hawk Films, Warner Bros. Stanley Kubrick.
THE MAN WHO WOULD BE KING, Columbia/Allied Artists. John Huston and Gladys Hill.
★ **ONE FLEW OVER THE CUCKOO'S NEST**, Fantasy Films, UA. Lawrence Hauben and Bo Goldman.
SCENT OF A WOMAN, Dean Films, 20th Century-Fox (Italian). Ruggero Maccari and Dino Risi.
THE SUNSHINE BOYS, Ray Stark, M-G-M. Neil Simon.

CINEMATOGRAPHY

★ **BARRY LYNDON**, Hawk Films, Warner Bros. John Alcott.
THE DAY OF THE LOCUST, Jerome Hellman, Paramount. Conrad Hall.
FUNNY LADY, Rastar, Columbia. James Wong Howe.
THE HINDENBURG, Robert Wise-Filmakers Group, Universal. Robert Surtees.
ONE FLEW OVER THE CUCKOO'S NEST, Fantasy Films, UA. Haskell Wexler and Bill Butler.

ART DIRECTION-SET DECORATION

★ **BARRY LYNDON**, Hawk Films, Warner Bros. Ken Adam and Roy Walker; Vernon Dixon.
THE HINDENBURG, Robert Wise-Filmakers Group, Universal. Edward Carfagno; Frank McKelvy.
THE MAN WHO WOULD BE KING, Columbia/Allied Artists. Alexander Trauner and Tony Inglis; Peter James.
SHAMPOO, Rubeeker, Columbia. Richard Sylbert and W. Stewart Campbell; George Gaines.
THE SUNSHINE BOYS, Ray Stark, M-G-M. Albert Brenner; Marvin March.

COSTUME DESIGN

★ **BARRY LYNDON**, Hawk Films, Warner Bros. Ulla-Britt Soderlund and Milena Canonero.
THE FOUR MUSKETEERS, Salkind, 20th Century-Fox. Yvonne Blake Ron Talsky.
FUNNY LADY, Rastar, Columbia. Ray Aghayan and Bob Mackie.
THE MAGIC FLUTE, Surrogate Releasing (Swedish). Henny Noremark and Karin Erskine.
THE MAN WHO WOULD BE KING, Columbia/Allied Artists. Edith Head.

SOUND

BITE THE BULLET, Brooks, Columbia. Arthur Piantodosi, Les Fresholtz, Richard Tyler and Al Overton, Jr.
FUNNY LADY, Rastar, Columbia. Richard Portman, Don MacDougall, Curly Thirlwell and Jack Solomon.
THE HINDENBURG, Robert Wise-Filmakers Group, Universal. Leonard Peterson, John A. Bolger, Jr., John Mack and Don K. Sharpless.

★ **JAWS**, Zanuck/Brown, Universal. Robert L. Hoyt, Roger Heman, Earl Madery and John Carter.
THE WIND AND THE LION, Herb Jaffe, M-G-M. Harry W. Tetrick, Aaron Rochin, William McCaughey and Roy Charman.

FILM EDITING

DOG DAY AFTERNOON, Warner Bros. Dede Allen.
★ **JAWS**, Zanuck/Brown, Universal. Verna Fields.
THE MAN WHO WOULD BE KING, Columbia/Allied Artists. Russell Lloyd.
ONE FLEW OVER THE CUCKOO'S NEST, Fantasy Films, UA. Richard Chew, Lynzee Klingman and Sheldon Kahn.
THREE DAYS OF THE CONDOR, De Laurentiis, Paramount. Frederic Steinkamp and Don Guidice.

MUSIC

(Song)
HOW LUCKY CAN YOU GET (*Funny Lady*, Rastar, Columbia); Music and Lyrics by Fred Ebb and John Kander.
★ **I'M EASY** (*Nashville*, ABC-Weintraub-Altman, Paramount); Music and Lyrics by Keith Carradine.
NOW THAT WE'RE IN LOVE (*Whiffs*, Brut, 20th Century-Fox); Music by George Barrie. Lyrics by Sammy Cahn.

RICHARD'S WINDOW (*The Other Side of the Mountain*, Filmways-Larry Peerce, Universal); Music by Charles Fox. Lyrics by Norman Gimbel.
THEME FROM MAHOGANY (DO YOU KNOW WHERE YOU'RE GOING TO) (*Mahogany*, Jobete, Paramount); Music by Michael Masser. Lyrics by Gerry Goffin.

(Original Score)
BIRDS DO IT, BEES DO IT, Wolper, Columbia. Gerald Fried.
BITE THE BULLET, Brooks, Columbia. Alex North.
★ **JAWS**, Zanuck/Brown, Universal. John Williams.
ONE FLEW OVER THE CUCKOO'S NEST, Fantasy Films, UA. Jack Nitzsche.
THE WIND AND THE LION, Herb Jaffe, M-G-M. Jerry Goldsmith.

(Scoring: Original Song Score and/or Adaptation)
★ **BARRY LYNDON**, Hawk Films, Warner Bros. Leonard Rosenman.
FUNNY LADY, Rastar, Columbia. Peter Matz.
TOMMY, Stigwood Organisation, Columbia. Peter Townshend.

SHORT FILMS

(Animated Films)
★ **GREAT**, Grantstern, British Lion Films Ltd. Bob Godfrey, producer.

Dog Day Afternoon (Warner Bros.; produced by Martin Bregman and Martin Elfand) starred John Cazale and Al Pacino (above), was directed by Sidney Lumet, and won an Oscar for Frank Pierson's Original Screenplay.

Barry Lyndon (Warner Bros.; produced and directed by Stanley Kubrick) won Academy Awards for Cinematography, Art Direction, Costume Design and Music Scoring: Adaptation. It was based on an 1844 novel by William Makepiece Thackeray and commented on morality and social structures in 18th-century England, with Ryan O'Neal (above, among the soldiers) and Marisa Berenson as its leading players.

Best Original Song: "I'm Easy" from *Nashville* (Paramount), with music and lyrics by Keith Carradine (right). Carradine became the first person to win an Oscar for composing a song he also introduced in a movie. In *Nashville,* directed by Robert Altman, he played a soft-spoken rock star briefly involved with a married woman (Lily Tomlin).

KICK ME, Swarthe Productions. Robert Swarthe, producer.
MONSIEUR POINTU, National Film Board of Canada. Rene Jodoin, Bernard Longpré and André Leduc, producers.
SISYPHUS, Hungarofilms. Marcell Jankovics, producer.

(Live Action)
★ ANGEL AND BIG JOE, Salzman Productions. Bert Salzman, producer.
CONQUEST OF LIGHT, Louis Marcus Films Ltd. Louis Marcus, producer.
DAWN FLIGHT, Lansburgh Productions. Lawrence M. Lansburgh and Brian Lansburgh, producers.
A DAY IN THE LIFE OF BONNIE CONSOLO, Barr Films. Barry Spinello, producer.
DOUBLETALK, Beattie Productions. Alan Beattie, producer.

DOCUMENTARY
(Short Subjects)
ARTHUR AND LILLIE, Department of Communication, Stanford University. Jon Else, Steven Kovacs and Kristine Samuelson, producers.
★ THE END OF THE GAME, Opus Films Ltd. Claire Wilbur and Robin Lehman, producers.
MILLIONS OF YEARS AHEAD OF MAN, BASF. Manfred Baier, producer.
PROBES IN SPACE, Graphic Films. George V. Casey, producer.
WHISTLING SMITH, National Film Board of Canada. Barrie Howells and Michael Scott, producers.

(Features)
THE CALIFORNIA REICH, Yasny Talking Pictures. Walter F. Parkes and Keith F. Critchlow, producers.
FIGHTING FOR OUR LIVES, A Farm Worker Film. Glen Pearcy, producer.

THE INCREDIBLE MACHINE, The National Geographic Society, Wolper Prods. Irwin Rosten, producer.
★ THE MAN WHO SKIED DOWN EVEREST, Crawley Films. F.R. Crawley, James Hager and Dale Hartleben, producers.
THE OTHER HALF OF THE SKY: A CHINA MEMOIR, MacLaine Productions. Shirley MacLaine, producer.

FOREIGN LANGUAGE FILM
★ DERSU UZALA, (U.S.S.R.).
LAND OF PROMISE, (Poland).
LETTERS FROM MARUSIA, (Mexico).
SANDAKAN NO. 8, (Japan).
SCENT OF A WOMAN, (Italy).

HONORARY AND OTHER AWARDS
TO MARY PICKFORD in recognition of her unique contributions to the film industry and the development of film as an artistic medium. (statuette)

SPECIAL ACHIEVEMENT AWARDS
For Sound Effects: PETER BERKOS for *The Hindenburg*, Robert Wise-Filmakers Group, Universal.
For Visual Effects: ALBERT WHITLOCK and GLEN ROBINSON for *The Hindenburg*, Robert Wise-Filmakers Group, Universal.

1975 IRVING G. THALBERG MEMORIAL AWARD
TO MERVYN LeROY

1975 JEAN HERSHOLT HUMANITARIAN AWARD
TO JULES C. STEIN

SCIENTIFIC OR TECHNICAL
CLASS I (statuette)
None.

CLASS II (plaque)
CHADWELL O'CONNOR of the O'Connor Engineering Laboratories for the concept and engineering of a fluid-damped camera-head for motion-picture photography.
WILLIAM F. MINER of Universal City Studios, Inc. and the WESTINGHOUSE ELECTRIC CORPORATION for the development and engineering of a solid-state, 500 kilowatt, direct-current static rectifier for motion-picture lighting.

CLASS III (citation)
LAWRENCE W. BUTLER and ROGER BANKS;
DAVID J. DEGENKOLB and FRED SCOBEY of Deluxe General Inc. and JOHN C. DOLAN and RICHARD DUBOIS of the Akwaklame Company;
JOSEPH WESTHEIMER;
CARTER EQUIPMENT CO., INC. and RAMTRONICS;
THE HOLLYWOOD FILM COMPANY;
BELL & HOWELL;
FREDRIK SCHLYTER.

★ INDICATES WINNER

1976 The Forty-Ninth Year

Three films dominated the 1976 Academy Awards: *Network* (with four awards), *All the President's Men* (also with four Oscars) and *Rocky* (with three awards, including the Best Picture of the Year statuette). It was also a triumphant night for Sylvester Stallone, although he didn't win an award; he was only the third person in the Oscar record books to be nominated in a single year both as an actor and as a screenwriter (preceded by Charles Chaplin in 1940 and Orson Welles in 1941).

It was a year for several records to be set. *Network* became the only motion picture other than 1951's *A Streetcar Named Desire* to win three awards for acting: Best Actress (Faye Dunaway), Best Supporting Actress (Beatrice Straight) and Best Actor (Peter Finch). Finch, who died two months before the Academy Awards winners were announced on March 29, 1977, was the first performer to win a posthumous Oscar. It was accepted by his wife.

Barbra Streisand, a Best Actress winner in 1968, became the first Oscar-winner performer to also be an Academy Award-winning composer; her song, "Evergreen" from *A Star Is Born,* written with Paul Williams, was named the year's Best Song. John Avildsen was named Best Director for *Rocky,* and among his competition was Lina Wertmuller, the first woman ever nominated in that category. Jason Robards in *All the President's Men* was chosen Best Supporting Actor, Pandro S. Berman was voted the Irving G. Thalberg Memorial Award and Special Visual Effects Awards went to both *King Kong* and *Logan's Run. Black and White in Color,* a film from the Ivory Coast, was chosen Best Foreign Language Film.

The show, originating from the Dorothy Chandler Pavilion of the Los Angeles Music Center, was telecast over ABC, produced by William Friedkin and directed by Marty Pasetta. Co-hosts for the evening were Richard Pryor, Jane Fonda, Ellen Burstyn and Warren Beatty. Among the show's entertainment highlights were Barbra Streisand, appearing on an Oscar show for the first time as a performer, and Muhammad Ali —unannounced and unexpected—good-naturedly sparring for an abbreviated round with a flabbergasted "Rocky" Stallone.

Best Actor: Peter Finch as Howard Beale (above) and **Best Actress: Faye Dunaway** as Diana Christensen (below) in *Network* (M-G-M/United Artists; directed by Sidney Lumet). *Network,* by Paddy Chayefsky, took a biting, semi-satirical look at television in the 1970s and its eagerness for high program ratings. Beale (played by Finch) was a fictional newsman who attracts high ratings by promising to commit suicide on camera; at the same time, he begs viewers to take a stand against current TV programming; Diana (Faye Dunaway) was a ruthless head of network programming, not above plotting an assassination, or other skulduggery, to hype her company's Nielsen numbers. Among the other Academy Awards won by *Network* was an Oscar to Chayefsky for Original Screenplay; he was, without question, a man highly gifted with words and ideas.

Best Picture: Rocky (United Artists; produced by Irwin Winkler and Robert Chartoff) and **Best Director: John G. Avildsen** for *Rocky*. It was the sleeper of the season, economically made for $960,000 in twenty-eight days, and it grew into the year's best-loved movie, the story of a likeable but deadweight fighter named Rocky Balboa (Sylvester Stallone, left, with Burgess Meredith) who miraculously gets picked for a heavyweight title bout and, in the final analysis, wins his own self-respect and dignity. Stallone also wrote the screenplay, and *Rocky* won a third Oscar for Film Editing. The cast also included Talia Shire, Burt Young and Carl Weathers.

Best Supporting Actor: Jason Robards as Ben Bradlee in *All the President's Men* (Warner Bros.; directed by Alan J. Pakula). Robards played the real-life Bradlee, editor of the Washington Post and the man who gave the final go-ahead (and continued support) to reporters Carl Bernstein and Bob Woodward in their investigation of the Watergate coverup in Washington, D.C. The film also won Academy Awards for Screenplay (based on material from another medium), Art Direction, and Sound.

Best Supporting Actress: Beatrice Straight as Louise Schumacher in *Network.* It took only three days of rehearsal and three more days of filming (at the classic old Althrop apartment building in New York City) for her role, but Beatrice Straight gave a superb Supporting Oscar performance in every sense of the word; she played the wife of William Holden, attempting to retain her dignity—and her sanity—when her husband admits he is in love with a younger woman.

Nominations 1976

PICTURE

ALL THE PRESIDENT'S MEN, Wildwood, Warner Bros. Produced by Walter Coblenz.
BOUND FOR GLORY, UA. Produced by Robert F. Blumofe and Harold Leventhal.
NETWORK, Gottfried/Chayefsky, M-G-M/UA. Produced by Howard Gottfried.
★ **ROCKY**, Chartoff-Winkler, UA. Produced by Irwin Winkler and Robert Chartoff.
TAXI DRIVER, Bill/Phillips-Scorsese, Columbia. Produced by Michael Phillips and Julia Phillips.

ACTOR

ROBERT DE NIRO in *Taxi Driver*, Bill/Phillips-Scorsese, Columbia.
★ **PETER FINCH** in *Network*, Gottfried/Chayefsky, M-G-M/UA.
GIANCARLO GIANNINI in *Seven Beauties*, Cinema 5 (Italian).
WILLIAM HOLDEN in *Network*, Gottfried/Chayefsky, M-G-M/UA.
SYLVESTER STALLONE in *Rocky*, Chartoff-Winkler, UA.

ACTRESS

MARIE-CHRISTINE BARRAULT in *Cousin, Cousine*, Northal Films (French).
★ **FAYE DUNAWAY** in *Network*, Gottfried/Chayefsky, M-G-M/UA.
TALIA SHIRE in *Rocky*, Chartoff-Winkler, UA.
SISSY SPACEK in *Carrie*, Redbank Films, UA.
LIV ULLMANN in *Face to Face*, Paramount (Swedish).

SUPPORTING ACTOR

NED BEATTY in *Network*, Gottfried/Chayefsky, M-G-M/UA.
BURGESS MEREDITH in *Rocky*, Chartoff-Winkler, UA.
LAURENCE OLIVIER in *Marathon Man*, Evans-Beckerman, Paramount.
★ **JASON ROBARDS** in *All the President's Men*, Wildwood, Warner Bros.
BURT YOUNG in *Rocky*, Chartoff-Winkler, UA.

SUPPORTING ACTRESS

JANE ALEXANDER in *All the President's Men*, Wildwood, Warner Bros.
JODIE FOSTER in *Taxi Driver*, Bill/Phillips-Scorsese, Columbia.
LEE GRANT in *Voyage of the Damned*, ITC, Avco Embassy.
PIPER LAURIE in *Carrie*, Redbank Films, UA.
★ **BEATRICE STRAIGHT** in *Network*, Gottfried/Chayefsky, M-G-M/UA.

DIRECTION

★ **JOHN G. AVILDSEN** for *Rocky*, Chartoff-Winkler, UA.
INGMAR BERGMAN for *Face to Face*, Cinematograph, A.B., Paramount (Swedish).
SIDNEY LUMET for *Network*, Gottfried/Chayefsky, M-G-M/UA.
ALAN J. PAKULA for *All the President's Men*, Wildwood, Warner Bros.
LINA WERTMULLER for *Seven Beauties*, Medusa Distribuzione, Cinema 5 (Italian).

Special Award: King Kong (Paramount; produced by Dino De Laurentiis) was voted a Special Achievement Award for its visual effects by the Board of Governors, and presented to Carlo Rambaldi, Glen Robinson and Frank Van der Veer. From 1939 through 1971 (excluding a three-year period, 1951-1953), Visual Effects were honored via a regular Awards category; between 1972 and 1976, such achievements were saluted by a Special Award, not mandatory each year, voted "at such times as in the judgment of the Board of Governors there is an achievement which makes an exceptional contribution to the motion picture for which it was created, but for which there is no annual Awards category."

Bound for Glory United Artists; produced by Robert F. Blumofe) featured David Carradine (above) in a biography of the late Woody Guthrie, a spirited and sensitive troubadour deeply affected by America's Depression era of the 1930s. The film received Academy Awards for Haskell Wexler's Cinematography, and for Leonard Rosenman's Scoring: Adaptation.

WRITING

(Screenplay Written Directly For The Screen)

COUSIN, COUSINE, Northal Film Distributors Ltd. (French). Jean-Charles Tacchella and Daniele Thompson.

THE FRONT, Columbia. Walter Bernstein.

✱ NETWORK, Gottfried/Chayefsky, M-G-M/ UA. Paddy Chayefsky.

ROCKY, Chartoff-Winkler, UA. Sylvester Stallone.

SEVEN BEAUTIES, Medusa Distribuzione, Cinema 5 (Italian). Lina Wertmuller.

(Screenplay Based On Material From Another Medium)

✱ ALL THE PRESIDENT'S MEN, Wildwood, Warner Bros. William Goldman.

BOUND FOR GLORY, UA. Robert Getchell.

FELLINI'S CASANOVA, Universal (Italian). Federico Fellini and Bernadino Zapponi.

THE SEVEN-PER-CENT SOLUTION, Herbert Ross/Winitsky-Sellers, Universal. Nicholas Meyer.

VOYAGE OF THE DAMNED, ITC Entertainment, Avco Embassy. Steve Shagan and David Butler.

CINEMATOGRAPHY

✱ BOUND FOR GLORY, UA. Haskell Wexler.

KING KONG, De Laurentiis, Paramount. Richard H. Kline.

LOGAN'S RUN, Saul David, M-G-M. Ernest Laszlo.

NETWORK, Gottfried/Chayefsky, M-G-M/ UA. Owen Roizman.

A STAR IS BORN, Barwood/Peters-First Artists, Warner Bros. Robert Surtees.

ART DIRECTION-SET DECORATION

✱ ALL THE PRESIDENT'S MEN, Wildwood, Warner Bros. George Jenkins; George Gaines.

THE INCREDIBLE SARAH, Helen M. Strauss-Reader's Digest, Seymour Borde & Associates. Elliot Scott and Norman Reynolds.

THE LAST TYCOON, Spiegel-Kazan, Paramount. Gene Callahan and Jack Collis; Jerry Wunderlich.

LOGAN'S RUN, Saul David, M-G-M. Dale Hennesy; Robert de Vestel.

THE SHOOTIST, Frankovich/Self-De Laurentiis, Paramount. Robert F. Boyle; Arthur Jeph Parker.

COSTUME DESIGN

BOUND FOR GLORY, UA. William Theiss.

✱ FELLINI'S CASANOVA, Universal (Italian). Danilo Donati.

THE INCREDIBLE SARAH, Helen M. Strauss-Reader's Digest, Seymour Borde & Associates. Anthony Mendleson.

THE PASSOVER PLOT, Coast Industries-Golan-Globus, Atlas Films. Mary Wills.

THE SEVEN-PER-CENT SOLUTION, Herbert Ross/Winitsky-Sellers, Universal. Alan Barrett.

SOUND

✱ ALL THE PRESIDENT'S MEN, Wildwood, Warner Bros. Arthur Piantadosi, Les Fresholtz, Dick Alexander and Jim Webb.

KING KONG, De Laurentiis, Paramount. Harry Warren Tetrick, William McCaughey, Aaron Rochin and Jack Solomon.

ROCKY, Chartoff-Winkler, UA. Harry Warren Tetrick, William McCaughey, Lyle Burbridge and Bud Alper.

SILVER STREAK, Frank Yablans, 20th Century-Fox. Donald Mitchell, Douglas Williams, Richard Tyler and Hal Etherington.

A STAR IS BORN, Barwood/Peters-First Artists, Warner Bros. Robert Knudson, Dan Wallin, Robert Glass and Tom Overton.

FILM EDITING

ALL THE PRESIDENT'S MEN, Wildwood, Warner Bros. Robert L. Wolfe.

BOUND FOR GLORY, UA. Robert Jones and Pembroke J. Herring.

NETWORK, Gottfried/Chayefsky, M-G-M/ UA. Alan Heim.

✱ ROCKY, Chartoff-Winkler, UA. Richard Halsey and Scott Conrad.

TWO-MINUTE WARNING, Filmways/ Peerce-Feldman, Universal. Eve Newman and Walter Hannemann.

MUSIC

(Song)

AVE SATANI (*The Omen*, 20th Century-Fox); Music and Lyrics by Jerry Goldsmith.

COME TO ME (*The Pink Panther Strikes Again*, Amjo, UA); Music by Henry Mancini. Lyrics by Don Black.

✱ EVERGREEN (Love Theme from a Star Is Born) (*A Star Is Born*, Barwood/ Peters-First Artists, Warner Bros.); Music by Barbra Streisand. Lyrics by Paul Williams.

GONNA FLY NOW (*Rocky*, Chartoff-Winkler, UA); Music by Bill Conti. Lyrics by Carol Connors and Ayn Robbins.

A WORLD THAT NEVER WAS (*Half a House*, Lenro Productions, First American Films); Music by Sammy Fain. Lyrics by Paul Francis Webster.

(Original Score)

OBSESSION, Litto, Columbia. Bernard Herrmann.

✱ THE OMEN, 20th Century-Fox. Jerry Goldsmith.

THE OUTLAW JOSEY WALES, Malpaso, Warner Bros. Jerry Fielding.

TAXI DRIVER, Bill/Phillips-Scorsese, Columbia. Bernard Herrmann.

VOYAGE OF THE DAMNED, ITC Entertainment, Avco Embassy. Lalo Schifrin.

(Original Song Score and Its Adaptation or Best Adaptation Score)

✱ BOUND FOR GLORY, UA. Leonard Rosenman.

BUGSY MALONE, Goodtimes Enterprises, Paramount. Paul Williams.

A STAR IS BORN, Barwood/Peters-First Artists, Warner Bros. Roger Kellaway.

SHORT FILMS

(Animated Films)

DEDALO, Cineteam Realizzazioni. Manfredo Manfredi, producer.

✱ LEISURE, Film Australia. Suzanne Baker, producer.

THE STREET, National Film Board of Canada. Caroline Leaf and Guy Glover, producers.

(Live Action)

✱ IN THE REGION OF ICE, American Film Institute. Andre Guttfreund and Peter Werner, producers.

KUDZU, A Short Production. Marjorie Anne Short, producer.

THE MORNING SPIDER, The Black and White Colour Film Company. Julian Chagrin and Claude Chagrin, producers.

NIGHTLIFE, Opus Films, Ltd. Claire Wilbur and Robin Lehman, producers.

NUMBER ONE, Number One Productions. Dyan Cannon and Vince Cannon, producers.

DOCUMENTARY

(Short Subjects)

AMERICAN SHOESHINE, Titan Films. Sparky Greene, producer.

BLACKWOOD, National Film Board of Canada. Tony Ianzelo and Andy Thompson, producers.

THE END OF THE ROAD, Pelican Films. John Armstrong, producer.

✱ NUMBER OUR DAYS, Community Television of Southern California. Lynne Littman, producer.

UNIVERSE, Graphic Films Corp. for NASA. Lester Novros, producer.

(Features)

✱ HARLAN COUNTY, U.S.A., Cabin Creek Films. Barbara Kopple, producer.

HOLLYWOOD ON TRIAL, October Films/Cinema Associates. James Gutman and David Helpern, Jr., producers.

OFF THE EDGE, Pentacle Films. Michael Firth, producer.

PEOPLE OF THE WIND, Elizabeth E. Rogers Productions. Anthony Howarth and David Koff, producers.

VOLCANO: AN INQUIRY INTO THE LIFE AND DEATH OF MALCOLM LOWRY, National Film Board of Canada. Donald Brittain and Robert Duncan, producers.

FOREIGN LANGUAGE FILM

✱ BLACK AND WHITE IN COLOR, (Ivory Coast).

COUSIN, COUSINE, (France).

JACOB, THE LIAR, (German Democratic Republic).

NIGHTS AND DAYS, (Poland).

SEVEN BEAUTIES, (Italy).

HONORARY AND OTHER AWARDS

None given this year.

SPECIAL ACHIEVEMENT AWARDS

For Visual Effects: CARLO RAMBALDI, GLEN ROBINSON and FRANK VAN DER VEER for *King Kong*, De Laurentiis, Paramount.

For Visual Effects: L.B. ABBOTT, GLEN ROBINSON and MATTHEW YURICICH for *Logan's Run*, Saul David, M-G-M.

1976 IRVING G. THALBERG MEMORIAL AWARD

TO PANDRO S. BERMAN

1976 JEAN HERSHOLT HUMANITARIAN AWARD

None given this year.

SCIENTIFIC OR TECHNICAL

CLASS I (statuette)

None.

CLASS II (plaque)

CONSOLIDATED FILM INDUSTRIES and the BARNEBEY-CHENEY COMPANY for the development of a system for the recovery of film-cleaning solvent vapors in a motion-picture laboratory.

WILLIAM L. GRAHAM, MANFRED G. MICHELSON, GEOFFREY F. NORMAN and SIEGFRIED SEIBERT of Technicolor for the development and engineering of a continuous, high-speed, Color Motion Picture Printing System.

CLASS III (citation)

FRED BARTSCHER of the Kollmorgen Corporation and to GLENN BERGGREN of the Schneider Corporation.

PANAVISION INCORPORATED;

HIROSHI SUZUKAWA of Canon and WILTON R. HOLM of AMPTP Motion Picture and Television Research Center;

CARL ZEISS COMPANY;

PHOTO RESEARCH DIVISION of the KOLLMORGEN CORPORATION.

✱ INDICATES WINNER

1977 The Fiftieth Year

Here it was at last: fifty years after that initial gathering at the Hollywood Roosevelt Hotel, the Academy celebrated its first half-century birthday, stronger than ever, with Oscar the acknowledged final word on motion picture achievement. The celebration took place April 3, 1978, again at the Dorothy Chandler Pavilion of the Los Angeles Music Center, with a stage full of stars, including the first Oscar winner Janet Gaynor, two-time champions such as Bette Davis and Olivia de Havilland, plus current box office names like John Travolta and Sylvester Stallone taking part. The show was telecast on ABC-TV, produced by Howard W. Koch and directed by Marty Pasetta, and it attracted the largest television audience for any Oscar show.

Star Wars won six statuettes for the biggest award total of the night, all of them in the technical divisions; it also received a seventh award, voted by the Academy Board of Governors, for its Special Achievement by Benjamin Burtt, Jr. in the creation of alien creature and robot voices. *Annie Hall* received four awards, including Best Picture, Best Actress (Diane Keaton), Best Director (Woody Allen) and Best Original Screenplay (Woody Allen and Marshall Brickman). Richard Dreyfuss was chosen Best Actor (for *The Goodbye Girl*), France's *Madame Rosa* was selected Best Foreign Language Film, Vanessa Redgrave was named Best Supporting Actress in *Julia* and Jason Robards was chosen Best Supporting Actor (for *Julia*). Robards, winner in the same category last year, became the fourth performer in Academy history to win in subsequent years (following Luise Rainer in 1936-1937, Spencer Tracy in 1937-1938 and Katharine Hepburn in 1967-1968). Miss Redgrave caused controversy when she used her acceptance speech to criticize "militant Zionist hoodlums" for protesting her political beliefs and actions.

It was a star-studded night for Oscar, and a fitting finale to those first fifty years of activity. The motion picture industry had changed drastically since that initial organizational banquet on May 11, 1927— and the world outside had changed even more—but the Academy had kept step, and kept strong.

Star Wars (20th Century-Fox; produced by Gary Kurtz) was the blockbuster of the year, a sweeping, energetic, and absolutely splendid space-adventure-fantasy which reawakened the world's interest in sci-fi films and showed what movies could do better than any other entertainment medium. The film won six Awards, the most of any film of 1977: for Costume Design, Film Editing, Art Direction, Sound, Original Music Score, Visual Effects plus a Special Achievement Award, voted by the Academy's Board of Governors.

Best Actor: Richard Dreyfuss as Elliot Garfield in *The Goodbye Girl* (M-G-M/Warner Bros.; directed by Herbert Ross). Dreyfuss, with words written by Neil Simon, played an aspiring actor in New York, sharing a Manhattan apartment with a grumbling mother (Marsha Mason) and her precocious young daughter (Quinn Cummings), and concurrently struggling to star in an off-Broadway and off-beat version of *Richard III*. It was his first Academy nomination.

Best Picture: Annie Hall (United Artists; produced by Charles H. Joffe), **Best Director: Woody Allen** and **Best Actress: Diane Keaton** as Annie (below, with Allen as Alvy Singer) in *Annie Hall*. Annie's a budding singer, and Alvy is a TV-nightclub comic; they meet in Manhattan, have a brief entanglement, then split. Told with penetrating insights into relationships (and generously sprinkled with Woody Allen's unique deadpan humor), *Annie Hall* won four Oscars, including two for Mr. Allen, as director and as co-author (with Marshall Brickman) of the Original Screenplay, and one for the infectious title performance by Miss Keaton.

Nominations 1977

PICTURE

★ **ANNIE HALL**, Rollins-Joffe, UA. Produced by Charles H. Joffe.
THE GOODBYE GIRL, Stark, M-G-M/Warner Bros. Produced by Ray Stark.
JULIA, 20th Century-Fox. Produced by Richard Roth.
STAR WARS, 20th Century-Fox. Produced by Gary Kurtz.
THE TURNING POINT, Hera Productions, 20th Century-Fox. Produced by Herbert Ross and Arthur Laurents.

ACTOR

WOODY ALLEN in *Annie Hall*, Rollins-Joffe, UA.
RICHARD BURTON in *Equus*, Winkast, UA.
★ **RICHARD DREYFUSS** in *The Goodbye Girl*, Stark, M-G-M/Warner Bros.
MARCELLO MASTROIANNI in *A Special Day*, Canafox Films, Cinema 5 (Italian).
JOHN TRAVOLTA in *Saturday Night Fever*, Stigwood, Paramount.

ACTRESS

ANNE BANCROFT in *The Turning Point*, Hera Productions, 20th Century-Fox.
JANE FONDA in *Julia*, 20th Century-Fox.
★ **DIANE KEATON** in *Annie Hall*, Rollins-Joffe, UA.

SHIRLEY MacLAINE in *The Turning Point*, Hera Productions, 20th Century-Fox.
MARSHA MASON in *The Goodbye Girl*, Stark, M-G-M/Warner Bros.

SUPPORTING ACTOR

MIKHAIL BARYSHNIKOV in *The Turning Point*, Hera Productions, 20th Century-Fox.
PETER FIRTH in *Equus*, Winkast, UA.
ALEC GUINNESS in *Star Wars*, 20th Century-Fox.
★ **JASON ROBARDS** in *Julia*, 20th Century-Fox.
MAXIMILIAN SCHELL in *Julia*, 20th Century-Fox.

SUPPORTING ACTRESS

LESLIE BROWNE in *The Turning Point*, Hera Productions, 20th Century-Fox.
QUINN CUMMINGS in *The Goodbye Girl*, Stark, M-G-M/Warner Bros.
MELINDA DILLON in *Close Encounters of the Third Kind*, Columbia.
★ **VANESSA REDGRAVE** in *Julia*, 20th Century-Fox.
TUESDAY WELD in *Looking for Mr. Goodbar*, Fields, Paramount.

DIRECTION

★ **WOODY ALLEN** for *Annie Hall*, Rollins-Joffee, UA.

GEORGE LUCAS for *Star Wars*, 20th Century-Fox.
HERBERT ROSS for *The Turning Point*, Hera Productions, 20th Century-Fox.
STEVEN SPIELBERG for *Close Encounters Of The Third Kind*, Columbia.
FRED ZINNEMANN for *Julia*, 20th Century-Fox.

WRITING

(Screenplay Written Directly for the Screen)

★ **ANNIE HALL**, Rollins-Joffe, Woody Allen and Marshall Brickman.
THE GOODBYE GIRL, Ray Stark, M-G-M/Warner Bros. Neil Simon.
THE LATE SHOW, Lion's Gate, Warner Bros. Robert Benton.
STAR WARS, 20th Century-Fox. George Lucas.
THE TURNING POINT, Hera Productions, 20th Century-Fox. Arthur Laurents.

(Screenplay Based on Material from Another Medium)

EQUUS, Winkast Company, UA. Peter Shaffer.
I NEVER PROMISED YOU A ROSE GARDEN, Scherick/Blatt, New World Pictures. Gavin Lambert and Lewis John Carlino.
★ **JULIA**, 20th Century-Fox. Alvin Sargent.
OH, GOD!, Warner Bros. Larry Gelbart.
THAT OBSCURE OBJECT OF DESIRE, First Artists (Spain). Luis Bunuel and Jean-Claude Carriere.

CINEMATOGRAPHY

★ **CLOSE ENCOUNTERS OF THE THIRD KIND**, Columbia. Vilmos Zsigmond.
ISLANDS IN THE STREAM, Bart/Palevsky, Paramount. Fred J. Loenekamp.

JULIA, 20th Century-Fox. Douglas Slocombe.
LOOKING FOR MR. GOODBAR, Freddie Fields, Paramount. William A. Fraker.

THE TURNING POINT, Hera Productions, 20th Century-Fox. Robert Surtees.

ART DIRECTION-SET DECORATION

AIRPORT '77, Jennings Lang, Universal. George C. Webb; Mickey S. Michaels.
CLOSE ENCOUNTERS OF THE THIRD KIND, Columbia. Joe Alves and Dan Lomino; Phil Abramson.
THE SPY WHO LOVED ME, Eon, UA. Ken Adam and Peter Lamont; Hugh Scaife.
★ **STAR WARS**, 20th Century-Fox. John Barry, Norman Reynolds and Leslie Dilley; Roger Christian.
THE TURNING POINT, Hera Productions, 20th Century-Fox. Albert Brenner; Marvin March.

COSTUME DESIGN

AIRPORT '77, Jennings Lang, Universal. Edith Head and Burton Miller.
JULIA, 20th Century-Fox. Anthea Sylbert.
A LITTLE NIGHT MUSIC, Sascha-Wien/Elliott Kastner, New World Pictures. Florence Klotz.
THE OTHER SIDE OF MIDNIGHT, Frank Yablans, 20th Century-Fox. Irene Sharaff.
★ **STAR WARS**, 20th Century-Fox. John Mollo.

SOUND

CLOSE ENCOUNTERS OF THE THIRD KIND, Columbia. Robert Knudson, Robert J. Glass, Don MacDougall and Gene S. Cantamessa.
THE DEEP, Casablanca Filmworks, Columbia. Walter Goss, Dick Alexander, Tom Beckert and Robin Gregory.
SORCERER, Friedkin, Paramount/Universal. Robert Knudson, Robert J. Glass, Richard Tyler and Jean-Louis Ducarme.
★ **STAR WARS**, 20th Century-Fox. Don MacDougall, Ray West, Bob Minkler and Derek Ball.

Best Supporting Actress: Vanessa Redgrave as Julia (right, with Jane Fonda) in *Julia* (20th Century-Fox; directed by Fred Zinnemann). *Julia* was based on Lillian Hellman's *Pentimento,* with Jane Fonda playing author Hellman, reminiscing about her early life and, especially a childhood friend (played by Miss Redgrave), who grew into an impassioned activist in World War II Europe, and was eventually murdered by Nazi factions. Previously, Vanessa Redgrave had been an Academy nominee for *Morgan!* (1966), *Isadora* (1968) and *Mary, Queen of Scots* (1971).

Best Supporting Actor: Jason Robards as Dashiell Hammett in *Julia.* For the second year in a row, Jason Robards won the Academy's Supporting Actor Award; for the second year in a row, he was also portraying a real-life person, this time, Dashiell Hammett, the author of *The Thin Man* and *The Maltese Falcon,* and—as portrayed in *Julia*—the man who helped Miss Hellman evolve into a noted playwright.

THE TURNING POINT, Hera Productions, 20th Century-Fox. Theodore Soderberg, Paul Wells, Douglas O. Williams and Jerry Jost.

FILM EDITING

CLOSE ENCOUNTERS OF THE THIRD KIND, Columbia. Michael Kahn.
JULIA, 20th Century-Fox. Walter Murch and Marcel Durham.
SMOKEY AND THE BANDIT, Rastar, Universal. Walter Hannemann and Angelo Ross.
★ STAR WARS, 20th Century-Fox. Paul Hirsch, Marcia Lucas and Richard Chew.
THE TURNING POINT, Hera Productions, 20th Century-Fox. William Reynolds.

VISUAL EFFECTS

CLOSE ENCOUNTERS OF THE THIRD KIND, Columbia. Roy Arbogast, Douglas Trumbull, Matthew Yuricich, Gregory Jein and Richard Yuricich.
★ STAR WARS, 20th Century-Fox. John Stears, John Dykstra, Richard Edlund, Grant McCune and Robert Blalack.

MUSIC

(Song)
CANDLE ON THE WATER (*Pete's Dragon,* Disney, Buena Vista); Music and Lyrics by Al Kasha and Joel Hirschhorn.
NOBODY DOES IT BETTER (*The Spy Who Loved Me,* Eon, UA); Music by Marvin Hamlisch. Lyrics by Carole Bayer Sager.

THE SLIPPER AND THE ROSE WALTZ He Danced With Me/She Danced With Me) (*The Slipper and the Rose—The Story of Cinderella,* Paradine Co-Productions, Universal); Music and Lyrics by Richard M. Sherman and Robert B. Sherman.
SOMEONE'S WAITING FOR YOU (*The Rescuers,* Disney, Buena Vista); Music by Sammy Fain. Lyrics by Carol Connors and Ayn Robbins.
★ YOU LIGHT UP MY LIFE (*You Light Up My Life,* Session Company, Columbia); Music and Lyrics by Joseph Brooks.

(Original Score)
CLOSE ENCOUNTERS OF THE THIRD KIND, Columbia. John Williams.
JULIA, 20th Century-Fox. Georges Delerue.
MOHAMMAD-MESSENGER OF GOD, Filmco International, Irwin Yablans Company. Maurice Jarre.
THE SPY WHO LOVED ME, Eon, UA. Marvin Hamlisch.
★ STAR WARS, 20th Century-Fox. John Williams.

(Original Song Score and Its Adaptation or Best Adaptation Score)
★ A LITTLE NIGHT MUSIC, Sascha-Wien/ Elliott Kastner, New World Pictures. Jonathan Tunick.
PETE'S DRAGON, Disney, Buena Vista. Al Kasha, Joel Hirschhorn and Irwin Kostal.
THE SLIPPER AND THE ROSE—THE STORY OF CINDERELLA, Paradine Co-Productions, Universal. Richard M. Sherman, Robert B. Sherman and Angela Morley.

SHORT FILMS

(Animated Films)
THE BEAD GAME, National Film Board of Canada. Ishu Patel, producer.
THE DOONESBURY SPECIAL, Hubley Studio. John and Faith Hubley and Gary Trudeau, producers.
JIMMY THE C, Motionpicker Production. James Picker, Robert Grossman and Craig Whitaker, producers.
★ SAND CASTLE, National Film Board of Canada. Co Hoedeman, producer.

(Live Action)
THE ABSENT-MINDED WAITER, Aspen Film Society. William E. McEuen, producer.
FLOATING FREE, Trans World International. Jerry Butts, producer.
★ I'LL FIND A WAY, National Film Board of Canada. Beverly Shaffer and Yuki Yoshida, producers.
NOTES ON THE POPULAR ARTS, Saul Bass Films. Saul Bass, producer.
SPACEBORNE, Lawrence Hall of Science Production for the Regents of the University of California with the cooperation of NASA. Philip Dauber, producer.

DOCUMENTARY

(Short Subjects)
AGUEDA MARTINEZ: OUR PEOPLE, OUR COUNTRY, Esparza Production. Moctesuma Esparza, producer.
FIRST EDITION, Sage Productions. Helen Whitney and DeWitt L. Sage, Jr., producers.
★ GRAVITY IS MY ENEMY, Joseph Production. John Joseph and Jan Stussy, producers.
OF TIME, TOMBS AND TREASURE, Charlie/Papa Production. James R. Messenger and Paul N. Raimondi, producers.
THE SHETLAND EXPERIENCE, Balfour Films. Douglas Gordon, producer.

(Features)
THE CHILDREN OF THEATRE STREET, Mack-Vaganova Company. Robert Dornhelm and Earle Mack, producers.
HIGH GRASS CIRCUS, National Film Board of Canada. Bill Brind, Torben Schioler and Tony Ianzelo, producers.

HOMAGE TO CHAGALL—THE COLOURS OF LOVE, CBC Production. Harry Rasky, producer.
UNION MAIDS, Klein, Reichert, Mogulescu Production. James Klein, Julia Reichert and Miles Mogulescu, producers.
WHO ARE THE DeBOLTS? AND WHERE DID THEY GET NINETEEN KIDS? Korty Films/Charles M. Schulz, Sanrio Films. John Korty, Dan McCann and Warren L. Lockhart, producers.

FOREIGN LANGUAGE FILM

IPHIGENIA, (Greece).
★ MADAME ROSA, (France).
OPERATION THUNDERBOLT, (Israel).
A SPECIAL DAY, (Italy).
THAT OBSCURE OBJECT OF DESIRE, (Spain).

HONORARY AND OTHER AWARDS

TO MARGARET BOOTH for her exceptional contribution to the art of film editing in the motion picture industry.
GORDON E. SAWYER and SIDNEY P. SOLOW in appreciation for outstanding service and dedication in upholding the high standards of the Academy of Motion Picture Arts and Sciences. (medal of commendation)

SPECIAL ACHIEVEMENT AWARDS

For Sound Effects Editing: FRANK WARNER for *Close Encounters Of The Third Kind,* Columbia.
For Sound Effects Creations: BENJAMIN BURTT, JR. for *Star Wars,* 20th Century-Fox.

1977 IRVING G. THALBERG MEMORIAL AWARD

TO WALTER MIRISCH

1977 JEAN HERSHOLT HUMANITARIAN AWARD

TO CHARLTON HESTON

SCIENTIFIC OR TECHNICAL

CLASS I (statuette)
GARRETT BROWN and the CINEMA PRODUCTS CORP. ENGINEERING STAFF UNDER THE SUPERVISION OF JOHN JURGENS for the invention and development of Steadicam.

CLASS II (plaque)
JOSEPH D. KELLY, EMORY M. COHEN, BARRY K. HENLEY, HAMMOND H. HOLT and JOHN AGALSOFF of GLEN GLENN SOUND for the concept and development of a post-production audio processing system for motion picture films.
PANAVISION, INCORPORATED for the concept and engineering of the improvements incorporated in the Panaflex Motion Picture Camera.
N. PAUL KENWORTHY, JR. and WILLIAM R. LATADY for the invention and development of the Kenworthy Snorkel Camera System for motion picture photography.
JOHN C. DYKSTRA for the development of the Dykstraflex Camera and ALVAH J. MILLER and JERRY JEFFRESS for the engineering of the Electronic Motion Control System used in concert for multiple exposure visual effects motion picture photography.
THE EASTMAN KODAK COMPANY for the development and introduction of a new duplicating film for motion pictures.
STEFAN KUDELSKI of Nagra Magnetic Recorders, Incorporated, for the engineering of the improvements incorporated in the Nagra 4.2L sound recorder for motion picture production.

CLASS III (citation)
ERNST NETTMANN of the Astrovision Division of Continental Camera Systems, Inc.;
EECO (ELECTRONIC ENGINEERING COMPANY OF CALIFORNIA;
DR. BERNARD KUNTZ and WERNER BLOCK of OSRAM, GmbH;
PANAVISION, INCORPORATED (2 citations);
TO PICLEAR, INC.

★ INDICATES WINNER

The First Fifty Years Awards Ceremonies

1st Awards: May 16, 1929
honoring 1927-28 achievements
Hollywood Roosevelt Hotel (banquet)

Participants included: Frank Borzage, Cecil B. DeMille, William C. deMille, Douglas Fairbanks, Janet Gaynor, William Cameron Menzies, Prof. W.R. Miles, Lewis Milestone, Conrad Nagel, Fred Niblo, Mary Pickford, Winfield Sheehan, Karl Struss, King Vidor, Darryl F. Zanuck, Adolph Zukor.

2nd Awards: April 3, 1930
honoring 1928-29 achievements
Ambassador Hotel, Los Angeles (banquet)

Participants included: Warner Baxter, William C. deMille, Frank Lloyd, Mary Pickford.

3rd Awards: November 5, 1930
honoring 1929-30 achievements
Ambassador Hotel, Los Angeles (banquet)

Participants included: John Cromwell, Jack Cunningham, Arthur Edeson, Lawrence Grant, Carl Laemmle Sr., Louis B. Mayer, William Cameron Menzies, Norma Shearer, Nugent H. Slaughter, Darryl F. Zanuck.

4th Awards: November 10, 1931
honoring 1930-31 achievements
Biltmore Hotel, Los Angeles (banquet)

Participants included: George Arliss, Lionel Barrymore, United States Vice President Charles Curtis, Marie Dressler, Lawrence Grant, William K. Howard, William LeBaron, Van Nest Polglase, J. Theodore Reed, B.D. Schulberg, Norma Shearer, Nugent H. Slaughter, Karl Struss, Norman Taurog, Waldemar Young.

5th Awards: November 18, 1932
honoring 1931-32 achievements
Ambassador Hotel, Los Angeles (banquet)

Participants included: Lionel Barrymore, Wallace Beery, Frank Borzage, Walt Disney, Howard Estabrook, Helen Hayes, William LeBaron, Fredric March, Louis B. Mayer, Conrad Nagel, John M. Nickolaus, Max Ree, Hal Roach, Mack Sennett, Norma Shearer, Karl Struss, Norman Taurog.

May 16, 1929: The Academy's second anniversary banquet, and first presentation of Awards

Participants

6th Awards: March 16, 1934
honoring 1932-33 achievements
Ambassador Hotel, Los Angeles (banquet)

Participants included: B.B. Kahane, Frank Lloyd, Will Rogers, Winfield Sheehan.

7th Awards: February 27, 1935
honoring 1934 achievements
Biltmore Hotel, Los Angeles (banquet)

Participants included: Frank Capra, Irvin S. Cobb, Harry Cohn, Claudette Colbert, Clark Gable, Shirley Temple.

8th Awards: March 5, 1936
honoring 1935 achievements
Biltmore Hotel, Los Angeles (banquet)

Participants included: Frank Capra, Harry Cohn, Bette Davis, Walt Disney, D.W. Griffith, Nathan Levinson, Victor McLaglen, Rouben Mamoulian, Robert Riskin, Pete Smith, Irving G. Thalberg, Henry B. Walthall.

Victor McLaglen, Bette Davis, Paul Muni

Charles Laughton, Norma Shearer, Fredric March

9th Awards: March 4, 1937
honoring 1936 achievements
Biltmore Hotel, Los Angeles (banquet)

Participants included: Walter Brennan, Frank Capra, Dr. Lee DeForest, Walt Disney, George Jessel, Frank Lloyd, Victor McLaglen, Louis B. Mayer, Paul Muni, Luise Rainer, Gale Sondergaard, Leopold Stokowski.

10th Awards: March 10, 1938
honoring 1937 achievements
Biltmore Hotel, Los Angeles (banquet)

Participants included: Edgar Bergen and Charlie McCarthy, Irving Berlin, Bob Burns, Frank Capra, Cecil B. DeMille, Walt Disney, Howard Estabrook, Douglas Fairbanks, W.C. Fields, Nathan Levinson, Leo McCarey, Louella O. Parsons, Luise Rainer, Robert Riskin, Joseph Schildkraut, Dr. Arnold Schoenberg, Mack Sennett, C. Aubrey Smith, Mrs. Spencer Tracy, Jack L. Warner, Darryl F. Zanuck.

Walt Disney, Shirley Temple

11th Awards: February 23, 1939
honoring 1938 achievements
Biltmore Hotel, Los Angeles (banquet)

Participants included: Fay Bainter, Edgar Bergen and Charlie McCarthy, Walter Brennan, Frank Capra, Harry Cohn, Bette Davis, Walt Disney, Lloyd C. Douglas, Deanna Durbin, Sir Cedric Hardwicke, Bob Hope, Jerome Kern, Frank Lloyd, Fred Niblo, Tyrone Power, James Roosevelt, Joseph M. Schenck, Shirley Temple, Spencer Tracy, Hal Wallis, Harry M. Warner.

12th Awards: February 29, 1940
honoring 1939 achievements
Ambassador Hotel, Los Angeles (banquet)

Participants included: Fay Bainter, Gene Buck, Douglas Fairbanks Jr., Y. Frank Freeman, Judy Garland, Jean Hersholt, Bob Hope, Dr. Ernest Martin Hopkins, Mervyn LeRoy, Vivien Leigh, Sinclair Lewis, Hattie McDaniel, Thomas Mitchell, Basil O'Connor, Mickey Rooney, Victor Saville, David O. Selznick, Spencer Tracy, Walter Wanger, Darryl F. Zanuck.

13th Awards: Feburary 27, 1941
honoring 1940 achievements
Biltmore Hotel, Los Angeles (banquet)

Participants included: Walter Brennan, Frank Capra, Jane Darwell, B.G. De Sylva, Walt Disney, Bob Hope, Lynn Fontanne, Mervyn LeRoy, Alfred Lunt, Major Gen. J.O. Mauborgne, Quentin Reynolds, Ginger Rogers, *President Franklin D. Roosevelt, Rosalind Russell, David O. Selznick, James Stewart, Preston Sturges, Walter Wanger, Darryl F. Zanuck.

*Via direct-line radio address from Washington, D.C.

14th Awards: February 26, 1942
honoring 1941 achievements
Biltmore Hotel, Los Angeles (banquet)

Participants included: Mary Astor, George Barnes, Gary Cooper, Donald Crisp, Cecil B. DeMille, B.G. DeSylva, Walt Disney, John Farrow, Joan Fontaine, John Grierson, Bob Hope, Mervyn LeRoy, William Pereira, Ginger Rogers, David O. Selznick, James Stewart, Preston Sturges, Wendell L. Wilkie, Darryl F. Zanuck.

15th Awards: March 4, 1943
honoring 1942 achievements
Ambassador Hotel, Los Angeles (banquet)

Participants included: Irving Berlin, Charles Boyer, James Cagney, Frank Capra, Gary Cooper, Walt Disney, Joan Fontaine, Mrs. Sidney Franklin, Y. Frank Freeman, Greer Garson, William Goetz, Van Heflin, Bob Hope, James Wong Howe, Alan Ladd, Mervyn LeRoy, Mary McCall Jr., Louis B. Mayer, William Cameron Menzies, Tyrone Power, David O. Selznick, Carey Wilson, Teresa Wright, Mrs. William Wyler.

16th Awards: March 2, 1944
honoring 1943 achievements
Grauman's Chinese Theatre, Hollywood
(first presentation in a theater)

Participants included: Jack Benny, Charles Coburn, Donald Crisp, Michael Curtiz, Howard Estabrook, Sidney Franklin, Y. Frank Freeman, Greer Garson, James Hilton, Jennifer Jones, Carole Landis, Paul Lukas, George Murphy, George Pal, Katina Paxinou, Rosalind Russell, Mark Sandrich, Dinah Shore, Hal Wallis, Walter Wanger, Jack L. Warner, Teresa Wright, Darryl F. Zanuck.

17th Awards: March 15, 1945
honoring 1944 achievements
Grauman's Chinese Theatre, Hollywood
Producer: Mervyn LeRoy
Musical director: Franz Waxman

Participants included: Ingrid Bergman, Hugo Butler, Charles Coburn, Gary Cooper, John Cromwell, Bing Crosby, B.G. DeSylva, Barry Fitzgerald, Bob Hope, Jennifer Jones, Charles Koerner, Mervyn LeRoy, Leo McCarey, Margaret O'Brien, Norma Shearer, Hal Wallis, Walter Wanger, Teresa Wright, Darryl F. Zanuck.

1942 Awards banquet

Hattie McDaniel, Fay Bainter

18th Awards: March 7, 1946
honoring 1945 achievements)
Grauman's Chinese Theatre, Hollywood
Producer: Dore Schary
Musical director: Johnny Green

Participants included: Ingrid Bergman, Charles Boyer, Frank Capra, Michael Curtiz, Bette Davis, James Dunn, Y. Frank Freeman, Peggy Ann Garner, Henry Ginsberg, D.W. Griffith, Van Heflin, Bob Hope, Eric Johnston, Ray Milland, George Murphy, Donald Nelson, Anne Revere, Ginger Rogers, Frank Sinatra, James Stewart, Walter Wanger, Billy Wilder, Esther Williams, William Wyler.

19th Awards: March 13, 1947
honoring 1946 achievements
Shrine Civic Auditorium, Los Angeles
Producer: Mervyn LeRoy
Musical director: Leo Forbstein

Participants included: Lionel Barrymore, Anne Baxter, Jack Benny, Hoagy Carmichael, Olivia de Havilland, Douglas Fairbanks Jr., Joan Fontaine, Greer Garson, Samuel Goldwyn, Rex Harrison, Dick Haymes, Jean Hersholt, Claude Jarman Jr., Deborah Kerr, Van Johnson, Eric Johnston, Ernst Lubitsch, Ray Milland, Robert Montgomery, Donald Nelson, Cathy O'Donnell, Maureen O'Hara, Anne Revere, Andy Russell, Harold Russell, Ann Sheridan, Dinah Shore, Shirley Temple, Lana Turner, Billy Wilder, William Wyler.

Olivia de Havilland, Ronald Colman

20th Awards: March 20, 1948
honoring 1947 achievements
Shrine Civic Auditorium, Los Angeles
Producer: Delmer Daves
Musical director: Ray Heindorf

Participants included: James Baskette, Anne Baxter, Ingrid Bergman, Ken Carpenter, Ronald Colman, Donald Crisp, Dennis Day, Olivia de Havilland, Edmund Gwenn, Jean Hersholt, Celeste Holm, Elia Kazan, Frances Langford, Gordon MacRae, Fredric March, Johnny Mercer, Robert Montgomery, Agnes Moorehead, George Murphy, Ken Murray, Larry Parks, the Pied Pipers, Dick Powell, Dinah Shore, Jean Simmons, Shirley Temple, Carey Wilson, Loretta Young, Darryl F. Zanuck.

21st Awards: March 24, 1949
honoring 1948 achievements
Academy Award Theater, West Hollywood
Producer: William Dozier
Musical director: Johnny Green

Participants included: Harry Babbitt, Ethel Barrymore, Ann Blyth, Frank Borzage, Ronald Colman, Wendell Corey, Jeanne Crain, Arlene Dahl, Doris Day, Douglas Fairbanks Jr., Glenn Ford, Ava Gardner, Sid Grauman, Kathryn Grayson, Edmund Gwenn, Jean Hersholt, Celeste Holm, John Huston, Walter Huston, Louis Jourdan, Deborah Kerr, Gordon MacRae, Robert Montgomery, George Murphy, Jane Russell, Robert Ryan, Jo Stafford, Elizabeth Taylor, Claire Trevor, Jerry Wald, Walter Wanger, Gloria Wood, Jane Wyman, Loretta Young, Fred Zinnemann.

22nd Awards: March 23, 1950
honoring 1949 achievements
RKO Pantages Theatre, Hollywood
Producer: Johnny Green
Musical director: Robert Emmett Dolan

Participants included: June Allyson, Gene Autry, Anne Baxter, Ann Blyth, Charles Brackett, James Cagney, Cass Country Boys, Broderick Crawford, Arlene Dahl, Olivia de Havilland, Mrs. Cecil B. DeMille, Paul Douglas, Peggy Dow, Bobby Driscoll, Joanne Dru, Jose Ferrer, Betty Garrett, Barbara Hale, John Hodiak, Dean Jagger, John Lund, Ida Lupino, Mercedes McCambridge, Joseph L. Mankiewicz, Dean Martin, Ray Milland, Ricardo Montalban, George Murphy, Patricia Neal, Donald O'Connor, Cole Porter, Dick Powell, Micheline Prelle, Ronald Reagan, Mark Robson, Ruth Roman, Ginger Rogers, Robert Rossen, Red Skelton, Jack Smith, James Stewart, Claire Trevor, Jane Wyman.

23rd Awards: March 29, 1951
honoring 1950 achievements
RKO Pantages Theatre, Hollywood
Producer: Richard L. Breen
Musical director: Alfred Newman

Participants included: Fred Astaire, Lex Barker, Ethel Barrymore, Charles Brackett, Dr. Ralph Bunche, Ruth Chatterton, Broderick Crawford, Arlene Dahl, Gloria DeHaven, Marlene Dietrich, *Jose Ferrer, Coleen Gray, Jane Greer, Helen Hayes, *Judy Holliday, Josephine Hull, Dean Jagger, Gene Kelly, Phyllis Kirk, Frankie Laine, Jerry Lewis, Leo McCarey, Mercedes McCambridge, Joseph L. Mankiewicz, Dean Martin, Louis B. Mayer, Robert Merrill, Marilyn Monroe, George Murphy, Lucille Norman, Georg Sanders, Jan Sterling, David Wayne, Alan Young, Darryl F. Zanuck.

*Via radio from New York City

24th Awards: March 20, 1952
honoring 1951 achievements
RKO Pantages Theatre, Hollywood
Producer: Arthur Freed
Writers: Sylvia Fine, Richard L. Breen
Musical director: Johnny Green

Participants included: Lucille Ball, Humphrey Bogart, Charles Brackett, Kay Brown, Leslie Caron, Marge and Gower Champion, Cyd Charisse, Ronald Colman, Bette Davis, Stanley Donen, Sally Forrest, Arthur Freed, Zsa Zsa Gabor, Greer Garson, Dick Haymes, Barry Jones, Danny Kaye, Howard Keel, Jesse L. Lasky, Sol Lesser, Clare Booth Luce, Karl Malden, Joseph L. Mankiewicz, George Murphy, Donald O'Connor, Nancy Olson, Jane Powell, Janice Rule, George Sanders, Constance Smith, George Stevens, Claire Trevor, Vera-Ellen, Jane Wyman, Darryl F. Zanuck.

25th Awards: March 19, 1953
honoring 1952 achievements
RKO Pantages Theatre, Hollywood
    and NBC International Theatre, New York
Producer: Johnny Green
Writer: Richard L. Breen
Musical director: Adolph Deutsch
NBC-TV director: William A. Bennington

Participants included: Irwin Allen, Anne Baxter, Edgar Bergen and Charlie McCarthy, Jacques Bergerac, Shirley Booth, Charles Brackett, Frank Capra, Charles Coburn, Ronald Colman, Merian C. Cooper, Broderick Crawford, Joan Crawford, Donald Crisp, Billy Daniels, Jane Darwell, Olivia de Havilland, Cecil B. DeMille, Walt Disney, Bobby Driscoll, Joan Fontaine, Greer Garson, Janet Gaynor, Gloria Grahame, Edmund Gwenn, Jean Hersholt, Celeste Holm, Bob Hope, Kim Hunter, Dean Jagger, Piper Laurie, Peggy Lee, Harold Lloyd, Victor McLaglen, Fredric March, Marilyn Maxwell, Johnny Mercer, Ray Milland, Paul Muni, George Murphy, Conrad Nagel, Mary Pickford, Katharine DeMille Quinn, Luise Rainer, Ronald Reagan, Tex Ritter, Ginger Rogers, Dore Schary, James Stewart, Gloria Swanson, Claire Trevor, John Wayne, Teresa Wright, Jane Wyman, Loretta Young, Darryl F. Zanuck.

1956 Awards telecast

26th Awards: March 25, 1954
honoring 1953 achievements
RKO Pantages Theatre, Hollywood
    and NBC Century Theatre, New York
Producer: Mitchell Leisen
Writer: Hal Kanter
Musical director: Andre Previn
NBC-TV directors: William A. Bennington
    and Gray Lockwood

Participants included: Buddy Adler, Phyllis Applegate, Lex Barker, Ann Blyth, *Shirley Booth, Charles Brackett, Keefe Brasselle, Joseph I. Breen, Walter Brennan, Marge and Gower Champion, **Gary Cooper, Cecil B. DeMille, Walt Disney, Kirk Douglas, Irene Dunne, Marla English, Marilyn Erskine, Arthur Freed, Mitzi Gaynor, Gloria Gordon, Audrey Hepburn, Jean Hersholt, William Holden, Virginia Leith, Mercedes McCambridge, Ann McCree, Fredric March, Dean Martin, Marjie Millar, Kim Novak, Merle Oberon, Donald O'Connor, Tyrone Power, Donna Reed, Connie Russell, David O. Selznick, Sara Shane, Frank Sinatra, Pete Smith, George Stevens, Elizabeth Taylor, Gene Tierney, Lana Turner, Jack Webb, Joan Weldon, Margaret Wilding, Michael Wilding, Esther Williams, Darryl F. Zanuck, Fred Zinnemann.

*Live cut-in from Philadelphia

**Cooper appeared in a special segment specifically filmed for the Oscar telecast, as other personalities have subsequently done from time to time.

27th Awards: March 30, 1955
honoring 1954 achievements
RKO Pantages Theatre, Hollywood
    and NBC Century Theatre, New York
Producer: Jean Negulesco
Writers: Richard L. Breen, Melville Shavelson,
    Jack Rose
Musical director: David Rose
NBC-TV directors: William A. Bennington,
    Gray Lockwood

Participants included: Buddy Adler, Lauren Bacall, Humphrey Bogart, Charles Brackett, Marlon Brando, Sarah Churchill, Rosemary Clooney, Lee J. Cobb, Bing Crosby, Dorothy Dandridge, Bette Davis, Johnny Desmond, Walt Disney, Nina Foch, *Audrey Hepburn, William Holden, Bob Hope, Jeanmaire, Katy Jurado, Danny Kaye, Elia Kazan, Grace Kelly, Nancy Kelly, Peggy King, Karl Malden, Muzzy Marcellino, Dean Martin, Tony Martin, Conrad Nagel, Edmond O'Brien, Dan O'Herlihy, Merle Oberon, Donna Reed, Tommy Rettig, Thelma Ritter, Eva Marie Saint, George Seaton, Frank Sinatra, Sam Spiegel, Rod Steiger, Jan Sterling, Claire Trevor, Tom Tully, Jane Wyman.

*Pre-filmed

28th Awards: March 21, 1956
honoring 1955 achievements
RKO Pantages Theatre, Hollywood
    and NBC Century Theatre, New York
Producers: Robert Emmett Dolan, George Seaton
Musical director: Andre Previn
Writers: Melville Shavelson, Jack Rose, Richard L.
    Breen
NBC-TV directors: William A. Bennington,
    Richard Schneider

Participants included: Harry Belafonte, Ernest Borgnine, *Marlon Brando, James Cagney, *Cantinflas, Maurice Chevalier, Claudette Colbert, Paddy Chayefsky, Mel Ferrer, Eddie Fisher, Susan Hayward, Harold Hecht, Audrey Hepburn, *Jennifer Jones, Grace Kelly, Peggy Lee, Jack Lemmon, Jerry Lewis, *''Mr. Magoo,'' *Anna Magnani, Joseph L. Mankiewicz, Delbert Mann, Joe Mantell, Dean Martin, Sal Mineo, Edmond O'Brien, Arthur O'Connell, Eleanor Parker, Marisa Pavan, Jane Powell, Eva Marie Saint, Frank Sinatra, Claire Trevor, Jo Van Fleet.

*Pre-filmed

29th Awards: March 27, 1957
honoring 1956 achievements
RKO Pantages Theatre, Hollywood
    and NBC Century Theatre, New York
Producers: Valentine Davies, Robert Emmett
    Dolan
Writers: Arthur Phillips, Harry Crane, Hal Kanter
Musical director: Johnny Green
NBC-TV directors: William A. Bennington,
    Max Miller

Participants included: Buddy Adler, Carroll Baker, *Ingrid Bergman, Ernest Borgnine, Yul Brynner, Eddie Cantor, Marge and Gower Champion, *Bing Crosby, *Kirk Douglas, the Four Aces, Y. Frank Freeman, Janet Gaynor, Hermione Gingold, Cary Grant, Gogi Grant, Celeste Holm, *Rock Hudson, Nancy Kelly, Deborah Kerr, Jack Lemmon, Jerry Lewis, Mercedes McCambridge, Patty McCormack, Anna Magnani, Dorothy Malone, Rita Moreno, Anthony Quinn, Mickey Rooney, Eva Marie Saint, Tommy Sands, George Seaton, Robert Stack, George Stevens, Elizabeth Taylor, Michael Todd, Claire Trevor.

*Pre-filmed

Elizabeth Taylor at 1960 post-Awards party

30th Awards: March 26, 1958
honoring 1957 achievements
RKO Pantages Theatre, Hollywood
Producer: Jerry Wald
Writers: Richard L. Breen, Melville Frank, John
  Michael Hayes, Hal Kanter, Norman Panama,
  Jack Rose, Melville Shavelson
Musical director: Alfred Newman
NBC-TV director: Alan Handley
(first year without simultaneous telecast in New York City)

Participants included: Anna Marie Alberghetti, June Allyson, "Broncho Billy" Anderson, Fred Astaire, Ann Blyth, Ernest Borgnine, Charles Brackett, Red Buttons, Marge and Gower Champion, Cyd Charisse, Maurice Chevalier, Joan Collins, Gary Cooper, Wendell Corey, Vic Damone, Bette Davis, Doris Day, Kirk Douglas, Donald Duck, Anita Ekberg, Taina Elg, Rhonda Fleming, Clark Gable, Zsa Zsa Gabor, Samuel Goldwyn, Betty Grable, Cary Grant, Myrna Hansen, Bob Hope, Rock Hudson, Tab Hunter, Harry James, Van Johnson, Jennifer Jones, Pat Jones, Shirley Jones, B.B. Kahane, Burt Lancaster, Hope Lange, David Lean, Janet Leigh, Jack Lemmon, Sophia Loren, Shirley MacLaine, Dorothy Malone, Dean Martin, Tony Martin, Guiletta Masina, Johnny Mathis, Paul Newman, David Niven, Sheree North, Kim Novak, Hugh O'Brian, Fess Parker, Gregory Peck, Vincent Price, Anthony Quinn, Ronald Reagan, Debbie Reynolds, Jimmie Rodgers, Rosalind Russell, Robert Ryan, Eva Marie Saint, Tommy Sands, Victoria Shaw, Jean Simmons, Sam Spiegel, James Stewart, Russ Tamblyn, Lana Turner, Miyoshi Umeki, John Wayne, Mae West, Joanne Woodward, Dana Wynter.

31st Awards: April 6, 1959
honoring 1958 achievements
RKO Pantages Theatre, Hollywood
Producer: Jerry Wald
Writers: Richard L. Breen, Harry Crane, I.A.L.
  Diamond, Hal Kanter, Mort Lachman, Arthur
  Phillips, Jack Rose, Melville Shavelson
Musical director: Lionel Newman
NBC-TV director: Alan Handley

Participants included: Nick Adams, Buddy Adler, Anna Maria Alberghetti, Eddie Albert, June Allyson, Ingrid Bergman, Dirk Bogarde, Red Buttons, James Cagney, Christine Carere, Marge and Gower Champion, Cyd Charisse, Maurice Chevalier, Joan Collins, Gary Cooper, Wendell Corey, Tony Curtis, Arlene Dahl, James Darren, Bette Davis, Doris Day, Sandra Dee, Irene Dunne, Tania Elg, Felicia Farr, Eddie Fisher, Rhonda Fleming, Joan Fontaine, Anthony Franciosa, Arthur Freed, Mitzi Gaynor, Cary Grant, Jon Hall, Susan Hayward, Harold Hecht, Van Heflin, Charlton Heston, Bob Hope, Rock Hudson, Burl Ives, Carolyn Jones, Dean Jones, Louis Jourdan, Howard Keel, Ernie Kovacs, Angela Lansbury, Janet Leigh, Jerry Lewis, Sophia Loren, Shirley MacLaine, Jayne Mansfield, Dean Martin, Tony Martin, Vincente Minnelli, Joanna Moore, Terry Moore, Lori Nelson, David Niven, Kim Novak, Erin O'Brien, Laurence Olivier, George Pal, Vincent Price, Anthony Quinn, John Raitt, Tony Randall, Barbara Rush, Rosalind Russell, Mort Sahl, Eva Marie Saint, Victoria Shaw, Jean Simmons, Robert Stack, George Stevens, Inger Stevens, Jacques Tati, Elizabeth Taylor, Constance Towers, Peter Ustinov, Robert Wagner, Jean Wallace, Jack L. Warner, John Wayne, Tuesday Weld, Shelley Winters, Natalie Wood, Jane Wyman, Dana Wynter.

32nd Awards: April 4, 1960
honoring 1959 achievements
RKO Pantages Theatre, Hollywood
Producer: Arthur Freed
Directors: Vincente Minnelli, John Houseman,
Joe Parker
Writers: Richard Breen, Hal Kanter, Jack Rose,
  Melville Shavelson
Musical director: Andre Previn
ABC-TV director: Richard Dunlap

Participants included: Anna Maria Alberghetti, Ann Blyth, Jack Clayton, Richard Conte, Isabell Cooley, Gary Cooper, Edward Curtis, Tony Curtis, Arlene Dahl, Sammy Davis Jr., Doris Day, Olivia de Havilland, Angie Dickinson, Ella Fitzgerald, Mitzi Gaynor, Gogi Grant, Haya Harareet, Susan Hayward, Charlton Heston, Bob Hope, Rock Hudson, Linda Hutchins, Joni James, Eric Johnston, B.B. Kahane, Buster Keaton, Gene Kelly, Frankie Laine, Fernando Lamas, Hope Lange, Barbara Lawson, Janet Leigh, Diane McBain, Yvette Mimieux, Yves Montand, Jo Morrow, Edmond O'Brien, Julie Payne, Carl Reiner, Ziva Rodann, Barbara Rush, Simone Signoret, Stella Stevens, Frankie Vaughn, Robert Wagner, Nancy Walters, John Wayne, Shelley Winters, Cindy Wood, Natalie Wood, William Wyler, Mrs. Sam Zimbalist.

33rd Awards: April 17, 1961
honoring 1960 achievements
Santa Monica Civic Auditorium, Santa Monica
Producer: Arthur Freed
Directors: Vincente Minnelli, John Houseman,
  Joe Parker
Writers: Richard Breen, Hal Kanter, Jack Rose,
  Melville Shavelson
Musical director: Andre Previn
NBC-TV director: Alan Handley

Participants included: Elizabeth Allen, Steve Allen, Brigid Bazlen, Polly Bergen, Brothers Four, Yul Brynner, Kitty Carlisle, Cyd Charisse, Carol Christensen, Betty Comden, Wendell Corey, Tony Curtis, Vic Damone, Bobby Darin, Valentine Davies, Sandra Dee, Connie Francis, Annette Funicello, Greer Garson, Adolph Green, Hugh Griffith, Moss Hart, Audrey Hepburn, The Hi-Los, Bob Hope, Jim Hutton, Eric Johnston, Shirley Jones, Danny Kaye, Burt Lancaster, Janet Leigh, Sol Lesser, Gina Lollobrigida, Tina Louise, Tony Martin, Asa Maynor, Jayne Meadows, Joyce Meadows, Margo Moore, Jane Morgan, Julie Palmer, Paula Prentiss, Juliet Prowse, Tony Randall, Juli Reding, Barbara Rush, Eva Marie Saint, Robert Stack, Barbara Steele, James Stewart, Susan Strasberg, Elizabeth Taylor, Shirley Temple, Vicki Trickett, Peter Ustinov, Sarah Vaughan, Jerry Wald, Richard Widmark, Billy Wilder, William Wyler.

Frank Sinatra, Sophia Loren

Vincente Minnelli, Liza Minnelli

34th Awards: April 9, 1962
honoring 1961 achievements
Santa Monica Civic Auditorium, Santa Monica
Producer: Arthur Freed
Writers: Richard Breen, Hal Kanter
Musical director: Johnny Green
ABC-TV director: Richard Dunlap

Participants included: Eddie Albert, Harriet Anderssen, Ann-Margret, Roxanne Arlen, Fred Astaire, Carroll Baker, Sue Barton, Charles Brackett, Brooke Bundy, Macdonald Carey, George Chakiris, Richard Chamberlain, Cyd Charisse, Wendell Corey, Joan Crawford, Angie Dickinson, Vince Edwards, Anthony Franciosa, Arthur Freed, Greer Garson, Gogi Grant, George Hamilton, Anne Helm, Bob Hope, Rock Hudson, Sharon Hugueny, Anne Jeffreys, Glynis Johns, Eric Johnston, Carolyn Jones, Shirley Jones, Howard Keel, Gene Kelly, Stanley Kramer, Burt Lancaster, Jack Lemmon, Patricia McNulty, Tony Martin, Johnny Mathis, Dina Merrill, Rita Moreno, Karla Most, Gene Pitney, Lee Remick, Debbie Reynolds, Jerome Robbins, Rosalind Russell, Maximilian Schell, George Seaton, Rod Taylor, Natalie Trundy, Nancy Walters, Andy Williams, Shelley Winters, Robert Wise, Joanne Woodward, Lang Yun.

35th Awards: April 8, 1963
honoring 1962 achievements
Santa Monica Civic Auditorium, Santa Monica
Producer: Arthur Freed
Writers: George Axelrod, Richard Breen, Hal Kanter,
  Stanley Roberts
Musical director: Alfred Newman
ABC-TV director: Richard Dunlap

Participants included: Robert Anderson, Ed Begley, Ingrid Bergman, Serge Bourguignon, Steve Broidy, George Chakiris, Wendell Corey, Joan Crawford, Bette Davis, Olivia de Havilland, Patty Duke, Eddie Fisher, Robert Goulet, Van Heflin, Audrey Hepburn, Anne Jeffreys, David Lean, Sophia Loren, Carol Lynley, Karl Malden, Ethel Merman, Rita Moreno, David Niven, Laurence Olivier, Gregory Peck, Donna Reed, Ginger Rogers, Eva Marie Saint, Maximilian Schell, Simone Signoret, Frank Sinatra, Sam Spiegel, Robert Stack, Robert Sterling, Miyoshi Umeki, Shelley Winters.

Sidney Poitier, Anne Bancroft

36th Awards: April 13, 1964
honoring 1963 achievements
Santa Monica Civic Auditorium, Santa Monica
Producer: George Sidney
Writers: George Axelrod, Richard Breen, Mort
   Lachman, Stanley Roberts, Melville Shavelson
Musical director: John Green
ABC-TV director: Richard Dunlap

Participants included: Julie Andrews, Annabella, Anne Bancroft, Anne Baxter, Ed Begley, James Darren, Sammy Davis Jr., Brandon de Wilde, Angie Dickinson, Patty Duke, Dame Edith Evans, Federico Fellini, Arthur Freed, Rita Hayworth, Rock Hudson, Shirley Jones, Jack Lemmon, Jack Lord, Shirley MacLaine, Fred MacMurray, Steve McQueen, Gregory Peck, David V. Picker, Sidney Poitier, Harve Presnell, Katina Ranieri, Donna Reed, Debbie Reynolds, Edward G. Robinson, Frank Sinatra, Sam Spiegel, James Stewart, Peter Ustinov, Tuesday Weld, Andy Williams.

37th Awards: April 5, 1965
honoring 1964 achievements
Santa Monica Civic Auditorium, Santa Monica
Producer: Joe Pasternak
Writers: Richard Breen, Hal Kanter, Milt Rosen
Musical director: John Green
ABC-TV director: Richard Dunlap

Participants included: Julie Andrews, Elizabeth Ashley, Fred Astaire, Claudia Cardinale, Macdonald Carey, Richard Chamberlain, Gladys Cooper, Alex Cord, Joan Crawford, George Cukor, Arlene Dahl, Alain Delon, Angie Dickinson, Jimmy Durante, Vince Edwards, Anthony Franciosa, Judy Garland, Greer Garson, Peter Gennero, Rex Harrison, Audrey Hepburn, Bob Hope, Rock Hudson, Jack Jones, Lila Kedrova, Deborah Kerr, Angela Lansbury, Joe Levine, Steve McQueen, Karl Malden, New Christy Minstrels, Merle Oberon, Patti Page, Gregory Peck, Sidney Poitier, Martha Raye, Debbie Reynolds, Rosalind Russell, Jean Simmons, William Tuttle, Dick Van Dyke, Jack L. Warner, Andy Williams, Nancy Wilson, Jonathan Winters.

38th Awards: April 18, 1966
honoring 1965 achievements
Santa Monica Civic Auditorium, Santa Monica
Producer: Joe Pasternak
Writer: Hal Kanter
Musical director: John Green
ABC-TV director: Richard Dunlap
(first Oscar show telecast in color)

Participants included: Julie Andrews, Martin Balsam, Warren Beatty, *Ingrid Bergman, Milton Berle, Macdonald Carey, Saul Chaplin, Cyd Charisse, Julie Christie, James Coburn, *Olivia de Havilland, Edmond L. DePatie, Angie Dickinson, Phyllis Diller, Patty Duke, Arthur Freed, James Garner, Robert Goulet, Kathryn Grayson, George Hamilton, Rex Harrison, Bob Hope, Richard Johnson, Jan Kadar, Lila Kedrova, Don Knotts, *Burt Lancaster, David Lean, Bill Lee Singers, Michel Legrand, Jack Lemmon, Virna Lisi, *Sophia Loren, Shirley MacLaine, Barbara McNair, Dorothy Malone, Lee Marvin, Yvette Mimieux, Liza Minnelli, James Mitchell, Jane Morgan, *Patricia Neal, *David Niven, Kim Novak, Gregory Peck, George Peppard, Debbie Reynolds, Jason Robards, *Simone Signoret, Smothers Brothers, Elke Sommer, Connie Stevens, Inger Stevens, Ivan Tors, Lana Turner, Peter Ustinov, Shelley Winters, Natalie Wood, Joanne Woodward, William Wyler.
*Pre-filmed

39th Awards: April 10, 1967
honoring 1966 achievements
Santa Monica Civic Auditorium, Santa Monica
Producer: Joe Pasternak
Writers: Hal Kanter, I.A.L. Diamond, Mort Lachman
Musical director: John Green
ABC-TV director: Richard Dunlap

Participants included: Ann-Margret, Fred Astaire, George Bagnall, Anne Bancroft, Candice Bergen, Yakima Canutt, Macdonald Carey, Diahann Carroll, Julie Christie, John Davidson, Olivia de Havilland, Jackie DeShannon, Irene Dunne, Arthur Freed, Y. Frank Freeman, Mitzi Gaynor, Richard Harris, Audrey Hepburn, Wendy Hiller, Bob Hope, Rock Hudson, Dean Jones, Bill Lee Singers, Claude Lelouch, Anita Louise, Fred MacMurray, Dean Martin, Lee Marvin, Walter Matthau, Robert Mitchum, Mary Tyler Moore, Mike Nichols, Patricia Neal, Sidney Poitier, Vanessa Redgrave, Lee Remick, Ginger Rogers, Barbara Rush, Rosalind Russell, Omar Sharif, James Stewart, Jack Valenti, Dick Van Dyke, Dionne Warwick, Raquel Welch, Roger Williams, Jonathan Winters, Shelley Winters, Robert Wise, Young Americans, Fred Zinnemann.

40th Awards: April 10, 1968
honoring 1967 achievements
Santa Monica Civic Auditorium, Santa Monica
Producer: Arthur Freed
Writers: Hal Kanter, I.A.L. Diamond, Mort Lachman,
    Daniel Taradash
Musical director: Elmer Bernstein
ABC-TV director: Richard Dunlap

Participants included: Julie Andrews, Louis Armstrong, *Anne
Bancroft, Claire Bloom, Brasil '66, Macdonald Carey, Leslie
Caron, Diahann Carroll, Carol Channing, Richard Crenna, George
Cukor, Sammy Davis Jr., *Olivia de Havilland, Angie Dickinson,
Patty Duke, Dame Edith Evans, Arthur Freed, Audrey Hepburn,
*Katharine Hepburn, Alfred Hitchcock, Dustin Hoffman, Bob
Hope, Rock Hudson, Shirley Jones, Danny Kaye, Lainie Kazan,
Gene Kelly, *Grace Kelly, George Kennedy, Stanley Kramer,
Angela Lansbury, Walter Matthau, Sergio Mendes, Jiri Menzel,
Walter Mirisch, Robert Morse, Mike Nichols, Estelle Parsons,
Gregory Peck, Sidney Poitier, Katharine Ross, Barbara Rush,
Rosalind Russell, Eva Marie Saint, Elke Sommer, Rod Steiger,
Barbra Streisand, Robert Wise, Natalie Wood.
*Pre-filmed

41st Awards: April 14, 1969
honoring 1968 achievements
Dorothy Chandler Pavilion, Los Angeles
Producer-director: Gower Champion
Writers: Tom Waldman, Frank Waldman
Musical director: Henry Mancini
ABC-TV director: Richard Dunlap

Participants included: Jack Albertson, Ingrid Bergman, Mel
Brooks, Macdonald Carey, Diahann Carroll, John Chambers,
Tony Curtis, Jose Feliciano, Jane Fonda, Aretha Franklin, Ruth
Gordon, Anthony Harvey, Bob Hope, Paula Kelly, Burt Lancaster,
Mark Lester, Abbey Lincoln, Henry Mancini, Walter Matthau,
Marni Nixon, Gregory Peck, Sidney Poitier, Martha Raye, Carol
Reed, Don Rickles, Rosalind Russell, Ludmila Savelyeva, Frank
Sinatra, Barbra Streisand, UCLA Marching Band, Onna White,
Natalie Wood, John Woolf.

Rosalind Russell, Gregory Peck

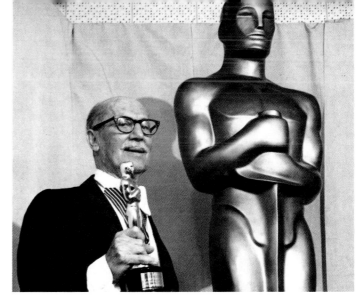

Groucho Marx

42nd Awards: April 7, 1970
honoring 1969 achievements
Dorothy Chandler Pavilion, Los Angeles
Producer: M.J. Frankovich
Director: Jack Haley, Jr.
Writers: Hal Kanter, Frank Pierson, Mary Loos
Musical director: Elmer Bernstein
ABC-TV director: Richard Dunlap

Participants included: Fred Astaire, Candice Bergen, *Ingmar
Bergman, Elmer Bernstein, *Sergei Bondarchuk, Glen Campbell,
Claudia Cardinale, Macdonald Carey, Clint Eastwood, *Federico
Fellini, Alice Ghostley, Elliott Gould, Cary Grant, Jerome Hellman,
Bob Hope, George Jessel, James Earl Jones, *Akira Kurosawa,
*David Lean, Michel Legrand, Myrna Loy, Ali MacGraw, Barbara
McNair, Burch Mann's Ballet America, *Mike Nichols, Jacques
Perrin, Hamed Rachedi, Lou Rawls, Cliff Robertson, Katharine
Ross, Mrs. Arthur Rubenstein, The Sandpipers, *John Schlesinger,
Frank Sinatra, Barbra Streisand, Elizabeth Taylor, B.J. Thomas,
Jon Voight, Shani Wallis, John Wayne, Raquel Welch, *Billy
Wilder, Gig Young, *Franco Zeffirelli.
*Pre-taped

43rd Awards: April 15, 1971
honoring 1970 achievements
Dorothy Chandler Pavilion, Los Angeles
Producer: Robert E. Wise, with Saul Chaplin
Writers: I.A.L. Diamond, Leonard Spigelgass,
    William Bowers
Musical director: Quincy Jones
NBC-TV director: Richard Dunlap

Participants included: Burt Bacharach, Harry Belafonte, Richard
Benjamin, Joan Blondell, Jim Brown, Genevieve Bujold, Glen
Campbell, Macdonald Carey, Leslie Caron, Petula Clark, Angie
Dickinson, Melvyn Douglas, Lola Falana, Janet Gaynor, Lillian
Gish, Goldie Hawn, Bob Hope, John Huston, James Earl Jones,
Shirley Jones, Sally Kellerman, Burt Lancaster, Frank McCarthy,
Donald McKayle Dancers, Steve McQueen, Karl Malden, John
Marley, Walter Matthau, Sarah Miles, John Mills, Juliet Mills,
Ricardo Montalban, Jeanne Moreau, Merle Oberon, Ryan O'Neal,
Gregory Peck, Paula Prentiss, Juliet Prowse, Rosalind Russell,
Eva Marie Saint, George Segal, Frank Sinatra, Maggie Smith,
Daniel Taradash, Liv Ullmann, Gig Young, Orson Welles.

44th Awards: April 10, 1972
honoring 1971 achievements
Dorothy Chandler Pavilion, Los Angeles
Producer: Howard W. Koch
Director: Marty Pasetta
Writers: Leonard Spigelgass, William Ludwig,
  Hal Kanter
Music director: Henry Mancini
NBC-TV director: Marty Pasetta

Participants included: Ann-Margret, Karen Black, Timothy Bottoms, Red Buttons, James Caan, Frank Capra, Macdonald Carey, Leslie Caron, The Carpenters, Richard Chamberlain, Charlie Chaplin, Paddy Chayefsky, Philip D'Antoni, Sammy Davis Jr., Sandy Duncan, Jane Fonda, William Friedkin, John Gavin, Betty Grable, Joel Grey, Gene Hackman, Richard Harris, Helen Hayes, Isaac Hayes, Dick Haymes, Joey Heatherton, Ben Johnson, Sally Kellerman, Alan King, Cloris Leachman, Jack Lemmon, Henry Mancini, Johnny Mathis, Walter Matthau, Liza Minnelli, Mitchell Boys Choir, Joe Namath, Jack Nicholson, Jennifer O'Neill, Charley Pride, Debbie Reynolds, Richard Roundtree, Jill St. John, Franklin J. Schaffner, Cybill Shepherd, Daniel Taradash, Jack Valenti, Raquel Welch, Tennessee Williams, Natalie Wood, Michael York.

45th Awards: March 27, 1973
honoring 1972 achievements
Dorothy Chandler Pavilion, Los Angeles
Producer: Howard W. Koch
Director: Marty Pasetta
Writers: Leonard Spigelgass, William Ludwig
Musical director: John Williams
Telecast on NBC-TV

Participants included: Eddie Albert, Edward Albert, Julie Andrews, Bea Arthur, Marisa Berenson, Candice Bergen, Cher Bono, Sonny Bono, Charles A. Boren, Peter Boyle, Carol Burnett, Michael Caine, Glen Campbell, Dyan Cannon, Macdonald Carey, Diahann Carroll, Mike Curb Congregation, Robert Duvall, Clint Eastwood, Bob Fosse, Greer Garson, John Gavin, Joel Grey, Gene Hackman, Laurence Harvey, Eileen Heckart, Charlton Heston, Rock Hudson, Michael Jackson, Angela Lansbury, Cloris Leachman, Jack Lemmon, Sacheen Littlefeather, Liza Minnelli, Roger Moore, Merle Oberon, Burt Reynolds, Mrs. Edward G. Robinson, Katharine Ross, Albert Ruddy, Rosalind Russell, Frank Sinatra, Elke Sommer, Springfield Revival, Connie Stevens, George Stevens, Daniel Taradash, Liv Ullmann, Jack Valenti, Robert Wagner, Richard Walsh, Raquel Welch, Billy Dee Williams, Natalie Wood.

46th Awards: April 2, 1974
honoring 1973 achievements
Dorothy Chandler Pavilion, Los Angeles
Producer: Jack Haley, Jr.
Director: Marty Pasetta
Writer: Marty Farrell
Musical director: Henry Mancini
Telecast on NBC-TV

Participants included: Elizabeth Allen, Ann-Margret, Burt Bacharach, Richard Benjamin, Candice Bergen, Tony Bill, Linda Blair, Cher Bono, Ernest Borgnine, Charles Bronson, Yul Brynner, James Caan, Dyan Cannon, Angie Dickinson, Peter Falk, Daniel Fortus, Jodie Foster, Melvin Frank, Marvin Hamlisch, Susan Hayward, Katharine Hepburn, Charlton Heston, George Roy Hill, Alfred Hitchcock, Steven Hood, John Houseman, John Huston, Jill Ireland, Gene Kelly, Henri Langlois, Peter Lawford, Peggy Lee, Jack Lemmon, Shirley MacLaine, Henry Mancini, Marcel Marceau, Groucho Marx, Marsha Mason, Walter Matthau, Jason Miller, Liza Minnelli, Roger Moore, Gary Morgan, David Niven, Donald O'Connor, Tatum O'Neal, Irwin Pearl, Gregory Peck, Julia Phillips, Michael Phillips, Paula Prentiss, Burt Reynolds, Debbie Reynolds, Diana Ross, Telly Savalas, Cybill Shepherd, Sylvia Sidney, Neil Simon, Connie Stevens, Elizabeth Taylor, Francois Truffaut, Twiggy, Cicely Tyson, Jack Valenti, Lew Wasserman, Lawrence Weingarten, Raquel Welch, Johnny Whittaker, Billy Dee Williams, Paul Winfield.

**Diane Keaton, Oscar's 50th "First Lady,"
greets the initial one: Janet Gaynor**

47th Awards: April 8, 1975
honoring 1974 achievements
Dorothy Chandler Pavilion, Los Angeles
Producer: Howard W. Koch
Director: Marty Pasetta
Writers: Hal Kanter, William Ludwig, Leonard
  Spigelgass
Musical director: John Green
Telecast on NBC-TV

Participants included: Lauren Bacall, Warren Beatty, Ingrid
Bergman, Susan Blakely, Joseph Bottoms, Macdonald Carey,
Art Carney, Diahann Carroll, Francis Ford Coppola, Sammy
Davis Jr., Peter Falk, Aretha Franklin, Susan George, John
Green, Howard Hawks, Goldie Hawn, Bob Hope, Lauren Hutton,
Glenda Jackson, Jack Jones, Gene Kelly, Arthur Krim, Frankie
Laine, Jack Lemmon, Roddy McDowall, Shirley MacLaine, James
A. Michener, Ryan O'Neal, Tatum O'Neal, Jennifer O'Neill,
Deborah Raffin, Katharine Ross, Bert Schneider, Martin Scorcese,
O.J. Simpson, Frank Sinatra, Danny Thomas, Brenda Vaccaro,
Jack Valenti, Jon Voight, John Wayne, Raquel Welch, Robert Wise.

48th Awards: March 29, 1976
honoring 1975 achievements
Dorothy Chandler Pavilion, Los Angeles
Producer: Howard W. Koch
Director: Marty Pasetta
Writers: Hal Kanter, William Ludwig, Leonard
  Spigelgass
Musical director: John Williams
Telecast on ABC-TV

Participants included: Isabelle Adjani, Burt Bacharach, Marisa
Berenson, Jacqueline Bisset, Linda Blair, Robert Blake, Ray
Bolger, Beau Bridges, Charles Bronson, George Burns, Art
Carney, Keith Carradine, Stockard Channing, Angie Dickinson,
Michael Douglas, Verna Fields, Louise Fletcher, Milos Forman,
William Friedkin, Kelly Garrett, Elliott Gould, Lee Grant, Joel
Grey, Marilyn Hassett, Goldie Hawn, Margaux Hemingway,
Audrey Hepburn, Charlton Heston, Anthony Hopkins, Jill Ireland,
Ben Johnson, Madeline Kahn, Diane Keaton, Gene Kelly,
Steve Lawrence, Mervyn LeRoy, Rod McKuen, Walter Matthau,
Walter Mirisch, Jack Nicholson, Jennifer O'Neill, Bernadette
Peters,*Mary Pickford, Charlotte Rampling, **Diana Ross, Telly
Savalas, Roy Scheider, George Segal, Robert Shaw, O.J.
Simpson, Jules Stein, Marlo Thomas, Jack Valenti, Gore Vidal,
Billy Dee Williams, William Wyler, Saul Zaentz.

*Pre-taped
**Live by satellite from The Netherlands

Bob Hope

49th Awards: March 28, 1977
honoring 1976 achievements
Dorothy Chandler Pavilion, Los Angeles
Producer: William Friedkin
Director: Marty Pasetta
Writers: Ray Bradbury, Hal Kanter
Musical director: Bill Conti
Telecast on ABC-TV

Participants included: Eddie Albert, Muhammad Ali, Ann-Margret,
John Avildsen, Pearl Bailey, Warren Beatty, Pandro S. Berman,
Ellen Burstyn, Robert Chartoff, Chevy Chase, Paddy Chayefsky,
Neil Diamond, Tamara Dobson, Faye Dunaway, Marty Feldman,
Mrs. Peter Finch, Louise Fletcher, Jane Fonda, Lillian Hellman,
William Holden, Tom Jones, Marthe Keller, Donald McKayle
Dancers, Norman Mailer, Jeanne Moreau, Jack Nicholson,
Tatum O'Neal, Richard Pryor, Jason Robards, Roy Scheider,
Red Skelton, Sylvester Stallone, Beatrice Straight, Barbra
Streisand, Donald Sutherland, Cicely Tyson, Liv Ullmann, Ben
Vareen, Lee Vivante, Paul Williams, Irwin Winkler.

Fiftieth Annual Academy Awards Presentation

HOWARD W. KOCH
Producer

MARTY PASETTA
Director

HAL KANTER
WILLIAM LUDWIG
LEONARD SPIGELGASS
Writers

HAL KANTER
Special Material

BUZ KOHAN
Special Musical Material

MICHAEL B. SELIGMAN
Associate Producer

ALLAN CARR
Executive Talent Consultant

TOM H. JOHN
Production Designer

NELSON RIDDLE
Musical Director

PAT BIRCH
ROB ISCOVE
Choreographers

MOSS MABRY
Costume Designer

DANETTE HERMAN
Production Coordinator

LAURIE ABDO
SKIP WARD
Assistants to the Producer

ROBERT F. METZLER
Business Manager

BOB HOPE
Master of Ceremonies

AWARD PRESENTERS
Fred Astaire
Michael Caine
Paddy Chayefsky
Bette Davis
Olivia de Havilland
Kirk Douglas
Farrah Fawcett-Majors
Joan Fontaine
Jodie Foster
Greer Garson
Janet Gaynor
John Green
Mark Hamill
Goldie Hawn
William Holden
Stanley Kramer
Henry Mancini
Marcello Mastroianni
Walter Matthau
Olivia Newton-John
Jack Nicholson
Gregory Peck
Eva Marie Saint
Maggie Smith
Sylvester Stallone
Barbara Stanwyck
John Travolta
Cicely Tyson
Jack Valenti
King Vidor
Jon Voight
Raquel Welch
Billy Dee Williams
Paul Williams
Henry Winkler
Natalie Wood
and
Artoo Deetoo
Mickey Mouse
See Threepio
(Anthony Daniels)

PROGRAM PARTICIPANTS
Jack Albertson
Irwin Allen
Edward Anhalt
Patty Duke Astin
John Avildsen
Priscilla Barnes
Anne Baxter
Tony Bill
Ernest Borgnine
Karen Black
Debby Boone
Margaret Booth
Red Buttons
Frank Capra
George Chakiris
Stockard Channing
Cyd Charisse
George Cukor
Starr Danias
Sammy Davis, Jr.
Richard Dreyfuss
Kermit Eller
Louise Fletcher
Aretha Franklin
Susan George
Joel Grey
Conrad Hall
Marvin Hamlisch
Edith Head
Charlton Heston
Burl Ives
Charles H. Joffe
Diane Keaton
George Kennedy
Cloris Leachman
Michele Lee
Gloria Loring
Dorothy Malone
John Meehan
Walter Mirisch
Rita Moreno
Edmond O'Brien
Eleanor Parker
Jane Powell
Deborah Raffin
Vanessa Redgrave
Donna Reed
Debbie Reynolds
Cliff Robertson
Mickey Rooney
Gale Sondergaard
Camilla Sparv
Beatrice Straight
Claire Trevor
Haskell Wexler
John Williams
Teresa Wright

Index

The First Fifty Years of Academy Awards Nominees

Compiled by George Jewell

The following index lists each individual and motion picture achievement nominated for and/or receiving an Academy Award during the fifty year period, 1927-28 through 1977, followed by the year of the nomination and/or Award.

Academy of Motion Picture Arts and Sciences

JAMES M. ROBERTS
Executive Director

DON J. YOTT
Administrator, Finance and Operations

DANIEL ROSS
Assistant to the Executive Director
Technical Branches and
Theater Operations

DEPARTMENT SUPERVISORS
Margaret Herrick Library:
BONNIE ROTHBART
Head Librarian

Publications:
MAXINE MARTIN
MELINDA PETTIT
Assistant Co-editors, Players Directory

VERNA RAMSEY
Editor, Screen Achievement
Records Bulletin

Educational and Cultural Activities
Program Administrator:
KAREN ARANDJELOVICH
Student Film Awards and
Visiting Artists Program

Coordinator:
ANTHONY SLIDE
National Film Information
Service and Exhibits

Film Archive and Production:
RODNEY RECOR
Executive Assistant

Legal Counsel:
GYTE VAN ZYL
Doggett & Van Zyl

Public Relations Counsel:
MARTIN M. COOPER
Harshe-Rotman & Druck, Inc.

Certified Public Accountants:
PRICE WATERHOUSE & CO.

1977-78 OFFICERS

HOWARD W. KOCH
President

FAY KANIN
First Vice President

MARVIN E. MIRISCH
Vice President

CHARLES M. POWELL
Vice President

HAL ELIAS
Treasurer

DONALD C. ROGERS
Secretary

1977-78 BOARD OF GOVERNORS

Jeff Alexander	Ruby R. Levitt
Gene Allen	Mike Medavoy
Edward Asner	Marvin E. Mirisch
Tony Bill	Walter Mirisch
John Cacavas	Donald O. Mitchell
Linwood G. Dunn	Ronald Neame
Hal Elias	Gregory Peck
Julius J. Epstein	Charles M. Powell
Verna Fields	William H. Reynolds
John C. Flinn	Donald C. Rogers
George Folsey	Frank E. Rosenfelt
June Foray	Tex Rudloff
Regina Gruss	William Schallert
Arthur Hamilton	John H. Senter
T. Hee	Leonard South
Fay Kanin	Robert Towne
Howard W. Koch	Ralph E. Winters
Stanley E. Kramer	Robert E. Wise

ACADEMY EXECUTIVE SECRETARIES*
FRANK WOODS, 1927-1931
LESTER COWAN, 1931-1933
DONALD GLEDHILL, 1934-1942
MARGARET HERRICK, 1942-1950

ACADEMY EXECUTIVE DIRECTORS
MARGARET HERRICK, 1950-1970
SAM E. BROWN, 1971
JAMES M. ROBERTS, since 1971
* designation changed to "Executive Director" under June 1950 Academy bylaw

ACKNOWLEDGEMENTS
Special thanks to the following for their invaluable assistance in helping
research and contribute to this history of the Academy's first fifty years:
Martin M. Cooper, editing; Darryl Lyman, editing; Russell Adams,
Rick Sandford; the staff of the Academy of Motion Picture Arts and
Sciences; Ron Yates, calligraphy; ABC-TV and George Long, photography;
Jim Britt, cover photo; Colormation Inc.; Frye & Smith Lithographers;
National Bindery; the staff of South Coast Typesetting; and last but
foremost, a special acknowledgement to the memory of co-publisher
Anna Lee Schworck for the support and interest that
made this project possible.